The Counselor's Companion: What Every Beginning Counselor Needs to Know

Authors' Purpose

In our interactions with counselor trainees, we often hear them express uncertainty about how to proceed after graduation. While they are in the midst of their counseling programs, students are surrounded by support systems comprised of professors, supervisors, and peers; yet, once in the field, novice clinicians often experience a sense of loss and can even become overwhelmed with questions that arise in their clinical interactions. Although we sincerely hope beginning counselors will create a support system with other professionals, we also recognize the harsh reality that not every counselor works in an environment with other trained mental health professionals and that there are few written resources that provide comprehensive and practical information for counselors who are just getting started. The goal of this project is to provide novice counselors with a reference tool or "friend" of sorts where they can turn when questions related to areas such as professionalism, ethics, research, and day-to-day clinical work arise in their practices. The journey to becoming a successful professional counselor is one that should not be walked alone. We hope that this book will become a faithful companion for students who have left their supervisors and teachers behind after graduation and that being able to reference the knowledge base of counselor educators and seasoned practitioners will ensure a journey to professionalism that is a little less bumpy!

Jocelyn Gregoire and Christin M. Jungers
Duquesne University

The Counselor's Companion: What Every Beginning Counselor Needs to Know

by Jocelyn Gregoire and Christin M. Jungers
Duquesne University

Ideal for use in practicum or graduate capstone courses, this book includes …

Cutting-Edge Topics: In addition to a focus on the traditional CACREP curriculum areas, readers will also find chapters on important and cutting-edge trends in the counseling field. Some of these areas include the use of neuroscience in counseling practice (chapter 28), bioecological approaches to practice (chapter 27), crisis counseling, pastoral counseling, and addictions counseling.

NCE Preparation Tool: Key chapters reflect specific content areas that students preparing for the NCE will need to know. Also included is a 200-question sample exam to test knowledge, application, and analysis of key concepts and information in the counseling field.

Case Examples: Throughout the book, readers will find example boxes that highlight important points or provide case examples to clarify counseling theory and bring counseling models into day-to-day practice.

Web References: Each chapter includes Web references that readers can use to find more information, download articles, and retrieve full documents, such as the ACA Code of Ethics, about relevant counseling-related topics.

Concise, Heart-of-the-Matter Format: The format is intentionally concise and presented in an outline form so that counselors can easily grasp and retain main points of each topic area without getting lost or distracted by peripheral details.

SPECIAL OFFERS!

Online Counseling Case Management Software: Athena Software, producer of Penelope, a Web-based case management software package designed especially for counseling and human services practitioners, is offering a special package for anyone who purchases this book. For only $7.95, you can subscribe for 120 days to the Penelope program. It is a great way for students in their practicum and internships to become familiar with the reality of the electronic revolution in counseling practice (e.g., the program supports online record keeping, note summary, appointment calendars, and evaluations). Visit www.athenasoftware.net/index.html for more information.

Titles of Related Interest From Lawrence Erlbaum Associates, Inc.

- *Advancing Social Justice Through Clinical Practice*
  Etiony Aldarondo

- *Countertransference and the Therapist's Inner Experience: Perils and Possibilities*
  Charles J. Gelso & Jeffrey A. Hayes

- *Handbook of Posttraumatic Growth: Research & Practice*
  Lawrence G. Calhoun & Richard G. Tedeschi

- *Empathy in Counseling and Psychotherapy: Perspectives and Practices*
  Arthur J. Clark

- *Handbook of Culture, Therapy, and Healing*
  Uwe P. Gielen, Jefferson M. Fish, & Juris G. Draguns

- *Half in Love With Death: Managing the Chronically Suicidal Patient*
  Joel Paris

- *Group Counseling and Psychotherapy With Children and Adolescents: Theory, Research, and Practice*
  Zipora Shechtman

- *An ADHD Primer, Second Edition*
  Lisa L. Weyandt

- *Neuropsychotherapy: How the Neurosciences Inform Effective Psychotherapy*
  Klaus Grawe

- *The Professional Counselor as Administrator: Perspectives on Leadership and Management of Counseling Services Across Settings*
  Edwin L. Herr, Dennis E. Heitzmann, & Jack R. Rayman

- *The Mind in Therapy: Cognitive Science for Practice*
  Katherine D. Arbuthnott & Dennis W. Arbuthnott

- *Emotionally Intelligent School Counseling*
  John Pellitteri, Robin Stern, Claudia Shelton, & Barbara Muller-Ackerman

- *The New Handbook of Counseling Supervision*
  L. DiAnne Borders & Lori L. Brown

- *Working With Troubled Men*
  Morley D. Glicken

- *Counseling and Therapy With Clients Who Abuse Alcohol or Other Drugs: An Integrative Approach*
  Cynthia E. Glidden-Tracey

- *Multicultural Assessment: Principles, Applications, and Examples*
  Richard H. Dana

- *The Great Psychotherapy Debate: Models, Methods, and Findings*
  Bruce Wampold

The Counselor's Companion: What Every Beginning Counselor Needs to Know

Jocelyn Gregoire
Christin M. Jungers
Duquesne University

Routledge
Taylor & Francis Group
New York   London

Lawrence Erlbaum Associates, Inc., Publishers
10 Industrial Avenue
Mahwah, New Jersey 07430
www.erlbaum.com

Cover design by Tomai Maridou

Interior design by Wendy MacRobbie

Library of Congress Cataloging-in-Publication Data

The counselor's companion : what every beginning counselor needs to know / edited by Jocelyn Gregoire, Christin Jungers.
        p. cm.
Includes bibliographical references and index.
ISBN 978-0-8058-5683-5 — 0-8058-5683-8 (cloth)
ISBN 978-0-8058-5684-2 — 0-8058-5684-6 (pbk.)
ISBN 1-4106-1674-6 (e book)
1. Counseling psychology. 2. Counseling psychology—Practice. I. Gregoire, Jocelyn. II. Jungers, Christin.
BF636.6.C68 2007
158'.3—dc22   2006030183
                                                                      CIP

Books published by Lawrence Erlbaum Associates are printed on acid-free paper, and their bindings are chosen for strength and durability

Printed in the United States of America
10 9 8 7 6 5 4 3

Brief Contents

Preface   xxxv

Acknowledgments   xxxix

Meet the Contributors   xli

---

part one

What Are the Primary Roles and Responsibilities of the Professional Counselor?   I

chapter 1   On Being a Professional Counselor   2

chapter 2   The Demands and Obligations of Ethical Counseling   18

chapter 3   The Legal Intrigues of Counseling Practice   32

chapter 4   Multicultural Intricacies in Professional Counseling   52

chapter 5   Supervision: An Essential for Professional Development   72

chapter 6   Collaborative Supervision for the Novice Supervisor   86

part two

What Are the Essential Elements of Counseling With Which All Counselors Must Be Familiar?   111

chapter 7   **Understanding Human Growth and Development**   112

chapter 8   **Counseling Across the Lifespan**   136

chapter 9   **Major Forces Behind Counseling Approaches**   154

chapter 10   **Individual and Social Aspects of the Helping Relationship**   194

chapter 11   **The Cultural Kaleidoscope: Eyeing Diverse Populations**   218

chapter 12   **Approaches to Group Work**   246

chapter 13   **Fundamentals of Group Work**   274

chapter 14   **Multicultural Components of Group Work**   298

chapter 15   **Counseling in the World of Work**   314

chapter 16   **Multicultural Issues in Career and Lifestyle Counseling**   340

chapter 17   **Fundamentals of Professional School Counseling**   360

chapter 18   **Approaches to Family Counseling**   376

chapter 19   **Understanding and Assessing Psychopathology**   404 part three

What Are the Fundamental Components of Appraisal and Research that New Counselors Should Use in Their Practice?   433

chapter
20   **Foundations of Measurement and Psychometrics**   434

chapter
21   **Testing and Assessment in Counseling Practice**   458

chapter
22   **Quantitative Research Designs**   486

chapter
23   **Fundamentals of Qualitative Research**   512

part four

What Are the Special Topics and Important Trends That Counselors Might Encounter?   527

chapter
24   **A Look at Consultation**   528

chapter
25   **Crisis Intervention in Counseling**   550

chapter
26   **Addictions Counseling**   568

chapter
27   **Ecological-Transactional and Motivational Perspectives in Counseling**   586

chapter
28   **Neuroscience in Psychotherapeutic Practices**   606

chapter
29   **Developmental Counseling and Therapy**   624

chapter
30
Counseling for Wellness   642

chapter
31
Spirituality and Pastoral Counseling Practices   658

appendix
A
Preparing for the National Counselor Exam:
What You Need to Know   675

appendix
B
Your Online Companion in Electronic Case Management:
An Introduction to Penelope Software   721

appendix
C
Hints, Helps, and FAQs About Working in a Managed Care
Environment   731

References   741

Index   785

Contents

Preface   xxxv

Acknowledgments   xxxix

Meet the Contributors   xli

---

part one

What Are the Primary Roles and Responsibilities of the Professional Counselor?   1

chapter

1

On Being a Professional Counselor   2

A Brief History of the Counseling Profession   3
 ■ Theoretical Shifts; Specialization; Professionalization

The Counselor's Identity   4
 ■ The Diversity of Counselor Identities; How Counseling Differs From
   Psychology and Social Work; Characteristics of an Effective Counselor

Professionalism   8
 ■ Training for Professional Counselors; Licensure; Certification; Professional
   Associations; Advocacy; Ethical Principles in Professional Counseling

Personal Health and Wellness   15
 ■ Countertransference; Burnout; Networking

chapter

2

The Demands and Obligations of Ethical Counseling   18

The Basics of Ethics in Counseling   19
 ■ Definition of Ethics; Ethical Codes; Ethical Codes and Cultural Diversity;
   Development of Ethical Codes; ACA Code of Ethics; Mandatory
   and Aspirational Ethics

Ethical Theory   22
■ Epicureanism; Utilitarianism; Kantianism; Situationalism

Ethical Principles and Decision Making   24
■ Nonmaleficence; Beneficence; Autonomy; Fidelity; Justice; An Ethical
Decision-Making Model

Common Ethical Concerns for Professional Counselors   28
■ Confidentiality; Dual Relationships and Potentially Beneficial Interactions;
Sexual Misconduct; Transference; Countertransference

Summary   31

chapter

3

The Legal Intrigues of Counseling Practice   32

Basics of Professional, Ethical, and Legal Practice for Counselors   33
■ A Look at Professions, Professionalism, and Professional Identity; Legal
Issues Related to Counselors' Professional Identity; Ethical Codes and
Standards of Practice; What Is Law?; Contracts in Counseling: Informed
Consent; Torts and Counselor Negligence

Professionalism for School Counselors   38
■ Building Collaborative Relationships; Facing the Political Barriers of the
School System; Community Standards in School Counselor Practice;
Protecting Students' Best Interests

Legal and Ethical Aspects of Competence   40
■ Consultation; Continuing Education; Malpractice

Record Keeping   42
■ School Records: Family Education Rights and Privacy Act (FERPA); ASCA
Ethical Guidelines on Educational Records; Agency Records: Health
Insurance Portability and Accountability Act (HIPAA)

Dual Relationships in School and Community Settings   45
■ Ethical and Legal Considerations of Dual Relationships; Complexity of
Dual Relationships in Schools; Safeguarding Clients' Emotional Health

Confidentiality, Privacy, and Privileged Communication   46
■ Ethical Standard of Confidentiality; Confidentiality for School Counselors;
Privacy; Legal Facets of Privileged Communication; Duty to Warn: Limit to
Privileged Communication; Duty to Protect

chapter
4

Multicultural Intricacies in Professional Counseling 52

Cultural Influences in Counseling 53
- Influence of Eurocentric Perspectives on Counseling; Rationale for a Multicultural Approach in Counseling; Multicultural Competencies for Professional Counselors

Essential Factors in Culture-Sensitive Counseling 54
- Culture Defined; Cultural Convergence; Etic and Emic Cultural Viewpoints; Cultural Encapsulation; Ethnocentrism; Acculturation and Assimilation; Alloplastic and Autoplastic Viewpoints

Cultural Constructs: A Closer Look 60
- Sex and Gender; Sexuality and Affectional Orientation; Race; Age; Ability; Religion and Spirituality

Bias, Prejudice, Discrimination, and Oppression 64
- Bias; Prejudice; Discrimination; Oppression; Privilege

Cultural Identity Development 67
- Racial and Cultural Identity Development Model; White Racial Identity Development

Multicultural Theories in Counseling 69
- Multicultural Counseling and Therapy; Benefits of Multicultural Counseling and Therapy

chapter
5

Supervision: An Essential for Professional Development 72

Basics of Clinical Supervision 73
- Supervision: A Key to Professionalism; Benefits of Supervision; Supervision Defined

Models of Supervision 75
- Developmental Models of Supervision; Theory-Specific Supervision Models; Social Role Models of Supervision: Discrimination Model; Integrated Model of Supervision; A Supervision Videotaping Method: Interpersonal Process Recall

chapter
6

Collaborative Supervision for the Novice Supervisor 86

A Look at Supervision 87
- Purposes of Supervision; Importance of Supervision to the Counseling Profession; Supervision, Professional Development, and Credentialing

Becoming a Supervisor: Some Starting Points   89
  ▪ Training Through Doctoral Programs; Self-Developed Supervision Skills:
    Modeling as a First Step; Self-Developed Supervision Skills: Gathering
    Other Resources

A Collaborative Model of Supervision: An Overview   91
  ▪ Constructivist Roots of the Collaborative Model; Meeting Competencies
    Through the Collaborative Model; Advantages of the Collaborative Model

Professional Development of Novice Supervisors: Knowledge Competency   92
  ▪ Theoretical Foundations; Ethical and Legal Considerations; Multicultural
    Impact

Professional Development of Novice Supervisors: Disposition   97
  ▪ Collaborative, Learner-Focused Stance; Supportive and Critical
    Dispositions: Coexisting Roles

Professional Development of Novice Supervisors: Strategies   99
  ▪ The Inquiry Learning Cycle; Building the Therapeutic Alliance; Using the
    FERA Inquiry Model in the Therapeutic Alliance; Promoting the
    Construction of Meaning; Using the FERA Inquiry Model in the
    Construction of Meaning; Evaluating the Work of the Counselor; Using the
    FERA Inquiry Model for Evaluating the Work of the Supervisee

Summary   109

part two

What Are the Essential Elements of Counseling With Which All Counselors Must Be Familiar?

What Are the Essential Elements of Counseling With
Which All Counselors Must Be Familiar?   111

chapter 7   **Understanding Human Growth and Development**   112

Prenatal Development   113
  ▪ Influences on Prenatal Development; Genetic Makeup; Prenatal
    Developmental Periods; Risks During Prenatal Development

Infancy: The First 2 Years of Life   114
  ▪ Physical Development in Infancy; Cognitive Development in Infancy;
    Social-Emotional Development in Infancy

Early Childhood: The Preschool Period   119
  ▪ Physical Development in Early Childhood; Cognitive Development in Early
    Childhood; Social-Emotional Development in Early Childhood

Middle Childhood: Elementary School Years   123
- Physical Development in Middle Childhood; Cognitive Development in Middle Childhood; Social-Emotional Development in Middle Childhood

Adolescence: Transition From Childhood to Adulthood   127
- Physical Development in Adolescence; Cognitive Development in Adolescence; Social-Emotional Development in Adolescence

Adulthood   130
- Physical Development in Adulthood; Cognitive Development in Adulthood; Social-Emotional Development in Adulthood

Death, Dying, and Bereavement   133
- Death and the Young; Theory of Dying Process; Grief and Bereavement

chapter 8   **Counseling Across the Life Span**   136

Perspectives in Human Growth and Development   137
- Nature and Nurture; Continuity and Discontinuity; Developmental Domains

Psychodynamic Theories of Human Development   139
- The Psychoanalytic Approach; The Psychosocial Approach

Behavioral and Learning Theories of Human Development   143
- Classical Conditioning; Stimulus–Response Model; Law of Effect; Skinnerian Approach; Social Learning Theory

Cognitive Theories of Human Development   146
- Piagetian Theory of Cognitive Development; Theory of Moral Development; Sociocultural Theory of Development

Ethological and Maturational Theories of Human Development   150
- Konrad Lorenz; Attachment Theory; Theory of Genetic Determination

Humanistic Theories of Human Development   152
- Maslow's Hierarchy of Needs

chapter 9   **Major Forces Behind Counseling Approaches**   154

Psychodynamic Approaches: Psychoanalysis   156
- View of Human Nature; Theory of Personality; Key Theoretical Concepts; Goals of Therapy; Therapeutic Techniques; Role of Therapist; Strengths and Limitations

Psychodynamic Approaches: Analytic Psychology   159
- View of Human Nature; Theory of Personality; Key Theoretical Concepts; Goals of Therapy; Therapeutic Techniques; Role of Therapist; Strengths and Limitations

Psychodynamic Approaches: Individual Psychology   161
- View of Human Nature; Theory of Personality; Key Theoretical Concepts; Goals of Therapy; Therapeutic Techniques; Role of Therapist; Strengths and Limitations

Psychodynamic Approaches: Transactional Analysis   164
- View of Human Nature; Theory of Personality; Key Theoretical Concepts; Goals of Therapy; Therapeutic Techniques; Role of Therapist; Strengths and Limitations

Cognitive-Behavioral Approaches: Behaviorism   167
- View of Human Nature; Theory of Personality; Key Theoretical Concepts; Goals of Therapy; Therapeutic Techniques; Role of Therapist; Strengths and Limitations

Cognitive-Behavioral Approaches: Neo-Behaviorism   169
- View of Human Nature; Theory of Personality; Key Theoretical Concepts; Goals of Therapy; Therapeutic Techniques; Role of Therapist; Strengths and Limitations

Cognitive-Behavioral Approaches: Cognitive Therapy   172
- View of Human Nature; Theory of Personality; Key Theoretical Concepts; Goals of Therapy; Therapeutic Techniques; Role of Therapist; Strengths and Limitations

Cognitive-Behavioral Approaches: Rational-Emotive Therapy   176
- View of Human Nature; Theory of Personality; Key Theoretical Concepts; Goals of Therapy; Therapeutic Techniques; Role of Therapist; Strengths and Limitations

Cognitive-Behavioral Approaches: Reality Therapy   179
- View of Human Nature; Theory of Personality; Key Theoretical Concepts; Goals of Therapy; Therapeutic Techniques; Role of Therapist; Strengths and Limitations

Cognitive-Behavioral Approaches: Multimodal Therapy   182
- View of Human Nature; Theory of Personality; Key Theoretical Concepts; Goals of Therapy; Therapeutic Techniques; Role of Therapist; Strengths and Limitations

Existential-Humanistic Approaches: Person-Centered   185
- View of Human Nature; Theory of Personality; Key Theoretical Concepts; Goals of Therapy; Therapeutic Techniques; Role of Therapist; Strengths and Limitations

Existential-Humanistic Approaches: Gestalt   187
  ▪ View of Human Nature; Theory of Personality; Key Theoretical Concepts;
    Goals of Therapy; Therapeutic Techniques; Role of Therapist; Strengths
    and Limitations

Existential-Humanistic Approaches: Logotherapy   190
  ▪ View of Human Nature; Theory of Personality; Key Theoretical Concepts;
    Goals of Therapy; Therapeutic Techniques; Role of Therapist; Strengths
    and Limitations

c h a p t e r   **Individual and Social Aspects of the Helping Relationship**   194
  10

The Helping Relationship   195
  ▪ Why Bother With Theories?; Theory Defined; Theories With Which
    Helpers Need to Be Familiar; A Word About Eclecticism; Helping Defined;
    The Helping Process; Frameworks Within Which the Helping Process
    Occurs; Helping Helpees Meet Their Needs

What Constitutes Effective Helping?   199
  ▪ Professional Helpers as Growth Facilitators; Personal Characteristics of
    Effective Helpers; Helpers' Skills; Helpers and Diversity Issues

Training Models for Coping Skills Development   203
  ▪ People-in-System Model; Life Skills Education Model; Structured Learning
    Therapy Model; Social Skills

Training Models for Interpersonal Skills Development   207
  ▪ Skilled Helping: Problem Management Model; Relationship Enhancement
    Therapy Model; Microskills Counseling Model; Interpersonal Process
    Recall; Human Resources Development Model; The Politics of Giving
    Therapy Away: Listening and Focusing

Social-Psychological Approaches to Helping   211
  ▪ Symbolic Interaction; Role Theory; Social Exchange; Cognitive Consistency;
    Dissonance Theory; Heider's Balance Theory; Congruity Theory;
    Newcomb's A-B-X Model of Interpersonal Attraction; Attributions

c h a p t e r   **The Cultural Kaleidoscope: Eyeing Diverse Populations**   218
  11

Opening up to Multicultural Realities in Counseling   220
  ▪ Implications of a Multicultural Worldview to Counselors' Training;
    Implications of a Multicultural Emphasis for Counselor Educators;
    Implications of Multicultural Counseling for Program Development;
    Cross-Cultural Differences in Counselor–Client Relationships; What Is
    Cultural Context?; A Model for Understanding Differences; Avoiding
    "Preferred" Clients Only; The Notion of White Privilege

Challenges for Children of Specific Populations   224
- Examining the Influence of Ethnicity on Children; Additional Concerns
  When Working With Children of Different Ethnic Groups

Native American Population   225
- Historical and Demographic Factors; Family Characteristics; Value
  Orientations; Stereotypes; Communication Styles; Mental Health Issues

African American Population   228
- Historical and Demographic Factors; Value Orientations; Family
  Characteristics; Communication Styles; Mental Health Issues;
  Considerations When Counseling

Asian American Population   231
- Historical and Demographic Factors; Family Values; Common Stereotypes;
  Mental Health Issues; Communication Styles; Effective Counseling
  Approaches

Latin American Population   234
- Historical and Demographic Factors; Family Characteristics;
  Communication Styles; Value Orientations; Mental Health Issues

Arab American Population   236
- Historical and Demographic Factors; Family Characteristics; Value
  Orientations; Stereotypes; Counseling Issues

Elderly Population   239
- Demographic Factors; Stereotypes; Mental Health Issues; Approaches to
  Counseling

Ableism and Disability   241
- Demographics; Stereotypes; Rehabilitation Counseling; Counseling Issues

Gay, Lesbian, Bisexual, and Transgendered Population   243
- The Process of "Coming Out"; Counseling Issues

Conclusion   244

chapter
12   **Approaches to Group Work**   246

Psychoanalytic Approach to Group Work   247
- Key Theoretical Concepts; Goals and Stages; Therapeutic Techniques; Role
  of Group Leader; Strengths and Limitations

Adlerian Approach to Group Work   249
- Key Theoretical Concepts; Goals and Stages; Therapeutic Techniques; Role
  of Group Leader; Strengths and Limitations

Transactional Analytic Approach to Group Work 251
 ■ Key Theoretical Concepts; Goals and Stages; Therapeutic Techniques; Role
 of Group Leader; Strengths and Limitations

Psychodramatic Approach to Group Work 254
 ■ Key Theoretical Concepts; Goals and Stages; Therapeutic Techniques; Role
 of Group Leader; Strengths and Limitations

Behavioral Approach to Group Work 257
 ■ Key Theoretical Concepts; Goals and Stages; Therapeutic Techniques; Role
 of Group Leader; Strengths and Limitations

Rational-Emotive Behavior Therapy Approach to Group Work 260
 ■ Key Theoretical Concepts; Goals and Stages; Therapeutic Techniques; Role
 of Group Leader; Strengths and Limitations

Reality Therapy Approach to Group Work 262
 ■ Key Theoretical Concepts; Goals and Stages; Therapeutic Techniques; Role
 of Group Leader; Strengths and Limitations

Person-Centered Approach to Group Work 264
 ■ Key Theoretical Concepts; Goals and Stages; Therapeutic Techniques; Role
 of Group Leader; Strengths and Limitations

Gestalt Approach to Group Work 267
 ■ Key Theoretical Concepts; Goals and Stages; Therapeutic Techniques; Role
 of Group Leader; Strengths and Limitations

Existential Approach to Group Work 270
 ■ Key Theoretical Concepts; Goals and Stages; Therapeutic Techniques; Role
 of Group Leader; Strengths and Limitations

chapter **13** **Fundamentals of Group Work** 274

History of Group Counseling 275
 ■ Theoretical Influences; Uses of Groups; Ethical and Legal Considerations

Fundamentals of Group Work 276
 ■ Definition of Group Work; Types of Group Work; Group Member
 Activities; Leader Interventions

Group Dynamics 278
 ■ Group Processing; Group Conflict; Group Cohesiveness; Therapeutic
 Factors in Groups; Group Typology

Group Leadership 281
 ■ Leadership Styles; Group Leader Attributes; A Framework for
 Intervention; Concerns of Beginning Group Leaders; Coleadership

Cultural Considerations for Group Leaders   284
- Influences on Diversity; Non-Western Values in Group Work;
  Characteristics of Culturally Competent Leaders; Benefits of Multicultural
  Awareness

Pregroup Planning   287
- Logistics; Site Considerations; Defining the Group's Purpose; Selection of
  Members

Beginning Phase   288
- Structure; Group Norms; Role of the Leader in the Beginning Phase; Goal
  Setting Feedback in the Beginning Phase

Middle Phase   292
- Conflict in the Middle Phase; Group Interactions; Role of the Leader in the
  Middle Phase; Feedback in the Middle Phase

Final Phase   295
- Final Phase Resistance; Generalization of Learning; Role of the Leader in
  the Final Phase

chapter

14

Multicultural Components of Group Work   298

History of Multicultural Group Work   299
- Goals of Group Work; Culture and Group Work; Multicultural Group
  Work Defined; Multicultural Group Work and Ethical Practice

Core Competencies of Multicultural Group Work   301
- Individual Competencies of Multicultural Group Workers; Principles for
  Diversity-Competent Group Workers

Theory and Multicultural Group Work   303
- Diversity and Multicultural Framework; Failure to Recognize Diversity
  Issues in Theory; Flexibility to Operate Within Multicultural Worldviews

Assessment and Group Ideologies   305
- Assessment in Multicultural Group Work; Process of Assessment; Delivery
  of Assessment Decisions; Communication Styles; Thematic
  Communication in Assessment; Individual and Cultural Values in
  Assessment

A Diversity-Competent Model of Multicultural Group Work   311
- How to Choose a Model of Multicultural Group Work; Images of Me: An
  Afrocentric Approach to Group Work

c h a p t e r **Counseling in the World of Work** 314
15

Career Counseling Overview 315
- Historical Development of Career Counseling; Nature of Career Counseling; Important Terminology in Career Counseling

Career Development Theory 317
- Frank Parsons: Trait and Factor Theory; John Holland: Theory of Vocational Choice and Adjustment; Eli Ginzberg: Developmental Career Theory; Donald Super: Life-Span Theory; Anne Roe: Needs Theory; E. Bordin: Psychoanalytic Career Theory; Tiedeman and O'Hara: Choice and Adjustment Theory Gottfredson: Theory of Circumscription and Compromise; John Krumboltz: Social Learning Career Theory; Socioeconomic Career Theories; Career Theories for Women

Process of Career Counseling 325
- Stage 1: Dealing With Change; Stage 2: Developing Career Focus; Stage 3: Exploring Career Options; Stage 4: Preparing for Job Search; Stage 5: Obtaining Employment

Use of Assessment Tools in Career Counseling 328
- History of Assessment: Trait and Factor Model; Interest Inventories; Personality Inventories; Values/Lifestyle Inventories; Qualitative Tools

Special Issues in Career Counseling 332
- Job Loss; Dual-Career Considerations; Displaced Homemakers; Individuals With Disabilities; Midlife Career Changes

Technological Competencies for Career Counselors 336
- ACES Technology Competencies; Need for Technological Skills

c h a p t e r **Multicultural Issues in Career and Lifestyle Counseling** 340
16

Understanding Cultural Issues in Career Counseling 341
- Historical Approaches to Multicultural Career Counseling; Important Terminology: Cross-Cultural and Multicultural

Multicultural Career Development: Traditional Theoretical Approaches 342
- Holland's Person–Environment Fit Theory; Roe's Theory of Occupational Classifications; Super's Life Span-Life Space Theory; Gottfredson's Theory of Circumscription and Compromise; Social Cognitive Career Theory; Theories Summary

Culture-Specific Variables 349
- Acculturation; Racial and Cultural Identity Development; Racial Salience; Loss of Face

Culturally Appropriate Career Counseling Models   351
- Integrative Sequential Model of Career Counseling Services; Culturally
  Appropriate Career Counseling Model; Developmental Approach Career
  Development Assessment and Counseling; Integrative Multidimensional
  Model

Future Research and Theory Development   356
- Key Concepts in Career Counseling Research; Recommendations for
  Future Research

chapter **Fundamentals of Professional School Counseling**   360
17

Foundations of Professional School Counseling   361
- What Is School Counseling?; Brief Historical Background; Professionalism
  for School Counselors

ASCA National Standards   364
- Domain 1: Academic Development; Domain 2: Career Development;
  Domain 3: Personal and Social Development

ASCA National Model   367
- The Foundation; The Delivery System; The Management System; The
  Accountability System; Programmatic Approach: A New Paradigm for
  School Counseling; Collaboration and Systemic Support

The Transforming School Counseling Initiative   371
- Implications for School Counselor Practice; The Counseling Process;
  Consultation; Coordination of Services; Leadership; Advocacy;
  Collaboration and Teaming; Managing Resources; Use of Data

School Counseling in the 21st Century   374
- Functions and Responsibilities of the School Counselor; The Transformed
  School Counselor

chapter **Approaches to Family Counseling**   376
18

Behavioral and Cognitive-Behavioral Family Therapy   378
- Key Concepts in Behavioral and Cognitive-Behavioral Therapy; Role of
  Therapist in Behavioral and Cognitive-Behavioral Therapy; Goals of
  Treatment in Behavioral and Cognitive-Behavioral Therapy; Therapeutic
  Techniques in Behavioral and Cognitive-Behavioral Therapy; Strengths and
  Limitations of Behavioral and Cognitive-Behavioral Therapy

Bowenian Family Therapy 380
- Key Concepts in Bowenian Therapy; Role of Therapist in Bowenian Therapy; Goals of Treatment in Bowenian Therapy; Therapeutic Techniques in Bowenian Therapy; Strengths and Limitations of Bowenian Therapy

Constructivist Family Therapy 383
- Key Concepts in Constructivist Therapy; Role of Therapist in Constructivist Therapy; Goals of Treatment in Constructivist Therapy; Therapeutic Techniques in Constructivist Therapy; Strengths and Limitations of Constructivist Therapy

Experiential Family Therapy 385
- Key Concepts in Experiential Therapy; Role of Therapist in Experiential Therapy; Goals of Treatment in Experiential Therapy; Therapeutic Techniques in Experiential Therapy; Strengths and Limitations of Experiential Therapy

Feminist Family Therapy 387
- Key Concepts in Feminist Therapy; Role of Therapist in Feminist Therapy; Goals of Treatment in Feminist Therapy; Therapeutic Techniques in Feminist Therapy; Strengths and Limitations of Feminist Therapy

Psychodynamic Family Therapy 389
- Key Concepts in Psychodynamic Therapy; Role of Therapist in Psychodynamic Therapy; Goals of Treatment in Psychodynamic Therapy; Therapeutic Techniques in Psychodynamic Therapy; Strengths and Limitations of Psychodynamic Therapy

The Satir Growth Model of Family Therapy 391
- Key Concepts in the Satir Growth Model; Role of Therapist in the Satir Growth Model; Goals of Treatment in the Satir Growth Model; Therapeutic Techniques in the Satir Growth Model; Strengths and Limitations of the Satir Growth Model

Solution-Focused Brief Family Therapy 394
- Key Concepts in Solution-Focused Brief Therapy; Role of Therapist in Solution-Focused Brief Therapy; Goals of Treatment in Solution-Focused Brief Therapy; Therapeutic Techniques in Solution-Focused Brief Therapy; Strengths and Limitations of Solution-Focused Brief Therapy

Strategic Family Therapy 396
- Key Concepts in Strategic Therapy; Role of Therapist in Strategic Therapy; Goals of Treatment in Strategic Therapy; Therapeutic Techniques in Strategic Therapy; Strengths and Limitations of Strategic Therapy

Structural Family Therapy   398
- Key Concepts in Structural Therapy; Role of Therapist in Structural
  Therapy; Goals of Treatment in Structural Therapy; Therapeutic
  Techniques in Structural Therapy; Strengths and Limitations of Structural
  Therapy

Systemic Family Therapy   400
- Key Concepts in Systemic Therapy; Role of Therapist in Systemic Therapy;
  Goals of Treatment in Systemic Therapy; Therapeutic Techniques in
  Systemic Therapy; Strengths and Limitations of Systemic Therapy

chapter

19

Understanding and Assessing Psychopathology   404

Understanding Psychological Disorders   406
- What Is Abnormality?; Models of Abnormality

Assessment of Psychopathology   407
- Diagnostic Classification Systems; The Assessment Process; Gathering
  Information: Written, Verbal, and Observational Methods; Assessment
  Results

The Diagnostic System: Some Considerations   411
- Uses and Advantages of the DSM Classification System; Limitations of the
  DSM System; Dimensional Diagnoses: A New Approach to Diagnosing

Disturbances Related to Anxiety   412
- Approaches to Understanding Anxiety; Generalized Anxiety Disorder;
  Phobias; Panic Disorder; Obsessive-Compulsive Disorder; Stress Disorders

Disturbances With Mood   415
- Approaches to Understanding Depression; Unipolar Depression; Bipolar
  Disorder; Suicide

Disturbances Related to Eating and Weight Loss   418
- Approaches to Understanding Eating Disorders; Anorexia Nervosa;
  Bulimia Nervosa (Binge–Purge Syndrome)

Disturbances in Substance Use   419
- Distinctions Between Abuse and Dependence; Approaches to
  Understanding Substance Abuse; Some Drugs of Choice

Disturbances With Sexuality and Gender Identity   421
- Approaches to Sexual Dysfunction; Sexual Dysfunction; Paraphilias; Gender
  Identity Disorder; Sex Therapy

Disturbances of Psychosis, Memory, and Other Cognitive Functions   424
- Approaches to Understanding Schizophrenia; Symptoms of Schizophrenia;
  Dissociative Disorders

Disturbances in Personality   426
- ■ Approaches to Understanding Problems With Personality; Odd Personality
  Disorders; Dramatic Personality Disorders; Anxious Personality Disorders

Disturbances in Childhood   428
- ■ Approaches to Understanding Childhood Disturbances; Mental Health
  Problems in Childhood; Elimination Disorders; Chronic Disorders
  Beginning in Childhood

Disturbances Related to Aging and Cognition   431
- ■ Problems With Cognition and Neurology in Older Adults; Mood
  Disorders in Older Adulthood

part three

What Are the Fundamental Components of Appraisal and Research That New Counselors Should Use in Their Practice?

                                                                                       433

chapter
20

Foundations of Measurement and Psychometrics   434

Statistics: A Brief Introduction   435
- ■ Ethics in Statistical Research; Differentiation Between Descriptive and
  Inferential Statistics: Some Basics

Descriptive Statistics   436
- ■ Scales of Measurement; Measures of Central Tendency: Mean, Median, and
  Mode; Measures of Dispersion: Range, Variance, and Standard Deviation;
  Distribution; Percentile

Inferential Statistics   441
- ■ Probability; Standard Scores; Tests of Significance

Reliability   445
- ■ Classical Test Theory; Importance of Reliability; Measurement of Reliability;
  Methods of Estimating Reliability; Standard Error of Measurement; The
  Confidence Interval

Validity   449
- ■ Content Validity; Face Validity; Construct Validity; Criterion-Related
  Validity

Test Construction   453
- Methods of Test Development; Writing the Items; Item Try-Out;
  Normative Sample; Writing the Manual

chapter 21   **Testing and Assessment in Counseling Practice**   458

Overview of Assessment   460
- Uses of Assessments; Professional Organizations Supporting Assessment

Assessment Process   461
- Review Referral Information; Decide Whether to Take the Case; Obtain
  Background Information; Consider Systematic Influences; Observe the
  Client in Several Settings; Select and Administer an Appropriate Test
  Battery; Interpret Results; Develop Intervention Strategies; Document the
  Assessment; Meet With Concerned Individuals; Follow Up on
  Recommendations

Cognitive Assessment   463
- Nature of Intelligence; Stanford–Binet Intelligence Test; Wechsler Scales;
  Woodcock–Johnson Scales

Educational Assessment   468
- Achievement Tests; Aptitude Tests; Psychoeducational Test Batteries

Personality Assessment   472
- Rorschach Psychodiagnostic Test; Thematic Apperception Test; Minnesota
  Multiphasic Personality Inventory; MMPI-A; NEO Personality
  Inventory–Revised

Behavioral Assessment   475
- Self-Report; Direct Observation; Behavior Rating Scales

Neuropsychological Assessment   478
- The Mini Mental State Examination; The Wechsler Memory Scale–Third
  Edition; The Halstead–Reitan Neuropsychological Battery

NEPSY   480

Interest in Employment   480
- Strong Interest Inventory; Armed Services Vocational Aptitude Battery;
  General Aptitude Test Battery; Myers–Briggs Type Indicator

Assessment of Organizational Culture   483
- Discussion of Organizational Culture; Job Descriptive Index; Minnesota
  Satisfaction Questionnaire; Organizational Commitment Questionnaire

chapter
22
Quantitative Research Designs   486

Foundations of Research Design   487
- The Hypothesis; Types of Research Hypotheses; The Null Hypothesis; Decision to Reject or Accept the Null; Alpha or Significance Level; Point Estimates and Confidence Intervals; Hypothesis Testing

Experimental Research   491
- Manipulation; Random Assignment; Controlling for Confounds; Treatment Integrity; Manipulation Check; Settings for Conducting Experiments

Experimental Validity   495
- Internal Validity; External Validity

Basic Experimental Design   497
- One Group Posttest Only Design; Treatment–Control Posttest Only; One Group Pretest–Posttest Design; Pretest–Posttest Control Group Design; Posttest Only Design; Treatments and Concomitant Variables; Factorial Designs; Solomon Four-Group Design

Quasi-Experimental Designs   502
- The Nonequivalent Control Group Design; Interrupted Time-Series Design; Counterbalanced Designs; Single Case Experimental Designs; Multiple-Baseline Designs; Alternating Treatments Design and Changing Criterion Design

Nonexperimental Research Designs   507
- Classifications of Independent Variable; Purposes of Nonexperimental Research Design; Types of Nonexperimental Designs; Combining Experimental and Nonexperimental Designs; Interpretation of Nonexperimental Research; Longitudinal Research

chapter
23
Fundamentals of Qualitative Research   512

Roots of Qualitative Research   513
- Cultural Anthropology; Sociology; Education

Meaning in Qualitative Research   514
- The World Is Meaningful; Some Things Are Only Meaningful; Knowledge Depends on Understanding

How to Recognize Qualitative Research   516
- Natural Setting; Holistic Approach; Researcher Involvement

Basic Techniques of Qualitative Research   517
- Observation; Interviews; Participation; Interpretation

Basic Products of Qualitative Research   520
- Ethnography; Case Study; Grounded Theory; Material Analysis

The Role and Future of Qualitative Research in Counseling   524
■ Qualitative Research Tackles Complex Questions and Issues; Counselors and Qualitative Researchers Share Similarities; Qualitative Research Provides Possibility and Freedom

part four

What Are the Special Topics and Important Trends That Counselors Might Encounter?   527

chapter

24

A Look at Consultation   528

Historical Evolution of Consultation   529
■ Clinical or Expert Approach; Organizational Consultation; Client-Centered Consultation; Total Quality Management Approach; Social Work Perspective; Definition of Consultation; The Counselor as Consultant; Stages in Consultation

Theories of Consultation   533
■ Person-Centered Theory of Consultation; Learning Theory of Consultation; Gestalt Theory of Consultation; Psychoanalytic Theory of Consultation; Chaos Theory of Consultation

The Consultation Relationship   535
■ Consultant-Centered Orientation; System-Centered Orientation

Mental Health Consultation   536
■ Definition of Mental Health Consultations; Basic Characteristics of Mental Health Consultation; Psychodynamic Orientation of Mental Health Counseling; Types of Mental Health Consultation

Behavioral Consultation   539
■ Definition of Behavioral Consultation; Characteristics of Behavioral Consultation; Bergan and Kratochwill's Model of Behavioral Consultation

Organizational Consultation   542
■ Definition of Organizational Consultation; Use of Systems Theory; Diagnosing Organizational Problems; Content and Process Consultation; Organizational Paradigm; Paradigm Shift

School-Based Consultation   545
■ Collaboration; Types of School Consultation; Theoretical Approach to School Consultation

Chapter Summary   548

chapter
25

Crisis Intervention in Counseling 550

Understanding Crisis and Crisis Intervention 551
- Definition of Crisis; Types of Crisis; Crisis in Culture; Characteristics of an Effective Crisis Counselor

Differences Among Psychological Emergency, Crisis, and Trauma 555
- Psychological Emergency; Crisis; Trauma

Crisis Response: The Six-Step Model of Intervention 559
- Step 1: Define the Problem; Step 2: Ensure Safety; Step 3: Provide Support; Step 4: Examine Alternatives; Step 5: Make Plans; Step 6: Obtain Commitment

Crisis Assessment: Using the Triage Assessment Form 562
- Assessment of Crisis Reactions; Severity Scales

Trends in Crisis Intervention 564
- Contextual Models; Strength-Based Approach; Systemic Approach

chapter
26

Addictions Counseling 568

Fundamentals of the Addictive Process 569
- The Use–Dependence Continuum; Classifications of Dependence; Progression; Hallmarks of Addictive Behavior; Tolerance and Withdrawal

Models of Addiction 572
- Moral; Medical and Disease; Spirituality; Impulse Control; Genetic; Social Learning; Bio-Psycho-Social; Cultural Implications for Addiction Models

Screening and Assessment 574
- Physiological and Behavioral Assessment; Clinical Interviewing; Psychometric Instruments; Diagnosis and Co-occurring Disorders; Intervention Level Assessment

Intervention and Treatment Considerations 579
- Crisis Management; Stages of Behavioral Change; Treatment Modalities; Beyond Addiction Management; Dual Diagnosis; Pharmacological Interventions; Special Populations; Defining Successful Treatment; Legal, Ethical, and Professional Issues

chapter

27

Ecological-Transactional and Motivational Perspectives in Counseling   586

Background to the Ecological-Transactional Model   587
- Best Practices in Counselor Education: Emphasis on Context and Culture; Deficits of Traditional Theories in Counselor Education

An Ecological-Transactional Developmental Framework   588
- Learning Theory: Vygotsky; Attachment Theory: Bowlby; Bioecological Human Development: Bronfenbrenner

The Ecological-Transactional Model and Professional Counseling   591
- Developmental Psychopathology; Resilience; Assessing Risks and Protective Factors

Self-Determination Theory?   593
- Organismic and Dialectical Underpinnings of Self-Determination Theory; Basic Psychological Needs and the Social Context; Reasons for Nonintrinsic Actions; Motivation

Relating Self-Determination Theory to the Helping Professions   598
- Blocks to Clients' Motivation Toward Change; How Can Counselors Help Motivate Clients for Change?; Empirical Evidence for Self-Determination Theory and Autonomy Support; Recommendations for Providing an Autonomy Supportive Context

Conclusion   603

chapter

28

Neuroscience in Psychotherapeutic Practices   606

Neuroscience and Psychotherapeutic Practices   607
- Neuroscience and Psychotherapy: Early Connections; What Is Neuroscience and Why Is It Important to Therapists?

The Nervous System   607
- Systems Within the Nervous System; Neurons; Action Potential; Autonomic Nervous System

The Brain   609
- The Cerebral Cortex; The Forebrain; Midbrain; Hindbrain

Facilitating Neural Change   613
- How Does Neural Change Occur?; Principles for Brain-Based Psychotherapy; Understanding Schemas; Dealing With Problematic Schemas; Changing View About Incoming Stimuli; Impact of Stress on Neural Change; Utilizing the Hemispheres

Ensuring Lasting Neural Change   616
- Automization of Internalized Processes; Monitoring Change in Client Thinking; Monitoring Change in Clients' Executive State; Techniques for Engaging Emotional States

Clients With Processing Deficits   618
- Effectiveness of Cognitive Remediation Therapy; Cautions When Using Cognitive Rehabilitation

Attention-Related Processing Deficits   619
- Individualizing the Length of Therapy Sessions; Use of Cues

Memory-Related Processing Deficits   620
- Rehearsal; Mnemonic Strategies; Labels, Notebooks, and Calendars; Spaced Retrieval

Executive Functions Deficits   621
- Goal Management Training; Other Approaches to Helping Clients With Executive Functioning Deficits

Summary   622

chapter

29

Developmental Counseling and Therapy   624

Historical Context of Developmental Counseling and Therapy   625
- Influences of Piagetian Cognitive-Emotional Developmental Theory; Influences of Life-Span Developmental Theory; Influences of Postmodern Theory; Influences of Wellness Theory and Research; Impact of Traditional Theories of Counseling and Psychotherapy; Influence of Multicultural Counseling

Underlying Philosophy of Developmental Counseling and Therapy   626
- Developmental Nature of Being; Multidimensionality in Developmental Counseling and Therapy; Cultural Relevancy of Developmental Counseling and Therapy

Modes of Consciousness in Developmental Counseling and Therapy   628
- Sensorimotor-Elemental Style; Concrete-Situational Style; Formal-Operational Style; Dialectic-Systemic Style

Developmental Counseling and Therapy Approach to Wellness   632
- The Indivisible Self: Evidence-Based Model of Wellness; Core Factors of the Indivisible Self

Fundamentals of Systemic Cognitive Developmental Therapy   634
- Defining Disorder from the Systemic Cognitive Developmental Therapy Perspective; Assessment in Systemic Cognitive Developmental Therapy; Treatment in Systemic Cognitive Developmental Therapy

Developmental Counseling and Therapy Techniques: Developmental Strategies Questioning Sequence   636
- Questioning Strategies in the Opening Presentation of Issue; Questioning Strategies in the Sensorimotor-Elemental Style; Questioning Strategies in the Concrete-Situational Style; Questioning Strategies in the Formal-Pattern Style; Questioning Strategies in the Dialectic-Systemic-Integrative Style

Role of the Therapist in Developmental Counseling and Therapy   639
- Precision Matching; Active Engagement of the Therapist

Evaluation of Developmental Counseling and Therapy   640

chapter 30   **Counseling for Wellness**   642

Historical Context of the Wellness Movement   643
- Philosophical Groundwork of Wellness; Counseling-Based Approach to Wellness

Modern Definitions of Wellness   643
- Differentiation Between Health and Wellness; Multiple Understandings of Wellness; Wellness Defined From a Counseling Perspective

Wellness Models   645
- Wheel of Wellness Model; Indivisible Self (IS-WEL): Evidence-Based Model of Wellness

Assessment Tools for Examining Wellness   648
- The Wellness Evaluation of Lifestyle; The Five Factor Wellness Inventory

Counseling for Wellness   650
- Step 1: Introduction of the Wellness Model; Step 2: Assessment of the Components of the Wellness Models; Step 3: Intentional Interventions to Enhance Wellness; Step 4: Evaluation and Follow-Up; Strengths and Limitations

chapter 31   **Spirituality and Pastoral Counseling Practices**   658

The Importance of Spirituality in Counseling   659
- Spirituality in Professional Counseling and Psychology Organizations; Spirituality in American Society

Pastoral Counseling and Related Ideology   660
- Religion and Spirituality; Spirituality and Counseling; Evolution of Pastoral Counseling

Ethics, Spirituality, and Counseling 663
- Ethical Decision-Making Criteria; Purpose of Ethical Codes; Counselor Competence; Supervision

Psychodynamic Theories and Spirituality 665
- Freud and Psychoanalysis; Jungian Psychology

Existential and Phenomenological Theories and Spirituality 667
- Frankl and Logotherapy; May and Existentialism; Rogers and Client-Centered Theory; Perls and Gestalt Therapy

Behavioral Theories and Spirituality 671
- Watson and Behaviorism; Skinner and Behavioral Conditioning; Lazarus and Multimodal Therapy

Cognitive and Cognitive Behavioral Theories and Spirituality 673
- Glasser and Choice Theory; Ellis and REBT

Conclusion 674

appendix
A
**Preparing for the National Counselor Exam:
What You Need to Know** 675

appendix
B
**Your Online Companion in Electronic Case Management:
An Introduction to Penelope Software** 721

appendix
C
**Hints, Helps, and FAQs About Working in a Managed Care
Environment** 731

References 741

Index 785

Preface

THE STORY BEHIND *THE COUNSELOR'S COMPANION*

This book was born out of the belief that having a quick, reference-style resource can provide new counselors not only with valuable information but also with a sense of assuredness and a way to bridge the gap between what they learned in the classroom and the challenges they meet in their practice.

In our interactions with newly graduated counselors and with students soon to be completing their graduate programs, we often hear them express uncertainty about how to proceed after graduation. While they are in the midst of their counseling programs, students are surrounded by support systems. Professors encourage and coach them as they work toward the goal of graduating; supervisors and colleagues at practicum and internship sites provide critical feedback that counselors can rely on to fine-tune their techniques and skills. Yet, once these beginning practitioners are in the field and expected to fulfill their counseling role, they often experience a sense of loss and even can become overwhelmed with questions that arise in their clinical interactions. Each experience with a client may make counselors aware of lapses in their formation. Even if they are able to form a support system similar to the one they had in graduate school, there is still little succinct and practical information available to help counselors who are just getting started.

What students need is a reference tool to help them answer questions and provide them with the support they need after just graduating. This idea of a comprehensive reference book reminded us of similar books used in other fields, such as the *Physician's Desk Reference* (*PDR*) used by doctors or the *Monthly Index of Medical Specialties* (*MIMS*) that aids pharmacists. We both agreed that this type of overall reference book tailored to counseling topics would fill this gap for counselor trainees and so this text was begun.

ORGANIZATION OF *THE COUNSELOR'S COMPANION*

The contents of this book are guided by the core curriculum of the Council for Accreditation of Counseling and Related Programs (CACREP), and information is intentionally presented in brief form so that the main points of each section are concise, clear, visible, and easily accessible. Moreover, the information presented here is a collection of contributions from counselor educators and professionals in the field, each offering a chapter or chapters on the areas of their counseling expertise. The use of various contributors adds a diversity of viewpoints and ensures that knowledgeable and experienced counselor educators and practitioners provide quality content. We hope that this book will become a support system for students who have left their supervisors and teachers behind after graduation.

A wide variety of topics are introduced in this text that familiarize readers with more traditional theories and ideas as well as some cutting-edge areas as seen in the chapter on using neuroscience in counseling and the chapter describing an ecological approach to therapeutic interventions. Students and new counselors will find that this book is an important resource companion for the duration of their educational careers and beyond.

To help readers get acquainted with the layout of the book, we briefly outline the four main parts within which the contents are packaged. Each part is framed by a broad question that we believe new counselors may ask of themselves as they begin their professional endeavors.

Part I asks "What are the primary roles and responsibilities of the professional counselor?" To answer this question, the first part of the book looks at the following areas:

1. On Being a Professional Counselor.
2. The Demands and Obligations of Ethical Counseling.
3. The Legal Intrigues of Counseling Practice.
4. Multicultural Intricacies in Professional Counseling.
5. Supervision, an Essential for Professional Counselor Development.
6. Collaborative Supervision for the Novice Supervisor.

Part II asks, "What are the essential elements of counseling with which all counselors must be familiar?" In response to this question, the second part of the book addresses the following areas:

7. Understanding Human Growth and Development.
8. Counseling Across the Life Span.
9. Major Forces Behind Counseling Approaches.
10. Individual and Social Aspects of the Helping Relationship.
11. The Cultural Kaleidoscope: Eyeing Diverse Populations.
12. Approaches to Group Work.
13. Fundamentals of Group Work.
14. Multicultural Components of Group Work.
15. Counseling in the World of Work.
16. Multicultural Issues in Career and Lifestyle Counseling.
17. Fundamentals of Professional School Counseling.
18. Approaches to Family Counseling.
19. Understanding and Assessing Psychopathology.

Part III asks, "What are the fundamental components of appraisal and research that new counselors should use in their practice?" To answer this inquiry, the third part discusses the following areas:

20. Foundations of Measurement and Psychometrics.
21. Testing and Assessment in Counseling Practice.
22. Quantitative Research Designs.
23. Fundamentals of Qualitative Research.

Part IV asks, "What are the special topics and important trends that counselors might encounter?" In response to this final query, the fourth part addresses the following areas:

24. A Look at Consultation.
25. Crisis Intervention in Counseling.
26. Addictions Counseling.
27. Ecological-Transactional and Motivational Perspectives in Counseling.
28. Neuroscience in Psychotherapeutic Practice.
29. Developmental Counseling and Therapy.
30. Counseling for Wellness.
31. Spirituality and Pastoral Counseling Practices.

SPECIAL FEATURES OF *THE COUNSELOR'S COMPANION*

There are several features and enclosures in this book that make it especially appealing to newly graduating counseling students and beginning practitioners. These aspects transform the book from a text that counselors read to a tool they can readily use.

■ NCE Sample Exam

One of special features of *The Counselor's Companion* is the sample National Counselor Exam (NCE) that is included in Appendix A. Most states today use the NCE as the exam of choice in their licensure process. The types of questions that are posed and the topic areas that are covered in the sample exam are modeled after the NCE, and, as such, the sample exam is an invaluable preparation tool for graduating students and beginning counselors who are aimed at obtaining state licensure.

■ Penelope: Online Case Management Software

Another unique aspect of *The Counselor's Companion* is the cutting-edge software package to which users can subscribe at the introductory price of just $7.95 (for a

120-day trial period) with the purchase of this text. Penelope is an online case management software package suitable for human services professionals that is downloadable or accessible via the World Wide Web. This piece of software is an excellent example of the type of case management program that is utilized in counseling offices and agencies today. By interacting with Penelope, users, and especially newly graduating students, will have the chance to become familiar with how online case management works and increase their marketability as professionals. Penelope offers a multitude of unique features, only a few of which include a system for creating client case notes, assessment tools, billing features, and much more. Appendix B more fully introduces the software and walks users through some of the basic steps in interacting with the program.

■ Tips and Hints for Working in the World of Managed Care

Included in Appendix C is a set of helpful tips and answers to frequently asked questions about practical, day-to-day issues that practitioners encounter, such as, "How do I go about purchasing liability insurance? How do third-party reimbursements take place? How do I get approved as an insurance payee?" Many other similar questions also are addressed.

SENDING YOU FORTH WITH *THE COUNSELOR'S COMPANION*

We hope that readers will find that *The Counselor's Companion* complements their library of counseling books. In its usefulness and indispensability, we believe *The Counselor's Companion* will become the primary reference book for graduate counseling students, beginning counselors, and even practitioners in the field—a text they can access over and over again.

We encourage users to take full advantage of the special features of this book, such as the sample NCE, the opportunity to subscribe to Penelope at a minimal cost, and the helpful hints for working in a managed care environment. Most of all, we hope that *The Counselor's Companion* will be for you a reliable resource and tool that enhances your professional practice, knowledge, and skill as a counselor!

—*Jocelyn Gregoire & Christin M. Jungers*

Acknowledgments

First and foremost, we wish to express our sincere gratitude to all of the contributors who have so willingly offered their time, talents, and expertise in order to enrich the quality of this book. Moreover, their cooperation and conscientiousness helped to ensure that the entire editing process ran smoothly and in a timely manner.

A special vote of thanks goes to Steve Rutter, our editor, whose vision, experience, and excitement helped us to see "outside the box" of possibilities for this book, and also to Nicole Buchmann, our editorial and research coordinator, who provided her valuable input. Both Steve and Nicole have been our greatest supporters throughout the various phases of the writing, editing, and publication processes. A sincere thank also goes to Sara Scudder, the production supervisor, and the copy editing team at LEA, whose hard work and dedication not only contributed to the quality of the book, but also enabled us to stay on schedule with production.

Our appreciation also goes to all those whose input and feedback has been invaluable throughout the process of compiling this manuscript. We would like to thank Jonathan Impellizzeri and Jennifer Dougherty, who diligently helped us to get the manuscripts organized. Thank you, as well, to all those close to us—family and friends—who have supported and encouraged us throughout this process. To each and every one: Your support has been priceless!

Meet the Contributors

Elizabeth Antkowiak is a clinical counselor for the Perinatal Addiction Center, a division of Western Psychiatric Institute and Clinic. She instructs counselors at PAC in applying Dialectical Behavior Therapy to women who are pregnant and dually diagnosed. Elizabeth can be contacted at: antkowiakem@upmc.edu.

Paul Bernstein, PhD, is an Associate Professor at Duquesne University as well as the founder and President of Pennsylvania Psychological Services. He is a certified school psychologist, a licensed psychologist, and a licensed professional counselor. He can be contacted at: bernstein@duq.edu.

Dan-Bush Bhusumane, MEd, is a doctoral candidate in the Counselor Education and Supervision Program at Duquesne University and also teaches at the University of Botswana. He can be contacted at danbushnet@yahoo.com.

Kimberly A. Blair, PhD, is an Assistant Professor in the Department of Psychiatry, University of Pittsburgh School of Medicine. She also serves as the Director of the Matilda Theiss Child Development Center at Western Psychiatric Institute and Clinic, which is part of the University of Pittsburgh Medical Center. Dr. Blair's academic training is in applied developmental and school psychology, with a specialization in early childhood emotional and behavioral disorders. She can be contacted at: blairka@upmc.edu.

Dr. Lancelot I. Brown is an Assistant Professor in the Department of Foundations and Leadership at Duquesne University. His research interests focus on the Caribbean and address the role of school leadership and other organizational and wider systemic factors that impact the effectiveness level of the school. He is an Associate Editor for the journal *Educational Measurement: Issues and Practice*. Lancelot can be contacted at: brownli@duq.edu.

William J. Casile, PhD, is an Associate Professor in the Counseling, Psychology, and Special Education Department at Duquesne University. He also is the coordinator of the doctoral program in Counselor Education and Supervision at Duquesne. Dr. Casile can be contacted by email at: casile@duq.edu.

Pamela Cogdal, PhD, is an Assistant Professor in the Counseling, Educational Psychology and Research Department at the University of Memphis. Dr. Cogdal also serves as the coordinator of psychological assessment for the Center for Rehabilitation and Employment Research. Dr. Cogdal is a licensed psychologist and has been teaching in the field of counseling and counseling psychology since 1989. She can be contacted at the University of Memphis at (901) 678-4931.

Christian Conte, PhD, is an Assistant Professor in the Counseling and Educational Psychology Department at the University of Nevada, Reno. Questions or comments can be directed to conte@unr.edu; or by phone (775) 784-6637 ext 2068.

Hugh C. Crethar, PhD, is an Assistant Professor in the School Counseling and Guidance Program of the Department of Educational Psychology at the University of Arizona. He is on the Executive Board of the National Institute for Multicultural Competence, has served in numerous positions within the American Counseling Association, and is currently President Elect of Counselors for Social Justice. His work centers on promoting multicultural competence and advocacy competence in the field of counseling. He can be contacted at: crethar@email.arizona.edu.

Carol A. Dahir, EdD, is an Associate Professor in counselor education at the New York Institute of Technology (NYIT). Carol has co-authored of *The National Standards for School Counseling Programs (1997), School Counselor Accountability: A Measure of Student Success 2e (2007),* and *The Transformed School Counselor (2006)* and writes and presents extensively about school counseling programs and accountability. Carol can be contacted at NYIT, School of Education, 21 West 60th St. New York, NY 10023, 516 686-7777 or by e-mail at cdahir@nyit.edu

David L. Delmonico, PhD, is an Associate Professor at Duquesne University. He is the Editor-in-Chief of *Sexual Addiction and Compulsivity: Journal of Treatment and Prevention,* as well the co-founder of *Internet Behavior Consulting.* He can be contacted at delmonico@duq.edu.

Dr. Grafton Eliason is an Assistant Professor in the Department of Counselor Education and Services at California University of Pennsylvania. He has taught courses in death, dying, and spirituality and has a special interest in existential philosophy and religion. He also has earned an MDiv from Princeton Theological Seminary and an MEd in School Counseling from Shippensburg University. He is a National Certified Counselor (NCC), Licensed Professional Counselor (LPC) in Pennsylvania, Certified School Counselor (K-12) in Pennsylvania, and he is an Ordained Presbyterian Minister. He can be contacted through email at: graftoneliason@msn.com. Co-authors for Dr. Eliason's chapter are Colleen Triffanoff, a counselor at Thomas Jefferson High School, and Maria Leventis, who is associated with Pace University.

Tara Greene is a doctoral student in the School Psychology Program at Duquesne University. She earned her BS from Allegheny College in Neuroscience and Psychology and her Master's degree from Duquesne University in Child Psychology. She can be contacted by email at: greenet@duq.edu.

L. Jocelyn Gregoire, CSSp, EdD, co-editor of this text, is a Roman Catholic priest and an Assistant Professor in the Counseling, Psychology, and Special Education Department at Duquesne University. Dr. Gregoire splits his time between teaching at Duquesne University and working as a missionary in the Republic of Mauritius in the Indian Ocean. He can be contacted at: gregoire@duq.edu.

Elizabeth J. Griffin, MA, LMFT, is the co-founder of *Internet Behavior Consulting* and works as a therapist, consultant, and trainer in the area sexual addiction. She can be contacted at: ejgrif@aol.com.

Elizabeth A. Gruber is an Associate Professor in the Counselor Education and Services Department at California University of Pennsylvania. She serves as the field coordinator for the clinical experience in the department. She has been at California University since 1988. During that time, she also worked in the University Counseling Center and coordinated their drug and alcohol programs. She is currently a doctoral candidate at Duquesne University. She can be contacted at: Gruber@cup.edu.

Arpana Gupta, MEd, is a doctoral student in the Counseling Psychology program at the University of Tennessee, Knoxville. She obtained her Master's from Wake Forest University in counseling. Her research interests include cultural/racial identity issues, the process of acculturation, stereotype threat, and discrimination experienced by Asian Americans, mental health problems specifically related to suicide in Asian Americans, Asian American public policy, and quantitative research methods such as meta-analyses and structural equation modeling. She can be contacted at: rohit109@yahoo.com.

Erin E. Hardin, PhD, is an Assistant Professor in the Counseling Psychology Program in the Psychology Department at Texas Tech University. She is interested in multicultural psychology, with a focus on cultural differences in the self (e.g., self-construal, self-discrepancy) and implications for both career and personal counseling. She can be contacted at: erin.hardin@ttu.edu.

Stephanie D. Helsel, MS Ed, is pursuing a doctoral degree at Duquesne University, in the Counselor Education and Supervision program. Her clinical work currently is in the areas of chemical dependency as well as employee assistance counseling. She can be reached at: helsels@duq.edu.

Tammy L. Hughes, PhD, is an Associate Professor of School Psychology with Duquesne University and a certified school psychologist. Her work experience includes assessment, counseling,and consultation services in forensic and juvenile justice settings focusing on parent–school–interagency treatment planning and integrity monitoring. She can be contacted at hughest@duq.edu. Coauthors are currently associated with the Duquesne University School Psychology Program and include **Erinn Obeldobel, MS Ed,** EObeldobel@pressleyridge.org, **Susie**

Mclaughlin, EdD, susanbmclaughlin@comcast.net, and **Jamie King, MS Ed,** jmking0522@gmail.com.

Allen E. Ivey, EdD, ABPP is Distinguished University Professor at the University of Massachusetts, Amherst and is Courtesy Professor at the University of South Florida, Tampa. Allen also is the President of Microtraining Associates, Inc., and he is known for defining the microskills of the interview and the integative theory Developmental Counseling and Therapy. He is the author of over 40 books and 200 articles. Dr. Ivey's recent focus is on spirituality in counseling and on neuro-psychotherapy. He can be contacted at: ivey33@comcast.net.

Christin M. Jungers, MS Ed, co-editor of this text, is a doctoral candidate in the Executive Counselor Education and Supervision (ExCES) Program at Duquesne University. She is a Licensed Professional Counselor and a National Certified Counselor. Her research interests lie in the area of aging and adult development as well as counselor identity and development. She can be contacted by email at: chrissyjungers@hotmail.com.

Steven P. Kachmar, MA, is a PhD candidate in the School Psychology Program at Duquesne University. He received his Master of Arts degree in Counseling Psychology from Kutztown University of Pennsylvania in May 2003. His interests include early childhood care and education center quality, appropriate early childhood assessment and intervention, and therapeutic interventions across the lifespan. He can be contacted through email at: skachmar.msn.com.

Barbara Keaton, PhD, is the president and senior consultant of Keaton Resources. She can be contacted through email at: bkeatonphd@msn.com.

Mariellen Kerr is completing her doctoral studies at Duquesne University and can be contacted at mariellenkerr@yahoo.com. She has had the pleasure of serving as an elementary counselor and department head for 16 years and was awarded the Pennsylvania Elementary School Counselor of the Year award for 2006.

Maura Krushinski, EdD, is an Assistant Professor in the Counseling, Psychology, and Special Education Department at Duquesne University. Dr. Krushinski is the Coordinator of the Counseling Department at Duquesne; she also is a Licensed Psychologist, a Licensed Professional Counselor, and a National Certified Counselor. She can be contacted by email at: krushinski@duq.edu.

Stacie A. Leffard, MS Ed, is a doctoral student in the School Psychology Program at Duquesne University. She can be contacted at: sleffard@gmail.com.

Dr. Frederick T. Leong is Professor of Psychology at Michigan State University and is affiliated with the Industrial/Organizational and Clinical Psychology programs. He has authored or co-authored over 100 articles in various counseling and psychology journals, 50 book chapters, and also edited or co-edited 8 books. He is Editor-in-Chief of the *Encyclopedia of Counseling*, which is in preparation. Dr. Leong can be reached at: <u>fleong@msu.edu</u>.

Lisa Lopez Levers, PhD, is an Associate Professor in the Counseling, Psychology, and Special Education Department at Duquesne University. Her research interests include childhood trauma and, more recently, HIV/AIDS in Africa. She can be contacted by email at: <u>levers@duq.edu</u>.

Martin F. Lynch, PhD, is an Assistant Professor at the University of South Florida/ Sarasota-Manatee. He can be contacted by email at: <u>Lynch@banshee.sar.usf.edu</u>.

Jeffrey A. Miller, PhD, ABPP is an Associate Professor as well as the Associate Dean for Graduate Studies and Research at Duquesne University. He also is the Associate Editor for the *Journal of Psychoeducational Assessment*. He can be contacted by email at: <u>millerjeff@duq.edu</u>. **Nate Kegal** and **Julie Williams,** co-authors for Dr. Miller's chapters, are associated with the Duquesne University School Psychology Program.

Rick Myer, PhD, is an Associate Professor at Duquesne University and a licensed psychologist with primary research interests in the area of crisis intervention. He is the developer of the Triage Assessment Model, a tool widely used in crisis intervention. Dr. Myer can be contacted by email at: <u>myerra@duq.edu</u>.

Jane E. Myers, PhD, is a Professor in the Department of Counseling and Educational Development at the University of North Carolina-Greensboro. Jane can be reached through email at: <u>jemyers@uncg.edu</u>.

Sherlon P. Pack-Brown is a Professor in the Mental Health and School Counseling Program at Bowling Green State University, Bowling Green, Ohio. She received her doctorate in guidance and counseling from the University of Toledo, Toledo, Ohio. She is an Ohio licensed professional clinical counselor with supervisory status, a Fellow of the American Counseling Association (ACA), past president of the Association for Multicultural Counseling and Development, and past chair of the ACA Ethics Committee. She can be contacted at: <u>sbrown@bgnet.bgsu.edu</u>.

Sandra A. Rigazio-DiGilio, PhD, is a Professor in the Marriage and Family Therapy Program at the University of Connecticut's School of Family Studies. She can be contacted by email at: <u>srdigilio@comcast.net</u>.

Seth N. Rosenblatt is a doctoral candidate at Duquesne University in Pittsburgh, Pennsylvania where he serves as a counselor supervisor, adjunct professor, university counselor, and advisor. He received his master's degree in Student Personnel Services in Higher Education from Eastern Kentucky University. His dissertation investigates the application of counseling theory and the cognitive exploration process by which personal counseling philosophies are attained. He can be contacted by email at: <u>srosenblatt55@hotmail.com</u>.

Lori Russell-Chapin received her PhD from the University of Wyoming. She is a Professor of Education at Bradley University in Peoria, Illinois where she teaches graduate counseling practicum and internship courses and an introductory counseling survey course. Lori currently is the Associate Dean of the College of Education and Health Sciences. She has been conducting supervision workshops throughout the world. Please contact her at 309-677-3186 and lar@bradley.edu.

Dr. Gary Shank is a Professor of Educational Research at Duquesne University. He is the author of numerous articles on qualitative research and semiotics. He is also the author of *Qualitative Research: A Personal Skills Approach (2nd Ed)* and the co-author of *Exploring Educational Research Literacy* (forthcoming). Dr. Shank can be reached at: shank@duq.edu.

Leslie Slagel, MS Ed, is a doctoral candidate in the Counselor Education and Supervision Program at Duquesne University. She also is employed by the Women's Center and Shelter of Greater Pittsburgh where she counsels abused women. Leslie can be contacted through email at: coofran@aol.com.

Rex Stockton, EdD, is a distinguished Chancellor's Professor of Education at Indiana University, Bloomington. He has spent his career investigating aspects of group dynamics and factors of therapeutic change in groups. He can be contacted by email at: stocktor@indiana.edu.

Carolyn Stone, EdD, is an Associate Professor and co-program leader in the College of Education and Human Services at the University of North Florida. Dr. Stone specializes in the areas of counselor education and school counseling, with an emphasis on ethics and legal issues in school counseling. She is the president of the American School Counselor Association (2006/2007). She can be contacted at: cstone@unf.edu.

Ellen Swaney, MS Ed, has 12 years of experience in career counseling and corporate consulting. She obtained her Master's degree in counseling from Duquesne University, and her Bachelor's degree in business from Indiana University of Pennsylvania. She can be contacted by email at: ellenswaney@adelphia.net.

Thomas J. Sweeney, PhD, is a Professor Emeritus in Counseling and Higher Education at Ohio University. He can be contacted by email at: sweeneyt@ohio.edu.

Leann J. Terry is a doctoral student in counseling psychology at Indiana University, Bloomington. Her research and scholarly interests include group counseling trainings in Africa as a way to address psychosocial needs stemming from HIV/ AIDS and the unmet mental health needs of international students in the United States. She can be contacted at ljterry@indiana.edu or through writing at: 201 N. Rose Avenue, Bloomington, IN 47401.

Carol A. Thomas earned her master's degree in school counseling from Duquesne University and is currently a doctoral candidate in Duquesne University's Counselor Education and Supervision Program. She has worked as Director of School Counseling in the Western Beaver County School District for the last seven years. Carol can be reached by email at: cthomas400@comcast.net.

Laurie Vargas, MS, is a mental health counselor with the San Francisco Unified School District and spends much of her time working with the multi-cultural and social justice issues her families face. She can be contacted by email at: l.vargas@earthlink.net.

part one

What Are the Primary Roles and Responsibilities of the Professional Counselor?

On Being a Professional Counselor

Lisa Lopez Levers
Duquesne University

In This Chapter

▶ *A Brief History of the Counseling Profession*
  - Theoretical Shifts
  - Specialization
  - Professionalization

▶ *The Counselor's Identity*
  - The Diversity of Counselor Identities
  - How Counseling Differs From Psychology and Social Work
  - Characteristics of an Effective Counselor

▶ *Professionalism*
  - Training for Professional Counselors
  - Licensure
  - Certification
  - Professional Associations
  - Advocacy
  - Ethical Principles in Professional Counseling

▶ *Personal Health and Wellness*
  - Countertransference
  - Burnout
  - Networking

A BRIEF HISTORY OF THE COUNSELING PROFESSION

The counseling profession has evolved extensively from its early roots in the last century. These roots are shared with the other schools of helping practices that emerged from the works of 19th-century theoreticians like Freud, Jung, and Adler.

■ Theoretical Shifts

The field has seen four main theoretical phases:

1. Psychodynamic perspectives.
2. Person-centered therapy.
3. Behavioral and cognitive interventions.
4. Systemic and ecologically oriented approaches.

■ Specialization

During the latter half of the last century, counselor education programs moved from a generalized training model for professional counselors to one that emphasizes specialization while still preserving a core counseling curriculum.

■ Professionalization

The momentum toward passing counselor licensure laws across the country was one sign of professionalization. Another was the evolution of an association serving the field. The name changes that the association experienced represent the field's development:

1. The American Personnel and Guidance Association was inaugurated in 1952.
2. The name of the American Personnel and Guidance Association was changed in 1983 to the American Association of Counseling and Development.
3. In 1992, the American Association of Counseling and Development became the American Counseling Association (ACA).

It was not until relatively late in the 20th century that the terms *professional counseling* and *professional counselor* were used, largely to designate a credentialed profession and a licensed professional. The ACA (1997) adopted this definition:

Professional counseling: "The application of mental health, psychological or human development principles, through cognitive, affective, behavioral or systemic interventions, strategies that address wellness, personal growth, or career development, as well as pathology."

THE COUNSELOR'S IDENTITY

Professional counseling is an expanding field, with credentialed counselors providing a variety of mental health and human development services in a multitude of settings. Given such a broad spectrum of helping roles, it is difficult to succinctly characterize what a counselor is. However, some generalizations can be made.

Assumptions About Professional Identity

- Because we live and practice in diverse contexts, counselors strive to develop a mature multicultural perspective, one that includes sensitivity to race, ethnicity, class, gender, ability, religion, sexual orientation, and other issues of diversity.
- Because individual clients are whole persons with multiple and complex social and cultural connections, and because their problems cannot be compartmentalized easily, counselors tend to operate from more or less holistic or ecological frameworks and engage clients in a collaborative counseling process.
- Counselors largely operate from a strengths-based model, even though we routinely assist clients in working through problem areas, often involving diagnosis.
- Counselors are mandated to engage in ethical practices and are bound ethically to maintain confidentiality about clients, although privileged communication varies from state to state, depending on state legal codes.
- Effective counseling relies on the keen ability of the professional counselor to engage in self-reflection.
- Because such a significant portion of preservice training focuses on interpersonal skill building, counselors typically value empathy, trust, respect, therapeutic relationship building, empowerment, and process.

■ The Diversity of Counselor Identities

A number of specialty areas attract professional counselors, who provide services to clients in situations that are highly diverse. The following lists include some of the possibilities.

Specialty Areas

- Clinical mental health.
- Rehabilitation.
- Family and marriage.
- Pastoral counseling.
- Wellness counseling.
- Career counseling.
- School and college counseling.

- Student affairs leadership.
- Sports counseling.
- Consulting on gender issues.
- Gerontology.
- Addictions counseling.
- Forensics.

Specialty Populations

- Children.
- Adults.
- Elders.
- Couples.
- Families.
- Groups.
- Persons with disabilities (physical, developmental, cognitive, and psychiatric).
- Persons who have been traumatized.
- Persons with addictions.
- Persons who are or have been incarcerated.
- Other counseling professionals (clinical and administrative supervision).
- Business and policy organizations (consultation).

Settings

- Community-based agencies.
- Schools and institutions of higher education.
- Nonprofit agencies.
- Governmental organizations.
- Nongovernmental organizations.
- Hospitals.
- Outpatient clinics.
- Rehabilitation centers.
- Nursing homes.
- Respite care facilities.
- Penal institutions.
- Private practices.

■ How Counseling Differs From Psychology and Social Work

Many of the theories and techniques used by professional counselors (discussed elsewhere in this book) are the same as those used by other helping professionals. However, due to epistemological variations among different types of helpers, the ways in which counselors approach the helping process are often paradigmatically different from others. Van Hesteren and Ivey (1990) postulated that counseling falls somewhere between psychology and social work. The differences among the three professions might be explicated as follows:

Psychological paradigm: Approach to the helping relationship that emphasizes the etiology of psychopathology as intrinsic to the individual.

Sociological paradigm: Approach to the helping relationship that focuses on systems.

Professional counseling paradigm: Approach to the helping relationship that pays particular attention to the interface between clients and their cultural and systemic connections, with strong emphasis on interpersonal relationships.

It has been the province of professional counselors to focus on intra- and interpersonal factors, attending to both client risks and resiliencies.

An argument can be made that counseling is a highly interdisciplinary profession, influenced not only by psychology and sociology, but also benefiting historically from the influences of disciplines like education, anthropology, philosophy, theology, other humanities, and the biological sciences. This argument is enhanced by the fact that students matriculate into counseling master's degree programs from a wide variety of undergraduate disciplines (Zimpher, 1996; Zimpher & DeTrude, 1990).

> An argument can be made that counseling is a highly interdisciplinary profession, influenced not only by psychology and sociology, but also benefiting historically from the influences of disciplines like education, anthropology, philosophy, theology, other humanities, and the biological sciences.

Although counseling is a separate mental health and human development profession, there is a great deal of overlap among all helping professionals in terms of what we actually do with clients and in terms of the theories that drive our practices. These similarities and differences have been points of contention within the counseling profession for some time. Interested readers can peruse lengthier discussions on their own (e.g., Gale & Austin, 2003; Hanna & Bemak, 1997; Ivey & Ivey, 1998; Myers, Sweeney, & White, 2002; Skovholt, Rønnestad, & Jennings, 1997; Van Hesteren & Ivey, 1990). It is sufficient to say here that the identity of professional counseling is marked by its emphasis on pluralism and multidisciplinary influences, both in terms of service delivery and professional affiliation, as well as by its focus on clients' interpersonal relationships.

■ Characteristics of an Effective Counselor

The delivery of truly effective professional counseling requires the synthesis and synergy of many professional and personal characteristics. However, one primary and essential characteristic of the effective counselor is the mastery of at least baseline technical competencies. These technical competencies, when used properly, are enhanced by the infusion of certain values commonly adhered to within the profession.

Technical Competencies (Ivey & Ivey, 2003)

- Attending.
- Focusing.
- Listening actively.
- Questioning.
- Observing.
- Reflecting feelings.
- Confronting.
- Interviewing.
- Operating from an ethical framework.
- Influencing.
- Integrating technical skills.

Values

- Respect.
- Understanding.
- Warmth.
- Genuineness and authenticity.
- Client empowerment.

The effective counselor also has a strong knowledge of theory, with a demonstrated ability for application. Multicultural competencies and ethical competencies are infused throughout the counselor's skill level, values, and knowledge base.

The effective counselor is able to move beyond the mere technology of helping to a more tacit dimension. This includes less tangible skills, such as focusing on client meaning making and facilitating whatever form of self-actualization or self-efficacy the client desires or tolerates (Levers, 1997). The counselor must have a complex array of not only technical skills, but also sensitivity, recursion, timing, and maturity to manage this dimension. The counselor demonstrates an attitude of caring by empathy, trust, respect, empowerment, and diversity.

There are no cookbook recipes for addressing the integration of the tacit dimension of counseling with the technology of helping. Perhaps one of the most important nontechnical characteristics of an effective counselor, to embrace this array sufficiently, is therefore the capacity for honest self-reflection and self-discovery. Although some theorists attempt to dichotomize the counseling process as either art or science, the efficacious practice of counseling is probably best represented as a balance between mature self-knowledge and a keen mastery of theory and technique.

PROFESSIONALISM

The professional counseling literature offers divergent discussions of professionalism (e.g., Gale & Austin, 2003; Hanna & Bemak, 1997; Ivey & Ivey, 1998; Myers et al., 2002; Ritchie, 1990; Van Hesteren & Ivey, 1990). Most can agree on the following tenets of professionalism for individual counselors:

- Graduation from an accredited program.
- Acquisition of appropriate credentials.
- Membership in professional associations.
- Adherence to the profession's code of ethics.

See Chapter 5 for more on professionalism.

■ Training for Professional Counselors

The master's degree is the entry level for professional counselors. Most licensure laws and professional certifications require at least a master's degree from an accredited university program, as well as postdegree supervision, to qualify for application. Some licensure laws require additional graduate courses that address specified clinical areas (e.g., the Professional Clinical Counselor credential under Ohio's licensure law).

Some professional counselors return to the university to acquire a doctoral degree—a PhD or EdD—to enhance their clinical skills and theoretical knowledge. The doctoral degree is often a basic requirement for teaching in a university counselor education program (CEP) or in another related program. Nearly all instructors of counselor education have their doctorates; exceptions include when doctoral students teach or supervise master's students in their CEPs, under the supervision of their professors, or when counselors with master's degrees—and usually a lot of clinical experience—teach at universities at the instructor level.

A number of credentialing bodies govern the educational practices associated with the preservice preparation of professional counselors, and numerous credentials qualify counselors to practice.

Accreditation for Counselor Education Programs

- Universities are accredited by regional accrediting bodies—for example, the Middle States, New England, North Central, Northwest, Southern, and Western

Associations of Colleges and Schools—and CEPs are a part of the larger university environment.

- As a part of a school or college environment, usually a school or college of education, CEPs can be accredited, along with their schools or colleges, through the National Council for the Accreditation of Teacher Education or the Teacher Education Accreditation Council.
- If a CEP offers a school counseling program, state department of education accreditation is necessary.
- The accreditations of most specific concern to counselors and counselor educators are those of the Council for Accreditation of Counseling and Related Educational Programs (CACREP) and the Council on Rehabilitation Education (CORE).

CACREP and CORE govern both master's-level and doctoral programs.

 The CACREP and CORE Web sites offer guidelines for rigorous professional curricula and provide standards for academic training.

▶ www.cacrep.org

▶ www.core.org

■ Licensure

According to the ACA (2002), more than 80,000 professional counselors have been licensed throughout the country.

Licensure Requirements

- The applicant must have graduated from a master's or doctoral program in counseling or a closely related field.
- The applicant must have a graduate degree that includes supervised practicum and internship experiences.
- The applicant must have passed an examination.
- The applicant must have had 2 to 3 postdegree years of supervised clinical experience.

Licensure is a mandatory process for counselors who practice in states where the profession has been legally codified; however, criteria vary, depending on whether the law is a title-only law or a practice law. The licensee is responsible for understanding the mandates and restrictions of the particular law.

The primary reason for enacting laws that govern professional practices is to protect consumers. In addition, mental health-related laws, in general, facilitate the consumer's freedom of choice of services.

States Offering Licensure

- The first law aimed at licensing professional counselors in the United States was passed in Virginia in 1976.
- As of the summer of 2004, licensure laws had been passed in 48 states and the District of Columbia.
- Only California and Nevada have not yet passed state laws to license professional counselors (California has a Board of Behavioral Sciences, but it does not have a Professional Counseling Board, nor does it provide for the licensure of professional counselors).

Because so much variability exists across licensure laws, many counselors have experienced great difficulty when moving from one state to another. The American Association of State Counseling Boards (AASCB) has facilitated coordination among the state licensure boards. AASCB and other professional organizations have worked hard on the portability issues surrounding professional counseling credentials. *Portability* of a license means that once the counselor is licensed, he or she can practice with that license in another state without necessarily repeating the full application process. Because it is not unusual for a licensed counselor to move to a new state or practice regionally in multiple states, portability is important for professional development. Counselors need to be able to practice without unreasonable restrictions on mobility. States need to have reciprocal portability agreements, and the National Credentials Registry was recently inaugurated to address the portability needs of the profession.

✔ Keep tabs on the progress being made in coordinating the requirements of state licensure boards at the Web site of the National Board for Certified Counselors.

▶ www.nbcc.org

The American Counseling Association Web site provides information about the licensure laws in individual states.

▶ www.counseling.org

■ Certification

Certification is a voluntary process. Certifications tend to be based on best practice standards, as determined by experts in the particular area of certification. Whereas licensure has legal implications, certification usually is not encoded in the law, except regarding school counselors. All states require school counselors to hold state certifications (Bureau of Labor Statistics, 2004), but this is not the same as the national certification for school counselors.

National Certifications

- The National Certified Counselor, the National Certified School Counselor, and the Master Addictions Counselor, all endorsed by the National Board of Certified Counselors (NBCC).
- The Certified Rehabilitation Counselor, endorsed by the Council for the Certification of Rehabilitation Counselors.
- The Certified Clinical Mental Health Counselor, endorsed by the Academy of Clinical Mental Health Counselors and NBCC.

Obtaining a professional certification involves an application process; the requirements for each type of application are set by the governing body of the specific certification and vary greatly across certifications.

In addition to national certifications, individual states may have state-specific requirements for state-based certification of school counselors, addictions counselors, and those employed at various levels of the mental health service delivery system.

■ Professional Associations

The paramount professional association for counselors is the ACA, although numerous other professional affiliations are also available. Professional associations are important to the individual professional counselor's professional growth and development. Associations keep abreast of current issues in the field, mediate adherence to the professional code of ethics, assist in maintaining necessary levels of training, enhance professional identity, and advocate for needed changes in the field.

Professional Counseling Organizations

- ACA.
- American School Counselor Association (ASCA).
- National Rehabilitation Counseling Association.
- National Rehabilitation Association.

The ACA has 18 divisions under its organizational umbrella, representing a plethora of professional counseling interests.

Divisions of the ACA

- Association for Assessment in Counseling and Education.
- Association for Adult Development and Aging.
- Association for Creativity in Counseling.
- American College Counseling Association.

- Association for Counselors and Educators in Government.
- Association for Counselor Education and Supervision.
- Association for Gay, Lesbian, and Bisexual Issues in Counseling.
- American Mental Health Counselors Association.
- American Rehabilitation Counseling Association.
- American School Counselor Association.
- Association for Spiritual, Ethical, and Religious Values in Counseling.
- Association for Specialists in Group Work.
- Counseling Association for Humanistic Education and Development.
- Counselors for Social Justice.
- International Association of Addiction and Offender Counselors.
- International Association of Marriage and Family Counselors.
- National Career Development Association.
- National Employment Counseling Association.

In addition to the national organization and its divisions, the ACA has regional- and state-level associations and divisions. Most of the individual state associations have their own Web sites, offering more information about state-specific issues and activities.

Other Professional Associations

- Chi Sigma Iota is the international honor society for professional counselors. Membership in the society is contingent on academic achievement in a CEP. The society operates through university-based local chapters and has members throughout the world.
- The American Educational Research Association has Division E for Counseling and Human Development.
- American Psychological Association Division 17 is for counseling psychologists.

 Check out the following Web sites for basic information about each association's membership requirements and activities:

▶ www.counseling.org (ACA)

▶ www.schoolcounselor.org (ASCA)

▶ www.nrca-net.org (National Rehabilitation Counseling Association)

▶ www.nationalrehab.org (National Rehabilitation Association)

▶ www.csi-net.org (Chi Sigma Iota)

■ Advocacy

Client advocacy and professional advocacy are both significant elements of the counseling profession. These two types of advocacy are profoundly interconnected. It is difficult to advocate sufficiently for our clients if we have not advocated adequately for the profession and are therefore operating from a weak professional position.

Many people who seek counseling are marginalized or disenfranchised and might not be in a position to advocate for themselves; therefore, professional counselors often find themselves assuming an advocacy role with clients. Although not all professional counselors are positioned well to assume the role of client advocate, many counselors are attracted to the field precisely out of a strong sense of social justice. For these counselors, a social justice agenda might be nearly inseparable from their counseling objectives.

Altruism is always admirable, and advocating for clients is important. However, we must take a closer look when advocacy transgresses personal boundaries or goes unrecognized as countertransference. Proper clinical supervision can help the counselor avoid potential trouble in this area.

Aspects of Client Advocacy

- Client advocacy might be prompted by the inadvertent neglect of some clients or groups of clients on the part of an organization, agency, or school. It can be remedied easily by drawing attention to the resulting inequity or raising the consciousness of those involved.
- Client advocacy might be prompted by a benign acceptance of a more complex situation.
- Client advocacy might be prompted by cultural and social disparities arising from issues related to race, ethnicity, class, gender, ability, religion, and sexual orientation.

Wherever on the continuum the injustice might be found, counselors can have a profound impact on people's lives. Thus counselors have a duty to maintain dignity, integrity, and ethics while advocating for clients.

Counseling has been around for a long time, and counselors have provided services to people in need for a long time. However, the profession of counseling needs to catch up to other licensed professions in its self-advocacy. One dimension of professionalism is keeping abreast of current affairs that could have an impact on the profession, as well as on the profession's ability to provide quality services to clients.

The ACA, along with other counseling organizations, has initiated advocacy strategies designed to affect policy and legislation surrounding issues that are crucial to the profession.

Professional Advocacy Initiatives

- Of special historical significance is the ACA's 1990 appointment of the Professionalization Directorate, with a vision of guiding the progress of counselors' developing professionalism.
- The Directorate later became the Professionalization Committee, and since then the work of the former Committee has been divided among several of the ACA's national professionalism-related committees.

Counselors must continue to pursue a stronger and better coordinated professional advocacy agenda (Myers & Sweeney, 2004). Individual professional counselors have ample opportunities to become involved with the work of ACA's advocacy committees at state, regional, and national levels.

EXAMPLE

Importance of Advocacy for Counselors

The importance of professional advocacy cannot be overstated, especially in light of the fact that counselors arrived relatively late to the licensure table. Other licensed professionals have ensured that their services were encoded in state laws. Counselors need to attend to this lack of parity; while counselors continue high levels of advocacy for clients, counselors also need to engage in vigorous, systematic, and unrelenting advocacy for the profession.

■ Ethical Principles in Professional Counseling

Adherence to professional ethics is arguably the most important aspect of professionalism with which a counselor must deal on a day-to-day basis. Licensed counselors are required by state licensure laws to adhere to professional ethics.

Ethical Codes for Professional Counselors

- The ethical standards for professional counselors are codified by the *ACA Code of Ethics.* The Code was reauthorized recently (ACA, 2005).
- School counselors adhere to the *ACA Code of Ethics,* as well as the ASCA's (2004b) *Ethical Standards for School Counselors.* State-certified school counselors also must follow state-mandated ethical practices, often derived from ACA and ASCA ethical standards.
- The NBCC (2005b) requires board-certified counselors to adhere to the *ACA Code of Ethics.*

- Certified Rehabilitation Counselors follow the *Code of Professional Ethics for Rehabilitation Counselors,* as established by the Commission on Rehabilitation Counselor Certification (2002).

These various codes govern areas such as the counseling relationship, confidentiality, professional responsibility, relationships with other professionals, evaluation, assessment, interpretation, supervision, training, teaching, research, publication, and methods for resolving ethical issues.

Forester-Miller and Davis (1996) provided an excellent brief discussion of the moral principles on which the codes of ethics are constructed; they also offered a useful seven-step model for ethical decision making. Understanding the underlying moral principles of ethical practice and having a ready model when facing ethical dilemmas can reinforce counselors in maintaining higher standards of professionalism.

See Chapter 3 for more on ethical codes for counselors.

PERSONAL HEALTH AND WELLNESS

Although the work of counselors can be highly fulfilling and rewarding, it also can be challenging and stressful. Counselors see clients who are experiencing varying degrees of problems, dilemmas, and crises. Without a personal sense of wellness, accompanied by healthy outlets for stress, it is easier for counselors to become overburdened or to take on their clients' problems. Many senior members of the profession emphasize the importance of counselors taking care of themselves. The CACREP standards, and by extension, many CEPs, encourage counselors' continued self-development. In the face of stressful work environments, counselors must maintain optimum levels of personal health and wellness.

Refer to Chapter 30 for more information about wellness movements in counseling.

■ Countertransference

Countertransference arises from taking on client problems. It can potentially lead to therapeutic misadventures. It is usually when countertransference goes undetected or is denied that it becomes a potential clinical hazard.

Incidentally, countertransference is not necessarily a negative dynamic; it happens quite frequently in counseling, and the skilled and self-aware practitioner knows how to identify it and then process it with a clinical supervisor. With proper handling, a countertransference event can lead to dynamic and productive interventions with clients.

EXAMPLE

Encountering and Managing Countertransference in Practice

I can provide an example from my own clinical work. I once was counseling a client diagnosed with Borderline Personality Disorder. During one particular session, the client unleashed extreme anger that unnerved me. I began to experience my own anger in response, then caught myself engaging in countertransference. As soon as I was able to identify the countertransference, and quickly process it, my anger was replaced with compassion. I then was able to reframe my perspective on this client and to understand better what it must be like in the client's world—especially how other people receive the client's anger. Immediate acknowledgment and self-reflection about my countertransference response assisted me in understanding my client's dilemma from a more visceral perspective. Failure to understand the countertransference dynamic in this situation could have led to a less productive, or even counterproductive, response.

■ Burnout

When counselors do not take care of themselves—emotionally, spiritually, existentially, or physically—they run the risk of eventual professional **burnout.** Counselors burn out in response to constant levels of high or intense stress.

Effects of Burnout on Personal and Professional Levels

- Burned-out counselors can end up feeling helpless, hopeless, cynical, resentful, and depressed.
- Unchecked professional burnout eventually can affect job performance.
- One's health, career, and relationships with others could be threatened by high levels of stress.
- Unchecked professional burnout also easily progresses to professional impairment.

Counselor impairment is an ethical issue that must be taken seriously and addressed responsibly—by the counselor, by professional peers, and by those involved in supervisory relationships with the impaired counselor.

Counselors who work with survivors of trauma and clients with posttraumatic stress disorder (PTSD) run the risk of experiencing **secondary victimization,** or vicarious trauma. *Vicarious trauma* can occur when bearing witness to the results of extreme or unexpected harm or violence to another person. Counselors who offer trauma counseling need to be vigilant about protecting the integrity of their own emotional and existential constitutions.

In the case of professional burnout or vicarious trauma, the age-old dictum, "Doctor, heal thyself," easily can read "Counselor, heal thyself." The best line of defense is prevention.

Strategies for Preventing Burnout

- Seeking adequate clinical supervision.
- Varying the daily routine.
- Maintaining a healthy sense of humor.
- Having a stress management plan.
- Having a professional development plan.
- Having a personal development plan.
- Seeking personal counseling when needed

Knowing up front that counseling is a high-stress field can help the new counselor to maintain personal health and wellness.

■ Networking

Networking with other professionals is an important aspect of the counselor's sphere of work and contributes to both client advocacy and professional growth. Counselors can find opportunities to network with other professionals at workshops, conferences, and conventions, as well as through their professional associations.

Chapter 1:   Key Terms

- ► Professional counseling
- ► Psychological paradigm
- ► Sociological paradigm
- ► Professional counseling paradigm
- ► Burnout
- ► Secondary victimization

The Demands and Obligations of Ethical Counseling

2

Christian Conte
University of Nevada, Reno

In This Chapter

▶ *The Basics of Ethics in Counseling*
- Definition of Ethics
- Ethical Codes
- Ethical Codes and Cultural Diversity
- Development of Ethical Codes
- ACA Code of Ethics
- Mandatory and Aspirational Ethics

▶ *Ethical Theory*
- Epicureanism
- Utilitarianism
- Kantianism
- Situationalism

▶ *Ethical Principles and Decision Making*
- Nonmaleficence
- Beneficence
- Autonomy
- Fidelity
- Justice
- An Ethical Decision-Making Model

▶ *Common Ethical Concerns for Professional Counselors*
- Confidentiality
- Dual Relationships and Potentially Beneficial Interactions
- Sexual Misconduct
- Transference
- Countertransference

▶ *Summary*

THE BASICS OF ETHICS IN COUNSELING

Ethics defines counseling as much as theory and practice define it. Conscious or not, professional counselors all act under belief systems or ethical positions that help or hinder their clients. Over the course of two millennia, ethical thought in Western civilization has evolved into wide-ranging guidelines that provide a background against which the relationship between counselor and client can be assessed. This chapter provides an overview of ethical thought as it relates to counseling.

■ Definition of Ethics

Counseling is nothing if it is not about character, appropriate as the Greek word *ethos* means character. Ethics can be understood in two contexts:

1. Ethics sometimes refers to the study of morality and specific moral choices.
2. Ethics can be understood as a philosophical discipline concerned with the standards that govern conduct perceived to be acceptable by a culture or society.

Ethical thought related to the counseling profession falls primarily within the second context and has a direct impact on counselors' relationships with their colleagues and their former and current clients. For counselors, **ethics** can be defined as follows:

Ethics: The standards governing the conduct of members of the counseling profession.

■ Ethical Codes

If ethics are the standards that govern conduct, **ethical codes** can be understood in this way (Gladding, 2005):

Ethical codes: The written form of ethical conduct that is intended to improve professionals' ability to successfully and competently respond to clients' needs.

Although not all encompassing, ethical codes provide detailed guidelines to which counselors can refer when making decisions about their own behavior or actions taken on behalf of the client. Thoughtful consideration and implementation of the codes results in the protection of client welfare and the welfare of counseling professionals. The general public gains trust in the integrity of a profession that requires clinicians to live up to an ethical code, and professionals who act within the recommendations of the codes are safeguarded from unfounded lawsuits.

Consequences for breeches of the ethical code also ensure that the counseling process will be safe for the general public. The American Counseling Association (ACA) provides a governing body that establishes and enforces consequences for ethical code violations. Although the ACA has subdivisions, some of which have developed best practices statements, the national branch's ethical codes serve as the quintessential guidelines for all counselors.

■ Ethical Codes and Cultural Diversity

The general public the code of ethics strives to serve is recognizably diverse. Accounting for variances in moral standards, values, and a range of interpretation about human conduct is an important concern in developing ethical standards and codes. Thus, the ethical codes must be rooted in standards that, while mirroring some moral tenets, respect cultural diversity.

EXAMPLE

Cultural Issues and Ethical Codes

Respecting all cultures is a pragmatic contradiction. Some Satanic cultural ideals exonerate torture and pain, whereas the majority of other cultures do not condone such ideals. Incorporating ethical codes that equally consider all cultural codes of conduct is not possible.

■ Development of Ethical Codes

Ethical codes are not static. New research and expanding awareness both contribute to the need for constant revision of the ethical codes.

Revisions of the ACA Code of Ethics and Standards of Practice

- The American Personnel and Guidance Association adopted its first code of ethics in 1961.
- Since the first revision in 1974, the code has been revised every 7 years.
- The latest revision of the *ACA Code of Ethics* was released in 2005.

■ ACA Code of Ethics

The most recent revision of the *ACA Code of Ethics* (2005a) contains eight sections that address the following areas:

1. The counseling relationship.
2. Confidentiality, privileged communication, and privacy.

3. Professional responsibility.
4. Relationships with other professionals.
5. Evaluation, assessment, and interpretation.
6. Supervision, training, and teaching.
7. Research and publication.
8. Resolving ethical issues.

Each section includes an introduction that clarifies the conduct toward which counselors aspire and lets readers know what will be presented in the section. Briefly, goals of the standards outlined in the ACA code can be summarized as follows.

Aims of the ACA Code of Ethics (ACA, 2005a)

- Clarify the nature of ethical responsibility of ACA members.
- Support the mission of the ACA organization.
- Establish principles, ethical guidelines, and best practices for counselors.
- Assist counselors to make the best decisions on behalf of clients and to support the values of the profession.
- Provide a reference against which complaints about counselors can be evaluated.

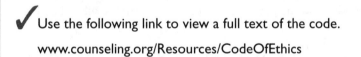

✓ Use the following link to view a full text of the code.

www.counseling.org/Resources/CodeOfEthics

■ Mandatory and Aspirational Ethics

When acting in response to the code of ethics, a difference exists between what a counselor has to do and what a counselor strives to do. That difference is summed up in the concepts of **mandatory ethics** and **aspirational ethics** (Remley & Herlihy, 2001).

Mandatory ethics: The level of functioning counselors must exhibit to fulfill the minimum ethical obligations.

Aspirational ethics: The highest standards of conduct to which counselors aim to meet ethical standards.

The concept of mandatory ethics suggests that there are minimal requirements if counselors are to act ethically. At the same time, the goal of ethical codes generally is not to outline specific behaviors. The following example provides more detail about the distinction between mandatory and aspirational ethics.

E X A M P L E

Intimate Relationships With Clients

Section A.5.a. Current Clients of the ACA Code of Ethics (2005a) states that counselors cannot have sexual intimacies with their clients. This code is a mandatory ethic. In other words, it does not need to be interpreted, only read literally.

A.5.b. Former Clients of the same section, however, describes guidelines by which a healthy length of time (5 years) is needed to pass before it is considered ethical to engage in sexual intimacies with former clients. Although 5 years is clearly stated, this code leaves room for counselors to aspire to make sound ethical choices about the nature of their relationships to former clients. It would be unethical, for example, to prematurely terminate counseling with a client only to begin waiting 5 years with the hope that at the end of that time a sexually intimate relationship can begin. It is hoped that counselors will use aspirational ethics when considering the most beneficial course of action when dealing with such issues.

It is imperative for counselors to contemplate and discuss current ethical issues, although the answers will not always be addressed by a code of ethics. Because codes of ethics are incomplete, counselors can benefit from understanding ethical theories and the ethical principles on which the ethical codes are based.

ETHICAL THEORY

Like counseling theories, ethical theories are the groundwork on which professional counselors build uncompromising clinical practices. The ethical theories presented here span more than 2,000 years and constitute only four of many possible views. Studying ethical theories in greater detail is essential to integrating personal beliefs with sound ethical reasoning.

In general, ethical systems or theories fall into four classes based on their foci, identified as follows:

1. The best interest of the self.
2. The best interest of others.
3. A rational approach that leads to universal principles.
4. The best interest of an individual within a specific circumstance.

■ Epicureanism

Epicurus (341–270 B.C.) advocated an ethical theory that focused on the individual. Tenets of Epicureanism include the following:

- Mental pleasures are emphasized over physical pleasures.
- Balance is the key to happiness.

- Happiness is the supreme good.
- The goal of human activity is pleasure.

Epicureanism as an ethical system is relevant for counselors because it supports phenomenology (i.e., it provides a philosophical rationale for accepting and supporting clients' desires). A drawback for counselors who accept Epicureanism as their ethical system is that they could easily focus on their own, rather than their clients' needs. Also, because Epicureanism technically supports pure relativism, it might be used to justify a client's decision to harm others.

■ Utilitarianism

John Stuart Mill (1806–1873) is an excellent envoy of utilitarian ethical theory. In the context of utilitarianism, performing the greatest good for the greatest number is the core of ethics. Accordingly, an action is considered good if it produces the greatest amount of happiness for the greatest number of people.

Using utilitarian ethical theory can be advantageous for counselors because this viewpoint encourages them to carefully consider whether or not their actions will benefit the maximum number of people. However, strict adherence to utilitarian ethical theory might not be practical if counselors must wait until all possible outcomes have been considered before they act.

■ Kantianism

For Westerners, Immanuel Kant (1724–1804) is the hallmark philosopher of ethics. Kant described a clear method for moral reasoning that can be summed up in this statement: Whatever decision individuals make, they must be comfortable having the decision become a universal law. In other words, people should make ethical decisions based on the principle that, given the same circumstances, everyone in the world would choose the same course of action.

Counselors may benefit from Kantian ethics because this viewpoint will push them to thoroughly evaluate the decisions they make. A criticism of Kantian ethics is that this perspective does not consider cultural differences that call into question the possibility of universal law.

■ Situationalism

In the middle of the 20th century, from the wellspring of contextualism sprang an ethical theory called situationalism. Joseph Fletcher (1905–1991) articulated this perspective in his classic work, *Situation Ethics: The New Morality* (1966). These principles characterize situationalism:

- Ethical decisions take into account individual circumstances.
- Ethical decisions reflect a balance between legalism (law as an absolute) and antinomianism (no laws whatsoever).
- Ethical decisions use maxims and principles as guides rather than answers.

Situationalism as an ethical system provides counselors with two advantages: It allows them to carry their own morals and values into the counseling process without imposing their beliefs on others, and it enables counselors to evaluate unique situations without violating laws or breaking professional codes. A criticism of situationalism is that it has the potential to enable people to rationalize any action, regardless of the consequences for self or others.

ETHICAL PRINCIPLES AND DECISION MAKING

Kitchener (1984) outlined the following five principles that serve as the basis of ethics in the counseling profession act as the foundation on which the *ACA Code of Ethics* is established:

1. Nonmaleficence.
2. Beneficence.
3. Autonomy.
4. Fidelity.
5. Justice.

■ Nonmaleficence

The first ethical principle, **nonmaleficence,** is the keystone of counselors' ethical obligations and can be defined in this way:

> **Nonmaleficence:** The ethical principle stating that counselors should do no harm.

Counselors must not knowingly engage in behavior they know will be harmful to their clients. Harm can come in many forms. Implementing the principle of nonmaleficence means everything from counselors not practicing outside the scope of their competence to counselors not attempting to use techniques that are inappropriate for addressing clients' needs.

■ Beneficence

In addition to the mandate not to cause harm, counselors have an ethical obligation to strive to do something beneficial for their clients.

> **Beneficence:** The ethical principle stating that counselors actively do something good for clients.

Beneficence can be as simple as providing referral numbers to clients who counselors decide they cannot ethically treat. Reading a book a client references time and again in the hope of gaining further insight into the client can also be an act of beneficence. At its zenith, counselors who most effectively uphold the ethical principle of beneficence are authentic and intellectually and psychologically prepared to engage in every counseling session.

■ Autonomy

Autonomy entails creating an atmosphere that allows clients to make well-informed choices about every aspect of their involvement with the therapeutic process. Counselors can adopt the following definition of **autonomy:**

> **Autonomy:** The ethical precept stating that counselors respect clients' right to be self-governed.

Counselors respect the ethical precept of autonomy when they dialogue with clients about treatment options and accept the choices their clients make.

■ Fidelity

The concept of **fidelity** encourages counselors to be honest with clients and faithful to the relationships they have established with them.

> **Fidelity:** The ethical principle stipulating that counselors act faithfully and honestly with their clients.

Counselors can adhere to this principle by being open with their clients. Kell and Mueller (1966) noted that glossing over issues (e.g., "Don't worry, everything will be okay.") trivializes clients' problems and provides a false sense of security that can be detrimental to clients' psychological health.

■ Justice

Counselors who follow the principle of **justice** treat their clients with equal respect for their religion, culture, ethnicity, gender, age, or any variable that visibly or invisibly differentiates clients from themselves. Justice can be defined as follows:

> **Justice:** The ethical precept specifying that counselors act fairly toward all potential, current, and past clients.

An example of implementing justice is granting pro bono service to a client who has no means of providing compensation. The ethical precept of justice ensures counselors strive to interweave equal treatment into every facet of their practice.

EXAMPLE

Giving Advice: Ethical or Unethical?

Have you ever heard of counselors being equated to advice givers? Have you ever heard people say they are going to counseling because they want someone to tell them how to get out of a tough situation?

Giving advice is not a regular part of the counseling process because it breaks the ethical principle of autonomy. If a client takes a counselor's advice and it works, the client is likely to return to the counselor to get further successful advice. This creates a dependence on the counselor, which disregards the client's autonomy. If the counselor's advice works out poorly, on the other hand, the client will likely blame the counselor for the resulting misfortune, thus eschewing responsibility for his or her actions. Either result of advice giving is generally not helpful. It should be noted, however, that never giving advice is an extreme position and also unethical. Many crisis situations warrant providing direct advice to clients to protect the safety of all involved.

The five underlying ethical principles are vital to the counseling profession. Although all five have distinct properties, every ethical dilemma can be viewed in light of these ethical principles. Professional counselors and counselor trainees should know the five underlying ethical principles well.

■ An Ethical Decision-Making Model

The awareness of ethical principles coupled with an ethical decision-making model provides counselors with a systematic way to approach ethical dilemmas. Because ethical decisions are often made in minutes, and sometimes seconds, stopping to reread a step-by-step ethical decision-making model is not practical. Thus, counselors should infuse into their everyday work an ethical decision-making process by which they choose to approach ethical dilemmas.

The following seven-step model, based on the work of Kitchener (1984) and Welfel (2002), is only one of many ethical decision-making models, but it provides a useful, systematic approach to making ethical decisions. The seven steps are as follows:

1. Recognize ethical situations.
2. Play out alternative solutions.
3. Refer to the ACA ethical codes.

4. Consider legal consequences.
5. Seek supervision.
6. Make a choice.
7. Reflect on your decision.

To understand the relevance of an ethical decision-making model, consider the following example; then, visualize applying this model in your own counseling situations.

E X A M P L E

Applying a Model of Ethical Decision Making

A 10th-grade student named Colton arrives in his guidance counselor's office and tells her two other students are picking on him by calling him names. His counselor, Miss Solana, knows the two students well and realizes that she has a good enough rapport with them to convince them to stop picking on Colton.

From her readings, course work, and training, Miss Solana adeptly follows Step 1 because she recognizes this situation as an ethical dilemma. In Step 2, she begins to formulate options. For instance, she realizes that if she approaches the other students, she might in fact help Colton to experience relatively quick relief from his current situation. Also, by addressing the other students, she might send a message, at least to the two antagonists, that bullying will not be tolerated in the school. In providing Colton with quick relief, however, she might also send an underlying message to Colton that he needs to rely on others to solve his problems. Furthermore, by addressing the bullies, it strikes Miss Solana that she will not be providing Colton any insight into what behavior he contributed (if any) to the situation. Lastly, Miss Solana considers that by addressing the bullies, she will not provide Colton with the skills necessary to handle future situations in which he is "picked on."

It is here that following Step 3 can be helpful. The *ACA Code of Ethics* encourages counselors to avoid fostering dependent counseling relationships. Miss Solana must ask then, "Will my decision respect Colton's autonomy?" Next, Step 4 leads her to consider any legal consequences. Applied to this case, gathering information on what specifically was said is the first step. If it turns out that no threats were made, this is not likely to be a situation that warrants legal consultation. Thus considered, Miss Solana can move on to Step 5 and seek supervision. If Colton stopped by her office only briefly, with the intention of sitting down with her at a later time, then she might in reality have an opportunity to seek supervision ahead of time. If not, discussing her decision with her supervisor ex post facto is strongly recommended.

After considering alternative solutions, consulting the ethical codes, taking into account unethical and illegal ramifications, it is time for Step 6: Make a decision and act on it. The final step of the ethical decision-making model, Step 7, entails reflecting on the decision made so that psychological growth might result from the counseling interaction.

Although following a decision-making model might appear to be a linear process, the actual decision-making process is often recursive. Counselors might need to revisit steps of the ethical decision-making model to reach a decision that is in the best interests of the client.

COMMON ETHICAL CONCERNS FOR PROFESSIONAL COUNSELORS

The scope of ethical dilemmas is vast and varied; however, some concerns are more frequently encountered than others. Some common ethical concerns are addressed next.

■ Confidentiality

Most people who have a secret betrayed by a close friend or confidant experience feelings of fear, anger, or sadness; this introduces an element of mistrust into the relationship. Preventing this type of psychological harm is just one reason confidentiality is recognized as an essential component of the counseling process. An equally important reason for maintaining confidentiality is to shield clients from the social stigma that historically has been associated with mental illness. Counselors, therefore, keep disclosed information confidential to assure clients that they are engaging in a safe process.

Confidentiality is not absolute, however, and clients have the right to understand its limits.

Limits to Confidentiality

- Client waiver of privilege for release of information to third parties (e.g., counselors' supervisors).
- Prevention of clear and imminent danger that clients pose to themselves or others.
- Court mandates that confidential information be revealed.

Clients must be made fully aware of the right to and limitations of confidentiality. At the onset of counseling, counselors provide such awareness to clients through a process called informed consent.

Informed Consent

- **Informed consent** is the written and verbal disclosure to clients of what takes place in the counseling process.
- Informed consent should include the purpose, goals, techniques, procedures, limitations, and potential risks and benefits of entering professional counseling.
- Informed consent should not stop after clients give their initial consent; rather, informed consent should be viewed as an ongoing process that holds the welfare of clients and their best interests in the foreground of treatment.

■ Dual Relationships and Potentially Beneficial Interactions

The *ACA Code of Ethics* states that counselors should avoid dual relationships when possible. **Dual relationships** are deleterious to therapeutic relationships because they can compromise counselors' objectivity.

Dual relationship: Any significantly different relationship a counselor has with a client outside of his or her counselor–client relationship.

Recent research, however, appears to indicate that dual relationships might not always be detrimental and at times can even be beneficial (Moleski & Kiselica, 2005). In some rural areas, dual relationships are often unavoidable. In such cases, the goal is not to go to extremes to avoid dual relationships, but rather to be keenly aware of the impact the nontherapeutic relationship has on the therapeutic one. *Section A.5.d. Potentially Beneficial Interactions* recognizes that in some circumstances, clients may profit from an ethically appropriate dual relationship. Engaging in close supervision can help counselors discern the impact of potentially beneficial interactions. Future ethical codes may consider the effect community size and contact inevitability have on dual relationships, but current ethical codes do not.

> Engaging in close supervision can help counselors discern the impact of potentially beneficial interactions. Future ethical codes may consider the effect community size and contact inevitability have on dual relationships, but current ethical codes do not.

Regardless of the stance one takes on dual relationships, **boundaries** in the counseling process must be clearly defined. Boundaries can be understood in this way:

Boundaries: The physical and psychological limits that frame a professional counseling relationship.

Boundaries such as professional language and mannerisms constitute a framework from which a professional relationship can begin and help professionals to establish and maintain objectivity. Clients can feel confused without clear boundaries, whereas counselors often feel overexposed when clear boundaries are not set.

■ Sexual Misconduct

Section A.5.a. Current Clients clearly states that sexual or romantic counselor–client interactions or relationships with current clients, their romantic partners, or their family members are prohibited.

Although clients enter counseling with their whole selves, counselors are encouraged to remain veiled throughout the therapeutic process (Kell & Mueller, 1966). In other words, by offering only relevant self-disclosures, counselors remain blank slates on whom clients project aspects of their unconscious. This is a great responsibility, as clients often project that counselors are capable helpers who only hold the best of intentions. Such projections set up vulnerabilities that do not exist in nontherapeutic relationships. Abusing the vulnerability of clients through sexual misconduct can be detrimental to clients in a number of ways.

Detriments of Sexual Misconduct

- When feelings of trust are used to elicit sexual activity, clients can feel overexposed, guilt ridden, and a general sense of mistrust of others.
- Clients' self-efficacy may become contingent on pleasing their counselors.
- As a whole, sexual activity with clients exploits clients, counselors, and the reputation of the counseling profession (Welfel, 2002).

■ Transference

The concept of **transference** was articulated by Sigmund Freud to specifically refer to the phenomenon whereby people project the dynamics of their response patterns to their parents onto their therapists. Perls (1973) expanded what is meant by transference to encompass all the dynamics of response patterns clients project onto their therapists, not just how clients reacted to their parents.

Transference: Projections clients cast on their counselors.

For example, consider the contemporary client that begins to describe her life using an antiquated form of formal English. If this is not a part of her daily communication to others, she might be transferring onto the counselor the way she responds to perceived authority figures. By recognizing transference, counselors can observe a historical chunk of a person's psyche and raise clients' awareness of their dynamics.

■ Countertransference

Countertransference is the antithesis of transference. The concept can be defined as follows:

Countertransference: Projections counselors cast on their clients.

In general, countertransference occurs when counselors project their own undiscovered psyches onto their clients. For instance, a counselor who experienced abuse in the past might be guarded and unable to empathize with a client who is in counseling to treat his abusive behaviors.

Countertransference is essential to a discussion of ethics because what counselors do not know about themselves can hurt their clients. In other words, when counselors are not aware of what clients stir up in them, their unconscious reactions hold no therapeutic intention, though, as Jung (1957) pointed out, the potential for therapeutic value is present in all human interaction. Countertransference is detrimental to the counseling process because counselor–client interactions are directed by unconscious agendas rather than systematic therapy. Understanding countertransference sheds a new light on the relevance of self-awareness as a vital part of the counseling process.

SUMMARY

The subject of ethics refers to the study of morals and the specific moral choices people make. These choices relate to the standards that govern human conduct that is perceived to be acceptable or not by a culture or society. Ethical codes are the written form of the codes. A written code of ethics provides the public some assurance that professional counselors are held accountable for their professionalism. The *ACA Code of Ethics* is rooted in five underlying ethical principles: nonmaleficence, beneficence, autonomy, justice, and fidelity.

Ethical decisions can best be made through the use of a sound ethical decision-making model. Although following the letter of the law enables counselors to perform mandatory ethics, it is hoped that counselors will follow the spirit of the law and aspire to go above and beyond for their clients. Counselors should avoid multiple relationships with their clients, unless doing so provides a benefit to their clients.

Chapter 2:   Key Terms

- ▶ Aspirational ethics
- ▶ Autonomy
- ▶ Beneficence
- ▶ Boundaries
- ▶ Countertransference
- ▶ Dual relationships
- ▶ Ethics
- ▶ Ethical codes
- ▶ Fidelity
- ▶ Informed consent
- ▶ Justice
- ▶ Mandatory ethics
- ▶ Nonmaleficence
- ▶ Transference

The Legal Intrigues of Counseling Practice

Carolyn Stone
University of North Florida

Christian Conte
University of Nevada, Reno

Elizabeth Antkowiak
Western Psychiatric Institute and Clinic

In This Chapter

▶ *Basics of Professional, Ethical, and Legal Practice for Counselors*
  ■ A Look at Professions, Professionalism, and Professional Identity
  ■ Legal Issues Related to Counselors' Professional Identity
  ■ Ethical Codes and Standards of Practice
  ■ What Is Law?
  ■ Contracts in Counseling: Informed Consent
  ■ Torts and Counselor Negligence

▶ *Professionalism for School Counselors*
  ■ Building Collaborative Relationships
  ■ Facing the Political Barriers of the School System
  ■ Community Standards in School Counselor Practice
  ■ Protecting Students' Best Interests

▶ *Legal and Ethical Aspects of Competence*
  ■ Consultation
  ■ Continuing Education
  ■ Malpractice

▶ *Record Keeping*
  ■ School Records: Family Education Rights and Privacy Act (FERPA)
  ■ ASCA Ethical Guidelines on Educational Records
  ■ Agency Records: Health Insurance Portability and Accountability Act (HIPAA)

▶ *Dual Relationships in School and Community Settings*
  ■ Ethical and Legal Considerations of Dual Relationships
  ■ Complexity of Dual Relationships in Schools
  ■ Safeguarding Clients' Emotional Health

▶ *Confidentiality, Privacy, and Privileged Communication*
  ■ Ethical Standard of Confidentiality
  ■ Confidentiality for School Counselors
  ■ Privacy
  ■ Legal Facets of Privileged Communication
  ■ Duty to Warn: Limit to Privileged Communication
  ■ Duty to Protect

BASICS OF PROFESSIONAL, ETHICAL, AND LEGAL PRACTICE FOR COUNSELORS

Professional counseling in the 21st century is a developing discipline. Because counseling involves working with complex human beings, the rapid growth and many changes the field has experienced since its inception are likely to continue. The professional, ethical, and legal principles that guide school and mental health counselors are especially prone to advancements and evolution. With an emphasis on this area, the aims of this chapter are to highlight professional, ethical, and legal concerns relevant to school and mental health counselors as well as to review legal and ethical obligations with respect to specific areas such as counselor competence, record keeping, dual relationships, and confidentiality.

■ A Look at Professions, Professionalism, and Professional Identity

When talking about the ethical and legal obligations of professional counselors, it is helpful to understand what is meant by both a profession and a professional. Professions often are distinguished from occupations or jobs in that the former tends to center on the betterment of others, whereas the latter tends to focus on the betterment of the self. Additionally, a profession usually is characterized by a body of specialized knowledge that a group of people commit to acquire, sustain, and promote (Sperry, 2007). Professionals, or individuals who commit themselves to a chosen profession, likewise have several notable characteristics. Krushinski (2005) described the characteristics of professionals this way:

Four Traits of Professionals

1. Professionals have a graduate degree.
2. Professionals practice in a field that focuses work on others.
3. Professionals belong to an organization representative of their field.
4. Professionals contribute academically to their fields.

The idea that professions are rooted in a helping mode of behavior sets the foundation for counseling as a profession and counselors as professionals. Professionalism in the counseling field suggests specific responsibilities of school and community counselors.

Obligations of Professional Counselors

- Attend to the welfare of others.
- Serve students' ongoing and ever-changing needs.
- Remain current with the latest research, theory, and techniques.
- Become members of counseling organizations.
- Contribute academically to the profession.
- Attend or present at local, state, and national conferences and workshops.

- Share experiences and clinical progress with both colleagues and the community.
- Adhere to the standards of competency set by the field.

Legal Issues Related to Counselors' Professional Identity

Counselors' professional identity is influenced by a number of legal and, in some cases political, arenas that affect how they represent themselves to the general public and the ways they practice; a few of these areas include job titling, testing and diagnosis, and reimbursement.

Professional counselors have an obligation to accurately represent themselves. Titling, such as "licensed professional counselor," is a legal matter reserved for individuals who have fulfilled licensure requirements established by state licensing boards. Moreover, counselors can only claim expertise in areas in which they received formal professional training. For example, a master's-level counselor who earns a PhD in English literature cannot use the title "Dr." to represent himself or herself as a counselor.

Historically, counselors have had to fight to establish the legal right to engage in testing and diagnosis practices. Yet most counselor education programs require course work in these areas, and counselors long have been involved in the process of testing and diagnosis. There is variation from state to state on counselors' legal right to use tests and diagnose mental and emotional disorders.

In the U.S. health care system, insurance reimbursements are often provided for mental health intervention, and counselors who offer these services have fought to be approved providers by insurance companies. Especially for private practitioners, the ability to receive third-party payment (i.e., from insurance companies) is crucial to their practices and clients.

Ethical Codes and Standards of Practice

Counseling professionals in all settings must comply with the ethical guidelines and legal statutes that bring scrutiny to their conduct. When the welfare of any member or group of the public is at stake, the law ultimately can override ethical guidelines; nonetheless, legal issues are closely tied to and complement ethical guidelines.

Two national organizations that have done a great deal to set the ethical standards counselors follow are the American Counselor Association (ACA) and the American School Counseling Association (ASCA). Adhering to the guidance offered by these organizations through their ethical codes and standards of practice is a means for counselors to avoid potential **liability,** defined as:

Liability: The legal responsibility one person has to another as a result of committing a negligent act.

The codes of these national counseling organizations are mentioned next.

Codes of Ethics in School and Community Practice

- The *Ethical Standards for School Counselors* were developed by ASCA (2004b) to clarify the ethical responsibilities of its members to students, parents, colleagues, the profession, the community, and school counselors.
- The *ACA Code of Ethics* (ACA, 2005a) developed by ACA for community counselors is set forth for the welfare of the public, profession, and individual practitioners.

Counselors have the responsibility to become knowledgeable and understand the ethical standards to which they are bound. Although the codes cannot be all-encompassing or directly address every ethical dilemma, they do serve a number of important purposes.

Functions of Ethical Codes

- Offer guidelines and standards with which counselors must be familiar before beginning their practices.
- Reflect changes in the practice of ethical conduct with which counselors must remain current and to which counselors can turn in times of uncertainty.
- Provide the community with a sense of security essential to a profession.
- Enable the field of counseling to have a composite understanding of such concepts as confidentiality, acceptance, and fairness.

Professionalism means knowing your professional association's codes as well as adhering to them. The ethical standards from ASCA that are most germane to being a professional school counselor are characterized by the following behaviors:

- Avoiding dual relationships when possible.
- Establishing healthy relationships with peers.
- Treating colleagues with respect, courtesy, and fairness.
- Having knowledge of resources for students.
- Establishing clear relationships with students' other counselors.
- Being a gatekeeper in regard to hiring new employees.
- Maintaining well-being.
- Not recruiting students for private practice clients.
- Contributing to the profession.
- Providing mentoring.
- Making sound ethical decisions.

See Chapter 1 for more on professionalism and professional identity and Chapter 2 for more on ethics in counseling.

Check out these sites for a downloadable version of the ASCA and ACA ethical codes:

http://www.schoolcounselor.org/files/ethical%20standards.pdf
http://www.counseling.org

■ What Is Law?

Professional counselors are bound to practice within ethical standards; likewise, counselors also must abide by federal and state laws that govern their professional behavior. Although law in the United States is complex and cumbersome, counselors can benefit from a cursory understanding of the law as it pertains to potential legal ramifications to their practice. Generally, **law** is defined as the rule of conduct established by society and enforced by that society's government. Two distinct types of law exist: **criminal law** and **civil law.** Anderson (1996) described the distinction between these two types of law this way:

> **Criminal law:** Involves crimes punishable by fine, imprisonment, or death and is prosecuted by the government.

> **Civil law:** Includes everything that does not fall under the category of criminal law and is exemplified by lawsuits resulting in sanctions (generally monetary awards).

According to Anderson (1996), counselors find that most of their legal involvements fall under the category of civil law. Contracts and the law of torts also are handled under civil law.

■ Contracts in Counseling: Informed Consent

Contracts are the soul of any commercial transaction (Bullis, 1993), and counseling can in some sense been seen as a commercial transaction, with informed consent serving as the contract between counselors and clients. More important, informed consent defines the basic treatment relationship (Anderson, 1996). It is imperative that clients participate in the process (Bullis) because informed consent is meant to protect clients' legal right to consent to or refuse treatment. Therefore, although informed consent should be written, counselors also have an ethical responsibility to explain the contract verbally. A special consideration with regard to informed consent involves minors, who cannot legally consent to treatment. Counselors are therefore required to obtain parental consent prior to treatment of minors.

E X A M P L E

What Are the Necessary Elements of an Informed Consent Document?

Duffy (2007b) defined at least 10 elements that should be included in an informed consent contract, as follows:

1. Type of treatment that will be offered.
2. Professional qualifications of the therapist.
3. Nature of the confidential client–therapist relationship and exceptions to confidentiality.
4. Risks and benefits of therapy.
5. Treatment alternatives.
6. Right to refuse treatment without recourse.
7. Client's statements of competence and lack of coercion.
8. Office hours, emergency and business contact information.
9. Fee schedule and payment options.
10. Privacy statement.

■ Torts and Counselor Negligence

Torts are civil wrongs recognized by law as grounds for a lawsuit. In regard to the counseling profession, negligent torts occur when counselors harm clients and the clients then seek compensation for the harm done. **Negligence** can be understood as follows:

> **Negligence:** Any conduct that does not meet the minimum requirements for acceptable professional behavior.

Torts essentially fall into the two categories (Anderson, 1996) described here:

1. Unintentional violation may involve counselors not using all of their skill in dealing with clients.
2. Negligence refers to a demonstrated failure to follow all the requirements of a protective statute.

According to Anderson, four factors come into play for plaintiffs pursuing negligent torts.

Factors That Define Counselor Negligence

1. A counselor–client relationship existed.
2. The clinical treatment fell below the minimally acceptable standard of care.
3. An actual loss or injury (harm) occurred.
4. The substandard treatment caused the harm.

PROFESSIONALISM FOR SCHOOL COUNSELORS

All counselors are equally subject to ethical and legal standards within their professional organizations and with respect to the laws of the states in which they practice. Additionally, school counselors have distinct professional responsibilities as a result of the setting in which they practice. In this section we look at some of the unique aspects that come into play in the practice of professional school counseling.

■ Building Collaborative Relationships

Collaboration is a critical skill in the counseling profession but especially critical in the school setting where optimum school counseling programs require that school counselors be part of the leadership team (Idol, Nevin, & Paolucci-Whitcomb, 2000). Relationship development with the principal, teachers, parents, and other stakeholders garners support for counselors and ultimately benefits the students. After all, school counselors need the input of as many stakeholders as possible to deliver programs that have the potential to reach as many students as possible. In difficult political relationships, the key to success is the genuine offering of respect and support to teachers within the sensitive positions in which they must operate.

> Collaboration is a critical skill in the counseling profession but especially critical in the school setting where optimum school counseling programs require that school counselors be part of the leadership team

Collaborative efforts build trust within relationships. Consequently, having firmly established confidences is important. When counselors have to share necessary information, students' privacy rights should be respected. Specifically, this means counselors should only provide germane information to teachers, facilitating their ability to support students' academic and social environments. If counselors are uncertain whether or not principals or teachers will deal deftly with a delicate situation, they should prepare alternative plans. Identifying allies, such as the assistant principal or someone who will use compassion and a nonjudgmental approach to problem solving, will help in the throes of a dilemma (Stone, 2005).

■ Facing the Political Barriers of the School System

Systemic barriers are a daily fact of life for school counselors. Effective school counselors are vigilant in understanding policies, practices, attitudes, and beliefs that stratify students' opportunities and act as systemic change agents to remove these barriers. Failure to understand the political climate will hinder a counselor's efforts to advocate for important policy changes. The ethical school counselor uses finesse and diplomacy to navigate the political landscape and advocate for the needs of students.

■ Community Standards in School Counselor Practice

Community and institutional standards can differ significantly from school to school and community to community. It is difficult to accept the fact that professional behavior varies depending on the prevailing standards of the community; however, it is counselors' ethical obligation to be aware of and respectful toward the standards of the community that the school serves (Stone, 2005).

EXAMPLE

Responding to Teen Pregnancy: Community Considerations

Community standards can have a significant impact on how counselors advocate for their students in moments of crisis. For example, it is acceptable behavior for school counselors in certain schools and communities to refer pregnant students to agencies that assist pregnant minors. Yet, in many other communities this would be considered a serious breach of ethics, infringing on parents' rights to be the guiding voice in their children's lives.

■ Protecting Students' Best Interests

Acknowledging the prevailing standards of a community does not mean unconditionally accepting the standards. School counselors are respectful of the values of their students and their families, diligently separating out their own values and beliefs and offering an objective voice in every situation. If school counselors believe a practice, policy, or law of a particular school or community is in any way detrimental to a student, their ethical imperative is to work in a responsible manner and be change agents to protect students (Stone, 2005). "The professional school counselor supports and protects the educational program against any infringement not in students' best interest" (ASCA, 2004, D.1).

EXAMPLE

Advocating Against Corporal Punishment Standards

If the school's discipline plan and the standards in the community accept the use of corporal punishment, school counselors might have a difficult time beginning the change process needed to promote the well-being of all students, and might also have a difficult time creating an inviting place for students to work. It is the duty of school counselors to explore what would be a good approach to influence the culture and climate of the school. School counselors, for instance, could discuss with the administration the idea of forming a committee to develop a revised discipline approach for the school that helps students feel "invited to work." School counselors could also involve community resources by interviewing supervisors in Child Protective Services to determine what constitutes abuse, the incidence of abuse in the community, the number of students who have been removed from homes for abuse, and per capita the number of children who have died at the hands of parents locally as compared to other parts of the United States. These data can inform and compare two communities in different locations with adverse views on the issue of corporal punishment. By actively directing community members' attention to the controversy of corporal punishment and using advocacy skills, school counselors can ignite important conversations about topics that need to be more thoroughly examined (Stone, 2005).

LEGAL AND ETHICAL ASPECTS OF COMPETENCE

Counselor competence is implied in the professional identity of helping practitioners. At the very least, counselors are charged with complying with minimum ethical standards such as, "Do no harm." However, because counselors are engaged in interpersonal and organizational work aimed at serving others, they should aspire to the maximum levels of competence. A couple recommendations for attaining and maintaining competence are provided first in this section; ethical and legal ramifications of incompetence also are mentioned.

■ Consultation

Mental health counselors who remain isolated in their clinical practice tend to limit their awareness and understanding of the healing process in counseling. Although experience is necessary for professional development, by itself, it is not sufficient for providing effective services to the community. Palmer (1998) noted that teachers who are isolated from each other in individual classrooms run the risk of becoming insipid; in the same way, counselors who are secluded (even for reasons of confidentiality) run a similar risk of limiting their ability to provide effective services. Thus, consultation is an important component of attaining a high level of competence. Counselors need to communicate with other professionals to continually broaden their understanding of counseling, treatment, client issues, and their own involvement in the therapeutic process.

See Chapter 24 for a more in-depth look at consultation.

■ Continuing Education

Continuing education is a means by which counselors can expand their knowledge while engaging in clinical practice and, additionally, ensure their competence as practitioners. Both ethical and legal codes inform the area of continuing education. The *ACA Code of Ethics* (ACA, 2005a), for example, specifies that counselors recognize the need for ongoing education, take the steps necessary to maintain competence in the skills they use, and keep current with the diverse populations with whom they work (*Section C.2.f*). This ethical standard reinforces public confidence in the profession because it ensures that professional counselors will continually strive to be informed on how to provide the best possible level of care.

Credentialing bodies, such as state licensing boards, dictate the legal requirements associated with how much continuing education licensed practitioners are required to have and which programs, workshops, or other activities (e.g., publications) are approved. There is no federal standard that addresses continuing education; therefore, individual states regulate how much continuing education is essential to maintain licensure. Despite state-to-state variability, counselors typically should expect to acquire around 30 continuing education units every 2 years.

■ Malpractice

On the continuum of counselor competence, the extreme of unethical behavior is incompetence, and counselors can be held legally accountable for malpractice. Malpractice includes any harm done to clients due to counselor negligence. Anderson (1996) provided examples of types of malpractice lawsuits that can be brought against counselors. Some of these cases are listed here.

Malpractice Suits Sometimes Brought Against Counselors

- Abuse (physical, sexual, mental) of a client.
- Sexual misconduct.
- Incompetent practice (e.g., practicing outside the scope of professional training, misdiagnosing clients).
- Violations of confidentiality (e.g., communicating information to a third party who has neither need or privilege to have the information).
- Failure to treat or refer clients.
- Breaches of the counselor–client contract.
- Defamation of character.
- Illegal search and seizure (e.g., attempting to unreasonably search a student or community member for drugs).
- Any act involving moral turpitude.

One way to avoid malpractice is to provide both written and verbal informed consent to clients, because it is a statute of case law, not simply an ethical standard (Crawford, 1994).

RECORD KEEPING

Counselors keep records known as case notes to validate the clinical treatment of clients. Record keeping is such an integral part of ethical behavior for counselors that the adage, "If it wasn't charted, it didn't happen" emerged. More important than the adage, however, is that counselors are charged with protecting the contents of client records. Protecting client information is important in both school and community settings. However, because the legislation defining record keeping in these sites is unique, in this section we look at record keeping in both settings.

■ School Records: Family Education Rights and Privacy Act (FERPA)

Ideally, school counselors should not be in charge of managing education records, but they still need a working knowledge of the legal guidelines to support their role in advocating for the legal and ethical protection of any written information kept on a student (ASCA, 2004). The 1974 **Family Education Rights and Privacy Act (FERPA)** is federal legislation that governs education records and dictates how all written information on a student will be handled and disseminated for the protection of the student and his or her family (Alexander & Alexander, 2005; Fischer & Sorenson, 1996; Imber & Van Geel, 2004). FERPA, also known as the Buckley Amendment, is administered by the Family Policy Compliance Office and has enacted safeguards so that parents can access their children's education records and have a voice in how that information is shared with others (Alexander & Alexander, 2005; Fischer & Sorenson, 1996; Imber & Van Geel, 2004).

Purposes of and Protections Outlined by FERPA
(Alexander & Alexander, 2005)

- FERPA was expressly written to identify parents' right to view their children's education records and to decide, within certain parameters, who has access to their child's records.
- Students who are at least 18 years of age or who are in postsecondary school are eligible to access their records.
- Noncustodial and certain stepparents are granted rights under FERPA (20 U.S.C. § 1232g; 34 CFR Part 99).
- The FERPA legislation allows parents and eligible students to request that corrections and amendments be made to records that could be erroneous or potentially misleading.
- FERPA requires that parents be given due process to protest the contents of records when they disagree with the school district about the accuracy of the record.

According to FERPA guidelines, schools must have written permission from parents or the eligible student before any information is released from a student's education record. There are, however, a number of exceptions to the regulations on disclosing information.

Exceptions to FERPA Standards Pertaining to Release of Information

- School officials with legitimate education interest (school counselors are considered school officials along with teachers).
- Other schools to which a student is transferring.
- Officials for purpose of audit or evaluation.
- Persons involved with the financial aid of the student.
- Those involved with conducting specific research studies for the school.
- Organizations involved in accreditation.
- Holders of a judicial order or lawfully issued subpoena.
- Persons involved with emergencies or in cases of health and safety.
- Local and state authorities in the juvenile justice system, in compliance with specific state law.

In addition to the exceptional cases in which release of information is permitted by FERPA, the federal act further allows for the dissemination of *directory information,* or public information on students such as their name, address, or telephone number without parent or eligible student consent. Within certain parameters, FERPA allows states to define what they will classify as directory information. School districts can establish policies and procedures regarding the release of directory information and decide not to participate. It should be noted, however, that the military cannot be excluded from directory information unless a student's parents have signed to opt out of releasing directory information (Alexander & Alexander, 2005).

 Check out the U.S. Department of Education Web site for more information about FERPA at:

http://www.ed.gov/policy/gen/guid/fpco/ferpa/index.html

■ ASCA Ethical Guidelines on Educational Records

The ethical standards from ASCA that are most germane to ethical and legal considerations for educational records pertain to some of the following areas.

ASCA Ethical Guidelines on Student Records

- Maintaining and securing student records, including electronic transmissions.
- Informing parents or guardians of the counselors' role.
- Making reasonable efforts to honor the wishes of parents or guardians.
- Understanding limits and rights of sharing information.
- Conducting appropriate research and protecting students' identity when using data.

■ Agency Records: Health Insurance Portability and Accountability Act (HIPAA)

In April 2003, with the implementation of the federal government's 1996 **Health Insurance Portability and Accountability Act (HIPAA),** protecting clients' records became a federal standard. HIPAA emerged to address the substandard level of care in place to address sharing and releasing of client information. HIPAA forced the Department of Health and Human Services to publish new standards ensuring the protection of clients' physical and mental health information. Essentially, HIPAA guidelines were developed to improve health care organizations by two primary means.

Ways HIPAA Protects Health Care Recipients' Private Information

1. Standardization of how electronic data is transferred and kept (including administrative and financial data).
2. Protection of the confidentiality, integrity, and security of individual health care information through setting and enforcing standards and penalties.

The seriousness with which the HIPAA regulations are enforced for providers of physical and mental health care becomes clear on examination of the fines and penalties associated with breaches of privacy.

Examples of Penalties for HIPAA Violations

- Fines up to $25,000 for multiple violations of the same standard in a calendar year.
- Fines up to $250,000, imprisonment up to 10 years, or both for knowing misuse of individually identifiable health information.

 Check out the U.S. Department of Health and Human Services Web site for HIPAA statutes and regulations at:

http://www.hhs.gov/ocr/hipaa

DUAL RELATIONSHIPS IN SCHOOL AND COMMUNITY SETTINGS

Dual or multiple relationships are potentially harmful to clients in either community or school settings because of the inherent power differential between counselors, who hold the position of power, and clients, who are more vulnerable.

■ Ethical and Legal Considerations of Dual Relationships

Some dual relationships, such as sexual relationships, are recognized as always unethical because they exploit clients' vulnerabilities (Duffy, 2007a). Sexual involvement between therapists and clients, moreover, potentially can represent negligence on the part of the counselor and be grounds for malpractice lawsuits. At the same time, literature on dual relationships also suggests that, at times, multiple relationships between counselors and clients might be unavoidable or potentially beneficial (ACA, 2005a; Duffy, 2007a).

See Chapter 2 for more information about dual relationships in professional counseling.

■ Complexity of Dual Relationships in Schools

The reality of multiple relationships is particularly present in schools. Therefore, counselors must be especially vigilant to maintain a professional distance with students and parents. *Professional distance* is the appropriate familiarity and closeness that a school counselor engages in with students and their family members (Stone, 2005). However, when professional distance is disregarded, dual relationships transpire (ASCA, 2004b, A.4.). For example, accepting an invitation to attend a special event might simply be a show of support for a student who needs to know someone cares. However, when a counselor accompanies this with behaviors such as trying to groom friendships with students and singling out a few on whom to lavish attention, that counselor violates professional distance.

Not only do dual relationships involve an inappropriate boundary crossing, but they also involve personal gains (Stone, 2005). Whereas professional school counselors work vigilantly to ensure that they do not gain any unfair advantages through their work, unethical counselors cross boundaries for personal gain.

Examples of Personal Gains From Boundary Crossing

- Using the dual relationship to boost one's ego or sense of self-worth.
- Using the dual relationship to receive benefits from select parents.

E X A M P L E

Dual Relationships in Schools: Whose Needs Is the Counselor Serving?

It is unethical for school counselors to nourish the belief they are "heroes" in advocating for students, currying favor with students or their parents, or establishing themselves as heroes for students (Stone, 2005). Professional school counselors must continually examine their actions and ask this question: Whose needs are being met by my behaviors? If the answer is "only a select few students with whom I work" or "I am feeding my own personal needs by my behavior," then these counselors are in the midst of a significant ethical violation.

■ Safeguarding Clients' Emotional Health

Both school and community counselors have a duty to guarantee the emotional safety of their minor students or their clients. Dual relationships are to be avoided because they have the potential to harm clients and the counseling profession, as well as put employers in jeopardy (Stone, 2005). Unfortunately, when counselors work in small communities and in closed settings like schools where everyone knows each other, dual relationships might be unavoidable. In such cases, the counselor is responsible for eliminating or reducing the potential for harm.

Safeguards Against Dual Relationships (ASCA, 2004b)

- Informed consent.
- Consultation.
- Supervision.
- Documentation.

CONFIDENTIALITY, PRIVACY, AND PRIVILEGED COMMUNICATION

Whether working in schools or community settings, counselors need to understand the meaning, implications, and limits of confidentiality as defined by their respective ethical standards (e.g., ACA or ASCA). To understand **confidentiality,** counselors also have to have a working knowledge of its legal aspects, encompassed in **privileged communication** and **privacy.** Corey, Corey, and Callanan (2003) defined these three concepts this way:

Confidentiality: An ethical standard that safeguards clients from unauthorized disclosures of information given in a counseling relationship.

Privileged communication: A legal concept that guards against compulsory disclosure in legal proceedings that breaks a promise of privacy.

Privacy: Refers to the constitutional right of people to decide the time, place, manner, and extent of personal disclosure.

■ Ethical Standard of Confidentiality

Confidentiality is first an ethical guideline that charges counselors to protect client disclosures in the therapeutic relationship. The ACA and ASCA codes regarding confidentiality are grounded in ethical principles of beneficence and nonmaleficence.

For more on confidentiality and ethical principles, see Chapter 2.

■ Confidentiality for School Counselors

The legal and ethical complexities of working with minors in schools require that school counselors remain vigilant to the rights and responsibilities of students and their parents, as well as to the implications of these rights on their work (ACA, 2005a; ASCA, 2004b; Imber & Van Geel, 2004). The numerous responsibilities school counselors have in a setting designed to deliver academic instruction further complicate the legal and ethical world of school counseling (Baker & Gerler, 2004; Gibson & Mitchell, 2003; Sink, 2005; Stone, 2001). These complications are acutely present in individual counseling (Thompson, Rudolph, & Henderson, 2004; Vernon, 2004) and even more so in group counseling, where confidentiality cannot be guaranteed and sensitive information about the private world of students and their families is often discussed (Corey, 2004b; Greenberg, 2003).

How School Counselors Can Protect Confidentiality

- School counselors gather informed consent at the beginning of the counseling relationship to inform the counselee of the purposes, goals, techniques, and rules of procedure under which she or he may receive counseling.
- The meaning of confidentiality is explained in developmentally appropriate terms.
- The limits of confidentiality are outlined and include exceptions of danger to self or others and court-ordered disclosures of information.

Confidentiality is difficult in school settings because of the competing interests and obligations that extend beyond the students to parents, administrators, and teachers. Working with clients who are minors poses special considerations with parents but never more so than in a setting designed for academic instruction and not counseling. In some instances, parents might demand and obtain information that their child is discussing.

Generally speaking, school counselors should feel free to discuss relevant but controversial issues with students such as drug and alcohol abuse, sexual experimentation, pregnancy, abortion, and birth control. When engaged in individual and group counseling, professionals must carefully consider the developmental and chronological levels, in loco parentis (to assume the responsibilities of the parents), and parents' rights to be the guiding voice in their children's lives.

EXAMPLE

Implications of Court Rulings on Confidentiality in Schools

In *Parents v. Williams-Port Area School District* (1991) a psychologist could not use his professional confidentiality as a basis for refusing to reveal to parents what was said in an individual counseling session recorded in individual case notes. This decision informs counselors that parents probably have a right to their child's information, especially information that is value laden and revealed to a school counselor in a setting designed for academic instruction. Other court cases have supported the school counselor's confidentiality to the extent possible; however, the courts tell counselors to be ready to defend their competence in addressing issues of interest with a student in isolation of his or her parents.

■ Privacy

Ensuring client privacy is the aim of confidentiality. A basic client right, privacy suggests that clients have the autonomy to choose how and when they will disclose personal information, and, additionally, that they are in control of their private health and mental health records. Thus, counselors must only give germane information when reporting to third-party payees to safeguard clients' privacy.

■ Legal Facets of Privileged Communication

All states have some form of privileged communication, although the details of that communication differ from state to state. Laws that address privileged communication ensure that in legal proceedings, client disclosures of personal information will be protected from exposure by therapists. In other words, based on privileged communication, therapists can refuse to produce a client's records in court. Despite the protections afforded to clients by the law, there are a number of exceptions to privileged communication.

Exceptions to Privileged Information

- A client consents to disclosure.
- Child or elder abuse is occurring.
- A duty to warn exists.
- Legal rules require disclosure.

- A client brings a lawsuit.
- In the case of an emergency.

Typically, groups and family therapy do not fall under privileged communication. Confidentiality, like privileged communication, also has limitations.

See Chapter 2 for more on the limits to confidentiality.

■ Duty to Warn: Limit to Privileged Communication

One of the most well-known and recognized limits to privileged communication is the **duty to warn,** and probably the most well-known legal battle upholding the duty to warn is the 1976 case of *Tarasoff v. Regents of the University of California*. Following the court decisions handed down in *Tarasoff* and similar landmark cases, mandates have been put into place that require mental health professionals to operate under the obligation to warn of clear and imminent danger to the client or any other identifiable persons that is disclosed in the process of counseling.

> **Duty to warn:** The responsibility of a counselor or therapist to breach confidentiality if a client or other identifiable person is in clear or imminent danger.

In situations where there is clear evidence of danger to the client or other persons, the counselor must determine the degree of seriousness of the threat and notify the person in danger and others who are in a position to protect that person from harm (Herlihy & Sheeley, 1988; Pate, 1992). For example, if a student tells the school counselor that another student is planning to commit suicide, the counselor is obliged to investigate and should not leave the indicated student alone until the parents or guardians have arrived (Davis & Ritchie, 1993).

EXAMPLE

Landmark Case: Implications of the *Tarasoff* Decision to the Duty to Warn

The *Tarasoff* case was monumental in the formulation of counselors' duty to warn others of impending danger. On October 27, 1969, Prosenjit Poddar murdered Tatiana Tarasoff. Following her death, Tarasoff's parents claimed that 2 months earlier Poddar had confided his intentions to kill their daughter to Dr. Lawrence Moore, a psychologist who was at that time a member of the staff at the Cowell Memorial Hospital at the University of California at Berkeley. They further claimed that on Moore's request the university police briefly detained Poddar but released him when he appeared, to them, to be rational. Finally, Tarasoff's parents claimed that Moore's supervisor, Dr. Harvey Powelson, directed that no further action needed to be taken to detain Poddar and that no one ever warned them, or Tarasoff, of her impending peril.

■ Duty to Protect

McWhinney, Haskins-Herkenham, and Hare (1992) noted the effects of the *Tarasoff* case, stating that the case imposed an affirmative duty on therapists to warn a potential victim of intended harm by the client. In short, the right to confidentiality ends when public peril begins. This legal decision sets an affirmative duty precedent in cases of harm to others that is generally accepted within the helping professions. According to Davis and Ritchie (1993), this case indicates that contacting the police in the event of a threat does not meet the burden of counselor responsibility under the duty to protect, and this action alone will not safeguard the counselor from lawsuit if the threat is realized. In keeping with ripple effect of these circumstances counselors must diligently and tirelessly labor under the obligation of being sentinels that safeguard others through what was originally labeled a duty to warn about possible harm and is now understood to be a duty to protect from the same threat.

Chapter 3:   Key Terms

- ▶ Liability
- ▶ Law
- ▶ Criminal law
- ▶ Civil law
- ▶ Torts
- ▶ Negligence

- ▶ Family Education Rights and Privacy Act (FERPA)
- ▶ Health Insurance Portability and Accountability Act (HIPAA)
- ▶ Confidentiality

- ▶ Privileged communication
- ▶ Privacy
- ▶ Duty to warn

Multicultural Intricacies in Professional Counseling

Hugh C. Crethar
University of Arizona

Laurie Vargas
San Francisco Unified School District

In This Chapter

▶ *Cultural Influences in Counseling*
  - Influence of Eurocentric Perspectives on Counseling
  - Rationale for a Multicultural Approach in Counseling
  - Multicultural Competencies for Professional Counselors

▶ *Essential Factors in Culture-Sensitive Counseling*
  - Culture Defined
  - Cultural Convergence
  - Etic and Emic Cultural Viewpoints
  - Cultural Encapsulation
  - Ethnocentrism
  - Acculturation and Assimilation
  - Alloplastic and Autoplastic Viewpoints

▶ *Cultural Constructs: A Closer Look*
  - Sex and Gender
  - Sexuality and Affectional Orientation

  - Race
  - Age
  - Ability
  - Religion and Spirituality

▶ *Bias, Prejudice, Discrimination, and Oppression*
  - Bias
  - Prejudice
  - Discrimination
  - Oppression
  - Privilege

▶ *Cultural Identity Development*
  - Racial and Cultural Identity Development Model
  - White Racial Identity Development

▶ *Multicultural Theories in Counseling*
  - Multicultural Counseling and Therapy
  - Benefits of Multicultural Counseling and Therapy

CULTURAL INFLUENCES IN COUNSELING

Our intent in this chapter is to introduce areas of cultural concern that are relevant to counseling professionals by focusing on the contributions of diversity-sensitive literature in the counseling profession. In particular, we will look at the impact of culture on the counseling relationship, provide an overview of key concepts of multicultural counseling, and address multiculturally sensitive approaches to counseling.

■ Influence of Eurocentric Perspectives on Counseling

The United States is a diverse, multicultural, and constantly evolving nation. However, despite numerous peoples and cultures having long coexisted in the United States, European and Western cultures traditionally have held a dominant position in defining cultural norms, rules, laws, and **mores,** or convictions about the moral rightness or wrongness of behavior. Early approaches to counseling, too, have been defined from a Eurocentric perspective and have reflected the customs, values, language, and philosophies of European cultures (Ponterotto & Casas, 1991).

■ Rationale for a Multicultural Approach in Counseling

Although the overwhelming majority of counseling and psychotherapy theories arose from the dominant cultures found in Europe and the United States (Ponterotto & Casas, 1991), increasing attention is being paid to the influence of minority groups and, thus, to the elements of cultural differences in counseling relationships. Ultimately every competent counselor is required to account for social and cultural factors in her or his clinical work. New awareness in the field of counselor education related to the need for a multicultural approach is grounded in a number of rationales for the shift to a multicultural perspective.

Why a Multicultural Worldview Is Necessary

1. Every client comes to the counseling relationship with a worldview that is distinct from that of the counselor due to personal experience within an array of cultural contexts (Ibrahim, 1991; Ivey & Ivey 2007).
2. Without cultural sensitivity, many counselors and psychologists fail to recognize that they are approaching the counseling relationship from a perspective that is quite different from their clientele.

To ground the rationales for adopting multicultural perspectives, one need only consider the example of counselors who might not have gained awareness that the great majority of cultures and societies in the world emphasize a collectivistic rather than an individualistic perception of identity. In cultures that operate out of collectivist values, individualism is seen more as a hindrance to healthy development than as evidence of healthy development (White & Parham, 1990). When working with clients from collectivist-minded backgrounds, counselors who adopt individualist perspectives must recognize the implications of differing values for the counseling process.

■ Multicultural Competencies for Professional Counselors

In an article that was published in both *The Journal of Counseling and Development* and *The Journal for Multicultural Counseling and Development*, Sue, Arredondo, and McDavis (1992) outlined multicultural competencies that are now an integral and foundational part of counselor training programs and practice. The authors outlined a number of rationales for adopting multicultural standards in the counseling field, among them the ever-increasing diversity of the United States and the historical Eurocentric approach to psychological theory. The multicultural standards can be summarized as follows.

Components of the Multicultural Standards for Counselors
(Sue et al., 1992)

1. Awareness of personal assumptions, values, and biases.
2. Knowledge about the worldview of the culturally different client.
3. Ability to develop appropriate strategies and techniques for culturally different clients.

 To download a copy of the multicultural competencies for professional counselors, see

www.counseling.org/Resources

ESSENTIAL FACTORS IN CULTURE-SENSITIVE COUNSELING

In this section, we focus on a review of concepts that provide a framework for talking about and understanding social and cultural approaches to the helping process.

■ Culture Defined

Pedersen (1991) described multicultural counseling as the fourth force in counseling. Today, it can be argued that all counseling is multicultural in nature and that all good counseling is multicultural in perspective (Pedersen). Understanding the complex arena of multiculturalism begins with creating a definition of culture that is suitable to the counseling field. For the purposes of this text, counselors can adopt this definition of culture:

> **Culture:** A combination of learned behaviors, thoughts, and beliefs as well as the results of learned behaviors, thoughts, and beliefs whose components and elements are shared and transmitted by the members of a particular society.

Every society that shares and transmits these factors to its members has a culture. The learned behaviors, thoughts, and beliefs supported by a culture also include some of the more specific dimensions mentioned later (see, e.g., Falicov, 1998; Lewis, Lewis, Daniels, & D'Andrea, 2003; Robinson & Howard-Hamilton, 2000).

Key Dimensions of Culture

- Race or ethnicity.
- Religion and spirituality.
- Language.
- Gender or sex.
- Affectional orientation.
- Age or cohort.
- Physical ability.
- Socioeconomic status.
- Education (formal and informal).
- Experience with trauma.
- Migration history (including region of upbringing).

■ Cultural Convergence

Each of the key dimensions of culture just mentioned is important in its own right and has a unique impact on individuals' experiences; yet, all of the dimensions of culture also overlap, interact, or converge. Robinson and Howard-Hamilton (2000) referred to convergence this way:

> **Convergence:** The phenomenon of overlapping cultural dimensions affecting experience and identity.

The dimensions of culture converge in different ways based on people's experiences, contexts, and interpersonal interactions. To understand culture and the effect it has on clients, counselors must strive to develop clear understandings of each cultural construct as well as awareness of the multiple ways in which the constructs converge.

EXAMPLE

Convergence in a Counseling Relationship

Mayra, a 21-year-old Latina working in child care, comes to a public agency seeking couple's counseling. A culturally competent counselor working with her would need to attend to a number of merging cultural constructs. Mayra is bicultural, as her mother was originally from El Salvador and father was originally from Mexico. A daughter of Spanish-speaking farm workers, Mayra was born and raised in the Central Valley of California. Reared as a Jehovah's Witness, Mayra attended religious services with her family on a weekly basis. She has a high school diploma and is now attending night classes at the local community college to obtain licensure to open her own child-care center. Because seeking help from a counselor is not in concert with the precepts of her religion, once she steps into the counseling office she must face how her actions reflect beliefs differing from those of her parents. Converging issues to consider in this case include (a) language differences (not raised in an English-speaking home), (b) religious differences (not raised in a mainstream Christian religion), (c) social class differences (not middle class), and (d) sex or gender differences (as a woman, she does not have male privilege). As each of these issues has an impact on the reality of Mayra's experiences, a culturally competent counselor needs to take into account each issue as well as the convergence of all issues when selecting a helping approach.

■ Etic and Emic Cultural Viewpoints

Literature that addresses multiculturalism recognizes two primary approaches to the helping process: cultural universality, often referred to as the etic perspective, and cultural relativism, known as the emic perspective. It is useful for counselors to understand the distinction between these approaches.

What Is Cultural Universality?

- **Cultural universality,** or the **etic perspective,** suggests that many aspects of human behavior are universal, and counselors, therefore, can apply therapeutic techniques similarly across cultures and contexts.
- The etic perspective attempts to find universal definitions of health and sickness, normality and abnormality, and effectiveness and ineffectiveness of treatment assessment across cultures.
- Counselors who approach clients from an etic perspective use their own cultural standards as the basis for interpretation.

What Is Cultural Relativism?

- **Cultural relativism,** or the **emic perspective,** suggests that cultural values, worldviews, and contexts all affect definitions of normal and deviant behavior.

- Counselors who function from this perspective are both receptive to and respectful of various cultures' meanings and evaluations of experiences.
- Emic perspectives allow counselors to account for clients' cultural contexts rather than rely solely on universal or even stereotypical assumptions.

Few counseling professionals embrace the extremes of either cultural universality or cultural relativism, as both have validity (Sue & Sue, 2003). Counselors who approach their work from a multicultural perspective maintain the awareness, knowledge, and skills necessary to adjust to multiple cultural and contextual variables, while responding to relatively universal psychological phenomena. Balancing these two approaches, counselors are able to accommodate diverse cultural groups, while acknowledging that their own cultural values come into play in the counseling relationship.

■ Cultural Encapsulation

As are all people, counselors are prone to being culturally encapsulated by their own perceptions and, therefore, hindered in recognizing their biases that may be harmful to clients. Skovholt and Rivers (2004) proposed this definition of cultural encapsulation that counselors can adopt:

> **Cultural encapsulation:** Counselors' reliance on a narrow model of helping that fails to account for cultural values, beliefs, and variables and interprets health and wellness the same across cultures.

Wrenn (1962, 1985) suggested that counselors are vulnerable to the experience of cultural encapsulation when five basic stances are present. The characteristics and behaviors of culturally encapsulated counselors are presented next.

Identifying Behaviors of Culturally Encapsulated Counselors

1. Define truth and reality on a rigidly maintained set of cultural assumptions that is presumed to be constant and unchanging.
2. Become trapped by their particular way of thinking that resists adaptation, rejects alternatives, and is insensitive to perspectives from other cultures.
3. Maintain perspectives based on unreasoned assumptions without proof and regard to empirical reality and, when confronted with evidence contrary to their encapsulated assumptions, ignore or otherwise invalidate the information presented.
4. Fail to carefully evaluate the viewpoints of others when those viewpoints are not similar their own and are not apt to accommodate the needs of others who are different from them.
5. Make judgments of others based on the viewpoint of their own criterion without regard for the cultural context of others.

To challenge culturally encapsulated perspectives and attitudes, counselors can engage in some of the following behaviors.

Ways to Challenge Culturally Encapsulated Perspectives
(Wrenn, 1962, 1985)

- Become aware of personal culture and worldviews.
- Seek out contact with groups of people that are culturally different than oneself.
- Search for ways to recognize unique qualities within various cultures.
- Avoid using one's own group as the standard by which appropriate behavior is assessed.

EXAMPLE

Vulnerability to Being Culturally Encapsulated

One of the challenges to confronting cultural encapsulation is the fact that many of the things people do on a daily basis inherently reinforce its existence. The criteria counselors use in self-referencing fosters ongoing cultural encapsulation because many of the labels that people use to define themselves are based on culturally laden concepts. For example, a man who consistently refers to himself as "self-made" and "independent" is choosing to define himself in terms that highlight specific culturally encapsulated values. In this case, the preferred value is individualism. The value-based use of such labels highlights one cultural perspective while deemphasizing or even denigrating other cultural perspectives (e.g., collectivism). Even if people do not say anything directly negative about another person or culture, their self-descriptions automatically place priorities on certain values, actions, thoughts, and attitudes.

■ Ethnocentrism

Counselors who are culturally encapsulated generally approach clients from an ethnocentric perspective. Ethnocentrism can be defined this way:

> **Ethnocentrism:** The tendency to use one's own cultural standards as the standards by which to evaluate other groups and to rank these standards higher than all others (Berry, Poortinga, Segall, & Dasen, 1992).

■ Acculturation and Assimilation

Although acculturation and assimilation frequently have been used interchangeably, the two terms represent two distinct forms of adaptation. The distinction between acculturation and assimilation can be understood this way (Roysircar-Sodowsy & Maestas, 2000):

> **Acculturation:** Suggests that minority groups adapt to the culture, values, and norms of the dominant group rather than the dominant group adjusting to the presence of the minority group.

> **Assimilation:** Refers to adaptations that are made by the minority group to the norms, values, and culture of the dominant group as well as structural adaptations made by the dominant group to include portions of the culture, values, and norms of the minority group.

Although people who are highly acculturated have adopted the values, norms, language, and behaviors of the core dominant society, the latter does not make any adjustments to meet those of the incoming people. In a fully assimilated society, conversely, members of various groups interact with each other as friends and equals to the extent that even marriage partners are selected without biased regard to ethnic or racial identities. The dominant culture in assimilated societies adjusts to include key elements of the incoming culture.

E X A M P L E

Differences in Assimilating Cultural Groups in the United States

A good example of the variance in how minority groups are assimilated to the dominant culture can be seen by examining the way that U.S. culture has adapted more to Irish customs, culture, and values than to Chinese customs, culture, and values. Despite the fact that large numbers of both populations have resided in the United States for approximately the same amount of time, assimilation has occurred to a greater extent with people of Irish descent than with people of Chinese descent.

◼ Alloplastic and Autoplastic Viewpoints

Related to the concepts of acculturation and assimilation are the concepts referred to as alloplastic and autoplastic viewpoints. The terms define two different levels of adaptation in society.

> **Autoplastic perspective:** Suggests that people focus on adapting to the regulations of the dominant social structure and setting.

> **Alloplastic perspective:** Suggests that people focus primarily on working to adjust society to better fit their needs and preferences.

Counselors may work with their minority clientele to adopt the dominant culture, make adaptations to it, or some combination thereof (Pedersen, 1976). Although intentionality in this viewpoint is important, any choice does not take away from the fact that assimilation will not occur without the dominant society adjusting to meet the norms, values, and behaviors of the incoming culture.

E X A M P L E

Autoplastic and Alloplastic Perspectives

A counselor who encourages her minority clientele to strive for acculturation is working from an autoplastic perspective. She is presuming that it is in the best interest of her clientele to change to fit into society. She is also presuming that mainstream society cannot or should not have to adjust to the diversity that her clientele bring. On the other hand, a counselor who encourages her minority clientele to strive for assimilation will help them develop heightened understanding and sharpened abilities to advocate for structural changes in society around their own culture, values, and norms.

CULTURAL CONSTRUCTS: A CLOSER LOOK

Counselors who strive to be multiculturally competent develop as clear an understanding of cultural constructs as possible. We present here a brief overview of some of the significant concepts that counselors must understand to practice competently.

■ Sex and Gender

Two important areas of cultural consideration are sex and gender. Because of the influence these facets of personhood have on clients' identity development and because of the role that sex and gender can play in the helping relationship, counselors need to be knowledgeable of these constructs. Additionally, counselors can increase their effectiveness in the therapeutic relationship when they are aware of and comfortable with their own sexual and gender identity. Although the terms *sex* and *gender* have at times been used interchangeably, they are distinct concepts and can be differentiated this way:

> **Sex:** The system of sexual classification based on biological and physical differences, such as primary and secondary sexual characteristics, which create the categories of male and female.

Gender: A system of sexual classification based on the social construction of the categories of men and boys and women and girls and usually refers to a person's masculinity or femininity.

Although sex and gender refer broadly to the physical characteristics of men and women or to the social construction of maleness and femaleness, there are also sex and gender groups with more ambiguous characteristics. These groups are known respectively as intersex and androgynous.

Intersex: A person who was born with genitalia, secondary sexual characteristics, or both of indeterminate sex, or with features combined from both sexes. A more archaic and less preferred term for people who are intersex is *hermaphrodite*.

Androgynous: A person who has both feminine and masculine qualities and who may assume female and male roles.

The area of gender, in particular, is receiving increasing attention in the helping field, as professionals are recognizing the impact of gender and gender identity on clients' experiences. The interplay between gender and culture can have a significant effect on the counseling relationship because the meaning of gender and gender roles are socially constructed and may be understood differently by the counselor and the client. Counselors can benefit from being aware of several more concepts related to the area of gender, including gender roles, gender stereotypes, transgender, cisgender, and androcentism.

Gender roles: Behaviors, attitudes, values, emotions, beliefs, and attire that a particular cultural group considers appropriate for males and females on the basis of their biological sex.

Gender role stereotypes: Socially determined models that contain the cultural beliefs about what the gender roles should be.

Transgender: A person whose gender identity does not match her or his assigned gender (gender assignment is usually based on biological physical sex).

Cisgender: People who possess a gender identity or perform a gender role society considers appropriate for one's sex.

Androcentrism: The practice, conscious or otherwise, of placing male human beings or the masculine point of view at the center of one's view of the world and its culture and history.

■ Sexuality and Affectional Orientation

The term *affectional orientation* is preferred today over the more traditional term *sexual orientation,* as it presumes that the orientation of a person's affections goes beyond sexuality.

> **Affectional orientation:** Orientation toward the type of person with whom a given individual is predisposed to bond emotionally and share personal affection.

Although sexual attraction plays a role in affectional orientation, it is not the sum of any relationship; therefore, a broader description of orientation allows for an inclusion of interpersonal affection as significant to the relational bonds people form.

■ Race

Race as a biological construct has become increasingly invalidated and controversial (Jackson & Sellers, 1997); however, it continues to be used as a nominal category within the human service fields (Helms & Cook, 1999). Viewed as an inherently biological construct, Zuckerman (1990) defined race this way:

> **Race:** "An inbreeding, geographically isolated population that differs in distinguishable physical traits from other members of the species" (p. 1297).

Scientists who interpret race biologically have created from as few as 3 categories of race (Caucasoid, Mongoloid, and Negroid) to as many as 200 distinct racial categories, suggesting that there is little agreement on the empirical groundings of race as a biological concept. With the completion of the human genome mapping, scientists have been able to assess genetic differences in racial distinctions and, on review of the empirical studies on race, have concluded that race as a biological construct is fictional, whereas race as a social construct is real (Cornell & Hartmann, 1997; Smedley & Smedley, 2005; Zuckerman, 1990).

Although race is more accurately considered a social construction, understanding the way it interfaces in society is key in developing empathic relationships with clientele. According to West (1993), racial distinctions have long been used as a method to differentiate, distinguish, separate, segregate, and oppress. The constructed variable of race is employed in decisions made by bankers, attorneys, law enforcement, parents, teachers, and policy writers. People make assumptions about others based on perceptions of race and ethnicity on a daily basis. Recently, it has become apparent that racially biased attitudes have evolved from an unconcealed and openly hostile approach to one that is more subtle and ambivalent (Brief, Dietz, Cohen, Pugh, & Vaslow, 2000).

■ Age

In U.S. society, the increasing need for competence in working with the aged is clear. The demographic of the U.S. population is shifting toward growing numbers of older adults, which suggests that counselors need to be aware of the issues and potential biases related to ageism. At the same time, stereotypes and myths about young adults also abound. Thus, the demographic factor of age also is of concern to counselors who work with youth who might experience a type of prejudice known as adultism.

■ Ability

Ability is another cultural dimension that is of immense concern to counselors because the profession is centered on helping individuals who experience impairment on cognitive, emotional, and, at times, physical levels. Ableism is the term that describes prejudice toward persons who are limited in ability. This type of prejudice creates a hostile, unfriendly, or unyielding environment for people whose mental, physical, and sensory abilities are not within the scope of what is defined as socially acceptable.

■ Religion and Spirituality

Although many forms of religious and spiritual bias and oppression exist, one of the most significant in history is that of anti-Semitism. Historically, there are two forms of anti-Semitism, religious anti-Semitism and racial anti-Semitism. Religious anti-Semitism, or anti-Judaism, predominated throughout history up until the mid-19th century. During this period of time, most anti-Semitism was primarily religious in nature, as Judaism was the largest minority religion in Christian Europe, as well as in the Muslim world. This form of prejudice was directed at the religion itself instead of at all people of Jewish ancestry.

By the late 19th century, racial anti-Semitism became the predominant form of prejudice against Jewish people, emerging largely out of conceptualizations of race that were prevalent during the Enlightenment. Racial anti-Semitism was based on the belief that Jewish people were a racially discrete group regardless of religious practice. This form of anti-Semitism effectively replaced the hatred of Judaism as a religion. As a result of this shift, Jewish people as a race became targets of discrimination, segregation, and persecution regardless of religious persuasion.

See Chapter 31 for more information about pastoral counseling and spirituality and counseling.

BIAS, PREJUDICE, DISCRIMINATION, AND OPPRESSION

To effectively treat a diverse population of clients, counselors need to be aware of the influences of bias, prejudice, discrimination, and oppression in their clients' lives. Moreover, counselors themselves consciously have to avoid biased viewpoints so that they can treat clients with the dignity and respect afforded them as humans.

■ Bias

Prejudice, discrimination, and oppression stem from worldviews that are biased. Skovholt and Rivers (2004) suggested that **bias** is a "preference, tendency, or inclination toward particular ideas, values, people, or groups" (p. 31). Bias tends to constrict a person's perspective and can lead to prejudiced beliefs or acts of discrimination.

■ Prejudice

Prejudice refers to generalizations or stereotypical beliefs about a group of individuals that are not grounded in empirical evidence (Skovholt & Rivers, 2004). There are countless examples of the effects of prejudice on minority groups in the United States, some of the most well known of which include prejudice against African Americans, women, and gay and lesbian persons. Like biased views, prejudicial perspectives can lead to misuses and abuses of power as well as overt or covert acts of aggression against groups who are seen as inferior.

■ Discrimination

Characterized by unfair and unequal treatment that systematically prevents certain groups from being afforded opportunities that are provided to other groups, **discrimination** can have deleterious effects (Skovholt & Rivers, 2004). One of the most widely recognized types of discrimination in the United States is racism, which can be defined this way:

> **Racism:** The belief that racial or ethnic groups other than one's own are psychologically, intellectually, or physically inferior (Ridley, 1989).

Racism is based on the view that there are qualitative differences across racial lines. This form of discrimination results in a pattern of behavior that denies access to opportunities or privileges to members of one racial or cultural group while favoring access to another racial or cultural group. There are at least three categories of racism, including individual, institutional, and cultural racism; these are described briefly next.

Types of Racism

1. *Individual racism* is comprised of personal attitudes, beliefs, and behaviors designed to convince oneself of the superiority of her or his race over other races.

Acts of individual racism include various forms of oppression, discrimination, and bias toward others based on conceptions of their race.

2. *Institutional racism* is manifested in the regulations, laws, public policy, and practices in decision making that serve to maintain the social and economic advantage of the racial group currently in power. This is accomplished through oppression, subjugation, and compulsory dependence on the larger society. Institutional racism is commonly legal, or at least customary, and, therefore, is embedded within laws, policy, traditions, and expectations throughout all levels of institutional organizations.

3. *Cultural racism* includes societal beliefs and customs that promote the assumption that the products of the dominant race (e.g., language, traditions, appearance) are superior to those of other races. Cultural racism results in rigid definitions of attractiveness, intellect, and capability and can curtail the range of a person's perceived choices, dreams, privileges, creative expression, and self-actualization.

Although racism is probably the best known type of discrimination, it is by no means the only kind of discrimination that is perpetuated by biased viewpoints and prejudiced beliefs. Some other forms of discrimination relate to a person's sexuality, gender, age, ability, and religion.

Forms of Discrimination

- **Sexism** is the belief that women and men are inherently and qualitatively different, with men being presumed superior to women.
- **Cultural heterosexism** is the stigmatization, repudiation, subjugation, or defamation of sexual minorities within societal institutions.
- **Psychological heterosexism** is the individual internalization of worldviews underlying cultural heterosexism resulting in prejudice against people who are not heterosexual.
- **Homophobia** is the expression of irrational fears about people who exhibit signs of accepting or using behaviors related to same-sex forms of sexual desire and orientation.
- **Affectional prejudice** subsumes homophobia as it incorporates negative attitudes and biases based on affectional orientation, including homosexuality, bisexuality, or heterosexuality.
- **Ageism** is systematic and stereotypic prejudice against people simply because they are old.
- **Adultism** is prejudice and accompanying systematic discrimination against young people.
- **Ableism** is a pervasive system of discrimination and exclusion that oppresses people who have mental, emotional, and physical disabilities.
- **Anti-Semitism** is the systematic discrimination against, hatred, denigration, or oppression of Judaism, Jews, and the cultural, religious, and intellectual heritage of Jewish people.

EXAMPLE

Combating Ableism

Eric is a 37-year-old man seeking counseling for help with career decisions and how his decisions will affect his family. Although Eric has attempted counseling in the past and thought it was not successful, a friend has referred Eric to a licensed marriage and family therapist. During the initial phone call, the therapist asked Eric if he required any modifications, which was a question that no other therapist had ever asked him. Susan, the therapist to whom Eric was referred, was not aware that Eric was born with vision impairment and was considered legally blind even with the aid of glasses. Asking about modifications was standard practice for Susan, who strives to be a culturally competent counselor.

Eric felt it was important to understand how his family history has played a role in his decision-making process. Susan understood that the use of a genogram would be helpful for Eric and designed one using art materials. Following the concepts of a basic genogram, Susan used pipe cleaners to represent males (squares) and females (circles). Sand was used to represent substance abuse and mental health diagnosis. String was used to represent the relationships between family members. Once presented to Eric, he was able to visually see some of the concepts and, most important, feel his family history. Susan understood the importance of being aware of ableism and discussed with Eric how this affected his decisions in the past.

■ Oppression

Counselors who approach their work from a multicultural perspective must take into account the experience of oppression in the lives of the people they serve. Oppression affects the daily realities of most minority groups in a given society and cannot be ignored as a significant part of clients' life experience.

Oppression: The unjust or cruel exercise of authority or power that functions to crush or burden by abuse of power, privilege, or authority; oppression may also be an act of physical or psychological violence that hinders a person from being entirely human or alive (Freire, 1988).

■ Privilege

Intentional oppression occurs when people are oppressive of others through actions they choose, or through choosing to overlook inequities in society. However, oppression also can be unintentional, as is elucidated in the concept of privilege.

Privilege: The state of being preferred or favored in society combined with a set of conditions that systematically empower select groups based on specific variables such as race and gender, while systematically not empowering others.

Counselors from privileged backgrounds commonly have difficulty acknowledging the privilege that they experience because they have been socialized not to recognize the results of privilege. Most White people do not make the effort to understand and respond to the privileges they experience due to their racial status. By ignoring the reality of privilege, White people take part in oppressing people of color and potentially can engage in a form of **unintentional racism**. This difference in rights and privileges is normative in society and commonly overlooked in discussions of racism. Privilege also exists in other arenas of oppression, such as gender differences, class differences, ability differences, and so forth. For a deeper understanding of White privilege, readers are referred to McIntosh (1992), who wrote of an invisible container of 46 unearned assets that a White person can count on cashing in each day, but about which she or he is generally unmindful.

EXAMPLE

White Privilege and the Counseling Relationship

When White privilege is present in the counseling relationship, a counselor may inadvertently harm the relationship and client. A counselor who is not aware of her or his own White privilege might not understand the full impact of the stories that are relayed. For instance, a counselor might not understand how difficult it is to be one of a handful of minorities in a large business and feel as if he or she does not have a voice. Similarly, the counselor might not understand the impact of a family living in an ethnocentric neighborhood having to drive two hours to obtain cultural foods. Culturally competent counselors acknowledge the privilege they hold and their responsibilities to those who are not equivalently privileged. Whether it is race, language, gender, or sexual orientation, the counselor remains aware of how the privilege may or may not impinge on the counseling process.

CULTURAL IDENTITY DEVELOPMENT

To begin to understand others accurately, counselors first need to understand themselves. A key area of awareness for counselors relates to their cultural identity development. Numerous scholars have developed models to clarify the existence of cultural identity development. Historically, these models were limited to describing the transformation that African Americans underwent in developing awareness of themselves as racial beings (Cross, 1972; Jackson, 1975). Cross (1995), for example, developed a model of African American development that begins with viewing the world through the dominant European-American lens, moves to viewing the world based on one's own personal experiences, progresses to full acceptance of the African American culture and nonacceptance of others (particularly European Americans), and culminates with the desire to end racism for all individuals, both people of color and European Americans. More recently, models have been developed that address the identity development of Latinos (Bernal & Knight, 1993), Whites (Helms, 1995), and biracial people (Kerwin, Ponterotto, Jackson, & Harris, 1993). Models such as these function well to aid counselors in understanding the behaviors and attitudes of their clients from culturally different backgrounds.

■ Racial and Cultural Identity Development Model

A few models have been developed that sum up the developmental process of racial and cultural identity (e.g., Atkinson, Morton, & Sue, 1998; Helms, 1995; Sue, Ivey, & Pedersen, 1996; Sue & Sue, 2003). Sue and Sue (2003) developed the racial and cultural identity development model (R/CID). The R/CID integrates the experiences of oppressed people of various racial and cultural backgrounds as they strive to understand themselves in relation to their own culture, the dominant culture, and the interface between these cultures. The model separates cultural identity development into five stages: (a) conformity, (b) dissonance, (c) resistance and immersion, (d) introspection, and (e) integrative awareness. These stages view development as moving from an ethnocentric perspective of self in relation to a multicultural perspective of self in system. A brief outline of each stage is mentioned.

R/CID Stages (Sue & Sue, 2003)

- In the *conformity stage,* people of minority backgrounds hold appreciative attitudes toward the dominant group, while holding deprecating or neutral attitudes toward themselves and others of the same minority group.
- In the *dissonance stage,* people of minority backgrounds are in a state of internal conflict about the dominant group as well as about themselves and others of the same minority group.
- In the *resistance and immersion stage,* people of minority backgrounds become more appreciative of themselves and others of their minority group and are less affirming toward the dominant culture.
- In the *introspection stage,* people of minority backgrounds question the validity of both blanket negativity toward the dominant group and unequivocal appreciation of the minority group.
- The *integrative awareness stage* of development is a period characterized by security in oneself and one's cultural background and selective trust in and appreciation for the dominant group.

The five stages within the R/CID suggest a progression from complete immersion in the dominant culture to complete immersion in the minority culture to, finally, an appreciation of both the minority and dominant cultures.

■ White Racial Identity Development

Racial identity is not limited to people of color. Helms's (1984, 1995) model of White racial identity development allows White Americans to assess their own beliefs and identity development. Helms's model is based on the idea that White Americans have had to acknowledge their own identity. When White Americans move through Helms's stages, they are able to recognize their beliefs about minorities and understand ways in which society views White Americans and people of color as being different. White Americans, then, can have a positive sense of their own culture, be able to question some of society's norms, and ultimately engage in ongoing internal dialogue on racial identity.

MULTICULTURAL THEORIES IN COUNSELING

Despite the increasing diversity that characterizes the United States—a nation where racial and ethnic minorities soon will become the numerical majority (Atkinson, Morton, & Sue, 1998)—traditional counseling theories do not address adequately the complexity of cultural diversity, social context, and ecological perspectives (Sue, 1995). Theories that do address social factors are overlooked in counselor education. The difficulty with approaching counseling relationships only from traditional theoretical approaches is that the worldviews inherent in these perspectives favor individualism and often are at odds with the worldviews of clients who do not embrace or originate from Euro-American cultures (Ibrahim, 1985; Sue et al., 1996). Therefore, the focus of this section is Multicultural Counseling and Therapy (MCT), an approach to understanding human behavior that specifically accounts for factors of culture and diversity.

> The difficulty with approaching counseling relationships only from traditional theoretical approaches is that the worldviews inherent in these perspectives favor individualism and often are at odds with the worldviews of clients who do not embrace or originate from Euro-American cultures.

■ Multicultural Counseling and Therapy

MCT (Sue et al., 1996) was designed as a metatheory (a theory about theories) to help counselors develop an organizational framework for applying the multicultural competencies to the counseling relationship. MCT is based on the accumulation of years of research and theoretical development on counseling clients in a diverse society. A forward-looking theory, MCT is responsive to past data and learning while calling for research to challenge and modify it in the future. The following are some key precepts followed by counselors who use MCT.

Key Behaviors of Counselors Employing MCT

- MCT-oriented counselors work with the clients instead of on the clients, thus helping them to serve as active and equal participants as they coconstruct definitions of both the problems and the goals in the counseling relationship.
- MCT-oriented counselors avoid overemphasizing either cultural differences or cultural similarities but, instead, approach clients from a combined perspective.
- MCT-oriented counselors are aware of and responsive to the fact that salient cultural features (individual, group, or universal) change for clients during counseling, and, thus, track and respond to the various cultural affiliations of their clients instead of presuming stagnant, oversimplified definitions of culture.
- MCT-oriented counselors are aware that cultural identity evolves in response to a person's experiences and context.
- MCT-oriented counselors avoid treating the individual, family, or group in isolation; therefore, the focus of work moves from a more traditional focus on self-concept to a focus on self-in-relation.
- MCT-oriented counselors avoid using theories of identity that disregard cultural context and instead understand that identity is learned within cultural context.
- MCT-oriented counselors realize that the client's perspective must be understood comprehensively and within historical context.
- MCT-oriented counselors realize that a linear approach to thinking is appropriate for some clients, whereas others are best served with a nonlinear approach.
- MCT-oriented counselors differentiate between individual differences and cultural differences.
- MCT-oriented counselors continually strive to expand their repertoire of helping responses as they realize that no single approach is equally effective across all populations and situations.
- MCT-oriented counselors realize that any theory or technique must be approached from a culturally appropriate frame of reference.
- MCT-oriented counselors follow the Golden Rule of counseling: Do unto others as they would have you do unto them. Avoid doing unto others as you would have them do unto you, as they may prefer something very different.
- MCT-oriented counselors approach helping from multiple roles, ranging from one-to-one remedial work to systemic intervention and prevention.

- MCT-oriented counselors value and incorporate Western methods of helping as well as traditional and non-Western methods.
- MCT-oriented counselors focus on developing critical consciousness, or the relation of clients to their entire context, thus teaching their clients about the underlying cultural, sociological, and historical dimensions of presenting concerns and creating potential liberation of consciousness.

■ Benefits of Multicultural Counseling and Therapy

Use of a metatheoretical approach such as MCT provides a number of benefits to culturally sensitive counselors. A few of these advantages are highlighted here:

- Allows for the understanding of multiple oppressions clients might experience.
- Promotes recognition of the collectivist identity crucial to many cultures.
- Allows clients to define wellness within their own context.
- Encourages counselors to recognize the multiplicity of strengths clients bring to bear from their diverse backgrounds.
- Recognizes the numerous roles counselors may have to fill in response to client diversity.

Chapter 4:   Key Terms

- Mores
- Culture
- Convergence
- Etic perspective
- Emic perspective
- Cultural encapsulation
- Ethnocentrism
- Acculturation
- Assimilation
- Autoplastic perspective
- Alloplastic perspective
- Sex
- Gender

- Intersex
- Androgynous
- Gender roles
- Gender role stereotypes
- Transgender
- Cisgender
- Androcentrism
- Affectional orientation
- Race
- Bias
- Prejudice
- Discrimination
- Racism

- Sexism
- Cultural heterosexism
- Psychological heterosexism
- Homophobia
- Affectional prejudice
- Ageism
- Adultism
- Ableism
- Anti-Semitism
- Oppression
- Privilege
- Unintentional racism

Supervision: An Essential for Professional Counselor Development

Lori Russell-Chapin
Bradley University

In This Chapter

▶ *Basics of Clinical Supervision*
- Supervision: A Key to Professionalism
- Benefits of Supervision
- Supervision Defined

▶ *Models of Supervision*
- Developmental Models of Supervision
- Theory-Specific Supervision Models
- Social Role Models of Supervision: Discrimination Model
- Integrated Model of Supervision
- A Supervision Videotaping Method: Interpersonal Process Recall

---

BASICS OF CLINICAL SUPERVISION

The counseling profession, like any discipline offering a public service, has a responsibility to assess continually its quality of service. Likewise, individual counselors have the responsibility to analyze the degree to which counseling helps clients and to evaluate the overall effectiveness and outcome of the counseling process (Nugent, 1990).

One of the most exciting and fruitful methods of achieving this professional attitude and behavior is to engage in clinical supervision throughout the life span of a counseling career.

■ Supervision: A Key to Professionalism

For many counselors, clinical supervision begins in graduate school, and once the program of study is completed, so too are the days of supervision. However, as Neukrug (2003) so eloquently stated:

> Embracing a professional lifestyle does not end once one finishes graduate school, obtains a job, becomes licensed, has ten years of experience or becomes a "master" therapist. It is a lifelong commitment to a way of being, a way that says you are constantly striving to make yourself a better person and a more effective counselor, committed to professional activities. (p. 72)

Engaging in regular clinical supervision is one method of maintaining and regulating counseling performance for the counselor and consumer. Additionally, many counselors enhance their professionalism by becoming credentialed supervisors who guide new counselors and trainees. Organizations such as the National Board of Certified Counselors (NBCC) and the American Counseling Association (ACA) support supervisory efforts, training, and practice.

 Visit the Center for Credentialing and Education site for information about the Approved Clinical Supervisor Credential:

▶ www.cce-global.org/credentials-offered/acs

■ Benefits of Supervision

Helping professionals who understand the importance of clinical supervision throughout the life span of counseling careers benefit in a number of ways:

- Committing to continual supervision adds to the professionalism of the counseling field as it keeps the supervisee and the supervisor on the cutting edge of best practice methods.
- Continued supervision allows for connectedness to others in the profession.
- Supervision provides resources for coping with the stressors that the counseling profession brings.

It does take a certain amount of courage to remain in supervision, expose and demonstrate individual skills, and share overall knowledge. If counselors allow supervision to enhance their counseling outcome and overall effectiveness, the profession will continue to thrive.

■ Supervision Defined

Russell-Chapin and Ivey (2004b) provided a concise definition of supervision:

> **Supervision:** A distinctive, structured approach in which an often more experienced professional counselor responds to a counselor trainee or supervisee's needs with attention to the supervisee's differing developmental and competency levels.

The supervisor usually will clarify and combine three aspects throughout supervision: roles, expectations, and functions. A brief description of the supervisor's roles, the joint expectations of the supervisor and supervisee, and functions of the supervision process are given here.

Supervision Roles

- Among the roles that supervisors assume, a number of common stances include that of teacher, consultant, evaluator, and encourager (Bernard & Goodyear, 1998).
- Based on an informal or formal assessment of the supervisee's needs, the supervisor decides which role or "hat" is most appropriate to the supervisee's needs.

Supervision Expectations

- Prior to every supervision session, the expectations of supervisor and supervisee must be clarified because it is essential to know what is expected from each of the team members.
- The expectations of the supervisor and supervisee are shared throughout the lifetime of supervisory experience.

Supervision Functions

- The functions of supervision will vary based on the supervisee's needs.
- Major responsibilities of supervision include administration, education, and support.

Holloway and Carrol (1999) suggested that it is the supervision tasks and roles plus the functions of those tasks that equal the supervision process. In other words, when the roles and responsibilities of the supervisor are combined with the need of the counselor in training, then a supervision process has begun.

E X A M P L E

Clarifying Expectations in Supervision

An example of a clarifying question that can be used to open the supervisory process is this: "What do you need and want out of supervision today?"(Russell-Chapin & Ivey, 2004a, 2004b). This simple question is an effective way to illuminate the expectations of supervisees in the supervision session.

MODELS OF SUPERVISION

Most supervision models emphasize the value of a healthy supervisee–supervisor relationship, stress the importance of feedback and communication, and describe a variety of supervisor tasks and functions. Four supervision models and one supervision method are presented here, including the following:

1. Developmental models.
2. Theory-specific models.
3. Social role models.
4. Integrated models.
5. Interpersonal Process Recall method.

■ Developmental Models of Supervision

A developmental model of supervision usually is selected if a major goal of supervision is to assess and better understand the developmental level and process of the supervisee. One of the underlying assumptions of developmental models is that supervisees grow at individual paces with differing needs and unique learning styles. Some other generalizations about this approach also can be made.

Assumptions About the Developmental Approach to Supervision

- There seem to be predictable stages or levels through which many supervisees progress as they learn the skills of the counseling process.

- The work of supervision is to discover and articulate the individualized needs of the supervisee (Stoltenberg, McNeill, & Delworth, 1998).
- Strategies should maximize the supervisee's strengths and minimize the liabilities (Russell-Chapin & Ivey, 2004b).

In the developmental model, change and growth are not only assessed for the individual supervisee, but are also reflected in the supervisory relationship. Supervisees strive for cognitive advances and skills acquisition. As that growth takes place, the interaction between supervisee and supervisor must evolve to meet the demands of the supervisee. Another way of conceptualizing the developmental aspect of the supervision relationship is to look at parallels between the supervision and counseling relationships. In individual counseling, assessing the developmental level of the client is essential to choosing an appropriate, corresponding intervention (Ivey & Ivey, 2003). A parallel process occurs within developmental supervision.

Two key figures who gave a detailed description of the characteristics of supervisees' developmental phases and parallels in the supervisory relationship are Stoltenberg and Delworth (1987; see also Stoltenberg, 1981). They formulated a supervision model describing four distinct assessment levels of supervisee growth. Table 5.1 provides a brief synopsis of the four levels outlined by Stoltenberg and Delworth along with the corresponding supervisee and supervisor behavior for each level.

During each level or stage, the job of the supervisor is to structure supervision so that it moves from imitative and demonstrative functions at the beginning level to more competent and self-reliant functions at the advanced levels (Stoltenberg et al., 1998). In this model, a strong emphasis is placed on understanding the supervisee's world, motivational levels, and degree of autonomy, as each of these is described in the beginning, intermediate, advanced, and master counselor levels. Additionally, nine growth areas are identified in each of the four levels.

TABLE 5.1 Developmental Levels of Supervisees		
Levels	*Supervisee Behavior*	*Supervisor Behavior*
Beginning—Level 1	Little experience; dependent on the supervisor	Models needed skills and behaviors; teacher role
Intermediate—Level 2	Less imitative; strives for independence	Provides some structure but encourages exploration
Advanced—Level 3	More insightful and motivated; more autonomous sharing	Listens and offers suggestions when asked
Master Counselor—Level 4	Skilled interpersonally, cognitively and professionally	Provides collegial and consultative functions

Supervisee Growth Areas in the Developmental Model

1. Intervention.
2. Skill competence.
3. Assessment techniques.
4. Interpersonal assessment.
5. Client conceptualization.
6. Individual differences.
7. Theoretical orientation.
8. Treatment goals and plans.
9. Professional ethics.

To evaluate the supervisee's level of performance correctly and support the supervisee throughout the supervision process, the supervisor who works from a developmental approach engages in a number of tasks.

Supervisor Tasks in the Developmental Model (Stoltenberg, 1981; Stoltenberg & Delworth, 1987)

- Use the supervisee's questions and general skills to assess the supervisee's developmental level of functioning from Levels 1 through 4 (e.g., if supervisees seem to be aware of their impact on the client, functioning is likely at Level 2 and 3).
- Attend to the supervisee's levels of awareness of self and others, motivation toward the developmental process, and the ability to think independently.
- Highlight client conceptualization and treatment goals and plans.
- Encourage the supervisee to gain confidence in skill development (Levels 2 and 3).
- Listen more than lead and be collegial in nature (Level 4).

■ Theory-Specific Supervision Models

Helping professionals who adhere to a specific therapeutic orientation (e.g., cognitive-behavioral, psychodynamic, person-centered) may believe it is wise to supervise from the same theoretical orientation. If supervisors choose to operate from a discipline-specific perspective, the supervisor is typically guided by the tenets of the chosen theory throughout the supervisory process. Theory-specific supervision is selected when there is a need for expansion of knowledge of theory and its corresponding techniques. There are a number of benefits to using theory-specific approaches to supervision.

Major Advantages of Theory-Specific Supervision Models

- Supervisors and supervisees who share the same theoretical orientation can maximize modeling that occurs in supervision (Bernard & Goodyear, 1998).
- Supervisors can demonstrate discipline-specific skills as well as integrate necessary theoretical constructs.

The link between the counselor role and the tasks and function of the supervisor in theory-specific supervision are highlighted next through a brief description of Rational Emotive Behavioral Therapy (REBT), psychodynamic, and person-centered models of supervision.

Key Components of REBT Supervision

- The supervisor identifies the problem and irrational thinking of both the supervisee and the client.
- The supervisor and supervisee select ways to dispute and challenge the irrational thoughts as a method for changing and learning new, productive thoughts and behaviors (Ellis, 1989; Woods & Ellis, 1996).
- Behavioral and cognitive-behavioral supervisors emphasize and expect demonstration of more technical mastery than most supervisors (Bernard & Goodyear, 1998).

Using REBT as a supervisory approach will require the supervisor to incorporate the general tenets of Ellis's theory as outlined for counseling. Similarly, the psychodynamic approach to supervision also reflects some of the main ideas that underlie the psychodynamic theory of counseling.

Tenets of Psychodynamic Supervision Model

- **Parallel process** (Doehrmann, 1976), or the dynamic that occurs in the client–therapist relationship that is played out in the supervisee–supervisor relationship, is emphasized.
- The supervisor focuses on client resistance during the session and investigates the resistance the supervisee may have toward the client.

As is true of REBT and the psychodynamic approaches, a person-centered supervision model also is highly reflective of the person-centered approach to counseling.

Principles of Person-Centered Supervision Model

- The supervisor ensures that the basic facilitative conditions are in process throughout the supervision session.
- The supervisor emphasizes establishing unconditional positive regard, building trust, and creating a genuine environment for the supervisee to express self-doubts and fears about confidence in the counseling process (Hackney & Goodyear, 1984).

Whatever discipline-specific supervisory orientation is chosen, the continuity from counseling to supervision will assist the supervisee in expanding skills, constructs, and self-confidence.

■ Social Role Models of Supervision: Discrimination Model

The main premise of social role models is that the supervisor emphasizes the varying roles and foci required during the supervisory process. An example of one social role model of supervision is the discrimination model. The model has been widely researched, and its supporters believe it is an inclusive approach to supervision. Its roots are in technical eclecticism (Bernard & Goodyear, 1998).

A main goal of the discrimination model is to focus on the needs of the supervisee by having the supervisor respond flexibly with appropriate strategies, techniques, and guidance. To respond to supervisees' needs, the supervisor emphasizes two primary functions during each supervision session, namely the supervisor's role and the focus of the session. There are three possible supervisor roles and three possible supervision functions identified in the discrimination model.

Supervisor's Roles in the Discrimination Model
(Bernard & Goodyear, 1998)

1. The teacher role is used to directly instruct or demonstrate constructs and skills.
2. The counselor role is used to help supervisees locate "blind spots" or become aware of countertransference issues.
3. The consultant role is used when the supervisor needs to act as a colleague or during times when bouncing around intervention ideas about the client is required.

During the supervision process, the roles and focus of the work can change. The supervisor might decide that the teacher's role, a counselor's role, or a consultant's role is best suited to a supervisee's particular needs. Each of the supervisor roles accordingly emphasizes different foci of the session.

Supervision Foci in the Discrimination Model

1. The process focus is used to examine the communication between client and counselor.
2. The conceptualization focus is used to explore intentions behind the chosen skill intervention.
3. The personalization focus is used to identify mannerisms employed in interactions with clients, such as body language and voice intonation.

The elegance of discrimination supervision is that as the supervisor continues to supervise, the foci and roles change across and within sessions (Bernard & Goodyear, 1998). Supervisors may choose to focus on basic intervention skills by being in the role of teacher and counselor during a first session, and they may actually teach new skills and work on the supervisee's influence on the client. In later sessions, the supervisor's role may reflect that of a consultant more than a teacher. Throughout the process, supervisors decide which foci to select and which role to use to accomplish identified supervision goals.

■ Integrated Model of Supervision

Much like eclectic orientations to counseling, integrated models of supervision tend to be atheoretical but still operate from an organized framework. Supervisory integrationists blend the best from each model and its corresponding interventions. An example of an integrated model of supervision is the microcounseling supervision model (MSM). Highlighted here are some of the key points in the history of MSM's development.

Evolution of MSM

- The use of microcounseling skills was first reported by Ivey, Normington, Miller, Morrill, and Haase (1968).
- Baker and Daniels (1989) analyzed 81 studies on microcounseling skills training and concluded that the microcounseling training surpassed both the no-training and attention placebo control comparison.
- Daniels (2003) continued his work by following microcounseling training over a period of decades and identified more than 450 data-based studies on microcounseling skills training.
- The research into microcounseling skills eventually led to an investigation into the benefits of microcounseling skills and supervision (Russell-Chapin & Ivey, 2004b).

The initial goal of MSM is to help supervisees learn to identify and classify essential interviewing counseling skills. Once that goal has been achieved, the supervisor or supervisory team and supervisee can begin to process the flow of the sessions and focus on case conceptualization, diagnosis, strengths, and liabilities. Supervisors will select the MSM when essential micro- and macrocounseling skills are not utilized effectively.

There are several terms that are unique to MSM, including intention, basic mastery, and active mastery. Understanding these concepts is necessary for supervisors who choose to use the MSM approach. The terms can be defined as follows:

Intention: Choosing the best potential response from among the many possible options (Russell-Chapin & Ivey, 2004b).

Basic mastery: The ability to demonstrate chosen counseling skills during the counseling interview.

Active mastery: The ability to produce specific and intentional results from the chosen counseling skill.

Supervisors who use the MSM model should be familiar not only with key terminology, but also with the three major stages of MSM:

1. Reviewing microcounseling skills with intention.
2. Classifying skills with mastery.
3. Summarizing and processing supervisory needs.

The first stage of MSM begins by practicing, defining, and reviewing all the microcounseling skills and understanding how they are used with intention. Other steps include those listed here.

Steps in Stage 1 of MSM: Reviewing Microcounseling Skills With Intention

- Supervisees review each of the basic interviewing skills and understand their intention until they are comfortable with how the skills are defined and used.
- Supervisees learn not to look for the "right" solution and skill, but to select responses that adapt individual counseling style to the needs and culture of clients (Ivey & Ivey, 2003).

Once the supervisee has illustrated an understanding of the microcounseling skills and intention, the supervisor can assist the supervisee in rapidly entering into the second phase of the supervision model.

Steps in Stage 2 of MSM: Classifying Skills With Mastery

- Supervisors begin to teach mastery by having supervisees watch someone demonstrate the microcounseling skills and their uses.
- Supervisees are introduced to the Counseling Interview Rating Form (CIRF; see Russell-Chapin & Sherman, 2000), an instrument designed to identify all the micro- and macrocounseling skills plus the five stages of the counseling interview.
- Once supervisees are familiar with the CIRF, they can observe another counselor conducting a counseling session and use the CIRF to identify and classify skills being used with mastery and intention.
- The supervisor and supervisee begin to observe tapes from the supervisee using the CIRF as an evaluative tool.

The final stage of the MSM begins by summarizing and later processing the demonstrated skills on the CIRF as well as other important dimensions of the session.

Steps in Stage 3 of MSM: Summarizing and Processing Supervisory Needs

- The supervisee presents the interview video and case presentation ahead of time and is asked to formulate supervisory questions and concerns, which are addressed as a team in a round-robin fashion going over supervisory concerns, strengths, and areas of improvement.
- Using the CIRF and the interview video, supervisees summarize skill usage with frequency tallies for each of the counseling responses.
- At the end of the session or during each response, the counselor's responses are categorized as basic mastery or active mastery.
- The CIRF is tallied by the members of the supervisory team so that the processing aspect of microcounseling supervision can begin.
- The counselor's rating is compared with the supervisor's rating and results are discussed.
- Scores can be assigned to the entire counseling session or tape or used just to identify which skills are being used correctly and which skills are not being practiced at all.
- The very last question asked during the process is, "What did you learn in supervision today that will assist you in more effectively working with this client?"

MSM successfully combines many skills from a variety of counseling theories and supervision models and can be used in supervision with all orientations (Russell-Chapin & Ivey, 2004b). The cardinal rule of any integrative supervision is to customize supervision to meet the needs of the individual supervisee. In other words, "the 'how' of supervision should parallel the 'what' of supervision" (Norcross & Halgin, 1997, p. 210).

■ A Supervision Videotaping Method: Interpersonal Process Recall

Four main supervisory models have been presented. Many of these models require videotaping of counseling interviews or conducting counseling sessions in an actual live observation setting either digitally or with telephones. One of the most widely used videotaping supervision methods is Kagan's interpersonal process recall (IPR; Haynes, Corey, & Moulton, 2003). Borders and Leddick (1998) conducted a national survey of counselor educators and found IPR to be one of two distinct methods used during supervision courses.

Supervisors select IPR when immediacy is called for in a supervision session. Kagan believes that most people act diplomatically and often do not say what they actually mean or feel. This assumption is reflected in the goals of IPR.

Goals of IPR

- Create a supervision environment where supervisees can safely analyze their communication styles and strategies.

- Encourage the supervisee to reflect on and interpret his or her experience in the counseling session (Kagan, 1980).
- Generate discussion of essential personal or counseling issues through the use of a videotaped counseling session that can be stopped at opportune moments.

Besides its distinctive use of videotaping, another hallmark of IPR is its focus on raising awareness about supervisees' communication styles as well as their own processes and affect during the counseling session. IPR employs a variety of questions to tease out the supervisee's feelings and thoughts during the counseling session.

Questions Germane to IPR (Bernard & Goodyear 1998, p. 102)

- What were your thoughts, feelings, and reactions? Did you want to express them at any time?
- What would you like to have said at this point?
- What was it like for you in your role as counselor?
- What thoughts were you having about the other person at that time?
- Had you any ideas about what you wanted to do with that?
- Were there any pictures, images, or memories flashing through your mind then?
- How do you imagine the client was reacting to you?
- How do you think the client was seeing you at this point?
- Did you sense that the client had any expectations of you at that point?
- What did you want to hear from the client?
- What message did you want to give the client? What prevented you from doing so?

These questions can be used with or without a videotaped counseling session in almost any of the supervision models presented in this chapter. Indeed, the flexibility of the IPR method allows it to continue to be adapted and extended to many supervision needs. Examples of how IPR is used by or inspired the development of other supervision approaches are given next.

Extensions of IPR to Other Supervision Needs

- The work of Kagan (1980) and Ivey and Ivey (2003) inspired the development of the MSM.
- The creation of the CIRF for use while videotaping is an extension of Kagan's work of analysis and processing of the counseling interview.
- IPR inspired the newly advanced supervision technology using Landro Play Analyzer, which is a customized program that allows for digital, tapeless counseling sessions that have been created to assist supervisors in coding frame-by-frame performance analysis of supervisees' skills (Dandeneau & Guth, 2005).

Our main purpose in this chapter was to present the main tenets of four supervision models and one supervision approach. Using this information, supervisees and supervisors can ascertain how certain models might be more appropriate with specific supervisee needs. Determining which approach might fit the supervisee's learning and counseling style is a journey that constantly changes as the supervisee progresses and grows.

Chapter 5: Key Terms

- ▶ Supervision
- ▶ Parallel process
- ▶ Intention
- ▶ Basic mastery
- ▶ Active mastery

Collaborative Supervision for the Novice Supervisor

William J. Casile
Duquesne University

Elizabeth A. Gruber
California University of Pennsylvania

Seth N. Rosenblatt
Duquesne University

In This Chapter

▶ *A Look at Supervision*
- Purposes of Supervision
- Importance of Supervision to the Counseling Profession
- Supervision, Professional Development, and Credentialing

▶ *Becoming a Supervisor: Some Starting Points*
- Training Through Doctoral Programs
- Self-Developed Supervision Skills: Modeling as a First Step
- Self-Developed Supervision Skills: Gathering Other Resources

▶ *A Collaborative Model of Supervision: An Overview*
- Constructivist Roots of the Collaborative Model
- Meeting Competencies Through the Collaborative Model
- Advantages of the Collaborative Model

▶ *Professional Development of Novice Supervisors: Knowledge Competency*
- Theoretical Foundations
- Ethical and Legal Considerations
- Multicultural Impact

▶ *Professional Development of Novice Supervisors: Disposition*
- Collaborative, Learner-Focused Stance
- Supportive and Critical Dispositions: Coexisting Roles

▶ *Professional Development of Novice Supervisors: Strategies*
- The Inquiry Learning Cycle
- Building the Therapeutic Alliance
- Using the FERA Inquiry Model in the Therapeutic Alliance
- Promoting the Construction of Meaning
- Using the FERA Inquiry Model in the Construction of Meaning
- Evaluating the Work of the Counselor
- Using the FERA Inquiry Model for Evaluating the Work of the Supervisee

▶ *Summary*

A LOOK AT SUPERVISION

This chapter is intended as a resource for counselors who find themselves in a supervisory role for the first time. Although all master's programs in counseling have a supervision component during which counselor trainees are monitored, programs normally do not include formal training in counselor supervision. Thus, graduates of a counselor training program typically have experienced supervision only as a supervisee and have no specific training on how to be an effective clinical supervisor. Although endorsing the profession's efforts to establish training and practice standards for counselor supervisors, we also recognize the immediate and very practical needs of counselors faced with the day-to-day challenge of providing clinical supervision (Borders, Bernard, Dye, Fong, & Nance, 1991; Campbell, 2000). In response to those needs, this chapter, although not intended to be a comprehensive training program for counselor supervisors, introduces the collaborative model of supervision as a starting point for novice or untrained supervisors who need resources in their search for competency.

■ Purposes of Supervision

In their definition of supervision, Bernard and Goodyear (2004) incorporated three equally important and essential purposes for this distinct intervention:

1. Enhance the professional competence of the supervisee.
2. Monitor the quality of counseling offered to the client.
3. Serve as a gatekeeper to the profession of counseling.

It is assumed that in the supervisory relationship, the supervisor, a more experienced, better trained, more complete professional, will serve as a teacher, consultant, counselor, and evaluator for a less experienced counselor, the supervisee (Bernard, 1997). The ability to discriminate when and how to apply these multiple roles to accomplish supervisory goals distinguishes the competent from the novice supervisor (Bernard & Goodyear, 2004).

■ Importance of Supervision to the Counseling Profession

The place of clinical supervision in the process of providing professional counseling or any professional service is indisputable. The concern for the ethical, legal, and effective professional practice of counseling and other related human services requires that professionals participate in supervision of their work (Bernard & Goodyear, 2004). Prudent counselors need supervision to ensure that their clients receive appropriate and effective treatment and that they continue to engage in personal and professional development, a hallmark of being a professional counselor. The *Ethical Guidelines for Counseling Supervisors* (Hart, Borders, Nance, & Paradise, 1995) substantiate the need for supervision by outlining some necessary responsibilities of supervision.

Responsibilities of Supervision (Hart et al., 1995)

- Monitoring client welfare.
- Ensuring compliance with applicable legal, ethical, and professional standards of practice.
- Evaluating clinical performance and professional development of supervisees.
- Gatekeeping, or assuming responsibility to certify supervisee performance and potential for academic selection, employment, and credentialing.

■ Supervision, Professional Development, and Credentialing

The counseling profession has consistently recognized the supervision of counselors as an essential component to the development of competent counselors and the delivery of therapeutic services (Bernard & Goodyear, 2004; Bradley & Ladany, 2001).

State and Board Requirements for and Endorsements of Supervision

- In each state that offers a professional license for counselors, the established procedures require all applicants to practice counseling for a significant number of hours under the direct supervision of a licensed counselor capable of supervising their work (ACA, 2006).
- The National Board of Certified Counselors (NBCC) recognized the unique practice of supervision by publishing the *Standards for Ethical Practice of Clinical Supervision* (NBCC, 1999).
- The NBCC developed the Approved Clinical Supervisor (ACS) credential in 1997, a credential that identifies mental health professionals who have met the national supervision standards, promoted professional identity, and encouraged the professional growth of clinical supervisors. This certificate is now available from the Center for Credentialing and Education, Inc. (CCE, 2001).

Clearly, the essential role of supervision in the development of a capable professional counselor is irrefutable.

 Visit the CCE site for more information on the ACS credential and to download an application form at:

▶ www.cce-global.org

BECOMING A SUPERVISOR: SOME STARTING POINTS

In the counseling profession, many practitioners are promoted to the supervisory position as a result of their seniority, exceptional work as a counselor, or desire to be a supervisor. Moreover, successful counselors often are promoted to supervisory positions without systematic, formal training on how to supervise, despite the fact that there is increasing agreement in the professional literature that counselor supervision is a unique process requiring specific preparation and training and that practicing supervision without appropriate training is an ethical violation (Haynes et al., 2003). There are numerous obstacles counselors face to receiving the formal supervisory training recommended by the profession.

Barriers to Professional Supervisory Training

- Master's-level counselor education programs typically do not prepare graduates to be supervisors.
- Most counselors work in organizations that do not provide their employees with adequate clinical supervision.
- Agencies or organizations that employ counselors normally do not commit the resources to train counselors to become supervisors. Although essential to the quality of treatment, supervisory training usually is not seen as a billable part of the treatment model.

Counselors who want to develop supervision skills are practically limited to two choices. They can join a doctoral program in counselor education and supervision, or they can self-define and construct a personal route to competency.

■ Training Through Doctoral Programs

Most doctoral programs in counselor education emphasize a strand devoted to developing the knowledge base and skills needed to be successful as a counselor supervisor. However, doctoral work is a long and expensive route of continuing education that is available to only a few professional counselors. More frequently, the novice supervisor is left alone to identify a course of self-development activities that he or she deems appropriate.

■ Self-Developed Supervision Skills: Modeling as a First Step

Because all professionally trained counselors have at least experienced supervision as a supervisee, they can begin the journey of becoming competent supervisors by modeling the practice of past supervisors they have experienced. However, reliance on modeling has several obvious limitations.

Limitations of Modeling as the Predominant Supervisory Training Experience

- Many counselors in private practice, schools, or some agencies may not have a current supervisor to model.
- When available, there is no assurance that the existing supervision experiences are worthy of emulation.
- The power of a learning model that relies solely on modeling without the clarification of reflection, feedback, and guided practice is undoubtedly a highly unreliable approach to preparing professionals for the complex demands of supervision (Schön, 1987).

■ Self-Developed Supervision Skills: Gathering Other Resources

Because of the limitations of modeling as a primarily approach to learning how to supervise, counselors may attempt to assemble some combination of seminars, workshops, conferences, and contracted supervision of supervision to enhance their skills as a supervisor. This informal and self-structured approach of learning to become a supervisor typically begins with many questions that emphasize learning needs.

Self-Inquiries That Guide Learning Needs of Untrained Supervisors

- What is my role as a supervisor?
- What are my ethical responsibilities and legal liabilities?
- What theory and model of supervision do I use?
- Do I focus on the client or the supervisee?
- What do I have to document in supervision?
- How do I supervise multiple supervisees?
- Am I creating dual relationships with my supervisees?
- How do I obtain supervision?

Unfortunately, these questions usually are generated out of desperation as novice supervisors attempt to learn their new role and do not support a systematic approach to becoming a supervisor (Allstetter-Neufeldt, 1999; Falendar & Shafranske, 2004). Rather, reflections and questions generated in moments of stress or desperation tend to promote a hodge-podge of activities cobbled together by the aspiring supervisor. What counselors need, therefore, is a simple framework or model of supervision that guides professional development and that can be used by novice supervisors who might not have had the opportunity to receive formal supervisory training. A collaborative approach to supervision offers the most effective map that beginning supervisors might use on their journey toward proficiency.

A COLLABORATIVE MODEL OF SUPERVISION: AN OVERVIEW

The collaborative model of supervision described in this and subsequent sections is a tool to assist experienced counselors in becoming effective supervisors. The model borrows generously from the developmental and constructivist elements of existing theories of supervision to provide novice supervisors with a structural frame to begin constructing a personal approach to the practice of supervision. Novice supervisors can gain confidence quickly as they discover that their prior learning to become effective counselors also will support their learning to become competent supervisors. Additionally, the use of a constructivist approach to learning helps novice supervisors understand their new roles and responsibilities by emphasizing the isomorphic relation between counseling and supervision. Finally, this model of supervision can assist novice supervisors in laying the philosophical groundwork for their supervisory tasks and conceptualizing how and why they respond the way they do in supervision sessions.

■ Constructivist Roots of the Collaborative Model

Constructivism is concerned with the nature of how knowledge is created and is based on the assumption that people actively create meaning by connecting previous knowledge to new information gained through experience (Fosnot, 1996). The result is the creation of new understanding and meaning (McAuliffe, Eriksen, & Associates, 2000). The collaborative model of supervision takes advantage of the constructivist theory of learning and acts like a conceptual scaffold that helps the counselor acquire the knowledge, disposition, and skills needed to become a supervisor. The model allows competent counselors to begin conceptualizing their practice of supervision by building on their current understanding of the developmental processes in counseling. That is, the model encourages counselors to become active creators of new meaning by helping them relate what they already know about counseling to similar processes found in supervision.

■ Meeting Competencies Through the Collaborative Model

The collaborative model of supervision focuses on the fact that in both counseling and supervision, one of the most important outcomes is that both supervisees and clients develop, learn, and change in ways that allow them either to practice more effectively or live healthier lives without the risk of harm in the process of growth. Counselor education prepares counselors to facilitate and monitor this process with clients. The collaborative model helps to bridge existing counseling competencies to the competencies required of successful supervisors.

Knowledge, Disposition, and Strategies Competencies

1. *Building a knowledge base:* In the collaborative model, novice supervisors build a knowledge base for supervision by beginning with what they have learned to become effective professional counselors. Specifically, supervisors must explore, understand, and apply theoretical foundations, ethical and legal principles, and cultural awareness to the process of supervision.
2. *Promoting a collaborative disposition:* The collaborative model encourages supervisors to approach supervision with a disposition that promotes a collaborative partnership, the nature of which is characterized by a critical friendship.
3. *Identifying strategies:* The collaborative model identifies three essential tasks or strategic areas that must be addressed to discharge the major responsibilities or obligations of the supervisor. These tasks are building a therapeutic or working alliance, promoting the construction of meaning, and evaluating and monitoring the work of the counselor.

■ Advantages of the Collaborative Model

The use of this model has several advantages derived from its premise that the competent counselor already has learned much that can be applied to supervision. First, it provides a solid theoretical platform on which the novice supervisor can stand confidently. Second, it encourages supervisors to emphasize the collaborative perspective of supervision over the evaluative component in their relationships with supervisees. Third, the model emphasizes the supervisor's responsibility, parallel to that of the counselor, to create a safe environment where supervisees become active partners, empowered to reflect and examine their own resources, performance, and needs for development.

PROFESSIONAL DEVELOPMENT OF NOVICE SUPERVISORS: KNOWLEDGE COMPETENCY

The knowledge base of the successful counselor can form a sturdy foundation on which to build the new learning needed for working as a supervisor. Trained counselors have assimilated much information about (a) theoretical foundations, (b) ethical and legal principles, and (c) the impact of cultural variables on the process of counseling; thus, these three areas are essential starting points for novice supervisors to construct the knowledge needed to become effective clinical supervisors.

■ Theoretical Foundations

Counseling theories are the basis of successful clinical work; theoretical foundations of supervision are equally essential to competent supervision. Supervisors must be grounded in a supervisory theory that speaks to their beliefs about how supervisees and clients think, learn, grow, and change. The process of theory exploration lays the foundation for how the novice supervisor begins to conceptualize supervision. The emergence of an individualized theory of supervision ultimately structures the practice of supervision, guiding what the supervisor attends and responds to during the supervisory session.

> Supervisors must be grounded in a supervisory theory that speaks to their beliefs about how supervisees and clients think, learn, grow, and change.

To develop a personalized supervision theory, practitioners first must read and reflect on currently proposed theories. Most prevalent supervision theories in the counselor supervision field have their roots in counseling theory. Only relatively recently have dedicated theories of supervision been described. Bernard and Goodyear (2004) presented a concise overview of three classifications of counselor supervision models that are a useful starting point for creating a theoretical foundation to supervision; the three categories are psychotherapy-based models, developmental models, and social role models.

Three Classifications of Counselor Supervision Models (Bernard & Goodyear, 2004)

1. Psychotherapy theory-based supervision models are grounded in assumptions about human change, what change means, and how it occurs in the counselor–client therapeutic alliance. These beliefs about the therapeutic alliance are applied to the supervisor–supervisee relationship.
2. Developmental supervision models focus on how supervisees grow and change during their personal and professional lives. The major tenet of the developmental philosophy holds that individual stages of growth occur among the diverse pool of supervisees. The supervisor must recognize the individual needs and growth potential of supervisees and then create an environment tailored to fit the individual, developmental needs of each supervisee.
3. Social role supervision models recognize that supervisors and supervisees bring a variety of professional role experiences, learned knowledge, and conceptualizations about the process of counseling and supervision to the supervisory experience. Social role theories presuppose that supervision acts as a metarole used to monitor supervisee needs and guide the supervisor in the selection of the most efficacious role (e.g., teaching, consulting, and counseling roles) to meet supervisee needs.

Although there is not space to describe the various theories that comprise the three categories of supervision theory, a list of theories is given here for interested readers.

Psychotherapy-Based Supervision Models

- Psychodynamic model (Frawley-O'Dea & Sarnat, 2001; Gill, 2001).
- Person-centered model (Lambers, 2000; Patterson, 1997).
- Cognitive-behavioral model (Liese & Beck, 1997; Rosenbaum & Ronen, 1998).
- Systemic/family therapy model (Liddle, Becker, & Diamond, 1997; Montgomery, Hendricks, & Bradley, 2001).
- Narrative model (Clifton, Doan, & Mitchell, 1990).
- Solution-focused model (Marek, Sandifer, Beach, Coward, & Protinsky, 1994; Rita, 1998)
- Feminist model (Carta-Falsa & Anderson, 2001; Prouty, Thomas, Johnson, & Long, 2001).

Developmental Theories of Supervision

- The Littrell, Lee-Borden, and Lorenz model (Littrell, Lee-Borden, & Lorenz, 1979).
- The Stoltenberg model (Stoltenberg, 1981).
- The Loganbill, Hardy, and Delworth model (Loganbill, Hardy, & Delworth, 1982).
- The Stoltenberg and Delworth model (Stoltenberg & Delworth, 1988).
- The Skovholt and Rønnestad model (Rønnestad & Skovholt, 1993; Skovholt & Rønnestad, 1992).

Social Role Theories of Supervision

- The discrimination model (Bernard, 1979, 1997).
- The Hawkins and Shohet model (Hawkins & Shohet, 1989, 2000).
- The Holloway systems model (Holloway, 1995, 1997).

■ Ethical and Legal Considerations

No counselor can practice without a thorough understanding of the legal and ethical principles that guide appropriate professional behavior. Similarly, no supervisor can operate responsibly without adhering to the principles that define legal and ethical supervisory practice. The *ACA Code of Ethics* (2005a) outlines ethical issues of importance for supervisors and supervisees. Additionally, the Association for Counselor Education and Supervision (ACES), the professional organization for counselor educators and supervisors, has developed Ethical Guidelines for Clinical Supervisors (ACES, 1993).

ACES Guidelines for Ethical Supervisory Behavior (ACES, 1993)

- Observe ethical and legal protection of clients' and supervisees' rights.
- Meet the training and professional development needs of supervisees in ways consistent with clients' welfare and programmatic requirements.
- Establish policies, procedures, and standards for implementing programs.

These same Ethical Guidelines for Clinical Supervisors (ACES, 1993) also describe the functions of the supervisory role.

Functions of the Ethical Supervisor (ACES, 1993)

- Monitor client welfare.
- Encourage compliance with relevant legal, ethical, and professional standards for clinical practice.
- Monitor supervisee clinical performance and professional development.
- Evaluate and certify current performance and potential of supervisee.

Bernard and Goodyear (2004) categorized the major ethical issues facing counselor supervisors. A summary of these issues is given here.

Key Ethical Issues Facing Counseling Supervisors

- *Due process* refers to the procedures that guarantee notice and fair hearing prior to the removal or abridgment of a person's rights.
- *Informed consent* is the client's right to be fully informed of the parameters of treatment, including potential harm.
- *Dual relationship* refers to a relationship a supervisor forms with a client or supervisee in addition to the therapeutic or supervisory relationship.
- *Competence* is the ability to practice (therapy and supervision) effectively and within the limits of the professional's training and ability.
- *Confidentiality* is the ethical responsibility of the counselor or supervisor not to disclose information obtained in professional relationships with clients, except when required to ensure safety or meet a judicial order.

Borders and Brown (2005) added to this list the issue of *evaluation*. Supervisors have an ethical responsibility to provide their supervisees with continuous feedback based on regular face-to-face review of actual performance samples.

It is clear that supervisors are both ethically and legally responsible for the quality of their supervisee's work (Bernard & Goodyear, 2004; Borders & Brown, 2005; Disney & Stephens, 1994; Falvey, 2002). Supervisors may be directly or vicariously liable for the actions of the supervisee. Therefore, it is critical that supervisors learn how to maintain careful documentation of their work so that they can promote the professional development of their supervisees, ensure the appropriateness of treatment for clients, and manage their own exposure to professional liability (Falvey).

Allstetter-Neufeldt (1999), Campbell (2000), and Falvey et al. (2002) all provide valuable information on documentation in supervision.

For more information on ethical and legal issues in counseling, see Chapters 2 and 3.

■ Multicultural Impact

Multicultural awareness and competence is perhaps the most important force shaping the practice of counseling and supervision today. The recent revision of the ACA *Code of Ethics* (ACA, 2005a) focused on the inclusion of multicultural and diversity issues to all aspects of the counseling professional's work. Indeed, the code states, "Counseling supervisors are aware of and address the role of multiculturalism/diversity in the supervisory relationship" (ACA, 2005a, F.2.b). By maintaining contact with the ACA, the ACES, and the Association for Multicultural Counseling and Development, supervisors integrate and reinforce the multicultural aspects of relevant ethical standards into their work with supervisees.

According to Sue and Sue (2003), the first step to becoming a multiculturally competent counselor is increasing awareness of one's own assumptions, values, and biases that may affect the therapeutic alliance. Likewise, cultural competence is central to the supervisory relationship to ensure that supervisors will not allow cultural assumptions, values, and biases to interfere with the supervisee's development, affect the welfare of the supervisee's clients, or interfere with the working alliance.

Ways to Ensure Cultural Sensitivity in the Supervisory Relationship

- Identify and discuss explicitly multicultural issues present in both counseling and supervisory relationships (Neufeldt, 1999).
- Use the working alliance between supervisor and supervisee to collaboratively and authentically examine the impact of culture on the supervisory work.
- Develop trusting, open, and congruent avenues of communication about culture in the supervisory relationship to help counselors and supervisees construct parallel discussions around culture in their therapeutic relationships with clients.
- Respond respectfully to differences and use culturally appropriate interventions.

Counselors and supervisors must understand and integrate into practice the critical skills needed to be multiculturally competent professionals. Ignoring multicultural issues potentially can lead to ineffective supervision or result in harm to the supervisee or client. Thus, it is essential that cultural awareness and competence underlie both counseling and supervision practice. Ladany, Brittan-Powell, and Pannau (1997); Ladany, Inman, Constantine, and Nutt (1997); and Pope-Davis and

Coleman (1997) all provided useful and more detailed reflections on multicultural awareness in supervision.

See Chapter 4 for more information about multicultural competence in counseling.

PROFESSIONAL DEVELOPMENT OF NOVICE SUPERVISORS: DISPOSITION

Constructing a wide knowledge base is one aim of the collaborative model of supervision; additionally, the model suggests that novice supervisors will be most successful if they consciously cultivate a professional disposition characterized by an amalgam of support and critique. Through supportive, yet critical partnerships, supervisees will be able to receive the feedback needed for their development, the assurance that their practice will do no harm to their clients, and the validation that their performance meets the standards demanded by the profession. Whether working in the role of teacher, consultant, counselor, or evaluator, supervisors' effectiveness will be enhanced if they are able to frame their work from a supportive or critical or collaborative perspective.

■ Collaborative, Learner-Focused Stance

The collaborative model of supervision is consistent with a postmodern view of learning and development in that it emphasizes an epistemological shift from objectivism to constructivism. Implications of the shift to a constructivist philosophy in the supervision relationship are mentioned here.

Characteristics of a Collaborative Supervisory Relationship

- The "learners" or the clients and supervisees, as well as their social contexts, are accentuated over the "content" that emerges during the supervision sessions (Neufeldt, 1997; Sexton, 1997).
- The expert authority, didactic, and abstract instructional paradigm that presupposes "expert" supervisors know what the novice supervisees need is deemphasized.
- A collaborative disposition that creates a culture of trust, openness, and the mutual or shared responsibility for the well-being and development of the client, counselor, and supervisor is emphasized (Casile & Davison, 1998).
- Supervisors working from a collaborative disposition do not abandon their evaluative responsibility; rather, they invite the supervisee to treat it as another problem to be solved and another mutual opportunity for learning.

One way to understand the collaborative disposition is to examine the fundamental nature of the relationship between supervisor and supervisee that serves the developmental and evaluative aims of supervision.

■ Supportive and Critical Dispositions: Coexisting Roles

To simultaneously assume a supportive, friendly role and a critical stance in the same supervisory relationship seems to be a contradiction. Indeed, combining the roles and norms of both a critic and a friend may appear to pose a dilemma (Achinstein & Meyer, 1997; Bambino, 2002; Hill, 2002). However, current conceptualizations of the supervisory process are unable to avoid the merging of developmental and evaluative roles that are both critical and supportive. It is, in fact, the role of supervisors to be the critical friend of counselors who promote development by holding counselors' work up to the ethical and professional practice standards that define competency. Costa and Kallick (1993) described the critical friend as follows:

> **Critical friend:** "[A] trusted person who asks provocative questions, provides data to be examined through another lens, and offers critiques of a person's work as a friend. A critical friend takes the time to fully understand the context of the work presented and the outcomes that the person or group is working toward. The friend is an advocate for the success of that work" (p. 50).

Hill (2002) introduced a competency model for framing the work of a successful critical friend in terms of knowledge, skills, and attitudes.

Characteristics of the Competent Critical Friend (Hill, 2002)

- The critical friend is knowledgeable about a critical framework and how assumptions underpin people's justification for their practices.
- The critical friend is skillful at reflective responding, scholarly and investigative reframing, facilitated silence, encouraging documentation and data collection, scholarly reading, articulating an inquiry paradigm, big-picture facilitation, and encouraging publication.
- The critical friend's attitude is intricately linked to beliefs about one's provision of critical friendship, the value of reflection as a professional skill, and oneself.

Interactions between a supervisor and counselor should be a true dialogue between eager listeners, not a struggle between contending and defensive interests. The critical friend or the supervisor who assumes a collaborative disposition encourages the creation of effective therapeutic working alliances, the construction of meaning, and the shared, formative evaluation of the practicing supervisor.

PROFESSIONAL DEVELOPMENT OF NOVICE SUPERVISORS: STRATEGIES

As mentioned in the overview of the collaborative model, there are three strategies employed by all supervisors:

1. The collaborative supervisor is the consultant or counselor who creates a supportive and developmental relationship with the supervisee.
2. The collaborative supervisor is the teacher who cultivates the supervisee's personal and professional growth by fostering new meaning and understanding in the work.
3. The collaborative supervisor is the evaluator who assesses the supervisee's competence and effectiveness, ensuring that the work does no harm.

Although not meant to be an exhaustive description of supervisor tasks, these three strategies are necessary and essential components of effective supervision. In addition, they provide a structural parallel between what counselors do and what supervisors must learn to do. Thus, the novice supervisor can begin to construct or learn the tasks of supervision by building on what he or she already knows about the tasks associated with the counseling process.

Effective counselors have the ability to engage clients in working relationships, similar to Bordin's (1994) concept of a working alliance in supervision. The construction of meaning through the exploration and understanding stages of the counseling process described by Egan (1998, 2002) and others parallels the meaning-making aspect of supervision facilitated in the collaborative model of supervision through the inquiry learning cycle (Hill & O'Brien, 1999). Finally, counselors must develop strategies to evaluate and monitor the work and progress of their clients. Supervisors, too, must learn how to evaluate their supervisees' work, its impact on their clients, and the supervisors' fitness for the profession.

These three strategies—developing the working alliance, generating new meaning, and evaluating the work—are central to the work of collaborative supervision. However, each of these functional tasks is dependent on the context of the unique interpersonal role relationship that evolves between the supervisor and supervisee. This supervisory relationship, like any other relationship, is susceptible to interpersonal interferences such as transference and countertransference (Ladany et al., 2000), attachment styles (Watkins, 1995), and power and influence (Holloway, 1995). To mitigate the effects of these and other factors that influence the working alliance, the collaborative model of supervision uses the inquiry learning cycle as a tool to guide the novice supervisor through the stages associated with learning and

development. For more information on factors that influence the supervisory relationship, see Bernard and Goodyear (2004), Frawley-O'Dea and Sarnat (2001), and
Gill (2001).

■ The Inquiry Learning Cycle

In the collaborative model of supervision, the skills of inquiry learning are used to
structure and support the primary tasks of supervision in developing a working
relationship, constructing deeper meaning, and evaluating the performance of
supervisees and their impact on clients.

Collaborative supervisors can effectively address the developmental or learning
tasks and the evaluative tasks of supervision by applying the stages of the FERA
learning cycle—focusing, exploring, reflecting, and applying—to monitor their
work with counselors in supervision.

In the collaborative model, the process of supervision can be conceptualized as a
continuously recursive learning cycle that includes the use of the following stages
and associated methods to address the primary tasks of building the relationship,
fostering insight, and evaluating the work.

Stages of the FERA Learning Model in Supervision

1. **Focus** by engaging the counselor and determining what is known and what is
   not known about both content and process. The supervisor must listen for and
   determine what is explicit and what is implied in the counseling or supervision
   relationship.
2. **Explore** by encouraging the counselor to frame questions, develop hypotheses,
   and predict consequences of action that might be taken. This stage promotes
   the investigation of issues and processes that are emerging in the counseling or
   supervisory relationships.
3. **Reflect** through facilitating dialogue that promotes shared or mutual understanding and insight into the counseling and supervising experiences. New
   learning and the removal of blind spots help both the counselor and the supervisor gain different perspectives on the work and the relationships.
4. **Apply** by monitoring the implementation of new learning as it is used in the
   practice of counseling and supervision. Each decisive action plan or action can
   become the target of an investigation to determine if it is working and if the
   practice is effective.

These stages of the FERA learning cycle can be applied to each task of supervision
identified in the collaborative model of supervision. One way to demonstrate the
use of the FERA model in the development of collaborative supervision is to examine some case examples. Each of the following three case studies provides examples of supervisor probes to move the work of supervision toward the accomplishment of one of the primary tasks of supervision: building the therapeutic alliance,
promoting the constructing of meaning, and evaluating and monitoring the work

of the counselor. It is important to note that some of the probes target the supervi-sory relationship, and some questions are directed at the counseling relationship. Although these are not addressed simultaneously, it is important for the supervisor to ensure that both of these systems are examined in the course of supervision.

■ Building the Therapeutic Alliance

To best serve the purposes of supervision, the relationship between the supervisor and supervisee must function as a therapeutic working alliance (Bordin, 1983). In the context of supervision, the therapeutic working alliance can be described as fol-lows:

> **Therapeutic working alliance:** A supervisee-centered, collaborative relation-ship driven by the clinical and developmental needs of the supervisee, in which the process of identifying and addressing the supervisee's needs as they arise must be the mutual responsibility of both professionals.

The creation of a working alliance between the supervisor and supervisee that emphasizes mutual responsibility for the work of supervision is the foundation of collaborative supervision. This relationship is a precursor and necessary condition to the construction of meaning and evaluation of outcomes in supervision. It is the formation of this alliance that supports authentic learning for the supervisee, as well as the supervisor, and it ensures that the supervisee's and clients' learning and welfare are held to the highest level of professional standards of accountability.

The relationship or working alliance in collaborative supervision is fostered by explicitly creating a safe and secure environment through the application of the core Rogerian conditions for effective helping: genuineness, respect, and empathy (Rogers, 1951). This parallels the relationship that the counselor is attempting to develop with the client. However, the parallels also extend to the threats to these re-lationships. Both are susceptible to defense mechanisms, projections, and other in-terpersonal processes that can interfere with awareness and expression.

The inquiry learning cycle applied to the process of relationship development will establish a supervision culture that emphasizes the development of healthy supervisor–counselor attachments and decreases the probability that the attach-ments will be anxious or compulsive as a result of an excessive emphasis on the hi-erarchical power structure in the counseling or supervisory relationship. Spe-cifically, as the counselor and supervisor move through the FERA cycle, their awareness, or the ability to perceive what is going on with the client, counselor, and supervisor systems, will be increased. The supervisor must learn to model and fa-cilitate expression, or the willingness to verbalize questions, interpretations, and confrontations that invite the pair into deeper, more accurate, and complete under-standing of their experiences. The combination of increased awareness and risked expression fuels the developmental process in supervision in the same way it does in counseling.

EXAMPLE

The Case of Gwen: Building the Relationship

Gwen was promoted to clinical supervisor 3 months ago. She has been with her agency for 4 years as a clinician. Gwen has a master's degree in community counseling and is well respected by her peers as a clinician. One of her supervisees presented the following case: Margarita (supervisee) is counseling an 11-year-old female who was referred to counseling by her grandmother. The client lost her mother about 6 months ago and is currently living with her grandmother. She is suffering from sleep deprivation, grief and loss, panic attacks, and separation anxiety. The separation anxiety intensifies when she is at school due to her fear that if she is not with her grandmother, she may pass away like her mother. Margarita hopes in presenting this case she can deal with her confusion of where to focus with this client, as well as receive feedback on how effective she has been in forming a relationship with this client.

Gwen and Margarita have a positive working alliance. They have been colleagues for 2 years and discussed their new supervisor and supervisee roles. There is trust in their relationship and agreed-on goals in the supervision contract. Margarita, the counselor, is not sure if she knows how to develop the relationship with a client this young. She wants to develop a safe and trusting environment with the client. However, when she presents the case in supervision, she focuses on the content of the child's narrative. Gwen, the supervisor, wants the counselor to focus more concretely on the counselor's relationship with the client and with her as the supervisor.

■ Using the FERA Inquiry Model in the Therapeutic Alliance

The first step in the FERA model is to focus, by engaging the counselor and determining what is known and what is not known, about both content and process. The supervisor chooses interventions that first promote focusing on the mutual goals of the supervisory dyad.

Probes That Focus on the Goals of the Supervisory Alliance

- How do you perceive your relationship with me in supervision?
- I feel that our supervisory relationship has benefited by our shared experience as peer counselors.
- Tell me about your relationship with this client.
- What is not safe or trusting in your relationship with the client?
- What are your thoughts when an 11-year-old tells you of her recent loss?

The second step in the inquiry model is to explore by encouraging the counselor to frame questions, develop hypotheses, and predict consequences of action that might be taken. Once the supervisor feels the counselor is focused on an aspect of one of the relationships, the supervisor might shift to encouraging the counselor to experiment with the situation.

Probes That Help Supervisees Explore Their Relationships

- How do you feel aspects of your culture affect your working relationship with me in supervision?
- What do you want to ask me about our work together in supervision?
- Tell me what you need from me in supervision.
- How do you explain the part of our work together that is least effective?
- How might supervision be different if I did live supervision of your next session?
- What questions have you formed or asked your client about her culture?
- Does your ethnicity affect your working relationship with this client?
- What are you curious about in your relationship with this client?
- What might get in the way of building a trusting relationship with your client?
- What might happen if you stopped taking responsibility for suggesting things she could talk about?
- What questions do you think you need to ask your client?

The third step in the FERA model is to reflect, which can be done by facilitating dialogue that promotes a shared understanding of the counseling and supervising experiences. After exploring the supervisee's experience and their shared experience, the supervisor poses interventions that invite the counselor to derive new meaning from these experiences. The supervisee constructs new meaning by building on what is already known. Where appropriate, the supervisor adds meaning from alternative perspectives.

Probes That Can Add Meaning to the Supervisory Experience
and the Working Alliance

- Tell me what you have learned about our working relationship.
- What has been difficult for you in our supervision?
- How have you become more aware of yourself in supervision?
- How have you become more aware of yourself in counseling?
- How has this work been the same or different than your work with other clients?
- What have you learned about your relationship with your client?
- What do you think about most frequently when you see this client?
- I am wondering what you hold back and do not say to your client.

In the last step, apply, the supervisor monitors the implementation of new learning into the counseling and supervision process.

Probes That Facilitate the Use of New Learning About
the Therapeutic Alliance

- What will you do to acknowledge cultural differences in supervision?
- How will we know if we are addressing your issues and concerns in supervision?

- What are the most helpful ways for me to give you feedback on your responses to this client?
- How do you evaluate your effectiveness as a supervisee?
- What have you learned about strengthening the therapeutic relationship with this client?
- What will you do to acknowledge cultural differences in counseling?
- What techniques are you considering using in your next counseling session?
- How will you know if you are developing a safer, more trusting relationship with this child?

■ Promoting the Construction of Meaning

Inquiry-based learning utilizes questioning or probing techniques that promote an applied research or active inquiry approach to learning. Examples of similar techniques in current supervision practice include Kagan's interpersonal process recall (IPR) (1976, 1980) and Anderson's (1987) use of reflecting teams. Inquiry is designed to uncover or help construct meaning and promote insight in the use of interventions, conceptualization of case issues, and the process of therapy and supervision.

In this phase of supervision, the supervisory alliance turns its attention to developing effectiveness. Focusing on the skills of counseling and supervision (Rønnestad & Skovholt, 1993) and brainstorming possible and alternative responses to the expressed and implied content, as well as the process emerging in the relationships between client and counselor and counselor and supervisor, new insight and the possibility of a more effective future emerges.

EXAMPLE

The Case of Penina: Promoting Insight

Penina (supervisee) is working with a 19-year-old female college student who is abusing alcohol and other substances at least four times a week. Her grades have dropped over the past semester and she is contemplating changing her major. She missed 30% of her classes before 11:00 a.m. She is in a verbally abusive relationship. She also reports mood swings and signs of depression. Penina refers her for an assessment at an alcohol and drug treatment facility but the client refuses to go, and she denies she has a problem with substances. The client believes alcohol and drug use and abuse is just part of the college culture. The client's goal for counseling is to control the mood swings to help her relationship improve. She has expressed an interest in continuing to work with Penina. Penina is frustrated because the client will not follow through with the recommendations she makes. She is seeking supervision to help her deal with her frustration in this case.

■ Using the FERA Inquiry Model in the Construction of Meaning

The questions in this section and the following three sections attempt to guide supervisees in the construction of new meaning in the supervisory process. Focus, the first step in the FERA model, calls supervisors to engage the counselor and determine what is known and what is not known, about both content and process.

Probes That Help Focus the Counselor on Alternative Meanings

- What are the major reasons for presenting this case in supervision?
- What do you need from me?
- How do I frustrate you?
- How does the client frustrate you?
- What do you know about substance abuse?
- What do you know about the developmental levels of college students and the norms of the college culture?
- What is the client not telling you?

Next, the supervisor explores with the supervisee ways to frame questions, develop hypotheses, and predict consequences of action that might be taken.

Probes That Explore New Meanings

- What more do you need to know about me as your supervisor?
- How has our progress been affected by working with a supervisor of a different race or gender?
- What ethical issues need to be addressed?
- What are the challenges for you in this case?
- How do you feel about addicts … this addict?
- Tell me about your frustrations.
- What more do you need to know about your client?
- What are your concerns about the relationship your client is in?
- What theories help you understand what this client is doing in therapy?

After exploring the supervisee's experience and their shared experience, the supervisor poses interventions that invite the counselor to reflect and to derive new meaning for these experiences. The supervisee constructs new meaning by building on what he or she already knows. The supervisor facilitates this process and, where appropriate, adds meaning from alternative perspectives.

Probes That Add Meaning for the Counseling and Supervisory Experience

- What have you learned about working with me?
- What do you struggle with in supervision?
- How can we be more effective in supervision?

- What have you learned about working with this client?
- How is your theory of counseling giving you a foundation to work with this client?
- How has new awareness changed your goals?

In the last step, apply, the supervisor monitors the implementation of new learning into the counseling and supervision.

Probes That Facilitate the Use of New Learning

- What can we do in supervision to deal with the frustration you feel when this client does not follow through?
- How do you evaluate your ability to understand your client's behavior?
- What have you learned working with this client that might help you with the other clients we discuss?
- How will you begin your next session with this client?
- What homework can you do to gain more knowledge about this client's addiction?
- What techniques will you use with this client?
- What are the options and possible outcomes you have considered?

■ Evaluating the Work of the Counselor

One of the roles that a counselor supervisor must assume is that of an evaluator. Evaluation in supervision can be defined this way:

> **Evaluation:** The "objective appraisal of the supervisee's performance based on clearly defined criteria that are realistic and attainable" (Kadushin, 1992).

In the collaborative model of supervision, the process of evaluation can still be promoted as a collaborative process and a shared responsibility. There is no question that supervisors have the authority and ethical responsibility to evaluate counselors' effectiveness and fitness for the professional practice of counseling (Bernard & Goodyear, 2004; Borders & Brown, 2005). However, that does not preclude the use of collaborative methods to discharge this functional duty.

Characteristics of Effective Coevaluation in a Collaborative Supervisory Relationship

- Coconstructed evaluation agendas, goals, and targets (What will be learned?).
- Jointly selected performance criterion (How well will it be learned?).
- Mutually agreed-on observable samples and products of performance (What will be the evidence of learning?).

This disposition toward evaluation promotes the explicit intention and reasons for the assessment of the supervisee's level of competency demonstration. It invites supervisees to claim their level of competency by comparing evidence of their performance to the competencies they have helped to construct. This approach to evaluation fosters the use of self, peer, and expert data collection and behavioral assessment in formulating a conclusion about the effectiveness of the work. The use of a written supervision agreement, mutually developed, fosters growth of the supervisee and provides critical documentation of the supervision.

EXAMPLE

The Case of Marquel: Coevaluation and Feedback

Marquel (supervisee) is working with a 27-year-old woman who is engaged to be married. She entered counseling to deal with anxiety she has been experiencing. The client recently reported she was sexually abused as a child. Because the client feared no one would believe her, she never disclosed this to anyone before, but she feels she is not able to keep it in any longer. The perpetrator was a neighbor and the abuse occurred when she was 7 years old. The client reports that she feels okay and believes this experience will not affect her relationship with her fiancé, although she is worried that her fiancé may have difficulty with her past sexual abuse and leave her. She wonders whether or not to tell him. Marquel has worked with other survivors of sexual abuse, but he is concerned about this client and unable to stop thinking about this situation. Marquel seeks supervision from his supervisor to help him with this case and deal with his concerns for his client.

■ Using the FERA Inquiry Model for Evaluating the Work of the Supervisee

The first step in using the FERA process, again, is to focus, this time on the counselor's performance in both the counseling and supervisory relationships.

Probes That Help Focus on the Counselor's Performance

- What are your goals for supervision in this case?
- What aspects of your work do you want to address?
- What role do your discomfort or concerns for this client play in your work?
- How do you judge if your concerns for this client inhibit or promote your effectiveness with her?
- What criteria do you use to evaluate your effectiveness with this goal?
- How do you judge the effectiveness of your interventions with this client?
- What does this client do to let you know if you are accurately empathic?

The second step, exploration, encourages the counselor to frame questions, develop hypotheses, and predict consequences of action that might be taken. Once the supervisor feels the counselor is focused on an aspect of evaluation, he or she might shift to encouraging the counselor to test the situation.

Probes That Test the Counselor's Evaluation

- What criteria should we choose to evaluate your work in supervision?
- Where do you begin with your self-evaluation of your performance in this area?
- What can we do differently to enhance the supervision experience for you?
- What can we look at to evaluate your ability to … ?
- What do you need to know next?
- What skills do you want to develop next?

The third step in the FERA model, reflect, is engaged by facilitating dialogue that promotes a shared understanding of the counseling and supervising experiences. After exploring shared experiences regarding evaluation, the supervisor poses interventions that invite the counselor to derive new meaning from these experiences.

Probes That Add New Meaning for the Supervisee in Relation to Evaluation

- What does my evaluation of your work mean to you?
- What have you learned about yourself today?
- What have you learned about how you use or ignore your theoretical orientation?
- How much do you trust your self-evaluation of your effectiveness with this client?
- What might you want to do differently with this client?
- How have your goals for working with this client changed?
- Tell me what you have learned about yourself working with someone from a different or similar culture.
- Do you see this client differently?
- How congruent has your behavior been with the goals you set with this client?

The final step, apply, calls on the supervisor to monitor the implementation of new learning in the counseling and supervision.

Probes That Enhance the Use of New Learning About Evaluation

- I am going to do … to improve my supervisory skills.
- What outside work will you do for professional development in this area?
- What are you going to do to improve your counseling skills?

- How will you gain the needed knowledge?
- How will you integrate new learning into supervision? Counseling? Other areas?
- What are your plans for your new learning with your client?
- How can this supervision support your professional or career goals?

SUMMARY

It was our intent in this chapter to provide novice supervisors with a framework to begin the formal professional development training needed if they are to become ethical and effective supervisors. The collaborative model of supervision, like all attempts to model complex human interactions, is a simplistic attempt to explain the intricate process of supervisor development. However, it has been proposed as one way to establish the essential elements of a map to guide the journey toward supervisor maturity. The model suggests the needed knowledge acquisition, a strategy for skill development, and the promotion of a collaborative disposition toward the work of a supervisor. The model incorporates the application of an inquiry learning cycle, from focus through exploration, to reflection and application, as a strategic approach to the tasks of supervision: building the therapeutic alliance, constructing meaning, and evaluating the work of the supervisee.

It is through the application of a tangible model of supervision, in this case, the collaborative model of supervision, that novice supervisors can begin to chart a course of professional development that will promote their sense of self-as-supervisor (Alonso, 1983; Hess, 1986). The concrete structure of this model allows beginning supervisors to move quickly through the mechanical operations of acting like a supervisor to a more fully integrated and autonomous supervisor, representative of a more advanced stage of supervisor development (Stoltenberg et al., 1998). Although the model may only be an outline for the first few steps on a much longer and continuing journey, it provides clear indicators to ensure that the novice supervisor gets off on the right foot and in the right direction.

Chapter 6: Key Terms

- ► Therapeutic working alliance
- ► Evaluation

- ► Focus
- ► Explore
- ► Reflect

- ► Apply
- ► Critical friend

What Are the Essential Elements of Counseling With Which All Counselors Must Be Familiar?

Understanding Human Growth and Development

Kimberly Blair
University of Pittsburgh

Stephen P. Kachmar
Duquesne University

In This Chapter

▶ *Prenatal Development*
- Influences on Prenatal Development
- Genetic Makeup
- Prenatal Developmental Periods
- Risks During Prenatal Development

▶ *Infancy: The First 2 Years of Life*
- Physical Development in Infancy
- Cognitive Development in Infancy
- Social-Emotional Development in Infancy

▶ *Early Childhood: The Preschool Period*
- Physical Development in Early Childhood
- Cognitive Development in Early Childhood
- Social-Emotional Development in Early Childhood

▶ *Middle Childhood: Elementary School Years*
- Physical Development in Middle Childhood

- Cognitive Development in Middle Childhood
- Social-Emotional Development in Middle Childhood

▶ *Adolescence: Transition From Childhood to Adulthood*
- Physical Development in Adolescence
- Cognitive Development in Adolescence
- Social-Emotional Development in Adolescence

▶ *Adulthood*
- Physical Development in Adulthood
- Cognitive Development in Adulthood
- Social-Emotional Development in Adulthood

▶ *Death, Dying, and Bereavement*
- Death and the Young
- Theory of Dying Process
- Grief and Bereavement

PRENATAL DEVELOPMENT

The study of human growth and development begins before an infant is ever born, and, indeed, the development that occurs during prenatal periods has a significant impact on a person's health and well-being. Our aim in this chapter is to highlight the significant physical, cognitive, and socioemotional gains that are part of the life stages, beginning with the prenatal period and concluding with old age.

■ Influences on Prenatal Development

An individual's genetic makeup and environmental influences combine to determine physical and behavioral characteristics and course of development. Reaction range (Gottesman, 1963) and canalization (Waddington, 1957) are concepts that attempt to explain the degrees of genetic and environmental influence on development. These concepts are defined along with two other terms—genotype and phenotype—that are key to understanding prenatal development.

Genotype: The underlying genetic makeup of an organism.

Phenotype: An organism's manifest physical and psychological characteristics, which are determined by both genetic makeup and environmental factors.

Canalization: Refers to situations in which the environment has little impact on inherited characteristics.

Reaction range: The range of possible phenotypes for a particular genotype across all environmental influences (Scarr, 1984).

To understand development, it is necessary to know about the basic building blocks of growth, such as genotypes and phenotypes. Additionally, one must understand something about the developmental process. Two terms that address the 'how' of development are critical period and sensitive period, defined as followed:

Critical period: A limited time frame in which an organism is biologically predisposed to acquire certain behaviors in the presence of the appropriate environmental stimuli.

Sensitive periods: In humans, the periods that are optimal, but not exclusive, for certain aspects of development.

■ Genetic Makeup

Genes are the basic unit of heredity and are carried on rod-shaped structures called *chromosomes*. Each normal human has 46 chromosomes or 23 pairs of chromosomes, with each pair having one chromosome from each parent. Of the 23 chromosomal pairs, 22 are matched pairs called autosomes; the 23rd pair is the sex chromosome. Genes also come in matched pairs (one from each parent), but may have different forms called *alleles*. If the alleles from each parent are alike, that trait is homozygous; if the alleles are different, then the trait is heterozygous. Heterozygous pairings can be dominant–recessive, in which the dominant gene determines the pattern of genetic inheritance, or codominant, in which both alleles influence genetic inheritance. Many traits appear to be polygenetic, a pattern of genetic inheritance in which many genes affect the characteristic in question. Genetic mutations and chromosomal abnormalities are major causes of serious developmental problems.

■ Prenatal Developmental Periods

Prenatal development can be divided into three periods:

1. During the period of the ovum (Weeks 1–3 of pregnancy) implantation occurs and the neural tube forms.
2. During the period of the embryo (Weeks 4–8 of pregnancy) most organ systems develop, moving in **cephalocaudal** (from head to feet) and **proximodistal** (from center of the body to extremities) directions.
3. During the fetal period (Week 8–birth) the reproductive system forms and other systems mature.

■ Risks During Prenatal Development

During the prenatal stage of life, disruptions known as teratogens can occur that have adverse effects on development. The term *teratogen* can be defined as follows:

Teratogens: Environmental agents capable of causing developmental abnormalities in utero.

Examples of teratogens that may cause immediate structural damage during prenatal development include drugs, alcohol, environmental pollutants, and infectious diseases, as well as other maternal factors such as diet and stress. Some health problems or neurological impairments caused by teratogens may not become evident until later in development.

INFANCY: THE FIRST 2 YEARS OF LIFE

Once an infant is born, the developmental domains expand beyond the largely biological aspects. Beginning with this section on infancy, we look at the physical, cognitive, and socioemotional developmental domains in which changes and transitions occur across the life span.

Physical Development in Infancy

When infants are born, they enter the world with a number of reflexes in place. Some of these reflexes are necessary for survival and adaptation, and others do not have apparent survival value and disappear during the first few months of life. A number of survival and primitive reflexes are provided in the lists that follow.

Survival Reflexes

- Breathing.
- Rooting.
- Sucking.
- Papillary.
- Eye blink.
- Primitive Reflexes
- Moro (startle).
- Palmar.
- Plantar.
- Babinski.
- Stepping.
- Swimming.

As in prenatal development, physical and motor development in infancy continues to follow cephalocaudal and proximodistal patterns of development. Gross motor development generally follows a specific sequence. Some of the major accomplishments in gross and fine motor development during infancy are outlined here.

Gross and Fine Motor Skills Development in Infancy

- Following a proximodistal pattern, infants first raise their heads and chest, and then turn over, sit, crawl, stand, and walk.
- Between 11 and 15 months of age, infants typically can walk unaided.
- Fine motor skills such as uncoordinated reaching and grasping with the palm (ulnar grasp) are initially evident and later transform into more coordinated pincer grasping using thumb and forefinger.

In addition to making gains in motor ability, infants' physical development in the areas of vision and hearing also is significant. Infants are sensitive to a wide range of sounds and can be soothed, alerted, or distressed depending on the frequency or rhythm of the tones.

Facets of Auditory Development in Infancy

- Infants can discriminate between speech and nonspeech sounds.
- Infants show a preference for human voices.

- Infants tend to prefer their mother's voice as compared to other voices by 4 months of age.

Vision also improves dramatically early in infancy. Some of the more prominent gains are listed here.

Facets of Visual Development in Infancy

- Infants develop abilities for focusing, color discrimination, and visual acuity during the first few months.
- Depth perception develops early in infancy, and studies using the "visual cliff" demonstrate that infants can interpret spatial cues for depth.
- Infants show a preference for human faces as compared to objects.

■ Cognitive Development in Infancy

Two of the more well-known approaches to understanding cognitive development are the Piagetian theory of child development and the information processing perspective.

Piaget termed the developmental period of early infancy the sensorimotor stage. This stage is characterized primarily by reflexive learning; one of the most important achievements children make in this stage is known as object permanence.

Object permanence: The understanding that objects continue to exist even when out of sight.

A number of other achievements that appear during the sensorimotor stage are listed next.

Sensorimotor Stage: Cognitive Learning Gains in Infancy

- Learning is reflexive and occurs through exploration with eyes, ears, hands, and other sensorimotor equipment.
- Toddlers become goal-oriented and capable of symbolic thought.
- Young children achieve object permanence.
- Infants develop the ability to categorize objects first perceptually, then conceptually during play.

By the second year of life, young children have achieved a number of cognitive gains that require more than just reflexive learning. Some of the more salient concepts promoted by the information processing perspective include deferred imitation, habituation, and dishabituation. These are defined as follows:

Deferred imitation: An infant's ability to imitate an adult's sounds or behaviors after a delay of several hours or days.

Habituation: An infant's waning interest in a stimulus that is repeatedly presented.

Dishabituation: An infant's restored interest in a known stimulus.

A range of information processing developments are listed next.

Information Processing: Key Learning Gains in Infancy

- Infants' ability to understand and process information includes speed of habituation and dishabituation, visual novelty preference, and cross-modal transfer.
- Infants become increasingly able to sustain and shift attention.
- Toddlers are capable of recognition early in infancy and are able to engage in recall by the end of the first year.

   Another aspect of cognitive development is communication and linguistic ability. Prior to the use of words, babies' communication is prelinguistic and includes crying, cooing, babbling, and imitating language sounds. Two theories of language development have tried to explain how infants move from a prelinguistic to linguistic stage. The first, learning theory, emphasizes the influence of reinforcement and imitation, whereas the second, nativism, maintains that the ability to learn language is innate. Today, both genetic and environmental influences on language development are recognized, and early communication between caregivers and children, such as **motherese** or child-directed speech, is seen to play a crucial role. Between 9 months and 3 years, a significant amount of linguistic development occurs.

Timeframe for Linguistic Development in Infancy

- Babies are able to understand meaningful speech around 9 or 10 months of age.
- Between 10 and 14 months of age, a baby typically says the first word that is often considered **holophrastic,** or the expression of a complete thought as a single word.
- Between 16 and 24 months a child's vocabulary explodes.
- Between 18 and 24 months the emergence of two-word sentences, or **telegraphic** expressions, generally occurs.
- By age 3, grammar and syntax are fairly well developed; however, they are characterized by the overregularization, underextending, and overextending of word meanings.

■ Social-Emotional Development in Infancy

The foundation of early social-emotional development is built on the concepts of temperament and attachment.

Temperament: A child's typical way of behaving and responding to the environment.

Attachment: The bond between a child and the primary caregiver.

Although there are several theories of temperament, three patterns are typically described.

Temperament Patterns (Santrock, 1999)

1. Easy tempered children usually respond positively to the environment.
2. Difficult tempered children typically respond negatively to the environment.
3. Slow-to-warm-up tempered children often have low activity levels.

Temperament characteristics appear to be largely innate but can be affected by environmental circumstances. The goodness of fit between a child's temperament and the environment provided by caregivers is important for early emotional adjustment and the development of emotional bonds or attachments. As well, the responsiveness of a child's primary caregiver predicts the quality of early attachment. Three main patterns of attachment (Ainsworth, 1979) have been identified as follows:

1. Secure attachment.
2. Anxious-ambivalent (resistant) attachment.
3. Avoidant attachment.

A secure attachment is generally evident when parenting is warm and nurturing, resulting in a child who trusts that his or her needs will be met.

Characteristics of Children With Secure Attachments

- Show distress at separation from their mother.
- Can be easily comforted on the mother's return.
- Use the primary caregiver as a secure base from which to explore their world.

Ambivalent attachments are a type of insecure attachment often found to be associated with inconsistent caregiving.

Characteristics of Children With Ambivalent Attachments

- Show distress at separation.
- Cannot be easily comforted.
- Alternate between approaching and resisting the mother.

In the case of avoidant attachment, also considered an insecure attachment, caregivers typically show less warmth and affection to their babies as compared to other mothers.

Characteristics of Children With Avoidant Attachments

- Do not appear distressed by separations from the mother.
- Actively avoid or ignore the mother.

A fourth pattern of attachment, called disorganized (Main & Solomon, 1986), is thought to be the most insecure and most likely to be related to later social-emotional adjustment difficulties.

During the second half of the first year, the issue of attachment becomes strikingly prominent with the emergence of separation and stranger anxiety, which is most intense around 18 months of age.

General emotional development is thought to be externally influenced by the responsiveness of parents during infancy and, over time, self-regulation becomes internalized. Self-awareness also emerges during the first few years of life; a few key gains are noted here.

Sense of Self: Developmental Gains

- Infants learn that they have their own existence, separate from others.
- Infants begin to discover that their actions can have predictable effects on the world around them.
- During toddlerhood children become aware of their own physical features.

EARLY CHILDHOOD: THE PRESCHOOL PERIOD

Early childhood typically refers to the period between 3 and 5 years of age. In general, children's physical as well as cognitive and social-emotional gains are quite outstanding. In this section, we look at the physical, cognitive, language, and social-emotional development.

■ Physical Development in Early Childhood

The general growth curve reflects rapid growth during infancy and adolescence and slower, although noticeable gains in body size in early and middle childhood. Some of the typical physical changes that occur in children from ages 3 to 5 are mentioned here.

Gross Motor and Fine Motor Gains in Early Childhood

- Skeletal development includes the gradual hardening of bones through ossification.
- Individual differences in body size, including height and weight, become more apparent.
- Gross motor skills advance and become better coordinated with a shift of the center of gravity toward the trunk.
- Gaits become smooth and rhythmic, and gross motor skills show signs of automaticity.
- Fine motor skills also begin to show automaticity.

EXAMPLE

Gross Motor and Fine Motor Skill Development: Age 3 to 5

The gross and fine motor gains that girls and boys make in early childhood are manifested in the new abilities that emerge on the scene. Preschoolers gradually begin to dress and feed themselves with more ease. Children's drawings show more complexity and realism and their writing becomes more controlled. Handedness emerges during early childhood and children begin to utilize a typical pencil grip for writing.

■ Cognitive Development in Early Childhood

Cognitive development in early childhood reflects what Piaget termed the preoperational level of thinking. Young children display thought processes that are characterized by animism, reification, and egocentrism. These concepts can be understood in this way:

Animism: Attributing live characteristics to inanimate objects.

Reification: Treating concepts or abstractions as if they were real, concrete things.

Egocentrism: A self-centered view of the world in which everything is perceived in relation to oneself.

Some generalizations can be made about thought processes during the preoperational level of cognition in early childhood.

Preoperational Stage: Cognitive Learning Gains in Early Childhood

- Symbolic thinking, which began during infancy, continues to be refined.
- Because thinking is not yet logical, children's problem solving is concrete.

- Thinking is characterized by centration and irreversibility, which leads to difficulties with conservation and hierarchical classification.

In addition to the important contributions Piaget made about thought and thought processes in early childhood, there are also gains in the information processing abilities of young children. Around age 4, children are beginning to construct a "theory of mind" and are becoming knowledgeable of their own metacognitions. Metagcognition can be defined in this way:

> **Metacognition:** The process of monitoring one's own process of thinking and memory.

Some highlights of development relative to information processing include the following.

Information Processing Achievements in Early Childhood

- Although preschool-age children are considered to have relatively short attention spans, sustained and selective attention continues to advance during this period of development.
- Memory capacities improve, although recall memory is less well developed than recognition memory at this age.
- Episodic memory is well developed.
- Young children become able to approach challenging tasks by trying out a variety of strategies, interpreting the individual success of different strategies, and eventually selecting strategies that will work best in similar situations.

Vygotsky's sociocultural theory also has applications to early childhood. Vygotsky considered language to be the foundation of cognition, and private speech to be important for helping children master challenging tasks within the zone of proximal development. The processes known as fast mapping, syntactic bootstrapping, and semantic bootstrapping (Gleitman, 1990) are explanations for the explosion in language and vocabulary development that occurs in preschool-age children. These processes can be understood this way:

> **Fast mapping:** The ability to build vocabularies very quickly by learning to connect new words with their underlying concepts after only brief encounter.

> **Syntactic bootstrapping:** The process of discovering the meaning of words by observing how the words are used in syntax.

> **Semantic bootstrapping:** A process of relying on word meanings to learn grammatical rules.

A number of other important linguistic gains that appear in early childhood are noted here.

Linguistic Gains in Early Childhood

- Grammar and syntax are fairly well developed by age 3.
- Young children become more skilled at pragmatics, appropriately adapting their speech to their listeners as the situation demands.

■ Social-Emotional Development in Early Childhood

The social-emotional development in early childhood begins to expand as the child develops, including not just gains in the sense of self, but also influences from peer relations and parenting styles.

Sense of Self: Early Childhood Advances

- Preschoolers' self-concepts primarily reflect observable characteristics and beliefs.
- Self-esteem, which is high in preschool, begins to differentiate or become associated with emerging skills.
- Children feel good about themselves for having successfully accomplished certain tasks and judge themselves poorly for failures in performing other tasks.

Along with the development of self-understanding, the emergence of emotions such as empathy, shame, and guilt reflect a child's developing self-consciousness and emotional and social competence. As children's self-understanding and emotional understanding improves, and, as children become more self-conscious, their social behavior is affected. Empathetic emotional experiences, combined with the influence of temperament and parenting styles, promote the expression of sympathy and prosocial behavior.

A child's propensity to exhibit prosocial behavior is often observable in peer interactions. During early childhood, social interactions with peers primarily occur in the context of play. Parten (1932) described the process of increasing social interaction in the context of five types of play. These categories of play include solitary play, onlooker play, parallel play, associative play, and cooperative play; each type of play is described briefly.

Types of Play

- *Solitary play* involves children playing by themselves.
- *Onlooker play* involves children who are playing passively while watching and talking to other children.
- *Parallel play* refers to instances where the child is playing alongside or in the midst of other children, but remains engaged in his or her own independent play activity.

- *Associative play* is interactive, yet not coordinated with regard to play objectives.
- *Cooperative play* refers to play interactions between children that are organized and have specific goals, as in the case of games.

Positive peer interactions exhibited during children's play may reflect their social problem-solving ability, whereas negative peer interactions may involve some form of aggressive behavior. During early childhood, instrumental aggression declines, whereas hostile aggression tends to increase. Hostile aggression may be in the form of overt aggression or relational aggression.

Relational aggression: More common in girls and involves the act of damaging social relationships and status.

Overt aggression: More common in boys and involves physically aggressive acts.

Parents directly and indirectly influence a child's early peer relationships and socially competent behavior. Four parenting styles are commonly recognized: authoritative, authoritarian, permissive, and uninvolved.

Parenting Styles

- *Authoritative* parents tend to be highly accepting and involved, setting clear limits and appropriate control techniques that help children observe the consequences of their behavior in the emotional reactions of others.
- *Authoritarian* parents tend to be cold and rejecting and adopt a coercive approach to controlling child behavior.
- *Permissive* parents are warm and accepting, but may exert little control on their children, opting instead to be overindulging or inattentive.
- *Uninvolved* parents (Maccoby & Martin, 1983) are emotionally detached, inattentive, and indifferent to their children's behavior.

According to Baumrind (1971) authoritative parents are the most successful, promoting empathy and prosocial behavior as well as psychological adjustment. Authoritarian, permissive, and uninvolved approaches to parenting are likely to increase the possibility of maladaptive psychological adjustment in children, including behaviors that are oppositional, anxious, or unhappy.

MIDDLE CHILDHOOD: ELEMENTARY SCHOOL YEARS

Middle childhood refers to the period of development that typically ranges from ages 6 to 11. This period is marked especially by more sophisticated advances in cognitive development and increasingly greater influences from the peer and social spheres.

■ Physical Development in Middle Childhood

Physical development in middle childhood reflects slowed rates of body growth; however, there are wide differences in growth rates that vary based on genetics, nutrition, emotional health, ethnicity, and culture. Marked improvements are observed in gross and fine motor skills, strength, and agility. Gender differences in physical development are apparent during this period.

■ Cognitive Development in Middle Childhood

During middle childhood, children enter Piaget's concrete operational stage of cognitive development. The ability to understand conservation is a major gain in middle childhood. Conservation can be defined as follows:

Conservation: The ability to understand an object's stability despite a change in appearance.

Some other advances in cognitive ability noted by Piaget for this stage are provided here.

Concrete Operational Stage: Cognitive Gains in Middle Childhood

- Children are beginning to be able to engage in logical thinking to solve problems.
- Reasoning is concrete and limited to tangible objects or concepts.
- With the ability to think logically comes the ability to solve conservation problems, which includes identity conservation, reversibility, and decentration.
- Children advance in their understanding of classification and class inclusion.
- Children are not only better able to organize objects and concepts into logical groups or categories, but they are beginning to understand seriation and transitivity, demonstrated by their ability to compare objects and organize them according to logical hierarchies or levels.

From an information processing perspective, middle childhood signals a time of growth for children in their ability to learn new and more efficient strategies for processing information.

Advances in Information Processing in Middle Childhood

- Selective and sustained attention continues to improve.
- Older children are better able to filter out irrelevant information to focus on what is necessary.
- Although children may begin using memory strategies in early childhood, they do not begin using strategies such as rehearsal and organization efficiently until middle childhood.
- Children have a more advanced understanding of how learning and memory occur.

An enhanced understanding of metacognition benefits the school-age children by aiding them in academic skill development, such as reading, comprehension, writing, and problem solving. A sense of metacognition also helps developing children become better at approaching problems and critical thinking.

By middle childhood, children demonstrate a comprehensive knowledge and use of language. During this period there continue to be significant gains in vocabulary, grammar, and pragmatic skills.

Refinements in Linguistic Ability in Middle Childhood

- Children expand the number, richness, and complexity of the words available to them.
- Grammatical mistakes made in early childhood such as overregularization are corrected.
- Pragmatic skills increase in early childhood.
- Children begin to understand how best to communicate with others given the context.
- Code switching is utilized as children learn to adapt their language to the individual with whom they are speaking (Shatz & Gelman, 1973).

EXAMPLE

Code Switching in Middle Childhood

Interactions with peers may call for a restricted code or informal speech, whereas communications with adults may call for a more formal or elaborated code. Older children are able to process hidden meanings in communications (i.e., idioms) as opposed to just the literal meaning of words.

■ Social-Emotional Development in Middle Childhood

Children's self-concepts continue to be refined and move beyond observable characteristics and beliefs to include psychological traits. Some of the salient gains in self-understanding are noted here.

Self-Concept: Developmental Gains in Middle Childhood

- Children begin to make social comparisons, interpreting their own abilities and behaviors in relation those around them.
- The high self-esteem typical during early childhood drops to a more realistic level as older children begin to incorporate feedback about their own skills and competencies in comparison to the skills and abilities of others.
- Self-esteem also differentiates in middle childhood, yielding at least four separate categories including academic competence, social competence, physical and athletic competence, and physical appearance.

Emotionally, older children's experience of self-conscious emotions is associated with personal responsibility and occurs without adult prompting. Gains in cognitive development and emotional understanding make possible better developed social perspective taking. Children become able to interpret what others are thinking and feeling. Gradually, they become able to understand another's perspective and subsequently engage in third-party perspective taking.

Children make significant gains in their ability to self-regulate emotions during middle childhood. Emotion regulation has been linked to numerous aspects of social functioning in preschoolers, including socially appropriate behavior, popularity with peers, adjustment, shyness, empathy, sympathy, and prosocial behavior (Eisenberg, Fabes, Guthrie, & Reiser, 2002). Two general strategies are outlined as a way to cope with stress and regulate negative emotions.

Strategies for Emotional Regulation in Middle Childhood (Lazarus & Lazarus, 1994)

1. Problem-centered coping suggests that children appraise the situation causing the distress and, through problem solving, identify ways in which to change the situation.
2. Emotion-centered coping strategy occurs within the individual.

By middle childhood, peer groups become increasingly important. Children tend to choose friends who are similar to themselves in terms of age, gender, race, ethnicity, socioeconomic status, popularity, achievement, and social behavior. Research in which children report which peers they like and dislike suggests that peer acceptance is organized into four basic groups of children: those who are popular, rejected, controversial, and neglected.

> Children tend to choose friends who are similar to themselves in terms of age, gender, race, ethnicity, socioeconomic status, popularity, achievement, and social behavior.

Common Classifications of Peer Groups in Middle Childhood

1. Popular children are typically well liked by other children; two subtypes of popular children reflect behavior that is popular-prosocial or popular-antisocial. The popular-prosocial children tend to be socially competent, whereas popular-antisocial children, although accepted by peers, tend to be highly aggressive boys.
2. Rejected children are actively disliked and also tend to fall into two subtypes: rejected-aggressive and rejected-withdrawn. Both groups often experience adjustment problems. The rejected-withdrawn group consists of children who

tend to be socially awkward, passive, and are often victims of peers' aggression.

3. Controversial children, who are liked by some peers and disliked by others, often engage in both prosocial behavior and bullying of peers to maintain social dominance.

4. Neglected children are typically not reported as liked or disliked by peers and, although they appear to have limited social contacts, are often well adjusted and socially skilled.

ADOLESCENCE: TRANSITION FROM CHILDHOOD TO ADULTHOOD

The transition from middle childhood to adolescence begins to occur around age 12 and continues through age 19. This often tumultuous time is a period of great advancement, particularly in adolescents' physical development and social-emotional development as they strive to form their sense of identity.

■ Physical Development in Adolescence

The beginning of adolescence is marked by puberty. Growth hormone released from the pituitary gland stimulates the release of other hormones by other glands. Two basic types of physical pubertal changes occur as a result of the hormone changes that direct puberty: sexual maturation and body growth.

Aspects of Sexual Maturation

- Estrogens and androgens are released and trigger sexual maturation.
- Bodily changes affect primary sexual characteristics such as the reproductive organs and secondary sexual characteristics, such as external physical changes.
- Menarche in girls and spermarche in boys are signals of sexual maturation.

Physical changes not directly related to sexual maturation also occur in adolescence and tend to reflect a trend in reverse of the cephalocaudal growth characteristic of childhood. When thyroxine is released by the thyroid gland, rapid gains in height and weight take place. Some of the salient physical gains related to adolescence are noted here.

Aspects of Physical Maturation in Adolescence

- Adolescents grow 10 to 11 inches and gain 50 to 75 pounds.
- Hands, legs, and feet grow first.
- Boys' shoulders broaden and girls' hips broaden.

- Boys add more muscle and girls add more fat.
- Gross motor skills improve, with boys demonstrating larger gains than girls.

The timing of maturation can have psychological effects. Early-maturing boys and late-maturing girls tend to have more positive body images and psychological adjustment. Early-maturing girls and late-maturing boys tend to experience more emotional and social difficulties.

■ Cognitive Development in Adolescence

With adolescence comes the capacity for abstract, scientific thinking, or what Piaget called formal operations. Although not all adolescents or adults become capable of logical and abstract thought, a majority show the cognitive abilities described next.

Formal Operations: Cognitive Learning Gains in Adolescence

- Adolescents are able to engage in complex problem solving with hypothesis testing, or hypothetico-deductive reasoning.
- Adolescents are able to engage in propositional thought, reasoning without the need for real-world evidence.

The information processing perspective is consistent with Piaget's view of adolescent cognitive development. Although other aspects of information processing, such as attention, strategy use, knowledge, cognitive self-regulation, and processing speed continue to advance, metacognition is thought to be central to the development of abstract thought and scientific reasoning (Kuhn, 1999).

Adolescent argumentativeness, self-consciousness, and idealism appear to be related to their newfound capacity for abstract thought. Two terms that describe teenagers' self-consciousness and self-centeredness are imaginary audience and personal fable (Elkind & Bowen, 1979; Inhelder & Piaget, 1958).

Imaginary audience: A form of egocentrism that describes an adolescent's impression that he or she is the center of everyone's attention and judgment.

Personal fable: Adolescents' inflated opinion of themselves and their importance.

Although with adolescence often comes the advanced capacity of abstract thinking, adolescents also may have difficulty with everyday planning and decision making (Berk, 2004).

■ Social-Emotional Development in Adolescence

As in other stages of development, adolescents make some characteristic strides in self-concept.

Gains in Self-Concept During Adolescence

■ Adolescents begin to use qualifiers to describe themselves and their self-concepts become more organized.

■ They begin to recognize that their self-concepts may change depending on the situation.

■ Most adolescents lose some of the confidence and high self-esteem characteristic of childhood.

■ Self-esteem continues to expand and differentiate to include dimensions such as close friendship, romantic appeal, and job competence (Harter, 1999).

Adolescence is typically a time when teenagers search for their identity by exploring their values and life goals. The search for identity is classified into four categories of identity status: identity achievement, moratorium, identity foreclosure, and identity diffusion.

Categories of Identity Status (Marcia, 1980)

1. Identity achievement reflects a commitment to self-chosen values and future goals.
2. Identity moratorium refers to adolescents who have not yet made a commitment—they are exploring possibilities and roles to find those that best fit them.
3. Identity-foreclosed adolescents have accepted another's values and goals, often those of their parents.
4. Identity diffusion is characterized by a lack of direction; the identity-diffused adolescents have not committed to any goals and are not actively trying to determine what their future goals are to be.

Of the four identity statuses, identity achievement and moratorium are most indicative of psychological well-being and a healthy search for a sense of self.

The influence of peers becomes increasingly significant during adolescence as teenagers search for their sense of identity and belonging to a larger group. Some of the more important manifestations of peer relations in adolescence are noted here.

Aspects of Peer Relations in Adolescence

■ Generally, adolescent friendships foster self-concept, perspective taking, identity, and the capacity for intimate relationships (Connolly & Goldberg, 1999).

■ Girls tend to place more emphasis on emotional bonds, whereas boys tend to emphasize status and mastery.

- **Cliques** are small groups of five to seven members who tend to resemble one another in family background, interests, and social status, and form.
- With the increased importance of peer affiliation, peer pressure and conformity increases.
- Adolescent romantic relationships serve as practice for the more mature bonds of adulthood, although most dating relationships established during adolescence dissolve or become less satisfying after identity formation occurs (Shaver, Furman, & Buhrmester, 1985).

Adolescent emotional development includes the search for autonomy. As noted, part of this search typically involves a shift away from the influence of the family to include the greater influence of peers. However, parent–child relationships continue to be important. Parent–child conflict during adolescence is not unusual, but serious relationship difficulties tend to have their roots earlier in childhood, rather than being a product of adolescent turmoil.

E X A M P L E

Parenting Through Adolescence

Parenting styles and cultural identity can affect self-esteem. Adolescents with authoritative parents tend to have higher self-esteem and are more able to resist unfavorable peer pressure. African American culture, which benefits from large, warm, extended families and a sense of ethnic pride tend to produce adolescents with higher self-esteem (Gray-Little & Hafdahl, 2000).

ADULTHOOD

The longest period of development, adulthood begins in the early 20s and extends into late life and eventually to the point of death. Highlights of physical development and decline, as well as facets of cognitive and social-emotional development in adulthood are presented.

■ Physical Development in Adulthood

Body structures reach maximum capacity and efficiency in the teens and 20s. After this period, biological aging or **senescence,** which refers to genetically influenced declines in the performance of organs and systems, begins to occur (Cristofalo, Tresini, Francis, & Volker, 1999). Individual variation in biological aging is great and is influenced by many factors such as genetics, lifestyle, and living environment. Some of the genetic factors related to aging are mentioned here.

Genetic Factors Contributing to Aging

- Biological aging may result from a complex blend of both the programmed effects of specific genes and the random events that may cause cells to deteriorate.
- Age-related damage to DNA is thought to be due to the release of highly reactive free radicals.
- Genetic and cellular deterioration also affects organs and tissues when, over time, protein fibers form links and become less elastic, producing declines in many organs.
- Endocrine and immune system declines may also contribute to aging.

Most of the gradual sensory changes that occur in adulthood begin around age 30, whereas other gradual changes in physical health begin to take place in early adulthood and later accelerate. Some examples of common declines seen in adulthood are mentioned next.

Common Physical Declines in Adulthood

- Athletic gross motor skills requiring speed, strength, and coordination peak in the early 20s and begin to decline gradually.
- Skills requiring endurance peak in the late 20s and early 30s before showing gradual declines.
- When tendons and ligaments stiffen with age, speed and flexibility of movement diminishes.
- **Presbyopia,** a major change in vision, results in diminished color discrimination, night vision, and visual acuity of marked decline between ages 70 and 80.
- Hearing loss, or **presbycusis,** usually affects a person's ability to detect higher frequencies first. Age-related hearing loss appears to begin earlier and show more rapid declines for men than for women.
- Reduced capacities of cardiovascular and respiratory systems occur, particularly in late adulthood, as stiffening takes place in the connective tissues of the lungs, chest muscles, and heart muscle.
- After age 35, women's reproductive capacity declines significantly and ends with the occurrence of menopause.
- For men, a gradual decrease is observed in the concentration and motility of sperm after age 40 and reproductive capacity declines rather than ends.

■ Cognitive Development in Adulthood

A focus on intellectual ability is common to an examination of cognitive ability in adulthood. Some theories of intelligence include the following.

Understandings of Intelligence in Adulthood

- A classic pattern of intelligence suggests that intelligence increases until early adulthood and then declines through late adulthood in an inverted U-shaped pattern (Botwinick, 1977).
- Crystallized intelligence shows fewer age-related declines than fluid intelligence.
- Schaie's (1996) Seattle Longitudinal Study has shown that intellectual declines in adulthood do not occur significantly until late in life or evenly across intellectual abilities.

Information processing continues to be a relevant area of interest in adulthood. For example, speed of cognitive processing slows with age. Also, different memory systems reflect differences in cognitive aging effects.

Effects of Aging on Memory

- Episodic memory typically shows declines with advancing age, although some research indicates that lifestyle may have an impact on how much decline occurs.
- Semantic memory shows little in the way of age-related declines; in fact, research has often discovered that the vocabulary of older adults is often better than younger adults, although they may access the information more slowly.
- Procedural memory appears to be relatively unaffected by aging.
- Working memory for brief and simple tasks shows less in the way of age-related declines than does working memory for tasks that involve processing more complex information.

■ Social-Emotional Development in Adulthood

Adult development theorists describe social-emotional development throughout adulthood in similar ways. Like Erikson, Levinson's seasons of life theory (1978) and Valliant's (1977) psychosocial theories describe early adulthood as a time when development is focused on the search for intimacy. Middle adulthood is characterized by generativity—reaching out to others by giving to and guiding the next generation, as well as becoming guardians of their culture (Valliant, 1977). During late adulthood, the goal for individuals becomes looking back on their lives and coming to terms with and being satisfied with their achievements.

Theories of Adult Development

- Levinson described adult development in terms of a person's life structure—with the underlying design of life consisting of relationships with significant others.
- Valliant also explained development as being shaped by the quality of relationships with important people.

- Sternberg (1987, 1988) proposed a triangular theory of romantic love in which there are three components that shift in emphasis as relationships develop: intimacy, passion, and commitment. The passionate love presents at the beginning of a relationship giving way to intimacy and commitment, and forming the basis of companionate love.

   Another important influence on adult development is the **social clock** (Neugarten, 1968, 1979), which refers to life events such as marriage, a first job, a first child, and so on, that follow age-graded patterns based on societal and cultural expectations. According to the family life cycle, the development of families progresses in a series of phases that is consistent in most families around the world. Marriage, childbearing, and rearing occur in early adulthood. Children leave home, diminishing parenting responsibilities in middle age. Retirement, growing old, and the death of one's spouse characterize late adulthood (Framo, 1994; McGoldrick, Heiman, & Carter, 1993).

   The changes that occur in our social networks as people age may be referred to as the **social convoy.** Some bonds become closer, others are added, and still others become more distant. There are a number of psychosocial theories that describe the aging process. A few of these are briefly described next.

Psychosocial Theories of Aging

- Disengagement theory describes this social withdrawal as a result of the desires of the elderly to withdraw from society in anticipation of death (Cumming & Henry, 1961).
- Activity theory states that social barriers cause the decline in social interaction late in life (Maddox, 1963).
- Socioemotional selectivity theory proposes that social interaction does not suddenly decline in late adulthood, but that it is the physical and psychological changes that occur over time that lead to changes in social interaction (Lang, Staudinger, & Carstensen, 1998).

Overall, the goal of adult development is successful aging, which is defined as maximizing gains and minimizing losses.

DEATH, DYING, AND BEREAVEMENT

Like all other phases of life, death and dying have physical, cognitive, and emotional implications for the dying person and for that person's loved ones. From a physical perspective, there are generally three phases to the dying process:

1. The *agonal* phase refers to the initial moments in which the body can no longer sustain life.

2. *Clinical death* refers to a short interval in which resuscitation is still possible although circulatory, respiratory, and brain functioning have stopped.
3. *Mortality* refers to death that is final and without possibility of resuscitation.

■ Death and the Young

To grasp the cognitive component of death, dying, and bereavement, it is helpful to consider the age-related differences that exist with regards to understanding concepts of and attitudes toward death. Young children typically rely on the magical thinking characteristic of early childhood to make sense of death. However, between the ages of 7 and 10 (Kenyon, 2001), most children have mastered the three primary concepts related to death.

Major Concepts Related to Death and Dying

1. The concept of permanence emerges first.
2. Children next come to the understanding of universality, or an acceptance that all things eventually die.
3. Nonfunctionality emerges last, as children come to the understanding that all living functions cease at death, including thought, feeling, and movement.

Although these three primary concepts are mastered during childhood, adolescents often fail to apply their understanding that death can occur to anyone at any time. Adolescents tend to not apply the possibility of death to their own personal experiences, choosing instead to embrace ideas about life after death or reincarnation.

■ Theory of Dying Process

Kübler-Ross (1969) developed a five-stage theory through which dying individuals typically pass: denial, anger, bargaining, depression, and acceptance. These stages should not be viewed as a fixed sequence and not all individuals display each response.

■ Grief and Bereavement

The grief and bereavement process is a highly emotional one. *Bereavement* refers to the experience of losing a loved one. Many theorists have concluded that the grieving process usually unfolds through several phases. One phase is characterized by avoidance, shock, or disbelief, which may last for hours, days, or weeks. Another phase involves the individual's confronting the loss and experiencing a number of emotional reactions, which may include but are not limited to anxiety, sadness, anger, depression, and yearning for the lost loved one. As grief subsides, the individual adjusts to life without the loved one and begins to engage again in the normal processes of daily life.

Chapter 7: Key Terms

- Genotype
- Phenotype
- Canalization
- Reaction range
- Critical period
- Sensitive periods
- Cephalocaudal
- Proximodistal
- Teratogens
- Object permanence
- Deferred imitation
- Habituation

- Dishabituation
- Motherese
- Holophrastic
- Telegraphic
- Temperament
- Attachment
- Animism
- Reification
- Egocentrism
- Metacognition
- Fast mapping
- Syntactic bootstrapping

- Semantic bootstrapping
- Relational aggression
- Overt aggression
- Conservation
- Imaginary audience
- Personal fable
- Cliques
- Senescence
- Presbyopia
- Presbycusis
- Social clock
- Social convoy

Counseling Across the Life Span

8

Stephen P. Kachmar
Duquesne University

Kimberly Blair
University of Pittsburgh

In This Chapter

▶ *Perspectives in Human Growth and Development*
- Nature and Nurture
- Continuity and Discontinuity
- Developmental Domains

▶ *Psychodynamic Theories of Human Development*
- The Psychoanalytic Approach
- The Psychosocial Approach

▶ *Behavioral and Learning Theories of Human Development*
- Classical Conditioning
- Stimulus–Response Model
- Law of Effect
- Skinnerian Approach
- Social Learning Theory

▶ *Cognitive Theories of Human Development*
- Piagetian Theory of Cognitive Development
- Theory of Moral Development
- Sociocultural Theory of Development

▶ *Ethological and Maturational Theories of Human Development*
- Konrad Lorenz
- Attachment Theory
- Theory of Genetic Determination

▶ *Humanistic Theories of Human Development*
- Maslow's Hierarchy of Needs

PERSPECTIVES IN HUMAN GROWTH AND DEVELOPMENT

Understanding human growth and development is a blend of scientific study and human reflection on the process of life-span development. This chapter highlights some long-held, and at times opposing, opinions about development, describes the main developmental domains, and, finally, outlines key tenets of various theories of human development.

■ Nature and Nurture

One of the longest standing debates in the study of human development is the theoretical nature and nurture controversy. This debate reflects competing notions about which forces drive development. Listed here are some of the assumptions held by strict naturists and nurturists.

Assumptions of Naturists

- Individual development is dictated by inherent genetic composition.
- Development occurs unwaveringly, neither hastened nor thwarted by environmental interactions.
- People achieve developmental milestones at a similar pace, as prescribed by genetic composition.

The naturist position contrasts with that held by nurturists and can be summarized as follows.

Assumptions of Nurturists

- Environmental interactions are the main force in determining development.
- The types of interactions one has with the environment have an impact on an individual's simple and complex behaviors.

An environmental factor that plays a significant role in explaining variations in development is sociocultural context, which can be defined in this way:

> **Sociocultural context:** A precise set of cultural, physical, socioeconomic, and historical circumstances that have an impact on variations in human development.

The variety of influences that are encompassed in a socio-cultural context includes (a) interactions with parents, guardians, and caregivers, (b) interactions with societal institutions such as schools, religious entities, and community organizations, and (c) compliance with cultural norms such as sleeping rituals.

Generally, theorists today believe that both genetic elements and environmental interactions act in concert to shape development across the life span. Additionally, the overall impact of individual differences is of colossal importance to development across the life span. Variations in lived experience, individual genetic predisposition, and personal characteristics ultimately lead to differences in development.

E X A M P L E

Twins in the Nature–Nurture Debate

Identical twins are always of interest to researchers. Apart from having the same genetic makeup, one might expect identical twins to share cultural background and socioeconomic status and to be exposed to similar environmental factors. Yet, development of identical twins is itself never absolutely identical. If one considers the phenomenon of twins from inside the debate between nature and nurture, the role of individual differences is very powerful; ultimately, the individual's physical abilities, intellectual propensities, and quality of environmental exposures must be taken into account.

See Chapter 7 for more information on genetics.

■ Continuity and Discontinuity

Related to the nature–nurture debate is the discussion about continuous and discontinuous development. Whether or not development happens fluidly or in distinct stages is summed up in the contrasting beliefs in continuous and discontinuous development.

Continuous development: Development that occurs gradually over the course of the life span in a fashion that may be thought of as cumulative or quantitative in nature.

Discontinuous development: Development that occurs in distinct stages throughout the life span.

E X A M P L E

Continuous and Discontinuous Development

The gradual growth that characterizes continuous development is exemplified in a child's ability to speak. When a child says a first word, it may be thought of as part of a continuous process that has included listening to others, babbling, and making many attempts to vocalize. Although such an event is monumental to parents and caregivers, it is, in fact, the result of years of auditory processing, cognitive growth, and physical maturation.

On the other hand, developmentalists often use the example of a caterpillar changing into a butterfly to point to discontinuous development. Each stage of change in the butterfly's evolution is different from that of the previous stage, and, as such, may be viewed as qualitative rather than quantitative.

■ Developmental Domains

Across the life span, development occurs in physical, cognitive, and socioemotional domains.

Physical development: Involves growth of a physical nature, including gains in muscular strength and fine and gross motor skill development.

Cognitive development: Involves changes in inherent intellectual and linguistic abilities through stimulating interactions with the surrounding environment.

Socioemotional development: Involves changes in the ability to initiate and maintain interactions with others, changes in personality, and emotional regulation.

Cognitive development is a lifelong process that is enhanced by environmental interactions; however, stimulation in early childhood is essential to overall lifetime achievement. Likewise, physical development is a long-term process; gains are seen in the main areas of fine and gross motor skills. **Fine motor skills** are physical abilities that require the use of small muscles and are needed for activities such as reaching and grasping in infancy and early childhood and skills such as typing in later development. **Gross motor skills** are physical abilities that require the use of large muscles; these skills are necessary in infancy for crawling and are required for walking from early childhood through adulthood. Socioemotional development is central to a person's ability to form new and lasting relationships with other as well as to respond appropriately to the ups and downs of life experiences.

PSYCHODYNAMIC THEORIES OF HUMAN DEVELOPMENT

Psychodynamic approaches to human development include Freud and Erikson's psychoanalytic and psychosocial theories. Both theorists conceptualized development in terms of stages and, thus, represent discontinuous approaches to development. Developmental progress is determined by the degree of success one has in resolving intrapersonal, unconscious conflicts germane to each stage.

■ The Psychoanalytic Approach

Freud's psychoanalytic or psychosexual theory of development proposed that children progress through a series of distinct developmental stages in which they must manage disparity between societal expectations and their own biological drives and sexual energy. How an individual resolves these dilemmas ultimately determines development.

Three structures—the id, ego, and superego—comprise the personality in the psychoanalytic perspective. Zimbardo, Weber, and Johnson (2000) understood these systems this way:

> **Id:** Structure of personality that is present at birth and may be considered the primitive, unconscious segment of personality that motivates individuals to seek immediate gratification of inherent desires (sexual, physical, emotional) without regard for potential consequences.

> **Ego:** Component of personality that relies on the reality principle to weigh the desires of the id against the demands of the superego and the external world.

> **Superego:** Structure of personality that serves as an individual's conscience, represents a moral code handed down from parent to child, and guides behavior to reflect rules that closely resemble societal norms or expectations.

In the psychoanalytic approach, emphasis is placed on parental management of children's sexual and aggressive drives. Freud suggested that parents are responsible for moderating the degree of gratification a child receives at each stage of development. Becoming stuck in a developmental stage is possible; the terms fixation and arrestment explain how stagnation in development occurs (Berk, 1997).

> **Fixation:** Inability to move to a higher level of development because of excessive gratification.

> **Arrestment:** Inability to move to a higher level of development because of inadequate gratification.

Balance in gratification is the key to preventing fixated or arrested development. Indeed, healthy development is a function of successful navigation through the five stages of psychosexual personality development. Key tenets of each stage are outlined here.

Oral Stage (Birth–1 Year)

- The child is focused on the oral cavity and receives gratification through sucking, babbling, eating, and crying.

- Oral fixation, or arrestment, manifests in habits including nail-biting and smoking and interpersonal conflicts such as lack of trust and difficulty forming close relationships.

Anal Stage (Ages 1–3)

- Stimulation and function of one's bowels and bladder provide gratification.
- Too many or too few parental discipline demands related to toilet training and bodily self-control can cause fixation or arrestment.
- Excessive demands contribute to anal-retentive tendencies, whereas an absence of discipline leads to anal-expulsive traits, such as messiness, reckless, and disorderliness.

Phallic Stage (Ages 3–6)

- Gratification centers on the genital area and is characterized by finding pleasure in stimulation of this bodily region and great interest in the genitals of others.
- The child experiences incestuous desire for the opposite-sexed parent and wishes for the removal of the same-sexed parent (known as the Oedipus complex in males, Electra complex in females).
- To remedy the Oedipus or Electra complex, the child abandons sexual desires and adopts the characteristics and values of the same-sexed parent (Berk, 1997), allowing the superego to form.

Latency Stage (Ages 6–11)

- Sexual desires that were present in the phallic stage recede.
- The primary focus turns away from the stressful conflicts of the phallic stage to asexual pursuits such as school, athletics, and friendships.

Genital Stage (Ages 11–18)

- Patterns of behavior that emerged as a result of the resolution of previous stages are apparent.
- Sexual desires that were repressed during the phallic stage reemerge to help further mature sexual relationships, marriage, and the parenting of children.

Full development ultimately allows individuals to pursue the goals of love and work and only can be attained if the dilemmas in each stage are successfully resolved.

For more information on the id, ego, and superego, and the application of this approach to counseling, see Chapter 9.

■ The Psychosocial Approach

Erikson accepted the general principles underlying psychoanalytic personality theory. However, he expanded the framework to emphasize the importance of psychosocial aspects of human development. Additionally, Erikson conceptualized personality development as extending beyond adolescence into a lifelong phenomenon marked by crises needing to be resolved.

The psychosocial approach includes eight stages, the first five of which parallel those proposed by Freud, especially with regard to the approximate age of engagement. Individuals acquire new skills at each stage that allow them to be active, productive members of society (Berk, 1997). A description of the psychosocial stages follows.

Erikson's Psychosocial Stages of Development

1. In the *Basic Trust Versus Mistrust* stage, children learn to trust the world through warm and responsive interactions with caregivers, particularly through maternal relations; mistrust forms from unresponsive and cold caregiver relationships.
2. In the *Autonomy Versus Shame and Guilt* stage, a sense of autonomy is formed when parents allow children to use newly developed gross and fine motor skills to explore the surrounding world; shame and guilt results when parents stifle free choice by fostering dependency or by shaming children for their behavior.
3. In the *Initiative Versus Guilt* stage, initiative is fostered when parents support experimentation of newly developed skills through self-initiated activities; however, when such actions are met with parental scolding due to a lack of self-control, the child may form a sense of inadequacy or guilt (Zimbardo, Weber, & Johnson, 2000).
4. In the *Industry Versus Inferiority* stage, a sense of industry forms when, in the context of home or school environment, children employ skills that allow them to complete tasks collaboratively with others; however, if such attempts are coupled with negative experience, feelings of inferiority or incompetence may emerge.
5. In the *Identity Versus Identity Diffusion* stage, teenagers attempt to define themselves in relation to society, test limits, and form an identity; unsuccessful resolution of identity development leads to identity confusion.
6. In the *Intimacy Versus Isolation* stage, young adults attempt to establish meaningful, intimate relationships with others; failure to establish such relationships may result in a sense of isolation and a lack of meaningful interactions.
7. In the *Generativity Versus Stagnation* stage, adults strive to give to the next generation through productive work (Berk, 1997); a sense of stagnation or self-absorption occurs when an individual fails to achieve a sense of meaningful accomplishment.
8. In the *Integrity Versus Despair* stage, older adults who can identify value and significance in their existence develop a sense of integrity, whereas adults who believe their lives were dissatisfying or without value may develop a sense of despair.

BEHAVIORAL AND LEARNING THEORIES OF HUMAN DEVELOPMENT

Unlike Freud and Erikson, who advocated a psychodynamic approach to understanding human development, some psychologists viewed mental structures and intrapersonal conflicts as arbitrary. Behaviorists assumed that because personality structures cannot be observed, their existence neither can be validated nor supported as a legitimate influence on human development. Subsequently, theorists, such as Pavlov, Watson, Thorndike, Skinner, and Bandura, advocated for approaches that utilized the scientific method as a means to gather tangible—and largely behavioral—data for observation, analysis, and interpretation about human growth and development. Some of the most well-known behavioral theories of development briefly are described here.

■ Classical Conditioning

Pavlov is famous for the experiment in which he conditioned dogs to salivate at the sound of a bell after the bell was repeatedly paired with the presence of meat powder. Pavlov's classical conditioning theory posited that when an unconditioned stimulus (UCS) is presented, that stimulus elicits a response or reflex. If such a response-provoking stimulus is paired with a nonprovoking stimulus over repeated trials, the second, conditional stimulus will elicit an identical response when the UCS is removed.

Unconditioned stimulus (UCS): Stimulus that evokes an unconditioned response.

Conditioned stimulus (CS): Stimulus that is paired with the UCS with the goal of evoking the same response as the UCS.

Unconditioned response (UR): The natural response an organism makes to the UCS.

Conditioned response (CR): The response that is elicited in the presence of the CS.

■ Stimulus–Response Model

Following Pavlov, Watson's work in the early 1900s launched a new behavioral movement in psychology that focused primarily on the use of objective, scientific methods to explain human behavior. Watson's stimulus–response model (S–R) to human behavior and development is based on the premise that all human action, even the most complex behavior, is a response to particular stimuli. Stimuli and behavior are inextricably linked in the S–R model, which almost wholly negated the influence of mental phenomena.

■ Law of Effect

Thorndike conducted numerous experiments on animal intelligence over the early half of the 20th century that led him to conclude that behavior is learned by trial and error. Thorndike is known for describing the law of effect and the law of exercise.

> **Law of effect:** Behavior has a higher propensity to be repeated if the consequence of that behavior is positively reinforcing.

> **Law of exercise:** A behavior will occur more frequently if connections between the behavior and reinforcer or consequence routinely are practiced; conversely, failure to support connections between the behavior and reinforcer through practice will result in weaker associations and a decreased likelihood of reoccurrence.

■ Skinnerian Approach

Skinner used operant conditioning procedures to explain how people respond to the environment and how behavior changes. A key component of Skinner's theory of development is operant conditioning, which can be defined this way:

> **Operant conditioning:** Learning that relies on consequences that follow behavior.

Skinner suggested that learning occurs only through the presence of a reinforcing stimulus that follows arbitrary behavior. Reinforcers, which can be either positive or negative, increase the likelihood that a behavior will be repeated.

> **Positive reinforcement:** Provision of a valued stimulus following a desired behavior.

> **Negative reinforcement:** The application of a desirable stimulus to decrease a behavior.

Skinner proposed five schedules of reinforcement. These are described briefly next.

Skinnerian Reinforcement Schedules

1. A continuous schedule provides constant reinforcement, which tends to elicit a high frequency of the preferred behavior.
2. A fixed-interval schedule provides reinforcement only after a predetermined time interval has elapsed, despite the frequency of behavioral displays.
3. Fixed ratio schedules use a reinforcing stimulus only after a predetermined frequency of the behavior has been demonstrated.
4. A variable interval schedule involves the constant alteration of reinforcing time intervals.
5. A variable ratio schedule involves the adjustment of the behavior frequency required for the provision of the reinforcing stimulus.

Skinner is well known for his conceptualization of positive and negative reinforcement, which increase the probability of certain behavioral occurrences. Along with other behavioralists, Skinner proposed several other methods of behavioral modification, including extinction, shaping, and aversive conditioning.

Extinction: Withholding reinforcement from a formerly reinforced behavior.

Shaping: Reinforcing behaviors that increasingly resemble the desired behavior until the desired behavior is attained.

Aversive conditioning: An undesirable stimulus is presented after a target behavior to decrease the probability that such behavior will happen again.

EXAMPLE

Behavioral Techniques in Practice: Using Extinction Methods

Consider the example of a first-grade teacher who has a student who continually gets out of her seat to wander around the classroom. The teacher's initial responses were either to lead the child back to her seat or verbally to request that the child sit down. When these tactics failed to work, the teacher began to implement the behavioral technique known as extinction. The teacher consciously chose not to reinforce the child's misbehavior with verbal or behavioral attention. Eventually, the teacher's approach of not reinforcing the behavior led the child to stop wandering around the classroom.

See Chapter 9 for more information about behavioral modification.

■ Social Learning Theory

Bandura believed that early childhood experiences have a profound influence on personality development (Mazur, 2002). To explain these influences, Bandura developed social learning theory, which suggests that learning occurs not only through classical and operant conditioning, but also as a result of observational learning or imitation. Observational learning is based on vicarious reinforcement, which can be understood as follows:

> **Vicarious reinforcement:** Learning that occurs vicariously or as a result of watching someone model a particular behavior.

Bandura's theory of social learning and vicarious reinforcement is linked closely to studies he conducted on childhood aggression. The famous Bobo doll studies involved a scenario in which a young woman treated an inflatable doll aggressively and received favorable consequences. Bandura discovered that children who watched the woman imitated her behavior by treating the doll similarly. Because the children did not receive reinforcement for their behavior, Bandura concluded that learning took place as a result of their observing how the young woman acted and by noting the consequences of her behavior.

Bandura identified the following four factors that are essential to imitative behavior (Mazur, 2002):

1. Attention to what is being modeled.
2. Retention or the ability to remember what was demonstrated.
3. Ability to reproduce the behavior.
4. Motivation or drive to reproduce modeled behaviors.

COGNITIVE THEORIES OF HUMAN DEVELOPMENT

Cognitive theories of human development focus primarily on the development of mental and verbal abilities. Piaget, Kohlberg, and Vygotsky's theories have been extremely influential in the fields of education and related sciences.

■ Piagetian Theory of Cognitive Development

Piaget viewed the developing child as an active organism who is constantly trying to make sense of the world. Learning begins when children engage in a process of either assimilation or accommodation. Both processes help children adjust to and understand new experiences. As well, when they are adapting to new knowledge, children form new schemas that promote learning by helping them understand new experiences. Assimilation, schemas, and accommodation are described as follows:

Assimilation: Process of using preexisting knowledge to make sense of new experiences.

Schemas: New ways of thinking that change with age, experience, and exposure to new environmental circumstances.

Accommodation: Process of altering current ways of thinking or creating new ways of thinking to understand new knowledge.

Through research and observation, Piaget determined that the development of increasingly complex cognitive structures corresponds with four distinct, age-related stages of cognitive development:

1. Sensorimotor stage.
2. Preoperational stage.
3. Concrete operational stage.
4. Formal operational stage.

Cognitive gains in which children learn to think qualitatively differently about the world characterize the movement through the four developmental stages.

Sensorimotor Stage (Birth–2 Years)

- Understands the world primarily through physical and sensorimotor experiences.
- Begins to recognize familiar faces, coordinate simple movements, and engage in goal-directed behavior.
- Exhibits capacity for forming mental representations of objects and events and forging primary memory.
- Exhibits evidence, at the end of the stage, of grasping **object permanence,** or the understanding that an object continues to exist even when it is out of sight.
- Shows capacity for **symbolic substitution,** or the utilization of a word or other symbol in the place of a specific action.

Preoperational Stage (Ages 2–7)

- Exhibits monumental advances in the ability to make mental representations of objects and events and to use those representations to solve simple problems.
- Shows signs of being able to distinguish himself or herself from others.
- Manifests increased language skills.
- Remains limited by preoperational **egocentrism,** a self-centered view of the world in which everything is perceived in relation to oneself; **animistic thought,**

or the belief that inanimate objects possess living qualities; and **centration,** or a narrow topical focus.

Concrete Operational Stage (Ages 7–11; Berk, 1997)

- Employs increasingly organized and logical thought processes.
- Displays an understanding of **conservation,** or the ability to recognize that an object's physical properties remain constant despite alteration to the object's appearance.
- Exhibits the ability to use mental operations to solve problems through mental manipulation.
- Comprehends the concept of **seriation,** or the arrangement of items on a quantitative dimension, and uses **cognitive maps,** or mental representations of large-scale spaces.

Formal Operational Stage (Ages 12 and up)

- Develops the ability to think about complex concepts abstractly and determine potential outcomes through hypothetico-deductive reasoning.
- Exhibits egocentric qualities by believing that he or she is the focus of attention.
- Displays a sense of personal importance that extends beyond realistic levels, thus intensifying the experience of success and failure.

■ Theory of Moral Development

Kohlberg's theory of moral development is very similar to Piaget's cognitive-developmental stage theory in that both theories recognize the developing child's attempt to reason through new situations by applying experienced ethical convention. However, Kohlberg believed that the development of just, fair, and moral reasoning was more complex than the process proposed by Piaget, a belief reflected in his more intricate theory of moral development.

Kohlberg's theory identifies three levels of moral development, each of which is comprised of two distinct stages. Preconventional morality, conventional morality, and postconventional morality, the three broad levels of moral development, can be described as follows:

Preconventional morality: The first level of moral development in which moral judgments reflect considerations for personal needs, but place little emphasis on societal needs.

Conventional morality: The second level of moral development in which ethical decision making is based on societal expectations and necessities for the purpose of maintaining social norms.

Postconventional morality: The third level of moral development in which moral conclusions are internalized, and individuals make moral choices based on their evaluation of alternate moral codes and ultimate subscription to a personal moral code.

Six Stages of Moral Development (Green & Piel, 2002)

1. *Heteronomous morality* emphasizes compliance to rules and norms established by authority figures, and decisions characteristically are made to avoid punishment.
2. *Individualistic morality* reflects a level of development in which moral decision making is based on fulfilling personal needs and desires.
3. *Morality of interpersonal expectations, relations, and interpersonal conformity* reflects a value on maintaining peer expectations and, therefore, decisions are made to please others, despite consequences.
4. *Morality of social systems and conscience* is characterized by moral decisions made in consideration of the universal social system and with the aim of bettering society, and not simply of fulfilling individual desires or those of an immediate peer group.
5. *Morality of social-contract, utility, and individual rights* is a developmental level at which individuals recognize and obey societal norms and rules and, concurrently, are capable of evaluating law in light of the individual, inherent rights, such as life and liberty.
6. *Morality of ethical principles* is the highest level of development in which an individual recognizes and abides by social laws but also is willing to break those laws if they violate ethical standards.

■ Sociocultural Theory of Development

Vygotsky suggested that cognitive development is a product of the interaction between a child and the environment. By accounting for the dual influences of inherent ability and the environment, Vygotsky differentiates his theory from that of Piaget, in which inherent ability is believed to be the most influential variable in development.

From a sociocultural perspective, once the child forms the ability mentally to depict objects and events and develops language, the child actively can engage his or her environment and further cognitive development. Vygotsky's concept of the zone of proximal development highlights the degree of the importance he placed on social influences to development (Thomas, 1992).

Zone of proximal development: The dynamic and interactive process between what a child is capable of doing by him or herself and what a child can do with the assistance of a parent, teacher, or mentor.

By completing tasks with the help of skilled individuals, children become more capable of independently completing demanding enterprises. Two other constructs are related to the skilled assistant–child interaction learning partnership. **Intersubjectivity** is the process through which two individuals with differing views modify their views to come to a mutual understanding. **Scaffolding** reflects the altering degree of assistance that a child receives from the skilled adult to suit his or her level of competence (Berk, 1997).

ETHOLOGICAL AND MATURATIONAL THEORIES OF HUMAN DEVELOPMENT

Ethological theories of human development, such as those of Lorenz and Bowlby, are based on Darwinian evolutionary theory and propose that behavior is the direct result of biological factors. Maturational approaches to human development, like that of Gesell, also focus primarily on growth trends that are dictated by biology. Maturational approaches adequately describe the behaviors that may be expected by an individual at a particular developmental stage, however, they are void of information relevant to how or why the changes in one's development occur.

■ Konrad Lorenz

Through studies with the greyleg goose, Lorenz is credited with discovering the phenomenon of imprinting, a specialized learning process that occurs extremely early in life (Schwartz, 1989).

> **Imprinting:** A learning process driven by innate propensities to establish social bonds in the form of permanent attachments with the first living, moving organisms a young animal or human notices and shadows.

Lorenz's research showed that once initial bonds are formed with the first organism, even if it is of a varying species, the relationship with the imprinting organism is irreversible. Additionally, Lorenz pioneered the concept of a critical or sensitive period, defined as follows (Green & Piel, 2002; Lafreniere, 2000):

> **Critical period:** Brief stage of development during which a developing child is predisposed to learn a specific ability or function because of heightened susceptibility to particular environmental stimuli.

Critical periods are crucial to a child's development. In the presence of learning opportunities, children can experience tremendous gains that prepare them for greater cognitive, social, and emotional advances in later stages of development.

■ Attachment Theory

Bowlby incorporated ideas from a number of distinct fields and his own work with children and families to formulate attachment theory. Attachment theory emphasizes the importance of positive child–mother relations to healthy development. To become a well-adjusted adolescent and adult, a child and mother must bond through warm, intimate interactions that satisfy both the parent and child.

> Attachment theory emphasizes the importance of positive child–mother relations to healthy development. To become a well-adjusted adolescent and adult, a child and mother must bond through warm, intimate interactions that satisfy both the parent and child.

Although Bowlby emphasized the place of attachment in development, he did so primarily with regard to the mother–child bond. Paternal relations are considered second in importance to the relationship between a mother and child. Ethological research out of which the concept of separation anxiety grew supported his views about the mother–child bond. Separation anxiety can be defined as follows:

Separation anxiety: Extreme stress experienced by infants or young children when they are separated from their mother.

The result of separation is infant or child protest or behavioral tantrums, a response that suggests that the concept of attachment is viable. Bowlby also posited the concept of despair as an elevated separation and grief response that occurs prior to detachment.

■ Theory of Genetic Determination

A maturational approach, Gesell's theory of genetic determination suggests that biology determines natural maturation and is considered the greatest force directing one's development. He posited that the development of all humans occurred in a relatively predetermined fashion, allowing for developmental comparisons to be made. Further, Gesell proposed that a child's development might be viewed as cyclical, with children continuously alternating between better and worse stages, with the better implying a balance between the child and his or her environment, and worse implying the child's unhappiness and confusion in relation to the physical and social realms (Thomas, 1992).

HUMANISTIC THEORIES OF HUMAN DEVELOPMENT

Humanistic theories of human development are based on the premise that people are intrinsically good and make decisions that are in their best interest.

■ Maslow's Hierarchy of Needs

Maslow proposed a needs hierarchy based on the notion that the drive to respond to individual needs motivates behavior. The highest level in the hierarchy is self-actualization, which Maslow considered the goal of human existence. However, before people can achieve self-actualization, they must satisfy their most primitive needs, which have the greatest influence and serve as the strongest motivating force on behavior. Once basic needs are satisfied, the individual may move to higher levels of the hierarchy in an effort to satisfy the needs at those respective levels.

Levels of Maslow's Hierarchy (Maslow, 1943)

- The most primitive needs identified by Maslow are biological or physiological needs, such as the need for sustenance, relaxation, and sex.
- The second tier of Maslow's hierarchy is safety, which may be characterized as an individual's need for security or an absence of danger.
- Once physiological and security needs are met, people seek love and companionship with others to fulfill the need for love and belongingness.
- Esteem needs emerge next and are characterized by an individual's desire to view himself or herself in a positive light and to be seen positively by others.
- The highest level of need is self-actualization, or the drive to develop one's fullest potential and do what one must do to experience happiness.

Chapter 8:   Key Terms

- Sociocultural context
- Continuous development
- Discontinuous development
- Cognitive development
- Physical development
- Socioemotional development
- Fine motor skills
- Gross motor skills

- Id
- Ego
- Superego
- Fixation
- Arrestment
- Unconditioned stimulus
- Conditioned stimulus
- Unconditioned response
- Conditioned response
- Law of effect

- Law of exercise
- Operant conditioning
- Positive reinforcement
- Negative reinforcement
- Extinction
- Shaping
- Aversive conditioning
- Vicarious reinforcement
- Assimilation
- Schemas

- ▶ Accommodation
- ▶ Object permanence
- ▶ Symbolic substitution
- ▶ Egocentrism
- ▶ Centration
- ▶ Animistic thought

- ▶ Conservation
- ▶ Seriation
- ▶ Cognitive maps
- ▶ Imprinting
- ▶ Critical period
- ▶ Preconventional morality

- ▶ Conventional morality
- ▶ Postconventional morality
- ▶ Zone of proximal development
- ▶ Intersubjectivity
- ▶ Separation anxiety

Major Forces Behind Counseling Approaches

Paul Bernstein
Carol Thomas
Duquesne University

In This Chapter

▶ *Psychodynamic Approaches: Psychoanalysis*
- View of Human Nature
- Theory of Personality
- Key Theoretical Concepts
- Goals of Therapy
- Therapeutic Techniques
- Role of Therapist
- Strengths and Limitations

▶ *Psychodynamic Approaches: Analytic Psychology*
- View of Human Nature
- Theory of Personality
- Key Theoretical Concepts
- Goals of Therapy
- Therapeutic Techniques
- Role of Therapist
- Strengths and Limitations

▶ *Psychodynamic Approaches: Individual Psychology*
- View of Human Nature
- Theory of Personality
- Key Theoretical Concepts
- Goals of Therapy
- Therapeutic Techniques
- Role of Therapist
- Strengths and Limitations

▶ *Psychodynamic Approaches: Transactional Analysis*
- View of Human Nature
- Theory of Personality
- Key Theoretical Concepts
- Goals of Therapy
- Therapeutic Techniques
- Role of Therapist
- Strengths and Limitations

▶ *Cognitive-Behavioral Approaches: Behaviorism*
- View of Human Nature
- Theory of Personality
- Key Theoretical Concepts
- Goals of Therapy
- Therapeutic Techniques
- Role of Therapist
- Strengths and Limitations

▶ *Cognitive-Behavioral Approaches: Neo-Behaviorism*
- View of Human Nature
- Theory of Personality
- Key Theoretical Concepts
- Goals of Therapy
- Therapeutic Techniques
- Role of Therapist
- Strengths and Limitations

In This Chapter (*continued*)

▶ *Cognitive-Behavioral Approaches: Cognitive Therapy*
  - View of Human Nature
  - Theory of Personality
  - Key Theoretical Concepts
  - Goals of Therapy
  - Therapeutic Techniques
  - Role of Therapist
  - Strengths and Limitations

▶ *Cognitive-Behavioral Approaches: Rational-Emotive Therapy*
  - View of Human Nature
  - Theory of Personality
  - Key Theoretical Concepts
  - Goals of Therapy
  - Therapeutic Techniques
  - Role of Therapist
  - Strengths and Limitations

▶ *Cognitive-Behavioral Approaches: Reality Therapy*
  - View of Human Nature
  - Theory of Personality
  - Key Theoretical Concepts
  - Goals of Therapy
  - Therapeutic Techniques
  - Role of Therapist
  - Strengths and Limitations

▶ *Cognitive-Behavioral Approaches: Multimodal Therapy*
  - View of Human Nature
  - Theory of Personality
  - Key Theoretical Concepts

  - Goals of Therapy
  - Therapeutic Techniques
  - Role of Therapist
  - Strengths and Limitations

▶ *Existential-Humanistic Approaches: Person-Centered*
  - View of Human Nature
  - Theory of Personality
  - Key Theoretical Concepts
  - Goals of Therapy
  - Therapeutic Techniques
  - Role of Therapist
  - Strengths and Limitations

▶ *Existential-Humanistic Approaches: Gestalt*
  - View of Human Nature
  - Theory of Personality
  - Key Theoretical Concepts
  - Goals of Therapy
  - Therapeutic Techniques
  - Role of Therapist
  - Strengths and Limitations

▶ *Existential-Humanistic Approaches: Logotherapy*
  - View of Human Nature
  - Theory of Personality
  - Key Theoretical Concepts
  - Goals of Therapy
  - Therapeutic Techniques
  - Role of Therapist
  - Strengths and Limitations

PSYCHODYNAMIC APPROACHES: PSYCHOANALYSIS

In 1856, Sigmund Freud was born to a lower-middle-class Jewish couple. Spending most of his life in Vienna, Freud excelled in academics and, in 1811, earned a medical degree. During this time, he married Martha Bernays, with whom he eventually had six children. Freud began to formulate psychoanalysis while working with Josef Breuer, a pioneer in hypnosis and talk therapy. Freud's career exploded with the publication of a book on dream interpretation, which ultimately lead to his foundational contributions to the psychology field and Western culture. In 1938, under Nazi occupation, Freud fled Vienna for London, England, where he died a year later.

■ View of Human Nature

In the first 6 years of life, individuals progress through libidinally induced psychosexual stages of development.

Freud's Stages of Development

1. Oral stage: 0 to 12 months.
2. Anal stage: 12 months to 3 years.
3. Phallic stage: 3 to 4 years.
4. Latency period: 6 years to puberty.
5. Genital stage: Puberty to death.

One's success in progressing through these early stages determines the quality of psychological health throughout life (Seligman, 2006). People utilize various defense mechanisms to block the unconscious because its drives are socially unacceptable and, at times, dangerous (Gladding, 2000).

■ Theory of Personality

In the Freudian tradition, the personality has three segments; these are briefly outlined.

Three Essential Structures of Personality

1. *Id* includes the unconscious, primal urges motivated by unmitigated libido and a demand for pleasure regardless of consequence.
2. *Ego* is the conscious, rational conduit for healthy behavior influenced by both id and superego.
3. *Superego* is the socially constructed body of internalized rules and approved behaviors, thoughts, and feelings that motivates guilt and shame.

An individual who is psychologically healthy has an ego that safely can regulate the pressures of the selfish demands of the id and the perfectionistic ideals of the superego to achieve a logic-based balance between the two (Seligman, 2006).

■ Key Theoretical Concepts

To conduct psychoanalysis, the analyst understands that humans are driven by un-controllable, unconscious forces—*libido*—directed by psychosexual crises in the first 6 years of life (Corey, 2005). By using techniques to work through the repression of the unconscious, the analysand (i.e., patient or client) becomes conscious of the unconscious forces and, thereby, resolves the symptoms that brought him or her to therapy. Thus, therapy revolves largely around two key ideas: the conscious and the unconscious. These terms can be defined this way:

Conscious: The smallest part of the mind that contains the thoughts and feelings of which a person is aware.

Unconscious: The largest part of the mind that contains thoughts and feelings of which a person is unaware or has repressed.

■ Goals of Therapy

The goal of psychoanalysis is to make the unconscious conscious (Gladding, 2000). Analysis increases the patient's awareness of his or her uncontrollable, unconscious drives and allows the patient to relive incomplete resolutions of the psychosexual stages through transference. As the analyst explains the basis for the behavior, the patient gains the cognitive understanding and actual experience, via transference, of a more satisfying resolution to the past, thus gaining the skills to deal with unresolved psychosexual issues (Prochaska & Norcross, 2003).

■ Therapeutic Techniques

The psychoanalyst uses the following four techniques to raise the patient's awareness. For effective technique use, the patient must be completely honest.

Techniques Common to Psychoanalysis

- *Free association* occurs when the analyst encourages the patient to talk without censorship about whatever comes to his or her mind (Corey, 2005).
- *Dream interpretation* in classic psychoanalysis is the primary means to encountering the unconscious and revealing otherwise-repressed experiences. Dreams

have **manifest content,** the obvious narrative of the dream, and **latent content,** the unconscious meaning hidden behind the manifest meaning.

- *Transference* allows the patient to work through his or her symptoms by reliving past situations through the current relationship with the analyst. The patient chooses new coping skills instead of repeating damaging unconscious behavior patterns (Corey, 2005).
- *Analysis of resistance* requires the analyst to examine a patient's reluctance to work toward unconscious awareness. Denial of the analyst's interpretations and self-censorship are common forms of resistance (Gladding, 2000).

EXAMPLE

Working in Free Association

A patient who is free associating may begin by talking about a conversation he had with his father about music. The patient then mentions a time in childhood when his uncle made a similar comment to him, which the patient then explores further. The analyst uses this unconscious guidance to search for clues about the repression blocking the patient's awareness. The technique's challenge is ensuring the uncensored flow of unconscious-inspired information.

■ Role of Therapist

The analyst approaches the client *tabula rasa* to focus singularly on the client. One way the analyst focuses on the client is to sit behind the client, who is physically relaxed, to eliminate visual cues that may create bias. There are a number of other stances that characterize the role of the psychoanalyst; a few are listed here.

Tasks of the Analyst (Prochaska & Norcross, 2003)

- Reflect to the patient the truth about himself or herself and remain personally uninvolved.
- Assume most of the work in the course of treatment.
- Analyze and interpret the patient's revelations.
- Educate the patient about his or her condition in psychoanalytic terms.

■ Strengths and Limitations

The greatest strength of classical psychoanalysis is recognizing the importance of the early years of life in creating a "blueprint" for emotional development and attachment. Its most crippling limitation is the outmoded belief that people are passive observers of their own lives, waiting for either an unconscious urge or an analyst's insight to decide their fate.

PSYCHODYNAMIC APPROACHES: ANALYTIC PSYCHOLOGY

Carl Gustav Jung was a Swiss psychiatrist who began his professional career in 1900 at the Burgholzi Mental Hospital, working under the tutelage of the eminent psychiatrist, Eugene Bleuler. In 1909, Jung traveled with Sigmund Freud to Clark University in Worcester, Masssachusetts, and introduced psychoanalysis to the American intelligentsia. Before his personal and professional break with Freud in 1911 to 1913, Jung was considered the successor and crown prince of the psychoanalytical movement (Nystul, 2003).

■ View of Human Nature

Jung believed the individual, the culture, and the human species can find positive values in their nature (Jung, 1928; Nystul, 2003). Some other thoughts central to Jung's view of human nature are provided here.

Jungian Assumptions About Human Nature (Nystul, 2003)

- People follow a natural path of development that promotes psychological and spiritual health.
- The psyche is viewed as a dynamic system that is used to discover meaning in and find solutions to life's conflicts.
- Humankind not only attempts to fulfill instinctual desires, but establishes a healthy relationship with the world by increasing self-understanding.

Despite his optimistic outlook, Jung was no apologist for humanity. He opined that unless the race confronts the psychological causes of its pathological behavior, it will continue to enact cruelty on its own members.

■ Theory of Personality

Believing nature has as much to do with nurture in the creation of the person, Jung suggested the following ideas about the personality.

Key Assumptions of Jungian Personality Theory

- Basic, common personality traits exist in the culture, transhistorically.
- Jung initially believed that people are extroverted or introverted and later expanded the typology to include such types as sensate, thinker, and intuitive.
- Psychological types underscore the manner in which individuals experience and relate to the world.

Jung's typology became the foundation of the Myers–Briggs Personality Inventory, an instrument in popular use today. Jung's term *personality* is descriptive of more than typology and is elaborated on later in this overview.

■ Key Theoretical Concepts

Arguably, the most important contribution to theoretical psychology was Jung's formation of the archetypes of the collective unconscious.

Archetypes: A priori structures in the psyche that form the building blocks of psychological reality; they are primordial images that contain psychic energy and assign meaning to experience.

Collective unconscious: The unconscious memories and common images, such as mother, earth, or death, shared by all of humanity that are inherited from the ancestral past.

Client narratives, life scripts, and most basic values conform to archetypal patterns. Archetypes propose a broad sweeping claim about the nature of awareness. Human experience is understood by life motifs that appear historically in symbol and myth, carrying a remarkable similarity to one another (Hall & Lindzey, 1978).

■ Goals of Therapy

A goal of Jungian analysis is to help clients understand how their maladaptive behaviors are attempts to gain personal autonomy and well-being. Jung named the uncovering of the unique self individuation.

Individuation: The movement of the personality toward its fullest creative potential.

A natural process, individuation occurs throughout life. The goals of Jungian analysis are similar to the goals of pastoral counseling. Each emphasizes the concept of soul and self. One is moved along the individuation process by uncovering uncomfortable truths and understanding latent unconscious personality structures (personal and archetypal). By discovering the tensions, conflicts, and opposites in their myths, clients may achieve an individuated sense of self.

■ Therapeutic Techniques

Although there are a number of techniques that Jungians can use to encourage the individuation process, one important technique is dream interpretation. Dreams contain archetypes that underlie the client's reality and, if correctly interpreted, the dream's meaning and symbols can hasten individuation. Other techniques also are mentioned here.

Common Jungian Techniques

- Dream interpretation.
- Art therapy.
- Bibliotherapy.
- Play therapy.
- Free association.

■ Role of Therapist

When Jung practiced, there were few systems of psychotherapy aside from Freud's *talking cure,* a process through which the analyst related past experiences to present conflicts. The model of exploration into the unconscious was something Jung never abandoned. He, however, altered the paradigm to fit his understanding of unconscious material and its relation to a healthy self.

Tasks of the Jungian Analyst

- Aid the client in the individuation process.
- Return the client to unconscious material by helping him or her to face uncomfortable, personal truths that, although denied, are part of the unconscious.

■ Strengths and Limitations

A strength of the Jungian system is its completeness. Jung accounted for the development of personality, past conflicts, and present experience; treatment is tailored to the client. Jung's theory reaches deep within the client's life to provide a transformative experience. Jungian analysis allows for the promotion of natural life processes (e.g., aging), and, as in the existential school, personal meaning through experience is identified. Limitations of the Jungian system are its length of treatment, expense, and the vigorous training of its practitioners.

PSYCHODYNAMIC APPROACHES: INDIVIDUAL PSYCHOLOGY

Alfred Adler was born in Vienna, Austria, in 1870 to a middle-class Jewish family. His life and work were, in part, shaped by an unhappy childhood. After receiving a medical degree from the University of Vienna, Adler went into practice as an ophthalmologist. It was through his research in neurology that, in 1899, Adler met Freud. Because of significant theoretical differences with psychoanalysts, in 1912, Adler left Freud's inner circle to found the Society of Individual Psychology. After Hitler's rise to power, Adler settled in New York City, where his work with immigrants gave rise to the creation of settlement houses; he was instrumental in initiating the field of social work. On May 28, 1937, while lecturing in Aberdeen, Scotland, Adler died of a heart attack.

■ View of Human Nature

Individual psychology presumes a holistic view of human beings. A number of key tenets characterize this tradition's view of humanity.

Themes in Individual Psychology's View of Humanity

- People are complete, integrated, complex beings, not merely a cluster of psychiatric symptoms identified by a diagnosis.
- Many facets comprise a person's life, including early experiences, beliefs, and future aspirations.
- Much of one's personality is formed in early childhood; however, people are continually creating themselves.
- With maturity, opportunities to choose one's own beliefs and behaviors exist through transcending the past, becoming more aware of the present, and establishing goals for the future.

■ Theory of Personality

In his conceptualization of personality, Adler emphasized the holistic nature of the human person. Unlike his predecessor, Freud, who proposed that personality is comprised of the three major components—id, ego, and superego—Adler described a unified personality that emerges within a specific familial and cultural context and that develops through the process of striving for a valued life goal (Corey, 2005). The role of the social context is especially important to development and cannot be understood apart from social influences. Thus, the role of human relationships in the formation of personality is more important than that of the intrapsychic dimension (Corey).

■ Key Theoretical Concepts

Adler's contributions to counseling are extensive; a few of his more salient ideas such as social interest, birth order, family constellation, and the creative self are described here (Nystul, 2003).

Social interest: The need humans have to experience a sense of belonging and to emphasize overall concern for humanity.

Birth order: A child's chronological or psychological birth position that influences the child's behavior and eventual perception of his or her world.

Family constellation: Variables such as personality, developmental issues, family attitudes and values, and structural factors that influence a child's interaction with and perception of the family compilation, and the ways in which a child views himself or herself outside of the family.

Creative self: Each person's ability to overcome his or her limitations and use personal attributes, abilities, and talents to contribute positively to society.

■ Goals of Therapy

The primary goal of individual psychology is to help clients become well-functioning individuals. There are also a number of ancillary goals, some of which are mentioned here.

Ancillary Goals of Individual Psychology (Adler, 1963)

- Gain insight.
- Establish realistic goals.
- Prevail over feelings of inferiority.
- Overcome neurotic symptoms and irrational cognitions.
- Increase client's motivation to contribute positively to society.

■ Therapeutic Techniques

Adlerian therapy is flexible, providing clients with support and encouragement. Encouragement builds self-confidence and stimulates courage. The techniques of this tradition correspond to four phases of therapy that the client and counselor use fluidly and revisit if necessary (Corey, 2005).

Phases of Adlerian Therapy

- Establish a therapeutic relationship by making contact with the client and attending to the client's experience.
- Explore client dynamics by gathering subjective information about the key issue(s) and objective data including family background, medical history, activating events.
- Encourage self-understanding and insight that leads clients to find purpose in their struggle.
- Assist clients in acting on their insights by encouraging new behaviors.

■ Role of Therapist

Adlerian therapists typically are attributed with having positive attitudes, encouraging demeanors, and helpful stances in helping clients establish clear, attainable goals. Other tasks of the therapist are provided here.

Tasks of the Adlerian Therapist (Corey, 2005)

- Explore the client's dynamics by using a Lifestyle Assessment to determine how the client is dealing with life tasks, to assess birth order and family constellations, to examine priorities and behaviors, and to analyze early recollections.
- Encourage, offer interpretation, and gently confront the client.
- Help reorient or clarify client goals related to solving existing problems.
- Provide emotional support in the therapeutic alliance.

■ Strengths and Limitations

The strength of individual psychology is its focus on mental health, not mental illness. Group counseling, parent education, and family systems therapy are rooted in Adler's theory. Individual psychology helped humanize education and contributed to the community mental health movement (Ansbacher, 1974). Adlerian therapy is flexible, integrative, and offers brief therapeutic approaches. Limitations of Adlerian therapy include its rigid birth order stereotypes, which may prove to be more harmful than helpful. This system is limited to those willing to openly examine their lifestyle. Normal intelligence is required, as this approach involves logic and insight.

 Check out the North American Society of Adlerian Psychology for more information on this approach to therapy and for other links to useful sources:

▶ www.alfredadler.org

PSYCHODYNAMIC APPROACHES: TRANSACTIONAL ANALYSIS

In 1910, Eric Berne was born in Canada to Dr. David and Mrs. Sara Gordon Bernstein. Berne's father died of a heart attack at age 38, leaving Berne and his younger sister to be raised by their mother. Berne attended McGill University, and in 1935 received his medical degree. Transactional analysis (TA) was developed in an attempt to simplify psychoanalysis so that it could be easily understood by the lay person.

■ View of Human Nature

TA emphasizes the influence of childhood experiences to describe human nature. However, the theory also posits that if people want to change and are given the tools and assistance to do so, change will occur. According to TA, people develop and live out life scripts that are first formed from parental or societal messages.

■ Theory of Personality

Berne (1964) believed that individuals begin life in an autonomous state (i.e., capable of awareness, spontaneity, and intimacy). He believed people were influenced by the messages of their parents and their childhood experiences. These messages and experiences have an impact on one's decisions and personality throughout life, unless the person chooses to change. Emotional disturbances result from negative messages, lack of messages, or negative early childhood experiences. Berne also believed that emotional problems could be successfully treated if one desired to change and if necessary tools for change were provided.

■ Key Theoretical Concepts

The basic concepts of TA revolve around what Berne termed the ego state, defined in this way:

Ego state: "A system of feelings accompanied by a related set of behavior patterns" (Berne, 1964, p. 23).

Berne identified three distinct ego states—parent, adult, and child. Each of these states exists within all individuals and can be observed in clients' dynamic interactions with others (Gladding, 2000). The three ego states are defined as follows:

Parent ego state: Consists of the *critical parent* and the *nurturing parent*. The critical parent acts to protect and is filled with values, shoulds, and ought to's. The nurturing parent acts as a nurturer and caregiver.

Adult ego state: Acts much like a computer, taking in and regulating information from the parent, the child, and the environment. This ego state is the logical and realistic part of a person and makes the best possible decision in a given situation.

Child ego state: Consists of the *adapted child* and the *free child* (or *natural child*). The adapted child conforms to the rules and wishes of the parent ego state and basically is compliant. The free child is spontaneous, fun, creative, and curious, caring for its needs without regard for others.

In addition to the three ego states, there are four life patterns recognized in TA.

Life Patterns in TA

- I'm not OK, you're OK.
- I'm not OK, you're not OK.
- I'm OK, you're not OK.
- I'm OK, you're OK.

These patterns explain the strengths and weaknesses of interpersonal relationships and are developmental in nature.

Goals of Therapy

An important goal of TA is for the client to develop greater autonomy, become more independent of parental messages, and become more spontaneous and capable of intimacy. The individual, with the help of therapy, rewrites a more positive life script to become more balanced and healthy (Gladding, 2000).

Therapeutic Techniques

TA assumes that people are born with positive tendencies to grow and develop, but this potential must be nurtured if it is to become a reality. The emphasis of TA work is on participatory learning and cognition through the utilization of homework assignments, structural analysis, life script analysis, transactions analysis, and analysis of games people play.

Role of Therapist

The role of the therapist in TA is to help clients become autonomous and self-aware of the games they play with others in their transactions that either help them or hinder them in their lives. Some approaches TA therapists might engender are mentioned here.

Goals of the TA Therapist

- Help clients learn how to communicate positively with others by giving strokes, or genuine, positive feedback.
- Help clients become aware of the games they play with others.
- Increase clients' awareness of their preferred ego state.
- Aid clients in rewriting their life scripts to meet their personal life goals.

■ Strengths and Limitations

TA is partner to the client and flexible enough to adapt to individual needs. Clients are perceived as good and capable of change. Occasionally, therapists will assume the role of parent and assist clients in recapturing past experiences. By so doing, clients may transcend former experiences and be better positioned to make improved choices. TA, according to Berne, simplified and modernized psychoanalytic concepts. Limitations of TA include its narrow application. Clients must be able to grasp its terms and concepts for therapy to be effective. TA sometimes is misused because of its simplistic nomenclature (Corey, 2005).

COGNITIVE-BEHAVIORAL APPROACHES: BEHAVIORISM

A graduate of Harvard College, B. F. Skinner had a profound impact on the psychological landscape in the mid-20th century as a chief proponent of behaviorism. Behaviorism, although a largely deterministic, historical movement, is dramatically different from the psychodynamic understanding of human behavior. Troubled by his psychodynamic predecessors' emphasis on the past, unconscious drives, and intrapsychic dynamics, Skinner attempted to simplify the panorama by focusing on objective, measurable phenomena—a return, in fact, to scientific respectability.

■ View of Human Nature

Skinner's view of human nature can be reduced to that of a fine-tuned machine. The complexity and mystery of the individual is traded for a behavioral mechanism that can be controlled strictly through the efficacy of environmental titillation. Human nature succeeds insofar as it can learn to survive and adapt to its environment. In a Skinnerian paradigm, human nature is a passive agent in that the locus of control is placed outside the individual, relegating one's destiny as utterly contingent on external stimuli (Skinner, 1953).

■ Theory of Personality

Behaviorists are not interested in personality theory, per se, but rather in how people learn.

Key Assumptions in Behaviorism About Human Learning

- The person is a fluid construct dependent on the environment for one's functioning.
- For change to occur, one must change the contextual forces in a relevant way.

Notwithstanding the behaviorist's reluctance to venture into the client's past, a behavioral therapist may inquire about the past, but only to explore the behavioral repertoires that one has learned to apply environmental implications to the here and now.

■ Key Theoretical Concepts

Skinner's most widespread influence on the field is the result of his theory of operant conditioning. Skinner posited that one can shape behavior by way of consequences that take form in two ways: reinforcement and punishment (Skinner, 1959).

Reinforcement: Increases the probability that a behavior will occur through a desirable consequence.

Punishment: Applies an aversive stimulus to diminish the likelihood of occurrence of a behavior.

Positive reinforcement: Increases a behavior by introducing a desired stimulus.

Negative reinforcement: The application of a desirable stimulus to decrease a behavior.

Thus, desired behavior can be brought to fruition through environmental modulation.

■ Goals of Therapy

The primary goal of behaviorism is to modify behavior. The system does not repudiate feelings, thoughts, or choices—all of which Skinner (1971) referred to as *mentalism.* Conversely, behavioral change is the precursor to altering one's thoughts or feelings. The behaviorist's notion of change posits that by changing an individual's behavior, changes in thought and affect are imparted (Skinner, 1971).

■ Therapeutic Techniques

Therapy utilizing behaviorism includes the following well-known techniques.

Common Therapeutic Behavioral Tools

- *Flooding* is an intentional overexposure to an aversive stimulus to decrease the stress associated with that stimulus. This technique is effective in treating client phobias.

- *Shaping* is the modification of behavior by means of incremental steps toward a desired end behavior, or to reword, successive approximations toward the desired goal (Skinner, 1953).
- *Extinction* is the removal of stimuli that sustains an undesirable behavior that, in turn, will diminish that behavior (Skinner, 1953).

Many other therapeutic techniques exist under this model, all of which are designed to change behavior. Some of these techniques include relaxation training, systematic desensitization, and assertion training.

■ Role of Therapist

The role of the therapist in behavioral therapy is pivotal to the point that client outcomes hinge on the therapist's competence. A few qualities and tasks of behavioral helpers are noted here.

Characteristics of Behavioral Therapists

- Therapists are highly directive.
- Therapists model appropriate behavior for their clients.
- The therapist rewards desired behavior with appropriately positive stimuli, increasing the probability that the desired client behavior will increase.

■ Strengths and Limitations

The primary strength of this approach is its proven effectiveness in bringing about change in behavior. Due to the quantifiable nature of the theory, there is a preponderance of scientific evidence substantiating the behavioral system as a viable therapeutic option. Limitations of this approach to therapy include the lack of encouragement for clients to express their emotions; the lack of focus on client insights, which has been deemed critical to outcome; and the control and manipulation of clients by the therapist.

COGNITIVE-BEHAVIORAL APPROACHES: NEO-BEHAVIORISM

Albert Bandura was born in 1925 in a small town in northern Alberta, Canada. He received his bachelor's degree in psychology from the University of British Columbia in 1949. He went on to the University of Iowa, where he received his PhD in 1952. There, he came under the influence of the behaviorist tradition and learning theory. In 1953, Bandura started teaching at Stanford University. While there, he collaborated with his first graduate student to write his first book on adolescent aggression.

■ View of Human Nature

Bandura's view of human nature is grounded in the behaviorists' perspective on human nature.

Neo-Behaviorist Assumptions of Human Nature

- An individual is the producer and the product of his or her environment (Corey, 2005).
- Individuals have a capacity to affect their own environments.

■ Theory of Personality

Bandura's theory of personality consists of an interaction among three things: the environment, behavior, and the person's psychological processes. Self-regulation—controlling one's own behavior—is the other "workhorse" of human personality. Bandura suggests that three steps that comprise self-regulation.

Steps in Self-Regulation

1. *Self-observation* entails looking at one's behavior and keeping mental notes of it.
2. *Judgment* suggests that people compare what they see with a standard. For example, people can compare their performance with traditional standards, such as rules of etiquette, or create arbitrary standards, like "I'll read a book a week."
3. *Self-response* is the reaction that people make to their standards. If people do well in comparison with their standards, they give themselves rewarding self-responses. If they do poorly, people give themselves punishing self-responses.

■ Key Theoretical Concepts

A key theoretical concept of the behavioral approach is that all behavior, emotions, and cognitions have been learned, and all behaviors can be changed or modified by new learning. Change occurs through acquisition of new behavior or modification of existing behavior. As this happens, emotions and attitudes also are shifted. Two other important concepts developed by Bandura (1986) are those of reciprocal determinism and self-efficacy.

Reciprocal determinism: An individual's behavior both is influenced by and influences an individual's personal factors and the environment.

Self-efficacy: People's judgments of their capabilities to organize and execute courses of action required to attain designated types of performances.

Just as behavior is determined reciprocally, the same is true of the relation between personal factors such as cognitive skills or attitudes and behavior or the environment. Each can have an impact on and be influenced by the other.

■ Goals of Therapy

At the outset of therapy, clients, with the assistance of a therapist, determine specific goals that they would like to meet throughout the therapeutic process. Throughout the counseling process, the therapist and client continually assess the client's goals to determine which goals are being met. The therapist has a strong role in helping the client formulate specific, measurable treatment goals. These goals drive the counseling process as the therapist and client work toward meeting the goals through discussion, creating the circumstances that best facilitate change, and creating a plan of action (Corey, 2005).

■ Therapeutic Techniques

Several techniques are utilized that incorporate what Bandura termed *self-control therapy* and what today is known as *social learning theory*. These techniques have been quite successful in treating problems, such as smoking, overeating, and poor study habits.

Common Neo-Behavioral Techniques

- *Behavioral charts* are self-observations that clients use to keep close tabs on their behaviors, both before beginning changes and as change occurs.
- *Environmental planning* evolves out of behavioral charts and diaries and allows clients to begin to alter their environment by, for example, avoiding some of the cues that lead to bad behaviors.
- *Self-contracts* are explicitly written contracts by which clients arrange to reward themselves when they adhere to the plan and, possibly, punish themselves when they do not.

Other people may be involved in the rewards and punishments if clients are not strict enough with themselves.

EXAMPLE

Behavior Charts: A Pathway to Change

Behavior charts can be as simple as counting how many cigarettes are smoked in a day and as complex as keeping detailed behavioral diaries. With the diary approach, clients keep track of the specifics of their problem in question. This allows them to make a connection between the kinds of cues that are associated with the habit. For example, they note if they are smoking more after meals, with coffee, with certain friends, in certain locations, and so on. The specificity of the contract enhances the chances of the client becoming aware of and changing the identified behavior.

■ Role of Therapist

Bandura (1969, 1971) maintained that most learning that occurs through direct experiences also can be learned indirectly through the observation of others. Therefore, the role of the therapist centers around a number of tasks related to the assumption that modeling is a central part of learning.

Key Tasks of the Neo-Behaviorist (Corey, 2005)

- Act as a role model that the client can imitate and, thereby, alter their behaviors.
- Exhibit values, beliefs, attitudes, and behaviors of high integrity that clients can observe.
- Approach counseling with caution and be aware of the potential for abuse of the influence that counselors may have over their clients.

■ Strengths and Limitations

Strengths of this theory include its ease of comprehension and implementation. Clients can grasp fairly easily the concepts of behavior charts, action plans, and self-contracts. Yet, there must be some level of cognition for this to occur. Limitations include the possibility for cultural insensitivity with regard to goal planning. For some ethnically diverse clients, it is difficult to separate behavioral problems from the cultural environment in which they live, and they may have difficulty viewing therapeutic issues as being individualistic.

COGNITIVE-BEHAVIORAL APPROACHES: COGNITIVE THERAPY

Aaron Temkin Beck was born in Rhode Island in 1921 to Russian immigrant parents who were devout Jews. Beck graduated from Brown University and pursued a medical degree at Yale University, where he abandoned his first interest, neurology, for studies in psychiatry. While studying depressed patients, Beck observed that clients often had a negative bias against themselves and in the foresight of their futures. He termed these negative biases *cognitive distortions.* In the early 1960s, Beck termed his system of psychotherapy *cognitive therapy,* which primarily deals with logical errors in client thinking.

■ View of Human Nature

Cognitive theorists believe that the most prominent and influential aspect of the human person is the cognitive component (Beck, 1976). A concise review of cognitive theory's assumptions about humankind is provided here.

Key Assumptions About Human Nature in the Cognitive Tradition

- Basic human needs, including preservation, reproduction, dominance, and sociability are controlled by cognitions or thoughts.
- People have a biological tendency toward creating distorted perceptions.
- Improvements in mental health are related to people's ability to change their thinking.

■ Theory of Personality

Cognitive theory views personality as reflecting the individual's cognitive organization and structure—based both on genetic endowment and social influences. Emotions and behavior are determined by how we perceive, interpret, and place meaning on our experiences, all of which, according to Beck (1976), are cognitive functions. Psychological distress develops when one creates maladaptive cognitive structures known as schemas, beliefs, or modes.

■ Key Theoretical Concepts

Cognitive therapy emphasizes recognizing and changing negative thoughts and maladaptive beliefs that, ultimately, lead to dysfunctional behavior. Some of the central concepts to cognitive therapy that are used to describe dysfunctional behaviors or, more specifically, cognitive distortions, are defined here (Corey, 2005).

Arbitrary interferences: The conclusions that people make about situations without due cause.

Overgeneralization: The tendency to apply conclusions or beliefs about a specific instance to other nonrelated instances.

Personalization: Interpreting events and reactions as related to oneself even if there is no evidence of the connection.

Polarized thinking: The tendency to view events as either completely negative or positive, or thinking that is dualistic and characterized by either–or traits.

Another concept of Beck's theory is that thought processing exists in three domains: the automatic or preconscious, the conscious, and the metacognitive (Corey, 2005). The term automatic thoughts is defined here because it is so integral to this perspective.

Automatic thoughts: Deep-seated, personal beliefs that are triggered by the environment and typically result in maladaptive feelings and behaviors.

■ Goals of Therapy

There are a number of goals that characterize cognitive therapy. Corey (2005) summarizes them this way.

Aims of Cognitive Therapy

- Help clients unravel their distortions in thinking and learn more realistic ways to formulate healthy cognitive experiences.
- Aid clients in distinguishing between false perceptions and accurate beliefs.
- Alter automatic or preconscious thoughts that lead to undesirable behaviors and feelings.
- Provide relief of symptoms.
- Deal with current issues.
- Support the client in the prevention of relapse.

■ Therapeutic Techniques

Therapeutic techniques are employed to assail dysfunctional thoughts in an approach called *cognitive restructuring.* The center of attention is placed on altering dysfunctional schemas and beliefs, regardless of the domain in which they exist. The following techniques are used in cognitive therapy.

Therapeutic Practices Germane to Cognitive Therapy

- Homework assignments.
- Questioning.
- Thought recording.

- Behavioral experiments.
- Imagery and role playing.
- Problem solving.

■ Role of Therapist

The role of the therapist involves a series of structured steps incorporated into each session.

Primary Therapist Tasks in Sessions

- Create a session agenda and administer a test of mood.
- Allow clients to present their problems.
- Establish agreed-on goals.
- Educate the client about the cognitive model.
- Develop a diagnosis and give homework assignments.
- Provide a summary of the session and feedback for the client.

To meet the goals of therapy and for the therapeutic alliance to be successful, a therapist must first develop trust with the client as well as a positive rapport. To aid in the development of this alliance, the counselor employs empathy, warmth, and genuineness.

■ Strengths and Limitations

One of the major strengths and contributions of cognitive therapy is its focus on thinking. Cognitive therapy sparked a movement by taking a scientific approach to understanding cognition and behavior. Research has proven the use of this form of therapy in the treatment of depressed clients. One limitation is that, for one to be a competent and effective practitioner, extensive training, skill, and hard work are necessary. Also, many debate the effectiveness of focusing solely on thinking as a means of altering one's behavior and question the reliance on the power of positive thinking as a primary function of change (Corey, 2005).

 Check out the Web site for the Association for Cognitive and Behavioral Therapies for more information on practitioners' issues and research:

www.aabt.org

COGNITIVE-BEHAVIORAL APPROACHES: RATIONAL-EMOTIVE BEHAVIOR THERAPY

Albert Ellis was born in 1913 in Pittsburgh, Pennsylvania, and has lived the majority of his life in rural New York. Originally trained in psychoanalysis, Ellis eventually came to experience it as a superficial and unscientific treatment method. In the mid-1950s, Ellis combined physiological, humanistic, and behavior therapy to create rational-emotive therapy (now known as rational-emotive behavior therapy [REBT]). He is known around the world as the grandfather of cognitive behavior therapy.

■ View of Human Nature

A number of presuppositions characterize REBT. Key assumptions about REBT's perspective on human nature are summarized here.

Assumptions About Human Nature in REBT

- Humans are born with two potentials: one for rational thinking and one for irrational thinking.
- All people have inherent tendencies toward growth and self-actualization (Ellis, 1999, 2000).
- Emotional disturbance is primarily self-inflicted, born out of the continued repetition of irrational thoughts and beliefs about the self.
- Blame is the cause for the propensity of humans to internalize negative thoughts and beliefs.

According to REBT, people must learn to accept themselves despite any imperfections that may exist and stop blaming others for any experienced unhappiness.

■ Theory of Personality

REBT explains personality through the A-B-C theory. Corey (2005) described this theory as follows:

A-B-C model of personality: Suggests that A (the activating event) does not cause C (the emotional consequence). Instead, B, which is the person's belief about A, largely causes C, the emotional reaction.

Thus, humans are responsible for creating their own irrational beliefs and reactions. According to Corey (2005), philosophical restructuring needs to occur to change dysfunctional personalities. The steps of this process are detailed next.

Steps in Philosophically Restructuring Dysfunction (Corey, 2005)

1. Fully acknowledge that we create our own emotional problems.
2. Accept that we have the ability to change these problems.
3. Acknowledge that emotional disturbances stem from irrational and negative beliefs.
4. See value in disputing irrational and negative beliefs.
5. Accept that change can only occur through hard work directed at changing irrational and negative beliefs.
6. Utilize REBT methods as a life practice.

■ Key Theoretical Concepts

The main premise of REBT is that a person's thinking about an event or situation, not the events or situations themselves, produces feelings. REBT posits that persons who have irrational and negative thoughts become emotionally unbalanced and behave in nonproductive ways; persons who think rationally tend to have calmer thoughts and behave in productive ways. Therefore, for people to behave productively, they must first control their thoughts. If people are successful at controlling their thoughts, they feel happy and are able to enjoy their lives (Ellis, 1973).

■ Goals of Therapy

The main goals of REBT theory are threefold and can be summarized as follows:

1. Assist clients in learning to separate the evaluation of their behaviors from the evaluation of their self-worth.
2. Encourage clients to accept themselves in totality and in spite of any imperfections that may exist.
3. Help clients replace irrational beliefs and behaviors with rational ones.

■ Therapeutic Techniques

Techniques utilized in REBT combine cognitive and emotive practices; a few common techniques are described here.

Cognitive Techniques

- *Disrupting irrational beliefs* entails therapists actively disputing irrational thoughts in an effort to help clients learn how to do the same.
- *Doing cognitive homework* is used to help clients become aware that they often create negative, self-fulfilling prophecies. Homework may include making lists of

problems, identifying absolute (usually irrational) beliefs, or completing the REBT Self Help Form.

- *Changing one's language* encourages clients to replace shoulds, oughts, and musts with their personal preferences, in an effort to think, behave, and, eventually, feel differently.

Emotive Techniques

- *Rational-emotive imagery* is a technique wherein clients imagine themselves thinking, feeling, and believing in exactly the way they wish they were thinking, feeling, and behaving. This assists in client development of new emotional patterns.
- *Role playing* allows clients to rehearse certain behaviors for productive feedback from a therapist.
- *Use of force and vigor* is meant to help clients use forceful internal dialogues with themselves to eradicate self-defeating thoughts.

Behavioral techniques, such as assertiveness training and skill building, also can be employed when utilizing REBT.

■ Role of Therapist

Consistent with the assumptions about human nature and the A-B-C model outlined in this approach, therapists embrace a number of roles to help clients:

- Help clients understand how their shoulds, oughts, and musts contribute to irrational thinking.
- Aid clients in understanding how their own unrealistic and illogical thought patterns contribute to their dysfunctional behaviors and emotional turmoil.
- Support clients in shedding irrational thoughts and replacing them with productive, rational thinking in an effort to break the cycle of a nonproductive and negative thought process.
- Educate the client in an effort to elucidate understanding around how one's irrational thoughts contribute to one's emotional state of unrest.

■ Strengths and Limitations

A strength of REBT is its emphasis on putting newly acquired insights into action. Here, it is not enough just to experience new insights; rather, the focus is on applying what has been learned in a productive, health-promoting way. Comprehensive and eclectic techniques make REBT a useful tool for therapists and allows them to draw from cognitive, behavioral, and emotive techniques, depending on the situation at hand. A limitation of REBT can be its confrontational nature. Not all clients respond well to a confrontational style and some may be frightened off by this type of therapy. Similarly, REBT therapists can misuse their power with clients by imposing their own ideas on the client. Clients must not feel pressured to assume the beliefs and values of the therapist. A cooperative, trusting, and balanced client–therapist relationship is essential for a beneficial outcome.

COGNITIVE-BEHAVIORAL APPROACHES: REALITY THERAPY

Born in 1925 in Cleveland, Ohio, William Glasser was first trained as a chemical engineer and later received graduate degrees in clinical psychology and medicine from Case Western Reserve University. Board certified in psychiatry in 1961, Glasser worked in private practice until 1986. In 1965, Glasser's objections to psychoanalysis led him to develop reality therapy, expounded on in his work, *Reality Therapy* (Glasser, 1965). In 1967, Glasser established the Institute for Reality Therapy, and, in 1998, he expanded on his earlier ideas and termed his new concept choice theory.

■ View of Human Nature

Glasser (1965, 2000) contended that people are born with fundamental needs but are not endowed necessarily with the ability to fulfill these needs.

Five Basic Human Needs Recognized in Reality Therapy

1. Survival.
2. Power.
3. Love and belonging.
4. Freedom.
5. Fun.

If, at an early age, people learn to fulfill their needs in a healthy, responsible way, they will be positioned better to form strong relationships. Failure to fulfill the five needs results in conflict and pain (Corey, 2005; Glasser, 1965). Glasser believed that love and belonging are paramount to positive mental health.

■ Theory of Personality

According to Glasser (1998), personality is partially fixed at birth. The five basic needs dictate what Glasser termed *total behavior,* the elements of which are listed next.

Four Elements of Total Behavior

- Acting.
- Thinking.
- Feeling.
- Physiology.

Glasser believes that people can control how they act and think, which then affects how people feel. What people want from life and from the significant relationships they form are encompassed in what Glasser (1998) termed a *quality world*. This quality world—although often idealized—is a person's view of how life would be if all human needs were sufficiently fulfilled. Conflict is seen as an inconsistency between the quality world (how things should be) and reality (how things are).

■ Key Theoretical Concepts

Reality therapy is an active and directive model that stresses a person's present behavior and an individual's personal responsibility (Glasser, 1984).

Personal responsibility: The concept that people have no power over others' behaviors, but they do have control over their own behavior, for which they are responsible.

> Reality therapy is grounded in the assumption that people create their inner worlds, which is more important than the "real" world. Thus, therapy focuses on the way people perceive the world to exist.

The focus of reality therapy, therefore, is behavior, not attitude, insight, feelings, one's past, or unconscious motivation. Reality therapy is grounded in the assumption that people create their inner worlds, which is more important than the "real" world. Thus, therapy focuses on the way people perceive the world to exist. Glasser (1984) believed that "all behavior is generated within ourselves for the purpose of satisfying one or more basic needs" (p. 323). Glasser further suggested that struggles arise when individuals are not able to meet one or more of the five psychological needs.

■ Goals of Therapy

The primary goal of reality therapy is to help clients learn more productive ways to fulfill their needs (Glasser, 2000). Clients are encouraged to evaluate their needs and behaviors and clarify what it is that they want. By establishing (or reestablishing) satisfying relationships, clients choose to take charge of their lives (Glasser, 1965, 1998, 2000).

■ Therapeutic Techniques

For clients to evaluate themselves effectively and accurately discern their needs, a therapeutic alliance must first be established. This alliance will model satisfying relationships (Corey, 2005). In addition to building a strong relationship, reality therapy uses a number of therapeutic techniques or guides to practice; some are listed next.

Techniques Germane to Reality Therapy

- Little attention is given to the past.
- Present concerns and behaviors are addressed (Glasser, 1965, 1998, 2000).
- Questions focus on what the clients are doing, not why they are doing it (Glasser, 1965, 1998).
- The therapist guides the clients' self-evaluations, although it is ultimately the clients' responsibility to determine if their behavior helps fulfill their needs.
- The therapist helps clients develop a plan that will allow for acquisition of therapeutic goals (Corey, 2005; Glasser, 1965, 1998).

■ Role of Therapist

The primary role of the therapist is to establish a satisfying relationship with the client (Corey, 2005; Glasser, 1965). Glasser rejected the objective role of the Freudian analyst, believing that the client is more amenable to self-evaluation if judgment does not exist. The therapist helps the client behave realistically by focusing on the present and learning to satisfy responsibly his or her needs (Glasser, 1965, 1998, 2000).

■ Strengths and Limitations

Strengths of realty therapy include the attention paid to the present, client accountability, and the brevity of treatment (Corey, 2005; Glasser, 1998). Failure to appreciate the influence of the past, rejection of unconscious determinants, objection to psychotropic medication, and denial of neurologically influenced mental disorders, such as schizophrenia, bipolar disorder, and personality disorders are some of the system's limitations.

COGNITIVE-BEHAVIORAL APPROACHES: MULTIMODAL THERAPY

Arnold A. Lazarus earned a PhD in clinical psychology from the University of the Witwatersrand in Johannesburg, South Africa, and after 6 years as a private practitioner, immigrated to the United States. He has taught at Stanford University, Temple University Medical School, Yale University, and Rutgers University, where he has held the rank of Distinguished Professor of Psychology since 1972. Currently the Executive Director of The Lazarus Institute in New Jersey, Lazarus has maintained an active psychotherapy practice since 1959. As a graduate student in psychology, Lazarus first developed a therapy based on behavioral psychology. In the 1980s, he expanded this into cognitive behavior therapy, and later into a multifaceted system of therapy called *multimodal therapy.*

■ View of Human Nature

Multimodal therapy views human nature from a behaviorist perspective. That is, at birth, each person is like a blank slate with no presumed innate drives, motives, needs, or tendencies, except the aptitude to learn behavior. All behaviors are learned in response to environmental contingencies. According to Fall and Holder (2003), behaviorists consider personality to be "the sum total and the interaction of voluntary and involuntary behaviors in one's response repertoire at any given time" (p. 275).

■ Theory of Personality

This theory suggests that humans are all fallible and have both limitations and assets. Other key tenets of the approach's view of personality are mentioned here.

Assumptions About Personality in Multimodal Therapy

- Personality is the result of an interaction between genetic makeup, the physical environment in which an individual was raised, and an individual's social learning history (Fall & Holder, 2003).
- All people are equal to one another, regardless of social status or notoriety in the world.
- People with superior skills in certain areas are not viewed as superior human beings.

Lazarus described human personality through the BASIC I.D. model, comprised of seven specific modalities, described next.

■ Key Theoretical Concepts

Multimodal therapy is a comprehensive, systematic, and holistic approach to behavior therapy. It is based on the idea that humans are biological beings who think, feel, act, sense, imagine, and interact and that all seven modalities should be addressed in treatment. Treatment is built around the BASIC I.D. framework (Lazarus, 1989). The BASIC I.D. acronym represents the following concepts.

BASIC I.D.

- *Behavior* refers to all that we say or do, including our actions, reactions, and responses.
- *Affect* refers to all emotions that humans experience.
- *Sensation* refers to all five senses: touch, taste, smell, sight, and hearing.
- *Imagery* refers to thoughts born out of dreams and other auditory images.
- *Cognition* refers to thoughts, values, attitudes, beliefs, and ideas.
- *Interpersonal relationships* refers to all of our social experiences, including those with family, peers, coworkers, and friends.
- *Drugs/biology* refers to all aspects of physical well-being, including diet, health, sleep, exercise, fitness, as well as any physical ailments.

If change takes place within any one of the seven modalities, the functioning of the remaining modalities is affected; therefore, for optimal development and change to occur, all seven modalities must be addressed.

■ Goals of Therapy

The overall goals of multimodal therapy include a reduction of psychological difficulties and a promotion of personal growth (Fall & Holder, 2003). Problems within each of the seven modalities are examined in conjunction with a client's wishes for change within each modality. Multimodal therapists assist clients in setting obtainable goals so that hope can be instilled and success can be reached. Vague or obtuse goals are discouraged in favor of specific, concrete goals.

■ Therapeutic Techniques

Unlike many other forms of therapy, multimodal therapy does not assume that the client will fit the therapy; rather, it draws from a wide repertoire of techniques to ensure that the client's needs are being met. Thus, a key idea in this approach is technical eclecticism.

Technical eclecticism: The idea that treatment can and should consist of techniques from a variety of theoretical perspectives without the therapist necessarily adopting a theoretical basis for those techniques.

Because individuals bring a wide variety of problems to therapy, it is appropriate for the therapist to bring a variety of treatment strategies. Multimodal therapy is psychoeducational in nature and contends that many client problems arise from either misinformation or missing information.

Sampling of Techniques Used in Multimodal Therapy

- Bibliotherapy.
- Assertiveness and communication training.
- Social and cognitive learning techniques.

■ Role of Therapist

Multimodal therapists tend to be very active and participatory during sessions with clients, as well as very flexible and adaptable. A description of the roles and tasks is provided here.

Variety of Mulitmodal Therapist Roles

- Therapists act as consultant, educator, trainer, and role model.
- Therapists draw from a wide range of techniques and therapeutic styles depending on the differing styles, personalities, and needs of the client.
- Therapists, usually in concert with the client, determine which specific problems across the BASIC I.D. framework are most salient and then focus attention on those specific issues.
- Therapists determine the relationship style that best fits for a particular client.

■ Strengths and Limitations

A strength of multimodal therapy is that it requires the client to do something, allowing therapists to draw from many behavioral strategies to assist the client in formulating a plan of action toward change. Behavior models have been researched well, are applicable to a wide variety of settings, and are easily understood by many clients. Given that multimodal therapy is behaviorally based, feelings are generally not dealt with as part of the overall treatment plan—a limitation of this therapeutic system. A second limitation is the amount of manipulation and control that the therapist might be perceived as having over the client, given their directive involvement in treatment.

EXISTENTIAL-HUMANISTIC APPROACHES: PERSON-CENTERED

Born in 1902 in a suburb of Chicago to parents who were strict Christian fundamentalists, Carl Rogers grew up lacking social skills and was isolated and self-contained until his first year of college. Rogers was educated at the University of Wisconsin in Madison and, after marrying, moved to New York City to attend Columbia University's Union Theological Seminary, where he changed his major area of study from theology to psychology. In 1931, Rogers earned a PhD in psychology from the Teachers College of Columbia University and accepted a position at a child guidance center in Rochester, New York. Rogers became known around the world for originating and developing the humanistic approach to psychotherapy.

■ View of Human Nature

The person-centered view of human nature is one of the most optimistic among the range of counselor theories. A few of the central assumptions of humankind made by Rogers are presented here.

Person-Centered Assumptions of Human Nature (Corey, 2005)

- Humans inherently have within themselves all of the assets needed to move forward in a positive, constructive manner.
- People are trustworthy, resourceful, able to make constructive changes, and capable of living useful and productive lives.
- People naturally move toward health if they believe a pathway is open for them to do so.

■ Theory of Personality

The person-centered theory of personality mirrors its view of human nature. That is, Rogers believed that humans have within themselves, as part of their inherent makeup, everything necessary for them to move forward in their lives.

■ Key Theoretical Concepts

Unlike earlier methods of therapy that largely were directive, Rogers's (1961, 1980) form of counseling was nondirective. Three fundamental concepts define Rogers's person-centered theory: genuineness, unconditional positive regard, and empathy, defined as follows:

Genuineness: The congruence or "realness" of the therapist that increases the likelihood of growth and change in the client.

Unconditional positive regard: The nonjudgmental, caring, and accepting attitude of the therapist toward the client.

Empathy: Ability of the therapist both to enter the world of the client without being influenced by his or her own personal values or beliefs and to communicate understanding genuinely and effectively.

■ Goals of Therapy

Essentially, the goals of person-centered therapy are twofold; the dual aims are presented next.

Aims of Person-Centered Therapy

1. Providing a climate conducive to helping clients shed the "masks" or facades they wear and become fully functioning people.
2. Assisting clients in their growth process so they are able to cope better with current and future problems that may arise in their lives.

■ Therapeutic Techniques

Person-centered therapy does not utilize specific techniques. Rather, it posits that the quality of the therapeutic relationship, not the administration of specific techniques, is the primary agent of growth for the client. Person-centered therapists rely heavily on the reflection of clients' feelings. This does not mean simply restating what a client has shared. Rather, according to Corey (2005), there exists the belief that the "relational attitudes and fundamental ways of being with the client constitute the heart of the change process" (p. 174).

■ Role of Therapist

Because of the foundational belief in the client's ability to move toward growth under the proper conditions, the role of the therapist reflects a radical departure from the traditional (i.e., psychoanalytic and behavioral) approaches to treatment.

Tasks of the Client-Centered Clinician

- Create an environment of emotional safety, warmth, and understanding in an effort to facilitate client growth and change.
- Avoid giving advice, making suggestions, and interpreting the meaning of client disclosure.
- Listen and reflect back the client's sharing.

With unconditional positive regard comes client insight and positive action. Reflective listening increases insight and self-regard.

■ Strengths and Limitations

Strengths of the person-centered approach to therapy include its focus on the therapist–client relationship—not specific techniques. This allows the therapy to be productive in a variety of settings, including individual, couples, families, and groups. Research consistently shows that empathy, one of person-centered therapy's hallmarks, is the most powerful predictor of client progress. However, a limitation of the approach emerges when person-centered therapists focus primarily on empathy and support and not on challenging the client. Additionally, therapists may be challenged to remove their hopes for the client from the therapeutic process and allow clients to chart their own course, even when therapists feel choices are being made that are not in the best interest of the clients.

EXISTENTIAL-HUMANISTIC APPROACHES: GESTALT

Frederick (Fritz) Perls was a native of Berlin, Germany, and in his youth, a student of psychoanalysis. After moving to the United States in 1964, Perls began to create his approach to therapy, known as Gestalt therapy. The impact of his work is seen in that it continues to be studied and practiced today at the Gestalt Institutes in New York and Cleveland, among other places. Two of Perls's most well-known works are entitled *Gestalt Therapy Verbatim* (1969a) and *In and Out of the Garbage Pail* (1969b). Perls died in 1970 while preparing to open another institute of Gestalt study in British Columbia.

■ View of Human Nature

A basic tenet of Gestalt therapy is that clients are capable of self-regulation within their environments when they are fully aware of what is happening both internally (within themselves) and externally (in the surrounding environment). Perls believed that clients only make productive change when they become aware, and that knowledge is the product of what immediately is evident in the clients' perceived experiences.

■ Theory of Personality

The Gestalt view of personality largely is influenced by existential philosophy and highlights such concepts as living in the here and now, increasing self-awareness, and integrating all aspects of one's way of being into a gestalt or whole.

■ Key Theoretical Concepts

The main objective of Gestalt therapy is for an individual to gain awareness, a necessary component in the process of integration into a whole (gestalt). According to

Latner (1973), there are four fundamental principles of Gestalt therapy: the principle of holism (integration), the principle of awareness, the principle of figure/ground, and the principle of polarities. These principles drive the work one does in Gestalt therapy and lead to self-actualization.

Principle of holism: Clients experience a sense of completeness when they tie up problematic situations, or loose ends, from the past that cause anxiety and prevent integration (Perls, Hefferline, & Goodman, 1951).

Principle of awareness: Clients gain insight when they become aware of and take responsibility for their sensations, thoughts, and behaviors in the here-and-now (Perls et al., 1951).

Principle of figure/ground: Clients address their most pressing needs first and as these are resolved, previously less evident needs emerge to be dealt with.

Principle of polarities: Clients acknowledge the opposite or hidden aspects of a problematic situation to promote resolution of conflicts.

■ Goals of Therapy

The fundamental goal of Gestalt therapy is for clients to gain awareness. Only when clients become aware can they be positioned to make selective choices. Other specific goals of therapy include those listed here.

Aims of Gestalt Therapy

- Assuming ownership of one's experiences.
- Developing skills necessary for the satisfaction of needs without violating the rights of others.
- Developing a heightened awareness of one's senses.
- Learning to accept responsibility and consequences for one's actions.
- Moving from reliance on external supports to reliance on internal supports.

■ Therapeutic Techniques

Gestalt techniques rely heavily on experiments, identified by Corey (2005) as "useful tools to help the client gain fuller awareness" (p. 210). Some of the more common experiments are mentioned next.

Gestalt Therapeutic Experiments (Corey, 2005)

- *Internal dialogue exercise* is used to promote integration between the polarities of conflict that exist in everyone, bringing a new sense of awareness to the client.
- *Making the rounds* happens in group settings when a client approaches each member and speaks or does something to experiment with new behavior.
- *The reversal exercise* involves the client in playing the role opposite of what is normal for that individual. By clients doing the very thing that causes anxiety, they might gain attributes they have denied in the past.
- *Staying with the feeling* happens at a point when a client experiences an unpleasant or negative feeling, and he or she is encouraged to stay with the feeling to make way for higher levels of personal growth.

Many techniques exist in the Gestalt therapy that all aspire to bring a greater awareness to the client.

■ Role of Therapist

The role of the Gestalt therapist is to help clients develop awareness by learning to express what it is they are experiencing in the present moment. A few other methods Gestalt therapists use to heighten awareness are noted here.

Tasks of the Gestalt Therapist

- Notice for the clients what is in the foreground and what is in the background of their experiences.
- Point out notable body language.
- Challenge clients with interventions aimed at awareness of their language patterns.

■ Strengths and Limitations

Gestalt therapy allows for a high level of creativity. A client's past can be reenacted in the present in very creative and lively ways. A key strength of this approach, according to Corey (2005), is Gestalt therapy's attempt to integrate practice, theory, and research. A criticism of Gestalt therapy is that it focuses too heavily on emotion and too little on cognition. Also, there is potential for abuse of power by the therapist who is typically highly active and directive. Because of its complexity, Gestalt therapy requires adequate training and supervision of therapists if it is to help people lead healthier and more fulfilling lives.

EXISTENTIAL-HUMANISTIC APPROACHES: LOGOTHERAPY

Viktor Frankl was born in Vienna, Austria, in 1905 and died there in 1997. Under Nazi rule, his immediate and extended family was taken to concentration camps where, although Frankl and one sister survived the 3-year ordeal, his entire family was murdered. Postliberation, Frankl reclaimed his career as a neurologist and psychiatrist and founded The Third Vienna School of Psychotherapy: Logotherapy. Over the span of his life, Frankl published more than 30 books, lectured across the globe, and received 29 honorary degrees.

■ View of Human Nature

Frankl's view of human nature includes a couple of core ideas that are mentioned here.

Tenets of Human Nature Proposed in Logotherapy

- Individuals have the capacity to accept fate (that which is presented and confronted in its immediacy of life experiences) and give it meaning and connectedness to one's memories, environment, and other individuals with whom there exists a relationship of love and care.
- A sense of humor although grim in the face of hardship helps people to momentarily escape life's burdens and find an attitude of meaning.

■ Theory of Personality

This existential theory does not offer a particular theory of personality. One of Frankl's most poignant awarenesses about personality was the identification of love as the ultimate and highest goal to which humans can aspire (Corey, 2005).

■ Key Theoretical Concepts

With respect to logotherapy, three key propositions summarize the basic dimensions of the human condition.

Key Philosophical Concepts in Logotherapy

1. *Will to meaning* is the fundamental driving force of humanity and is characterized by the search for meaning in all situations, especially in times of pain and suffering.
2. *Freedom of will* suggests that despite circumstances, people always have the ability to choose how they will interpret and respond to their situations.

3. *Meaning in life* is the proposition that life is fundamentally a meaningful endeavor and existence that calls people to respond to it in the most responsible and productive ways they can.

Goals of Therapy

Clients often are not living full and meaningful lives. Therefore, the logotherapist and client work at accomplishing some of the following therapeutic goals.

Aims of Logotherapy

- Discern the meaning of the past, present, and future.
- Accept the freedom and responsibility to act.
- Move toward personal authenticity and become aware of how and when one is deceiving oneself.
- Relinquish a victim role for a freer sense of existence.

Therapeutic Techniques

As in other types of existential therapy, therapeutic techniques are secondary to the establishment of a trusting relationship that allows the therapist to challenge the client. However, logotherapy employs the following two techniques.

Two Techniques Used in Logotherapy

1. *Paradoxical intention* is used to encourage the client to manifest or desire what he or she fears.
2. *Dereflection* diverts the client away from problems toward something meaningful.

Role of Therapist

The logotherapist helps clients discern the meaning of past and present experiences in an effort to help them uncover new understandings and options. A central task of the therapist is to help clients uncover ways in which they are living restricted experiences and remaining "stuck." In this way, the therapist helps move clients toward accepting their personal responsibility for future changes.

Strengths and Limitations

Frankl's theory offer a foundation for understanding universal human concerns, provides a new conceptualization of death as holding meaning, and focuses on the human quality of the therapeutic relationship. Criticisms of Frankl's work include its vagueness and lack of empirical support. Philosophical insights may not be appropriate for some clients, and social factors that cause human problems may be ignored because the interventions are wholly individualistic.

 Visit the Web site of the Viktor Frankl Institute for more information on logotherapy at:

▶ http://logotherapy.univie.ac.at/e/indexe.html

Chapter 9:   Key Terms

▶ Conscious
▶ Unconscious
▶ Manifest content
▶ Latent content
▶ Archetypes
▶ Collective unconscious
▶ Individuation
▶ Social interest
▶ Birth order
▶ Family constellation
▶ Creative self
▶ Ego state
▶ Parent ego state

▶ Adult ego state
▶ Child ego state
▶ Reinforcement
▶ Punishment
▶ Positive reinforcement
▶ Negative reinforcement
▶ Reciprocal determinism
▶ Self-efficacy
▶ Arbitrary interferences
▶ Overgeneralization
▶ Personalization
▶ Polarized thinking
▶ Automatic thoughts

▶ A-B-C model of personality
▶ Personal responsibility
▶ Technical eclecticism
▶ Genuineness
▶ Unconditional positive regard
▶ Empathy
▶ Principle of holism
▶ Principle of awareness
▶ Principle of figure/ground
▶ Principle of polarities

Individual and Social Aspects of the Helping Relationship

Jocelyn Gregoire
Christin M. Jungers
Duquesne University

In This Chapter

▶ *The Helping Relationship*
- Why Bother With Theories?
- Theory Defined
- Theories With Which Helpers Need to Be Familiar
- A Word About Eclecticism
- Helping Defined
- The Helping Process
- Frameworks Within Which the Helping Process Occurs
- Helping Helpees Meet Their Needs

▶ *What Constitutes Effective Helping?*
- Professional Helpers as Growth Facilitators
- Personal Characteristics of Effective Helpers
- Helpers' Skills
- Helpers and Diversity Issues

▶ *Training Models for Coping Skills Development*
- People-in-System Model
- Life Skills Education Model
- Structured Learning Therapy Model
- Social Skills

▶ *Training Models for Interpersonal Skills Development*
- Skilled Helping: Problem Management Model
- Relationship Enhancement Therapy Model
- Microskills Counseling Model
- Interpersonal Process Recall
- Human Resources Development Model
- The Politics of Giving Therapy Away: Listening and Focusing

▶ *Social-Psychological Approaches to Helping*
- Symbolic Interaction
- Role Theory
- Social Exchange
- Cognitive Consistency
- Dissonance Theory
- Heider's Balance Theory
- Congruity Theory
- Newcomb's A-B-X Model of Interpersonal Attraction
- Attributions

THE HELPING RELATIONSHIP

People embrace a helping profession such as counseling for a wide variety of reasons. Underpinning their motives for entering the field of counseling also are their diversity of views and concepts about the nature of the helping process (Seligman, 2004). However, the practice of counseling and psychotherapy requires that professional helpers possess both the core skills and the experience necessary to become effective therapists (Sperry, Carlson, & Kjos, 2003).

■ Why Bother With Theories?

A common question that most potential helpers ask revolves around why they need to bother learning about or applying theories, because all they really want to do is help people. In response, professional helpers point both to their years of personal experiences and to research in the field of helping to testify to the importance of studying and functioning within conceptual frameworks (Kottler, 2000; Parsons, 2004). Other compelling reasons that attest to the value of theories are mentioned here.

Support for Theories

- They help organize data.
- They provide frameworks for actions.
- They help affirm credibility of the helpers.
- They are landmarks for the helpers' work.

■ Theory Defined

Santrock (1999) defined theory generically and also provided a definition of counseling theory as follows:

Theory: A set of principles that helps to explain a group of facts or a phenomenon and is used to make predictions.

Counseling theory: A framework for observing and understanding human behavior that allows for making predictions about the concerns, actions, perceptions, emotions, and motivations of human beings. It is also the basic platform from which counselors operate to make interventions.

■ Theories With Which Helpers Need to Be Familiar

Although it is not an easy task to master every single theory about helping that populates the field of counseling, there are still some basic frameworks helpers should grasp. Having theoretical frameworks at their fingertips helps counselors understand the ways people learn, grow through their life's experiences, and develop problems; additionally, theories aid counselors in deciding which path to follow to help people get back on their feet. Kottler (2000) proposed that helpers be familiar with following basic conceptual models.

Core Counseling Theories

- Developmental theories.
- Learning theories.
- Theories of intervention.
- Psychoanalytic theories.
- Client-centered theories.
- Existential theory.
- Gestalt theory.
- Adlerian theory.
- Behavioral theory.
- Cognitive-behavioral theory.
- Reality theory.
- Structural or systemic theory.
- Strategic or problem-solving theory.
- Narrative theory.

■ A Word About Eclecticism

Numerous helpers describe their therapeutic approach as eclectic. Kottler (2000) defined eclecticism this way:

> **Eclecticism:** Borrowing "from a variety of approaches depending on the presenting problem; the client's most important needs at a moment and time; how much time is available to initiate change; what objectives and goals have been agreed upon, the preferences, styles, and mood of the helper; and the philosophy of the organization" (pp. 26–27).

■ Helping Defined

Young (2001) defined helping in these terms:

> **Helping:** "[A] broad term that encompasses all the activities we use to assist another person, whether we have a professional relationship or not" (p. 24).

Helping requires a person seeking help (a client), another person who has the ability, as well as the desire, to give help (the helper), and an appropriate setting where the helping process can take place (Cormier & Hackney, 2005).

■ The Helping Process

The main elements that constitute the helping process can be summarized as the personality of the helpers, which, when coupled with their use of specific skills, produce growth conditions that have an important impact on the helpees, the helpers, and society as a whole. More specifically, the process of helping is aimed at a number of goals.

Goals of the Helping Process (Brammer & MacDonald, 1999)

- Promoting changes in behaviors and lifestyle.
- Transforming thoughts and self-perceptions.
- Developing awareness and understanding.
- Bringing relief from suffering.

Parsons (2004) viewed helping as a special kind of interpersonal process and response that implies the involvement of at least two persons. He proposed the following as the operational elements of this special process.

Elements of the Helping Process

- The helping dynamic.
- The helping participants.
- The helping relationship.
- The helping focus.
- The helping outcome.

■ Frameworks Within Which the Helping Process Occurs

Skovholt and Rivers (2004) postulated that the helping process generally takes place within the following simple framework in spite of the variability that exists in helping.

Skovholt and Rivers's (2004) Conceptualization of the Helping Process

1. Beginning.
2. Maintenance.
3. Ending.

Parsons (2004) seemed to concur with this conceptualization when he declared, "[T]heorists may differ in their opinions about the specific number of stages, but most will agree that helping proceeds through at least three fundamental stages" (pp. 20–21).

Parsons's (2004) Description of the Helping Process

1. Coming together or developing and building a helping alliance.
2. Exploring together or reconnaissance.
3. Acting together or intervention.

Although recognizing that the course of psychotherapy comprises a beginning, middle, and end point, Sperry et al. (2003) offered a four-phase model of the helping process.

Sperry et al.'s (2003) Phases of Helping

1. Engagement.
2. Assessment.
3. Intervention.
4. Maintenance and termination.

Finally, Young (2001) proposed a five-stage structure as a road map for the helping process, which is described here.

Young's (2001) Stages of Helping

1. Relationship building and opening up.
2. Assessment and planning information.
3. Treatment planning and goal setting.
4. Intervention and action.
5. Evaluation and reflection.

■ Helping Helpees Meet Their Needs

To provide help means to set up the necessary conditions that will assist helpees to meet their needs. These needs can be understood by considering the work of Maslow (1962), who offered a five-level hierarchy of needs that has to be satisfied to attain optimum development or actualization. The classification of these human needs suggests that higher order needs only will emerge when the lower ones have been reasonably satisfied.

Maslow's Hierarchy of Human Needs

1. Physiological and biological needs.
2. Safety needs.

3. Love needs.
4. Self-esteem needs.
5. Self-actualization needs.

See Chapter 8 for more information on Maslow's needs hierarchy.

WHAT CONSTITUTES EFFECTIVE HELPING?

The 1995 annual survey of *Consumer Reports* about the effectiveness of helping concluded that, regardless of modality, most people benefited greatly from therapy (Seligman, 1995). Research findings on the effectiveness of helping indicate that "the personal qualities of helpers are as significant for positive growth of helpees as are the methods they use" (Brammer & MacDonald, 1999, p. 26). What follows are some of the criteria that define the role of professional helpers as growth facilitators and the personal characteristics that contribute to making helping effective.

■ Professional Helpers as Growth Facilitators

Rogers (1980) saw the following personal characteristics as essential for helpers' effectiveness.

Rogers's (1980) Characteristics of Effective Helpers

- *Congruence* is the ability to be genuine with the client or the ability of the helper to maintain a consistency among personal feelings, thoughts, and behavior.
- *Unconditional positive regard* is the counselor's ability to accept and respect each client as a person and to believe in the inherent worth of every individual.
- *Empathy* is the helper's ability to understand another person's feelings and frames of reference and to suspend personal judgment while entering into the subjective worldview of the client.

Expanding on Rogers's theoretical framework, Carkhuff and Berenson (1967), Truax and Carkhuff (1967), Carkhuff (1968), and Combs (1982) all identified the following facilitative traits in which helpers can be trained to influence helpees' growth.

More Traits of Effective Counselors

- *Empathy:* Helpers attempt to view the world with the eyes of their helpees, by stepping into their internal frame of reference.

- *Warmth and caring*: Helpers attempt to express friendliness and consideration toward their helpees and to show compassion and genuine concern about their helpees' welfare.
- *Openness*: Helpers are willing to disclose their own personal views to their helpees in a genuine and honest way as a means to gain the trust of their helpees.
- *Respect and positive regard*: Helpers not only communicate deep concern for their helpees' welfare, but also manifest toward them respect for their individuality and worth as persons.
- *Concreteness and specificity*: Helpers attempt to be unambiguous and precise instead of general and vague while communicating with their helpees.
- *Communication competence*: Helpers are able to communicate to their helpees better ways to describe themselves as well as provide them with clearer descriptive insights about their problems and are able to function within the multicultural verbal and nonverbal language framework of their helpees.
- *Intentionality*: Helpers are capable of navigating through and choosing from a wide range of possible responses to their helpees' situations.

Seligman (2001) viewed the following as essential conditions of effective therapeutic relationships.

Conditions of Successful Therapeutic Relationships (Seligman, 2001)

- Empathy.
- Trustworthiness.
- Caring.
- Genuineness and congruence.
- Persuasiveness.
- Hope.

Finally, according to Parsons (2004), the effective helpers are those that display the following characteristics.

Qualities of Effective Helpers (Parsons, 2004)

- Self-aware.
- Exhibit facilitative attitudes and values.
- Maintain emotional objectivity.
- Employ an investigative approach to helping.

■ Personal Characteristics of Effective Helpers

Combs (1982) coined the term *self as instrument* to "indicate that our principle helping tool is ourselves acting spontaneously in response to the rapidly changing interpersonal demands of the helping relationship" (Brammer & MacDonald, 1999, p. 36). The following are personal helpers' characteristics that determine the nature of this relationship.

Traits of Helpers That Influence the Counseling Relationship

- Awareness of self and values.
- Awareness of cultural experiences.
- Ability to analyze personal feelings.
- Ability to serve as model and influencer.
- Altruism and compassion.
- Strong sense of ethics.
- Responsibility.
- Ability to empower others.

Regardless of the settings and the theoretical framework from which they operate, effective helpers embody certain, basic qualities. Cormier and Hackney (2005) identified the following personal qualities of successful counselors.

Personal Qualities of Transformative Helpers

- Self-awareness and understanding.
- Good psychological health.
- Sensitivity to and understanding of racial, ethnic, and cultural factors in self and others.
- Open-mindedness.
- Objectivity.
- Ability to promote the welfare of the client.

Moreover, Okun (2001) suggested the following characteristics as important to the success of the helping relationship.

Skills and Characteristics That Make Good Helpers (Okun, 2001)

- Helpers can operate easily with a multitude of approaches and strategies.
- Helpers are self-aware of their personal beliefs and values to help their clients become familiar with their own belief and value systems.
- Helpers are able to instill trust within the helping relationship through proper use of emphatic communication skills.
- Helpers are sensitive to multicultural variables in their choice of strategies and interventions when working with culturally diverse clients.
- Helpers are familiar with strategies that will address the affective domain (feelings and emotions), the cognitive domain (thoughts and intellectual processes), and the behavioral domain (actions and deeds) of the clients.

Based on a study conducted by Jennings and Skovholt (1999) of peer-nominated outstanding therapists, Seligman (2004) reported the nine qualities that characterize effective clinicians.

Recognized Qualities of Effective Clinicians (Seligman, 2004)

1. They are eager to learn.
2. They draw heavily on their extensive experience.
3. They value and can deal with ambiguity and complex concepts.
4. They can recognize and accept people's emotions.
5. They are emotionally healthy and nurture their own emotional well-being.
6. They are self-aware and can assess the impact their own emotional health has on their work.
7. They have strong interpersonal skills.
8. They believe in the importance of and value in the therapeutic alliance.
9. They can use their good interpersonal skills to develop a positive therapeutic alliance.

■ Helpers' Skills

Corey (1995) proposed a list of skills that group leaders need to be familiar with to be effective; these skills are equally necessary in individual therapy. The following list outlines the skills that professional helpers need to master to be successful.

Skills of Effective Helpers (Corey, 1995)

- Active listening.
- Restating.
- Clarifying.
- Summarizing.
- Questioning.
- Interpreting.
- Confronting.
- Reflecting feelings.
- Supporting.
- Empathizing.
- Facilitating.
- Initiating.
- Setting goals.
- Evaluating.
- Giving feedback.
- Suggesting.

- Protecting.
- Disclosure.
- Modeling.
- Terminating.

■ Helpers and Diversity Issues

Neukrug and Schwitzer (2006) pointed out that research has consistently supported the view that minority clients with non-White backgrounds often are misdiagnosed, shun counseling, terminate counseling prematurely, and find therapy of little or no help. Arredondo (1999) saw clinicians' biases, stereotypes, and lack of genuine information about clients from minority groups as one of the reasons for these situations. Neukrug and Schwitzer (2006) offered a number of counselors' negative attitudes that contribute to the failure of counseling with minority non-White clients.

Helpers' Negative Attitudes Influencing "Minority Clients"

- Holding onto the melting pot myth.
- Having different expectations about counseling than the client.
- Not understanding the impact of social forces.
- Maintaining an ethnocentric worldview.
- Being ignorant of one's own racist attitudes and prejudices.
- Not understanding differences in the expression of symptomatology.
- Not realizing that assessment and research instruments may be culturally insensitive.
- Being unaware of institutional racism.

For more on diversity issues in counseling, see Chapters 4, 11, 14, and 16.

TRAINING MODELS FOR COPING SKILLS DEVELOPMENT

At one time, psychological knowledge, skills, and strategies were the sole property of expert psychologists. However, a paradigm shift started to occur within the mental health field when helpers discovered that for psychology to be of any relevance to human welfare, it must be given away (Larson, 1984). With this revelation, the professional helping field began to witness the conversion of psychological principles and approaches into skills that were teachable and propagated through systematic methods and programs. In the next two sections, we present some of the models that have been developed over the years to train both professionals and nonprofessionals.

In this section, we present models that constitute coping skills that are taught directly to clients. These include the following:

- People-in-system model.
- Life skills education model.
- Structured learning therapy model.
- Social skills model.

People-in-System Model

The people-in-system model, pioneered by Egan and Cowan (1979), is based on the equation $HD = f[(P \times S) \times (S \times S)]$, to signify that "human development (HD) is a function of (f) the interaction between ($\times$) people (P) and the human systems (S) in which they are involved, and this interaction system ($P \times S$) is in turn affected by ($\times$) other systems in the environment ($S \times S$)" (Larson, 1984, p. 25). The three elements that constitute the model are the same basic elements of the equations.

Central Elements of the People-in-System Model
(Egan & Cowan, 1979, p. 7)

1. *People* (*P*): Individuals journeying through the stages of life, facing lifelong and developmentally appropriate tasks and crises.
2. *Human systems* (*S*): Refer to the groups of which the individuals are members and in which they undergo life development experiences.
3. *Interaction* (×): A two-way interaction between individuals and the system and between the systems themselves.

For individuals in the systems to achieve a positive outcome from these interactions, they must possess a combination of working knowledge and skills. The people-in-system model offers the following framework from which counselors can be trained.

Elements of the Training Framework for Counselors

- A working knowledge of developmental processes across the life span.
- A working knowledge of the major human systems that affect people's lives.
- The kinds of life skills needed for individuals to effectively cope with developmental tasks within the social settings of their lives.

Life Skills Education Model

Working within a developmental and psychoeducational framework, Adkins (1984) developed the Life Coping Skills Program, which focuses on helping people learn how to become more aware of and perceptive about life crises as well as more educated and behaviorally competent to cope with these crises. The programs are designed to help the learners "clarify feelings and values, make decisions and choices, resolve conflicts, gain self-understanding, explore environmental opportunities and constraints, communicate effectively with others, and take personal responsibility for their actions" (Larson, 1984, p. 44). Central to the life skills approach to counseling are the four stages Adkins proposed for learning.

Learning Stages in the Life Skills Approach

1. In the *stimulus stage* there is a dramatic presentation of an emotionally loaded, provocative video vignette aimed at stimulating and focusing discussion.
2. In the *evocation stage,* the life skills educator (LSE) uses a structured pattern of questions to draw out elements of the problem presented from the group members, help them recognize the important issues, and invite them to identify with similar experiences they have had.
3. During the *objective-inquiry stage,* the LSE finds out through various activities what others know about the problem and how they relate to it.
4. In the *application stage,* the learner is encouraged to transfer the new understanding, insight, feelings, and knowledge into actual behavior in a simulated or real-life situation.

■ Structured Learning Therapy Model

Designed by Goldstein, Gershaw, and Sprafkin, the structured learning therapy model seeks to "meet the needs, lifestyles, and environmental realities of the lower class, since traditional methods of treatment have proved grossly inadequate and inappropriate for this population" (Larson, 1984, p. 70). The designers proposed two prescriptive approaches for the client from a lower socioeconomic background, which they termed *conformity presecription* (Goldstein, 1973).

Conformity prescription: Seeks to make clients fit the therapy by trying to enhance in them a positive appreciation for the therapeutic relationship.

Reformity prescription: Seeks to make the therapy fit the client through structured learning therapy so that it can be more consistent with the client's styles.

The following techniques are used in structured learning therapy.

Techniques of Structural Learning Therapy

- Modeling.
- Role playing.

- Performance feedback.
- Transfer of training.

Social Skills

Developed by Gambrill, social skills training is grounded in a **transactional model** that acknowledges that people are active creators of their social environments and, in turn, are influenced by it (Larson, 1984). Social competence is achieved when individuals can use cognitive processes to discern and perform appropriate behaviors relevant to specific situations. A process model of social skills is comprised of cognitive, psychological, and overt behaviors as major components. Any deficiency that occurs in any of these components can influence the following behavioral skills.

Components of Behavioral Skills

- *Goals/plans/feedback* suggests that social situations allow for pursuit of various goals attainable in different situations.
- *Perception* suggests that effective social behavior requires one to be particularly attentive to and make accurate observation of other people.
- *Translation* implies that although one must have accurate perception of the behavior of others, one also must interpret their behavior correctly.
- *Taking the role of others* implies that skilled observers of other people's point of view perform their social tasks more effectively than those who are less skilled.
- *Situations* are the specific contexts in which every effective social behavior occurs.
- *Verbal and nonverbal behaviors* suggest that socially effective behavior includes the implicit facility to begin, continue, and finish conversations.
- *Self-presentation* implies that information about our role, status, and claim for social identities is given to others by us.
- *Feedback* suggests that socially effective people make good use of feedback, are attentive to others' responses to their actions, and utilize these reactions to adjust subsequent behaviors.
- *Rewardingness and reinforcement* implies that when small reinforcements are offered through approval or disapproval and through pleasure or displeasure, people's lives are influenced.
- *Flexibility, creativity, and coping skills* suggest that effective social behavior is characterized by the ability to be flexible in choosing from a variety of options, as well as the skill to create new options and skills in specific situations.

Social skills training is designed to enhance observational, performance, and cognitive skills related to effective social behaviors in particular situations, and consists of a variety of components that include the following.

Components of Social Skills Training

- *Guidance* refers to instructions, prompting, and programming of change.
- *Demonstration* refers to modeled presentation and rehearsal.
- *Practice* suggests that participants practice the modeled behavior.
- *Constructive feedback* is the positive feedback offered after each rehearsal.
- *Homework assignments* are new behaviors that are tried out in real-life settings through assignments.

TRAINING MODELS FOR INTERPERSONAL SKILLS DEVELOPMENT

The following models have been developed to enhance interpersonal skills in helpers for effective helping and living:

- Skilled Helping: Problem Management Model.
- Relationship Enhancement Therapy.
- Microskills Counseling Model.
- Interpersonal Process Recall.
- Human Resources Development.
- Listening and Focusing.

■ Skilled Helping: Problem Management Model

Egan (2002) proposed a three-stage problem management framework for helping and helper training. The model also consists of a nine-step process that can be taught to clients so that they can become more effective in managing crisis situations in their lives. An "instrument for systematic and integrative eclecticism" (Larson, 1984, p. 133), the model can be used by all helpers, irrespective of their theoretical approach or school, as a tool to help clients identify, create, and utilize environmental resources to manage their problems.

Egan's Stages of the Helping Process

- Stage I asks, "What's going on?" and guides helpers to identify, clarify, and explore key issues and unused opportunities by reviewing the current scenario.
- Stage II asks, "What solutions make sense for me?" and suggests that helpers identify and determine outcomes for a better future or a preferred scenario.
- Stage III asks, "What do I have to do to get what I need or want?" and guides helpers to develop strategies for accomplishing therapeutic goals.

Each of the three stages Egan identified is further divided into three steps. These steps are outlined next.

Steps Within Stage I

1. Help client tell their stories.
2. Help clients break through blind spots in themselves, their problems, and missed opportunities.
3. Help clients choose the right issues to work on.

Steps Within Stage II

1. Help clients discover for themselves possibilities for a better future.
2. Help clients select realistic and challenging goals.
3. Help clients find the incentives for commitment to change.

Steps Within Stage III

1. Help clients see the multiplicity of ways for accomplishing goals.
2. Help clients opt for strategies that are the best fit for them.
3. Help clients craft a plan.

All three stages are rooted in action, as they are only the planning for change, not change itself. In describing action, Egan (2002) asked how helpers can aid clients in making changes and implementing their plans. In other words, clients need to do something for themselves right at the onset of the helping process to promote change. Egan also proposed three basic communications skills he saw as necessary for the helping process.

Egan's (2002) Communication Skills

- *Attending*: The skill of visibly tuning to clients summarized in the acronym SOLER (squarely facing the client, open posture, leaning toward each other, eye contact is maintained, and relaxed appearance).
- *Active listening*: Paying attention both to verbal behavior and nonverbal behavior to really understand what clients are saying.
- *Empathy*: Ability to draw from personal experiences, emotions, and behaviors and to respond in ways that express to clients that their experiences, emotions, and behaviors are being understood.

■ Relationship Enhancement Therapy Model

Guerney (1977) is considered the father of relational enhancement therapy (RET). Influenced by the theoretical orientation of Rogers, Horney, Sullivan, Anna Freud, Skinner, and Bandura, this integrative model can be used as a therapy, a means of problem prevention, and a program that can enhance personal and vocational life (Guerney, 1977). Single individuals, family members, and organizational groups can benefit from the skills of RET to achieve their goals and improve their personal and interpersonal transformation. The following are some skills taught to clients in RET.

RET Therapist Skills

- *Expressive skills* enhance clients' awareness and knowledge of their own self-concept, emotions, conflicts, and issues, and increase their ability to communicate these effectively to others.
- *Empathic skills* increase clients' capacity to understand others' behaviors, feelings, conflicts, problems, needs, and goals.
- *Mode switching* increases clients' ability to move from empathic mode to expressive mode at the appropriate time and in relevant situations.
- *Interpersonal conflict or problem resolution* increases clients' capacity to solve conflicts and problems with self and with others.
- *Facilitation* increases clients' ability to trigger in others interpersonal reactions that can contribute to conflict and problem resolutions, enrichment of relationships, and personal growth.
- *Generalization and maintenance* enhances clients' capability to utilize RET in daily life situations on a permanent basis.

■ Microskills Counseling Model

Designed by Ivey and Galvin, the microcounseling program takes its roots in social learning theory and teaches specific interviewing skills (Larson, 1984). Because the model is transtheoretical, counselors can be effectively trained in it independent of their therapeutic orientations. The format for the microcounseling training is as follows:

- Brief introduction to the skill.
- Viewing of brief video vignette of the skill being demonstrated by an expert.
- Presentation of literature that elaborates on the concept just viewed.
- Group practice of skills with audiovisual equipment.

Several skills needed for the microcounseling model, taken from "Ivey's Microskill Hierarchy" (Larson, 1984, p. 210) are presented next.

The Microskills Hierarchy

- Attending behavior.
- Client observation skills.
- Open and closed questions.
- Encouragement, paraphrasing, and summarization.
- Reflection of feeling.
- Reflection of meaning.
- Focusing.
- Influencing skills.

- Confrontation.
- Skill sequencing and structuring the interview.
- Skill integration.

See Chapter 5 for more information on how microskills are used in supervision.

Interpersonal Process Recall

The interpersonal process recall (IPR) model was developed by Kagan (1980) primarily as a means to improve the reliability of training programs for mental health workers. The method consists of reviewing a videotape or audiotape to recall and increase counselor awareness of covert thoughts and feelings of client and self, practice expressing covert thoughts and feelings in the here and now without negative consequences, and, consequently, to deepen the counselor–client relationship.

Phases of IPR

1. Facilitating communication.
2. Affect simulation.
3. Counselor recall.
4. Inquirer training.
5. Client recall.
6. Mutual recall.
7. Transfer of learning.

Human Resources Development Model

The human resources development (HRD) model takes its roots from the work of Carkhuff, who, in the early 1960s, expanded on Rogers's core conditions of empathic understanding, unconditional positive regard, and genuineness to include many facilitative therapist skills (Cash, cited in Larson, 1984). Characteristics added to Rogers's core concepts are concreteness, confrontation, and immediacy.

The three stages of Carkhuff's counselee model and the helping skills employed to facilitate this process are as follows:

1. *Self-exploration* includes prehelping and responding.
2. *Understanding* involves personalizing the issue.
3. *Action* involves initiating, problem solving, and program development.

Additionally, HRD is a training program that is comprised of the six modules identified here.

The HRD Training Program

- Module I: Introduction to and overview of the training program.
- Module II: Prehelping skills.
- Module III: Responding skills.

- Module IV: Personalizing skills.
- Module V: Problem-solving processes.
- Module VI: Program-development steps.

■ The Politics of Giving Therapy Away: Listening and Focusing

Gendlin, pupil of the late Rogers, attempted to demystify the process of therapeutic change by treating it as a teachable skill. He defined focusing as the technique of "attending to the physically sensed border zone between the conscious and unconscious" (cited in Larson, 1984, p. 287). In other words, when the client actually can sense the change occurring in his or her body, the individual then can begin to recognize when change is occurring and act in ways that foster change.

> **Listening:** "[R]eceiving what someone wishes to convey and saying it back to the person exactly as it was meant" (p. Larson, 1984, p. 288).

> **Focusing:** Paying attention to a problem as a whole within one's body, as these bodily shifts and responses to problems or solutions often go unrecognized.

Listening on the part of the helper, then, serves as the precursor for the helpee to focus.

Preliminary steps to focusing include placing one's attention in the middle of the body and sensing the concerns that the body is carrying and imagining what the body would feel like without those concerns.

The Six Movements of Focusing

1. The preliminary space-making.
2. The felt sense coming.
3. The quality "handle."
4. The resonating.
5. The asking.
6. Protecting the little step that came.

SOCIAL-PSYCHOLOGICAL APPROACHES TO HELPING

Many of the training models and approaches mentioned thus far focus on the individual person in the helping relationship. In the final section, we highlight the social context that is important to change in the helping process by providing an overview of several key approaches to understanding human relationships from the viewpoint of social psychology. Social-psychological examinations of the human experience are grounded largely in sociological movements that long have been interested in the interactions of people with their environments. In line with the purposes of the chapter, in this section we look at how an appreciation of people-in-relation can be useful to professional counselors.

■ Symbolic Interaction

Symbolic interaction is a sociological theory of human behavior proposed by philosopher George Mead and more fully developed by Blumer in reaction to behaviorist explanations of human interaction (Slawski, 1981). From this perspective, human behavior is explained as indirect reactions to stimuli; that is, interactions are initiated on the basis of the interpretations (symbols) that one assigns to a behavior. Symbolic interactionism theorizes that individuals form their self-identity based on their interpretations of others' reactions to them in a social context. Thus, the human self is primarily a social construction rather than a biological creation or a product of unconscious drives as suggested by psychoanalysis. The following are core concepts in symbolic interaction.

Key Assumptions of Symbolic Interactionism

- Social acts are the core process of interaction between individuals and are the processes from which meaning is derived over a period of time and interactions.
- Symbols and language are a central part of communication.
- Humans are distinguished in the social world because of their ability to assign meaning to events and objects and to communicate through symbols.
- Change and adjustment is constant, therefore, people continually are reacting to others and redefining who they are based on interpersonal interactions.

To illuminate the power of symbols, it might be helpful to consider the impact the *Diagnostic and Statistical Manual of Mental Disorders IV–TR (DSM–IV–TR;* American Psychiatric Association, 2000) has had on the counseling profession and on clients.

EXAMPLE

Connecting Symbolic Interactionism to Counseling

The *DSM–IV–TR* is used widely in the human services field as a way of characterizing and categorizing mental disorders. From a symbolic interactionist perspective, the labels that are applied to individuals who display peculiar behaviors or ways of thinking encourage and support those behaviors because the label is a symbol that the individual internalizes, and the label influences the self to the extent that the self becomes the label.

See Chapter 19 for further critique of the DSM–IV–TR from a social constructivist perspective.

■ Role Theory

J. L. Moreno, founder of the group therapy intervention, psychodrama, is one of the early pioneers of role theory. Role theory developed out of symbolic interactionism and is based on the assumption that behavior is influenced by socially imposed role obligations, assuming social roles are a distinguishing characteristic of human be-ings (Slawski, 1981). Moreover, social roles constantly are changing over the course of a lifetime; as individuals enter new life stages with different expectations and as they develop varying significant relationships, they adopt new roles to fit their life stage and personal interactions. From this perspective, behavior is rewarded or punished based on evaluation of role performance.

■ Social Exchange

The social exchange approach has its roots in the behaviorist movement and posits that people consciously or unconsciously account for the exchange of costs and benefits in relationships and favor relationships with the greatest benefits (Slawski, 1981). Embedded in exchange theory is the law of reciprocity, which can be under-stood this way:

> **Law of reciprocity:** Suggests that resource outputs must be balanced by inputs.

The principal concepts that characterize social exchange theory were summarized by Call, Finch, Huck, and Kane (1999) and Koper and Jaasma (2001) this way:

- The exchange of gains and losses perceived to be connected to an interaction in-fluences decisions about social involvement.
- Individuals create and maintain social involvements based on rewards they receive.
- Exchange of costs and benefits should be balanced over time.
- People in positions of power can demand greater benefits than people who are not in positions of power.
- People act in ways that increase the chance of receiving items they value and de-crease the chance of receiving items they devalue.

The power of social exchange theory is seen in the many day-to-day applications it has to human experiences. The example of caregiving for older parents is just one case of social exchange in action.

EXAMPLE

Looking at Caregiver Burden From Exchange Theory

One highly stressful experience for family members is caring for aging and ill parents. Call and colleagues (1999) used exchange theory to propose that the burden of caring for older relatives can be perceived as part of a natural give and take that occurs in long-term family relationships. From the viewpoint of exchange theory, caregiving for the elderly is part of an ongoing relation-ship with a history of exchanges, rather than a time-limited intervention. Furthermore, caregiv-ing is an art of a reciprocal exchange in which the individual being cared for adds benefits to the relationship throughout the caregiving process, rather than being the sole recipient of benefits.

■ Cognitive Consistency

Written about by a number of theorists including Heider (1958), Newcomb (1953), and Osgood and Tannenbaum (1955), cognitive consistency suggests that people strive to make their thoughts, attitudes, and behaviors consistent with each other. The theory proposes that inconsistency results in psychological distress, which becomes a primary motivator for attitudinal or behavioral change. Cognitive consistency is developed more fully by dissonance theory.

■ Dissonance Theory

The theory of cognitive dissonance states that related cognitions exist in a state of consonance or dissonance. Festinger (cited in Forsyth, 1987) suggested that individuals experience psychological discomfort when they are aware of dissonance and, therefore, are motivated to resolve the conflict among ideas or beliefs to reestablish a state of consistency (Slawski, 1981). Dissonance theory, as a model for explaining motivation as well as attitude change, continues to be adjusted and disputed in research.

Terms that are central to an understanding of dissonance theory are defined here:

Dissonance: Occurs when there is inconsistency between two thoughts.

Consonance: Exists when two cognitions are aligned or consistent with one another.

The likelihood that dissonance will increase is related to several characteristics of the thoughts that are at odds with one another. Some of these factors are identified here.

Factors Increasing Dissonance

- Relative importance of the subject.
- Extent to which the thoughts are in conflict.
- Individual's capacity to ally discordant thoughts.

When cognitive dissonance occurs, psychological discomfort is relieved by taking one of several actions.

Ways to Relieve Dissonance (Slawski, 1981)

1. Increasing the number of thoughts that are consistent with the primary cognition.

2. Reducing the number of thoughts that are dissonant with the primary cognition.
3. Increasing the importance of the consonant thoughts.
4. Decreasing the importance of the dissonant thoughts.
5. Changing the environment that promotes dissonance.

Interpretations of cognitive dissonance imply that our beliefs about something become stronger after we are disproved because it is a way of protecting our self-image as well as compensating for the lack of consistency between what we believe to be true and what has been shown to be true in real-life situations when these two differ.

EXAMPLE

Applying Cognitive Dissonance to Help Stop Smoking Addiction

Counselors can apply dissonance theory as a motivator for change with clients by helping them become aware of inconsistencies in their thoughts and behaviors. According to dissonance theory, the discomfort of this inconsistency is an instigator for change. One common example is the inconsistency in smoking and the public knowledge that smoking is a health risk. The unknown factor, however, with which counselors have to deal is the varying levels of dissonance that different clients can absorb.

■ Heider's Balance Theory

In the social sciences, Heider's (1958) balance theory offers one way of understanding how interpersonal relationships maintain stability. Relationships in which two individuals have either an explicit or perceived agreement about a third object are balanced. Interactions in which partners disagree about a third object or issue are less stable due to the cognitive dissonance that results from the imbalanced relationship. Several concepts characterize balance theory.

Assumptions of Balance Theory

- The perceived agreement about an object or issue can be as powerful as an actual agreement in maintaining a cognitively balanced relationship.
- Assimilation occurs when partners overestimate actual agreement to ensure a balanced interaction.
- Individuals are inclined to inflate the level to which they believe they are understood by others to achieve a higher level of cognitive balance.

■ Congruity Theory

Congruity theory is a further development of Festinger's dissonance theory and Heider's balance theory. The concern of Osgood and Tannenbaum's (1955) congruity theory is the attitudes that an individual has toward two objects that are juxtaposed. Based on the same principle of congruency, the congruity theory proposes that people experience inner pressure to reconcile conflicting attitudes toward related objects.

Assumptions of Congruity Theory

- The relative strength or weakness of an attitude can be quantified.
- Weaker attitudes will be subject to change before stronger attitudes about objects.

■ Newcomb's A-B-X Model of Interpersonal Attraction

Newcomb's A-B-X model attempts to explain the processes involved in interpersonal attraction. Of primary importance in this model is the role of values, beliefs, and interests (Forsyth, 1987). Newcomb postulated that people with similar interests and backgrounds are more likely to form close relationships than those with dissimilar characteristics, backgrounds, or values. Furthermore, the stronger the bonds between two people, the more effort they will exert to reconcile differing attitudes toward an identified object (Psychology 200, 2005).

In the A-B-X model, *A* represents a person of primary interest, his or her ideas and behavior open to change. In the same model, *B* represents a second person in the triangle. The *X* in Newcomb's model represents the attitude object, which may be a value, norm, idea, or issue at hand. The terms *symmetry* and *dissymmetry* are used to talk about the relationship among the three components of Newcomb's model; they can be understood this way (Slawski, 1981):

Symmetry: The state of balance among A, B, and X (two individuals and an object).

Dissymmetry: Exists when either A and B have contradictory attitudes toward X; when dissymmetry exists, A and B change intensity of their attitudes toward X or their attraction toward one another until symmetry is reestablished.

■ Attributions

Attribution theories are a social-psychological attempt to explain the causes of people's behavior (Forsyth, 1987). Attributions or explanations for why people act in the ways they do are broadly classified as either internal or external influences

(Bemmels, 1991). Internal attributes suggest that motivation for a particular behavior is located within a person, whereas external attributes assign causation for behavior to outside forces. According to Kelley (1967), attribution is assigned based on three factors.

Factors Associated With Assigning Attributes

1. Consensus is the degree to which a behavior is exhibited only by an individual or by a larger contingent of individuals. The more a behavior is displayed only by an individual, the greater the likelihood that the behavior will be considered internally motivated.
2. Distinctiveness is the extent to which a behavior is situation specific or related to a particular entity.
3. Consistency is the frequency with which the behavior in question has been present over a period of time. A behavior that an individual exhibits with great frequency is likely to be attributed to the individual rather than to the environment.

EXAMPLE

Attribution Theory and Career Counseling

In dealing with a client who is seeking career counseling, a therapist may have to help the client resolve affective responses to work-related issues. From the perspective of attribution theory, the client who is frustrated by not receiving a promotion may evaluate the situation by making the following conclusions or attribution assignments to the boss:

1. The boss buys into a company mentality in which employees are not promoted.
2. The boss does not promote any employee in his or her division—the client is not the only person whose contribution to the company is underappreciated.
3. The boss consistently fails to give promotions to employees.

Chapter 10: Key Terms

- Theory
- Counseling theory
- Eclecticism
- Helping
- Conformity prescription

- Reformity prescription
- Transactional model
- Listening
- Focusing
- Law of reciprocity

- Dissonance
- Consonance
- Symmetry
- Dissymmetry

The Cultural Kaleidoscope: Eyeing Diverse Populations

Maura Krushinski
Duquesne University

In This Chapter

▶ *Opening up to Multicultural Realities in Counseling*
  - Implications of a Multicultural Worldview to Counselors' Training
  - Implications of a Multicultural Emphasis for Counselor Educators
  - Implications of Multicultural Counseling for Program Development
  - Cross-Cultural Differences in Counselor–Client Relationships
  - What Is Cultural Context?
  - A Model for Understanding Differences
  - Avoiding "Preferred" Clients Only
  - The Notion of White Privilege

▶ *Challenges for Children of Specific Populations*
  - Examining the Influence of Ethnicity on Children
  - Additional Concerns When Working With Children of Different Ethnic Groups

▶ *Native American Populations*
  - Historical and Demographic Factors
  - Family Characteristics
  - Value Orientations

  - Stereotypes
  - Communication Styles
  - Mental Health Issues

▶ *African American Population*
  - Historical and Demographic Factors
  - Value Orientations
  - Family Characteristics
  - Communication Styles
  - Mental Health Issues
  - Considerations When Counseling

▶ *Asian American Population*
  - Historical and Demographic Factors
  - Family Values
  - Common Stereotypes
  - Mental Health Issues
  - Communication Styles
  - Effective Counseling Approaches

▶ *Latin American Population*
  - Historical and Demographic Factors
  - Family Characteristics
  - Communication Styles
  - Value Orientations
  - Mental Health Issues

I would like to acknowledge Dr. Tom Petrone for his highly insightful suggestions as well as for his time and efforts in reviewing this chapter.

In This Chapter (*continued*)

▶ *Arab American Population*
  ▪ Historical and Demographic Factors
  ▪ Family Characteristics
  ▪ Value Orientations
  ▪ Stereotypes
  ▪ Counseling

▶ *Elderly Population*
  ▪ Demographic Factors
  ▪ Stereotypes
  ▪ Mental Health Issues
  ▪ Approaches to Counseling

▶ *Ableism and Disability*
  ▪ Demographics
  ▪ Stereotypes
  ▪ Rehabilitation Counseling
  ▪ Counseling Issues

▶ *Gay, Lesbian, Bisexual, and Transgendered Population*
  ▪ The Process of "Coming Out"
  ▪ Counseling Issues

▶ *Conclusion*

OPENING UP TO MULTICULTURAL REALITIES IN COUNSELING

At its beginning, the counseling field was dominated primarily by White theorists of European descent. Although these theorists provided the field with the strong theoretical foundations still taught in counselor education programs today, they, nonetheless, had a rather narrow view of cultural diversity that is reflected in their theories. The impact of such a narrow worldview on the counseling profession is that, at one time, it was appropriate to avoid acknowledgment of cultural differences, establish therapeutic neutrality, and counsel everyone as if they were of the same background. Gradually, minority groups began to proclaim their differences, which compelled the counseling profession to begin embracing the challenges of having an increased awareness of multicultural realities and making a determined effort to acknowledge and honor the cultural makeup of the client's experience.

As the profession continues to evolve, increasing attention is being paid to the need to adjust counseling approaches and methods to facilitate therapeutic work with clients from specific cultural and ethnic groups. The counseling ethics state purposefully that our primary concern is "the welfare of the client"; this means not some clients, but all clients. Therefore, in an attempt to help counselors increase their cultural competence, this chapter concentrates on the following specific populations that counselors likely are to encounter during their professional careers: Native Americans; African Americans; Asian Americans; Latin Americans; Arab Americans; elderly individuals; disabled persons; and gay, lesbian, bisexual, and transgendered persons.

■ Implications of a Multicultural Worldview to Counselors' Training

The fact that some counselors choose to ignore their obligation to multicultural competence and lack exposure to differing cultures has become a concern. Often, counselor trainees' greatest exposure to populations different than their own is not through direct contact but, rather, through the media. In a field where multicultural competence is essential, trainees must adhere to ethical and professional responsibilities.

How Counselor Trainees Can Build Multicultural Competence

- Develop the skills necessary to work with specific populations and incorporate them into all aspects of their counseling program.
- Recognize and honor clients' diverse cultural values and heritage.
- Assume an attitude of openness to the multicultural aspect of counselor training by acknowledging any lack of awareness or limited exposure to populations different than their own.

■ Implications of a Multicultural Emphasis for Counselor Educators

Expectations for providing a multiculturally sensitive learning experience for students also are placed on counselor educators.

How Counselor Educators Respond to Emphases on Multicultural Values

- Heighten their own awareness and examine their own experiences and attitudes with regard to multiculturalism.
- Present a wide array of available materials on counseling specific populations.
- Teach all aspects of culture, such as classism, racism, stereotypes, biases, issues with gender, age, religion, sexual preference, and ethnicity.
- Ensure that racial development models, the experience of race, and the experiences of the culturally different in the United States are seriously examined in the classroom.

■ Implications of Multicultural Counseling for Program Development

Until recently, multicultural issues and strategies were considered a specialized field in counselor education (Pedersen, Draguns, Lonner, & Trimble, 2002), and courses on multiculturalism often were offered as 1 credit hour electives. Recently, professional organizations such as the ACA, CACREP, The National Council for the Accreditation of Teacher Education (NCATE), the NBCC, and state licensing boards have defined the development of multicultural competence as an integral part of the counseling curriculum. Course requirements and standards for counseling diverse clients have been infused into counseling programs and appear on national counselor certification examinations, as well.

 Check out CACREP's (2001) standards for accredited counselor education programs on social and cultural diversity:

▶ http://www.cacrep.org/2001Standards.html

■ Cross-Cultural Differences in Counselor–Client Relationships

Cross-cultural and cross-class counseling implies that there are differences between the counselor and the client. Awareness of these differences may help the counselor avoid the many pitfalls that negatively influence good contact and effective helping in the counseling relationship. The Association for Advanced Training (AAT, 1991) recommends the following considerations for counselors to increase their multicultural awareness.

Recommendations for Increasing Cultural Awareness

- The counselor must acknowledge awareness of differences to the client in a supportive way.
- The counselor must be aware of factors that contribute to the client's orientation and values such as language, degree of assimilation, and socioeconomic status.

- The counselor must respect differences and avoid reference to negative stereotypes.
- The counselor must be aware of supportive referral sources for the client.
- The counselor must recognize that social, economic, and political discrimination and prejudice are real issues for minority groups in the United States.
- The counselor must avoid generalizations about all clients who belong to a particular group.

What Is Cultural Context?

All attitudes, behaviors, and feelings are learned within a cultural context. Cultural context was defined as follows by Pedersen et al. (2002):

> **Cultural context:** the totality of the context in which people live, "including ethnographic, demographic, status and affiliation variables" (p. 3).

Effective counseling interventions depend on an understanding of how variables that make up a cultural context blend with the counseling process. Indeed, "the search for professional excellence in counseling is closely linked with the search for multicultural competence" (Pedersen et al., 2002, p. 3). Cultural bias, intentional or unintentional, on the part of the counselor potentially can lead to inappropriate counseling goals and process for the culturally different client.

For more information on multiculturalism as well as cultural context, see Chapter 4.

A Model for Understanding Differences

Sue and Sue (1990) described the Kluckhohn and Strodtbeck (1961) model as "one of the most useful frameworks for understanding differences among individuals and groups" (p. 138). Their model presumes that there is a set of core human questions that are present for all cultures.

Core Human Orientations for Clients of All Cultures

- Perception of time: Some cultures emphasize the past, some the present, and some are future oriented. History and tradition, the here and now, and planning for the future are all value orientations related to time (Sue & Sue, 1990).
- Attitudes toward activity: Some cultures value doing over being, believing self-worth is determined by accomplishment.
- Definitions of social relationships: Relationships with others are a dimension of importance in all cultures (Sue & Sue, 1990). In some cultures, relationships are

authoritarian and hierarchical, whereas in other cultures equal or balanced relationships are important.

- The nature of people: Human nature is seen either as good or evil, and people generally are socialized into trusting or suspicious modes.

The model also discusses the ways in which cultures make assumptions about how their members relate to nature. Some cultures see themselves as "harmonious with Mother Earth" (Sue & Sue, 1990, p. 140), whereas some attempt to control nature.

■ Avoiding "Preferred" Clients Only

Skillful counselors understand that each worldview must be valued and that their role is to help the client integrate aspects of each worldview in a way that will maximize their psychological and physical well-being. They also recognize the potential biases that exist in their preferences for certain client populations. Hence, counselors working with clients different than themselves may embrace Schofield's concept that counselors prefer to work with the **"YAVIS" client,** that is, "one who is young, attractive, verbal, intelligent and successful" (cited in Sue & Sue, 1990, p. 33). Sue and Sue (1990) also discussed Sundberg's view that "therapy is not for the **'QUOID' client,** that is, one who is seen as quiet, ugly, old, indigent and dissimilar" (p. 33).

■ The Notion of White Privilege

While working with culturally different clients, the counselor also must take into account the presence of privilege, especially privilege of the dominant culture. McIntosh (1988) described one type of privilege, White privilege, this way:

> **White privilege:** "[A]n invisible knapsack of special provisions, unearned assets that put certain cultures at an advantage over others" (p. 1).

McIntosh pointed out a colleague's statement that "Whites are taught to think of their lives as morally neutral, normative and average, and also ideal, so that when we work to benefit others, this is seen as work which will allow 'them' to be more like 'us'" (p. 1). Counselors who have lived with the reality of invisible privileges are encouraged to be aware of their privilege, especially when working with clients who are or have been underprivileged.

For more on the concept of privilege, see Chapter 4.

CHALLENGES FOR CHILDREN OF SPECIFIC POPULATIONS

The issue of children of diverse populations is a topic that deserves special mention. Because their ethnic or social class backgrounds are different from those of the majority, children sometimes face challenges related to being rejected, receiving unfair treatment, being ridiculed, and being subjected to lower expectations. Juntunen, Atkinson, and Tierney (2003) described a 1998 study that identified stress from racial and ethnic discrimination and stress from the acculturation process as two major types of stress faced by children from differing ethnic groups. Additional stressors include those mentioned next.

> Because their ethnic or social class backgrounds are different from those of the majority, children sometimes face challenges related to being rejected, receiving unfair treatment, being ridiculed, and being subjected to lower expectations.

Stressors for Children From Differing Ethnic Groups

- They may experience difficulties in combining the roles and values of their specific culture with those of the dominant culture.
- They may incorporate roles and values from another culture more quickly than other family members, thereby creating clashes at home.
- They may have to contend with more limited opportunities to succeed.
- The adolescent's struggle for identity will include the variable of cultural difference as they struggle with defining self and meaning of life.
- They may be subjected to verbal rejection, discrimination, and even physical attacks.
- They may suffer social isolation and derisive labels.

■ Examining the Influence of Ethnicity on Children

There are three perspectives to consider when examining the influence of ethnicity on children:

1. A developmental perspective helps the counselor to consider the role an ethnic group has on a child's life.
2. An ecological perspective provides the counselor with the means to investigate the interaction of systems such as family, school, government, social and economic policies, and the impact on available risks and opportunities for the child.
3. A cross-cultural perspective compares the child's culture of origin to the dominant culture.

■ Additional Concerns When Working With Children of Different Ethnic Groups

Counselors must consider potential concerns of cultural variation when working with children of different ethnic groups. Those variations include the following:

- Country of origin.
- Immigration status.
- Languages spoken.
- Knowledge of English.
- Sleeping and eating patterns.
- Cultural expectations.
- Level of acculturation.
- Important holidays or celebrations.
- Family attitudes about play.
- Playmates.
- Toys.
- Discipline.

NATIVE AMERICAN POPULATION

The remainder of this chapter is dedicated to examining relevant aspects of specific cultural groups, beginning with Native Americans. Native Americans represent one of the most ethnically diverse cultural groups in the United States (Harper & McFadden, 2003). This population consists of numerous tribal groups that reside in cities or on reservations. Although many tribes encompass similar values and beliefs, the cultural practices, traditions, and social organization of Native American tribes vary and are influenced by such factors as geographic location and historical trauma experienced (Harper & McFadden, 2003).

■ Historical and Demographic Factors

The Native American population is 2,475,956, and represents 0.9% of the total U.S. population (U.S. Census, 2000). This group of individuals is organized into 561 American Indian and Alaskan native tribes that speak more than 252 different languages. Their history is characterized by military defeat, ethnic demoralization, and forced displacement, which resulted in the loss of millions of lives, land confiscation, and tribal dispersion. Historically, Native American children were removed from their families and placed in boarding schools so that they might be assimilated into the European culture. Furthermore, the Native American family often is faced with overwhelming poverty, unemployment, and family dissolution that is due, in part, to federal government policies and educational failures.

■ Family Characteristics

Although family values vary among the Native American population and are determined by the particular tribe, band, or clan to which the members belong, the family, including extended family, is still the center of Native American culture. Hence, "cousins are referred to as brother and sister and the primary relationship is not the parents but rather that of the grandparents" (McGoldrick, Giordano, & Pearce, 1996, p. 36). There are no distinctions made between natural family members and those who enter the family system through marriage. However, because each tribe has its own worldview, it is inappropriate for the counselor to view the Native American population as a homogeneous group.

■ Value Orientations

The Native American population is historically characterized as a "thriving, self-governing people living in harmony with nature" (Harper & McFadden, 2003, p. 66). Additionally, a number of other things can be said to be generally reflective of Native American value systems.

Commonly Held Values in Native American Populations

- They demonstrate deep reverence for the land and for their relationship with wildlife.
- They manage the environment with respect and great adaptability.
- They are a holistic and spiritual people, giving thanks for their blessings (Harper & McFadden, 2003).
- Religion, medicine men and women, spiritual forces, and traditional religious practices are essential in their lives.

■ Stereotypes

Historical stereotypes portray Native Americans as villains (Harper & McFadden, 2003) and violent savages whose aim was to slaughter White settlers. The culture was seen as inferior in comparison to the European lifestyle and culture. Current stereotypes portray this population as having a higher than normal incidence of alcoholism.

According to Harper and McFadden (2003), there are three things that make Native Americans dissimilar from other ethnic minority groups.

Dissimilarities Between Native Americans and Other Minority Groups

1. Each tribe holds power and authority over the people that reside on its lands.
2. Federally recognized tribes have a government-to-government relationship with the federal government.
3. Tribes that surrendered lands were relocated to reservations and were provided with housing, health care, food subsidies, and educational opportunities.

■ Communication Styles

Counselors working with the Native American population must be aware of some of the unique elements related to Native American communication styles.

Key Awarenesses About Native American Communication Styles

- Different tribal dialects exist.
- Time orientation to the present is common.
- Nonverbals and intuition are emphasized.
- The desire to satisfy present needs by understanding the world through mystical stories and folklore is important.
- Listening is highly valued.
- Long periods of silence indicate respect, the search for finding the right words to say, or waiting for the right time to speak, and must not be misconstrued as resistance.

■ Mental Health Issues

The most prevalent mental health issues of the Native American population are suicide and alcohol abuse. Essential treatment approaches are holistic and integrate indigenous and Western healing techniques. The therapeutic relationship must view healing as a spiritual journey and be open to including the tribal healer in the therapeutic process. Language, class, and cultural values are generic aspects of counseling that can interact with the characteristics and values of Native Americans and disrupt the therapeutic relationship.

Recommendations for Counselors Working With Native Americans (Richardson, cited in AAT, 1991)

- Use nondirective counseling approaches, specifically silence, acceptance, restatement, and verbal summarization.
- Be contained and focused on what the client is saying.
- Show openness to the client's thoughts and feelings.

- Repeat the client's statements for the purposes of clarification.
- Ask questions intended to clarify issues for the client.
- Summarize verbally what has been worked on in various sessions over an extended period of time.
- Acknowledge one's lack of experience or cultural understanding when appropriate.
- Approach sensitive topics such as alcoholism, history, suicidal tendencies, treaties, boarding schools, and reservations with caution.
- Honor the role of the medicine person in the counseling process.
- Appeal to the traditional healer as a cocounselor in the process, and treat elders and healers with respect.
- Make use of cognitive-behavioral interventions rather than psychodynamic or client-centered therapy because it can be adapted to the culture and the community.
- Include respected community and traditional leaders in the helping process.

In summary, counselors who provide counseling services to the Native American population must show respect for their history, current socioeconomic status, and the many varied aspects of the culture.

AFRICAN AMERICAN POPULATION

The African American population is among the largest minority groups in the United States. Coupled with the longevity of their presence in the United States as well as their history of oppression, it is imperative that counselors are well-educated on working with this group.

■ Historical and Demographic Factors

Although it is virtually impossible to fully describe the historical perspective of any culture, it is important to recognize that the history of African Americans is characterized by slavery. As a result, this population has struggled to develop a strong cultural identity, experienced adverse effects of racism and inappropriate value judgments, and has been unable to overcome the perception of being a problem in society.

The African American population numbers approximately 33.9 million people and 9 million families, representing 12% of the total U.S. population (U.S. Census, 2000). Nearly 80% of African Americans earn a high school diploma and 17% earn an undergraduate or graduate degree (Harper & McFadden, 2003). Despite educational achievement, the African American population continues to suffer from poverty-related challenges.

■ Value Orientations

African Americans share a strong sense of collective identity, kinship, or collective unity (AAT, 1991). Although all immigrant groups have had acculturation problems, African Americans continue to fight social, economic, and political hardships because of racial discrimination. They place less emphasis on childhood experiences as contributors to mental health, even though therapeutic philosophies often stress the role of childhood experiences in the development of personality and behavior. Concurrently, they value the role of family and church more than counseling when dealing with problems.

■ Family Characteristics

African Americans have a strong sense of family. Interactions with extended family members tend to get more intensive as African Americans turn toward each other in times of crisis. Discussion of family problems outside of the family generally is considered to be a breach of family ethics, which is an area of consideration for counselors trying to get African American clients to open up. Although it was believed at one time that African American families tended to be matriarchal, with the father taking a lesser, or absentee role, this notion has been disproved, as African American fathers are no less involved with the family than fathers of other cultures.

■ Communication Styles

Although therapists often view African American clients as being nonverbal and concrete (AAT, 1991), it is important to realize that the nonverbal African American client may actually be speaking a different language or using a lack of verbal clarity as a defense. Other common attributes of African American communication styles are mentioned next.

Emphases in African American Communication Styles

- Nonverbal communication.
- Lack of eye contact.
- High levels of emotional expressiveness.
- Brief, to-the-point communication.

See Chapter 14 for more information about African American communication styles.

■ Mental Health Issues

Providing counseling services to African Americans has raised concerns about therapist–client match, counselor preference, influence of racial identity development, and the most effective approaches to employ when working with the African

American population (Harper & McFadden, 2003). Working effectively with African Americans requires an awareness and recognition of the reality of the African American experience, which includes oppression and lack of privilege in the United States. Discussing the invisibility syndrome, Franklin (cited in Harper & McFadden, 2003) pointed out that the life of an African American is characterized by "chronic confrontations with racist, dehumanizing experiences" referred to as "microagressions" (p. 83). Consequently, the willingness to seek counseling services must be understood as a desire to heal "psychic abrasions" (p. 83).

■ Considerations When Counseling

The language, class values, and cultural values that may emerge in the counseling relationship with African American clients include the use of nonstandard English, emphasis on short-range goal planning, and utilization of nonverbal behaviors and reactions to oppression (Sue & Sue, 1990). They are more likely to be active and self-destructive when depressed; somatic complaints are more likely to be due to real physiological problems; and threats of homicide are more likely to be expressions of anger, not intent to kill (Block, 1981).

According to C. B. Block (1981), counselors typically make three mistakes when counseling the African American population.

Some Counselor Mistakes When Working With African Americans

1. Many non-Black counselors try to maintain the notion of color blindness, which avoids the importance of race to the African American client.
2. Counselors also may limit their effectiveness by assuming that issues of the African American client necessarily are related to historical and current oppression, and that oppression has produced permanent damage to the basic functioning of the African American population.
3. Counselors who display a patronizing attitude toward the client may miscommunicate the power differential, which may lead the African American client to mistrust the counselor.

Given potential mistakes counselors can make when working with African American clients, there are a number of suggestions professional helpers can follow to make the counseling experience positive and useful to this population.

Counseling Strategies for Counselors Working With African Americans

■ Use a socioecological approach that emphasizes an understanding of how economic status, education, health care, housing, racism, and other ecological factors affect the African American population.

- Avoid a medical model approach because it may focus on weaknesses and deficits and, as a result, cause counseling to be perceived as a punishment rather than a helpful process.
- Provide specific guidance to the client and assume a directive and active stance in the process within a time-limited, problem-solving approach.

Research (Griffith & Jones, cited in AAT, 1991) has indicated that client race is a factor in counseling and psychotherapy. Studies have found that African American clients often disguise their real problem to see if the counselor is able to see beyond the disguise. African American clients also may deny their need for help or the seriousness of the problem. This prevents the African American client from appearing dependent or helpless in the counseling relationship. To treat an African American client effectively, the counselor must pay careful attention to nonverbal behaviors and implied meanings to understand the client's problems (AAT, 1991).

ASIAN AMERICAN POPULATION

Asian Americans and Pacific Islanders include 43 ethnic groups with more than 100 languages and dialects. This population may have roots in countries including China, Japan, Korea, Vietnam, Cambodia, and the Philippines. Even though they are from differing countries, this population primarily is influenced by Old World and religious traditions passed down through generations.

■ Historical and Demographic Factors

According to the U.S. Census (2000), there are 10.2 million Asian Americans who represent 3.6% of the U.S. population, and 399,000 Pacific Islanders that account for 0.1% of the population. All Asian American groups have a complex immigration experience to the United States (McGoldrick et al., 1996) and are seen as a specific minority group with unique characteristics, values, needs, and challenges. Several of these groups have immigrated to the United State from war-ravaged countries seeking political asylum, and many may have to deal with lingering issues over World War II internment and other historical wartime concerns. Prior to coming to the United States, a good number of Asian American immigrants were exposed to losses, separation, torture, and other forms of trauma (McGoldrick et al., 1996). "Perceived discrimination, fear, stress from culture shock, perceived hate, homesickness and guilt" are major factors that contribute to the "acculturative distress" for new immigrants (Harper & McFadden, 2003, p. 101).

■ Family Values

The traditional Asian American family is patriarchal, where the father's authority is unchallenged and power is usually transferred from father to son. Females traditionally have been less valued than males, and their role is primarily domestic. It is common for Asian Americans to live with several generations in a single household. Additionally, Asian American families value the family unit over the individual, who usually is seen as the product of generations of the family. Thus, individual members' actions reflect not only on themselves, but also on their extended family and ancestors (McGoldrick et al., 1996).

■ Common Stereotypes

Stereotypes include the belief that all adults are hard working and successful and that all children are high academic achievers. However, the reality is that for many in this population, poverty is a concern, and failure is shaming; seeing a counselor may be embarrassing. The result is that the number of clients from the Asian American population in treatment is low, and research on effective therapeutic interventions is limited. Research suggests that for Asian Americans, certain coping mechanisms that were effective in their home country may appear dysfunctional in the new country.

■ Mental Health Issues

McGoldrick et al. (1996) reported six predictors of mental health problems for Asian Americans. These factors are outlined here.

Predictors of Mental Health Problems

1. Employment or financial status.
2. Gender (Asian women appear to be more vulnerable than men).
3. Old age.
4. Social isolation.
5. Recent immigration.
6. Refugee trauma and adjustment.

Although the need for counseling services is not less than for other populations, the process of going to counseling is not easy for Asian Americans. Because of some of the following factors, Asian Americans tend to use counseling resources as a last option.

Contributing Factors for Underutilization of Counseling by Asian Americans

- Lack of familiarity with Western mental health concepts.
- Problem-solving approaches that are internally oriented because using resources outside of the family can be seen as shameful.
- Social stigmatism with regard to the status of the family.

■ Communication Styles

Asian Americans traditionally have been taught to utilize nondirective styles of communication and to avoid direct confrontations. The counselor must avoid appearing too direct or insensitive to this communication style. An expression of little emotion must not be mistaken for denial or a lack of affect.

■ Effective Counseling Approaches

Asian American clients typically underutilize mental health resources because of cultural values related to privacy and nondisclosure of problems outside the family system. According to Sue and Sue (1990), the cultural conflicts Asian Americans experience in life may be mimicked in the counseling session. Specifically, Asian American clients may suppress emotional expressions, tend to focus more on educational and vocational complaints than emotional ones, and manifest a dislike of unstructured counseling processes. For counseling effectiveness with Asian American populations, the following recommendations are proposed.

Recommendations for Counseling Asian Americans

- Include the family in the counseling process, when appropriate, and allow the client to determine which family members may be included.
- Incorporate Asian values and characteristics in the counseling process and guard against using traditional Western counseling approaches such as self-disclosure and long-term counseling, as these approaches are likely to counter the Asian American values of self-repression and short, result-oriented solutions (McGoldrick et al., 1996).
- Be aware of how to facilitate self-disclosure of clients who highly value privacy.
- Explain the counseling process in such a way that the Asian American client feels confident.
- Use a counseling approach that provides a structured counseling situation (AAT, 1991).

Many members of this population are survivors of war, political unrest, and transitions. As with clients from all cultures, the Asian American must be understood and respected from this context.

LATIN AMERICAN POPULATION

The Latino American population is one of the fastest growing ethnic groups in the United States. McGoldrick et al. (1996) reported that the words *Hispanic* or *Latino* have been used to describe this group of people who come from many different countries, cultures, and religions, and who would never describe themselves using those terms. The use of *Hispanic* by the U.S. Census may be interpreted as an attempt to take away the Latinos' nationality. Latino or Latina is more accepted because this label allows for gender.

■ Historical and Demographic Factors

The history of Latinos in the United States is characterized by experiences of conquest, oppression, defeat, and struggle for freedom. For Latinos, the United States represented an opportunity to be free. Yet, they have become victims of discrimination and disrespect in the midst of their many contributions to the United States (Harper & McFadden, 2003).

According to the U.S. Census (2000), 13% of the U.S. population, or approximately 13.3 million people, are Latino. These numbers, however, do not reflect accurately the number of undocumented migrants that come into the United States daily. Moreover, the growing Latino population has not resulted in higher economic or political power; rather, Latinos, especially those who have come to the United States illegally, experience increased oppression. Indeed, the U.S. Census (2000) reported that this group is the most underinsured of all cultural groups in the United States. As a result, their access to medical and mental health services has been limited.

■ Family Characteristics

Latino American families, mostly patriarchal, are characterized by respect for and obedience to the father, who dominates and rules the household. The mother is accorded loyalty and love as she acts as the unifying force in the system. In this tradition, gender roles tend to be rigid. Latina females are seen as passive, dependent, and needing to be protected, whereas Latino males are permitted greater freedom and have higher expectations placed on them. Latino men also are expected to display dignity, love for their family, and respect for others (AAT, 1991).

■ Communication Styles

Most Latinos value cooperation rather than competition. Many Latino Americans tend to speak quietly, avoid eye contact when encountering those they see as having a higher status, and rarely interrupt others. Their manner of expression is often considered low key and indirect (Sue & Sue, 1990).

■ Value Orientations

Robinson (2005) outlined the primary Latin American cultural orientation and values system as noted next.

Primary Latin American Values

- *Personalismo* (intimacy).
- *Dignidad* (personal honor).
- *Familism* (faith in friends and family).
- *Respeto* (respect).
- *Confianza* (the development of trust).
- *Simpatia* (gentleness and simplicity).
- *Carino* (demonstration of endearment in verbal and nonverbal communication).
- *Orgullo* (pride).
- Loyalty of family.
- Collectivism.
- Service to others.
- Education as a means of development.

■ Mental Health Issues

Researchers have concluded that Latino Americans significantly underutilize counseling services. This tendency can be attributed to several factors.

Contributing Factors for Underutilization of Counseling by Latino Americans

- Lack of bilingual counseling programs.
- Traditional counseling models do not address the needs of Latino American clients.
- Latino Americans often perceive mental health problems as manifestations of physical problems.
- The Latino culture discourages self-referral to counseling services.

For counseling effectiveness with Latino American populations, the following recommendations are proposed.

Recommendations for Counselors Working With Latino Americans

- Establish rapport by utilizing small talk, first names, and personal greetings.
- Take an active, goal-oriented approach that will lead to a rapid solution to the presenting problem.
- Recognize the importance of differentiating the variety of ethnic identities and emphasizing values related to spirituality, family unity, welfare, and honor (McGoldrick et al., 1996).
- Understand and incorporate the strong sense of family commitment, obligation, and responsibility into counseling interventions for effective treatment.
- Solicit and listen to stories about the impact of living in the United States.
- Validate the strengths and positives elements of the culture to help reduce feelings of shame, promote dignity, and build a stronger sense of community.

As with any group, the Latin American population wants to improve their lives in this country. Many experience intense feelings of loss for family left behind. Feeling isolated and pressured to change may cause disruption and conflict.

ARAB AMERICAN POPULATION

As with other minority populations, the culturally competent counselor must commit to respect the customs, traditions, history, and values of the Arab American population. Some cultural, social, and historical factors related to the Arab American population are mentioned in this section.

■ Historical and Demographic Factors

In the 2000 U.S. census, Arab Americans are reported to number fewer than 1.5 million. The Arab American Institute (AAI) believes that more than 3.5 million people in the United States have Arab ancestry. The AAI (2006a) reported that Arab Americans are underreported on the U.S. Census due to lack of understanding of the importance of the census or concerns about confidentiality.

Arab Americans living in the United States include descendants from Arabic-speaking countries of southwestern Asia and North Africa and have been settling in the United States since the 1880s. According to the AAI (2006b) more than 80% are U.S. citizens. The Arab heritage reflects a culture that is thousands of years old and includes 22 Arab countries such as Egypt, Lebanon, Morocco, Yemen, Tunisia, and Palestine. The majority of Arab Americans are Christian.

■ Family Characteristics

The Arab world is complex in its social, religious, and political culture and traditions. One of the most important aspects in this culture is the role of family.

Cultural Influences on the Arab American Family

- Family is seen as more important than the individual and more influential than the nationality. Traditionally, large Arab families are an issue of pride and the larger the family, the more economic security is provided (AAI, 2006a).
- Birth order is important; the firstborn is closest to the parents, and individuation that separates family members is not encouraged.
- Arab Americans see family honor and status as an important goal.
- Patrilinearity, a system of descent where rights are inherited through the father, supports the man as the head of the household. Women are influential in the family and, contrary to stereotype, are not severely dominated by their husbands and fathers.
- Extended family is valued, and two or three generations of Arab Americans may reside in the same household.
- Immigration of other family members is encouraged and often paid for by the families in the United States.

■ Value Orientations

The Arab American population values collectivism, the good of many over the good of one. They respect authority and their elders, expect their children to be obedient, and value modesty and obedience as important traits in females. Arab Americans value harmony within their homes and communities and strive to work hard.

■ Stereotypes

Arab Americans are the victims of negative stereotypes. This population often is seen as oil-rich, fanatical, keeping their women in harems, or oppressive to women. The predominant view of Arab Americans in the United States is influenced by post-9/11 concerns of terrorism.

■ Counseling

Jaschik (2005) reported that when counseling the Arab American population, the counselor should be visible outside of the counseling office to encourage a higher comfort level for those seeking help. Carmichael (2004) recommended that the counselor not focus on insight-oriented strategies that may create more anxiety in members of this population. Because this culture is a collective or tribal-based culture, emphasis on the individual may create conflicts in the family or community system.

Carmichael (2004) cited Nassar-McMillan and Hakim-Larson in determining the factors that contribute to successful counseling, especially when working with Arab American children.

Recommendations for Counseling Arab American Children

- Build a relationship with the family system, which may include home visits or attendance at social gatherings.
- Use religious leaders as consultants.
- Request a reasonable fee for services so that the Arab American views the service as worthwhile.
- Thoroughly explain the therapeutic process, especially aspects of confidentiality.
- Carefully provide professional advice so it is not seen as a challenge to patriarchal authority.
- Do not confront or criticize in front of family or community members, especially when silence is present. Silence may not mean agreement.
- Rather than offend the family or individual, ask what items or assessment tools are permitted. Some systems that adhere to Islamic faith may not allow use of items or drawings that reflect human figures.

The American-Arab Anti-Discrimination Committee (1993) educational guide references Jackson, who recommended that group counseling be utilized with this population because it supports the Arab value of collectivism and that the group be comprised of the same gender. A cognitive approach is suggested because it allows the client to refrain from discussing personal feeling with a counselor who may be perceived as a stranger. The counselor must continuously demonstrate respect for the sanctity of the nuclear and extended family. Inviting the family to be part of the process can be very useful. Treating Arab Americans in a way that minimizes shaming or loss of face is important, as is helping the client or the family cope with issues related to acculturation, language differences, and acclimation.

Lastly, it is important for the counselor to demonstrate a respect for and acknowledgment of the differing Arabic populations and especially to be prepared to discuss the ways in which anti-Arab biases have affected the client. Arab Americans may express stress over the conflicts in their home countries and worry about extended family members living there. Adolescents trying to fit into the U.S. culture may deny their heritage as a way of avoiding discrimination. Conflict between traditional values and contemporary realities may create anxiety in the family system as women and children struggle with cultural restraints and men feel pressure to keep the family system intact.

ELDERLY POPULATION

Increased numbers of older people and a continued lengthening of the life span indicate the need to be aware of the special skills needed to provide counseling services to the older adult population. Although elderly people are healthier and better educated than ever before, there is a concern about their quality of life in their later years.

■ Demographic Factors

The U.S. Census (2000) reported the following statistics about the aging population in the United States, which provides evidence of the large and growing population of elders in the United States.

Demographic Characteristics of Older American Adults

- 34,991,753 are age 65 and above.
- 18,390,986 are age 65 to 74.
- 12,361,180 are age 75 to 84.
- 3,902,349 are age 85 to 94.
- 337,238 are 95 and older.

■ Stereotypes

Older adults in the United States have long been subjected to negative stereotypes, myths, and even prejudice. Schmidt (2006) described ageism this way:

Ageism: "[S]ystematic and stereotypic prejudice against people simply because they are old" (p. 143).

In general, a number of negative stereotypes and myths about American elders are pervasive in this culture.

Stereotypical Descriptors of Older Adults

- Slow movers and thinkers.
- Mentally and physically impaired.
- Sexually inactive.
- Committed to the past.
- Cranky.
- Depressed.
- Burden on society.

- Conservative.
- Judgmental.

A counselor must not hold the same mistaken stereotypes of the elderly. To be effective, the counselor must recognize the facts about older adults' experiences and needs and not rely on stereotypes.

■ Mental Health Issues

The AAT (1991) stated that, "perhaps the most critical error made by mental health professionals when counseling elderly clients is presuming that the elderly are simply preparing to die" (p. 11). Although death may emerge as an issue in counseling, more often elderly clients are seeking direction and meaning for this phase of their lives. Several factors lead to an increased need for counseling services among older Americans.

Factors Leading to the Need for Counseling Services Among Elders

- Spousal death.
- Retirement.
- Children leaving the home.
- Isolation.
- Institutionalization.
- Financial concerns.

■ Approaches to Counseling

Typical counseling issues with the elderly include identity transition, sexuality issues, depression, and awareness and acceptance of death. Identity transition is triggered by the realization that they are less physically active, their relationships have changed, and their previous self-identity has been lost. The first objective of the counselor is to offer empathy and provide coping skills to help the client adjust to life changes. This may lead to acceptance of change and the creation of a new identity, which may include goal planning for retirement and other social activities. Other areas of focus in counseling may include attention to sexual needs, treatment for depression, intervention related to suicidal ideations, and acceptance of death (AAT, 1991).

Working with the elderly may include individual, family, and group counseling, as well as social planning, advocacy, and community organization. General recommendations for working successfully with the elderly client are provided next.

Strategies for Working With Elders

- Help elders look for satisfaction in relationships and mentally creative activities.
- Offer support through role changes and identity transitions.
- Have a general respect for the elderly, a history of positive experiences with the population, and a deep sense of caring for elderly individuals.
- Understand the biological effects of aging and have a desire to learn from the elderly population.
- Understand and have patience for the repetition of stories.
- Be sensitive to older adults' burdens and anxieties and the special biological, psychological, and social needs of the aged.

Helping the elderly recognize that aging is a natural process can foster healthier perspectives and lifestyles. The counselor can serve as a strong, positive force in helping the aged client achieve this goal.

ABLEISM AND DISABILITY

Throughout time and across cultures, people with impaired physical, mental, and emotional abilities have faced discrimination. Impaired people "have been shunned at best and discarded at worst" (Schmidt, 2006, p. 134) by all societies. *Ableism* is a term used to describe the discrimination faced by individuals who are impaired in any way. Schmidt (2006) defined ableism this way:

> **Ableism:** "[A] pervasive system of discrimination and exclusion that oppresses people who have mental, emotional and physical disabilities" (p. 134).

■ Demographics

Smart and Smart (2006) reported that signs of disability are becoming increasingly common in a larger portion of the U.S. population. They cite the Americans With Disabilities Act (1990), which reported that people live longer with disabilities because of medical advances, technology, insurance, and a higher quality of living and support. The U.S. Census (2000) reported that 49.7 million Americans are living with a long-lasting condition or disability, and that disability has become "a natural part of human existence" (Smart & Smart, 2006, p. 29).

■ Stereotypes

People with disabilities are seen as a minority group because they are treated as a specific category of people. This leads to several stereotypes, one of the most negative of which is that disabled people are not capable of directing the course of their lives (AAT, 1991).

Rehabilitation Counseling

The majority of clients with disabilities who seek counseling are involved in some type of rehabilitation counseling. The AAT (1991) described rehabilitation counseling this way:

> **Rehabilitation counseling:** "[T]he maintenance of, or the improvement in, the physical, mental, and emotional states of a person, of any age, suffering from the effects of congenital mishap, crippling disease, injury, accident, or surgical intervention" (p. 15).

A client with a disability who seeks counseling should be treated from a proactive and rehabilitative perspective. The client also must be involved in creating the treatment plan.

Counseling Issues

Common issues with the population of disabled people include anxiety, depression, physical pain, stress, and chronic illness. Smart and Smart (2006) linked feelings of inferiority with loss, physical or emotional impairment, lifestyle changes, and the relative permanence of the disability. Pain can be a continual reminder of what has happened to the client's physical self. An important counseling goal with this population is to help them find a direction in life that brings satisfaction and feelings of self-worth, to look beyond their limitations and not sacrifice their uniqueness. Recommendations and consideration for working with the disabled population are described next.

Recommendations for Counselors (AAT, 1991)

- Become aware of and learn to manage personal fears and attitudes toward disability.
- Help clients create high expectations with appropriate measures of success.
- Facilitate supportive family caregiving and appropriate referrals to ancillary services.
- Become advocates to fight discriminatory practices and programs to aid clients in increasing self-acceptance and positive self-regard.
- Become educated about clients' specific disabilities.

GAY, LESBIAN, BISEXUAL, AND TRANSGENDERED POPULATION

Over time, a variety of theorists have attempted to attribute sexual orientation to family structure, mental health, dysfunctional behavior, rebellion, and hormonal imbalance (Schmidt, 2006). The oldest theory related to sexual orientation and, specifically to homosexuality, linked homosexuality to mental illness; however, this theory was disputed by Hooker's (1957) study. Today the *Diagnostic and Statistical Manual of Mental Disorders* (4th ed., text revision; American Psychiatric Association, 2000) no longer lists homosexuality as a disorder requiring treatment. Continuing research does indicate a possible relation between sexual orientation and certain biological factors.

■ The Process of "Coming Out"

Schmidt (2006) outlined several processes a member of the gay, lesbian, bisexual, and transgendered (GLBT) population may experience when coming out, a term that Schmidt defined this way:

> **Coming out:** The process through which individuals have accepted and announced their homosexuality.

A person going through the coming out process can experience such stages as these:

- Awareness of confusion and conflict.
- Identity comparison.
- Group association and social isolation.
- Exploration, tolerance, and acceptance.
- Satisfaction and integration.

Finally, the process of coming out can be hindered by a society that has little tolerance for and is even fearful of the GLBT population. The fears, attitudes, and resulting behaviors of those who react negatively to the GLBT population usually are related to *homophobia,* a term Schmidt (2006) defined as follows:

> **Homophobia:** The expression of "irrational fears about people who exhibit signs of accepting or using behaviors related to same-sex forms of sexual desire and orientation" (p. 106).

■ Counseling Issues

There are a number of mental health issues that seem to characterize the GLBT population encounters; these are noted here.

Potential Counseling Issues With the GLBT Population

- Oppression.
- Prejudice.
- Fear of lifestyle disclosure.
- Concerns about family and friends' judgment.
- Personal safety concerns.
- Grief associated with perceived loss of a traditional lifestyle.
- Drug and alcohol abuse related to the pressure of living a GLBT lifestyle.

In addition to being able to deal with some of these concerns, counselors should be prepared to face the challenges of working with a GLBT client. They should be aware that GLBT clients may anticipate prejudice on the part of the counselor unless they learn otherwise through the therapeutic relationship.

Given the variety of core issues that counselors and GLBT clients may encounter, there are some suggestions for working effectively with the GLBT population.

Recommendations for Counselors Working With the GLBT Client

- Become aware of personal biases, attitudes, and values related to the GLBT population.
- Respect and become knowledgeable of the challenges that are faced by the client.
- Create a safe and accepting environment for GLBT clients to share their concerns and confusion, as well as their own misconceptions about homosexuality.
- Separate myth from fact related to negative attitudes, including homophobia and counselor fear or stereotypes about the GLBT population.
- Focus on encouraging clients to accept and explore new beginnings.
- Realize that the GLBT community exists because of the need for other GLBT people to find support.
- Help clients access community resources, especially GLBT teenagers, who are just coming out, and those who live in rural areas where support systems are not likely to exist.

All clients must be supported in their growth and development toward health and life satisfaction. GLBT clients deserve encouragement as they face a society that does not hold much tolerance for their population.

CONCLUSION

The cultures of the world are many and varied. People of diverse cultural backgrounds who reside in the United States often are strongly connected with their cultural roots and, concurrently, are drawn to adapt to living in the United States. When serving the many, vital ethnic and cultural groups living in the United States, counselors must strive to appreciate and respond to the deeply embedded cultural traditions and values of these groups. By doing so, counselors can continue to help diverse clients who face personal, interpersonal, and systemic challenges in the United States live healthier lives and experience fullness of well-being.

Chapter 11: Key Terms

- ▶ Cultural context
- ▶ YAVIS client
- ▶ QUOID client

- ▶ White privilege
- ▶ Ageism
- ▶ Ableism

- ▶ Rehabilitation counseling
- ▶ Coming out
- ▶ Homophobia

chapter

12 Approaches to Group Work

Carol Thomas
Duquesne University

In This Chapter

▶ *Psychoanalytic Approach to Group Work*
  ■ Key Theoretical Concepts
  ■ Goals and Stages
  ■ Therapeutic Techniques
  ■ Role of Group Leader
  ■ Strengths and Limitations

▶ *Adlerian Approach to Group Work*
  ■ Key Theoretical Concepts
  ■ Goals and Stages
  ■ Therapeutic Techniques
  ■ Role of Group Leader
  ■ Strengths and Limitations

▶ *Transactional Analytic Approach to Group Work*
  ■ Key Theoretical Concepts
  ■ Goals and Stages
  ■ Therapeutic Techniques
  ■ Role of Group Leader
  ■ Strengths and Limitations

▶ *Psychodramatic Approach to Group Work*
  ■ Key Theoretical Concepts
  ■ Goals and Stages
  ■ Therapeutic Techniques
  ■ Role of Group Leader
  ■ Strengths and Limitations

▶ *Behavioral Approach to Group Work*
  ■ Key Theoretical Concepts
  ■ Goals and Stages
  ■ Therapeutic Techniques
  ■ Role of Group Leader
  ■ Strengths and Limitations

▶ *Rational-Emotive Behavior Therapy Approach to Group Work*
  ■ Key Theoretical Concepts
  ■ Goals and Stages
  ■ Therapeutic Techniques
  ■ Role of Group Leader
  ■ Strengths and Limitations

▶ *Reality Therapy Approach to Group Work*
  ■ Key Theoretical Concepts
  ■ Goals and Stages
  ■ Therapeutic Techniques
  ■ Role of Group Leader
  ■ Strengths and Limitations

▶ *Person-Centered Approach to Group Work*
  ■ Key Theoretical Concepts
  ■ Goals and Stages
  ■ Therapeutic Techniques
  ■ Role of Group Leader
  ■ Strengths and Limitations

▶ *Gestalt Approach to Group Work*
  ■ Key Theoretical Concepts
  ■ Goals and Stages
  ■ Therapeutic Techniques
  ■ Role of Group Leader
  ■ Strengths and Limitations

▶ *Existential Approach to Group Work*
  ■ Key Theoretical Concepts
  ■ Goals and Stages
  ■ Therapeutic Techniques
  ■ Role of Group Leader
  ■ Strengths and Limitations

PSYCHOANALYTIC APPROACH TO GROUP WORK

Freud (1959) was the father of psychoanalytic counseling, however, he never utilized groups in his psychoanalytic practice. Freud believed that groups acted as a reconstructed family unit through which members revisit unresolved childhood experiences. Alexander Wolf, a psychiatrist and psychoanalyst, is credited with adapting the psychoanalytic approach to groups in 1938. Generally, individual therapy within a group context is the most commonly practiced form of psychoanalytic group work.

■ Key Theoretical Concepts

The psychoanalytic approach to group work incorporates the tenets of classic psychoanalytic theory, utilizing specific techniques, such as free association, transference, and interpretation in aiding to free unconscious thoughts and make the unconscious more conscious. Unlike in individual psychoanalytic work, processes such as transference can be much more intense in group settings because of the interactions among group members. Even in a group setting, the focus of the psychoanalytic approach is generally on the individual, and the analysis of the individual's unconscious is a goal of psychoanalytic group work (Whitaker & Lieberman, 1965).

See Chapter 9 for more detail on theoretical concepts germane to psychoanalytic therapy.

■ Goals and Stages

Because psychoanalytic practitioners believe that people spend their lives trying to work out childhood experiences, both unresolved psychosexual and psychosocial issues are addressed. Additional goals of psychoanalytic group work include the following:

- Bringing the unconscious into conscious.
- Restructuring the group members' personalities.
- Strengthening egos through analysis of transference and resistance.

Unlike many types of therapeutic groups that concentrate on the development and process of the group, psychoanalytic groups emphasize development of the individuals within the group. Six stages of treatment characterize psychoanalytic group therapy.

Stages of Psychoanalytic Group Therapy

1. Preliminary individual analysis is used to screen out overly anxious individuals.

2. Free association about dreams and fantasies is used to establish rapport among members.
3. Analysis of client resistance and defense mechanisms is used to facilitate therapeutic growth.
4. Analysis of transference helps uncover members' projections of feelings onto the group leader, other members, or significant others.
5. Translating insights into actions occurs when group members challenge each other to promote growth.
6. Reorientation and social integration occurs when group members effectively and appropriately are able to manage anxiety and deal with the realities and pressures of life.

■ Therapeutic Techniques

To allow members' unconscious processes to surface, techniques such as free association, dream work, interpretation, and the analysis of transference and resistance are utilized. A description of each of these techniques follows.

Purposes of Psychoanalytic Techniques

- *Free association* or "free floating discussion" (Foulkes & Anthony, 1965) allows members to give and receive personal perceptions, an important aspect of the development of the human personality.
- *Dream analysis* allows members to learn more about one another and become more concrete in handling any feelings associated with their dreams.
- *Interpretation* is utilized in the early stages of group work to help group members gain insight into their behaviors and to model what members should be doing in later stages.
- *Resistance* is confronted immediately—usually first by the group leader but later by group members—to ensure that the group continues making progress.
- *Transference* is an effective technique that leads to individual and group insights.

■ Role of Group Leader

The primary role of the leader is to help group members work through issues of transference and bring repressed memories to conscious awareness. The group leader recognizes each member's potential to contribute positively to the good of the group and attempts to transfer leadership from the leader to group members, when appropriate (Wolf & Schwarz, 1962). Generally speaking, psychoanalytic group leaders should be warm, objective, and relatively anonymous (Corey, 2004b).

■ Strengths and Limitations

Advantages of psychoanalytic groups include their ability to help members experience and work through transference feelings toward the leader and other group members. Working through the broad range of feelings that are generated within a group can help members learn more about themselves than they might otherwise have an opportunity to do. Group members resolve current problems by working within the group on past issues—helping progress more quickly to occur.

A limitation of psychoanalytic group work is that group leaders are encouraged to be in therapy or to have completed a lengthy analysis. Likewise, psychoanalytic groups typically run longer than other forms of therapeutic groups, which can involve much time, energy, and cost to members. Finally, because the emphasis in a psychoanalytic group is often on childhood trauma, social, cultural, and interpersonal self-responsibility factors may be ignored.

ADLERIAN APPROACH TO GROUP WORK

In the early 1900s, Adler ended a 9-year association with Freud and Jung to develop his own theory of psychology. His contributions were brought to the United States in the late 1930s by Dreikurs (1950; Terner & Pew, 1978), who refined Adler's concepts into a clear, teachable system applicable to a variety of educational and mental health settings.

■ Key Theoretical Concepts

Unlike his predecessor, Freud, Adler emphasized social aspects of human development. The more well-known concepts associated with Adlerian therapy include **birth order,** the creative self, inferiority and superiority, and **social interest**. Moreover, Adler suggested that the human person is an individual whole and was interested in how the person integrates the various facets of his or her experience.

See Chapter 9 for more detail on Adlerian theoretical concepts.

■ Goals and Stages

Goals of Adlerian counseling include overcoming feelings of inferiority, nurturing social interests, identifying mistaken goals, changing faulty assumptions, and encouraging clients to become contributing members of society. Adlerian groups, likewise, have several common factors (Corey, 2004b).

Aims of Adlerian Group Therapy

- Establishing and maintaining a quality relationship between the counselor and group members.
- Identifying and clarifying members' individual "styles of life" and personal goals.
- Interpreting a person's early history to encourage insight.
- Reorienting members' perceptions, thoughts, and feelings.

According to Sonstegard and Bittner (1998), Adlerian groups typically have four stages.

Stages of Adlerian Group Work

1. Developing and maintaining the proper therapeutic relationship between leaders and members.
2. Assessing the dynamics that operate within individual members.
3. Working toward increasing individual insight and self-understanding.
4. Assisting the individual to discover new alternatives and make new choices.

Working through these stages should result in group members overcoming feelings of inferiority, reducing levels of discouragement, identifying mistaken goals, changing faulty assumptions that group members may have about themselves, and helping group members to become contributing members of society.

■ Therapeutic Techniques

The following Adlerian techniques are not limited to any one stage of the group process and can aid the leader in the development and growth of the group members throughout the life of the group.

Adlerian Group Techniques

- Modeling appropriate social skills.
- Showing interest to demonstrate acceptance.
- Utilizing active listening skills such as reflection, summarization, and restatement.
- Eliciting early recollections to aid in the identification of problematic emotional patterns and feelings that have been carried from childhood into adulthood.
- Assessing members' goals and translating them into individual lifestyles.
- Observing members' social interactions within the group as an interpretation of how members potentially behave outside of the group.

■ Role of Group Leader

Based on Adlerian concepts, the group leader should provide the following:

- A working relationship that promotes equality between leader and members.
- Communication based on mutual trust and respect.
- Assistance in the exploration of personal goals, feelings, beliefs, and motives that are determining factors in members' "styles of life."
- Assistance in gaining insight into self-defeating behaviors that impede the formulation of effective and attainable goals.
- Assistance in the practice of self-acceptance with all the assets and liabilities that comprise the self.
- Assistance in exploring new insights and encouragement to test new behaviors.

The Adlerian group leader uses gentle confrontation, self-disclosure, interpretation, and analysis of regular behavior patterns to challenge members' beliefs and goals. The Adlerian group leader pays close attention to the social context of members' behaviors. Finally, the Adlerian group leader encourages members to translate behaviors and insights learned within the group to behaviors and insights outside the group.

■ Strengths and Limitations

One of the strengths of Adlerian group counseling is that it encourages growth by giving members concrete ways to handle specific, problematic situations. This approach encourages democratic participation—useful for promoting openness and conversation. Another strength of Adlerian therapy is its eclectic nature (Corey, 2004b). Adlerian groups stress the value of social interests, the importance of **family constellations**, and the usefulness of goal-directed behaviors without being tied to a particular method or procedure.

A limitation in Adlerian group work may be its use of a detailed interview about family background. Adlerian group leaders must be sensitive to cultures where disclosing personal family information is divergent and must respect a member's right to forego disclosure concerning family matters. Additionally, for Adlerian group work to gain prominence, more research must document the effectiveness of this therapy (Manaster & Corsini, 1982).

TRANSACTIONAL ANALYTIC APPROACH TO GROUP WORK

Transactional analysis (TA) began during World War II when its founder, Eric Berne, developed his cognitive therapeutic model while working with soldier patients in discussion groups. Although Berne was trained as a psychoanalyst, his TA approach to group work differed from psychoanalytic group work in a number of ways.

Points of Differentiation Between TA and Psychoanalysis

- The "unconscious" is a concept not utilized in TA.
- Much less time is required with TA then with psychoanalysis—groups meet once a week for weeks or months, not every day for a year or more.
- The group leader is considered equal among group members, although he or she must know more about TA than group members.
- TA can be used with a broad range of clients, including children, mentally handicapped, and persons with a drug or alcohol addiction.

■ Key Theoretical Concepts

More than his predecessors, Berne stressed the importance of interpersonal communication or transactions to mental health. Transactions are influenced by a person's **ego state**. Berne defined three ego states—**parent ego state, adult ego state, and child ego state**—that, respectively, reflect Freud's personality constructs of the superego, ego, and id. Additionally, Berne identified four life stances.

Life Stances in TA

1. I'm OK, you're OK.
2. I'm not OK, you're OK.
3. I'm OK, you're not OK.
4. I'm not OK, you're not OK.

See Chapter 9 for more detail on theoretical concepts germane to TA.

■ Goals and Stages

The goal of TA group work is for members to let go of harmful critical parent messages and self-defeating child scripts (Gladding, 2002b), become more capable of responding to others from the adult ego state, and adopt the I'm OK, You're OK stance. For these goals to be met, group members must get in touch with their feelings, the structure of their personality, and their transactions with others. Group members accomplish this through gained awareness of their own ego states and understanding which ego state they are operating out of at any given moment. This awareness empowers group members to assess the interactions they most likely are to have and take corrective action, if needed.

The group process as described by Woollams and Brown (1979) involves seven stages or steps of development.

Steps of Development in TA Groups

1. Trust in others.
2. Trust in self.
3. Integration into the group.
4. Work.
5. Redecision.
6. Reintegration.
7. Termination.

These steps in development are sometimes overlapping and intermingle with each other so that they are not always distinct.

■ Therapeutic Techniques

TA group techniques include the concepts of games, life scripts, and therapeutic contracts to aid group members in understanding the complexities of the three ego states and the four life patterns.

Games: "[A]n ongoing series of complementary ulterior transactions progressing to a well-defined, predictable outcome" (Berne, 1964, p. 48).

Life scripts: Plans for life developed in early childhood that are reinforced by parents. Members are encouraged to rewrite their programmed scripts into scripts that offer more productive interactions.

Therapeutic contracts: Contractual forms completed by group members who indicate what it is they wish to accomplish as a result of participating in the group. Goals must be concretely defined so that group members can take responsibility for working toward them.

When either the group leader or a member notices that a game is being played, he or she will bring it to the attention of the group, who then will attempt to analyze it.

■ Role of Group Leader

The group leader in a TA therapeutic group should be a well-trained professional who has a good understanding of group dynamics and a mastery of the terminology used in TA. Operating from an "I'm OK" life position also is essential for a leader to be able to build rapport with members and teach them how to recognize and understand self-destructive messages or behavior patterns. Additionally, the TA group leader has four other duties.

Tasks of the TA Group Leader (Berne, 1966; Gladding, 1992)

- Protecting the group from physical or psychological harm.
- Giving permission to group members to behave against the directives of their parent ego.
- Acting with potency, or appropriate counseling techniques in certain situations.
- Using operations or very specific techniques that include interrogation, specification, confrontation, and illustration.

■ Strengths and Limitations

A strength of TA is its stress on intellectual insight as the basis for doing things differently. TA can help group members become aware of how they function interpersonally and intrapersonally and how their life decisions were made. The language used to explain the TA concepts is very clear and offers a highly structured approach to group work. Groups can be tailored to include many cultural differences and value systems. TA offers a short-term approach to group counseling, and its concepts can be very effective in group communication processes, such as those between employer and employees and those among coworkers (Nykodym, Ruud, & Liverpool, 1986).

A criticism of the TA approach to group work is its reliance on cognitive concepts. Persons of limited cognitive ability might not flourish in a group that utilizes TA concepts and language. Another limitation is the lack of attention to the group process (Yalom, 1985). TA groups are usually member–leader centered and often ignore the importance of other group dynamics such as interpersonal learning, cohesiveness, and universality.

PSYCHODRAMATIC APPROACH TO GROUP WORK

Psychodramatic therapy was founded in Vienna in 1921 by Jacob Moreno. After reflecting on the reactions of the actors and the audience to his "Theatre of Spontaneity," Moreno recognized that people experienced a release of pent-up feelings after the performances. Thus, Moreno developed a theory of psychology around the cathartic use of dramatic performance. In 1925, Moreno moved to New York and began utilizing his ideas of spontaneous drama with hospitalized individuals, and in 1942, Moreno founded the American Society of Group Psychotherapy and Psychodrama.

■ Key Theoretical Concepts

The psychodramatic method of therapy consists of the following five components: the director, a protagonist, the auxiliary egos, the audience, and the stage.

Director: The psychodramatic group leader, who encourages intense emotional participation by a protagonist, helps delineate what occurs after the psychodramatic enactment and helps the protagonist gain insight and emotional resolution through group feedback.

Protagonist: The group member who has chosen to enact a life situation or relationship in an effort to experience a cathartic release of emotions, gain insight, and learn new and productive ways of managing future situations or relationships.

Auxiliary ego: Group members selected by the protagonist to represent inanimate objects, pets, or persons who are dead, alive, real, or imagined.

Audience: Remaining group members who witness an enactment and hopefully experience a release of feelings and increased insight into their own struggles while observing the performance.

Stage: The formal stage area or large open room in which the enactment takes place.

■ Goals and Stages

Facilitating the release of pent-up feelings, providing insight, and assisting clients in developing innovative and more effective behaviors all are goals of psychodramatic therapy. By enacting a situation or relationship, the protagonist and observing group members will gain insight, experience a cathartic emotional release, and learn new ways of behaving in similar future situations (Gladding, 1999). There are three distinct phases of psychodramatic therapy.

Phases of Psychodramatic Therapy

1. The *warm-up phase* prepares members through various techniques for the experience as well as fosters feelings of security and trust.
2. The *action phase* occurs when the protagonist, directed by the group leader, acts out a situation, relationship, or other concern.
3. The *discussion or sharing phase* involves constructive and emotion-based feedback from group members, discussion about the entire experience, and closing remarks by the group leader.

■ Therapeutic Techniques

The nature of psychodramatic therapy supports a multitude of techniques. A number of the most common techniques are listed next.

Common Techniques in Psychodrama

- *Creative imagery* is a warm-up exercise that invites group members to imagine neutral or pleasant objects or scenes (Ohlsen, Horne, & Lawe, 1988).
- The *magic shop* is an exercise that utilizes the idea of a magic shop where items can be bartered for (e.g., if one wishes for better relationship skills, he or she may have to give up irrational anger in exchange for the desired skills).
- *Sculpting* occurs when group members arrange one another into physical configurations of persons with whom they have issues, such as family members, peers, or coworkers.
- The *soliloquy technique* encourages the protagonist to daydream out loud by giving a monologue about his or her situation as he or she is acting it out.
- *Role reversal* occurs when the protagonist switches roles with another person on stage as a way to view his or her situation from another perspective.
- The *mirror technique* entails an auxiliary ego mirroring the protagonist's posture, gestures, and words while the protagonist watches from offstage.
- The *double technique* requires an auxiliary ego to stand behind the protagonist and act with or speak for him or her as a way to help the protagonist gain awareness of internal processes.

■ Role of Group Leader

The primary role of the group leader or the director is to encourage emotional participation by group members. According to Moreno (1964), the director takes on the roles of producer, catalyst or facilitator, and observer or analyzer.

Functions of the Director (Haskell, 1975)

- Planning the session so various group members have an opportunity to be the protagonist.
- Creating a tolerant atmosphere that leads to spontaneous expression.
- Providing support and direction for the protagonist.
- Asking for clarity when necessary.
- Ensuring that the roles are being properly enacted.
- Protecting the protagonist from being verbally attacked by other group members or from being subjected to simplistic directives or advice.
- Leading a group discussion that encourages supportive feedback.
- Providing closure by summarizing the protagonist's experience on the basis of feedback.

There are several personal qualities that enhance the effectiveness of the psychodramatic group leader's work.

Characteristics of Psychodramatic Leaders

- Creative.
- Courageous.
- Innovative.
- Improvisational.

■ Strengths and Limitations

Corey (2004b) appreciated the use of psychodramatic therapy for individuals who cannot see alternatives for dealing with the significant people in their lives. Acting out alternative responses allows people to gain a different perspective on relating to problematic individuals or situations. When used correctly, this action-oriented form of therapy has group members doing something, rather than endlessly talking about problems in a detached, story-telling fashion.

A principal limitation of psychodrama is that the expression of feelings through cathartic theatrics and the enacting of past problems can be extremely threatening. Group leaders must use caution when encouraging members to display intense feelings in the group context. The danger of leaders using psychodramatic therapy to gratify their own psychological needs also exists. Therefore, it is crucial that leaders be aware of their own needs to prevent them from interfering with the group process.

 Check out the American Society on Group Psychotherapy and Psychodrama for more information at:

▶ www.asgpp.org

BEHAVIORAL APPROACH TO GROUP WORK

The behavioral approach to individual and group counseling is attributable to theorists such as Watson (1913), Bandura (1969), and Skinner (1974). Behavior theories began to emerge at the beginning of the 20th century (Wilson, 1989) and generally emphasize overt processes, learning, ways to change nonproductive actions, and goal definition.

■ Key Theoretical Concepts

A key theoretical concept of the behavioral approach to group work is that all behavior, emotions, and cognitions have been learned, and all behaviors can be changed or modified by new learning. Change occurs through acquisition of new behavior or modification of existing behavior. As this happens, emotions and attitudes are also shifted.

Methods to Encourage Change in Behavioral Group Work (Berkowitz, 1982)

- Behaviors that need to be changed are identified.
- Specific behavioral alterations are discussed.
- Events in the environment that maintain the behavior are studied.
- Intervention strategies for behavior modification are employed.
- Plans for maintaining and generalizing new behaviors are created.

■ Goals and Stages

The primary focus in behavioral groups is behavior, and the ultimate goal of therapy is to change nonproductive behaviors. Rose (1977, 1983) and Hollander and Kazaoka (1988) named seven specific stages that are universal to behavioral groups and support the goal of behavior modification.

Seven Stages of Behavioral Group Work

1. Forming the group and addressing organizational details.
2. Establishing group attraction and identity through the leader's determination of members who exhibit similar goals and potential connectedness (Rose, 1980).
3. Promoting openness and sharing through the leader's ability to model appropriate group behavior as well as through the discussion of members' expectations.
4. Creating behavioral frameworks that members can use as tools to evaluate and monitor their behavioral modifications.
5. Establishing and implementing behavioral models that address specific members' individual goals for group therapy.
6. Transferring treatment outside of the group is the beginning of the end of a working group (Wilson, 1989).
7. Maintaining behavior change and fading out of the need of the group's support.

At the final stage, a group leader may ask members to self-monitor by keeping records of behaviors or psychological reactions (Wilson, 1989). This allows members to chart their progress once they have departed from the group environment.

■ Therapeutic Techniques

Therapeutic techniques utilized in behavioral groups focus on group members' unproductive or unwanted behaviors. Behavior therapists believe that if they understand the group members' presenting problems, they can select a technique for changing the behavior. Techniques specific to behavioral therapy include the following:

Systematic desensitization: The gradual exposure to an aversive stimulus that eventually allows a person to overcome a specific fear.

Assertion training: Training that increases individuals' behavioral repertoire so they are better able to choose whether or not to behave more assertively in a given situation.

Modeling: A group leader or members exhibit behaviors and social skills that other group members can observe and then apply to their own lives.

■ Role of Group Leader

At the beginning stages of a behavioral group, the leader takes on a directive and active role, but eventually becomes a participant-observer, allowing the other group members to assume more responsibility as the group proceeds (Hansen, Warner, & Smith, 1980; Rose, 1983).

Leader Responsibilities in Behavioral Group Therapy (Corey, 2004b)

- Screening group members.
- Teaching members about the group process.
- Assessing members' progress within the group.
- Reinforcing group members' achievement of specific goals.
- Determining the effectiveness of techniques.
- Instructing members to use a particular social skill.
- Providing positive or negative feedback to members who use new skills.
- Giving homework assignments.

■ Strengths and Limitations

The primary strength of a behavioral approach to group work is its focus on helping members learn new ways of functioning (Corey, 2004b). Behavioral groups are relatively short term and focused (Hollander & Kazaoka, 1988), allowing specific goals to be met in a manageable amount of time. Additionally, behavioral group work is a well-researched way to treat alcoholism, drug addiction, and juvenile delinquency. Finally, behavioral groups can be integrated into many cultural settings.

Limitations of the behavioral approach to group work include the possibility that members can become overly dependent on the group for support, the limited attention given to past experiences, and the lack of attention given to group members' feelings (Rose, 1977).

RATIONAL-EMOTIVE BEHAVIOR THERAPY APPROACH TO GROUP WORK

Rational-emotive behavior therapy (REBT) is an extension of Ellis's A-B-C-D-E model first known as rational emotive therapy (RET). REBT groups are cognitively based and assume that group members have the potential to become rational thinkers.

■ Key Theoretical Concepts

The underlying premise of REBT is that irrational cognitions result in mental health issues or general unhappiness. Ellis proposed that a person's illogical cognitive interpretations about events, rather than the events themselves, produce negative feelings and are people's core problem.

See Chapter 9 for more on the A-B-C-D-E model.

■ Goals and Stages

There are two primary goals of REBT—challenging members' irrational thoughts and helping members realize that reactions to events, and not necessarily the events themselves, cause consternation. Ellis identified at least 15 irrational thoughts; a sampling is listed here.

Irrational Thoughts Identified in REBT

- It is a "dire necessity" for an adult to be loved or approved of by every important person in the community.
- A person needs to have someone stronger than himself or herself on whom to depend.
- A person's past behavior is a determinant of present behavior, and past experiences should continue to effect the present.
- Unhappiness is externally based, and a person has little control over his or her pains.
- There is one correct answer and one solution to a problem, and, if it is not found, trauma will ensue.
- The world should be fair, just, and impartial.

There are two primary stages in REBT group work. In the first stage, group members learn the difference between irrational and rational beliefs. At this stage, known as intellectual insight, members' convictions about their rational beliefs stay at the level of intellectual understanding because the beliefs are not sufficiently strong to influence how members feel and act. During the second stage, known as emotional insight, group members' convictions about their rational beliefs are influential enough to alter how members feel and act.

■ Therapeutic Techniques

Therapeutic techniques of REBT group work are similar to those utilized in many other cognitive or behavioral types of group work; the aim of these techniques is to teach members how to become more rational thinkers.

REBT Interventions

- Persuasion.
- Challenges.
- Role playing.
- Confrontation.
- Group discussion.

Group leaders listen for irrational beliefs and dispute them. Group members are taught how to identify the irrationality of shoulds, musts, and oughts, and group leaders help address any irrational thoughts that may arise.

■ Role of Group Leader

The REBT group leader's role primarily is to encourage rational thinking. This is accomplished in several ways:

- The group leader teaches members about the origin of emotions.
- The group leader is active in the group process by challenging members to look at their irrational thought patterns.
- The group leader encourages other members to assist each other thinking rationally.
- The group leader assigns homework and performs activity-based experiences.

The group leader acts as a positive role model and reveals how he or she practices REBT in his or her daily life. Additionally, the group leader looks to other group members to act as auxiliary counselors once a member has shared a problematic issue (Ellis & Dryden, 1987).

■ Strengths and Limitations

REBT groups stress members' capacity to control their own destiny. The approach works well in multicultural groups by helping members of any ethnicity examine their beliefs. Through the utilization of the A-B-C-D-E system, Ellis has demystified the process of REBT group therapy. Members have a clear system from which to work and can apply it to their own issues, as well as issues of fellow group members. Finally, homework assignments between group sessions promote action.

Limitations to REBT groups are their attention to the individual, not the group (Wessler & Hankin, 1988). Members learn the importance of controlling their own thoughts, emotions, and behaviors but learn little about the group process or about group dynamics. Another limitation is that group leaders may exert too much power or control over the group members in determining what they believe to be irrational thinking. Also, because REBT is cognitively based, this type of counseling would not be appropriate for persons of limited cognitive ability.

REALITY THERAPY APPROACH TO GROUP WORK

Glasser developed reality therapy while working at the Ventura School for Girls in California during the late 1950s and early 1960s. There, Glasser utilized reality therapy (originally called control theory) in group settings with inpatient adolescent girls and eventually began using reality therapy in his work with individuals. The essence of reality therapy is that people all are responsible for what they choose to do. The basic assumption of reality therapy is that people only can control their lives in the present moment. Reality therapy, then, is a behavioral approach that focuses on what clients do, not what they feel.

■ Key Theoretical Concepts

Underlying Glasser's approach to therapy are the concepts of **personal responsibility** and choice. By emphasizing a client's ability to choose to meet his or her own needs, Glasser simultaneously deemphasizes blaming behaviors that prevent personal responsibility. Positive choices help people create their quality world in which needs for love, survival, belonging, power, and freedom are met.

■ Goals and Stages

Reality therapy assumes that change does not come from insight alone. Rather, group members have to act differently if they wish to experience change. The goal of therapy is to identify what members can do about their own behaviors, assuming that they cannot change the behavior of others. By challenging noneffective ways of thinking and acting, group leaders are able to aid members in developing plans of action for new ways of thinking and behaving that are productive and useful.

Individual Goals in Reality Therapy

- Giving up nonproductive and self-defeating behaviors for productive and attainable action plans.
- Gaining control of one's life and acquiring realistic behaviors.

These goals can be achieved when group leaders practice a series of eight basic steps (Glasser, 1984; Glasser & Zunin, 1973):

1. Make friends or establish a meaningful relationship with group members.
2. Emphasize present behaviors by asking, "What are you doing now?"
3. Question whether or not clients' actions are getting them what they want.
4. Assist clients in making a positive plan to do better.
5. Get a commitment to follow the positive plan.
6. Accept no excuses—responsibility lies with each group member.
7. Deliver no punishment—consequences occur naturally.
8. Never give up! Group members are assured continual support.

The use of open-ended questions and a focus on positive behaviors support group members in achieving their goals. Eventually, group members come to acknowledge their own basic needs and develop successful ways of meeting those needs.

■ Therapeutic Techniques

The main technique utilized in reality therapy is the encouragement by group leaders for group members to face reality, to discontinue behaviors that are not productive or are self-defeating, and to help group members find alternative ways of behaving that are productive. This is accomplished through the eight-step process outlined above.

■ Role of Group Leader

The role of the group leader, according to Glasser (1965), is fourfold and includes the following responsibilities.

Tasks of Reality Group Therapists

1. Group leaders must be responsible persons who are aware of and able to fulfill their own needs.
2. Group leaders mentally must be strong individuals who can resist pleas for sympathy and excuses for nonproductive behavior from group members.
3. Group leaders must practice acceptance of all group members.
4. Group leaders must be supportive and emotionally involved with each group member and, at the same time, use gentle confrontation to move members toward responsible living.

Reality therapy group leaders continue to explore and challenge their own values in an effort to strive toward their own personal growth.

■ Strengths and Limitations

Realty therapy has a short-term focus, making it an appropriate and effective therapy under today's health care system. Additionally, it relies heavily on accountability, which allows the group process to be member driven. Finally, the straightforward and clear approach characteristic of reality therapy makes it appropriate for parent groups, children's or adolescents' behavior management groups, teacher groups, addiction groups, groups for incarcerated men and women, and crisis intervention.

Austin (1999) criticized reality therapy as being more of a "process model" or technique rather than an actual theory. Other criticisms suggest that reality therapy is too simplistic and discounts valuable tactics, such as gaining insight and dream interpretation and analysis. Also, because reality therapy is very value laden, a manipulative group leader easily can disregard a group member's goals and impose his or her own values and beliefs. For change to be successful and permanent, group members need the opportunity to struggle with issues and reach their own conclusions (Corey, 2004b).

 For further information on reality therapy, visit William Glasser's Web site:

▶ www.wglasser.com

PERSON-CENTERED APPROACH TO GROUP WORK

Person-centered group work is linked directly to the counseling theory the Rogers (1967, 1970, 1980) developed; he termed his groups *basic encounter groups*. Rogers's interest in group work evolved in the early 1950s, during the proliferation of group experiences. Hobbs (1951) and Gordon (1951) developed Rogers's approach to therapy and applied it to specialty groups, including those for physically and mentally handicapped children and their parents, mothers requiring government assistance, persons receiving individual counseling, and mental-health professionals (Raskin, 1986a).

■ Key Theoretical Concepts

One of the most important concepts in person-centered therapy is indicated in its name—*person*-centered. The therapist best can understand and help the client by trying to comprehend the client's frame of reference or worldview. The well-known adage, "The client knows best," is an accurate representation of Rogers's approach to therapy. Additionally, there are three conditions for the therapeutic relationship that advance its effectiveness; namely, the counselor's **unconditional positive regard** toward the client, empathic stance, and **genuineness**.

See Chapter 9 for more information on Rogers's theoretical concepts.

■ Goals and Stages

Rogers believed that clients are the experts of their own lives and improve faster when they direct their actions. Goals of person-centered group counseling may include such things as enhancing self-esteem, reducing conflict with others, and increasing the overall productive functioning of group members. After gaining insight through experiencing the three fundamental conditions of person-centered therapy, members should be able to set their own goals and work toward achieving those goals.

Rogers (1970) defined 15 stages of the group process that include the following patterns.

Client Behaviors in Group Therapy Development

1. Milling around.
2. Resisting.
3. Revealing past feelings.
4. Expressing negative feelings.
5. Expressing personally meaningful material.
6. Communicating immediate personal feelings.
7. Developing a healing capacity in the group.
8. Accepting oneself.
9. Cracking facades.
10. Giving feedback.
11. Confronting.
12. Helping relationships outside the group.

13. Making a basic encounter.
14. Expressing closeness.
15. Changing behavior.

These group stages do not always occur in a clear-cut sequence and vary from group to group.

Therapeutic Techniques

Little emphasis is placed on specific techniques when conducting person-centered groups. Because the therapeutic process is relationship based, not technique centered, a group leader must display genuineness, unconditional positive regard, and **empathy** in addition to practicing good listening skills, possessing a positive outlook, and demonstrating effective interpersonal responses within the group setting. Rogers (1970) believed that the group environment leads to self-exploration and self-acceptance that eventually results in change.

Role of Group Leader

The person-centered group leader is known as the facilitator, which may be understood as follows:

> **Facilitator:** A leader who participates genuinely in the group process as a member of the group without using gimmicks or planned procedures (Bozarth, 1981).

Skills of the Person-Centered Facilitator

- Active listening.
- Supporting.
- Reflecting.
- Sharing.
- Affirming.
- Clarifying.
- Summarizing.
- Engaging.

Person-centered facilitators must maintain an optimistic and positive view—core qualities that are intervention tools for self-exploration, personal growth, and positive group experiences.

■ Strengths and Limitations

Personal encounter groups can help people enhance their interpersonal relationships and communication skills. Because the emphasis of a person-centered group is on relationship building, this theory is especially effective with expressive people and those who need to feel understood.

Limitations of person-centered groups include their tendency to discount the impact of past experiences on behaviors, values, and feelings. Because there are no techniques to guide members, the group may stagnate. The lack of structure and direction make encounter groups less useful for persons with mental disabilities, severe brain damage, or serious emotional disabilities.

GESTALT APPROACH TO GROUP WORK

Gestalt group work is attributed to Perls, who was trained as a psychoanalyst in his native Germany. In the early 1930s, Perls fled to South Africa during the Nazi regime. There, Perls refined his theory and, after immigrating to the United States, coauthored his first book, *Gestalt Therapy* (Perls, Hefferline, & Goodman, 1951), which outlined the fundamental tenets of Gestalt theory. The German word *gestalt* means a complete pattern or configuration. A gestalt is a perceived whole; as such, Gestalt therapy is rooted in Perls's belief in perceptual holism.

■ Key Theoretical Concepts

Grounded in an existential perspective, Gestalt group work is characterized by an effort to encourage clients to put meaning to their lives. Specifically, Perls advocated helping people become a gestalt or fully integrated by bringing to awareness their hidden or shadow side. To facilitate increased awareness, Gestalt therapy focuses primarily on the here and now.

■ Goals and Stages

Goals in Gestalt therapy address both the needs of individual group members and the group as a whole.

Individual Goals for Gestalt Group Members (Zinker, 1978)

- Integrating polarities within oneself.
- Learning to provide self-support instead of looking to others.
- Becoming aware of what one is sensing, feeling, thinking, fantasizing, and doing in the present.

- Defining one's boundaries with clarity.
- Translating insights into action.
- Learning about oneself by engaging in creative experiments.

Group Process Goals for Gestalt Groups

- Learning to ask clearly and directly for what members want or need.
- Learning how to deal with one another in the face of conflict.
- Learning how to give support and energy to one another.
- Being able to challenge one another to push beyond the boundaries of safety and what is known.
- Learning how to make use of resources within the group rather than relying on the group leader as the director.

There are three basic stages that occur in Gestalt groups:

1. Identity and dependence.
2. Influence and counterdependence.
3. Intimacy and interdependence.

During the first stage, identity and dependence, the group leader outlines the purpose and expectations of the group, and group members learn about contracting and boundary setting and develop relationships. In the second stage, influence and counterdependence, the primary issues are power, influence, authority, and control; members are encouraged to challenge group norms. During the second stage members also begin to take on roles, such as the "scapegoat" or the "victim," and learn to separate the role from the individual. In the third stage, intimacy and interdependence, group members begin to take risks of an interpersonal nature and use one another, as well as the leader, for support and understanding. After the group has moved through these three stages, there is a closing process that allows members to begin thinking about leaving the group.

■ Therapeutic Techniques

Gestalt therapy utilizes a wide variety of action-based techniques designed to intensify the experience of the present moment and increase awareness. Gestalt group work is unique in that the group leader's primary focus and interaction is with one group member at a time—someone who is willing to work. While the group leader is working with a particular member, other group members act as observers, gaining awareness through witness of another's experience. Two well-known techniques used in Gestalt group work are the following:

Empty chair technique: A technique designed to help members work through unfinished business. A member sits directly across from and speaks to an empty chair that he or she envisions holding the person with whom he or she is in conflict.

Paradoxical intention: A technique used to aid group members to exaggerate or magnify the behaviors that are causing concern for the purpose of bringing awareness to the underlying feelings related to distressing behaviors.

Other techniques that a group leader may utilize to achieve awareness include role playing, projection, dream interpretation, guided imagery and fantasy, and encouragement to focus on here-and-now feelings.

E X A M P L E

Using the Empty Chair Technique

Maria's mother died when she was only a child, and for years, Maria has been unable fully to face the grief of not having had the chance to grow up with her mother's presence. After several months of participating in a Gestalt-oriented personal growth group, during which time Maria talked extensively about her mother's death, she was challenged by a group member who noticed that Maria seemed angry when she talked about her mother. To facilitate a moment in which Maria might deal with unresolved anger at her mother for having passed away, the therapist asked Maria to imagine that her mother was sitting in a chair that he positioned in front of her. Although timid at first, Maria closed her eyes and began conversing to the chair as if her mother were sitting there in front of her. Guiding the process, the therapist supported Maria's release of sadness and anger at her mother for having left her alone during her childhood, teen, and adult years. At the close of the exercise, the group was invited to respond to Maria and to their own feelings at watching the exercise.

■ Role of Group Leader

To help group members focus on the here and now and more intensely experience their feelings, the Gestalt group leader asks "how" and "what" questions and rarely asks "why" questions.

Group Leader Questions

- "What are you experiencing now?"
- "What's going on inside you as you're speaking?"
- "How are you experiencing your anxiety in your body?"
- "What's your feeling at this moment—as you sit there and try to talk?"

Gestalt group leaders help members fully utilize their senses by focusing attention on their posture, voice, hand gestures, language patterns, and interactions with others. Sharing immediate experiences that are felt either by the group member or the group leader helps to raise awareness.

■ Strengths and Limitations

Gestalt therapy is particularly effective when used by counselors who have a humanistic, existential approach to helping others. Gestalt therapy allows for a high level of creativity on the part of the group leader and puts responsibility for personal growth on group members—more so than other forms of group therapy.

A criticism of Gestalt therapy is that it focuses too heavily on emotion and too little on cognition. There is also a danger of misusing Gestalt techniques, which can have detrimental effects if misused with volatile clients. Additionally, if techniques are used in a mechanical or gimmicky way by an inexperienced or untrained leader, the group may become passive, and the goals of creating self-supporting individuals may be defeated.

 Check out the following Web sites for more information about Gestalt therapy:

► www.gestaltreview.com

► www.gestaltcleveland.org

EXISTENTIAL APPROACH TO GROUP WORK

Kierkegaard, a 19th-century Danish theologian and philosopher, was the first to develop a philosophy based on the formulation of "truth" as a guide to becoming a whole individual. German and French theorists Martin Heidegger and Jean Paul Sartre later named Kierkegaard's approach *existentialism*. Swiss psychiatrist Ludwig Binswanger is credited with moving existentialism from a philosophy to a therapeutic process. Prominent contemporary contributors to existential therapy include Frankl, May, Bugental, and Yalom.

■ Key Theoretical Concepts

Existential therapy is a philosophical approach to counseling that stems from the fundamental belief that people are not victims of circumstance and always have a choice. Existential therapy also views people as constantly changing, emerging, and developing. Philosophical questions such as "Who am I?," "What can I hope for?," and "Where am I going?" are central to therapy under this model. According to the existential therapeutic model, there are six basic dimensions to the human condition (Corey, 2005).

Basic Dimensions of the Human Condition

- The capacity for self-awareness.
- Freedom and responsibility.
- Establishment of identity and meaningful relationships.
- The search for meaning, purpose, values, and goals.
- Anxiety as a condition of living.
- Awareness of death and nonbeing.

With the help of the group leader, the existential group members work toward developing clear understandings of these human conditions and their own meaning for life. Group members also develop a healthy awareness of the barriers preventing them from reaching their ultimate life goals.

■ Goals and Stages

The primary goal of existential therapy groups is to provide members with conditions that maximize self-awareness and reduce blocks to personal growth. This is done by helping group members discover and see freedom of choice in any situation and enabling members to assume responsibility for their own choices, thereby giving them the responsibility to act. May (1981) stated, "the purpose of psychotherapy is not to 'cure' the clients in the conventional sense, but to help them become aware of what they are doing and to get them out of the victim role" (p. 210). The existential approach to groups, unlike many other styles of group therapy, does not include specific stages of development.

> Unlike most other models of group work, existential group therapy does not utilize techniques. Group leaders employ interventions based on their philosophical views about the fundamental nature of humanity.

■ Therapeutic Techniques

Unlike most other models of group work, existential group therapy does not utilize techniques. Group leaders employ interventions based on their philosophical views about the fundamental nature of humanity. Van Deurzen-Smith (1990) emphasized that the existential approach is well known for its deemphasis on techniques. This does not mean that techniques never are used; rather, the group leader's self becomes the core of the group therapy. The group leader is free to draw from other therapeutic models if a particular technique proves useful.

Role of Group Leader

The role of the group leader in existential therapy groups is to view each group member as a "total person," who is the product of his or her choices, rather than of external circumstances (Austin, 1999).

Leader Tasks in Existential Group Work

- Helping group members see where, when, and how they have failed to realize their potential.
- Assisting members in identifying and clarifying their assumptions about the world and how it works.
- Encouraging members to examine their beliefs, values, and assumptions in an effort to determine their validity.
- Helping group members transform their new understanding into concrete action, which ultimately should result in group members' living a purposeful existence.

Strengths and Limitations

Existential therapy allows group members to view themselves honestly and with an understanding that their concerns are universal. According to Corey (2005), one of the main strengths of existential therapy is "its emphasis on the human quality of the therapeutic relationship" (p. 155). A second strength of this therapeutic model is the freedom that is given to group members to redesign their lives based on their awareness of choice.

A limitation to existential therapy is its perceived vagueness. Some critics find terms such as *self-actualization, authenticity,* and *being-in-the-world* unclear and elusive. As such, it becomes difficult to research the process or the outcomes of existential therapy. Another limitation is that the philosophical insight that is necessary for growth may not be appropriate for some group members. People with serious emotional disturbances may not be able to understand an approach that primarily is insight based.

 For further information on existential therapy visit

► www.go.to/existentialanalysis

Chapter 12: Key Terms

- ▶ Social interest
- ▶ Birth order
- ▶ Family constellation
- ▶ Genuineness
- ▶ Unconditional positive regard
- ▶ Empathy
- ▶ Facilitator
- ▶ Gestalt

- ▶ Empty chair technique
- ▶ Paradoxical intention
- ▶ Personal responsibility
- ▶ Director
- ▶ Protagonist
- ▶ Auxiliary ego
- ▶ Audience
- ▶ Stage
- ▶ Ego state

- ▶ Parent ego state
- ▶ Adult ego state
- ▶ Child ego state
- ▶ Games
- ▶ Life scripts
- ▶ Therapeutic contracts
- ▶ Systematic desensitization
- ▶ Assertion training
- ▶ Modeling

Fundamentals of Group Work

13

Rex Stockton
Leann Terry
Indiana University

Dan-Bush Bhusumane
University of Botswana

In This Chapter

▶ *History of Group Counseling*
- Theoretical Influences
- Uses of Groups
- Ethical and Legal Considerations

▶ *Fundamentals of Group Work*
- Definition of Group Work
- Types of Group Work
- Group Member Activities
- Leader Interventions

▶ *Group Dynamics*
- Group Processing
- Group Conflict
- Group Cohesiveness
- Therapeutic Factors in Groups
- Group Typology

▶ *Group Leadership*
- Leadership Styles
- Group Leader Attributes
- A Framework for Intervention
- Concerns of Beginning Group Leaders
- Coleadership

▶ *Cultural Considerations for Group Leaders*
- Influences on Diversity
- Non-Western Values in Group Work

- Characteristics of Culturally Competent Leaders
- Benefits of Multicultural Awareness

▶ *Pregroup Planning*
- Logistics
- Site Considerations
- Defining the Group's Purpose
- Selection of Members

▶ *Beginning Phase*
- Structure
- Group Norms
- Role of the Leader in the Beginning Phase
- Goal Setting
- Feedback in the Beginning Phase

▶ *Middle Phase*
- Conflict in the Middle Phase
- Group Interactions
- Role of the Leader in the Middle Phase
- Feedback in the Middle Phase

▶ *Final Phase*
- Final Phase Resistance
- Generalization of Learning
- Role of the Leader in the Final Phase

HISTORY OF GROUP COUNSELING

In 1905, Joseph Pratt inadvertently started the counseling group when he brought patients together who suffered from an infectious disease (Gazda, Ginter, & Horne, 2001). His intention was to save time by not seeing each patient individually. These groups, however, turned into a valuable addition to typical treatment due to their interpersonal focus and support (Hadden, 1955). Pratt's group intervention generally is thought of as the start of formal group counseling, which today is set up for specific therapeutic purposes.

■ Theoretical Influences

Over the years, group work has evolved in several dimensions and through various theoretical approaches. The development of group work has been influenced by theoretical contributions from psychoanalysis to psychodrama and by methodologies ranging from empirical to anecdotal (Barlow, Fuhriman, & Burlingame, 2004). The work of social psychologists such as Lewin (1951) and his students also have had an impact on the development of group work. Social psychologists' interest in group work has cycled through various levels of interest, but it always has been one of the foci in the discipline. Since this original inception of group work, the field has grown tremendously and several professional societies have formed to support group therapy.

Professional Organizations for Group Work

- American Psychological Association, Group Psychology and Group Psychotherapy (Division 49).
- American Society of Group Psychotherapy and Psychodrama.
- American Group Psychotherapy Association.
- Association for Specialists in Group Work (ASGW).

✓ Check out these Web sites from the APA, the American Society of Group Psychotherapy and Psychodrama, the American Group Psychotherapy Association, and the ASGW:

  ▶ www.apa49.org
  ▶ www.agpa.org
  ▶ www.asgpp.org
  ▶ www.asgw.org

◼ Uses of Groups

Since Pratt's time, the use of groups has expanded exponentially into a wide range of populations, problems, and settings. As a testament to the wide application of groups, the *Handbook of Group Counseling and Psychotherapy* (DeLucia-Waack, Gerrity, Kalodner, & Riva, 2004) discusses in depth more than 32 types of therapeutic groups, including specialized approaches for different cultural groups, settings, client difficulties, and client demographics. For example, task groups increasingly are used in industries and large governmental organizations; Forsyth (1998) stated that 80% of large organizations use group work. With the demonstrated efficacy, efficiency, and applicability of therapeutic groups and with the advent of managed care, it is reasonable to conclude that groups will continue to be a major mode of counseling and psychotherapy.

◼ Ethical and Legal Considerations

Rapin (2004) stated, "One of the defining tenets of a profession is that it has a code of ethics" (p. 151). Ethical guidelines that normally correspond with the law (although not in every case) are considered to be the province of the respective professional organization. However, it is not unusual for courts of law to be guided by the published code of ethics from the relevant professional organization.

In the case of counselors, the relevant organization is the ACA with its *Code of Ethics and Standards of Practice* (ACA, 2005a). Just as in any other form of counseling, ethical and legal considerations in group work are extremely important. Indeed, the unique nature of groups, in which therapists work with multiple clients, makes ethical and legal considerations all the more crucial. Each state has its own laws concerning practice, and it is the responsibility of the practitioner to be familiar with those laws. The group work division of ACA, the ASGW (2000), offers guidelines that assist in the training of group leaders in a document entitled *Professional Standards for the Training of Group Workers*.

See Chapter 2 for more on ethics in counseling.

FUNDAMENTALS OF GROUP WORK

The impact that groups have on human beings is tremendous. Even in an individualistically oriented society such as the United States, groups serve important functions. Whether people gather in informal groups for purposes such as exercising, celebrating special occasions, and grieving, or in formal groups such as mental health agencies, schools, and a large variety of other organizations, groups serve as a means of satisfying the need people have to feel accepted and part of a larger community.

■ Definition of Group Work

The ASGW (2000) defined group work in the following way:

> **Group work:** A broad professional practice involving the application of knowledge and skill in group facilitation to assist people in reaching mutual goals, which may be intrapersonal, interpersonal, or work-related.

In addition to providing professional counselors with an understanding of group work, the ASGW also outlined some basic goals of group work, as listed next.

Goals of Group Work (ASGW, 2000)

- Accomplishment of work-related tasks.
- Education.
- Personal development.
- Personal and interpersonal problem solving.
- Remediation of mental and emotional disorders.

■ Types of Group Work

There have been a number of attempts to classify types of professional group work. Perhaps the most relevant and widely accepted classification is the division of group work into four specific areas: task, psychoeducational, counseling, and psychotherapeutic groups. A brief description of these groups based on the ASGW (2000) definitions follows.

Four Classifications of Group Work

1. Task groups are used to accomplish group tasks and goals.
2. Psychoeducational groups are based on educational and developmental strategies and often are used for personal growth to prevent future difficulties.
3. Counseling groups promote personal and interpersonal methods for growth and often use a here-and-now interactional focus.
4. Psychotherapeutic groups focus on personal and interpersonal difficulties similar to counseling groups and also can be used to address dysfunctional behavior and cognitive distortions.

These four categories are not mutually exclusive, and, at times, there is considerable overlap in the problems addressed, populations served, group leadership styles, skills, interventions, and strategies used for each type of group.

■ Group Member Activities

Stockton and Toth (2000) described effective counseling groups as providing members with a number of important experiences, opportunities for exploring the activities of life, and the chance to learn authentic ways of relating. In effective groups, members engage in basic but necessary activities.

Common Group Member Tasks

- Meet other members.
- Share their lives.
- Learn about rules for membership.
- Learn to trust and confront one another.
- Share a variety of feelings.
- Say goodbye.

■ Leader Interventions

Basic therapeutic skills used in individual counseling are also important for counselors who engage in group work. These skills include, but are not limited to the following:

- Active listening.
- Reflection.
- Clarification.
- Summarizing.
- Questioning.
- Paraphrasing.

However useful these are, they are not the only interventions available to group leaders. Because of the nature of groups, a variety of other tasks need to be considered by group leaders.

GROUP DYNAMICS

The dynamics of groups are ever evolving; they have a substantial impact on group members and represent the interdependence among all members in a group. Marcus (1998) described group dynamics this way:

Group dynamics: The way "in which the members interact with each other and mutually influence one another's perceptions and behavior" (p. 230).

Two concepts that are fundamental to a discussion about group dynamics are content and process. Understanding the difference between content and process is an important task of counselors who work as group leaders. The distinction has been described by Yalom (1995) this way:

> **Group content:** The words that are spoken between individuals in a group.

> **Group process:** "Nature of the relationship between interacting individuals" (p. 130).

Working with content and process, leaders focus on the relationship between members, or the *process,* as well as what is directly said, or the *content,* that might influence the relationship. In addition to referring to content and process, the umbrella concept of group dynamics encompasses a number of other key ideas in the study and practice of group work; these are addressed in this section.

■ Group Processing

It is important to differentiate the group process from the act of processing that occurs in group. The content and process of the group provide fodder for the processing, which usually is facilitated by the leader. Ward and Litchy (2004) described the activity of processing this way:

> **Processing:** "[A]n activity in which individuals and groups regularly examine and reflect upon their behavior in order to extract meaning, integrate the resulting knowledge, and thereby improve functioning and outcome" (p. 104).

Although processing may be a spontaneous intervention, it is always a purposeful attempt to derive meaning from the group. Stockton, Morran, and Nitza (2000) described a "cognitive map" for processing that contains four interrelated steps.

Cognitive Map for Processing

1. Identify critical incidents that are important to the group members.
2. Examine the event and the group member reactions.
3. Derive meaning and self-understanding from the event.
4. Apply the new understandings for personal change outside the group.

■ Group Conflict

According to Boulding (1962), conflict is found in almost all situations of life and, "in an actual conflict situation, then, there must be awareness, and there must also be incompatible wishes or desires" (p. 6). Thus, group leaders should not be surprised that conflict inevitably occurs, but, rather, should use their skills to manage the conflict so it can be used for the benefit of the group.

■ Group Cohesiveness

When members begin to feel like they are a part of the group and want to remain in the group, they are more likely to overcome any potential conflict and other issues that might motivate members to drop out. Given the complexity of cohesion in a group, the leader's role is crucial in understanding, balancing, and facilitating the development of cohesion.

> **Group cohesiveness:** The attractiveness of a group to the members that can be developed between individual group members, between the member and the group, and between the members and the group leader (Burlingame, Fuhriman, & Johnson, 2001).

■ Therapeutic Factors in Groups

Understanding the factors that help people develop as a result of therapeutic groups is exceedingly important. Yalom (1975, 1985, 1995), the premier figure in therapeutic factor theory and research, and a number of others (e.g., Crouch, Bloch, & Wanlass, 1994; Kivlighan & Mullison, 1988; MacKenzie, 1987) have tackled the subject of therapeutic factors in groups. Bloch and Crouch (1985) provided a useful definition of a therapeutic factor:

> **Therapeutic factor:** "[A]n element of group therapy that contributes to improvement in a patient's condition and is a function of the actions of the group therapist, the group members, and the patient himself" (p. 4).

Throughout a group experience, the therapeutic factors take on more or less salience depending on the stage of the group's development. Yalom (1995) listed 11 therapeutic factors or elements that contribute to member improvement.

Therapeutic Factors in Group

1. Instillation of hope.
2. Universality.
3. Imparting information.
4. Altruism.
5. Corrective recapitulation of the primary family group.
6. Development of socializing techniques.
7. Imitative behavior.
8. Interpersonal learning.
9. Group cohesiveness.

10. Catharsis.
11. Existential factors.

Group Typology

Kivlighan and Holmes (2004), utilizing cluster analysis, analyzed numerous studies that focused on the importance of therapeutic factors and developed "a typology of groups based on their therapeutic mechanisms" (p. 26). The analysis resulted in two dimensions—affective/cognitive and support/insight—that emerge in groups and that operate to create four types of group experiences.

Four Typologies of Group Experiences (Kivlighan & Holmes, 2004)

1. Affective support.
2. Affective insight.
3. Cognitive support.
4. Cognitive insight.

GROUP LEADERSHIP

Achieving positive outcomes from group therapy relies in large part on the skills, style, and personality of the group leader. When skills, style, and personality of the leader are combined appropriately with the aims of the group, a helpful atmosphere is created for member growth.

Leadership Styles

Leadership is one of the most studied areas in social psychology. It has implications for all who work with groups, whether they are military psychologists who are concerned with group dynamics at the squad level, organizational psychologists who focus on understanding how to make groups more effective in large organizations, or, more relevant to our purpose, counselors and researchers who wish to understand therapeutic small group leadership.

According to Napier and Gershenfeld (1993), leadership style simply is another word for "a collection of behaviors in a particular situation" (p. 241). In therapeutic group work the task is for members freely to discuss their concerns. To do this, they must feel secure enough to risk telling others their inner thoughts and concerns. Thus, leaders need to tailor their behaviors to the task.

One of the most quoted, as well as replicated, classic leadership research studies was conducted by Lewin, Lippitt, and White (1939) who investigated the effect of different styles of leadership on the social climate of three groups of 10-year-old boys in a camp setting. The leadership styles were divided into three categories.

Types of Leadership Styles (Lewin et al., 1939)

- Autocratic.
- Democratic.
- Laissez faire.

The study demonstrated major differences in the members' ability to deal effectively with a number of issues, most prominently stress. The democratic style clearly was best suited for the situation.

In yet another classic study directly related to counseling groups, Lieberman, Yalom, and Miles (1973) examined different leadership styles used in college student personal growth groups. The four styles of leadership were:

- Executive function (limit setting, time management, establishment of norms).
- Emotional stimulation (facilitation of expression of feelings and personal beliefs).
- Caring (demonstration of warmth and concern for group members).
- Meaning attribution (interpretation and providing framework for change processes).

Results of the study indicated that the most effective leaders are "moderate in stimulation, high in caring, utilize meaning-attribution, and are moderate in expression of executive functions" (Lieberman et al., 1973, p. 240). Readers will find a wealth of information on leadership styles in a variety of texts, including the *Handbook of Group Counseling and Psychotherapy* (DeLucia-Waack, Gerrity, et al., 2004).

■ Group Leader Attributes

Corey and Corey (2006) identified characteristics of group leaders that contribute to positive group experiences.

Effective Group Leader Attributes

- Courage.
- Willingness to model.
- Presence.
- Goodwill, genuineness, and caring.
- Belief in the group process.
- Openness.
- Nondefensiveness in coping with criticism.
- Self-awareness.

■ A Framework for Intervention

Stockton developed a tripartite framework for effective group leadership (Morran, 1992). The three dimensions are described next.

Dimensions of Effective Group Leadership

1. *Perceiving* refers to understanding the processes of the group, acquiring counseling group training, and possessing general human development knowledge.
2. *Selecting* refers to choosing appropriate interventions from a repertoire of possibilities.
3. *Risking* refers to having the courage to intervene even when there is the potential for less than successful results.

■ Concerns of Beginning Group Leaders

Novice group leaders usually are concerned about what will happen if no one talks and wonder how they will handle silence. Conversely, some novice leaders worry about what they will do with members who dominate the discussion or become confrontational. Some leaders may worry about actual physical violence.

EXAMPLE

Responding to Beginning Leaders' Fears

To respond to the trepidations of beginning group leaders or leaders in training, one can ask leaders at the beginning of a workshop or class, to make a list of their fears about group leadership. Typically, there is a great deal of universality in their fears that can be discussed. When the catastrophic fears are known, they can then be exorcized by having the leaders simulate anxiety-provoking situations, which detoxifies the expectations. The use of role play and simulations is one of the most powerful training techniques.

■ Coleadership

Coleaders are professionals who share the responsibility of facilitating a group experience. This approach to leadership offers many benefits, a few of which are listed here.

Benefits of Coleadership

- Beginning group leaders can learn from being paired with a more experienced leader.
- The knowledge, skills, and capabilities of two leaders are available to the group.
- Group members have a greater chance of being compatible with one of the leaders (Jacobs, Masson, & Harvill, 2002).
- The group can be more efficient and continue to run even if one leader is not present.

Although there are a number of benefits of coleadership to facilitators and members, there are also potential challenges worth mentioning.

Challenges of Coleadership

- Leaders may have different ways of resolving group differences (Riva, Wachtel, & Lasky, 2004).
- Different styles of leadership from the coleaders, such as one focusing on the process and the other focusing on content, can lead to tension and frustration in the group (Jacobs et al., 2002).

To deal with the challenges of coleadership, facilitators might want to interview each other before the group begins to identify their intrapersonal strengths and weaknesses and to share with each other their approaches to group counseling.

Research demonstrates that the relationship between the coleaders influences their effectiveness as a team (Okech & Kline, 2005). Thus, Okech and Kline encouraged coleaders to discuss their relationship, perceptions, and experiences of each other throughout the course of the therapeutic group. Supervisors can be particularly helpful in assisting coleaders to discuss their working relationship.

CULTURAL CONSIDERATIONS FOR GROUP LEADERS

There is a growing body of literature associating self-awareness with counselor effectiveness because it calls leaders to broaden their understanding of multicultural and diversity issues. In this section, we address a number of issues relevant to multiculturalism in group work.

■ Influences on Diversity

Culturally competent group leaders appreciate diversity and the difficulties associated with dealing with people from other cultures and cultural backgrounds (Sue & Sue, 1990). Cultural competence is necessary even when working with clients from the same culture because of differences related to subcultures (Vontress &

Jackson, 2004). Literature on multicultural counseling attributes cultural differences to a number of factors that play a role in the therapist–client relationship and, likewise, in the effectiveness of therapy (Goh, 2005).

Factors Associated With Cultural Differences

- Social orientation.
- Ethnicity.
- Race.
- Gender.
- Economic status.
- Social status.
- Family orientation.
- Sexual orientation.
- Religious affiliation.
- Spirituality.
- Language.
- Communication systems.
- Individual qualities.
- Mental and physical challenges.

■ Non-Western Values in Group Work

In group work, differences in traditional Western beliefs and non-Western values likely are to be found in communication styles, perception of power relations, concept of time, and other behaviors. These differences challenge the appropriateness of using the Western worldview as a yardstick for all acceptable behaviors. According to Pope (1999), various studies describe individualistic cultures as supporting winning in competition, achievement, freedom, autonomy, fair exchange, and challenging authority. Morris and Robinson (1996) argued that a critical examination of the traditionally accepted views may assist professionals in providing enhanced counseling experiences to members of diverse populations. Some of the non-Western ideals of which group leaders should be aware are listed here.

Common Non-Western Values

- Interdependence.
- Simplicity.
- Obedience.
- Hierarchy.
- Duty.
- Group survival.
- Nonlinearity of time.

- Group welfare.
- Family.
- Community.

Characteristics of Culturally Competent Leaders

Effective group leaders strive for cultural competence by developing expertise in handling multicultural and diversity issues (Goh, 2005). As the need for cultural competence continues to occupy center stage in group work, counselors face the challenge of learning new skills that enhance their cultural effectiveness and appropriateness in responding to experiences of group members. The following qualities define culturally competent group leaders.

Qualities of Culturally Competent Group Leaders

- Strive for self-awareness of personal assumptions about human behavior, biases, values, beliefs, and cultural heritage.
- Appreciate that one's worldview and that of the client inevitably are different.
- Acknowledge one's tendencies and views about other cultures and value the importance of acquiring sufficient knowledge about possible barriers to participation, family systems, and cultural practices of the members.
- Have the right attitude in terms of respect for members' religious beliefs, cultural values, and communication styles.
- Respect the different ways in which individuals and people from diverse cultures express feelings (Ivey & Ivey, 2003).
- Have training to work with cultural diversity and know when to individualize and generalize about characteristics of a client's cultural group, thereby developing a culture-specific expertise (Goh, 2005).
- Possess a working knowledge of members' cultures and reflect appreciation of the client's cultural experience and background.
- Use culturally relevant and appropriate intervention strategies (Sue & Sue, 1990).
- Exhibit openness to multiple methods or approaches to group facilitation and recognize that one's facilitation styles and approaches may be culture-bound.
- Anticipate and ameliorate the negative impact a culture-bound facilitation style may have by drawing on other culturally relevant skill sets (ASGW, 1998b).

For more on characteristics of multiculturally competent group workers, see Chapter 14.

Benefits of Multicultural Awareness

There are significant benefits of cultural competence in leading a group. A University of Notre Dame Counseling Center (2003) Web page lists the following benefits of becoming multiculturally aware.

Benefits of Cultural Competence to the Group Leader

- Increased self-awareness.
- Increased awareness of other cultures.
- Improved interpersonal communication.
- Improved likelihood of making appropriate interventions on stereotyping and prejudices.
- Increased openness to emotionally charged issues.
- Enhanced sensitivity to others' experiences.
- Minimized imposition of ones' own values and beliefs.
- Increased ability to promote living effectively in a diverse world.

Group members, especially those from a different cultural background, are likely to welcome the leader's interest in and appreciation for their culture. Cultural appreciation is only one of the benefits to members of a multicultually aware leader. Some of the other advantages to members include the following.

Benefits of Cultural Competence to Group Members

- Members feel safe and respected when their culture is appreciated.
- Members are likely to be able to forgive the leader when the leader makes honest mistakes in addressing their issues.
- Members are valued when leaders avoid stereotyping and instead highlight their uniqueness regardless of cultural backgrounds (Vontress & Jackson, 2004).

See Chapter 14 for more on multiculturalism in group work.

PREGROUP PLANNING

Before meeting with group members, leaders need to do preliminary planning. Dealing with basic logistics and site considerations, defining the purpose of the group, and selecting participants are some important tasks that leaders have to face in the preparation phase.

■ Logistics

Before any group begins to meet, the leader must address logistical issues. Seeking and receiving the required administrative approvals is one such issue that must be navigated. Administrators and other colleagues (e.g., nurses on a ward; teachers, counselors, and other nonteaching personnel in a school; or agency personnel) should know about the group and, more important, believe in the benefits offered.

In any organization, it is easy to hinder a good effort when individuals do not support the group as an important tool in responding to the needs of the clients. Ensuring that administrators support the activity and know necessary details facilitates easier resolution if any problems or outside questions arise.

■ Site Considerations

Basic but essential to a successful group experience are commodities such as a pleasant room, comfortable chairs, and a temperate environment. Ensuring that the space is private and free from interruptions is also crucial and cannot be taken for granted. There are numerous horror tales where any one of these important factors have not been met and later resulted in an untherapeutic situation.

■ Defining the Group's Purpose

One of the most important tasks of a leader is to define the focus of the group. In some settings, that already is done for the leader. Whether the leader or a larger entity, such as an agency, defines the goal of the group, there must be a good match between the leader's experience, knowledge, and skills and the proposed group purpose.

■ Selection of Members

Pregroup preparation entails providing information to prospective group members about the nature of the group and the likely course of activities before the first group meeting. In addition to providing information to prospective members, the leader also must obtain information about the members, and in some cases, decide not to select certain individuals for the group. The ACA (2005a) *Code of Ethics* requires that group leaders "to the extent possible … select members whose needs and goals are compatible with the goals of the group, who will not impede the group process, and whose well-being will not be jeopardized by the group experience" (Section A.8). The importance of preparing group members for their experience has received a great deal of empirical attention. The periodic reviews of Bednar and Kaul (1978, 1994) have demonstrated the importance of this concept. Burlingame et al. (2001) included pregroup preparation as one of the principles of the therapeutic relationship that empirically has been supported.

BEGINNING PHASE

A number of individuals have articulated stages of group development (e.g., Borgatta & Bales, 1953; Hare & Naveh, 1984), but the classic theoretical formulation was proposed by Tuckman (1965), who identified four stages: forming, storming, norming, and performing. Tuckman and Jensen (1977) later added a fifth stage of adjourning, thus giving importance to the affect that the members feel and express at the end of a group. Tuckman (1965) provided a definition of these stages that counselors can use:

Forming: The initial stage during which members are getting to know each other, the group leader, and the group boundaries.

Storming: The stage of group work characterized by inevitable conflict, mild disagreements, and resistance that can have positive or negative implications.

Norming: The stage in group work when the members develop "ingroup feeling and cohesiveness ... new standards evolve, and new roles are adopted" (p. 396).

Performing: Period of group work when the members have reconciled many of their differences and have developed enough trust and cohesion to examine themselves and their relationship to the group. During this stage "roles become flexible and function, and group energy is channeled into the task" (p. 396).

Adjourning: Refers to the termination stage when members may feel a sense of loss and a need to make sense of what has happened in the group.

There is no clear line between the various stages; however, the stages present a useful, metaphorical way of understanding the development of groups.

The focus of this section on the beginning phase corresponds to Tuckman and Jensen's (1977) stages of forming, with some characteristics of storming and norming. Typically, group members and beginning leaders are anxious in the beginning phase. Thus, in the early stages of a group, universality and the instillation of hope are two of the more prevalent therapeutic factors (Kivlighan & Holmes, 2004). They can be understood as follows:

Universality: Group members come to understand that others have similar problems, and they are not alone in their dilemma.

Instillation of hope: Members have a sense of hope about receiving help and learning how to better deal with their problems.

■ Structure

The beginning of a group is a crucial time not only for working with the anxiety that likely is to be present, but also for setting the tone and establishing the therapeutic ground rules. One of the main tasks of the leader in response to the beginning group issues is to provide an optimum amount of structure. Riva et al. (2004) defined structure this way:

> **Structure:** "[E]ncompasses many different techniques and interventions that have as their primary goal the development and maintenance of a healthy therapeutic group" (p. 40).

Techniques or interventions that provide structure can involve simple guidelines such as when the group will start and stop; structure also can refer to the leaders' interventions that help people feel safe.

EXAMPLE

Research Considerations for Group Structure

There was a period of time, especially in the early 1960s, when some theoreticians believed that the structure of a group should evolve with minimal input from the leader. Whitaker and Lieberman (1964) hypothesized that for a natural group culture to emerge, clients should be allowed to have their issues surface without interference, which would include leader-structured activities. However, Bednar, Melnick, and Kaul (1974) demonstrated that leaders can safely and beneficially provide structure. Researchers later supported the conclusion that an optimum amount of structure provides a facilitative atmosphere, whereas too much structure can be detrimental because it arouses resistance (Stockton, Rohde, & Haughey, 1992).

■ Group Norms

One of the variety of ways that a leader can create structure is through norm setting. Every group establishes its own set of norms, some of which are formal and others of which are informal; a succinct definition of these terms is provided here:

> **Group norms:** Informal and formal beliefs about group behavior, such as language, attendance, confidentiality, degree of self-disclosure, punctuality, content shared, and processes, expected to occur (Corey & Corey, 2001; Stockton & Toth, 2000).

> **Informal norms:** Group norms that influence individuals without the individuals necessarily being able to communicate the existence of the norms.

> **Formal norms:** Group norms that are communicated and agreed on.

Norms are the "rules of the game" (Stockton & Toth, 2000) established both by the members and the leaders of groups. The role of the leader in facilitating therapeutic norms at the beginning of any group experience, however, is extremely important.

One set of norms that leaders must address, for example, has to do with confidentiality. Establishing norms about confidentiality helps create structure and safety, both of which are important in the beginning phase of a group. A few generalizations about norms related to confidentiality are noted here.

Norm of Confidentiality

- The norm of confidentiality must be made explicit with the group members.
- Rather than instructing members to maintain confidentiality, the leader has to enlist their support in facilitating an understanding about why confidentiality is needed.
- Although the norm of confidentiality is established best through group discussion and consensus, the leader shapes this process by initiating and making his or her position clear.

E X A M P L E

Creating Appropriate Norms for the Setting

Students in a graduate classroom usually take their seats with a minimum of disruption and wait for the instructor to initiate a lecture or discussion. The same behavior would not be the norm for a group of small children entering a first-grade classroom. These both are examples of informal or implicit norms that reflect their own sense of appropriateness and their interpretations of societal expectations.

■ Role of the Leader in the Beginning Phase

In the beginning phase of groups, members have to feel safe before they can talk freely, and they need to be energized to share. The important aspects of leadership during the initial period are related directly to these member needs. Some of these are provided here.

Tasks of Group Leaders in the Beginning Phase

- Leaders work with the members to form a therapeutic milieu and establish optimum structure that encourages members to discuss issues.
- Leaders facilitate an environment of safety and encouragement so that members can feel secure in examining themselves freely and at their own pace.
- Leaders facilitate the process of members getting to know each other, by providing a structure that allows group members to feel relaxed and to begin talking about themselves in a safe way.

- Leaders use the intervention known as **protecting,** which is intended to protect the member from too much self-disclosure and subsequent feelings of regret, as well as pressure from others in the group to reveal more than that with which they may be comfortable.

Goal Setting

During the beginning sessions of a group, an important task for members is setting personal goals related to what they want to gain from the group experience. Especially in organizational literature (Locke & Latham, 1990; Mento, Steele, & Karren, 1987), research has found that task performance is increased when clear and challenging goals have been set. Discussion for goal setting can revolve around why the member is in the group and what he or she requires for making progress (Stockton & Toth, 2000). When a group member struggles with setting goals, the leader can paraphrase and narrow the focus of the member's goal as a way to operationalize the desired change.

Feedback in the Beginning Phase

Feedback is a very important part of therapeutic groups. The following is a definition of feedback that counselors can adopt:

> **Feedback:** A group member or leader's shared observations and reactions to another member's expressed feelings, thoughts, or behaviors.

Leaders help members understand the value of feedback by modeling appropriate feedback, which is especially important in the beginning stages of a group. A functional group has members who actively interact and provide feedback to each other and does not rely solely on a leader to give feedback to members. Initially, positive feedback is a useful technique to reinforce appropriate behavior. Corrective feedback is better accepted in the later stages of a group or sandwiched between two positive feedback statements (Morran, Stockton, Cline, & Teed, 1998).

MIDDLE PHASE

The middle period of a group corresponds to Tuckman's (1965) phases of storming and performing and also is considered the transition or working stage of a group. There are numerous characteristics of a group in the working stage.

Characteristics of a Group in the Working Stage

- Member-to-member interactions increase.
- Group members self-disclose more often and at a deeper level.
- Interpersonal feedback is appropriate and valued by the members.
- Members develop insight and create meaning from the process as they reflect on their experience.

■ Conflict in the Middle Phase

Storming is characterized by conflict between the members or directed toward the leader. The level of conflict ranges greatly depending on the situation and the personality of the individuals. How a group uses conflict influences whether it is viewed either positively or negatively. However, conflict in this phase can be thought of as inevitable in a freely evolving group. Indeed, it is very difficult for groups to move forward into a performing (working) phase without resolving conflicts.

The leader has a key role in facilitating the resolution of conflict. When done therapeutically, the resolution of conflict has a number of positive outcomes.

Outcomes of Positively Resolved Conflict

- Members learn to be more trusting of each other.
- Cohesion is strengthened.
- Members are better able to examine their values and concerns (Stockton & Toth, 2000).
- Members come to understand that disagreement is tolerated, and they still are accepted as valuable members of the group, even if they disagree with others.

■ Group Interactions

Interactions are especially important in therapeutic groups, where the task primarily is to examine oneself in relation to others. Thus, one of the leader's major tasks is to facilitate member-to-member interaction. When conflict is resolved appropriately, the members develop the cohesiveness and trust to risk sharing personal disclosures. Interactions among group members promote the development of facilitative relationships, a crucial ingredient for the efficacy of group work (Dies, 1983). Ideally, as the group develops, the members begin interacting with other members, and the leader plays a lesser role in the interactions. In this way, the group leaders facilitate interactions between members to foster the development of the necessary therapeutic factors (Yalom, 1995).

■ Role of the Leader in the Middle Phase

Some useful techniques that help group leaders to further interaction among group members are linking, drawing out, and blocking.

Linking: An intervention used by group leaders to connect the concerns or behaviors of one member with those of one or more other members (Morran, Stockton, & Whittingham, 2004).

Drawing out: The leader invites group members who find it difficult to share or who only share at a superficial level to participate at a level of involvement of the member's own choosing (Morran et al., 2004). It is important for the leader to identify possible reasons for a member's silence before deciding to intervene (Morran et al., 2004).

Blocking: "[A] specific type of protection that is used to stop a member from storytelling, rambling, or otherwise talking in a manner that runs counter to the purposes of the group" (Morran et al., 2004, p. 94). Blocking also can be used to stop members from scapegoating another member. A small hand gesture can serve to block a member from continuing without adding undue embarrassment.

In addition to using the interventions such as linking, drawing out, and blocking, group leaders will focus their attention on processing the group dynamics. Through the activity of processing, leaders "capitalize on significant happenings in the here-and-now interactions of the group to help members reflect on the meaning of their experience; better understand their own thoughts, feelings, and actions; and generalize what is learned to their life outside the group" (Stockton et al., 2000, p. 345).

■ Feedback in the Middle Phase

Feedback in the middle phase takes a different slant than in the beginning stages of a group. Leaders help members to give and receive more constructive feedback. Leaders guide members to provide feedback that reflects other characteristics that promote growth and self-reflection.

Characteristics of Feedback in the Working Stage (Stockton & Toth, 2000)

- Feedback should be relevant to members' individual goals.
- Feedback should reflect how members behave in the group.
- Feedback should deal with what members say about their actions outside the group to create a connection between insight into themselves and their personal growth within and outside the group.
- Feedback should help members learn more about themselves and how they are perceived by others.

FINAL PHASE

The final phases of group work are Tuckman and Jensen's (1977) stages of performing and adjourning. Leader and member tasks during this phase focus on summing up the learning of the group experience and saying goodbye.

■ Final Phase Resistance

To the degree that the group has played a meaningful role in the members' lives, they will experience loss at the conclusion of the group. One notable reaction to the loss is resistance, which may manifest in members reverting to earlier, maladaptive behavior. Leaders need to recognize and accept the resistance as well as process it to help the group make sense of their experience and to understand the inevitability of the end of the group.

Approaches to Dealing With Loss and Resistance

- Help members learn how to mourn and experience their sadness.
- Create an opportunity for members to talk about what they wished they had accomplished but did not accomplish.
- Honor what members have learned and can carry on in the future.
- Assist members in a process of letting go, as well as looking forward to new experiences.

■ Generalization of Learning

Generalization of learning is the summing up and making meaning of the learning that has taken place and how it can be applied to life outside the group. Transferring new knowledge, skills, and behaviors outside the group is a key process for the group members. Thus, the leader's task is to help the members discuss what they have learned and how they might use it beyond the life of the therapeutic group. In this way, a bridge to the future is constructed. Although the generalization of learning is particularly important to the final phase, it is also facilitative to engage members in such reflection at various points throughout the life of the group.

■ Role of the Leader in the Final Phase

The primary task of the leader in the termination or adjourning stage is to help the members make meaning of the experience. One intervention that assists leaders in this task is the go around.

Go around: A procedure during which members are asked either spontaneously or sequentially to discuss what they learned, what they wish they had accomplished but did not, and how they will use their new knowledge in the future.

To assist in the expression of feelings regarding the termination of a group, the leader may make a self-disclosure, which occurs when "therapists reveal their personal feelings, experiences, and here-and-now reactions to group members" (Morran et al., 2004, p. 98). They can share their reactions to what is happening in the group, model how to deal directly with conflict, or help members understand more about how they are perceived in a group. It is important to evaluate the purpose of a self-disclosure and to observe the group members' reactions afterward for a follow-up assessment. Leaders always must remember that the purpose of the group is to work on members' issues, not those of the leader. Any self-disclosure that does not facilitate this is self-serving and therefore not helpful.

In summary, group leaders do well to be aware of the characteristics of Tuckman's (1965) stages of group therapy to effectively lead counseling and psychotherapeutic groups. A grasp of other, key concepts that comprise the foundation of group interactions (e.g., group dynamics, processing, multicultural components, etc.) also is required of all good group leaders.

Chapter 13: Key Terms

- Group work
- Group dynamics
- Group content
- Group process
- Processing
- Group cohesiveness
- Therapeutic factor
- Forming

- Storming
- Norming
- Performing
- Adjourning
- Universality
- Instillation of hope
- Structure
- Group norms

- Informal norms
- Formal norms
- Protecting
- Feedback
- Linking
- Drawing out
- Blocking
- Go around

Multicultural Components of Group Work

Sherlon P. Pack-Brown
Bowling Green State University

In This Chapter

▶ *History of Multicultural Group Work*
  ▪ Goals of Group Work
  ▪ Culture and Group Work
  ▪ Multicultural Group Work Defined
  ▪ Multicultural Group Work and Ethical Practice

▶ *Core Competencies of Multicultural Group Work*
  ▪ Individual Competencies of Multicultural Group Workers
  ▪ Principles for Diversity-Competent Group Workers

▶ *Theory and Multicultural Group Work*
  ▪ Diversity and Multicultural Framework
  ▪ Failure to Recognize Diversity Issues in Theory
  ▪ Flexibility to Operate Within Multicultural Worldviews

▶ *Assessment and Group Ideologies*
  ▪ Assessment in Multicultural Group Work
  ▪ Process of Assessment
  ▪ Delivery of Assessment Decisions
  ▪ Communication Styles
  ▪ Thematic Communication in Assessment
  ▪ Individual and Cultural Values in Assessment

▶ *A Diversity-Competent Model of Multicultural Group Work*
  ▪ How to Choose a Model of Multicultural Group Work
  ▪ Images of Me: An Afrocentric Approach to Group Work

HISTORY OF MULTICULTURAL GROUP WORK

This chapter is intended to be a resource for group leaders by addressing the competencies of multicultural group work and offering a model sympathetic to multicultural group work. The foci will be (a) the history of group work, (b) core competencies, (c) culturally intentional assessment, and (d) a diversity-competent model of group work.

■ Goals of Group Work

Group work emerged to address the shortcomings of individual counseling. Three central aims of group work were and continue to be:

1. Sharing experiences among group members.
2. Bringing issues to the surface.
3. Building trust as group members collectively work to accomplish life tasks.

■ Culture and Group Work

Although the primary intentions of group work have remained the same over time, the process has evolved. Today, the culture and worldview of the leaders and members are recognized as important factors in successful group work. The terms *culture* and *worldview* can be defined in this way:

> **Culture:** A combination of learned behaviors, thoughts, and beliefs as well as the results of learned behaviors, thoughts, and beliefs whose components and elements are shared and transmitted by the members of a particular society.

> **Worldview:** A group worker's or member's presuppositions and assumptions about the makeup of her or his world.

More and more, researchers, scholars, and clinicians are giving voice to issues of multiculturalism and their effect on group process, dynamics, and training (Delucia-Waack & Donigian, 2004; Pack-Brown & Fleming, 2004). Professional associations, too, recognize the impact of culture on group work. The ASGW (1999), in the Preamble to its *Principles for Diversity Competent Group Workers*, stated its commitment to understand how issues of diversity affect all aspects of group work.

ASGW (1999) Areas of Commitment to Diversity in Group Work

- Training diversity-competent group workers.
- Leading research efforts into group work with diverse populations.
- Understanding how diversity affects group process and dynamics.

- Assisting group facilitators to increase their awareness, knowledge, and skills as they work with groups of diverse membership.

Multicultural Group Work Defined

Among the body of literature addressing group work, a solid definition of the practice of multicultural group work is lacking (DeLucia-Waack & Donigian, 2004; Pack-Brown & Fleming, 2004).

Factors Limiting an Understanding of Multicultural Group Work

- Traditional literature regarding group approaches has been slow to emphasize theoretical and assessment standards established with a select group of client characteristics, such as multiculturalism, diversity, and culture.
- Counseling professionals have diverse definitions of key terminology, such as multicultural, the meaning of which can vary depending on context.

In this chapter, the word *multicultural* emphasizes race and ethnicity, but also includes other human differences, such as age, gender, and sexual orientation. In spite of limiting factors, a definition of multicultural group work is offered here:

> **Multicultural group work:** The expansion of personal and group consciousness of "self-in-relation" by providing intentional, competent, and ethical helping behaviors that promote the mental health of group members.

Multicultural Group Work and Ethical Practice

Recent trends reflect the multicultural revolution to the degree that professional associations are updating their codes of ethics and standards of practice to guide group work professionals in this direction.

Multicultural Group Work in ACA Ethical Codes and ASGW Ethical Guidelines

- Section A.8.b. of the ACA (2005a) *Code of Ethics* states that in a group setting, counselors take reasonable precautions to protect clients from physical, emotional, or psychological trauma.
- Section 8.a., Equitable Treatment, in the ASGW Ethical Guidelines for Group Counselors states that group counselors recognize and respect differences (e.g., cultural, racial, religious, lifestyle, age, disability, gender) among group members (Capuzzi & Gross, 1992).

Although the ACA code is less explicit than the ASGW guidelines, the standard for group workers can be interpreted through a cultural lens. Given the inherent nature of culture to behavior, worldviews, and life experiences, group workers can understand Standard A.8.b. to mean that counselors use their cultural sensitivities as a tool to assist them in taking reasonable precautions to protect clients from physical, emotional, or psychological trauma.

The ethical guidelines of the ASGW are more explicit; group workers are encouraged to behave in a culturally intentional and ethical manner not only by recognizing but also by respecting diversity within the group setting to provide equitable treatment of all group members.

CORE COMPETENCIES OF MULTICULTURAL GROUP WORK

Multicultural group workers are guided by competencies that provide a basis for meeting group expectations and facilitating group process in the most professional manner possible. Applied to multicultural group work, competency can be defined this way:

> **Multicultural group worker competency:** A framework used by group workers to anchor group goals, expectations, and processes that support and promote culturally relevant and sensitive group work.

■ Individual Competencies of Multicultural Group Workers

As they prepare for, lead, and evaluate groups, culturally competent group workers look beyond their own worldview and value system to those of their clients by asking questions such as, "Through whose lens am I looking?" They recognize characteristics of multicultural group work that will help them facilitate effective process and dynamics.

Characteristics of Multicultural Group Workers

- Aware of personal biases, stereotypes, and prejudices that will affect their leadership.
- Knowledgeable of the cultural values, life experiences, and worldviews of group members.
- Skilled at identifying interventions that are more in line with the cultural purview of group members.

■ Principles for Diversity-Competent Group Workers

The 1999 *Principles for Diversity-Competent Group Workers* established by the ASGW serve a multitude of purposes, including helping group workers enhance their ability to be attentive to group members' verbal and nonverbal expressions and to factor in cultural connotations undergirding their communication. This ability is a skill that competent group workers exhibit. Competency, as outlined in the 1999 *Principles,* addresses not only the area of skill, but those of personal awareness and knowledge as well.

Awareness Competencies

- Diversity-competent group workers engage in activities to enhance personal awareness, knowledge, and skill of multicultural group work.
- Group workers reflect a high level of comfort in acknowledging the influence of realities, such as racial, ethnic, and cultural heritage; gender; socioeconomic status; sexual orientation; and religious and spiritual beliefs on group process and dynamics.
- Group workers are willing to value and respect (rather than ignore) differences among group members and between group workers and group members.

Knowledge Competencies

- Diversity-competent group workers are knowledgeable of the multicultural populations comprising their groups.
- Group leaders have knowledge of the thematic (common) life experiences, cultural heritage, and sociopolitical backgrounds of the members comprising their groups.
- Group workers possess information about identity development and subsequent effects on group process and dynamics in areas such as sexual orientation and physical, mental, emotional, and learning disabilities.

Skill Competencies

- Diversity-competent group workers offer a variety of verbal and nonverbal helping behaviors that parallel the diversity and development of group members.
- Leaders send and receive verbal and nonverbal messages within a culturally accurate context.
- Group leaders are not limited to one group approach and recognize that helping approaches may be culture bound.

Of significance is that group workers appreciate that diversity competencies, as a framework for securing group goals, expectations, and processes, are shaped by theory. That is, the facts, propositions, and principles analyzed in relation to each other and used to explain group work not only shape the competencies but also provide directives for performance. The skills and attributes inherent to the competencies are guided by theory.

Check out the Web site for the Association for Multicultural Counseling and Development for more information on diversity in counseling practice.

▶ http://www.bgsu.edu/colleges/edhd/programs/AMCD/

THEORY AND MULTICULTURAL GROUP WORK

Over the years, theoretical foundations for group work have been developed and tested. Until recently, few theories or theorists decisively have included culture in their theoretical tenets or considered the influence of cultural beliefs, values, life experiences, and worldviews on assessment and treatment.

■ Diversity and Multicultural Framework

Today group workers increasingly are directed to look at culture and the influence of both difference and similarity on group process and dynamics. Group workers operating within a multicultural framework embrace group work best practices related to diversity.

1998 ASGW Best Practice Guidelines on Diversity

- Group workers are sensitive to client differences, including but not limited to, ethnic, gender, religious, sexual, psychological maturity, economic class, family history, physical characteristics or limitations, and geographic location.
- Group workers become informed about the cultural issues of the diverse population with whom they are working, both by interaction with participants and from using outside resources.

One of the competencies outlined by the *Principles for Diversity-Competent Group Workers* (ASGW, 1999) is that a leader should be aware of the limits of a single theoretical approach to address the needs of all group members. In that vein, group workers should consider the following when choosing and evaluating theoretical approaches to group work.

Application of Multicultural Competencies to Group Theory

- Multiple worldviews exist among group members.
- Theories have underlying rules, ideas, principles, and techniques that may or may not be in line with those held in esteem by group members.
- Group workers must be able to discern how theory and practice merge within a cultural context and accept responsibility for aligning the values and world-

views of a theoretical orientation with those of group members to determine which theory and helping behaviors are more appropriate.

- Rather than being guided by one theoretical orientation, group workers investigate the accuracy of their theoretical approach by asking questions such as, "What are the cultural values of group members?" and "Are theoretical interventions commensurate with the cultural values of group members?"

■ Failure to Recognize Diversity Issues in Theory

Multiculturally competent group workers strive to appreciate the interrelatedness of traditional theory and culture and to understand that theories inherently rely on cultural values, assumptions, and worldviews to explain behavior and promote change. However, if group workers are insensitive to potential discrepancy between their espoused theoretical approach and the worldview of their clients, certain consequences may arise.

Implications of Insensitivity to Group Members' Worldview

- The group worker may unconsciously impose personal or theoretical values, beliefs, and attitudes on members.
- Group members holding a different worldview and value system may not be empowered to live life more fully.
- The group member(s) holding a different worldview and value system may physically or psychologically leave the group or get little to nothing from the group experience.

EXAMPLE

Person-Centered Approach From a Multicultural Framework

A group worker operating from a person-centered theoretical perspective is likely to be individualistically oriented and to operate from the assumption that group members should assume responsibility for their destinies and come to perceive "self" as a powerful change agent. Person-centered group process and dynamics, likewise, are guided by an individualistic worldview. Under the leadership of the person-centered group worker, members take control of their own lives to live life more fully by enhancing the member's self-concept and increasing their ability to see the power of the "self" to reach goals. If the group worker is facilitating a group comprised of diverse members and one or more of the members values a collectivistic worldview (i.e., "self-in-relation" approach to life), a leader may have to adjust his or her approach to meet those members in their own worldviews. Failure to do so can lead to miscommunications between leader and members, lack of trust, and a sense of alienation on the part of group members.

See Chapter 13 for more information on adverse effects of cultural insensitivity to group members.

Flexibility to Operate Within Multiple Worldviews

Depending on the cultural worldviews and value systems of group members, the worker may transition between working from individualistic and collectivistic worldviews and value systems. At times, the group worker may need to encourage group members to assume responsibility for their destinies and perceive self as an individual. At other times, the group worker may need to encourage group members to perceive self in relation to others and promote interdependence as a tool to live life more fully.

Advantages of Flexibility in Approaches to Group Work

- Group workers who are flexible with knowledge and skill are less apt to impose personal or theoretical values, beliefs, and attitudes on members of varying culture, values, belief, and attitudinal systems.
- Flexible group workers are positioned better to empower group members.
- Group members are positioned better to feel welcomed and appreciated, remain in-group, and get something from the group experience.

Group workers operating within a multicultural context are skilled at determining the effect of values, assumptions, and worldviews not only on theory selection and group membership but also on assessment and group ideology. In moving theory to practice, multicultural group workers pose and respond to the question, "How do assessment and group ideology intertwine?"

ASSESSMENT AND GROUP IDEOLOGIES

Assessment refers to a series of helping behaviors group workers use to determine the effectiveness of group work. The assessment process occurs at multiple levels and looks at the appropriateness of interventions, effectiveness of group workers, and issues and progress of group members.

Assessment in Multicultural Group Work

Multicultural group work assessment is challenging in that group workers are faced with questions about how the reality of culture has an impact on the group process. Assessment must address the screening process for group members, planning for sessions, and leading of groups. Much of the culturally related work around assessment involves a leader's ability to avoid cultural bias and send accurate messages about decisions made regarding the effectiveness or appropriateness of group work.

Bias: A preference, tendency, or inclination toward particular ideas, values, people, or groups.

E X A M P L E

Assessment Questions for Multicultural Group Work

During assessment of the group process, group workers may pose a number of questions. When evaluating factors leading to effective screening, workers may ask, "During screening, how do we predetermine the potential influence of diverse worldviews on group dynamics?" Group leaders examining plans for group sessions may ask, "What do we look for in group members to identify their cultural values?" Group workers determining leadership behaviors may ask, "What influence will members' cultural belief systems have on the way we lead the group?"

■ Process of Assessment

The process of assessment is culture bound and requires constant examination on the part of the group leader. For example, group workers must be skilled at identifying cultural biases underlying professional beliefs and assumptions about the process and dynamics of groups comprised of multicultural members. Pedersen (1987) shared 10 culturally biased assumptions that counselors exhibit in their work. Knowledge of these biases may help group workers diminish their potential for cultural bias during assessment. Following are two examples based on Pedersen's assumptions that are modified for group work and workers. Each assumption has recommendations to assist group workers in decreasing their cultural bias.

E X A M P L E

Diminishing Culturally Biased Assumptions in Group Work

Assumption 1: Some constant measure of "normal" behavior exists in groups.

Group workers can diminish cultural bias by recognizing that the norm for group members may or may not parallel their definition of normal behavior. To illustrate, an African American group worker observes a White group member expressing emotion with controlled affect. The worker assesses this behavior as abnormal and encourages the member to speak with more affect. A cultural bias may be evident if the African American group worker is unaware of the group member's cultural preference for expressing feelings. To diminish cultural bias, the group worker may ask himslef or herself, "Through whose lens am I looking as I assess normal behavior?" To respond effectively to this question, the group worker must possess knowledge of the cultural dictates about the expression of feelings within the African American and White communities.

Assumption 2: Neglect of support systems evident in the lives of group members has the potential for being culturally biased.

Group workers can diminish this bias by being aware of the effects of social support systems within some cultures. They can enhance the accuracy of assessment by intentionally factoring in the healing effects of support systems. To illustrate, a 25-year-old Chinese group member voices her desire to live with her parents while she is married. She expresses comfort in the support and knowledge her parents share with her husband and her. The group leader assesses that, within a cultural context, the group member is behaving in a culturally appropriate manner. The intervention chosen to help the member promotes interdependence and the healing power therein.

■ Delivery of Assessment Decisions

The delivery of assessment decisions during the group process necessitates that group workers send messages in a way that will be heard rather than resisted. Delivery can be challenging because group workers make decisions related to disputed, controversial, or doubtful matters on a regular basis. Communication under circumstances of controversy and doubt is difficult. When factoring in culture, communicating decisions becomes more daring. Group workers accurately must hear and understand the cultural values, communication styles, and worldviews of group members. They must determine how what was heard influences the dissemination of decisions and identify a way to get the information out.

■ Communication Styles

It is crucial that group workers who facilitate multicultural groups recognize and understand the communication styles of group members during assessment processes. If a group worker is unaware of the cultural communication dictates, a group member may physically, emotionally, or psychologically withdraw from the group. Even more critical, a group member may be denied the possibility of forward movement and growth if inappropriate assessment of communication behaviors is made. Finally, not to communicate well, on the same level, or in ways considered appropriate or respectful of group members may inhibit members from clearly understanding assessment decisions.

■ Thematic Communication in Assessment

Group workers operating within a culturally intentional, ethical, and competent framework pay close attention to communication style and values when assessing group members, process, and dynamics but also when determining how to deliver assessment decisions. Extensive research has been done to ascertain themes relevant to the values, beliefs, and worldviews of multicultural populations. Although no one population is homogeneous, group workers can use the themes to construct helping foundations that will (a) assist in more accurate communication with group members, and (b) facilitate the process of sharing assessment decisions. Group workers possessing knowledge of culturally thematic communication styles may use this information to guide them in transmitting decisions so that they are clearly heard and understood. Thematic communication styles can be understood as follows:

Thematic communication: Frequently observed styles of communication that are used within a particular ethnocultural community.

Table 14.1 reflects thematic communication styles of select ethnocultural populations.

The following example highlights the importance of understanding thematic communication styles to the delivery of assessment decisions.

TABLE 4.1
Select Communication Style Differences
for Four Ethnocultural Populations

African Americans	American Indians (Native Americans)	Asian Americans and Latino Americans	White Americans
Direct eye contact (prolonged) when speaking, less when listening	Indirect gaze when listening or speaking	Avoidance of eye contact when listening or speaking to high-status persons	Greater eye contact when listening
Affective, emotional interpersonal	Manner of expression is low key, indirect	Low key, indirect	Objective, task oriented

E X A M P L E

Relevance of Thematic Communication Styles to Screening Assessment

With the goal of assessing factors that will lead to the selection of members, group workers might pose the question, "During screening, how do we predetermine the potential influence of diverse worldviews on group dynamics?" The importance both of awareness and knowledge of communication styles is highlighted by the example of an African American, female, 60-year-old, PhD group worker who values prolonged, direct eye contact when speaking and diminished eye contact when listening. This group worker is screening a Chinese American woman who values avoidance of eye contact, particularly when speaking to high-status persons, such as elders. The group worker notices that the Asian American woman avoids eye contact with her throughout the screening process. She assesses the nonverbal language to reflect shyness and unassertive behavior. The group worker decides that the potential group member may be overpowered during a group if allowed to become a member. She concludes that the young woman is not ready for a group and recommends individual counseling to prepare the potential member to behave more assertively, thereby ensuring her success in a future group.

In this scenario, the group worker was not aware of the potential cultural communication style of the person being screened and made a decision about group membership based on her assessment of what might have been a cultural factor. Communication was blocked in that the group member believed she was behaving in a respectful manner and was punished by the group worker for her respectful behavior.

See Chapters 4 and 11 for more on communication styles with diverse populations.

■ Individual and Cultural Values in Assessment

Group workers are often familiar with ways to identify members' individual values. Many, however, are challenged when identifying cultural values. The difference between these two types of values can be described this way:

Individual values: The worth, importance, or usefulness of something to an individual group member. Group members share individual values when talking about self as the building block for living life more fully.

Cultural values: The worth, importance, or usefulness of something to a group member that is aligned with the member's cultural background. Cultural values contain a historical component in that they are passed from one generation to another and are highly esteemed by the individual as well as the community from which the individual comes.

TABLE 14.2			
Select Thematic Cultural Values for Four Ethnocultural Populations			
African American	*Asian American*	*White American*	*Latino American*
Group oriented	Group oriented	Individual oriented	Group oriented
Present oriented	Past oriented	Future oriented	Present oriented

Although no ethnocultural population is homogeneous, common cultural values exist among multicultural populations (Ivey, D'Andrea, Ivey, & Simek-Morgan, 2002; Pack-Brown & Whittington-Clark, 2002; Sue & Sue, 1999). Leaders can use their knowledge of these values, first, as a tool for discerning cultural underpinnings that may be significant to group assessment, process, dynamics, and planning, and, second, as a guide for deciding how to share assessments in a way that is likely to be heard and readily understood by group members. By acting on cultural knowledge, group workers enhance their flexibility in acquiring information about the group environment, process, and dynamics. Flexibility allows group workers to increase the potential for more accurate assessment of problems, issues, and life experiences expressed by multicultural group members. Table 2 reflects thematic values of select ethnocultural populations.

The following example is an illustration of how group leaders can identify and use cultural values in the assessment process.

EXAMPLE

How to Use Cultural Values in Assessments

An important task for group workers is assessing cultural values held by group members rather than making assumptions about values that are esteemed. Envision an African American adult group member by the name of Sadie sharing her thoughts about how adults behave. The member says, "It is important to me that my mother and I attend church together, even though I am married. She can join my husband and me." Another adult group member, Judy, who self-identifies as White states, "I think adults ought to be independent. For me, it is important to be able to stand on my own and not be dependent on my parents, whether it relates to religion or any other area of my life." The group worker listens to both members' thoughts about adult behavior. The worker hears that both self-identify as a member of a particular ethnocultural (racial and ethnic) population. Sadie self-identifies as African American and Judy self-identifies as White. The worker is familiar with thematic values of both populations and hears Sadie's values (culturally and individually) regarding a family orientation to life and Judy's values (culturally and individually) regarding an independent orientation to life. The worker understands that both orientations are viable and important to accurately assessing cultural values. The leader shares her assessment by stating that there are cultural definitions related to how each member identifies their orientation to life. Sadie appears to value an African American family-oriented approach to life. Judy appears to value a White independence orientation approach to life.

Using the knowledge gained from looking at the history of group work, core competencies associated with multicultural group work, and culturally intentional assessment, a model for a diversity-competent approach to group work is proposed.

A DIVERSITY-COMPETENT MODEL OF MULTICULTURAL GROUP WORK

Models of group work describe ways in which the group worker operates during group process and dynamics. Models address interpersonal processes, whereas theories provide an ideological structure for understanding group work. Although sparse, models of multicultural group work are emerging as the profession and professionals focus on culturally competent, intentional, and ethical group work. Estrada, Garrett, Pack-Brown, Molina, Monteiro-Leitner, and Torres-Rivera are among the clinicians and educators breaking ground in the area of diversity-competent group work.

■ How to Choose a Model of Multicultural Group Work

When choosing a model of multicultural group work, group workers must consider factors such as communication styles, cultural values, life experiences, and worldviews inherent to the members comprising their groups.

■ Images of Me: An Afrocentric Approach to Group Work

Images of Me (Pack-Brown, Whittington-Clark, & Parker, 2002) is a diversity-competent model of multicultural group work from an Afrocentric approach. Initially proposed by Pack-Brown in collaboration with Whittington and Parker, the model integrates theory of culture and group process and dynamics. Although the title suggests that this approach is applicable only to group work with African American women, it also may be useful for other populations. The Afrocentric approach to group work is built around the principles of the Nguzo Saba and includes four values.

Values Inherent to the Images of Me Diversity Model

1. Unity (*Umoja*, pronounced oo-MOH-jah).
2. Collective responsibility (*Kujichagulia*, pronounced Koo-ji-cha-goo-Lee-ah).
3. Faith (*Imani*, pronounced ee-MAH-nee).
4. Creativity of a new reality (*Kuumba*, pronounced koo-OO-Mbah).

A focus of the Afrocentric approach is to assist group workers in expanding their worldviews and building self-esteem as well as group pride among group members. There are three basic tenets of the Afrocentric approach to group work.

Tenets of the Afrocentric Approach

1. Spirit permeates everything, and everything in the universe is interconnected.
2. The collective (the group, the community) is the most significant element in existence.
3. Communal self-knowledge is the key to mental health.

Guided by these three tenets, group workers operate, first, from the assumptions that multicultural group work is grounded in the spirit, and everything in the group is interconnected. Second, group workers facilitate from the premise that multicultural group work is built on a foundation that is grounded in the unity within the group. Group workers believe that the group is the most significant element, and members are there to help each other (self-in-relation) live life more fully. Finally, group workers view multicultural group work as built on a foundation that purports that self-knowledge is informed by a communal stance. Group workers believe that communal self-knowledge is the key to mental health.

Techniques and strategies to assist group members in identifying and achieving goals are those that embrace the spirit, collectivity, and communal self-knowledge. The following is an example of a therapeutic approach to group work (drumming) that embraces these elements.

EXAMPLE

Drumming: An Afrocentric Diversity Model Technique

Drumming is a technique used in an Afrocentric approach to group work. Drumming integrates a therapeutic tool that serves multiple purposes, including, but not limited to, the following.

Eliciting emotional connections among group members.

Group members, via experiencing the beat of the drum, are able to feel their heartbeats connect with the beat of the drum. One way to accomplish this connection is to offer a *drum call;* that is, the group leader or a group member (skillful in drumming) singularly and rhythmically beats the drum while group members are encouraged to experience (be exposed to and become aware of the drum) and feel (to have a physical or emotional sensation) the beat of the drum.

Cultivating group identity and unity among group members.

As members feel connected to the heartbeat of the drum, they are encouraged to join the group leader or member who is drumming. In this case, the beat played by the skillful drummer is less complicated than the beat of the drum call although still rhythmic, so that group members each can beat their drums. Their task is to find the beat that the leader or member is playing and connect with the beat. As members work to identify the beat and simulate it, they find that there are struggles. Some are readily able to identify and play the beat. In this case, members readily unify. In other cases, members struggle with identifying and playing the beat. Their struggle may symbolically represent their abilities or inabilities to join the group, connect with the group, or maintain their own identify while in the group.

Strengthening the experience of the "here and now" among group members.

The sheer fact that group members are invited to play the drum collectively, experience the beat of the drum collectively, and find their places in the group via identifying the individual and collective beats forces them to focus on what is going on within them in the present. For example, they are in touch with the feelings, thoughts, and behaviors in the moment. Group workers can use this experience to help members who struggle with experiencing the "here and now" to get out their cognitive struggles and focus on other dimensions such as their feelings and behaviors.

Chapter 14: Key Terms

- ► Culture
- ► Worldview
- ► Multicultural group work
- ► Multicultural group worker competency
- ► Bias
- ► Thematic communication
- ► Individual values
- ► Cultural values

Counseling in the World of Work

Ellen Swaney
KSM Consultants

Barbara Keaton
Keaton Resources

In This Chapter

▶ *Career Counseling Overview*
  ■ Historical Development of Career Counseling
  ■ Nature of Career Counseling
  ■ Important Terminology in Career Counseling

▶ *Career Development Theory*
  ■ Frank Parsons: Trait and Factor Theory
  ■ John Holland: Theory of Vocational Choice and Adjustment
  ■ Eli Ginzberg: Developmental Career Theory
  ■ Donald Super: Life-Span Theory
  ■ Anne Roe: Needs Theory
  ■ E. Bordin: Psychoanalytic Career Theory
  ■ Tiedeman and O'Hara: Choice and Adjustment Theory
  ■ Gottfredson: Theory of Circumscription and Compromise
  ■ John Krumboltz: Social Learning Career Theory
  ■ Socioeconomic Career Theories
  ■ Career Theories for Women
  ■ The Lifecareer®/New Career Theory

▶ *Process of Career Counseling*
  ■ Stage 1: Dealing With Change
  ■ Stage 2: Developing Career Focus
  ■ Stage 3: Exploring Career Options
  ■ Stage 4: Preparing for Job Search
  ■ Stage 5: Obtaining Employment

▶ *Use of Assessment Tools in Career Counseling*
  ■ History of Assessment: Trait and Factor Model
  ■ Interest Inventories
  ■ Personality Inventories
  ■ Values/Lifestyle Inventories
  ■ Qualitative Tools

▶ *Special Issues in Career Counseling*
  ■ Job Loss
  ■ Dual-Career Considerations
  ■ Displaced Homemakers
  ■ Individuals With Disabilities
  ■ Midlife Career Changes

▶ *Technological Competencies for Career Counselors*
  ■ ACES Technology Competencies
  ■ Need for Technological Skills

CAREER COUNSELING OVERVIEW

A 1999 survey conducted by the Gallup Organization revealed that 1 in 10 adults seek assistance annually to support career-related changes. As the need for career counseling increases, counselors entering the field must be familiar with the theoretical constructs supporting the field, the nature and process of career counseling, the various assessment tools available to help counselors support clients, the psychoemotional concepts that can enter into the career counseling process, and the technical skills necessary for supporting clients in today's technological environment. Each of these areas is addressed in this chapter. First, however, a brief historical sketch of career counseling and vocational guidance is provided.

■ Historical Development of Career Counseling

The history of career counseling stretches back three centuries to the late 1800s, when a few pioneers began to implement their ideas about assisting individuals with vocational choice. Events from the evolutionary development of career counseling that signify the growth of the field are highlighted here.

Guidance Begins: The Late 19th Century

- In 1883, Richards advocated for **vacophers** (career counselors) to be placed in every town.
- In 1898, J. B. Davis instructed high school students in the world of work and later, as a principal, asked teachers to relate subject matter to particular vocations.

The turn of the century brought the posthumous publication of Parsons's (1909) *Choosing a Vocation,* in which he presented the first theoretical model for career choice; this publication signified the birth of vocational counseling and is one of Parsons's contributions that solidifies him as the "father of guidance." Other significant events that occurred during the 1900s are listed next.

Vocational Guidance Develops: The 20th Century

- In 1913, the National Vocational Guidance Association (NVGA) was established as the first counseling-related professional association in the United States.
- In 1939, the first *Dictionary of Occupational Titles* was published.
- Ginzberg, Ginsberg, Axelrad, and Herma (1951) published the first theory of career development in their book *Occupational Choice: An Approach to a General Theory.*
- Super (1953) published "A Theory of Vocational Development" in the *American Psychologist.*
- Roe (1956) published *The Psychology of Occupations.*

- Holland (1959) published "A Theory of Vocational Guidance" in the *Journal of Counseling Psychology.*
- In 1983, the NVGA established the National Certified Career Counselor Certification (Amundson, Harris-Bowlsbey, & Niles, 2004).
- In 1985, the NVGA became the National Career Development Association (NCDA), a branch of the ACA.
- In 1994, Congress enacted the Americans With Disabilities Act.

By the 21st century, the distinction between career counseling and the other counseling fields was solidified.

Career Counseling Continues to Evolve: The 21st Century

- In 2000, the National Board for Certified Counselors opted to decommission the National Certified Career Counselor Program.
- In 2001, the NCDA established the Master Career Counselor membership category as a means of credentialing career counselors.
- In 2006, NCDA supports research on career development and acts as a consultive body for government policies on career issues.

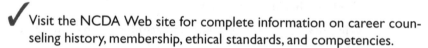

✓ Visit the NCDA Web site for complete information on career counseling history, membership, ethical standards, and competencies.

▶ www.ncda.org

■ Nature of Career Counseling

Despite its role as the cornerstone on which the counseling field was built, career counseling acquired a stereotype as being devoid of psychological process—a view that places the career counselor in a second-class category as compared to a personal-emotional counselor. Gysbers, Heppner, and Johnston (2003) refuted this stereotype, quoting Swanson's (1995) definition of career counseling:

> **Career counseling:** "[A]n ongoing, face-to-face interaction between counselor and client with the primary focus on work or career related issues; the interaction is psychological in nature, with the relationship between counselor and client serving an important function" (p. 3).

The bottom line in terms of the nature of career counseling is that the personal-emotional and career development realms intimately are connected. It is impossible to attend effectively to a client's career problems without exploring and resolving the client's specific personal-emotional issues, which influence the career development process.

Important Terminology in Career Counseling

For any counselor who wishes to practice competently in the career counseling field, basic proficiency in career-related concepts is required. The NCDA (2006) defined some key terms applicable to the career development field, including these:

Leisure: Relatively self-determined activities and experiences that are available because of discretionary income, time, and social behavior; activities may be physical, social, intellectual, volunteer, creative, or some combination of all five.

Career: The totality of work and leisure experiences one has in a lifetime.

Work: A conscious effort aimed neither at coping or relaxation that produces benefits either for oneself or for others.

Career development: The total constellation of psychological, sociological, educational, physical, economic, and chance factors that combine to shape the career of any given individual over the life span.

CAREER DEVELOPMENT THEORY

Career development theory has emerged over the course of the last century, beginning with Parsons's trait and factor theory. Today, career theories continue to be revised to account for new awarenesses, such as the need for multicultural approaches. In this section we outline the central tenets of classic theories of career counseling.

Frank Parsons: Trait and Factor Theory

Isaacson and Brown (2000) described the heart of trait and factor theory this way: "Trait and factor theories stress that individuals need to develop their traits, which include their interests, values, personalities, and aptitudes, as well as select environments that are congruent with them" (p. 21). As the major proponent of trait and factor theory, Parsons developed a conceptual framework in 1908 that ignited a national interest in career guidance. Three main components characterize Parsons's (1909) approach to helping an individual select a career.

Goals of Trait and Factor Theory

- Create a clear understanding of oneself and one's aptitudes, abilities, interests, resources, and limitations.
- Increase the knowledge of the requirements and conditions of success, advantages and disadvantages, compensations, opportunities, and prospects in different lines of work.
- Utilize "true reasoning" on the relations of these two groups of facts.

■ John Holland: Theory of Vocational Choice and Adjustment

One of the most prominent theorists in the career counseling field, Holland believed that an individual's heredity and experience lead to preferences for activities. These preferences in turn become interests that the individual pursues. As people pursue their interests, they develop necessary competencies for success. There are a number of assumptions on which Holland built his career theory. Understanding these principles helps illuminate the core of Holland's approach.

Assumptions of Holland's Career Approach (Isaacson & Brown, 2000)

- The individual's personality is the primary factor in vocational choice.
- Interest inventories are, in fact, personality inventories.
- Stereotypical views of occupations play a major role in occupational choice.
- Daydreams about occupations often are precursors to occupational choices.
- The clarity of an individual's perceptions of his or her goals and personal characteristics is related to having a small number of focused vocational goals.
- To be successful and satisfied, it is necessary to choose an occupation in which others in the work environment have similar characteristics as one's own.

Evident in the assumptions of Holland's theory is the connection between personality and career choice. Holland proposed that people can be grouped into six different personality types that correspond to careers and environments. When people place themselves in environments and careers that are similar or congruent to their personality type, they are likely to be satisfied with their choice. To assess personality types, Holland developed the Self-Directed Search (SDS; Holland, 1994), which is still one of the most frequently used career assessment tools today.

Holland's Six Personality Types

- Realistic.
- Investigative.
- Artistic.
- Social.
- Enterprising.
- Conventional.

Besides the SDS, Holland developed other, easy-to-administer assessment tools including *The Occupations Finder* and the *My Vocational Situation* tools. These instruments widely have been applied in the career counseling field. Additionally, his personality typology has been adjusted to fit the development of many other assessment instruments.

■ Eli Ginzberg: Developmental Career Theory

Developmental theories are based, first, on the belief that career development is a process that takes place over the life span (Zunker, 1998) and, second, on the assumption that biological, psychological, sociological, and cultural factors influence career choice, career changes, and career withdrawal across the stages of development. Ginzberg et al. (1951) proposed the first developmental theory in which they suggested that career choices span three chronological stages in an individual's lifetime.

Chronological Stages of Career Development

- The *fantasy stage* involves role playing and imagination.
- The *tentative stage* reflects a person's growing awareness of interests and abilities.
- The *realistic stage* entails the identification of a career choice.

Furthermore, the theory identified four factors that shape an individual's career decisions.

Factors That Have an Impact on Career Development

- Individual values.
- Emotional factors.
- Amount and kind of education.
- Effect of reality through environmental pressures.

■ Donald Super: Life-Span Theory

Like Holland's theory of personality–career fit, Super's (1953, 1990, 1992, 1994) life-span, life-space theory, which is both developmental and humanistic in nature, has been extremely influential in the career development field (Weinrach, 1996). Super viewed career development as a lifelong process occurring within the individual's psychosocial development, societal expectations, and occupational opportunities. Super defined three key components of career development:

Life-span: Career development is lifelong and occurs throughout five major life stages: growth, exploration, establishment, maintenance, and disengagement. Each stage has a unique set of career development tasks and accounts for the changes and decisions that people make from work entry to retirement.

Life-space: People have skills and talents developed through different life roles, making them capable of a variety of tasks and numerous occupations.

Self-concept: Understanding one's interests and skills is a key to career choice and satisfaction as people seek career satisfaction through work roles in which they can express themselves and implement and develop their self-concepts.

Super continued to rework and revise his career theory throughout his life, which is one reason the life-span, life-space model has sustained viability. One example of Super's adjustments is seen in his conceptualization of the life career rainbow. Originally based in a stage model suggesting that career mirrors a person's maturation, Super re-created the rainbow so that career exploration was seen as one facet of the overall human life exploration experience and to account for social and psychological factors (Blustein, 1997).

■ Anne Roe: Needs Theory

Roe (1956) developed a needs theory approach to career choice within which she conceptualized a two-way occupational classification system that involves person-oriented and non-person-oriented careers (Zunker, 1998). She identified the combination of early parent–child relations, environmental experiences, and genetic features as determinants in the need structure of the individual. Person-oriented and non-person-oriented careers can be understood this way:

Person-oriented career: The individual satisfies needs primarily through interactions with people.

Non-person-oriented career: The individual satisfies needs primarily by acting on things or ideas independently.

Two widely recognized components of Roe's theory are the eight categories of occupational groups and the six levels of complexity that exist within each grouping. These are listed here.

Roe's Occupational Groups

- Service.
- Business contact.
- Organizational.

- Technology.
- Outdoor.
- Science.
- General cultural.
- Arts and entertainment.

Roe's Levels of Complexity

- Professional and managerial I.
- Professional and managerial II.
- Semiprofessional and small business.
- Skilled.
- Semiskilled.
- Unskilled.

EXAMPLE

Identifying Some Person-Oriented and Non-Person-Oriented Careers

A client who is person-oriented would be encouraged to explore career options where the primary tasks and processes followed involve communicating and working collaboratively with others or where the results of the work have a direct impact on people. Examples of such careers are sales or teaching. A client who is non-person-oriented would be encouraged to explore career options where the work is self-involved, for example, an engineer or pet groomer.

■ E. Bordin: Psychoanalytic Career Theory

Bordin's psychoanalytic model related career choice to Freud's psychosexual stages with an emphasis on the role of play in adult work (Bordin, Nachmann, & Segal, 1963). Play is viewed as an important activity that brings about satisfaction. Bordin saw individuals as seeking to derive joy from their work. "This desire for satisfaction or joy in one's work will lead a person to select, unconsciously, an occupation that satisfies the need for enjoyment" (Sharf, 1997, p. 266).

■ Tiedeman and O'Hara: Choice and Adjustment Theory

Tiedeman and O'Hara (1963) described the stages of career decision from an individualistic perspective. Their approach includes two periods of decision making: anticipation and implementation. The anticipation stage of career decision is divided into four basic developmental phases.

Steps in the Anticipation Period of Career Development

- During the *exploration phase,* the client's focus is on understanding himself or herself in terms of career needs.
- In the *crystallization phase,* the client begins to develop options for career choice.
- In the *choice phase,* career options are defined and narrowed.
- During the *clarification phase,* the career choice is validated.

Based on the choices made in the anticipation phase, the client conducts a job search in the implementation phase. These phases form the foundation of many descriptions of the career development process today.

■ Gottfredson: Theory of Circumscription and Compromise

Gottfredson's (1981) theory of circumscription and compromise focuses on the development of career aspirations or how individuals become attracted to occupations. The theory of circumscription and compromise suggests that career choices are made in response to one's social and psychological self-image. Perhaps more than other theories, Gottfredson's approach to career development identifies gender roles and prestige as important parts of career development in childhood and adolescence. To understand the core of this theory it is necessary to define some key terms.

Circumscription: The process by which individuals gradually restrict the occupations they consider acceptable, based on their developing self-concept.

Compromise: The process by which individuals choose among available but imperfect occupational alternatives by compromising some needs for others.

Several generalizations highlight the groundwork of Gottfredson's theory.

Assumptions of the Theory of Circumscription and Compromise

- The career development process begins in childhood.
- Career aspirations are attempts to implement one's self-concept.
- Career satisfaction is dependent on the degree to which the career is congruent with self-perceptions.
- People develop occupational stereotypes that guide them in the selection process.

Gottfredson's theory proposes four stages of cognitive development that guide the way people match their self-concept with occupation. These stages are briefly outlined here.

Gottfredson's Stages of Cognitive Development

1. Orientation to size and power (ages 3–5) refers to children's classification of people as big and powerful or small and weak. During this stage, children make simple distinctions about people and their jobs and eliminate career possibilities that are incompatible with their gender.
2. Orientation to sex roles (ages 6–8) refers to a the stage of development during which children make classifications of jobs based on concrete distinctions, such as gender and eliminate vocations that are not gender appropriate.
3. Orientation to social valuation (ages 9–13) refers to the stage during which social class and prestige emerge as important factors in career choice, and vocations that are not class appropriate are eliminated.
4. Orientation to inique, internal self (ages 14 and older) refers to a level of cognitive development marked by adolescents' greater insight into vocational aspirations and how these match with the view of themselves, gender roles, and prestige. Adolescents begin to eliminate occupations that do not fit their self-image.

■ John Krumboltz: Social Learning Career Theory

Learning theories emphasize individualized learning processes that eventually lead to career interests and career choices. These theories differ from trait and factor and developmental theories in that they are more concerned with the impact of social influences on career choice than with the role of traits, values, or developmental stages. A proponent of learning theory, Krumboltz developed a theory of career selection based on Bandura's behavioral theory and reinforcement theory. A few assumptions characterize Krumboltz's view about the individual and, by extension, the career development process.

Assumptions of Social Learning Career Theory (Isaacson & Brown, 2000)

- People are born with certain factors that cannot be changed, such as genetic characteristics, race, gender, physique, and special abilities or disabilities.
- Learning over time occurs from encounters with the world and results in development of self-esteem and task skills that are applied to new situations.
- People select or avoid repetitive encounters that allow them to build skills in specific areas that lead to career choice through the reinforcement experienced in these encounters.

Krumboltz identified four factors that influence career decisions; these are mentioned next.

Factors Influencing Career Choice in Social Learning Theory

1. Genetic endowment and special abilities.
2. Environmental conditions and events.

3. Learning experiences.
4. Task approach skills.

■ Socioeconomic Career Theories

Numerous social and economic theorists have had an impact on the career counseling field. Their theories propose that institutional and impersonal market forces restrict decision making, which hinders the individual's career aspirations. Although socioeconomic theories place importance on the intellect as a factor in career choice, the theories' main focus is on the individual's socioeconomic status and the influence of sociological and economic factors on the choice.

Research Areas of Socioeconomic Career Theories (Sharf, 1997)

■ Status hierarchy of occupational structure.
■ Power and authority in the workplace.
■ Work socialization processes.
■ Labor unions and collective bargaining.
■ Operation of the labor market.
■ Sociology of professions.
■ Race and gender effects.
■ Family effects.
■ Chance encounters.

■ Career Theories for Women

Career self-efficacy theory, which is rooted in Bandura's social learning theory, emphasizes cognitive processes and focuses primarily on the effects of prior learning experiences on later learning experiences and, eventually, on career choice. Bandura (1986) gave this explanation of self-efficacy:

> **Self-efficacy:** The individual's "judgments of their capabilities to organize and execute courses of action required to attain designated types of performances" (p. 391).

Hackett and Betz (1981) recognized the role that environmental forces play in shaping women's beliefs about their ability to master certain types of knowledge and career areas. They suggested that a restricted range of options and underutilization of abilities hinder women's beliefs about the likelihood of their success in some career areas (Zunker, 1998). Hackett and Betz made the following recommendations for career counselors working with women.

Recommendations for Career Counseling With Women

- Help the female client understand how low self-esteem with regard to math and other areas is part of their socialization as women.
- Help the client explore how low self-esteem negatively affects interest in certain areas.
- Direct the client to observe female role models in the feared career to encourage pursuit of nontraditional academic courses or work.
- Reinforce clients' belief in their underused capabilities.
- Offer to guide clients through anxiety-reduction techniques.

■ The Lifecareer®/New Careering Theory

Miller-Tiedeman (1999) offered another perspective in her approach known as The Lifecareer®/New Careering Theory, which came out of her observation that career development should not be a *911* event. The theory suggests that a decision as important as a career path should not be forced on students in high school or even college but rather, should be supported as it naturally evolves over time as people discover their life mission. The best strategy for career counseling, therefore, is to offer principles for individuals to use as their life missions unfold. The job of the helper then becomes supporting individuals as they make their way for life.

PROCESS OF CAREER COUNSELING

Two widely accepted perspectives on the structure of career counseling are the client–counselor relationship and the career development process (Gysbers et al., 2003). As the career development process unfolds, so, too, does the client–counselor relationship. The following five stages describe a general approach to the career counseling relationship:

- Dealing with change.
- Developing career focus.
- Exploring career options.
- Preparing for job search.
- Obtaining employment.

Like any counseling process that proposes stages of movement or development, those described for the career counseling process also must be viewed as recursive. Counselors may have to revisit certain tasks in the counseling process and attend to the client's unique needs and development as they emerge in the counseling relationship. Whereas some clients need extra support in discovering new career options, other clients require additional help in following through on a job search.

In each stage of career counseling, there are three areas of focus: exploration, task, and developmental outcomes. A brief description of the stages of career counseling is provided with a focus on the explorations, tasks, and outcomes relevant to the stage.

■ Stage 1: Dealing With Change

During the first stage, the counselor builds the counseling relationship by providing unconditional positive regard, listening to the client's expressed needs, exploring the personal-emotional issues related to the career development process, and uncovering possible resistances to career exploration.

Foci of Stage 1 in Career Counseling

- Exploration revolves around understanding the client's reaction to the change process, personal career identity, and locus of control or resistances.
- Tasks include evaluating the client's wants, needs, and resistances, processing feelings, and identifying and implementing strategies for overcoming obstacles.
- Developmental outcomes of the first stage are realistic understandings of the challenges and opportunities for personal career change and the client's commitment to the career development process.

■ Stage 2: Developing Career Focus

When some of the outcomes of the first stage are achieved, the counselor begins to help the client develop career focus. The counselor guides the client in selecting and completing assessments and activities that help the client to pinpoint choices for career exploration.

The counselor builds the relationship during the second stage by guiding the client to gain insight into the relation between their personal wants and needs and the outcomes of their self-exploratory activities. The counselor also provides personal-emotional support to continually address and overcome resistances and builds client confidence by highlighting client strengths and accomplishments.

Foci of Stage 2 in Career Counseling

- Exploration centers on career accomplishments, relevant experience, career implications of personality traits, career implications of interest codes, values and lifestyle preferences, practical and financial considerations, and spiritual considerations.
- Tasks of the second stage include completing appropriate standardized and nonstandardized assessments, writing a personal career profile, writing or updating the résumé, and developing a plan for exploring career options.

- Developmental outcomes are a general preparation of the client for researching career options.

Once the client believes he or she adequately is prepared to explore career options, the career counselor focuses on building the client's confidence and helping the client overcome resistance to career exploration.

■ Stage 3: Exploring Career Options

At the third stage, the counselor takes on the added role of educator and helps the client gain a realistic understanding of the tasks involved in career exploration. This includes personal instruction and directing clients to other resources such as books, Web sites, or job search groups and clubs.

Foci of Stage 3 in Career Counseling

- Exploration focuses on clarifying myths and realities of the job search and the job market by using job advertisements and internet postings and agencies. Also job market resources are helpful in conducting research about career possibilities, and networking aids in uncovering potential positions.
- Tasks of the third stage involve reading about the job market and job search strategies, writing a personal job search plan, joining networking or job search clubs or chat groups, developing a list of target contacts for research, and conducting informational meetings with target contacts.
- Developmental outcomes related to the exploration phase are the development of an internal locus of control such that clients believe they have the ability to take action that will result in a positive career change, an understanding of the fit between personal career profile and job opportunities, and the completed target position and organization contact list.

■ Stage 4: Preparing for Job Search

While helping the client prepare for a job search, the career counselor continues in the role described in the third stage; however, it becomes important, again, for the counselor to support the client in interpreting career exploration experiences, gaining additional insight into his or her career identity, and fine-tuning career development goals. The counselor also continues to provide practical assistance to develop the client's job search skills. As well, the counselor begins to shift focus to necessary skills development that will aid the client in preparing for and obtaining employment.

Foci of Stage 4 in Career Counseling

- Skills development center on letter writing, e-mail and phone skills, and networking strategies.
- Tasks include conducting informational meetings with target position and organization contacts, and implementing job search plans to identify interviewing opportunities.
- Developmental outcomes are evidenced in a clear focus on appropriate job opportunities and interviews with potential employers.

■ Stage 5: Obtaining Employment

As the client begins to interview for specific positions, the counselor continues in the roles of supporter, educator, and practical helper as determined by the client's specific experiences and obstacles.

Foci of Stage 5 in Career Counseling

- Skills to be enhanced include interviewing and negotiating techniques.
- Tasks of the counseling process include practicing responses to difficult interviewing situations and determining compensation parameters.
- Developmental outcomes are very tangible and include job offers and negotiation of fair compensation.

The stages of the career counseling process depict a start-to-finish scenario. It is atypical, however, for a client to require full counseling support through the entire process. Most clients seeking a career counseling relationship do so for the same reasons clients seek any counseling relationship—to help them overcome perceived roadblocks and deal with the personal-emotional issues related to these roadblocks. Once clients have a clearer career focus and some degree of confidence, they usually can navigate the latter stages of the process independently using the vast array of published and online resources that are available to the job searching public. Although a career counselor cannot practice without the practical knowledge and skills found in the tasks of the latter stages of the career counseling process, the greatest value of the counselor to the client lies in the counselor's ability to help the client navigate the personal-emotional aspects of career development by providing support and insight and by nurturing a trusting, helping relationship.

USE OF ASSESSMENT TOOLS IN CAREER COUNSELING

Assessment tools are used in career counseling to gather diagnostic information about the client and to promote client self-awareness and exploration. There are a variety of tools that can be used in the beginning stages of the career counseling process to gather information about the client. After providing a brief historical look at career assessment, we focus in this section on three different types of assessment tools and inventories commonly used in career counseling:

- Interest inventories.
- Personality inventories.
- Values inventories.

■ History of Assessment: Trait and Factor Model

The use of assessment tools as part of career counseling originated with the work of Parsons, who was the first to emphasize the importance of personal analysis in career counseling. Parsons initiated a theoretical path that led to the trait and factor model of vocational development that the military used for intelligence testing during World War I. Utilizing assessment as part of the job selection process was firmly established by the military during World War II, when testing was used as an efficient way to match military personnel to jobs (Seligman, 1994). Additionally, the trait and factor model of vocational development focused the science of psychology on the development of tests and inventories to promote personal analysis. These tests had a pervasive influence on vocational counseling and became inextricably linked to the field of career counseling.

Since Parsons's innovative work around career testing, a variety of assessment tools have emerged in the field of career counseling. One simple way to categorize these career assessment tools is by their attention either to cognitive or affective variables.

Facets of Cognitive Tests

- Cognitive tests measure cognitive variables, such as aptitude or skills and typically pose questions that have correct or incorrect answers.
- Cognitive tests primarily are used for educational and placement purposes by school counselors, the military, and employers.

Facets of Affective Tests

- Affective tests measure ideas, preferences, self-descriptors, and opinions.
- The vast majority of diagnostic assessments in use by adult career counselors are affective tests that focus on self-awareness and discovery.
- Because there are no correct responses, affective tests more properly might be called inventories (Seligman, 1994).

■ Interest Inventories

Interest inventories identify an individual's self-reported interests, likes, dislikes, and preferred activities. Research into the connection between job choice and the interests of people in those jobs have suggested that employees of specific jobs often share similar interests. Interest inventories use shared interests as an indicator of potentially satisfying career fields.

Common Interest Inventories

- Strong Interest Inventory (SII; Campbell, Strong, & Hansen, 1991).
- SDS (Holland, 1994).
- Career Occupational Preference Survey (Knapp & Knapp, 1992).
- Career Decision-Making System (Harrington & O'Shea, 1992).
- Kuder Career Search with Person Match (Zytowski & Kuder, 1999).
- Jackson Vocational Interest Survey (Jackson, 1991).
- O*Net Interest Profiler (United States Employment Service, 2002).

O*Net, formerly *The Dictionary of Occupational Titles*, published by the federal government and the most widely used reference of job descriptions in the United States, is organized by Holland codes.

Among these inventories, the SII and the SDS frequently are used. Both inventories are based on Holland's six types, represented by the acronym RIASEC (realistic, investigative, artistic, social, enterprising, and conventional). The reports generated by these instruments provide three levels of detail.

Results of Interest Inventories

- General occupational themes summarize the client's interests by assigning a three-letter RIASEC type code (e.g., SEC) representing the top three types for which the client reported interest.
- Basic interest scales identify the top occupational categories, within their type code, for which the client reported interest.
- Occupational scales provide a detailed report of the client's interests in specific occupations within each of the RIASEC types.

The results of these inventories can be used to help the client think about the relation between his or her interests and job choice and to identify specific jobs that match the client's interests.

■ Personality Inventories

There are several well-known personality inventories used in career counseling, including the Sixteen Personality Factor, the Vocational Preference Inventory (Holland, 1985b), and the Myers–Briggs Type Inventory (MBTI; Myers & Briggs, 1993). Of these, the most commonly used inventory in adult career counseling is the MBTI, developed by Briggs-Myers and Briggs, and based on Jung's theory of personality. The goal of the MBTI is to help people discover, understand, and appreciate their natural styles (Seligman, 1994).

Advantages of the MBTI

- The premise of the MBTI is that all personality preferences equally are valuable; therefore, the test eliminates the trepidation some clients may have about taking a personality test.
- A vast array of support literature about MBTI is available to the career counselor and client.
- There are numerous career self-help books based on the MBTI that clients can use on their own.

The MBTI yields scores about personality type on four dimensions. Combinations of these scores are translated into 16 personality types.

MBTI Personality Types

- Introversion–extroversion.
- Sensing–intuition.
- Thinking–feeling.
- Judging–perceiving.

■ Values/Lifestyle Inventories

As the current trend for adult career counseling moves toward a more integrated approach to working with clients, an array of affective inventories are being used by career counselors to help clients search for personal meaning and career fit. Values inventories are an affective tool used to help match the client with a suitable job choice. Values inventories consider a client's intrinsic and extrinsic values. Intrinsic values are related the work and its contribution to society, whereas extrinsic values are related to the physical and environmental aspects of the job or earning potential. There are a number of values inventories available to career counselors; those that assess career maturity, self-concept, and self-esteem frequently are used. Examples of specific lifestyle inventories are listed next.

Commonly Used Values Inventories

- The Work Values Inventory (Super, 1964).
- Minnesota Importance Questionnaire (Rounds, Henly, Dawis, Loftquist, & Weiss, 1981).
- Work Importance Locator (2001).
- Work Importance Profiler (2002).
- Life Values Inventory (Crace & Brown, 1996).

■ Qualitative Tools

Qualitative tools aid the counselor and client in exploring the vast array of personal, social, spiritual, and economic factors that affect the client's career focus. Some of the most popular qualitative tools in use today include the following.

Common Qualitative Tools

- Genograms.
- Career-o-grams.
- Card sorts.
- Role plays.
- Assessments of career achievement.
- Assessments of transferable skills, knowledge, and ability.

The career counselor can develop or modify the qualitative tools to meet the needs of the particular client. In general, qualitative tools have three uses.

Applications of Qualitative Assessment Tools

- Help clients develop self-awareness.
- Assist in career decision making.
- Help in the development of a résumé or other job search communications.

SPECIAL ISSUES IN CAREER COUNSELING

Just as career counseling represents a niche in the counseling profession, there are some special issues that career counselors may face that require them to use extra sensitivity and a specialized knowledge base. We describe a few of these cases in this section.

■ Job Loss

Men and women experience the same degree of distress following the loss of a job; however, it appears that middle-aged men are more vulnerable to negative effects of job loss (Zunker, 1998). Physical and psychological effects of job loss are numerous.

Negative Effects of Job Loss

- Withdrawal.
- Decline of self-respect.

- Loss of identify and affiliation.
- Disruptive behavioral reactions.
- Depression.
- Suicidal ideations.

It is critical for career counselors to play a supportive role with individuals who have suffered the loss of a job, especially when the individual does not have a solid or extensive support system. Brammer and Abrego (1981) suggested some coping skills that assist individuals in managing transitions.

Counselor Skills for Coping With Job Loss (Zunker, 1998)

- Skills concerning perception and response to transitions such as developing self-control and a style for responding to change.
- Skills relating to assessing, developing, and utilizing external support systems as well as internal support system, such as attitudes and personal strengths.
- Skills relating to the reduction of psychological and emotional stress through relaxation exercises and the expression of feelings related to the distress.

■ Dual-Career Considerations

During the last 15 years, there has been a notable trend in the number of dual-career families. Families in this category can experience both positive and negative outcomes of a two-partner working household.

Positive Aspects of Dual-Career Families

- With both partners financially providing for families, one partner can take the opportunity to pursue other job interests, different career paths, or return to the educational arena while the other partner acts as the primary financial support.
- Families can enjoy the benefits of a higher socioeconomic position resulting from the combined income of the partners.

Although there are a number of benefits to dual-career families, there also may be some potential drawbacks to this lifestyle.

Potential Drawbacks of Dual-Career Families

- One spouse may lose job opportunities if the other partner is unwilling to resign from employment to relocate.
- Some dual-career families live in long-distance relationships because the spouses are employed in different parts of the country.
- Dual-career families can face problems with child care, finding time together, allocation of household chores, and parenting.

■ Displaced Homemakers

Displaced homemakers are people who are forced to replace their primary responsibility of taking care of the home and children with outside, paid work. Sudden or unexpected events that cause homemakers to become displaced include divorce, death of a spouse, abandonment, employment termination of a partner, and significant medical needs of children or elderly parents. Because of the often unexpected nature of the displacement, homemakers may benefit from personal counseling prior to career counseling to deal with issues that would have distracted them from their career exploration or search. Some displaced homemakers, however, quickly will jump into an employment relationship to avoid dealing with their emotional distress. Apart from dealing with mental health issues, the career counselor can address situational concerns presented by the displaced homemaker.

Counselor Responses to Situational Concerns of Displaced Homemakers

- Referral to financial professionals to deal with short-term or long-term financial problems.
- Exploration of support systems, including the expansion of those systems.
- Modification of self-concept to prepare individuals to assume responsibility for decisions perhaps previously made with a partner.
- Addressing day-to-day problems (e.g., yard care, car maintenance, cooking, etc.) so the client can afford to focus on career planning.

In addition to responding to the practical, contextual concerns that displaced homemakers may have, career counselors also need to explore a number of key issues that can have an impact on the client's job search.

Key Concerns in Counseling Displaced Homemakers

- Education about the world of work and the local labor market.
- Development of reasonable expectations as displaced homemakers sometimes set their work goals too low due to self-esteem issues.
- Consideration of immediate employment versus entry into a preparatory program.
- Assessment of the individual's energy.

■ Individuals With Disabilities

Career development issues frequently are the same for all individuals. However, "individuals with disabilities face specific barriers and challenges in their career development" (Feller & Walz, 1997, p. 243). Thus, special career development themes and issues need to be addressed with individuals with disabilities.

Career Counseling Issues for Persons With Disabilities

- Improving self-esteem.
- Accepting their disability.
- Implementing strategies for educating employers regarding accommodations.
- Developing interviewing skills equipping the individual to effectively answer questions related to his or her disability.
- Developing the ability to deal with insensitive questions during the selection process.
- Deciding when and how to disclose the disability to a prospective employer.

Counselors involved in the delivery of career development services also must review their own service delivery system. Although not exhaustive, counselors can use the following list of questions to begin reflecting on the accessibility of their services.

Questions for Evaluating Accessibility of Services for Disabled People

- Is the counselor's office accessible to the physically challenged individual?
- Is the restroom in the counselor's office adapted to meet the needs of individuals with disabilities?
- Does the career resource center include information about accommodations?
- Is the counselor aware of the Americans With Disabilities Act and its impact on the client and potential employers?

EXAMPLE

Americans With Disabilities Act and Counseling

Congress passed the **Americans With Disabilities Act** (ADA) to end discrimination against people with disabilities in the employment sector. The act states that "Employers must provide reasonable accommodations to qualified individuals with disabilities to enable them to do the essential functions of a job, unless the changes impose undue hardship upon the employer." Career counselors need to be aware of this law and need to educate their clients regarding protection afforded by the law. Subsequently, counselors will find their clients with disabilities pursuing positions often unexplored in the past.

■ Midlife Career Changes

At the midpoint of life, many people often question the purpose of their life and work and evaluate what they want to accomplish in their lifetime. Bradley (1990) noted that approximately 10% of adults between the ages of 30 and 44 transition from one job to another. Given the developmental issues relevant to midlife and the frequency with which people in this stage make job transitions, career counseling issues during the midlife stage often are intertwined with life issues. While pursuing career counseling, clients are encouraged to assess their values, goals, and life mission. To bring together the developmental and career issues that are so important to midlife career counseling, some specific questions can be asked.

Questions to Prompt Developmental and Career Reflection in Midlife

- What does the individual want to do with his or her life now?
- What are the dreams, vision, and interests that the client wants to pursue in the coming years?
- What are the most vital concerns related to midlife?
- How can the individual stop living to work and start working to live?
- How can the person bring a sense of balance to his or her life?
- In what ways can the individual use skills and abilities in new ways?
- What opportunities are available to individuals within their organization or with their current employer?

Four options available to individuals who wish to make a career change during their midlife stage (Feller & Walz, 1997) are encapsulated in the concepts of downshifting, moving sideways, moving up, and enriching the status quo. An understanding of these midlife career choices that can be adopted follows:

Downshifting: Individuals receive more for less by seeking positions within their present organizations, outside the organization, or in temporary positions that are challenging but pose less responsibility and fewer time demands than their current jobs.

Moving sideways: Individuals pursue lateral moves within their organization to positions providing them with more excitement and challenges.

Moving up: Individuals seek promotions or external positions with more responsibility and interest that can satisfy their needs.

Enriching the status quo: Individuals explore ways to live differently with what they have to resolve the conflict experienced by some adults during their midlife career development phase, including working flex time and carpooling or taking the bus to save money.

TECHNOLOGICAL COMPETENCIES FOR CAREER COUNSELORS

Today, career counselors cannot practice without competence in the use of the Internet and computer-based career resources and information. Technology related to Internet services and computer-assisted services has a direct impact on key components of the practice of career counseling.

Areas of Career Counseling Influenced by Technology

- Dissemination of career information.
- Career development assessment.
- Continuing education of workers.
- Job searches.
- Worker recruitment.

■ ACES Technology Competencies

The Association of Counselor Education and Supervision (ACES) established the following list of minimum technological competencies needed at graduation by counselor education students.

Technology Competencies for Professional Career Counselors

- Use productivity software to develop Web pages, presentations, résumés, letters, and reports.
- Use audiovisual equipment for presentations.
- Use computerized testing, diagnostic, and career decision-making programs with clients, on the Internet, in computer-assisted career guidance systems, and in career counseling centers.
- Use e-mail to contact employers and develop job-hunting networks.
- Help clients search for counseling-related information via the Internet, including information about careers, employment opportunities, educational and training opportunities, financial assistance and scholarships, treatment procedures, and social and personal information.
- Help clients prepare online résumés and conduct virtual job interviews.
- Subscribe to and participate in counseling-related listservs.
- Access and use counseling-related CD-ROM or DVD databases.
- Apply legal and ethical standards related to counseling services via the Internet.
- Identify the strengths and weaknesses of career development services offered on the Internet, including assessment and job placement services.
- Surf the Internet to find and use continuing education services.
- Use integrated technological systems.

 To obtain more details about ACES, check out their Web site:

▶ www.acesonline.net

■ Need for Technological Skills

Although competence in the use of computers and the World Wide Web is becoming increasingly important for all counselors, it is evident that professionals who enter the field of career counseling must have a very high level of technological skill. Some reasons for necessary technological competence are provided here.

Why Counselors Must Be Technologically Competent

- In 2005, the vast majority of information, resources, and job postings were accessed through the Internet.
- Web sites evolve rapidly and there are no quality controls in place to protect clients from misinformation or even fraud.
- It is incumbent on those in the career counseling field to stay up to date and aware of the frequent advances and changes in career-related technology.

Today's successful career counselor will gain and utilize expertise in a wide array of competencies including theoretical knowledge, assessment, research, and technology. As with all counseling fields, however, the counselor's effectiveness is determined by the development of a trusting counseling relationship, and the counselor's ability to support and guide the client through the stages of the counseling process.

Chapter 15: Key Terms

- ► Career counseling
- ► Americans With Disabilities Act
- ► Career
- ► Career development
- ► Person-oriented career
- ► Non-person-oriented career
- ► Circumscription

- ► Compromise
- ► Self-efficacy
- ► Displaced homemakers
- ► Interest inventories
- ► Leisure
- ► Vacophers
- ► Work

- ► Downshifting
- ► Moving sideways
- ► Moving up
- ► Enriching the status quo
- ► Life span
- ► Life space
- ► Self-concept

Multicultural Issues in Career and Lifestyle Counseling

Frederick T. Leong
Michigan State University

Erin E. Hardin
Texas Tech University

Arpana Gupta
University of Tennessee

In This Chapter

▶ *Understanding Cultural Issues in Career Counseling*
- Historical Approaches to Multicultural Career Counseling
- Important Terminology: Cross-Cultural and Multicultural

▶ *Multicultural Career Development: Traditional Theoretical Approaches*
- Holland's Person–Environment Fit Theory
- Roe's Theory of Occupational Classifications
- Super's Life Span–Life Space Theory
- Gottfredson's Theory of Circumscription and Compromise
- Social Cognitive Career Theory
- Theories Summary

▶ *Culture-Specific Variables*
- Acculturation
- Racial and Cultural Identity Development
- Racial Salience
- Loss of Face

▶ *Culturally Appropriate Career Counseling Models*
- Integrative Sequential Model of Career Counseling Services
- Culturally Appropriate Career Counseling Model
- Developmental Approach: Career-Development Assessment and Counseling
- Integrative Multidimensional Model

▶ *Future Research and Theory Development*
- Key Concepts in Career Counseling Research
- Recommendations for Future Research

UNDERSTANDING CULTURAL ISSUES IN CAREER COUNSELING

Multicultural issues are given increasing attention in the mental health field; the specialty area of career counseling is no exception. In light of the growing diversity of most societies, Western-based models of career counseling are being challenged; culturally appropriate career theories and models are being developed; and career counseling approaches are beginning to reflect issues of ethnicity, language, values, communication style, and time orientation (Fouad & Arbona, 1994; Leong, 1993), all in an effort to better serve culturally diverse clients. Because ethnic minorities also are most likely to seek counseling services that are related to career and educational issues (Sue & Sue, 1990), acknowledging the cultural context of the client is an important step in improving the process and outcome of career counseling for racial and ethnic minorities (Fouad & Bingham, 1995; Leong, 1993; Leong & Brown, 1995; Leong & Hartung, 1997).

■ Historical Approaches to Multicultural Career Counseling

Two approaches to ethnic minority development have arisen from vocational psychology and, today, influence multicultural career counseling and research. The first, cross-cultural counseling, has anthropological roots; the second, ethnic minority counseling, has a sociological foundation. Understanding the assumptions that underlie each approach is helpful to the discussion of multicultural career counseling.

Assumptions of Cross-Cultural Counseling

- The country of interest (e.g., the United States) and its majority population are the first unit of analysis in theory and research.
- Findings about the behaviors of people of the majority population (e.g., individuals of European American descent) are generalized to people of other cultures (Berry et al., 1992).
- An **etic perspective** that is concerned with universal laws that govern behavior across cultures is assumed.

Just as the cross-cultural approach is based on a set of assumptions, so the ethnic minority counseling approach is grounded in its own presuppositions.

Assumptions of Ethnic Minority Counseling

- Racial and ethnic groups are the first unit of analysis in theory and research.
- Racial and ethnic minority group behavior is not compared explicitly to that of the majority population.
- An **emic perspective** that focuses on culturally unique behaviors particular to certain groups is assumed.

■ Important Terminology: Cross-Cultural and Multicultural

It is important to clarify terminology relevant to the aims of this chapter, and specifically, the terms *multicultural* and *cross-cultural*, which often are used interchangeably. The career development literature suggests that both approaches are necessary. Leong and Brown (1995) understood the differences in terminology this way:

Multicultural career counseling: "[T]he study of career counseling in many cultures" (p. 145).

Cross-cultural career counseling: The study of how racial and ethnic minority groups adjust to European American majority work environments.

Both perspectives contribute valuable insights and can answer different questions about career counseling from a cross-cultural perspective. More frequently than not, though, researchers are interested in looking at cross-cultural career counseling, which can answer such questions as "To what extent do the predictions of established theories apply to minority groups?" or "What is the best way for a White counselor to work with a client of Asian American descent?"

> The absence of a comprehensive model for cross-cultural or multicultural career counseling suggests that scholars need to conceptualize career theories in ways that are more culturally appropriate, relevant, and effective.

MULTICULTURAL CAREER DEVELOPMENT: TRADITIONAL THEORETICAL APPROACHES

Vocational counseling and psychology scholars have begun to examine existing career theories and models from a multicultural context or with diverse clients in mind (e.g., Fitzgerald & Betz, 1994; Fouad, 1995; Leong, 1995; Savickas, 1995a, 1995b). A clear criticism that has arisen from these investigations is that most of the early research in career development relied on White undergraduate college participants and, thus, has limited applicability to career counseling with diverse populations. The absence of a comprehensive model for cross-cultural or multicultural career counseling suggests that scholars need to conceptualize career theories in ways that are more culturally appropriate, relevant, and effective. Although some scholars have made efforts to identify and describe variables that are specific to the career counseling of particular ethnic groups, such as African Americans (Cheatham, 1990) or Native Americans (Johnson, Swartz & Martin, 1995), no comprehensive career model exists. A number of both the traditional and more contemporary career theories have been modified to accommodate cultural variables important to diverse individuals (e.g., Gottfredson, 2002; Holland, 1985a; Lent, Brown, & Hackett, 1994, 2000; Roe & Lunneborg, 1991; Super, 1991). In this section, we summarize some traditional career development theories with specific emphasis given to cross-cultural criticisms as well as recommendations. Two theories—Gottfredson's theory of circumscription and compromise and the social cognitive career theory—are described in greater detail because they include elements that make them somewhat more sensitive to cultural issues in career counseling.

See Chapter 15 for more detail about career counseling theories.

■ Holland's Person–Environment Fit Theory

Holland's (1985a) person–environment fit theory emphasizes the impact of heredity and the environment on career choice and is among the most popular career theories. The cultural validity of the theory appears limited, however, when it is examined from a multicultural context. According to some researchers (Day & Rounds, 1998; Day, Rounds, & Swaney, 1998) Holland's hypothesized structure of interests (with, e.g., artistic interests being more similar to investigative than conventional interests) has been shown to be culturally appropriate among certain racial and ethnic groups. However, some cautions must be made.

Cross-Cultural Critique of Holland's Theory

- Research into the cultural validity of Holland's theory has produced mixed results for the theory's predictions about the relation between career interests and career choices.
- Among Asian Americans (Tang, Fouad, & Smith, 1999) and Mexican American girls (Flores & O'Brien, 2002), career interests were found not to be accurate predictors of career choice.
- The theory's concepts of **congruence,** the match between personal interest and work environment; **differentiation,** the difference between the highest and lowest interest; and **consistency,** the similarity between the top few interests, all showed differing degrees of validity with various ethnic and racial groups (Leong & Brown, 1995).

A number of recommendations need to be considered to increase the cross-cultural validity of Holland's career theory.

Recommendations for Holland's Career Theory

- Career counselors should be careful not to assume that a client's career interests are an accurate indicator of appropriate careers for the client (e.g., Asian Americans and Mexican American girls).
- A client's career should not be taken as evidence of the client's underlying interests.

■ Roe's Theory of Occupational Classifications

Roe (1956; Roe & Klos, 1972; Roe & Lunneborg, 1990) proposed a career theory that is based on a psychological classification system of occupations. She surmised that the evolution of one's personality eventually influences a career choice. Roe herself (Roe & Lunneborg, 1990) suggested that the occupational classification system does not address minorities or their cultural issues. One's family background, upbringing, family history, and genetic endowment all affect occupational choice. Because culturally based social and experiential factors are important in determining career choice, the generalizability of Roe's theory across various cultural, ethnic, and racial groups is limited by certain factors.

Cross-Cultural Critique of Roe's Theory

- Cultural concepts, although addressed by the theory, are in reality very difficult to measure accurately within the various ethnic groups.
- Differences in inherited abilities such as intelligence and temperament are difficult to interpret within cultural groups and need to be done with caution to avoid ethical dilemmas (Edwards & Polite, 1992; Helms, 1992).

Some recommendations can be made to strengthen this approach from a multicultural perspective.

Recommendations for Roe's Theory

- Roe's occupational classification system should be used with caution, if at all, with members of most racial and ethnic minorities because it fails to account for **occupational segregation,** or the tendency for members of particular groups to be overrepresented in some occupations and underrepresented in others.
- Counselors carefully should consider how external barriers and limited opportunities, rather than inherent deficiencies, might influence a client's apparent abilities and career choices.

■ Super's Life Span–Life Space Theory

Another highly influential career theory is that of Super (1990), who proposed that one's self-concept and the development of that self-concept over the life span are important factors in determining career choices. Super introduced the concept of career maturity, which he defined as follows:

Career maturity: The ability to perform the developmental tasks of life stages.

Critics argue that important factors influencing the development of the self-concepts of racial and ethnic minorities are unaccounted for in Super's theory

(Arbona, 1995, 1996; Carter & Cook, 1992). From a cross-cultural perspective, several other critiques of this theory can be made.

Cross-Cultural Critique of Super's Theory

- The life-span approach neither addresses the effects of disabling determinants such as poverty, socioeconomic status, and discrimination on self-concept, nor does the theory consider the restriction such determinants make on real and perceived occupational choices.
- The concept of career maturity has not been studied or validated with various cultural groups.
- A hallmark of career maturity in adolescence is the process of exploring career interests and crystallizing a vocational choice independent of the influence of significant others, such as family. The emphasis on independence is culturally inappropriate for members of many cultural groups that value collectivism and interdependence, such as Asian Americans (Hardin, Leong, & Osipow, 2001).
- The life-span theory may be most fitting to middle-class White men, who tend to have more educational and economic advantages than do members of other ethnic and racial groups who experience more limited opportunities due to institutional and individual discrimination (Arbona, 1995, 1996).

Several modifications to Super's model help to make it more cross-culturally relevant.

Recommendations for Super's Theory

- Counselors should explore with clients—especially those from lower socioeconomic backgrounds—how experiences of discrimination and poverty have affected their self-concept or led to restricted educational and vocational opportunities.
- Counselors should recognize that clients from more collectivist, family-oriented cultures (e.g., Asian Americans and Latinos) do not necessarily exhibit problematic dependence when they describe the importance of satisfying their family's wishes as part of choosing a career.
- Counselors should explore the preferences of significant others with clients rather than ignore them.
- Conflicts between a client's individual interests and those of his or her family should be handled in a way that respects both the client and family (Hardin et al., 2001).

■ Gottfredson's Theory of Circumscription and Compromise

According to Arbona (1995), Gottfredson's (2002) theory of circumscription and compromise, which proposes that the self-concept evolves as people pass through their own set of unique life stages, is a career model that accounts for cultural differences such as gender and social class. This theory posits that people develop perceptions over time of both the accessibility of certain jobs and the compatibility of those jobs with their values and roles. Two terms are key to understanding the tenets of this theory.

Circumscription: The process by which individuals gradually restrict the occupations they consider acceptable based on their developing self-concept.

Compromise: The process by which individuals choose among available but imperfect occupational alternatives by compromising some needs for others.

To further describe these terms, consider the example of an individual faced with two career choices: one that is gender "appropriate" but less prestigious and one that is more prestigious but gender "inappropriate." Of these two options, Gottfredson's theory predicts that the individual will choose the gender "appropriate" career.

Cross-Cultural Strengths of Gottfredson's Theory

- Gottfredson's (2002) reformed theory embraces a nature–nurture partnership theory in which both environment and heredity are important factors in individuals' career choices and decisions.
- Gottfredson's theory uses an understanding of the processes of circumscription and compromise to investigate whether individuals prematurely or unrealistically may have limited their career options. For example, the model explicitly acknowledges that one's perceptions of accessibility and one's self-concept are developed, in part, as a function of prevailing racial attitudes and discrimination.

The theory of circumscription and compromise accounts for environmental factors that strengthen its cross-cultural validity; however, several shortcomings—especially with regard to research results—still are evident.

Cross-Cultural Critique of Gottfredson's Theory

- The predictions made by the model of circumscription and compromise are difficult to test empirically, which has limited research on this theory.
- The few studies that have been conducted exhibited mixed results (Leung, 1993; Leung, Ivey, & Suzuki, 1994; Vandiver & Bowman, 1996).

Adjustments to Gottfredson's theory can build on its strengths as a culturally appropriate career model.

Recommendations for Gottfredson's Theory

- Counselors can help clients understand the role of environmental barriers in the processes of circumscription and compromise by exploring, for example, how experiences of discrimination, rather than their interests or abilities, may have led them to reject certain occupations as unacceptable or inaccessible.
- Continuing development on Gottfredson's theory should address issues of ethnic identity and socioeconomic class.

The practical applications of Gottfredson's theory continue to make it relevant to understanding the career development of culturally diverse individuals despite the lack of empirical evidence.

EXAMPLE

Research Considerations for Gottfredson's Career Model

Leung (1993) found that Asian Americans would compromise gender for prestige, which is contrary to Gottfredson's original predictions, but consistent with other research (Leong, 1995; Leung et al., 1994) that has demonstrated the importance of prestige to career decision making among Asian Americans.

■ Social Cognitive Career Theory

Social cognitive career theory (SCCT) builds on Bandura's (1977, 1986) work on self-efficacy, Krumboltz's (1996) social learning theory, and Hackett and Betz's (1981) application of self-efficacy theory to vocational psychology. Of the career theories discussed to this point, Lent et al.'s (1994) SCCT offers the most promise with regard to application to diverse cultural groups because it accounts for important culturally specific variables missing from many of the previously discussed career theories. Numerous studies in the literature focus on the cultural validity of this theory (e.g., Byars & Hackett, 1998; Hackett, Betz, Casas, & Rocha-Singh, 1992). Additionally, the theory focuses on other constructs that determine the extent of vocational choice within many groups, such as career interests, self-efficacy, and outcome expectations. Self-efficacy and outcome expectations are understood as follows:

Career self-efficacy expectations: Beliefs about one's own ability to perform occupationally relevant behaviors successfully; these expectations determine one's actions, effort, and persistence in regard to career behaviors.

Outcome expectations: Personal beliefs about the results of performance that are viewed as operating independently from efficacy expectations and dependent on actual performance.

Self-efficacy and outcome expectations are thought to be affected by learning experiences, which are, in turn, shaped by various background and personal factors, including race and ethnicity (see Lent et al., 1994, for more detailed discussion of the theory).

Cross-Cultural Critique of SCCT

- There is limited empirical evidence to support the theory's claim that career interests predict occupational choice for some ethnic groups (e.g., Asian Americans and Mexican American girls).
- Contextual variables such as barriers and outcome expectations still are understudied constructs, so their validity within various ethnic and racial cultures is difficult to evaluate (Lent et al., 2000).

To improve the cultural sensitivity of this approach, some recommendations can be made.

Recommendations for SCCT

- Career counselors should distinguish between collectivist and individualist cultural values and be aware of the role they may play in career behavior (Leong & Serafica, 1995).
- Counselors should acknowledge that variables such as acculturation can play a part in determining career choice (Leong & Chou, 1994), which is inconsistent with the original SCCT that suggests the effects of acculturation at the most are indirect (Lent et al., 1994).

EXAMPLE

Research Considerations for SCCT

Based on early work of Hackett and Betz (1981), numerous studies have tested the cultural validity of the hypothesis that self-efficacy beliefs influence interests and career choice (e.g., Dawkins, 1981; Hackett et al., 1992; Post, Stewart, & Smith, 1991; Post-Kammer & Smith, 1986). The general conclusion of these studies is that, "the extant research *does* suggest that career and academic self-efficacy significantly predict the academic achievement and career choice of people of color" (Byars & Hackett, 1998, p. 256).

However, in light of limitations of SCCT, Lent and his colleagues more recently have stated that "contextual factors may assert a *direct* influence on choice making or implementation. For example, particularly in collectivist cultures and subcultures, the wishes of influential others may hold sway over the individual's own personal career preferences," (Lent et al., 2000, p. 38). They went further, noting that "In individualistic cultures, as well, career interests or goals often need to be subjugated to economic or other environmental presses. Thus, SCCT posits that, when confronted by such presses, an individual's choice behavior may be guided less by personal interests than by other environmental and person factors" (p. 38).

■ Theories Summary

A review of some of the more key career models makes evident that, with the exception of SCCT, most models fail to consider seriously the cultural variables that influence career decisions and choices. Therefore, where traditional theories either are limited or not appropriate, new, more culturally sensitive career theories need to be developed and investigated. Before moving directly to a discussion about those theories, relevant, culture-specific variables that have been absent in traditional theories and that have attempted to be addressed by culturally appropriate career models will be examined.

CULTURE-SPECIFIC VARIABLES

A look at emic, or culture-specific variables that are germane to ethnic minority groups, can deepen the awareness of the impact of culture on career development, as well facilitate understanding of the processes involved when counseling culturally different individuals. A few of these variables are mentioned only briefly here due to space limitations. More information may be found in Leong and Brown (1995).

■ Acculturation

Acculturation is an important variable in understanding the process of career development among various ethnic minorities. Acculturation is understood as (Arbona, 1995; Johnson et al., 1995; Leong & Tata, 1990; Padilla, 1980):

Acculturation: The degree of identification an individual from an incoming cultural group makes with the host culture.

The following research about acculturation needs to be considered.

Key Areas of Research Around Acculturation

- Acculturation has been found to be related to work values (e.g., salary, task satisfaction, self-realization, object orientation, solitude, group cohesiveness and preference, or ideas–data orientation).
- Researchers have argued that different acculturation stages (i.e., separationist, assimilationist, integrationist, and marginalist) predict differing career outcomes (see Leong & Chou, 1994, for a detailed discussion of particular hypotheses regarding the relation between specific career outcomes and stage of acculturation for Asian Americans).

■ Racial and Cultural Identity Development

Racial and cultural identity development is another culture-specific variable that significantly influences career development. The process of racial and cultural identity development can be understood as follows:

> **Racial and cultural identity development:** The processes used by individuals of minority groups and oppressed peoples to understand their own identity in light of their culture, the culture of dominant groups, and the convergence of the two cultures.

Two of many racial identity models include the system Helms (1993) described for African Americans and a similar model Sue and Sue (1990) formulated for Asian Americans. Additionally, racial and cultural identity development models also exist for people of European descent (Helms, 1984, 1995). The career literature (Brown, 1995; Helms & Piper, 1994), provides evidence that racial identity can affect the vocational process, including career maturity, the perception of work environment and opportunities, work satisfaction, and satisfactoriness and racism at work (Parham & Austin, 1994).

See Chapter 4 for more information on racial identity development models and White racial identity development.

■ Racial Salience

A related factor that can influence the vocational process is racial salience, which can be understood as follows:

> **Racial salience:** The degree to which an individual perceives race as a factor affecting workplace options.

■ Loss of Face

Finally, the concept of loss of face or reputation must be considered and understood by counselors attempting to provide competent career interventions for numerous ethnic groups, and especially Asian Americans (Redding & Ng, 1982). This is a salient variable not only for understanding social behavior of the Asian American population, but also for shedding some light into the world of work for this population.

Emic approaches to career counseling that address these culturally specific variables can help counselors better understand the world of work for racial and ethnic minorities. Adjusting existing Western career models to incorporate multicultural elements will be helpful to a limited degree. For a more comprehensive understanding of vocational development for different ethnic and racial groups, these culturally specific, non-European constructs also will have to be thoroughly investigated on their own.

CULTURALLY APPROPRIATE CAREER COUNSELING MODELS

New career counseling models that are sensitive to cultural variables and issues are being developed. Four models that can guide career counseling with various groups and research efforts include the following:

- Integrative sequential model (ISM).
- Culturally appropriate model.
- Developmental approach.
- Integrative multidimensional approach.

■ Integrative Sequential Model of Career Counseling Services

The ISM is an ordered, comprehensive career model that accounts for the cultural context in which career counseling occurs (Leong & Hartung, 1997).

Characteristics of ISM

- Emphasizes the importance of culture, especially with regard to occupational issues.
- Includes four stages: problem emergence, help seeking, evaluation of vocational problems, and career intervention resulting in some counseling outcomes.
- Takes a sequential stage approach to career counseling that allows counselors to adjust their approach depending on the client's culture, preferences, and history.
- Highlights the role natural cultural history plays before, during, and after the career counseling process.

The following is a description of salient aspects of the stages of the ISM approach to career counseling.

First Stage of ISM: Emergence of the Career Problem

- The conceptualization of the career problem inextricably is linked to culture.
- Cultural values and ideals determine what is considered to be a normal work life and what is or is not a career problem.
- Counselors must approach career problems within clients' ethnic frameworks to avoid making faulty assumptions about clients and their career problems.
- Some cultures consider work to be a central part of one's identity, whereas other cultures view work primarily as a source of income. Individuals from these two cultures, therefore, are likely to conceptualize job satisfaction differently.

Clients may be reluctant to seek career counseling, may wait until the problems are serious, and may present their problems in the context of their impact on the family system.

Second Stage of ISM: Help Seeking

- The degree to which a particular racial and ethnic group seeks counseling, in general, is reflective of extent to which individuals in that group will seek career counseling services.
- Factors that increase reluctance to seek help include language barriers between counselors and clients and the traditional structure of therapy (i.e., self-disclosure by client) that is in opposition to values held by collectivistic cultures.
- Culturally diverse clients frequently seek services at the suggestion of family, friends, or clergy.
- Counselors are encouraged to discover how the referral source and other people close to the client influence the client's career options.

After clients have decided to seek assistance through career counseling, the counselor can begin to assess the vocational problems.

Third Stage of ISM: Evaluation of Vocational Problems

- Counselors conduct an intake to assess the nature of the career problem.
- Counselors may use career and personality tests to make a more accurate assessment of the client's career problems.
- Evaluation of career problems leads to career counseling if it is determined that the individual is in need of services.

In the final stage, the counselor uses assessment data and client input to make culturally appropriate interpretations of the problem and create interventions.

Fourth Stage of ISM: Career Intervention

- Counselors select traditional career assessment tools that help clarify clients' vocational needs as well as talk to clients about their subjective work needs that are influenced by cultural heritage.
- Accurate assessment is related to the counselor's multicultural competence.
- Interpretation of assessment data is made best by preparing the client for the results, presenting the results, and asking for client input about how the data fits with subjective experiences.

To illustrate the application of this career model across its various stages, we use an example about Asian Americans.

EXAMPLE

Using ISM With an Asian American Client

The first stage in career counseling from the ISM approach involves understanding the cultural and ethnic framework inside of which career problems emerge. When considering the situation of Asian Americans who seek career counseling, some basics about the culture must be recognized. First, because of the collectivistic, interdependent attitudes held by many Asian Americans, which lead to a sense of obligation to society and family, and because of cultural norms and values that stigmatize discussing problems outside the family, Asian Americans may be less comfortable than their White counterparts in discussing their career problems with others. Second, Asian Americans also are more likely to view their problems as complicated and connected to other members of their family or community. Recognizing and validating these cultural traits help counselors to appreciate the courage it may have taken the client to decide to seek services.

Asian Americans who eventually seek services often encounter counselors who use approaches in the second stage that stress autonomy and independence. For example, counselors may encourage clients to explore their personal career interests without regard for their parents' wishes. Such counselors are likely to be perceived by more interdependent Asian American clients as unhelpful and culturally inappropriate.

During the third stage, care must be taken not to interpret culturally appropriate interdependence as a sign of career immaturity or being too dependent on others. Research has demonstrated that this is an erroneous assumption with Asian Americans (Hardin et al., 2001).

Because many Asian American clients, particularly those with lower acculturation, expect a more directive and expert counselor, a nondirective and egalitarian counselor may cause further discomfort, puzzlement, and dissatisfaction. Thus, unfavorable outcomes may be obtained, the client may return to the community without resolving his or her problem and perceive the counseling process negatively. Counseling issues can be resolved from the perspective and values of the Asian American client. This means practicing within multiculturally competent ways specific to the client's culture.

Culturally Appropriate Career Counseling Model

The culturally appropriate model was introduced by Fouad and Bingham (1995) as an extension of Ward and Bingham's (1993) model for women from minority cultures. The underlying assumption of this model is that culture is an integral part of career counseling, so much so that it should be infused into every aspect of the counseling experience. Moreover, in response to the increasing amounts of cross-cultural and multicultural literature in the counseling field (e.g., Sue & Sue, 1990), the theory pays particular attention to factors such as racial identity development, discrimination, family role expectations, gender role expectations, and other worldview dimensions. Fouad and Bingham (1995) proposed seven steps to their culturally appropriate career counseling model; these are listed here.

Seven Steps of the Culturally Appropriate Model

1. Establish a culturally appropriate relationship with the client.
2. Identify career issues.
3. Assess the effects of cultural variables.
4. Set career counseling goals.
5. Design culturally appropriate counseling interventions.
6. Make career-related decisions.
7. Implement decisions and follow-up.

Each step of the model varies depending on the racial and ethnic identity of the client and needs to be adjusted to fit the culture of the client.

Developmental Approach: Career-Development Assessment and Counseling

The Career-Developmental Assessment and Counseling Model (C-DAC; Super, 1983) is a promising approach to career counseling because contextual and multicultural concepts, such as work role importance and values, are inherent to life span–life space theory from which the C-DAC model emerged. Hartung et al. (1998) proposed two modifications of the C-DAC model to increase its cultural relevance: (a) formally assessing the client's cultural identity in the first stage of the model, and (b) considering cultural identity throughout the process of implementing the C-DAC model. Because cultural identity is a key component of the C-DAC model, it is important to understand what is meant by this term. Hartung et al. (1998, p. 281) gave this definition:

> **Cultural identity:** "[I]nvolves taking account of cultural differences that may overlay … other components and influence individual career development and vocational behavior. These differences typically surface in attitudes and discriminatory practices in the current job market and world of work."

Characteristics of C-DAC

- The C-DAC model is especially beneficial for career counselors whose theoretical orientation is developmental in nature.
- Components of differential, developmental, and phenomenological theories (e.g., elements from Parsons's and Holland's theories, Super's theory, and narrative therapies, respectively) are blended into a comprehensive approach in C-DAC.
- C-DAC is implemented in a four-step process, a major component of which is assessment through a battery of career assessment tools that provides data about a client's career knowledge, values, and interests.
- The Multicultural Career Counseling Checklist (Bingham & Ward, 1996, 1997; Ward & Bingham, 1993) and the Career Counseling Checklist (Bingham & Ward, 1996, 1997; Ward & Bingham, 1993) are two recommended instruments.
- C-DAC is traditionally comprised of five dimensions that lead counselors to explore work and nonwork roles, understand career values and interests, identify life stages and tasks, assess career knowledge, and create plans of action.

Implementing the C-DAC model typically calls on the counselor to follow four main steps.

Four-Step Process of the C-DAC Model

1. Conduct initial interview to evaluate client's needs, review client records, assess the importance of work roles relative to other life roles, and create a preliminary plan.
2. Ask client to complete a battery of tests to determine the client's readiness, adaptability, interests, and values in making career decisions.
3. Review all the information gathered via formal and informal assessment techniques.
4. Begin the career counseling process in which data are explored and interpreted.

The C-DAC model intentionally is adjusted for cross-cultural validity; however, several recommendations can improve this approach's cultural competence.

Recommendations for Increasing Cultural Validity of the C-DAC

- Incorporate a sixth dimension to C-DAC that evaluates the cultural identity development of clients so that culture is recognized as a core component of the model. This modification would give consideration to such important cultural variables as acculturation, cultural value orientation, external career barriers such as racism, discrimination, and special racial group career development stages and behaviors.

- Conceptualize the developmental approach from universal (e.g., mainstream culture), group (e.g., specific cultural group), and individual (e.g., personality and behavior) levels.
- Encourage counselors to reflect on their own cultural values, beliefs, and behaviors, as well as examine their own career development from a culturally sensitive model such as C-DAC (Hartung et al., 1998).

■ Integrative Multidimensional Model

This model is an adaptation of cross-cultural counseling to the career counseling process. The integrative multidimensional model (IMM) was initially developed by Leong (1996) and then was extended to career counseling situations (Leong & Hardin, 2002; Leong & Hartung, 2003).

Characteristics of IMM

- IMM is based on the tripartite approach that considers and integrates career issues within the context of the individual, group, and universal dimensions.
- IMM increases the validity of the intervention and also provides a complete, comprehensive, and dynamic insight into the client's world.
- IMM is based on an eclectic style of therapy and can be applied to any career theory or model already established.

Past cross-cultural research efforts have focused only on one of these three dimensions, ignoring the others (Leong, 1995); the IMM is an attempt to address this shortcoming.

Emic or culture-specific approaches can be used to help explain anomalies within some of the older Eurocentric-based career models. However, it cannot be assumed that all variance observed with racial or ethnic minorities is due to cultural factors. Thus, care must be taken in making assumptions and in examining all three dimensions (individual, group, and universal) and how they interact to produce certain outcomes. Utilizing the IMM bodes well for cross-culturally competent career counselors.

FUTURE RESEARCH AND THEORY DEVELOPMENT

It appears from the preceding discussions that unless some significant strides are made to modify or develop culturally appropriate career models and theories, career counseling with racially and ethnically diverse clients will be both difficult and ineffective. It is obvious that there is still much that needs to be done in the investigation and creation of culture-specific factors and variables with regard to the career development and vocational behavior of various cultural populations.

Key Concepts in Career Counseling Research

A number of concepts have been identified by various scholars (Arbona, 1995; Brown, 1995; Leong, 1995, 1998; Leong & Serafica, 1995; Johnson et al., 1995) as important to future research on culturally appropriate career models.

Concepts of Relevance to Career Counseling Research

- Experiences of discrimination.
- Poverty (socioeconomic status).
- Acculturation.
- Gender.
- Cultural values.
- Ethnic identity.
- Cultural history.
- Reputation or loss of face.
- Migration status.
- Region or country of origin.
- "Colorism."
- Tribal identification and reservation versus nonreservation status of tribes.

Recommendations for Future Research

Once these culturally sensitive theories and models have been developed they need to be taken to the next level by being tested with various cultural groups. Suggestions for future research may address the following:

- Sufficiently documented studies that contribute to the growth of career literature.
- Attention to adequate sample sizes to obtain significant results.
- Between-group and within-group studies that apply across a wide range of racial and ethnic groups.
- Longitudinal and cross-sectional studies utilizing diverse cultural groups.
- Outcome studies that investigate new or modified career models.

Chapter 16: Key Terms

- Multicultural career counseling
- Cross-cultural career counseling
- Etic perspective
- Emic perspective
- Congruence
- Differentiation

- Consistency
- Occupational segregation
- Career maturity
- Circumscription
- Compromise
- Career self-efficacy expectations
- Outcome expectations

- Acculturation
- Racial and cultural identity development
- Racial salience
- Cultural identity

Fundamentals of Professional School Counseling

Mariellen Kerr
Duquesne University

Carol Dahir
New York Institute of Technology

In This Chapter

▶ *Foundations of Professional School Counseling*
- What Is School Counseling?
- Brief Historical Background
- Professionalism for School Counselors

▶ *ASCA National Standards*
- Domain 1: Academic Development
- Domain 2: Career Development
- Domain 3: Personal and Social Development

▶ *ASCA National Model*
- The Foundation
- The Delivery System
- The Management System
- The Accountability System
- Programmatic Approach: A New Paradigm for School Counseling
- Collaboration and Systemic Support

▶ *The Transforming School Counseling Initiative*
- Implications for School Counselor Practice
- The Counseling Process
- Consultation
- Coordination of Services
- Leadership
- Advocacy
- Collaboration and Teaming
- Managing Resources
- Use of Data

▶ *School Counseling in the 21st Century*
- Functions and Responsibilities of the School Counselor
- The Transformed School Counselor

FOUNDATIONS OF PROFESSIONAL SCHOOL COUNSELING

Entire semesters and textbooks are devoted to presenting detailed discussions of the various fundamental elements of school counseling. The purpose of this chapter is to present an overview of the major tenets of school counseling in a simple and concise manner for easy reference. Additionally, in this chapter we provide insight into the evolution of the profession and the recent initiatives that have significantly influenced the direction of professional school counseling in the 21st century.

■ What Is School Counseling?

The American School Counselor Association (ASCA) Governing Board adopted the following definition of **school counseling** (ASCA, 1997):

> Counseling is a process of helping people by assisting them in making decisions and changing behavior. School counselors work with all students, school staff, families, and members of the community as an integral part of the education program. School counseling programs promote school success through a focus on academic achievement, prevention, and intervention activities, advocacy and social-emotional and career development.

This definition shifted the focus of school counselors from the traditional approach of reactive and responsive services to one that influences the entire school community.

■ Brief Historical Background

Throughout time, young people have sought the counsel of elders regarding life issues. The roots of school counseling, arguably the oldest form of systematic counseling in the United States, if not the world, can be traced back to European research into individual differences, assessment techniques, psychological classifications, and explanations for behavior (Herr, 2003). The social and political climate in the United States during the late 19th century heightened awareness of human rights issues in response to massive immigration and the exploitation of children during the Industrial Revolution. These conditions spurred the need for a school-based professional to take an active role in child welfare and vocational guidance and set the stage for the emergence of systematized counseling within the schools. The birth and growth of school counseling thus has been influenced by many sociopolitical and professional occurrences. The following timeline represents some of these major events.

*Timeline of Major Events and Legislative Acts
in the Development of School Counseling*

- 1895: George Merrill develops first vocational guidance program in San Francisco.
- 1898: Jesse B. Davis encourages Detroit English teachers to include guidance lessons in character education, interpersonal relationships, and vocational interests.
- 1905: Alfred Binet develops first intelligence test to spearhead the testing movement and shape the content and methods of school counseling throughout the century.
- 1908: Frank Parsons, considered the father of vocational guidance, establishes the Bureau of Vocation in Boston. The term *vocational guidance* is first used and actions from this meeting launched vocational decision making in the schools (Zeran, Lallas, & Wegner, 1964).
- 1909: Parsons's book *Choosing a Vocation* is published posthumously. Parsons's most notable contribution may be his trait and factor approach to the vocational guidance process.
- 1930s: The Great Depression results in massive unemployment and the U.S. Employment Service and Bureau of Labor Statistics are established. Demand for career information prompts the publication of the *Dictionary of Occupational Titles* in 1939.
- 1940s: Expansion of testing was a hallmark of this decade, the result of the need for job classification in the armed forces. School counseling jobs continue to grow.
- 1952: American Personnel and Guidance Association (APGA) is formed.
- 1953: ASCA is established as a division of APGA, increasing credibility and advocating standards of practice and ethical guidelines for school counselors.
- 1957: Russia launches *Sputnik.* The U.S. education system is faulted for failing to produce students whose math and science skills were superior to Russian students.
- 1958: Considered to be the most important event in the history of school counseling, the National Defense Education Act (NDEA) is passed, providing federal funding for the training of secondary counselors, resources to establish and support guidance programs for the purpose of identifying students talented in math and science, and the guidance and advisement to pursue higher education.
- 1960s: In a decade of peak legislative support, the Elementary and Secondary Education Act (ESEA) is enacted in 1965, designating funding for guidance and in particular, for the training of elementary counselors. Along with amendments to NDEA and ESEA, amendments to the Vocational Education Act of 1963 expand funding for focus on career guidance for the disadvantaged, disabled, and the expansion into elementary schools.
- 1970s: Federal legislation continues support of guidance with specific focus on career and vocational education. Career Education Incentive Act of 1976 solidifies career guidance in schools by infusing it into the curriculum as part of the teaching and learning process. The 1976 amendment to ESEA includes major

support for guidance and counseling in the schools. Also in 1976 the National Occupation Information Coordinating Committee (NOICC) is established to provide career development resources to K–12 counselors.

- 1980s: Passage of the Carl D. Perkins Vocational Education Act in 1984 and subsequent amendments are the major source of funding and support for guidance in the schools during this decade.

- 1990s: The Perkins Act continues to provide major funding. The School to Work Opportunities Act of 1994 supports career and guidance counseling to assist students transitioning from school to the workplace. The Elementary School Counseling Demonstration Act of 1995, reauthorized in 1999 and 2001, provides funding to expand counseling programs and provide greater access for students by decreasing the counselor-to-student ratio, which was 1 school counselor to 561 students nationally in 1999.

- 1997: ASCA National Standards, content standards for student academic, career, and personal and social development are published as a proactive response to the GOALS 2000: The Educate America Act of 1994, which advocates for high expectations for all students regardless of race, ethnicity, and socioeconomic status.

- 1997: The Education Trust De Witt-Wallace Reader's Digest Transforming School Counseling Initiative defines a new vision for school counseling that emphasizes leadership, advocacy, use of data, and a commitment to support high levels of student achievement. This initiative also supports six institutions of higher education to develop a new model of school counselor preparation.

- 2001: No Child Left Behind (NCLB) Act passes to continue the work of school improvement in GOALS 2000 (1994), emphasizing accountability and high-stakes testing.

- 2002: National School Counselor Training Initiative is established by the Education Trust and the MetLife Foundation with the vision that school counselors are ideally situated in schools to serve as advocates for programs to promote success for all students.

- 2003: The ASCA National Model: A Framework for School Counseling Programs is published. ASCA collaborated with the Education Trust to infuse the themes of the Transforming School Counseling Initiative—advocacy, leadership, and systemic change—throughout the document.

■ Professionalism for School Counselors

The premier professional association for school counselors, the ASCA is a division of the American Counseling Association (ACA). This worldwide organization was founded in 1952 and represents more than 18,000 professional school counselors from pre-K to the college campus. With a motto of "One Vision, One Voice," the ASCA mission is to promote professionalism and ethical practices while focusing on professional development and researching effective practices aimed at improving school counseling programs (ASCA, 2004a).

See Chapter 3 for more information about professionalism in school counseling.

Check out the ASCA Web site for more information about this professional organization:

- ► www.schoolcounselor.org
- ► Or call (703) 683-ASCA (2722).

ASCA NATIONAL STANDARDS

The **ASCA National Standards** were developed in response to the GOALS 2000 (1994): Educate America Act and serve as the "single most legitimizing document in the [school counseling] profession" (Bowers, Hatch, & Schwallie-Giddis, 2001). The standards define what students should know and be able to do as the result of participating in a comprehensive, developmental K–12 school counseling program (Campbell & Dahir, 1997). Additionally, the National Standards served as the groundwork for the development of a national, comprehensive model for school counselor programs that today is known as the ASCA National Model. The goals of the National Standards include the following:

1. Promote equitable access to school counseling programs and services for all students.
2. Establish similar goals and expectations for all students.
3. Identify and prioritize the key content components for school counseling programs.
4. Position school counseling as an integral component of the academic mission of the school.
5. Identify the knowledge and skills that all students should acquire as a result of the pre-K through Grade 12 school counseling programs.
6. Ensure that school counseling programs are comprehensive in design and delivered in a systematic fashion for all students (Campbell & Dahir, 1997).

The ASCA National Standards address three domains of student development: academic development, career development, and personal and social development. Within each domain, three specific standards outline student competencies and indicators expressed as specific knowledge, attitudes, or skills obtainable as a result of participating in the school counseling program.

■ Domain 1: Academic Development

The program standards for academic development guide the school counseling program to implement strategies and activities to support and maximize each student's ability to learn (Campbell & Dahir, 1997). **Academic development** helps students achieve the attitudes, knowledge, and skills necessary to negotiate the landscape and landmines to succeed in schools.

Standards for Academic Development

1. *Standard A:* Students will acquire the attitudes, knowledge, and skills that contribute to effective learning in the classroom.
2. *Standard B:* Students will complete school with the academic preparation essential to choose from a wide variety of substantial postsecondary options, including college.
3. *Standard C:* Students will understand the relation of academics to the world of work, and to life at home and in the community.

EXAMPLE

Putting Domain 1 Standards Into Practice

Sample activities to address the standards for academic development include the following.

- *Elementary:* A classroom lesson focusing on development of a "Can do" attitude utilizing the book *The Little Engine That Could* by Watty Piper and age-appropriate activities meets Standard A.
- *Middle school:* A classroom lesson developed collaboratively with the math teacher estimating, calculating, and graphing present levels of time spent devoted to academic enhancement activities compared with leisure activities, including analysis and discussion of the results, meets Standards A and C.
- *High school:* Individual academic advisement and credit review sessions with students to determine course selection in accordance with postsecondary plans meets Standard B.

■ Domain 2: Career Development

The program standards for **career development** guide the school counseling program to provide the foundation for the acquisition of skills, attitudes, and knowledge that enable students to make a successful transition from school to the world of work, and from job to job across the life span (Campbell & Dahir, 1997).

Standards for Career Development

1. *Standard A:* Students will acquire the skills to investigate the world of work in relation to knowledge of self and to make informed career decisions.
2. *Standard B:* Students will employ strategies to achieve future career success and satisfaction.
3. *Standard C:* Students will understand the relation among personal qualities, education and training, and the world of work.

EXAMPLE

Putting Domain 2 Standards Into Practice

Sample activities to address the standards for career development include the following.

- *Elementary:* A classroom lesson focusing on the relation between personal qualities and the world of work utilizing the book *How Santa Got His Job* by Stephen Krensky meets Standards A and C.
- *Middle school:* A program in which students complete interview forms by choosing three presenters at the school's career exploration day meets Standard A and C.
- *High school:* The completion of a career portfolio over 4 years meets Standards A, B, and C.

■ Domain 3: Personal and Social Development

The program standards for **personal and social development** guide the school counseling program to provide the foundation for personal and social growth as students progress through school and into adulthood (Campbell & Dahir, 1997).

Standards for Personal and Social Development

1. *Standard A:* Students will acquire the attitudes, knowledge, and interpersonal skills to help them understand and respect self and others.
2. *Standard B:* Students will make decisions, set goals, and take appropriate action to achieve goals.
3. *Standard C:* Students will understand safety and survival skills. (All standards are reprinted by permission of the ASCA.)

EXAMPLE

Putting Domain 3 Standards Into Practice

Sample activities addressing the standards for personal and social development include the following.

- *Elementary:* A classroom lesson focusing on strategies to deal with teasing utilizing the book *Simon's Hook* by Karen Burnett meets Standards A, B, and C.
- *Middle school:* School-wide adoption of a peer mediation program for resolving conflicts between students meets Standards A and B.
- *High school:* Collaboration with English teachers to develop a unit on effective communication skills focusing on active listening and "I" messages meets Standards A and B.

The complete National Standards for Students are available from ASCA:

▶ www.schoolcounselor.org

ASCA NATIONAL MODEL

The **ASCA National Model** was created to assist school districts in designing school counseling programs that support the academic success of every student. The model itself serves as a framework for the development of a **comprehensive school counseling program,** taking into account individual state and local needs. The concept of the comprehensive school counseling program was developed by Gysbers and Moore (1981) and refined over the past 20 years by Gysbers and Henderson (2000). The ASCA National Model supports the overall mission of schools by promoting student achievement, career planning, and personal and social development for every student. In this model, the school counselor is defined as the program coordinator with an emphasis on counselor advocacy, collaboration, and leadership skills to effect systemic change. Finally, the design, development, implementation, and evaluation of a school counseling program are accomplished through effective collaboration with students, parents, faculty, administrators, and community, business, and higher education partners.

> The ASCA National Model was created to assist school districts in designing school counseling programs that support the academic success of every student. The model itself serves as a framework for the development of a comprehensive school counseling program, taking into account individual state and local needs.

To operationalize the overall goals of school counseling programs, the comprehensive model has an organizational structure that consists of four components (Gysbers & Henderson, 2000) adopted in the ASCA National Model (2003, 2005a). The four interrelated components that are the core of the model are foundation, delivery system, management system, and accountability. The model also accounts for the skills of leadership, advocacy, collaboration, and working toward systemic change as key philosophies and transformed skills (Education Trust, 1997), all criti-

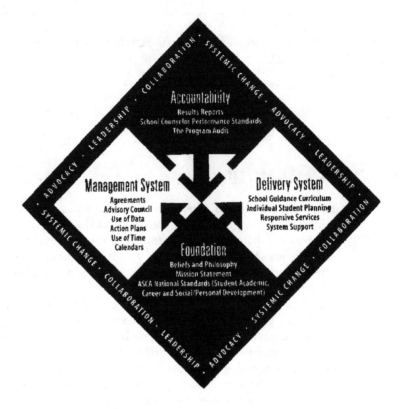

FIGURE 17.1 ASCA National Model. Reprinted by permission of the ASCA.

cal to the new mission of school counselors. See Figure 17.1 for a depiction of the National Model as developed by the ASCA (2003, 2005a).

■ The Foundation

The component of the model called the foundation addresses the belief and mission that every student will benefit from the school counseling program; it also houses the National Standards for School Counseling Programs, the foundation of the counseling program.

■ The Delivery System

The aspect of the model known as the delivery system defines several ways in which counselors can implement a standards-based program with students, such as teaching through a counseling curriculum, individual planning with students, and utilizing intervention, prevention, and responsive services. There are a number of components that comprise the delivery system.

Components of the Delivery System

1. *Guidance curriculum* is developmental, systematic programming delivered in classroom or small-group format and includes parent workshops. The suggested time for counselors to devote to guidance curriculum is 35% to 40% in an elementary school, 25% to 35% in a middle or junior high school, and 15% to 25% in a high school.
2. *Responsive services* include individual and group counseling, crisis intervention counseling, consultation, referral, and peer facilitation. The suggested time for counselors to devote to responsive services is 30% to 40% in an elementary school, 30% to 40% in a middle or junior high school, and 25% to 35% in a high school.
3. *Individual student planning* for individuals or groups of students includes advisement, assessment, placement, and evaluation of individual learning and attainment of academic, career, and personal and social competencies. The suggested time for counselors to devote to individual planning is 5% to 10% in an elementary school, 15% to 25% in a middle or junior high, and 25% to 35% in a high school.
4. *System support* is the establishment, maintenance, and evaluation of the school counseling program, including professional development of self and staff, community and public relations, district committees, consultation, and collaboration. Leadership and advocacy skills are used to promote systemic change. The suggested time for counselors to devote to system support is 10% to 15% in an elementary school, 10% to 15% in a middle or junior high school, and 15% to 20% in a high school.

■ The Management System

The management system is the part of the national model that deals with organizational processes and tools needed to deliver a comprehensive school counseling program. Included in this component are activities such as principal–counselor partnership plans, annual calendar, advisory council, and time and task analysis. It is the "who" and "when" of the counseling program.

Components Addressed by the Management System

- Management agreements.
- Action plans.
- Advisory council.
- Use of time.
- Use of data.
- Calendars.

The Accountability System

The accountability system is the facet of the national model that addresses the evaluation of the effectiveness of the school counselor's work in measurable terms, such as impact over time, performance evaluation, and a program audit. It answers the question, "How are students different as a result of the school counseling program?"

Some Measurable Means of Evaluating Counselors' Effectiveness

- Results reports—impact over time.
- Program audits.
- School counselor performance standards.

Programmatic Approach: A New Paradigm for School Counseling

The national model has shifted the focus of counseling from a student-by-student system of service delivery to a programmatic approach that is comprehensive and developmental. Through system support and collaboration with other professionals in the school building, school counselors influence policies and practices, and they advocate for students and the counseling program.

Collaboration and Systemic Support

School counselors are most successful when they engage others in the process of supporting every student in achieving his or her academic, career, and personal and social development. Furthermore, how successful a school or district is in reaching its improvement goals is highly dependent on the degree to which all school members collaborate and work as a team toward those goals. In a district with a comprehensive school counseling program, administration, faculty, staff, families, and community partners understand they have explicit roles and responsibilities in the program to ensure that every student benefits. Everyone interacts to assist students in achieving their goals.

Roles and Responsibilities of School Organization Personnel and Students

- School counselors provide proactive leadership to ensure that every student can succeed. They manage the comprehensive program and coordinate strategies and activities with others (teachers, support staff, parents, community agencies, business representatives) to meet the stated goals, standards, and competencies.
- Teachers are partners with school counselors. They develop and infuse guidance activities that are integral to good learning rather than extraneous, disconnected, or added material into the instructional program. Teachers can team or coteach

with counselors in the classroom. They may also serve as advisors or mentors to students.

- Students participate actively and assume responsibility for meeting the counseling standards and competencies. They can identify the skills, knowledge, and attitudes that they have gained in structured counseling sessions. Students and their families, working individually with counselors, develop learning plans for school and plan for life after high school.

- Pupil personnel services collaborate and team with the school counselors to ensure that school psychologists, school social workers, school nurses, student assistance counselors, and other support personnel are actively involved in supporting each student's academic, career, and personal and social development. They assist students with mental, physical, and social issues. They support students and families by providing in-school services, or referrals or information regarding outside agencies.

Specific counselor attitudes, knowledge, and skills facilitate the school counselor's positive impact on classrooms, schools, and families that most affect student development. School counselors must demonstrate strong communication, consultation, and leadership skills to effect systemic change. Together, the comprehensive program and the "new vision" skills of the school counselors will transform the school counseling program.

 For a more detailed description of the National Model visit the ASCA Web site at:

  ▶ www.schoolcounselor.org

THE TRANSFORMING SCHOOL COUNSELING INITIATIVE

The Education Trust, with support from the Dewitt-Wallace Reader's Digest Fund, began work in 1996 to identify what school counselors need to know to help all students succeed academically. A group of universities were funded to partner with the Education Trust to redesign counselor education programs to prepare school counselors as advocates, leaders, and systemic change agents in school improvement. The goals of the **Transforming School Counseling Initiative** (Education Trust, 1997) include those listed next.

Goals of the Transforming School Counseling Initiatives

- Point counselors in the direction of improving academic achievement and eliminating the achievement gap.

- Connect school counseling to each school district's mission and goals of school improvement.
- Provide school counselors with the tools to develop school counseling programs that include student competencies and outcomes based on the national standards (Campbell & Dahir, 1997) and aligned with state and district curriculum standards.
- Encourage school counselors to use data to develop measurable student outcomes. School counselors use school-based data to work collaboratively toward the goals of school improvement (Stone & Dahir, 2006a).

■ Implications for School Counselor Practice

In 2003, the Education Trust and MetLife Foundation established the National Center for Transforming School Counseling to deliver focused professional development to practicing school counselors and help all students achieve at high academic levels of success. The Transforming School Counseling initiative, with its more systemic approach to school counseling, resulted in a number of practical changes in the day-to-day practice of school counseling. Table 17.1 summarizes these changes.

Transformed school counselors deliver comprehensive school counseling programs by applying these skills in a "new vision" manner. In the following sections we provide a concise overview of the transforming role of school counselors as understood from the Transforming School Counselors Initiative.

<table>
<tr><td colspan="2" align="center">**TABLE 17.1**
Differences in Traditional and Transformed School Counselor Practices</td></tr>
<tr><td>*The Practice of the Traditional School Counselor*
(Service-Driven model)</td><td>*The Practice of the Transformed School Counselor*
(Data-Driven and Standards-Based Model)</td></tr>
<tr><td>
• Counseling
• Consultation
• Coordination of services
</td><td>
• Counseling
• Consultation
• Coordination of services
• Leadership
• Advocacy
• Collaboration and teaming
• Managing resources
• Use of data
• Use of technology
</td></tr>
<tr><td colspan="2">Education Trust (1997) and Stone and Dahir (2006b).</td></tr>
</table>

■ The Counseling Process

Counseling in schools is the process of assisting a student in understanding, assessing, and making a change in behavior. Students learn to make decisions to further improve their ability to achieve academic, career, and personal and social success in school (Stone & Dahir, 2006a). The combination of individual and group counseling increases the total number of student and counselor interactions.

Consultation

Consultation with teachers, administrators, and parents provides powerful solutions to improve the educational experience for all students. Whether in the classroom or in the conference room, collaboration offers a structure to identify issues and a team to find answers.

Coordination of Services

Coordination of services allows school counselors to manage and access resources for all students and families. Through community outreach, school counselors collaborate with agencies to provide a variety of services and opportunities to students and their families. These include mental health support, family counseling, wellness workshops, employment, volunteer positions, and service learning placements.

Leadership

Leadership encourages school counselors to examine the climate of a school to ensure a positive environment where all students can achieve academic, career, and personal and social success. As leaders, they have the primary responsibility for the comprehensive school counseling program. By participating in the School Improvement Team, district advisory boards, school safety teams, curriculum committees, or other decision-making bodies, school counselors help ensure that all district plans include school counseling programs.

Advocacy

Advocacy is a way of life. School counselors advocate for the students they serve. All students need advocates, especially those who do not have the skills to self-advocate and who are at risk for dropping out of school. School counselors work diligently for systemic change to eliminate practices that inhibit or stratify student opportunity.

Collaboration and Teaming

Collaboration and teaming is important with all school community members. Counselors collaborate most closely with teachers to deliver the school counseling curriculum to all students. In-service days or faculty meetings are the perfect venues to present information on the many aspects of the comprehensive school counseling program, including topics such as preventing bullying and sexual harassment. Teaming and collaboration demonstrates to members of the school community that the school counseling program supports each student in achieving her or his goals.

■ Managing Resources

Managing resources requires school counselors to serve as liaisons among teachers, parents, support personnel, and community resources to facilitate successful student development. School counselors secure the appropriate and necessary services and supports that are essential to every student's ability to achieve.

■ Use of Data

Use of data creates a picture of student needs and provides an accountable way to align the school counseling program with the school's academic mission. NCLB asks school counselors to demonstrate accountability and the impact of their work on student achievement (Stone & Dahir, 2006a). In this climate of accountability, connecting the work of school counselors to school improvement data is the most powerful indicator of the success of the school counseling program.

SCHOOL COUNSELING IN THE 21ST CENTURY

Professional school counselors play a vital role in maximizing student achievement and helping every student achieve success that ultimately will lead to high school graduation and the availability of a wide variety of postsecondary options on graduation (Campbell & Dahir, 1997).

■ Functions and Responsibilities of the School Counselor

The complex scope of practice of the professional school counselor encompasses a variety of functions and responsibilities. These include, but are not limited to, the responsibilities mentioned here.

Tasks of School Counselors

- Individual and group counseling.
- Classroom guidance lessons.
- Individual educational planning.

- Career exploration and planning.
- Crisis intervention.
- Advocacy for special-needs students.
- Assessment and interpretation.
- Staff development.
- Program planning.
- Multicultural awareness training.
- Consultation with parents, teachers, administrators, and mental health agencies.

Demands on time and services are often unrealistic when counselor-to-student caseloads can exceed 1:1,500. ASCA promotes the ideal ratio of 1:100, with 1:300 considered the maximum recommended ratio and 1:250 being the standard recommendation (ACA, 2001). The counselor-to-student ratio in the United States for the 2003–2004 school year was 1:488 (ASCA, 2006).

■ The Transformed School Counselor

ASCA and the Education Trust have called for a shift in the role of the professional school counselor. School counselors no longer are seen simply as service providers; rather, they are responsible for promoting optimal achievement for all students (Clark & Stone, 2000; Martin, 1998). The transformed skills of advocacy, leadership, collaboration and teaming, and use of data in addition to the art and science of counseling are essential to the successful delivery of the comprehensive school counseling program. Professional school counselors, rooted in the past, have taken hold of the present and continue to define the future.

Chapter 17: **Key Terms**

- ASCA National Standards
- ASCA National Model
- Academic development
- Career development

- Personal and social development
- Comprehensive school counseling program

- Transforming school counseling

Approaches to Family Counseling

18

Stephanie D. Helsel
Duquesne University

In This Chapter

▶ *Behavioral and Cognitive-Behavioral Family Therapy*
- Key Concepts in Behavioral and Cognitive-Behavioral Therapy
- Role of Therapist in Behavioral and Cognitive-Behavioral Therapy
- Goals of Treatment in Behavioral and Cognitive-Behavioral Therapy
- Therapeutic Techniques in Behavioral and Cognitive-Behavioral Therapy
- Strengths and Limitations of Behavioral and Cognitive-Behavioral Therapy

▶ *Bowenian Family Therapy*
- Key Concepts in Bowenian Therapy
- Role of Therapist in Bowenian Therapy
- Goals of Treatment in Bowenian Therapy
- Therapeutic Techniques in Bowenian Therapy
- Strengths and Limitations of Bowenian Therapy

▶ *Constructivist Family Therapy*
- Key Concepts in Constructivist Therapy
- Role of Therapist in Constructivist Therapy
- Goals of Treatment in Constructivist Therapy
- Therapeutic Techniques in Constructivist Therapy
- Strengths and Limitations of Constructivist Therapy

▶ *Experiential Family Therapy*
- Key Concepts in Experiential Therapy
- Role of Therapist in Experiential Therapy
- Goals of Treatment in Experiential Therapy
- Therapeutic Techniques in Experiential Therapy
- Strengths and Limitations of Experiential Therapy

▶ *Feminist Family Therapy*
- Key Concepts in Feminist Therapy
- Role of Therapist in Feminist Therapy
- Goals of Treatment in Feminist Therapy
- Therapeutic Techniques in Feminist Therapy
- Strengths and Limitations of Feminist Therapy

▶ *Psychodynamic Family Therapy*
- Key Concepts in Psychodynamic Therapy
- Role of Therapist in Psychodynamic Therapy
- Goals of Treatment in Psychodynamic Therapy
- Therapeutic Techniques in Psychodynamic Therapy
- Strengths and Limitations of Psychodynamic Therapy

In This Chapter (*continued*)

▶ *The Satir Growth Model of Family Therapy*
- Key Concepts in the Satir Growth Model
- Role of Therapist in the Satir Growth Model
- Goals of Treatment in the Satir Growth Model
- Therapeutic Techniques in the Satir Growth Model
- Strengths and Limitations of the Satir Growth Model

▶ *Solution-Focused Brief Family Therapy*
- Key Concepts in Solution-Focused Brief Therapy
- Role of Therapist in Solution-Focused Brief Therapy
- Goals of Treatment in Solution-Focused Brief Therapy
- Therapeutic Techniques in Solution-Focused Brief Therapy
- Strengths and Limitations of Solution-Focused Brief Therapy

▶ *Strategic Family Therapy*
- Key Concepts in Strategic Therapy
- Role of Therapist in Strategic Therapy
- Goals of Treatment in Strategic Therapy
- Therapeutic Techniques in Strategic Therapy
- Strengths and Limitations of Strategic Therapy

▶ *Structural Family Therapy*
- Key Concepts in Structural Therapy
- Role of Therapist in Structural Therapy
- Goals of Treatment in Structural Therapy
- Therapeutic Techniques in Structural Therapy
- Strengths and Limitations of Structural Therapy

▶ *Systemic Family Therapy*
- Key Concepts in Systemic Therapy
- Role of Therapist in Systemic Therapy
- Goals of Treatment in Systemic Therapy
- Therapeutic Techniques in Systemic Therapy
- Strengths and Limitations of Systemic Therapy

BEHAVIORAL AND COGNITIVE-BEHAVIORAL FAMILY THERAPY

Behavior therapy has been used in family settings since the 1970s. However, its impact on the field did not become significant until the 1980s, when cognitive principles were incorporated into behavioral techniques informed by learning theory (Nichols & Schwartz, 2004). There are few contemporary behaviorists who apply only behavioral techniques, and most utilize a combined cognitive-behavioral approach that draws on the work of Beck and Ellis. Due to the ease with which thoughts and behavior can be observed or rated, this approach enjoys scientific evidence of its efficacy with a wide range of populations and problems.

■ Key Concepts in Behavioral and Cognitive-Behavioral Therapy

How people perceive their environment determines how they experience it. Beliefs, attitudes, and behaviors are generated based on assumptions about one's family and world (Mytton, 2000; Nichols & Schwartz, 2004). Some of the central ideas in cognitive-behavioral family therapy include the following:

Reinforcement: If a behavior is immediately followed by a positive event or experience, the likelihood of that behavior recurring is increased (Lovell, 2000).

Empirical dictates: Interventions clinically proven to alter problematic behavior or thoughts that are used during therapy (Kalodner, 1995).

Outcome goals: Desired changes that are clearly defined as the goals of therapy. Progress toward outcome goals is often tracked by assessments that are completed throughout treatment.

■ Role of Therapist in Behavioral and Cognitive-Behavioral Therapy

Therapists focus on how the problem has an impact on the family in the present moment, even if the cause of the behavior is based on a past experience or event (Lovell, 2000). There are a number of approaches counselors can use to help families make concrete changes.

Therapist Strategies

■ The counselor works collaboratively with the family to define the problem and determine therapeutic goals and strategies that will help achieve desired outcomes (Lovell, 2000).
■ The therapist focuses on how the family reinforces problem behavior rather than on the problematic behavior specifically (Nichols & Schwartz, 2004).

- The therapist educates the family as to the role that thoughts play in behavior and emotion and provides instructions on how to monitor thoughts and modify beliefs or behavior (Mytton, 2000).
- The therapist provides communication and problem-solving skills training as needed (Dattilio, Epstein, & Baucom, 1998).

Goals of Treatment in Behavioral and Cognitive-Behavioral Therapy

Changing the way family members act as well as their dysfunctional attitudes or beliefs are central to cognitive-behavioral family therapy. A number of facets characterize this broad goal.

Goals of Cognitive-Behavioral Family Therapy

- Facilitating the family's ability to see patterns of behavior and to understand the interaction among cognitions, emotions, and behavior (Kalodner, 1995).
- Extinguishing problem behavior and increasing positive responses (Nichols & Schwartz, 2004).
- Improving each partner's level of functioning to improve the overall relationship (Weiss & Perry, 2002).

Therapeutic Techniques in Behavioral and Cognitive-Behavioral Therapy

To help families change their maladaptive attitudes and interactions, the following techniques may be utilized.

Cognitive-Behavioral Techniques

- Problematic behaviors or thought patterns are measured initially and throughout the therapeutic process to mark progress (Whisman & Weinstock, 2002).
- Through Socratic questioning, reframing, and reality testing, therapists challenge distorted ideas, thoughts, and behaviors and encourage families to try on new perspectives and ideas (Mytton, 2000).
- Material and social reinforcements, modeling, differential attention, and counterconditioning are used in behavioral parent training (Krumboltz & Thoresen, 1969).
- Family members are challenged to take turns offering positive reinforcement for others' attempts at behavior change.
- Couples negotiate specific behaviors that each will change (Nichols & Schwartz, 2004).

■ Strengths and Limitations of Behavioral and Cognitive-Behavioral Therapy

Behavioral and cognitive-behavioral techniques have been found to be effective for the treatment of several kinds of problems, including marital discord (Lovell, 2000). Assessment and evaluation methods whose reliability and validity have been empirically examined are also an asset in cognitive-behavioral treatment (Whisman & Weinstock, 2002).

There are a number of limitations of cognitive-behavioral work. First, more research is necessary to ascertain whether or not irrational or distorted beliefs are the cause of emotional disturbance rather than a symptom of such feelings (Dryden, 2000). Moreover, feelings and attitudes do not always change as a result of behavior alteration, and treatment goals may be reached without resolving underlying negative emotions (Nichols & Schwartz, 2004). Finally, cognitive-behavioral and behavioral approaches have received criticism for the lack of emphasis on insight or past experiences and because problems are addressed without understanding the context within which they developed (Kalodner, 1995).

BOWENIAN FAMILY THERAPY

Bowen is known as one of the founders of family therapy. He was the fist to examine family relationships from within the context of individual family member development (Knudson-Martin, 2002). He emphasized the importance of being emotionally connected to loved ones while maintaining independence of the self (Skowron, 2004). Bowen also examined the multigenerational nature of family dysfunction and encouraged people to investigate their family history to understand the context within which current patterns evolved. His primary focus was the emotional system within a family, and, specifically, whether or not members were too close and involved or too separate and closed off from one another.

■ Key Concepts in Bowenian Therapy

In Bowenian therapy, dysfunction is thought to be passed from one generation to the next through communication styles, ways of relating, and the degree of emotional connection between family members. Understanding Bowenian therapy necessitates a general appreciation of the following concepts:

Adaptability: The degree to which a person is able to manage life stress is dependent on the degree to which a person is emotionally dependent on others; attempting to manage stress by emotional dependence can lead to predictable problems (Bowen, 1976b).

Differentiation: The process of becoming an individual self who is not defined by family roles or expectations; the outcome of this process is emotional and intellectual clarity and low levels of anxiety (Skowron, 2004).

Triangulation: A basic, stable relationship system that can be healthy or unhealthy; unhealthy triangles form when family members lower stress by projecting the anxiety between two people onto a third person or thing.

Sibling position: Personality characteristics that are consistent with birth order and used to describe sibling position; failure to display the expected personality characteristics of birth order is attributable to family projections and triangulations (Bowen, 1976b).

■ Role of Therapist in Bowenian Therapy

The primary role of the therapist is to help family members become aware of family patterns of behavioral and emotional relating. Therapists increase awareness through asking appropriate questions, working with genograms, and encouraging emotional and intellectual autonomy of members.

Bowenian Therapist Characteristics

- The therapist has gone successfully through a process of differentiation; that is, the therapist has resolved his or her own family issues and is able to remain neutral, objective, and rational.
- Therapists are able to educate, coach, model behavior, and use Socratic questioning techniques.
- Therapists are capable of supporting the primary dyad (the couple) and disallow any attempts to be triangulated by them.

■ Goals of Treatment in Bowenian Therapy

A primary aim of Bowenian therapy is for family members to be objective and rational even in the midst of one another's emotionality. Members work toward remaining connected to one another in a supportive and autonomous manner (Kerr, 1985). Other goals include those listed here.

Bowenian Treatment Goals

- Gaining insight into multigenerational patterns that influence current relationships.
- Allowing differentiation among family members so that each individual member can express his or her own personality and become autonomous.

- Resolving projections and triangulations.
- Helping family members remain calm in the face of other members' emotionality and resolve conflicts using intellect rather than emotional reactivity.

Therapeutic Techniques in Bowenian Therapy

One of the purposes of techniques in the Bowenian approach is to help the therapist examine the tension between family members' basic desire for connection and community and the developmental process of becoming individuals. Therapists support self-differentiation by teaching communication skills and assertiveness. Therapy also focuses on stress management and upholding personal boundaries (Bowen, 1985). Some of the following techniques are used during the therapeutic process.

Bowenian Techniques

- Constructing genograms that graphically represent multiple generations of the family and the nature of the relationships between different members.
- Encouraging family members to talk directly to one another rather than to the therapist about their relationships.
- Asking questions that help members differentiate between thoughts and feelings and bring awareness to communication patterns (Bowen, 1976a).
- Focusing primarily on the couple to help them become a team and calling on other dyads or triads as needed to resolve issues affecting the family (Bowen, 1985).

Strengths and Limitations of Bowenian Therapy

A strength of Bowenian family therapy is that techniques are straightforward and practical. Members are encouraged to investigate their families of origin and understand the genesis of family patterns as a way to create a foundation for change and forgiveness (Gladding, 2002a). Empirical support also has been found for the relations among key concepts in this approach such as marital satisfaction, psychological well-being, anxiety, and degree of differentiation (Miller, Anderson, & Keala, 2004; Skowron, 2000).

A criticism of Bowen's approach is that the emphasis on differentiation may not be applicable to cultures in which interdependence is highly valued (McDermott, 1989). Feminist critiques posit that Bowen uses male standards to define healthy functioning and does not value the ways in which women typically relate to others (Knudson-Martin, 1994). Finally, there is no structure or system for developing relational capacities, which falsely implies that the process of differentiation develops such abilities (Knudson-Martin, 2002).

CONSTRUCTIVIST FAMILY THERAPY

The constructivist orientation is one of several postmodern reexaminations of the nature of knowledge, learning, and meaning making. In the constructivist perspective, the notions of scientific objectivity and external reality are rejected. Reality consists primarily of one's subjective experiences, interactions, cultural and linguistic influences, and cognitions. Key concepts in this movement draw on Piaget's developmental theories and Erickson's therapeutic techniques; philosophers such as Kant and Husserl are also central figures.

■ Key Concepts in Constructivist Therapy

From the constructivist position, there is no objective reality; each person creates his or her own worldview through experiences, memories, imaginations of the future, and, in the case of social constructionism, interpersonal relationships. It is through language that thoughts are conceptualized and processed. Because people perceive rather than just observe, the distinctions that are assigned to constructs, such as male and female, are arbitrary and not necessarily "real" in a definitive sense (Burr, 1995). Finally, action is derived from constructed knowledge; therefore, behavior is believed to be influenced by perceptions, which are culture bound (Burr, 1995).

■ Role of Therapist in Constructivist Therapy

A basic posture that therapists adopt in constructivist family therapy is to respect clients while still challenging their assumptions. Two primary tasks the leader undertakes are the following:

1. Creating a therapeutic alliance with the client devoid of a power hierarchy so that the client can be a partner in solution formulation (Hoyt, 1994).
2. Examining and testing clients' beliefs, thoughts, and language.

■ Goals of Treatment in Constructivist Therapy

The goals of treatment are very closely linked with the principal concepts of constructivism; they reflect an inherent respect for the client's worldview and reality and include the following.

Goals of Constructivist Family Therapy

- Supporting change through collaborative discourse that respects the client's values and reality.
- Allowing the client to dictate what changes will occur and what solutions will be applied to problems.

■ Therapeutic Techniques in Constructivist Therapy

To assist clients in developing new, positive meanings that lead to change, some of the following techniques may be used in constructivist family therapy.

Reframing: Offering a different perspective, usually a positive interpretation, of what the client has presented (Held, 1990).

Externalization: Conceptualizing problems as separate from the family to free members from the belief that they are problematic (Zimmerman & Dickerson, 1994).

Narrative or dramatic reenactment: Clients tell the story of their lives and create new ones for a desired future; couples act out scenes written by their partners to share perspectives and create new outcomes.

Reflecting team: A team of clinicians who observe family–counselor interactions and provide a "diagnosis" of family problems. The family is privy to all of the ideas and alternative viewpoints expressed by the team and is free to choose an interpretation that fits (Haley, 2002).

Circular interviewing: Family members are questioned about how others in the family connect to a problematic issue to illuminate a variety of perspectives and highlight the systemic nature of problems (Omer, 1996).

■ Strengths and Limitations of Constructivist Therapy

A positive aspect of the constructive approach is that the emphasis on multiple perspectives shifts the focus of therapy from pathologizing to empowerment (Minuchin, 1998). Additionally, constructive therapies have been described as socially responsible and appropriate for intercultural counseling, as therapists do not impose their worldview on clients (Hare-Mustin, 1994).

Refusing to take a dominant position, however, minimizes the expertise of the therapist and may leave clients feeling confused about the direction of therapy (Hoyt, 1994; Minuchin, 1998). Relational patterns of the family also can be overshadowed in the attempt to ensure that family members have an equal opportunity to voice their perceptions of reality (Minuchin, 1998). Finally, the concepts of constructivism (e.g., there is no definitive reality) at times seem paradoxical and confusing in that discussions of how therapy is best practiced are in fact making a claim that a certain reality is "better" than another (Held, 1990).

EXPERIENTIAL FAMILY THERAPY

Psychiatrist Carl Whitaker was a very dynamic, charismatic, and unconventional personality who first began working with families in 1945. He developed a therapeutic system called symbolic-experiential family therapy. Based on existential principles and philosophy, individuation is seen as a large part of the family therapy process. As his practice progressed, he began engaging multiple generations in his interventions. Despite the fact that Whitaker's rather idiosyncratic, intuitive approach has proven to be difficult to replicate, proponents such as Keith and Napier continue to utilize this approach with families (Framo, 1996).

■ Key Concepts in Experiential Therapy

Whitaker's approach maintains a systems perspective and views both change and causation as a circular process. Family therapy is seen as the ideal initial treatment response, regardless of the problem (Whitaker & Keith, 1981). Two assumptions characterize Whitaker's model. First, problems are dealt with in the present. All family conflict is brought into the "here and now" of the present moment (O'Hanlon & Weiner-Davis, 1989). Second, resistance is an expressed preference. Reflecting a conviction that the current situation is the best one available, resistance is dealt with by "inducing desperation" into the family by offering to end therapy (Whitaker & Keith, 1981, p. 214).

■ Role of Therapist in Experiential Therapy

The therapist seeks to cajole, inspire, or guide the family toward changing their behavior with one another. Insight is not believed to lead to change, but rather is seen as a result of change.

Leader Tasks in Experiential Family Therapy

- Taking an active and nondirective stance.
- Providing initial structure and control that lessens as therapy continues.
- Following the family's lead at all times.
- Becoming less directive as the family matures.
- Pointing out absurd behavior, teasing the family toward change, and confronting family members in a nonthreatening manner.

■ Goals of Treatment in Experiential Therapy

Linked with the existential concepts of balancing interconnectedness with individual expression, goals include the following (Whitaker & Keith, 1981).

Aims of Experiential Therapy

- Initiating change in the largest possible system is facilitated by inviting extended family members to the initial visit and working with multiple generations.
- Increasing family creativity, "craziness," and flexibility in problem solving.
- Maintaining intergenerational and family and community boundaries, especially between parents and children.
- Learning to play together as a family as a way to deal with the existential pressures of family life.

■ Therapeutic Techniques in Experiential Therapy

Techniques that illuminate the unconscious behavior and "life" of the family are used and families are encouraged to apply a playful attitude toward changing their dynamics (Gladding, 2002a).

Existential Family Therapy Techniques

- Anxiety is used as a motivating factor. Symptoms are reframed as system problems and multiple issues are brought to the family's attention (Whitaker & Keith, 1981).
- Play between parents and children is used during sessions to model affectionate behavior or draw in an isolated parent (Napier & Whitaker, 1978).
- Paradoxical statements in which the therapist argues for seemingly negative goals or offers absurd treatment suggestions are used to counter resistance (Napier & Whitaker, 1978).
- Extended family members, such as grandparents, are asked to act as "cotherapists" when family treatment is stalled (Whitaker & Keith, 1981).

■ Strengths and Limitations of Experiential Therapy

There are a number of strengths of experiential family therapy. First, multiple generations can be transformed by recognizing the importance of the multigenerational aspect of families and inviting extended family members into therapy. Additionally, nuclear families can learn to enlist the help of extended family members when crises are encountered. Families also can learn to improve their interactions and be playful and flexible in their roles (Napier & Whitaker, 1978). Finally, family members can become more fully individuated while enhancing their sense of belonging within the family (Napier & Whitaker, 1978).

A drawback of experiential therapy is that because this therapy relies heavily on the intuition and personality of the therapist, it can be difficult to teach (Framo, 1996). Playing with the family and using humor and absurdity when confronting members can have negative affects on individual members (Whitaker & Keith, 1981).

FEMINIST FAMILY THERAPY

Feminist therapy seeks to uncover the hidden effects of power, gender, and prejudice on interpersonal relationships (Corey, 2001). It is related to other postmodern perspectives in that it examines how knowledge is defined and owned in a given culture. Spurred by the political feminist movement of the 1960s and 1970s, female contributions to clinical and academic work have revealed sexism in the mental health field (Libow, Raskin, & Caust, 1982). This approach has helped to expand understanding of how external factors such as culture and world events affect individual well-being and functioning and the ways in which bias and counselor values can impact the counseling experience.

> Feminist therapy seeks to uncover the hidden effects of power, gender, and prejudice on interpersonal relationships (Corey, 2001). It is related to other postmodern perspectives in that it examines how knowledge is defined and owned in a given culture.

■ Key Concepts in Feminist Therapy

Problems that occur between couples cannot be addressed successfully unless the underlying inequality that exists between men and women is acknowledged and counteracted (Carter, 1992). Two assumptions are central to feminist family therapy. First, traditional gender roles are considered to be limitations both to men and women. Thus, rigid expectations regarding parenting and the division of labor must be expanded (Goldner, 1985). Second, therapy is most effective when it is client centered. To guard against hierarchical thinking or the misuse of authority, the client is considered to be the expert in his or her own experiences (Enns, 1997).

■ Role of Therapist in Feminist Therapy

The primary role of the therapist is to act as a guide or helper, eschewing the traditional hierarchical power structure. Therapists explore economic power, authority, and control issues within the family in an egalitarian and nonhierarchical way (Carter, 1992).

Tasks of Feminist Family Therapists

- Therapists are expected to shift family alliances and change dynamics in accordance with treatment goals rather than simply support the father as having final authority (Enns, 1997).

- Therapists model nonsexist behavior by encouraging independence, self-care, and maintenance of appropriate boundaries (Libow et al., 1982).
- Therapists are expected to maintain open and direct communication with clients; indirect or manipulative techniques are not tolerated (Libow et al., 1982).

Goals of Treatment in Feminist Therapy

A main function of feminist family therapy is to empower clients and help families to become more assertive. Clients are encouraged to expand their awareness of role inequities in society and become more assertive in changing society, not just adjusting to it (Libow et al., 1982). Specific goals of therapy include those listed next.

- Treatment aims from a feminist perspective.
- Facilitating flexibility in gender construction and family roles.
- Educating family members of the external social and cultural forces that dictate traditional gender roles and the effects of those forces on them (Enns, 1997).
- Supporting equality for women in the workplace and at home (Etaugh & Bridges, 2001).

Therapeutic Techniques in Feminist Therapy

To conduct therapy in a respectful and collaborative way, some of the following techniques may be used in feminist family therapy.

Techniques of Feminist Family Therapy

- Use contracts to negotiate goals, empower clients to take an active role in their process and keep them informed about the counseling process (Enns, 1997; Hare-Mustin, 1978).
- Reframe or relabel to help the client think beyond traditional views of symptoms or pathologies (Libow et al., 1982).
- Model egalitarian negotiation practices and nonstereotypical ways of being in the world for the client (Hare-Mustin, 1978).
- Help the family negotiate their responsibilities so that there is an equal amount of household work and parenting responsibilities delegated to the mother and father (Hare-Mustin, 1978).

Strengths and Limitations of Feminist Therapy

To its credit, feminist critiques of family therapy have spawned examinations of therapist bias and prejudice toward minority populations (May, 1998). In this model, each family member is ensured equal or appropriate degrees of power and respect. Additionally, members may experience greater satisfaction and quality of life as a result of challenging traditional gender roles.

However, this approach is limited in that simplistic examinations of power relationships between men and women can lead to a limited perspective of women as victims (Goldner, 1985). Moreover, feminist family therapists traditionally have not included the realities of minority and impoverished women in the therapeutic process (Etaugh & Bridges, 2001). Finally, gender sensitivity training has not typically included discussions of the traditional male gender role and its limitations (Framo, 1996).

PSYCHODYNAMIC FAMILY THERAPY

Psychodynamic family therapy grew from the psychoanalytic tradition established by Freud. The unconscious is seen as a motivating force for behavior, along with basic drives such as sexuality or aggression. In psychodynamic family therapy, to understand an individual, one must take into account the context within which an individual was raised and how this plays out in the present. The family is seen as the primary environment within which to work to effect change. This mode of family therapy was first developed in the 1950s by analysts Klein, Adler, Kohut, and Ackerman. Later well-known psychodynamic family therapists include Boszormenyi-Nagy, Kernberg, Framo, and Skynner (Gladding, 2002a).

■ Key Concepts in Psychodynamic Therapy

The key concepts for psychodynamic family therapy involve the role that the unconscious plays in childhood development and adult interpersonal functioning.

Object relations theory: A means of explaining how people relate to others based on early attachment experiences with a caregiver. The quality of our connection to the loved ones in our early lives influences what we expect in later life and explains how intergenerational relationships function (McGinn, 1998).

Transference: Occurs when the feelings an individual has for one person are attributed to another person.

Splitting: Individuals perceive people as either "good" or "bad" if their early experiences are unresolved (Nichols & Schwartz, 2004). These projections can be distorted and keep people from fully recognizing and dealing with the feelings behind these perceptions.

Projective identifications: The ways in which parents project unwanted aspects of their personalities onto their children, who in turn accept that identity and unconsciously agree to act out in such a way as to uphold those expectations (Nichols & Schwartz, 2004).

■ Role of Therapist in Psychodynamic Therapy

Psychoanalytic therapists work to slowly bring to the family's awareness the unconscious behavior patterns that are causing difficulties, starting with intrapersonal aspects before moving on to interpersonal family processes (Framo, 1970).

Psychodynamic Family Therapist Tasks

- Face personal unresolved issues related to family relationships to experience as little countertransference as possible (Boszormenyi-Nagy & Spark, 1973; Segal, 2000).
- Increase awareness of the projective identification that is being expressed in the family (Nichols & Schwartz, 2004).
- Assume the role of an imaginary parent to protect members from "interpersonal danger" and provide support and other elements that the members need and may never have gotten from their own parents (Ackerman, 1965/1982, p. 371).
- Focus on that which is most resisted, side with each member in turn, and become allies with different members at different times (Boszormenyi-Nagy & Spark, 1973).
- Model healthy behavior, educate clients about aspects of the unconscious, and act as a tool for reality testing (Ackerman, 1965/1982).

■ Goals of Treatment in Psychodynamic Therapy

The general goal for this approach is to resolve unconscious restrictions to allow free and meaningful interactions within the family or the couple (Nichols & Schwartz, 2004).

Goals of Psychodynamic Family Therapy

- Eradicate dysfunctional dependence or withdrawal by restructuring each family member's personality (Nichols & Schwartz, 2004).
- Resolve distorted fantasies developed in early childhood to perceive life realistically (Segal, 2000) and release other family members from idealized and projected identities (Framo, 1970).

■ Therapeutic Techniques in Psychodynamic Therapy

Rapport is valued as an essential tool in psychodynamic family therapy. Therefore, the therapist takes time to build a solid therapeutic relationship that will withstand challenge, confrontation, and restructuring (Segal, 2000). Once trust is established in the therapeutic relationship, the counselor may employ a number of approaches to bring unconscious and preconscious elements to consciousness.

Psychodynamic Therapeutic Techniques

- Each member is asked to discuss his or her experiences as part of the family; parents are asked about their families of origin (Framo, 1965).
- Parents are encouraged to identify unresolved feelings and memories of childhood so that they can be released and allow parents to treat their own children differently (Framo, 1965).
- Counselors reflect on preconscious feelings and defenses and use dream analysis to point out ways in which clients' behavior is not congruent with what is outwardly communicated (Framo, 1965), ways in which families exercise scapegoating, and ways they form alliances with and rescue one another (Ackerman, 1967; Frederickson, 1999).

■ Strengths and Limitations of Psychodynamic Therapy

An advantage of psychodynamic family therapy is that deep-seated conflicts and pain are transformed, resulting in a more independent and high-functioning couple or family (Segal, 2000). Removing the camouflage that couples and families employ, such as the avoidance of intimacy, can create authentic and satisfying relationships (Skynner, 1976; Wynne, Ryckoff, Day, & Hirsch, 1958).

A limitation of this approach, however, is that treatment is lengthy and expensive, as families are seen for a year or longer. Techniques, such as dream analysis, can become difficult if the family being counseled is large (Gladding, 2002a). This approach also requires that counselors and families have the intellectual capacity to understand concepts such as the unconscious and defense mechanisms (Gladding, 2002a). Little empirical evidence exists to support the efficacy of psychodynamic therapy (Segal, 2000).

THE SATIR GROWTH MODEL OF FAMILY THERAPY

Satir, creator of Conjoint Family Therapy, originally was a member of the Mental Research Institute and worked with schizophrenic patients and their families. The growth model focuses on communication patterns and structures and applies a systems perspective to the family. The therapeutic relationship is used as a model for family members, who are expected to engage in a process of maturation to increase levels of functioning. Satir's teachings are maintained today by the Avanta Network, a nonprofit organization that promotes personal and community well-being.

■ Key Concepts in the Satir Growth Model

Satir's model is contextual, taking into account the prescribed rules and particular communication styles of the family (Freeman, 1999). All behavior is seen as driven by the same basic needs of survival, connection to others, and growth (Satir, 1983). Along with the concept of universality, the five modes of communication are central to Satir's model and can be understood as follows (Satir, Stachowiak, & Taschman, 1975).

Universality: Change occurs when therapeutic work is done within the context of basic human needs, such as love and acceptance (Freeman, 1999).

Placating: Denying the self to agree with someone else.

Blaming: Declaring the self as in control and having power over others.

Super reasonable: Feelings are not acknowledged within the self or in others.

Irrelevant: Distracting the self and others by responding in a way that is not related to the context of the situation or to what is being felt, or to what has been previously said.

Congruent: Communication reflects the reality of the self and the other in that moment. Looks, feelings, tone of voice, and body language are all reflecting the same message.

■ Role of Therapist in the Satir Growth Model

In conjoint therapy, the counselor's use of self is the most important tool for facilitating change in a family. Thus, it is essential that the therapist be congruent in his or her thoughts, feelings, and actions when working with clients (Duhl, 1995). Conjoint therapy also stresses the importance of positive regard and empathy on the part of the therapist, as is typical in humanistic approaches (Duhl, 1995).

Skills of the Conjoint Family Therapist

- Initiating change through a leadership role in the beginning of the process (Satir et al., 1975).

- Modeling honest and healthy communication.
- Allowing all subjects to be equally addressed in therapy.
- Interpreting and responding to action appropriately (Satir, 1983).
- Using communication models to inform the therapy process.

■ Goals of Treatment in the Satir Growth Model

Once universal needs such as acceptance and connection are met, family members will have greater self-esteem and the ability to function in a healthier manner. An aim of therapy is to help family members communicate in a way that is congruent (Satir et al., 1975). Additionally, therapists and families work together to create a family system that is more open and operates with fewer internalized rules (Bandler, Grinder, & Satir, 1976).

■ Therapeutic Techniques in the Satir Growth Model

Some techniques of conjoint therapy are similar to those used in other therapies and require counselors to restate, reframe, and repeat clients' statements to challenge beliefs and communication styles in the family. There are also a number of recognized techniques that are specific to conjoint therapy. The aims of these techniques are to illuminate hidden agendas and rules of the family system to create freedom to change, and include the following (Gladding, 2002a; Satir, 1983).

Family map: A visual representation of three generations of the "star" or identified client's family that records adjectives to describe each person's personality or relationship to the larger family as well as general demographic information.

Life fact chronology: A detailed history of the family, including the history of the parents' romantic relationship, their respective family histories, any previous unions and divorces or deaths, a history of extended family members living with the family, or others who contribute financially or in other ways and figure prominently. Rates of contact with members who no longer live with the parents are obtained, and daily household schedules and regular activities are discussed (Satir, 1983).

Wheel of influence: A visual representation of all the influential people in the client's life.

Family time inventory: Members track their activities throughout the day to facilitate the scheduling of family time for at least 1 hour per day (Bandler et al., 1976).

■ Strengths and Limitations of the Satir Growth Model

Satir's approach to family therapy enables the family to use new communication styles to maintain healthy relationships after therapy has been completed (Bandler et al., 1976). Families have a renewed sense of their own value and appreciate the unique aspects of each of their members (Bandler et al., 1976).

Despite Satir's social contextual approach, it has been criticized for failing to account for the culturally prescribed roles of family members (Freeman, 1999). The existential goals of wholeness and increased enjoyment in one's family life may be vague and hard to conceptualize (Gladding, 2002a).

SOLUTION-FOCUSED BRIEF FAMILY THERAPY

There is no distinct founder of brief therapy, as counselors of all theoretical orientations have applied short-term techniques. Haley's strategic approach and the therapeutic concepts used by Erickson are strong influences of brief therapy and solution-focused therapy as it is practiced today (Stalker, Levene, & Coady, 1999). Solution-focused therapy, developed by former Mental Research Institute member Steve deShazer in 1986, shifts the clinical focus away from gaining insight into problems to creating preferred futures (O'Connell, 2003). Other brief therapy figures include Berg, Weiner-Davis, and O'Hanlon.

■ Key Concepts in Solution-Focused Brief Therapy

Brief and solution-focused therapy draws on systems and constructivist theories with an emphasis on language, perception, and the way in which changing one element in the family system often can transform the system itself (de Shazer & Molnar, 1984). With its deemphasis on problems, solutions become key, and different kinds of problems can be solved with the same solution (de Shazer & Molnar, 1984). When problems are recognized, they are attributed to flawed perceptions and understandings (O'Hanlon & Wilk, 1987). Therefore, a main concept in this approach is that perceptual changes—more than insight or emotional expression—contribute to solutions and ultimately to transformation (Cade & O'Hanlon, 1993).

■ Role of Therapist in Solution-Focused Brief Therapy

The therapist is singularly attentive to the negotiation of a specific definition of what the solution to the family or couple's problem will be (O'Hanlon & Wilk, 1987).

Tasks of the Solution-Focused Therapist

- Join in the family system as a way to influence clients (de Shazer, 1984; Stewart & Anderson, 1984).
- Take a collaborative stance by refraining from giving expert opinions or diagnosing the family's problems (O'Connell, 2003).
- Reframe the family situation positively by highlighting strengths, normalizing problems, and helping the family members see themselves in a new, more productive way (O'Hanlon & Weiner-Davis, 1989).

■ Goals of Treatment in Solution-Focused Brief Therapy

The specific goals of treatment are unique to the solutions that each family determines with the help of the therapist. Thus, success easily can be measured against the implementation of the solution into the family system (O'Hanlon & Weiner-Davis, 1989). Generally, though, therapy is aimed at helping families to make minimal initial changes. An assumption of solution-focused work is that subsequent, more substantial changes naturally follow the initial changes and are generated by the family itself (de Shazer & Molnar, 1984).

■ Therapeutic Techniques in Solution-Focused Brief Therapy

There are several techniques that are unique to the solution-focused approach.

Common Techniques in Solution-Focused Therapy

- Counselors identify strengths by asking the family to take note of the family dynamics they value and want to maintain (de Shazer & Molnar, 1984).
- Counselors look for exceptions to the problem by asking the family to recount times when the problem did not occur, and to account for why, to formulate a solution and highlight strengths (O'Hanlon & Weiner-Davis, 1989).
- Counselors use the "miracle question," which consists of asking the family or couple how they would know that the problem was gone. Specifically, they are asked, "If the problem were to be miraculously erased, what would be different?" (Berg & DeJong, 1996).

■ Strengths and Limitations of Solution-Focused Brief Therapy

One of the most beneficial aspects of brief therapy is that families experience change in a short period of time and benefit from the positive attitude of the therapist. In contrast to many therapeutic approaches, solution-focused therapy reconceptualizes clients' problems to allow for more healthy relationships. Finally, this limited time approach is complementary to the goals of managed care.

A limitation of this approach is that research done on this modality has been methodologically flawed; evidence exists that brief therapies are not effective in supporting lasting changes (Stalker et al., 1999). Also, solution-focused work does not account for the fact that some clients may not be able to resolve their problems without exploring their past (Nylund & Corsiglia, 1994).

STRATEGIC FAMILY THERAPY

Devised by Haley and Madanes, strategic family therapy is heavily influenced by the work of Erickson and focuses on problem solving rather than insight. The term *strategic,* coined by Haley, signifies interventions designed to influence clients to interrupt their problem behavior cycle, to promote a new perception of the problem, and to create an environment that encourages growth and change (Duncan & Solovey, 1989). Haley joined with clinician Madanes in 1976 to form the Family Therapy Institute in Washington, DC. Madanes added a gentle, playful element to creating change in families that expanded on Haley's more directive style (Corey, 2001).

■ Key Concepts in Strategic Therapy

The concepts of strategic family therapy reflect the assumptions of the strategic family therapeutic approach to change. The assumptions that underlie this approach are listed next.

Assumptions of Strategic Family Therapy

- The social context within which the presenting problem occurs is the primary focus.
- Symptoms or problematic behaviors are believed to stabilize the family (Braverman, 1986) and are seen as resulting from the interrelated actions of several people (Haley, 1987).
- Emotionally cathartic experiences are not necessarily helpful in meeting the therapeutic goals of resolving symptoms or problems (Haley, 1980).

■ Role of Therapist in Strategic Therapy

Therapists take on a leadership role, devising specific treatment strategies for each problem. Other responsibilities include those outlined as follows.

Responsibilities of Strategic Family Therapists

- Capitalizing on the family's desire for change by intervening during the initial session rather than spending time on fully understanding family dynamics or making diagnoses (Haley, 1973).

- Influencing the family to try new solutions and to conceptualize their problems in a new way.
- Working with emotions only when they can help inform treatment goals (Kleckner, Frank, Bland, Amendt, & Bryant, 1992).
- Treating the family as a whole rather than focusing on the symptomatic individual as a way to address the organizational nature of family dysfunction (Haley, 1973).

■ Goals of Treatment in Strategic Therapy

Reflecting the basic premise that the function of therapy should be to fix specific problems rather than heal deep emotional wounds or issues, the goals of treatment include the following:

- Recognizing the structure or hierarchy of family relationships so that no symptoms are needed to maintain it, and there is appropriate equity and authority (Braverman, 1986).
- Helping the family in perceiving problems as manageable and able to be solved (Haley, 1980).

■ Therapeutic Techniques in Strategic Therapy

This is a technique-laden approach, and many interventions exist for different problems. Ericksonian techniques such as the use of paradox are typical. The therapist may utilize prior coping strategies, observed patterns of behavior, and past attempts to solve problems as the foundation for treatment strategies (Coyne & Biglan, 1984). Other common techniques are described next.

The ordeal: Entails changing the family structure in a way that is beneficial by prescribing a difficult activity that is more severe than the problematic behavior. The technique is useful in creating negative consequences for problem behavior and in reinforcing appropriate boundaries and authority roles (Stone & Peeks, 1986).

Reframing: Describing problems in a positive or constructive way to enable the therapist to present interventions using language that promotes change (Coyne & Biglan, 1984).

Pretending: Performing the problematic behavior or symptom in the session and practicing coping skills (Madanes, 1981).

■ Strengths and Limitations of Strategic Therapy

Strategic family therapy may have cross-cultural implications because the approach is nonsexist (Braverman, 1986) and appears to be effective with clients from different cultures and ethnicities (Richeport-Haley, 1998). Strategic therapists do not pathologize the problems of their clients, which creates a nonthreatening and respectful environment (Braverman, 1986). Because success is measured distinctly by behavioral goals, improved functioning easily is charted and achieved.

However, the use of strong direction and influence to create changes in clients has been criticized as manipulative and disrespectful of clients (Duncan & Solovey, 1989). Also, strategic therapy's exclusion of intrapersonal variables such as early childhood experiences has been criticized as incomplete and limiting (Duncan, 1992).

STRUCTURAL FAMILY THERAPY

Structural family therapy, developed during the 1960s and 1970s by Minuchin, helped to bring family therapy to the attention of the larger psychological community. This approach is very technique driven and requires the therapist to take an active, dynamic role. The diagnostic process is very prominent, unlike other modes of therapy, and ingenious techniques have been devised to this end, such as family tasks that are observed through one-way mirrors (Elbert, Rosman, Minuchin, & Guerney, 1964). Restructuring family interactions is seen as a way to create healthy alliances and appropriate generational and relational boundaries.

■ Key Concepts in Structural Therapy

Structural family therapy maintains a systems perspective. Symptoms are seen as occurring within both an internal and external context (Minuchin, 1974). Dysfunctionality, additionally, is believed to result when family members of different generations form subsystems. Symptoms can be relieved by changing the family structure or patterns of relating that support or cause such behavior (Minuchin, 1974). Working through dysfunction is related to the two concepts of joining and accommodating.

Joining: The process through which the therapist enters the family system to diagnose the source of dysfunction, understand the way the family perceives reality, and form therapeutic goals (Minuchin, Colapinto, & Minuchin, 1998).

Accommodation: The process through which the therapist adapts to enter the family system, and the process that the family undergoes to make changes.

■ Role of Therapist in Structural Therapy

The attitude of the therapist is an essential element in structural family therapy. Adapting to the family's style and designing interventions that reflect each particular family is a key role.

Tasks of the Structural Family Therapist

- Joining the family system (Minuchin et al., 1998).
- Shifting attention to different subsystems, family members, and family dynamics either to draw attention to them or to maintain them as a family strength.
- Creating disequilibrium within the family to free up family dynamics and allow for the formation of new, healthy alliances between subsystem members (Minuchin, 1974).
- Stopping automatic responses by using interventions designed to disarm reactions that are triggered by existing structures or dynamics (Minuchin & Montalvo, 1967).

■ Goals of Treatment in Structural Therapy

One of the primary goals of structural family therapy is to create appropriate boundaries and hierarchies within the family (Gladding, 2002a). Changing unhealthy transactional patterns of the family and replacing inappropriate alliances and subsystems in favor of healthy ones is accordingly necessary (Minuchin, 1974). Finally, structural therapy aims at diminishing symptoms of family dysfunction, such as substance abuse or delinquency (Minuchin, 1974).

■ Therapeutic Techniques in Structural Therapy

To properly diagnose problematic relational patterns and change family structures, some of the following techniques are used in structural family therapy.

Structural Family Therapy Interventions (Minuchin et al., 1998)

- Constructing family maps.
- Restructuring the family.
- Enforcing boundaries.

■ Strengths and Limitations of Structural Therapy

As a very action-oriented therapy, stuctural therapy is usually successful in bringing about change (Minuchin et al., 1998). It is effective when working with a wide variety of families, including multicultural populations and families of all socio-economic levels (Gladding, 2002a). This approach easily can be learned and understood due to the clear and concise nature of the theory and techniques of which it is comprised (Minuchin & Fishman, 1981).

There is a possibility of oversimplifying the family subsystems when making family maps, as there is little emphasis on family development or past history. This can result in the therapist joining or aligning with some rather than all subsystems (Minuchin, 1974). Feminist therapists have pointed out that Minuchin's idea of a healthy family is based on a traditional hierarchy, where the father has the most power and authority (Hare-Mustin, 1986). Because joining is such an integral part of structural family therapy, there is the possibility that the therapist will become pulled into the family dynamics and not regain the distance necessary to properly diagnose problems or formulate treatment goals (Minuchin, 1974).

SYSTEMIC FAMILY THERAPY

The systemic approach significantly has influenced the way in which family therapy is currently practiced. The popularity of systems concepts has caused a shift in the way behavior is understood. Rather than being motivated by inner drives, as traditional psychoanalytic theories contend, the systems view describes behavior as being influenced by social and relational forces. Utilizing a contextual perspective, this approach encompasses elements of structural and strategic therapies and the work of Erickson and anthropologist, Bateson. Systemic therapy originally was developed by clinical research teams at the Mental Research Institute in California and at the Institute for Family Studies in Milan, Italy. As one of the first approaches to examine the nature of meaning, thought, and reality, systems theory laid the foundation for many of the postmodern perspectives that are being applied to therapy today.

■ Key Concepts in Systemic Therapy

Behavior is seen from within the context of the individual's relationships and family roles. Major concepts address the dynamic of family systems and communication within the family. First, systems are seen as self-regulating and are maintained by the particular way that characterizes that family. Whether or not a system interacts with the environment outside of itself determines whether or not it is open or closed (Nichols & Everett, 1986). Communication occurs through feedback, or the movement of information into and out of the system and either creates stability or change. Changes in the system alter the information that comes into the system, creating a recursive feedback loop (Nichols & Everett, 1986).

■ Role of Therapist in Systemic Therapy

The therapist recognizes that his or her presence alters the family system, and so presents a supportive, neutral face to the family. At times, teams of therapists work together to treat a family. In either case, the individual therapist or team of therapists adopt certain behaviors.

Behaviors of Systemic Family Therapists (Nichols & Everett, 1986)

- Taking a directive stance.
- Using specific strategies and interventions tailored to each family's circumstances.
- Setting goals.
- Determining which elements of the system require change (Martin, 1985; Watzlawick, Weakland, & Fisch, 1974).
- Defining symptoms as useful (Campbell & Draper, 1985).

■ Goals of Treatment in Systemic Therapy

Changing behaviors or eliminating symptoms are seen as the primary goals of therapy and come before the work of gaining insight (Nichols & Everett, 1986). This is accomplished by the following:

- Helping families to understand their interconnected nature.
- Enhancing families' communication skills and conflict resolution strategies.
- Teaching families to solve future problems with the interventions they have learned (Gladding, 2002a).

■ Therapeutic Techniques in Systemic Therapy

Competing subsystems and hierarchies within the family system are illuminated and the family is given tools for managing conflict and communication more effectively in the following ways.

Common Techniques in the Systemic Approach

- Circular questioning is used to address all members of a family to obtain their perspective on events and issues (Selvini Palazzoli, Boscolo, Cecchin, & Prata, 1980).
- Paradoxical interventions occur when the therapist invites the family to engage in the symptom rather than presenting a solution to a problem (Watzlawick et al., 1974).

- Reframing is used to free up the family myths or conceptualizations to make change possible (Watzlawick et al., 1974).
- Rituals are used to break the homeostasis, or balance of the system and require every family member to participate in an activity that directly addresses the essential symptom (Martin, 1985).

In addition to these techniques, longer session intervals frequently are used in systemic family therapy to allow the family to practice new behaviors and guard against the therapist becoming too integrated within the system. A characteristic of the Milan School of family therapy, sessions often were scheduled monthly.

■ Strengths and Limitations of Systemic Therapy

Systemic family therapy allows specific changes to be brought about in a brief period of time. Also, this approach helps family members themselves become capable of dealing with problems in the future. Problems and behaviors can be reconceptualized and can enable family members to be seen in a more positive light.

A drawback of the team approach sometimes adopted in systemic therapy is that working with teams of professionals can be expensive and impractical (Jones, 1993). Moreover, the directive stance required by strategic systemic therapists is contradictory to the premise that all members of a system co-construct all interactions (Cecchin, Lane, & Ray, 1993). Finally, because systemic therapy focuses on the resolution of one specific symptom, it might not contribute to overall insight or a deep-seated change in the family system.

 For more general information about marriage and family therapy, visit the International Association of Marriage and Family Counselors, a division of the ACA at:

▶ www.iamfc.com

Chapter 18: Key Terms

- ▶ Reinforcement
- ▶ Empirical dictates
- ▶ Outcome goals
- ▶ Adaptability
- ▶ Differentiation
- ▶ Triangulation
- ▶ Sibling position

- ▶ Reframing
- ▶ Externalization
- ▶ Narrative or dramatic reenactment
- ▶ Reflecting team
- ▶ Circular interviewing
- ▶ Object relations theory

- ▶ Transference
- ▶ Splitting
- ▶ Projective identifications
- ▶ Universality
- ▶ Placating
- ▶ Blaming
- ▶ Super reasonable

- ▶ Irrelevant
- ▶ Congruent
- ▶ Family map
- ▶ Life fact chronology

- ▶ Wheel of influence
- ▶ Family time inventory
- ▶ The ordeal
- ▶ Reframing

- ▶ Pretending
- ▶ Joining
- ▶ Accommodation

Tammy L. Hughes
Erinn Obeldobel
Susie McLaughlin
Jamie King
Duquesne University

In This Chapter

▶ *Understanding Psychological Disorders*
- What Is Abnormality?
- Models of Abnormality

▶ *Assessment of Psychopathology*
- Diagnostic Classification Systems
- The Assessment Process
- Gathering Information: Written, Verbal, and Observational Methods
- Assessment Results

▶ *The Diagnostic System: Some Considerations*
- Uses and Advantages of the *DSM* Classification System
- Limitations of the *DSM* System
- Dimensional Diagnoses: A New Approach to Diagnosing

▶ *Disturbances Related to Anxiety*
- Approaches to Understanding Anxiety
- Generalized Anxiety Disorder
- Phobias
- Panic Disorder
- Obsessive-Compulsive Disorder
- Stress Disorders

▶ *Disturbances With Mood*
- Approaches to Understanding Depression
- Unipolar Depression
- Bipolar Disorder
- Suicide

▶ *Disturbances Related to Eating and Weight Loss*
- Approaches to Understanding Eating Disorders
- Anorexia Nervosa
- Bulimia Nervosa (Binge–Purge Syndrome)

▶ *Disturbances in Substance Use*
- Distinctions Between Abuse and Dependence
- Approaches to Understanding Substance Abuse
- Some Drugs of Choice

▶ *Disturbances With Sexuality and Gender Identity*
- Approaches to Sexual Dysfunction
- Sexual Dysfunction
- Paraphilias
- Gender Identity Disorder
- Sex Therapy

In This Chapter (*continued*)

▶ *Disturbances of Psychosis, Memory, and Other Cognitive Functions*
- Approaches to Understanding Schizophrenia
- Symptoms of Schizophrenia
- Dissociative Disorders

▶ *Disturbances in Personality*
- Approaches to Understanding Problems With Personality
- Odd Personality Disorders
- Dramatic Personality Disorders
- Anxious Personality Disorders

▶ *Disturbances in Childhood*
- Approaches to Understanding Childhood Disturbances
- Mental Health Problems in Childhood
- Elimination Disorders
- Chronic Disorders Beginning in Childhood

▶ *Disturbances Related to Aging and Cognition*
- Problems With Cognition and Neurology in Older Adults
- Mood Disorders in Older Adulthood

UNDERSTANDING PSYCHOLOGICAL DISORDERS

Our intent in this chapter is to provide an overview of deviant behaviors and their treatments. We touch on three main areas. The first area deals with abnormality and the various theoretical perspectives on psychopathology. The second area describes the assessment of psychopathology, including the purpose, process, and different types of assessment strategies used in treatment planning and progress monitoring, as well as advantages and limitations of the current classification systems used in diagnosis and assessment. The third area deals with the main categories of psychological disorders by providing a review various theoretical perspectives on the causes of disorders, and mentioning the counseling techniques used in treating the disorder that are consistent with the causal theory.

■ What Is Abnormality?

Defining abnormality can be difficult. Because the meaning of specific cognitive, behavioral, and emotional manifestations often differs according to culture and varies across time in the same culture, the understanding of abnormality is not absolute. However, most definitions of psychological abnormality emphasize the four Ds: deviance, distress, dysfunction, and danger. Comer (2004) provided these explanations of the underlying facets of deviant behavior:

Deviance: Thoughts, emotions, or behaviors that are different for what is expected of that time and place.

Distress: Deviant thoughts, emotions, or behaviors that cause disruption and upset to the person experiencing them, and, at times, to others in contact with the individual experiencing distressing symptoms.

Dysfunction: Distress is so significant that it causes impairment in important daily activities (e.g., work or school) or relationships.

Danger: Distress may be so severe that a person becomes a danger to himself or herself (suicide) or to others (homicide).

Deviant, distressing, dysfunctional or dangerous thoughts, emotions, or behaviors are considered core symptoms of an abnormal psychological state.

■ Models of Abnormality

There are various approaches to understanding the origins of abnormal psychological symptoms; however, none of these adequately explains all abnormal symptoms or disorders. At the same time, it is important to understand how causes of problems are conceptualized, as these conceptualizations are used to inform treatment techniques that are prescribed to address the symptoms of the abnormality. A number of approaches to understanding abnormality, as well as the assumptions about dysfunction that undergird the core theoretical models, briefly are described here.

Approaches to Understanding Abnormal Behavior

- *Biological model:* Originates from a medical perspective in which abnormal behavior is viewed as an illness resulting from faulty portions of the brain or body. Depression, for example, is believed to be the result of an imbalance of brain chemicals.
- *Psychodynamic model:* Behavior is a result of underlying psychological forces of which people may or may not be aware, and abnormal behavior occurs when there is conflict between these internal forces.
- *Behavioral model:* Experiences that occur in proximity (operant and classical conditioning) result in learning, and inappropriate learning can result in abnormal behavioral responses to the environment.
- *Cognitive model:* Cognitive processes are at the core of behaviors, thoughts, and emotions, and distorted thoughts precede abnormal symptoms.
- *Humanistic-existential model:* Behavior extends from an understanding of and comfort in the human existence, and abnormal behaviors are a result of distraction from the pursuit of philosophical goals such as self-awareness, freedom of choice, and a sense of meaning in life.
- *Sociocultural model:* Abnormal behavior is a result of the social and cultural forces that influence people.

ASSESSMENT OF PSYCHOPATHOLOGY

Identifying psychological disorders begins with the important task of assessment, which can be defined as follows:

Assessment: The process of collecting and integrating data from interviews, case studies, observations, and psychometric tools for the purposes of informing clinical decisions.

In the assessment process, clinicians interpret the results from psychological tests and also evaluate the severity of abnormal symptoms. Factors such as age, context, setting, and reason for referral all are considered in the assessment process. The information that is gathered during the assessment process ultimately allows clinicians to diagnose disorders, recommend treatment, monitor the effectiveness of treatment services, and determine appropriate placement for clients (Sattler, 2001). Other key concepts in the assessment process are defined here.

Diagnosing: The process of matching an individual's observed and reported abnormal psychological symptoms to a cluster of symptoms known as a syndrome or a disorder.

Disorders or syndromes: Abnormal psychological symptoms that tend to occur together, present to a marked degree, and last for a significant amount of time.

Diagnosis: Statement made when psychological symptoms are consistent with a known mental health disorder or syndrome.

■ Diagnostic Classification Systems

The two main classification systems that list known psychological disorders or syndromes and that are used in making a diagnosis are the *Diagnostic and Statistical Manual of Mental Disorders* (4th ed., text revision [*DSM–IV–TR*]; American Psychiatric Association, 2000) and International Classification of Diseases (ICD; World Health Organization, 1992). A third system, the Individuals With Disabilities Education Act (IDEA), is used in schools as the classification system for children. Each of these systems contains lists of symptoms and criteria for determining if a symptom is typical to a particular disorder.

■ The Assessment Process

Assessment is a dynamic process in which clinicians gather data, formulate key questions that guide observations and data collection, make conclusions or diagnoses, and, at times, alter their decisions. Groth-Marnat (2003) and Sattler (2001) outlined eight steps to a thorough assessment.

Main Steps in the Assessment Process

1. Identify a reason for referral before beginning the assessment.
2. Obtain relevant information about physical, social, educational, and emotional history.
3. Observe the individual in a natural setting (home or classroom) when appropriate or in the therapy or testing sessions.
4. Develop a working hypotheses about nature of the symptoms.
5. Select and administer an appropriate battery of tests based on the hypotheses and the referral question.

6. Interpret the results in the context of all information obtained including the individual's history, the clinician's observations, test data, and information provided by others.
7. Reject, modify, or accept hypotheses.
8. Summarize the findings in a written report and make recommendations based on assessment results.

For more information on the assessment process, see Chapter 21.

■ Gathering Information: Written, Verbal, and Observational Methods

Counselors who are conducting assessments have at their disposal a variety of methods for gathering information. Two of the primary methods are written assessments, which commonly include paper-and-pencil questionnaires, and observational and verbal methods. Turning first to the written tools, counselors need to understand some basics of the written tools that they may use. In particular, counselors should be able to differentiate between broadband and narrowband instruments and have a working knowledge of these various types of tools.

Written Methods: Broadband and Narrowband Instruments

- **Broadband tools** simultaneously measure a wide range of characteristics, behaviors, and symptoms that can be used to diagnose one or several disorders (e.g., depression and anxiety). Broadband tools typically are used for initial diagnosis to rule out or simultaneously consider other disorders that may have overlapping symptoms. An example of a broadband instrument is the Minnesota Multiphasic Personality Inventory (MMPI; Butcher, Dahlstrom, Graham, Tellegen, & Kaemmer, 1989a).
- **Narrowband tools** measure a specific set of characteristics of only one disorder or syndrome (e.g., depression). Although they may be used for diagnosis, these instruments routinely are used for monitoring symptom severity once a diagnosis is established (e.g., the Beck Depression Inventory [BDI; Beck, Steer, & Brown, 1996]).

Not only should counselors understand the purpose and aims of a test, but they also need to know how the test was developed to determine its usefulness. Most tests that clinicians use are norm referenced; however they also may be criterion referenced.

Differences Between Norm-Referenced and Criterion-Referenced Tests

- A **norm-referenced test** is one that has been given in a standardized manner to a specific sample (group) of individuals, called the norm group. The sample is described in test manuals. Scores obtained represent performance ranks based on the studied norm group. The examiner compares the individual's scores to those of the representative group.

- A **criterion-referenced test** is one that is used to determine if an individual demonstrates a predetermined standard of performance.

Although tests are an integral component in accurate assessments, there are other forms of measuring behavior that can be equally effective. Interviews and observations offer crucial, dynamic, and contextual information about an individual. Drummond (2004) recommended clinical interviews to gather the following information.

Components of the Clinical Interview Assessment

- Demographic information includes age, education level, gender, and income status of clients.
- The chief complaint or the presenting symptom should be recorded in the client's words, and the clinician should note the client's insight into his or her problems, as well as the degree to which the client is prepared to accept help.
- Mental status is a record of individuals' functioning at the time of assessment, including observed cognitive functioning, emotional responsiveness and expression, social reciprocity, and stability of mood.
- Developmental and social history provides a detailed look into the family and developmental history, with emphasis on delays in development or maladaptive patterns of behavior that may be contributing to current difficulties.
- Past psychiatric history details difficulties experienced in the past and efforts taken to reduce symptoms and effectiveness of previous treatment.

The pieces of information just mentioned are all integral to making a sound assessment. Gathering this information, however, does not have to follow one standard method. In fact, there are several approaches that interviewers can use when conducting an evaluation.

Common Clinical Interview Styles for Making Assessments

- Structured interviews are characterized by a predetermined set of questions, followed sequentially, and often are symptom oriented.
- Semistructured interviews include a list of predetermined questions that are modified throughout the interview process based on an individual's reported experiences.
- Unstructured interviews have a flexible format, do not include a predetermined list of questions, and rely on observations as part of the information gathering process.
- Natural setting interviews occur in environments where the individual is comfortable and familiar, often without clients' foreknowledge that they are being observed.
- Therapeutic setting interviews occur in the context of the clinical relationship.

■ Assessment Results

Assessment results are the end product of the investigations into the referral question, initial and modified hypotheses, interview, observation, and test data that are considered in the context of an individual's life experience. In short, the assessment is a broad picture of an individual's thoughts, feelings, and behaviors that is interpreted in light of how most groups of people would act, think, or feel.

See Chapter 21 for more information on testing and assessment.

THE DIAGNOSTIC SYSTEM: SOME CONSIDERATIONS

The *DSM* has been a standard in the helping professions for years, and the organization of the manual, as well as its approach to describing the symptomatology that ultimately leads to diagnoses, is well known. Recently, new thought is emerging in the helping field with regard to this tool's approach to disorder diagnosis that raises questions about categorical diagnosis and introduces the idea of dimensional diagnosis, in which symptoms are understood as part of a continuum from health to problematic behavior.

■ Uses and Advantages of the *DSM* Classification System

The *DSM* classification system most widely is used by mental health professionals to describe psychological disorders. For a practicing clinician, the *DSM* provides a mechanism for categorizing behaviors into classification systems that are succinct in description, allowing for a more universal understanding of the kind of pathology experienced by patients. Diagnostic categories facilitate communication between mental health providers, assist in the process of securing access to mental health services (i.e., insurance), and also provide practitioners with a schema for understanding requisite symptom presentations for defining syndromes (e.g., depression). Additionally, the aim of the current diagnostic system is to offer clinicians a method for determining the presence and severity of the presenting problems for the purpose of identifying possible treatments to effectively alleviate symptoms.

■ Limitations of the *DSM* System

Although categorical classifications of symptoms and disorders can be helpful in understanding and working with clients with various difficulties, there are limitations to this approach. Difficulties inherent in the current diagnostic systems include (a) symptoms that are not specific to a single type of disorder (i.e., attention or concentration difficulties), (b) excessive comorbidity (co-occurring disorders), and (c) the limited ability to identify and characterize individuals with subclinical forms (failing to meet threshold for diagnostic criteria) of psychopathology (Widiger, 2005; Widiger & Samuel, 2005). Additionally, it should be noted that although diagnoses serve an important purpose, diagnoses alone do not always lead to effective treatment selection. In fact, many have argued that treating the underlying cause of the diagnosis (or presenting problems), rather than the manifesting behaviors that classifications rely on, will improve treatment effectiveness (McWilliams, 1999; Shirk & Russell, 1996).

■ Dimensional Diagnoses: A New Approach to Diagnosing

In response to difficulties found in the categorical approach to diagnosing, another perspective has been introduced from which symptoms of psychopathology are viewed dimensionally. From the dimensional perspective, symptoms are considered in light of a continuum of graded severity rather than as discrete clinical diagnostic categories. In light of the growing recognition that the current diagnostic practices are limited, professionals increasingly are advocating for the replacement of a categorical approach to diagnosing with a dimensional model of describing psychopathology. Currently, however, diagnoses continue to be made using categorical decisions indicating the presence or absence of psychopathology.

> In light of the growing recognition that the current diagnostic practices are limited, professionals increasingly are advocating for the replacement of a categorical approach to diagnosing with a dimensional model of describing psychopathology.

Given the current system for diagnosing psychopathology, in the next sections, we describe various clusters of disorders identified in the diagnostic manual and subsequently discuss related treatment issues. As described earlier, to meet criteria as a disorder, these symptoms must occur to a marked degree, for a long period, and impair daily functioning. Clinicians should refer to the current *DSM* to determine the number of symptoms and period of distress required to meet the threshold for diagnosis, as these details are subject to change.

DISTURBANCES RELATED TO ANXIETY

Anxiety disorder is a broad category that houses descriptions of specific manifestations of anxiety, such as generalized anxiety disorder, panic disorder, and obses-

sive-compulsive disorder, among others. The symptoms of anxiety that an individual exhibits determine the type of anxiety disorder experienced. Some of the more
common symptoms of anxiety disorders are listed here.

General Symptoms of Anxiety Disorders

- Tension.
- Fatigue.
- Sleep interruptions.
- Increased heart rate.
- High blood pressure.
- Perspiration.
- Adrenaline.
- Salivation.
- Pilo-erection (hair standing up on the back of the head and arms).
- Overactive startle instincts.

■ Approaches to Understanding Anxiety

As mentioned earlier in the chapter, there are a variety of approaches or schools of
thought as to the causation of psychological disorders. Table 19.1 summarizes
some theoretical approaches to understanding anxiety, its causes, and suggested
treatment regimens.

TABLE 19.1 Approaches to Anxiety		
Theory	**Cause of Anxiety**	**Treatment**
Biological	Not enough GABA (neurotransmitter)	Anti-anxiety medications, biofeedback
Psychodynamic	Suppression /redirect (to phobic object) id (primary) instincts	Appropriate expression of id impulses
Behavioral	Conditioning or learning, modeling	Exposure, systematic desensitization, relearning (social skills training)
Cognitive	Dysfunctional ways of thinking	Adopt functional thinking, relaxation
Humanists	Denying true emotions, thoughts, and behavior leads a person to be out of touch with true self	Get in touch with real or true self
Sociocultural	Environment is considered dangerous	Decrease poverty, oppression

■ Generalized Anxiety Disorder

Generalized anxiety disorder is characterized by severe, free-floating anxiety and excessive worry that may have no specific content and can occur under most circumstances. Treatment usually includes a combination of medication, cognitive, and behavioral approaches.

■ Phobias

Phobias are defined as persistent and unreasonable fears that can result in physical symptoms. Treatment usually includes cognitive and behavioral approaches. Some common types of phobias are mentioned here.

Categories of Phobias

- ■ Specific phobia is a fear of a particular object or situation (e.g., spiders).
- ■ Social phobia is the fear of embarrassment in social or performance situations.
- ■ Agoraphobia is a fear of going into public places, especially when alone.

Another aspect of phobias is the panic attack, which can be brought on by real fears or feelings of dread, or can occur without a causal source. Symptoms of a panic attack include heart palpitations, tingling of the hands and feet, sweating, hot or cold sweats, shortness of breath, trembling, chest pain, choking sensations, faintness, dizziness, and feelings of unreality. Treatment often includes medications and cognitive approaches.

■ Panic Disorder

A panic disorder is distinguished by dysfunction in thinking or behavior as a result of panic attacks, defined as sudden onset of anxiety symptoms that come on repeatedly, unexpectedly, and for no apparent reason. Panic disorder often is accompanied by agoraphobia. Treatment may include medication (antidepressants to manage norepinephrine), cognitive, or behavioral approaches.

■ Obsessive-Compulsive Disorder

Obsessive-compulsive disorder is characterized by recurrent and unwanted thoughts (obsessions), a need to perform repetitive and rigid actions (compulsions), or both. Compulsions are reported to reduce the anxiety associated with the obsessive thoughts. Treatment may include a combination of medicine aimed at increasing serotonin levels and cognitive approaches for stress management and life skills training.

▪ Stress Disorders

Stress disorders are characterized by lingering anxiety that continues well after a psychologically traumatic event is over (e.g., automobile accident, rape, war). These disorders are similar to anxiety disorders because anxiety symptoms are a primary concern, and people with both anxiety disorders and stress disorders tend to avoid activities associated with the anxiety. However, stress disorders also include symptoms such as flashbacks of the traumatic event, reduced responsiveness, and guilt. Both increased arousal (anxiety symptoms) and underarousal (numbness) can cooccur in stress disorders.

There are two main types of stress disorder that are distinguished primarily by time frame during which the anxiety occurs.

Types of Stress Disorder

- ▪ Acute stress disorder is identified when anxiety occurs close to the time of the event.
- ▪ Posttraumatic stress disorder occurs long after the event.

Treatment options for stress disorders include medication, behavioral exposure techniques, cognitive approaches such as insight therapy, and sociocultural interventions, in which family and group therapy are the focus.

DISTURBANCES WITH MOOD

Among the most prevalent psychological problems are those related to mood, and especially to depression. Other problems with mood are unipolar depression and bipolar disorder or manic depression. These diagnoses, along with suicide, which frequently is precipitated by a mood disturbance such as depression, are addressed in this section.

▪ Approaches to Understanding Depression

Because depression is potentially the most common among the mood disorders, Table 19.2 reflects various theoretical perspectives on the causes and treatment regimens for depression.

▪ Unipolar Depression

The diagnosis of depression is more specific than is depicted here, and clinicians use the battery of symptoms to accurately distinguish among the various manifes-

TABLE 19.2 Theoretical Perspectives on Depression		
Theory	**Causes of Depression**	**Treatment**
Biological	Genetic predisposition Low serotonin levels	Antidepressant drugs, electroconvulsive therapy (severe cases)
Psychodynamic	Traumatic event triggers anger and sadness (becomes self-directed)	Bring underlying issues to consciousness and work through
Behavioral	Life is a rewards and punishments system, and the right behaviors are not being rewarded	Reintroduce pleasurable activities, reward non-depressive behavior, social skills training
Cognitive	Pattern of thinking is irrational and negatively oriented	Recognize and change negative or irrational thought processes
Sociocultural	Social structure and social roles are oppressive	Interpersonal therapy, couples therapy

tations of depression. However, unipolar depression is typified by a sad state of mind accompanied by lack of energy, low self-worth, and guilt. Other common symptoms of depression are provided next.

Symptoms of Depression

- Feelings of worthlessness.
- Apathy.
- Decreased energy.
- Loss of feelings of pleasure.
- Thoughts of guilt and suicide.
- Sleep and appetite disruptions.

Treatment for depression typically combines medication to increase serotonin levels, cognitive techniques for eliminating negative self-talk, sociocultural techniques to improve relationships, behavioral rewards for appropriate thoughts and behaviors, and uncovering automatic (unconscious) triggers to self-directed hatred. Single symptoms of depression may be targeted by specific therapy techniques, and 70% of depression cases can remit without intervention.

■ Bipolar Disorder

Bipolar disorder is characterized by intermittent periods of depression and mania. Included in the symptom profile are cycles of depressive symptoms and cycles of manic symptoms, such as feelings of euphoria, pressured speech, and rapid flow of ideas that may not be coherent. Because the cause of bipolar disorder is believed to be related to neurotransmitter activity, ion activity, and genetic factors, medication is typically the first line of intervention. Lithium therapy is usually the treatment of choice, although antidepressants may be used to combat the depressive symptoms. Additionally, family support therapy and educational training may also be required to help identify the onset of cycles.

■ Suicide

Suicide is understood as intentional and self-directed death. Although the motives for suicide vary greatly from person to person and across cultures, some common precipitative factors are identifiable.

Precipitating Factors for Suicide

- Stressful events or situations (e.g., immediate loss of a loved one, natural disaster, serious illness, abusive environments, occupational dissatisfaction or distress).
- Changes in mood (increased sadness) and thinking (hopelessness, dichotomous thinking).
- Alcohol or drug use.
- Mental disorders, such as depression.
- Completed suicide by another person (e.g., in media, at work, in school).

Approaches to Suicide Prevention

- Taking all talk of death seriously (to coworkers, friends, family children in schools).
- Identifying parasuicidal behaviors such as cleaning of weapons, giving away belongings, saying goodbye, and getting finances in order.
- Conducting a suicide assessment.
- Signing a no-suicide contract in which people agree to a problem-solving sequence such as calling a friend, counselor, or 24-hour mental health hotline when they feel like hurting themselves.
- Resorting to involuntary commitment when psychiatric stabilization is required.

Clinicians frequently use an assessment as a prevention approach for suicide interventions. A suicide assessment should include a person's history of suicide attempts (previous attempts increase the likelihood of future attempts), level of detail present in his or her plans for death, access to a weapon, and lethality of the weapon. Additionally, clinicians should determine if the person has future-oriented thoughts that do not include his or her death and attempt to have the client sign a no-suicide contract. Reports of danger-to-self require all mental health workers to break confidentiality and to obtain a level of treatment that ensures the safety of that person.

DISTURBANCES RELATED TO EATING AND WEIGHT LOSS

Eating disturbances are characterized by overt attempts to alter body weight. Risk factors are multidimensional and include family pressures, co-occurring psychological problems (e.g., depression), and biological variables (e.g., body weight set points).

■ Approaches to Understanding Eating Disorders

Understanding eating disorders is a complex endeavor, and there are a variety of hypotheses related to the causes of this psychological issue that generally is recognized to be more than just a biological problem. Table 19.3 summarizes some of the perspectives used to explain and treat eating disorders.

■ Anorexia Nervosa

Anorexia is the term applied to the pursuit of thinness that results in extreme weight loss, to the extent that a person's health and, in severe cases, life, is jeopardized. Treatment options for anorexia include behavioral weight restoration programs that combine a high-calorie diet with positive reinforcement, cognitive techniques to address distorted thinking, and sociocultural techniques to increase positive family interactions.

TABLE 19.3
Approaches to Understanding Causes and Treatment of Eating Disorders

Theory	Cause of Eating Disorders	Treatment
Family environment	Overinvolved families do not allow the development of independence	Increase family harmony that allows for individual independence
Psychodynamic	Ego deficiencies result in poor autonomy and lack of control	Appropriate ego regulation with adequate separation from parents and balance superego (society) influences
Cognitive	Reliance on the views and wishes of others	Adopt thinking that values their own thoughts
Biological	Low serotonin body weight set point (going too low causes desire to binge eat)	Antidepressant medications
Sociocultural	Society overvalues thinness and humiliates the overweight person	Increase acceptance of a varied definition of female body sizes

■ Bulimia Nervosa (Binge–Purge Syndrome)

Bulimia is characterized by a person's engaging in repeated, uncontrollable episodes of extreme overeating followed by compensatory behaviors to avoid weight gain, such as forced vomiting, excessive exercise, and the use of laxatives. Treatment options for bulimia include a combination of individual insight therapy (cognitive and psychodynamic), behavioral therapy, medication to increase serotonin, and sociocultural support group techniques.

DISTURBANCES IN SUBSTANCE USE

Most often, substance use or addiction refers to the use of legal or illegal mood-altering substances in a manner that results in negative outcomes. Another recently recognized category of addiction in the counseling field is process addictions. Diagnostic criteria for most process addictions, however, are not found in the *DSM–IV–TR* classification system.

■ Distinctions Between Abuse and Dependence

The use and abuse patterns related to substances are best understood as part of a continuum of use. The least extreme usage patterns are known simply as substance use, and more extreme patterns of usage are considered abuse and dependence. These are defined here.

Substance abuse: A pattern of use that is chronic and excessive resulting in damage to relationships, work attendance or productivity, and health status.

Substance dependence: A pattern of use in which life activities are organized around the opportunity to consume a drug, and where psychological and physical tolerance (the need for more of the drug to get the same high) develops and withdrawal symptoms can result.

For more detailed information about substance and process addictions as well as the use–abuse continuum, see Chapter 26.

■ Approaches to Understanding Substance Abuse

There are a myriad of models that describe the causes of substance abuse. As mentioned previously, each of these models is laden with its own assumptions about why people become addicted and what they need to do to end their addictive behavior patterns. Table 19.4 summarizes just a few of these models.

For a brief description of other models of addiction and recovery, see Chapter 26.

TABLE 19.4 Theoretical Perspectives on Substance Disorders		
Theory	**Cause of Substance Disorders**	**Treatment**
Behavioral	Reinforcement is provided by decreasing tensions and inhibitions	Aversion therapy pairs punishments with drug use
Psychodynamic	Inadequate separation results in dependency	Increase awareness of underlying needs that result in drug use
Cognitive	Expectations that drug use will decrease tensions	Self-control of thoughts (changes behaviors)
Biological	Increased dopamine in the brain results in feelings of pleasure	Detoxification and antagonist drugs (block brain receptors so you do not experience a high even if you use the drug)
Sociocultural	Stress associated with poor living conditions, or environments support drug use	Support groups such as community prevention or Alcoholics Anonymous (AA)

■ Some Drugs of Choice

Counselors who work in the addictions field have to be well-educated on the numerous types of substances to which people can become addicted. The following list is a brief overview of some major drug categories.

Common Classes of Drugs

- Depressants such as alcohol, sedative-hypnotic drugs (e.g., benzodiazepines and barbiturates), and opioids (derivatives are morphine and heroin) slow functions of the central nervous system. This results in a reduction of tension and decreased inhibitions. Overdose decreases heart rate, slows breathing, and can result in death.
- Stimulants such as cocaine, amphetamines, caffeine, and nicotine increase activity of the central nervous system. Blood pressure, heart rate, alertness, and behavior and thinking are increased. Overdose can cause cardiac arrhythmia and death.
- Hallucinogens or psychedelics such as LSD, mescaline, peyote, psilocybin, and MDMA intensify sensory perception and can result in hallucinations, such as seeing things that are not there or blending of the five senses. Flashbacks or intrusive reexperiencing of events when using drugs or at a time when not using drugs can occur and may be reexperienced periodically over the course of months or years.

- Cannabis (e.g., hashish and marijuana) is produced from the hemp plant. The active chemical in cannabis is tetrahydrocannabinol, which can produce hallucinations.
- Designer drugs intentionally combine drug categories. Ecstasy, for example, is a combination of a stimulant and hallucinogen.

Treatment for substance users typically combines many theoretical perspectives where biological approaches (detoxification and antagonist drugs) are initial steps to getting sober. Cognitive-behavioral therapy can be used to address immediate needs for self-control, followed by psychodynamic therapy to address issues that brought individuals who are addicted to these patterns. Sociocultural support therapy such as Alcoholics Anonymous routinely is used in concert with each of these steps to provide daily support.

DISTURBANCES WITH SEXUALITY AND GENDER IDENTITY

Problems with sexuality encompass a wide variety of sexual dysfunctions and paraphilias, and, additionally, touch on the area of gender identity. In this section we outline some of the major sexual disorders and discuss sex therapy as one of the main treatment approaches to sexual dysfunction.

■ Approaches to Sexual Dysfunction

As with some other psychological problems, sexual dysfunctions can have a number of causes. Counselors who work with clients who have sexual dysfunction are encouraged to do a thorough assessment to explore the variety of attributes leading to the sexual disturbance. Table 19.5 summarizes a few of the possibilities.

■ Sexual Dysfunction

Sexual dysfunction refers to the inability to enjoy or participate in sexual intercourse or normal sexual activities. Moreover, when a sexual dysfunction is present, sexual activities are associated with pain or discomfort. There are a number of potential disorders or disturbances related to sexuality. A few are presented here.

Types of Sexual Disorders

- Hypoactive sexual desire occurs when an individual loses the desire for sexual interplay or intercourse. Sexual aversion disorder is characterized by an experiencing of sexual relations as aversive or unpleasant and an avoidance of genital contact and sexual intercourse.

| TABLE 19.5 | | |
| Perspectives on Understanding Sexual Dysfunction | | |
Theory	*Causes of Sexual Dysfunction*	*Treatment*
Biological	Abnormalities in hormone levels, comorbid chronic illness, pain medications, alcohol, cigarette smoking, diabetes, multiple sclerosis, antidepressant medications	Medication to target the identified difficulty (pain or depression), often paired with sex therapy
Psychological	Increase in anxiety, fears and trauma memories related to sexual interplay, depression, obsessive-compulsive disorder, performance anxiety	Sex therapy, often paired with appropriate medications
Sociocultural	Situational pressures and life stressors (death, new birth, job status change), relationship problems, sexual trauma, negative attitudes and beliefs about sex	Sex therapy, often paired with appropriate medications

- Erectile dysfunction disorder occurs when the male is unable to attain or maintain physiological sexual arousal marked by the lack of an erection through sexual intercourse.
- Female sexual arousal disorder is characterized by a female's inability to attain or maintain physiological sexual arousal, which is marked by the absence of vaginal lubrication or genital swelling throughout sexual intercourse.
- Male and female orgasmic disorders occur when the individual cannot reach sexual climax or is very delayed in reaching orgasm after the sexual excitement phase.
- Premature ejaculation is marked by recurrent episodes of reaching orgasm with minimal sexual stimulation and before the individual desires.
- Vaginismus refers to involuntary contractions of the third layer of muscles in the vagina leading to difficulties with sexual penetration during intercourse.
- Dyspareunia refers to recurrent experiences of genital pain during sexual intercourse for either males or females.

■ Paraphilias

Paraphilias are disorders typified by intense sexual urges or arousal that is associated with unconventional objects, including nonhuman objects, children, nonconsenting adults, or the experience of suffering and humiliation. A number of common paraphilias are listed here.

Well-Known Paraphilias

- Fetishism is marked by recurrent sexual fantasies, desire, or behaviors that involve nonliving objects over all other types of stimuli.
- Transvestitism is a desire to dress in clothes of the opposite sex to attain sexual arousal.
- Exhibitionism is sexual arousal obtained by exposing one's genitals to others.
- Voyeurism is a recurrent desire to view other unsuspecting individuals during intimate moments (e.g., watching an individual undressing or having intercourse).
- Frotteurism involves experiencing recurrent urges to rub against nonconsenting individuals to obtain sexual arousal.
- Pedophila refers to sexual gratification derived from watching, touching, or engaging in sexual activity with children.
- Sexual masochism refers to sexual arousal that occurs when the individual is humiliated or when physical pain or suffering is induced.
- Sexual sadism is sexual arousal that occurs when an individual inflicts pain on others through acts of domination, restraining, mutilating, and sometimes even killing another person.

■ Gender Identity Disorder

Another facet of sexual problems is gender identity disorders (GIDs), which are described as a person's excessive distress at feeling that the wrong sex was assigned at birth. Persons with this problem often are concerned with denying or getting rid of their primary sex characteristics (Comer, 2001). Treatment modalities for GID include sex-change therapy, hormone replacement treatments, and therapy.

■ Sex Therapy

Sex therapy was pioneered by Masters and Johnson in 1970 as a treatment used for most types of sexual disorders and encompasses the following principles and techniques.

Aspects of Masters and Johnson's Approach to Sex Therapy (Comer, 2001)

- Evaluating the problem by gathering information on the sex history of each partner, including other relevant information on past life events.
- Discussing the mutual responsibility of both partners for the sexual problems in their relationship.
- Providing education about sexuality through psychotherapy, bibliotherapy, and instructional videos.
- Challenging misinformed beliefs or myths about sexuality.

- Teaching methods of sexual interplay that deemphasize sexual intercourse and orgasm and redirect the attention to sexual pleasure experienced through exploration of one another's bodies.
- Increasing sexual and general communication skills.
- Changing destructive lifestyles and marital interactions that may be interfering with sexual intercourse.
- Addressing physical and medical factors to sexual dysfunction.

DISTURBANCES OF PSYCHOSIS, MEMORY, AND OTHER COGNITIVE FUNCTIONS

Schizophrenia, also known as psychosis, can be described as a loss of reality resulting in an inability to function at home, at work, in school, or in social relationships. An often severe and chronic problem, schizophrenia is characterized by disturbed thought processes, perceptions, and emotions that vary in responsiveness to treatment (Comer, 2001).

■ Approaches to Understanding Schizophrenia

Theorists in the biological, psychodynamic, behavioral, and sociocultural schools of thought all have considered the causes of schizophrenia, and although there may be a case for each of their attributions for psychosis, the biological explanations appear to be the best supported by research evidence (Comer, 2001). A summary of the differing perspectives on understanding this disturbance are mentioned in Table 19.6.

■ Symptoms of Schizophrenia

Symptoms of psychosis are classified by three themes, as described next.

Categories of Schizophrenic Symptomatology

- Positive symptoms are bizarre additions to a person's behavior, such as delusions and hallucinations.
- Negative symptoms are pathological behavioral deficits, such as blunted affect, social withdrawal, and loss of volition.
- Psychomotor symptoms include severely restricted movements such as catatonia.

There is general agreement that the diathesis stress model where a biological predisposition combined with other psychological and sociocultural factors is the best

TABLE 19.6
Approaches to Explaining and Treating Schizophrenia

Theory	Cause of Schizophrenia	Treatment
Biological	Biological predisposition (disorder manifests only when certain events or stressors are present) Excessive dopamine activity Abnormal brain structure	Regulate dopamine (medications)
Psychodynamic	Regression to pre-ego state and subsequent efforts to reestablish ego control due to poor (mother) parenting in early experiences	Insight into the causes and maintenance of symptoms
Behavioral	Reinforcement of bizarre responses to environment	Token economy systems where rewards are given for appropriate behaviors
Cognitive	Attempts to understand abnormal sensations that are triggered in the brain	Education about the symptoms of the disorder, insight into the causes of symptoms
Sociocultural	Social labeling Family dysfunction	Social support, daily living skills supported by family and community

explanation for the development of schizophrenia. Treatment of schizophrenia typically involves milieu therapy where medications, psychotherapy, and sociocultural support (either in a facility or in the community) are provided.

■ Dissociative Disorders

Some people experience marked disruptions in their memory, which is the key to knowing oneself and developing a stable identity. Interferences in memory are a form of dissociation, meaning that parts of an individual's memory are disconnected and independent from other parts of memory. There are many kinds of dissociative disorders; a few of these are mentioned here.

Categories of Dissociative Disorders

- Dissociative amnesia often appears after a trauma and is characterized by forgetfulness and inability to access memories containing important information.
- Dissociative fugue occurs when individuals forget their past and assume a new identity after geographically relocating.
- Dissociative identity disorder, formerly known as multiple personality disorder, occurs when an individual develops two or more distinct personalities with each subpersonality possessing different memories, feelings, and thoughts.

Although there are a number of perspectives on the causes of dissociative disorders, treatment regimens generally recommended include hypnotherapy, psychotherapy, and medication.

DISTURBANCES IN PERSONALITY

Personality disorders are patterns of rigid thoughts, feelings, and behaviors that differ dramatically from social norms. Disturbances with personality fall into three clusters: odd, dramatic, and anxious personality types (Comer, 2001), each of which is outlined in this section.

■ Approaches to Understanding Problems With Personality

Personality disorders of the three clusters are varied manifestations of inflexible patterns of being that are usually personally and socially problematic. The categories of disorders that fall within each of the three clusters are also unique, and to provide an analysis of the hypothesized causes of each disorder is beyond the bounds of this chapter. However, it is worth mentioning that the attributes of most of these personality disorders have not been empirically investigated and warrant further study from a variety of perspectives.

■ Odd Personality Disorders

Odd personality disturbances are characterized by odd or eccentric behaviors that are similar to those of schizophrenics. Paranoid, schizoid, and schizotypal are three types of odd disturbances that fall under this category.

Categories and Characteristics of Odd Personality Disorders

- Paranoid personality disorder is characterized by an avoidance of relationships due to chronic distrust and suspiciousness.
- Schizoid personality disorder is one in which a disinterest in and avoidance of relationships, as well as a lack of emotion, are manifest.
- Schizotypal personality disorder is characterized by extreme discomfort in close relationships, odd patterns of thinking and perceiving, and eccentricity in behavior; this is the most severe of the disorders in this cluster.

Treatment rarely is sought by individuals with paranoid personality disturbances. However, when treatment is desired, object relations therapy focusing on the importance of relationship and cognitive treatments focusing on managing distorted thoughts are used. Likewise, treatment rarely is sought for schizoid personality or schizotypal personality disorders, either. When sought, treatment for schizoid personality disturbances includes cognitive interventions dealing with the individual's inaccurate perceptions of others and behavioral measures that reward role playing. Treatment of schizotypal personality disorder focuses on connecting with others, cognitive interventions to correct inaccurate perceptions of others, and behavioral measures that reward role playing; at times, medications may be used.

■ Dramatic Personality Disorders

Dramatic personality disturbances are characterized by highly emotional and erratic behaviors, as well as extremely dysfunctional personal relationships. Dramatic personality disorders include antisocial, borderline, histrionic, and narcissistic personality disorders.

Categories and Characteristics of Dramatic Personality Disorders

- Antisocial personality disorder is typified by persistent disregard for the rights of others and often is accompanied by the lack of remorse.
- Borderline personality disorder is characterized by ongoing instability in relationships, self-image, and mood, as well as impulsive behavior.
- Histrionic personality disorder usually includes symptoms such as exaggerated, rapidly changing moods and attention-seeking behavior.
- Narcissistic personality disorder is characterized by a lack of empathy for others, grandiosity, and an insatiable need for attention and admiration from others.

A primary obstacle to treatment for antisocial personality disorder is the limited desire to change and lack of remorse for behaviors that usually are present in individuals with the symptoms that accompany the disorder. Most treatments are reported as ineffective, and sometimes traditional therapies are contraindicated. Treatment for borderline personality disorder usually includes a combination of psychodynamic, cognitive, behavioral, and sociocultural interactions. Medications may also be used. There is some evidence that sustained long-term treatment can result in some gains. People with histrionic traits typically do seek out treatment. However, they can quickly assimilate the therapist into their repertoire of inappropriate relationships. Thus, cognitive, psychodynamic, and sociocultural interventions all are aimed at creating a relationship that is not based on dependency. Narcissictic personality disorder is one of the most difficult psychological problems to treat. Psychodynamic interventions focus on recognizing and working through insecurities and defenses, whereas cognitive interventions focus on understanding others. None has shown substantive support.

■ Anxious Personality Disorders

Anxious personality disturbances are characterized by anxious and fearful behavior. Avoidant, dependent, and obsessive-compulsive personality disorders comprise this category of anxious-related disorders.

Categories and Characteristics of Anxious Personality Disorders

- Avoidant personality disorder is typified by excessive discomfort and inhibition in social situations, overwhelming feelings of inadequacy, and extreme sensitivity to negative evaluations.
- Dependent personality disorder manifests in a desperate, pervasive need to be taken care of. Individuals with this problem usually exhibit clingy behaviors and may develop an inability to carry out even the simplest tasks for themselves.
- Obsessive-compulsive personality disorder is characterized by a person's lack of flexibility, openness, and efficiency due to pervasive preoccupation with order, perfection, and control.

For persons with avoidant and dependent personality traits, cognitive and psychodynamic interventions focus on finding success in relationships. Additionally, behavioral exposure therapy, sociocultural support groups, medications (anti-anxiety), and family interventions sometimes are used. Treatment for obsessive-compulsive disorder rarely is sought, however, as individuals with this problem usually like their orderliness; that is, the symptoms are **ego syntonic** and cause these individuals little distress. When treatment is sought, cognitive and psychodynamic approaches often are combined in treatment, along with anti-anxiety and antidepressant medications.

DISTURBANCES IN CHILDHOOD

The varieties of psychological problems that arise in childhood include mental health oriented issues, such as separation anxiety and conduct disorder, as well as more biologically oriented problems, such as Down's syndrome and mental retardation. We outline a number of these disturbances in this section.

■ Approaches to Understanding Childhood Disturbances

There are a multitude of psychological problems that can manifest in childhood. Table 19.7 summarizes some of the biological, behavioral, and sociocultural perspectives on explaining and treating mental health issues in children and young adults.

	TABLE 19.7	
	Perspectives on Childhood Mental Health Problems	
Theory	**Causes of Childhood Mental Health Problems**	**Treatment**
Biological	Genetic inheritance, drug abuse	Medications
Behavioral	Learned through parent modeling and reinforcement, exposure to violence	Family therapy and parent training to redirect how parents reinforce appropriate patterns
Sociocultural	Poverty, traumatic events, troubled parent–child relationships, marital conflict, family hostility	Family therapy and parent training, play therapy, social support groups

■ Mental Health Problems in Childhood

Psychological disturbances not only are present in adulthood, but also are seen in childhood and adolescence. Indeed, some disturbances that arise in childhood may be indicative of potential issues in adulthood. Among the most widely recognized of childhood disorders today is attention deficit hyperactivity disorder; however, there are numerous other problems in childhood with which counselors should be familiar.

Categories and Characteristics of Childhood Disturbances

- Separation anxiety disorder is intense distress that occurs in a child when he or she is separated from the caregiver or home.
- Oppositional defiant disorder manifests as regular patterns of defiance, arguing, losing one's temper, and difficulty regulating emotions.
- Conduct disorder manifests in patterns of cruelty to others, lack of respect for authority, and repeated violations and exploitations on the rights of other people.
- Attention deficit hyperactivity disorder manifests in difficulty attending to stimuli, a tendency for overactivity and impulsive behaviors, or a combination of both.

■ Elimination Disorders

Elimination disorders are unique to childhood and are characterized by a pattern of behavior in which children either wet themselves or defecate in their clothing or in other inappropriate places in the home. Two categories of disturbance are identified as elimination disorders: enuresis and encopresis.

Types of Elimination Disorders

- Enuresis is marked by recurrent, involuntary episodes of bed-wetting.
- Encopresis is marked by recurrent, involuntary episodes of defecating while clothed.

Depending on the theoretical approach taken to understand this problem, treatment can include play therapy, family therapy aimed at reducing family stress that may be influencing the behavior, and medication, among other treatment regimens.

■ Chronic Disorders Beginning in Childhood

Autism, mental retardation, and Down's syndrome are all disorders that either begin or are diagnosed in infancy or childhood; all are long term and chronic in nature. Often, psychological and biological tenets explain the onset and etiological factors associated with each disorder.

Characteristics of Autism, Mental Retardation, and Down's Syndrome

- Autism manifests as a child's difficulty to communicate, patterns of interpersonal isolation, unresponsiveness to others, and repetitive and stereotypical movements. Symptoms emerge prior to age 3.
- Mental retardation is the term used for children whose cognitive functioning is well below average and who display deficits in adaptive behaviors.
- Down's syndrome is mental retardation caused by genetic abnormality in the 21st chromosome.

A leading theory on autism asserts that a form of mind blindness (i.e., problems with theory of the mind) interferes with the child's capacity for understanding others' perspectives, severely impairing the extent to which a child can engage interpersonally with others in the world. Research has suggested that psychoeducation, direct instruction in the classroom, and family therapy can be effective treatments for children with autism. Psychoeducational efforts should focus on teaching appropriate behaviors, social skills, self-help skills, and communicative skills in both the home and school environment.

For individuals with mental retardation or severe cognitive limitations resulting from other biological deficits or abnormalities, the main goal is to increase the person's capacity for independent living skills. Psychoeducation on issues associated with adaptive functioning (e.g., independent dressing, toileting, dating, sex education, job training) has been effective for many individuals with mental retardation.

DISTURBANCES RELATED TO AGING AND COGNITION

Perhaps the most common psychological problems associated with aging are those related to memory and cognition. In this section, we describe a number of disturbances that older adults encounter with regard to their cognitive ability. However, older adults also are susceptible to other mental health issues such as mood and anxiety disorders. Therefore, these also are addressed.

■ Problems With Cognition and Neurology in Older Adults

Although most older adults experience some type of memory loss as they age, symptoms of these disorders are recognized as more severe than what occurs in the normal process of aging. Some of those disturbances of cognition are outlined here along with other biopsychosocial problems.

Types of Psychological Problems Characteristic in Late Life

- Delirium is marked difficulty concentrating, attending to stimuli, and focusing leading to confusion, misinterpretations, and hallucinations.
- Dementia is marked memory loss combined with decreases in cognitive functioning and capacity for abstract thinking.
- Alzheimer's disease is the most common form of dementia resulting in loss of most cognitive faculties, disorientation, and decreased capacity for communication with others.
- Vascular dementia can be described as damage done to the brain subsequent to a stroke or accident, which leads to dementia.
- Pick's disease is a disorder affecting the frontal and temporal lobes that closely resembles Alzheimer's disease.
- Creutzfeldt–Jakob disease can be described as dementia associated with spasmodic movements.
- Huntington's disease is characterized by memory deficits that lead to personality changes and mood deregulation.
- Parkinson's disease is a neurological disease associated with tremors, rigidity, and dementia.

■ Mood Disorders in Older Adulthood

Depression and anxiety disorders are common mental health problems for older adults. Although the symptoms do not necessarily manifest in different forms for the elderly as compared with younger people, there are additional complications that should be noted. For example, older people who exhibit symptoms of depression or anxiety have a variety of medical sequelae that can increase the likelihood of suicidality. Research has suggested that individual therapies, group therapy, and medication therapies have been helpful in reducing the severity of depression and anxiety in older adults. At times, symptoms of depression, such as cognitive impairment, can be confused with normal aging or cognitive disorders in the elderly.

In conclusion, understanding deviant behaviors and how those behaviors are assessed, tallied for the purpose of diagnosis, and used in the tailoring of treatment is a primary role for clinicians. Comparing various theoretical perspectives side by side with treatments aids the clinician in clarifying intervention selections. That is, the connections between theoretical explanations of behaviors can direct the process of selecting treatments that correspond to the presenting problems of our clients. Through the combined use of clinical assessment and the knowledge of theories and interventions, practitioners more readily are able to identify the course of psychopathology at an individual client level, which increases the long-term capacity for positive client outcomes and effectiveness in treatment.

Chapter 19: Key Terms

- ▶ Assessment
- ▶ Deviance
- ▶ Distress
- ▶ Dysfunction
- ▶ Danger
- ▶ Diagnosing

- ▶ Disorders
- ▶ Syndromes
- ▶ Diagnosis
- ▶ Broadband tools
- ▶ Narrowband tools
- ▶ Norm-referenced test

- ▶ Criterion-referenced test
- ▶ Substance abuse
- ▶ Substance dependence
- ▶ Ego syntonic

part three

What Are the Fundamental
Components of Appraisal
and Research That New Counselors
Should Use in Their Practice?

Foundations of Measurement and Psychometrics

Tara Greene
Jeffrey A. Miller
Nate E. Kegal
Julie Williams
Duquesne University

In This Chapter

▶ *Statistics: A Brief Introduction*
  ■ Ethics in Statistical Research
  ■ Differentiation Between Descriptive and Inferential Statistics: Some Basics

▶ *Descriptive Statistics*
  ■ Scales of Measurement
  ■ Measures of Central Tendency: Mean, Median, and Mode
  ■ Measures of Dispersion: Range, Variance, and Standard Deviation
  ■ Distribution
  ■ Percentile

▶ *Inferential Statistics*
  ■ Probability
  ■ Standard Scores
  ■ Tests of Significance

▶ *Reliability*
  ■ Classical Test Theory
  ■ Importance of Reliability
  ■ Measurement of Reliability
  ■ Methods of Estimating Reliability
  ■ Standard Error of Measurement
  ■ The Confidence Interval

▶ *Validity*
  ■ Content Validity
  ■ Face Validity
  ■ Construct Validity
  ■ Criterion-Related Validity

▶ *Test Construction*
  ■ Methods of Test Development
  ■ Writing the Items
  ■ Item Try-Out
  ■ Normative Sample
  ■ Writing the Manual

STATISTICS: A BRIEF INTRODUCTION

Psychological measurement is based on core statistical principles that allow one to better understand, interpret, and conduct research, as well as make decisions using test data. Because counselors frequently are involved in testing and assessment of clients and then making decisions based on test results, they should at least be familiar and comfortable with the basics of descriptive and inferential statistics. Also important to the work of testing and assessment are the areas of reliability, validity, and test construction. Each of these topics is addressed in this chapter. First, however, it is necessary to mention the importance of ethical practice in statistical research.

■ Ethics in Statistical Research

Ethical practice is fundamental to all counseling-related endeavors, from the individual counseling relationship to research studies that are conducted in the field of counselor education. Adhering to high ethical standards is especially critical, because most research in the counseling field involves human participants. Thus, it is necessary that all researchers be aware of the various principles of ethical investigations. To ensure that students and professionals act within the specific guidelines that frame ethical research, they usually are required to complete online training in ethical practice in research, as well as secure approval from an institutional review board that independently reviews investigative proposals. A few terms that counselors who plan to conduct human-participant research may want to be familiar with include informed consent, voluntary participation, anonymity, and risk of harm. Trochim (2002) defined these concepts this way:

Informed consent: Participants must be made fully aware of the scope of expectations surrounding their participation in and the procedures of the study, and then freely give their consent to participate.

Voluntary participation: Participants are not coerced, forced, or deceived into participation.

Risk of harm: Participants will incur no physical or psychological harm as a result of taking part in the study.

Anonymity: A facet of protecting participants from risk of harm by which participants are ensured that their identities or any identifying information will not be revealed or used in the study.

To complete a tutorial on the protection of human participants in research, visit the following Web site:

► http://cme.cancer.gov/clinicaltrials/learning/humanparticipant-protections.asp

For a more detailed description of ethical codes surrounding research by professional counselors, refer to the ACA Code of Ethics at this Web site:

► http://www.counseling.org/Resources/CodeOfEthics

■ Differentiation Between Descriptive and Inferential Statistics: Some Basics

Basic statistical procedures can be classified as descriptive or inferential; it is important to understand the distinction between these two approaches to statistical inquiry. Rowntree (2004) made the following differentiation between these two types of statistics:

Descriptive statistics: Statistical inquiry that uses observations to describe or make summary statements about data.

Inferential statistics: Statistical inquiry that uses observations of a sample population to make predictions and generalizations about the wider population.

DESCRIPTIVE STATISTICS

This section of the chapter briefly addresses some key concepts in the area of descriptive statistics, including the following:

- Scales of measurement.
- Measures of central tendency.
- Measures of dispersion.
- Distribution.
- Percentiles.

■ Scales of Measurement

Scales of measurement are systems of ordinal or verbal descriptors that are used in statistics to describe the characteristics of a data set based on their empirical properties. There are four types of scales of measurement: nominal scales, ordinal scales, interval scales, and ratio scales. Because each scale measures different information, it is important to understand the purpose of each scale and when it is required; depending on the type of data and method of data collection, the scale of measurement will vary (Sprinthall, 2003). The measurement scales can be defined this way:

Nominal scales: The simplest form of measurement that assigns numbers to classify data into one or more categories (e.g., one type of nominal measurement is gender, and numbers can be assigned to the categories of male and female) to make observations about the frequency with which data fall into each category.

Ordinal scales: Like the nominal scales, data are classified into categories, and they are also rank ordered. The distance between the rankings, however, is not known and rankings are not necessarily equidistant. An example of an ordinal scale is the order of finishing in a race (first, second, third, etc.)

Interval scales: A form of measurement that also is rank ordered on a scale that contains equal intervals between numbers on the scale. However, there is no absolute zero point, indicating that no mathematical calculations can be done with the data set.

Ratio scales: Scales that have all the properties as the interval scale of measurement and also have an absolute or true zero point.

Increasingly more useful data are gleaned through the use of nominal, ordinal, interval, and finally ratio scales, with ratio scales providing for the most complex and valid comparisons of data. Examples of ratio scales include height, weight, speed, time, and distance. All mathematical operations can be done with these data because there is a true zero. For example, data can be compared, saying a bag with a weight of 40 pounds weighs twice as much as one that weighs 20 pounds.

■ Measures of Central Tendency: Mean, Median, and Mode

The most common measures of central tendency are the mean, median, and mode. Each of these measures represents a way of descriptively summarizing data without having to use complex methods of statistical analysis. The following are definitions of mean, median, and mode that counselors can adopt (Sprinthall, 2003):

Mean: A measure of central tendency that is represented by the mathematical average of a set of test scores from interval or ratio data. Symbolized by M, the mean is calculated by dividing the sum of all of the scores in a distribution (ΣX) by the total number of scores (N).

Median: The measure of central tendency that represents the midpoint in the distribution of data arranged either in ascending or descending order. The median is the point above which half of data lie and below which half of the data lie.

Mode: The measure of central tendency that represents the most frequently occurring score.

E X A M P L E

Calculating the Mean

The formula for finding the mean can be expressed this way: ($\Sigma X/N$). As an example, imagine that four students take a math test and their scores are 85, 90, 70, and 75. To find the average or mean score of the four students, it is necessary to add the scores together and divide the sum by the total number of scores. Expressed mathematically, the mean of the students' scores is: $(85 + 90 + 70 + 75) / 4 = 80$.

■ Measures of Dispersion: Range, Variance, and Standard Deviation

In addition to the measures of central tendency, measures of dispersion are another set of descriptive statistics that researchers have at their disposal for describing their data. Three of the most useful of these measures are range, variance, and standard deviation.

Range: Provides a quick assessment of the variability in the data by describing the uppermost and lowermost scores among the data.

Variance: Describes the spread of a distribution of scores by indicating how much variation there is in a set of scores from the mean. Variance is computed as the average squared deviation of each number from its mean.

Standard deviation (SD): The most commonly used measure of test score spread, also utilized in a wide variety of other, more complicated statistical analyses. Standard deviation is scaled in raw score terms and indicates how far individual scores are from the mean.

E X A M P L E

Calculating the Variance and Standard Deviation

Mathematically, s^2 is the variance, X is the observed score, M is the mean, and N is the total number of scores. The variance is calculated using the following equation:

Formula: $s^2 = \text{Sum} (X - M)^2 / N$

Example: $[(1 - 2)^2 + (2 - 2)^2 + (3 - 2)^2] / 3 = .667$

Standard deviation is calculated by taking the square root of the variance. The formula for the standard deviation is as follows:

$SD = \Sigma (X)^2 / N$

Example: $[(1 - 2)^2 + (2 - 2)^2 + (3 - 2)^2] / 3 = .667 = .817$

■ Distribution

Descriptive statistics, such as the mean, median, and mode, as well as measures of variance, help researchers begin to make sense of their data. Pictorial representations of distribution also are useful in providing an initial understanding of the data. Normally distributed data for a large group of test takers look like a bell-shaped curve (see Figure 20.1). The normal curve has several properties that allow for the standardized interpretation of individual test scores. The area underneath the normal curve is described using the mean, standard deviation, and percentiles.

Properties of the Normal Curve

- In the normal distribution curve, the mean is in the middle at the highest elevation of the curve.
- One standard deviation from the mean in both directions is found at the inflection point (the point where the curve changes from concave to convex).

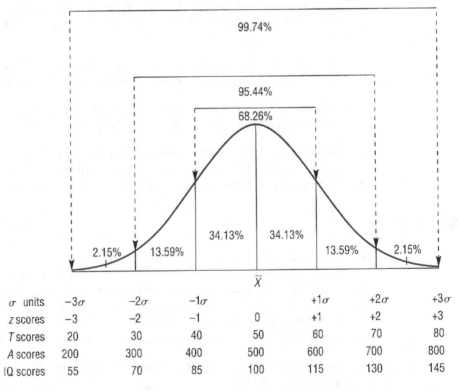

σ units	−3σ	−2σ	−1σ		+1σ	+2σ	+3σ
z scores	−3	−2	−1	0	+1	+2	+3
T scores	20	30	40	50	60	70	80
A scores	200	300	400	500	600	700	800
IQ scores	55	70	85	100	115	130	145

FIGURE 20.1 A normal distribution curve. From *Psychological testing and assessment: An introduction to tests and measurements* (5th ed., p. 97), by R. J. Cohen and M. E. Swerdlik, 2002, Boston: McGraw-Hill. Copyright 1999 by McGraw-Hill Company. Reprinted with permission.

- The normal curve is asymptotic (i.e., it never touches the x axis). All of the scores are represented under the curve, but there is no maximum or minimum score due to its asymptotic property.
- The normal curve is symmetrical, with 50% of the scores falling above the mean and 50% falling below the mean.
- Sixty-eight percent of the scores in a normal distribution fall within 1 standard deviation, and 95% of the scores fall within 2 standard deviations of the scores (see Figure 20.1).

The bell-shaped curve describes normally distributed data. However, in not all instances is the distribution of data symmetrical, and in these instances, data are considered to be either positively or negatively skewed. When data are skewed, most of the scores are found at one or the other end of the range of scores (Sprinthall, 2003).

Positively skewed data: Data contain few high scores and are comprised mostly of low scores. In this distribution, the tail of the curve goes out to the right.

Negatively skewed data: Data contain few low scores and are comprised mostly of high scores. In this distribution, the tail of the curve goes out to the left.

A final characteristic that researchers use to describe the distribution of data is kurtosis, which is defined by Abrami, Cholmsky, and Gordon (2001) this way:

Kurtosis: "[T]he extent to which a frequency distribution of scores is bunched around the center or spread toward the endpoints" (p. 99).

When data are clustered in the center, there is less variability, and when data are more widely spread to the endpoints (which results in a flat rather than a peaked distribution curve), there is greater variability in the distribution.

■ Percentile

The normal distribution can be thought of as a cumulative distribution of measured scores ranging from the lowest score at the left to the highest score at the right. Any score or point in this cumulative distribution can be described as a percentile, and in the normal distribution there are 100 percentiles. Percentiles are a way of organizing norm-referenced test results that provides information on how one person scored in relation to a group of people who took the same test.

Percentiles: Describe the percentage of people whose score falls at or below a particular raw score.

For example, if a child is at the 75th percentile, this child performed as well as or better than 75% of those that comprise the normal distribution.

E X A M P L E

Using Percentiles in Test Interpretation

The normal curve can be broken down into percentiles to help identify where a score falls on the normal distribution relative to other scores and the frequency of those scores. Ultimately, percentiles assist in score interpretation. Typically, test scores that fall between the 0 and 34th percentile represent below-average scores, those that fall above the 34th percentile and below the 84th percentile are classified as average, and those that are at the 84th percentile or above are above average. This is important information, especially for school counselors who have to interpret the aptitude, achievement, or intelligence tests they administer. If a student had a perfectly average intelligence score of 100 ($M = 100$, $SD = 15$) this student would be at the 50th percentile. The percentile allows the counselors to know that the person's score falls within the average range and is equal to or better than 50% of the scores that comprise the normal distribution.

INFERENTIAL STATISTICS

As already mentioned, inferential statistics are different from descriptive statistics in that they allow researchers to make predictions about a population based on a representative sample of that population. Additionally, inferential statistics allow researchers to test whether or not an experimental treatment has a significant effect on an identified dependent variable.

■ Probability

When utilizing inferential statistics, one of the basic building blocks researchers must be able to understand is probability. Abrami et al. (2001) defined probability in statistics as follows:

> **Probability:** the likelihood that an occurrence will take place given all other chance factors.

All researchers in and outside of human science investigations must decide how much chance for error they will allow in their study. Typically, in human science research, such as in the field of counseling, experts set the probability level or significance level at least at $p = .05$. This simple equation can be interpreted to mean that the researcher is willing to accept a 5% chance that the differences in sample means are due to chance factors. Expressed differently, the researcher is 95% certain that the differences are real and not due to chance factors.

■ Standard Scores

To deal with the reality that there is diversity among the means found in normal distributions from different tests, statisticians settled on one normal distribution that is considered the standard, with a mean of 0 and a standard deviation of 1. Values on the standard normal distribution are known as standard scores and are derived from the conversion of a raw or measured score from its original measurement scale to a new standard measurement scale. Standard scores remove negative scores and decimal points and are used because they more easily are interpreted than raw scores. Commonly used standard scores include the Graduate Record Examination (GRE), Scholastic Assessment Test (SAT), deviation IQ, ACT, *T* score, scaled score, and *z* score; each of the means and standard deviations for these standard scores are listed in Table 20.1 and are briefly described next.

Characteristics of the Z score

- The *z* **score** represents the number of standard deviations above or below the mean.
- The *z* score, or zero plus or minus one scale, is the primary standard score, and it precedes the construction of other standard scores.
- The *z* score is equal to the difference between a particular raw score and the mean divided by the mean standard deviation.
- The *z* score has a mean of 0 and a standard deviation of 1 and is calculated with the following equation: $x - M / s$ (Example: $75 - 80 / 15 = -0.33$).

Aspects of the GRE and SAT

- The GRE and SAT are two examples of tests that provide standard scores.
- These tests are commonly used for college and graduate school admission and have a mean of 500 and a standard deviation of 100.

Aspects of the Deviation IQ

- Deviation IQ is the standard measure for the intelligence quotient or IQ.
- Tests that use deviation IQ as their standard score have a mean of 100 and a standard deviation of 10.

Table 20.1
Scale Scores

Scale Name	Mean	SD
GRE, SAT	500	100
Deviation IQ	100	15
ACT	20	5
T-score	50	10
Scaled score	10	3
Z score	0	1

- The deviation IQ scores sometimes are referred to as standard scores, and so, the term *standard score* is used to describe both the general class of transformed scores and the specific instance of scores set to a mean of 100 and standard deviation of 15. If this is the case, 95% of deviation IQ scores fall between 70 and 130, or 2 standard deviations below and above the mean.
- Commonly used qualitative classifications used for deviation IQ scores include the following: > 129 = very superior; 120–129 = superior; 110–119 = high average; 90–109 = average; 80–89 = low average; 70–79 = below average; < 70 = well below average.

Aspects of the ACT

- The ACT is a standard score measure.
- Like the SAT, the ACT is used for college admission.
- The ACT has a mean set at 20 with a standard deviation of 5.

Aspects of the T Score

- The *T* score is another example of a standard score and should not be confused with the *t* test in statistics.
- The *T* score, which has a mean set at 50 and a standard deviation of 10, is a measure of how far a person's score is from the mean (Sprinthall, 2003).
- Traditionally, the *T* score was the measure used in reporting personality test scores such as the Minnesota Multiphasic Personality Inventory (MMPI; Hathaway & McKinley, 1983).

Aspects of the Scaled Score

- The scaled score has a standard deviation of 3 and a mean of 10.
- The scaled score often is used for subtest scores that are combined into composite scores.

EXAMPLE

Converting a Raw Score Into the Deviation IQ

This transformation of a raw score into a deviation IQ may be done because it is easier to understand and explain scores as well as compare scores from different tests when a standard score is used. In this example an individual has a raw score of 25. The test raw score mean is 18, and the raw score standard deviation is 5. It is necessary to compute the z score first, then the deviation IQ standard score.

$$z = (X - M) / SD$$
$$z = (25 - 18) / 5 = 1.4$$

Deviation IQ Standard score = Deviation ZQ M + (Deviation IQ SD * z score)

Example: Deviation IQ M = 100, Deviation IQ SD = 15, z score = 1.4

Deviation IQ Standard score = 100 (15 * 1.4)

Deviation IQ Standard score = 121

This individual would be classified in the superior range for deviation IQ.

■ Tests of Significance

Tests of significance, in inferential statistics, are the methods employed to compare two or more samples to determine whether or not true differences exist in the sample means. In other words, researchers want to see if the differences are big enough to indicate a true difference in sample means (Rowntree, 2004; Trochim, 2002). Tests of significance are chosen specifically to fit the research designs that investigators apply to their studies. Research designs can be categorized broadly as experimental and quasi-experimental designs and nonexperimental designs. Experimental and quasi-experimental designs typically deal with ordinal data and rely on parametric statistics, whereas nonexperimental designs usually involve categorical data (e.g., gender, educational level, etc.) and require nonparametric statistics, the most common of which is the chi-square test of significance. Although the statistical procedures that underlie each approach to analysis are not explored here, the following list identifies basic statistical procedures that researchers utilize.

Types of Parametric and Nonparametric Statistical Analysis

- The *t* **test** is a statistic that is used to determine whether or not there are true differences in two sample means for the same dependent variable.
- **One-way analysis of variance (ANOVA)** is statistically equal to the *t* test, but it can be used to test for true differences in two or more sample means on the same variable.
- The **repeated measures ANOVA** is used to analyze a single factor (independent variable) and a single dependent variable when the sample is the same for each treatment condition. The most common occasion in which this test is used is from pretest to posttest.
- **Analysis of covariance (ANCOVA)** also is used to test for statistically significant differences in sample means of three or more groups; however, by combining the ANOVA with a correlation, it also statistically removes the effects of identified **covariates** or confounding variables that potentially can influence the dependent variable.
- **Tests of linear regression** or **correlations** are used to indicate the strength of the relationship between two variables and to determine the extent to which the be-

havior of one variable can predict that of another variable. A strong correlation does not mean that one variable causes another, but rather, suggests that the relationship between two variables is strong and one variable may be used to make predictions about another.

- **Factor analysis** is used to analyze the effects of more than one independent variable as well as the interaction effects of the independent variables on a dependent variable.

- The **chi-square statistic** is a measure of goodness of fit or independence. It allows researchers to infer if two nominal variables are independent of one another or are related. The chi-square is a nonparametric statistic.

RELIABILITY

When deciding to use a testing instrument, practitioners need to evaluate two important factors: test reliability and validity. Validity is addressed in the next section, while some key aspects of reliability are described in this section. Reliability can be defined as follows:

> **Reliability:** An indication of the consistency of test scores over repeated test administrations.

A test that is highly reliable provides about the same score for the same person when given repeatedly, whereas an unreliable test yields quite different scores for the same person when repeatedly administered (Abrami et al., 2001; Sprinthall, 2003). The reason reliable tests yield consistent results is because they primarily measure individuals' true scores as opposed to error. This reasoning is explained further by the classical test theory.

> A test that is highly reliable provides about the same score for the same person when given repeatedly, whereas an unreliable test yields quite different scores for the same person when repeatedly administered.

■ Classical Test Theory

According to the classical test theory, tests measure two things: (a) the attribute being measured, also called *true score*, and (b) *random error*. The combination of the values of the true score and the random error is known as the *observed score*. The classical test theory is represented in the equation, $x = T + E$, in which x is the observed score, T is the true score or the reliability coefficient, and E is the random error. The sum of T and E is 1. In the absence of error, $x = T$, and the test score is said to be perfectly reliable. T and E, therefore, can be described as a percentage variance in the observed score accounted for by either the true score or error. The reliability coefficient ranges from 0 to 1, and tests with satisfactory reliability have reliability coefficients greater than .8. Stated differently, in tests that are adequately reliable, at least 80% of the observed score is due to the attribute being measured, or the true score.

■ Importance of Reliability

When a test has little error, the same approximate score will be observed for repeated administrations. On the other hand, when there is a lot of error, repeated administrations of the test will result in quite different scores because error contributes heavily to the observed score and the error is random. Researchers in the field of counselor education who choose to conduct quantitative investigations always will be interested in the reliability of the instruments they choose to use. The greater the reliability of the instrument, the more certain they can be of their test results and the more able they will be to draw strong conclusions about their outcomes.

■ Measurement of Reliability

Reliability can be described by the reliability coefficient, which is, fundamentally, the correlation of the test with itself. The reliability coefficient can be estimated through a variety of strategies, including test–retest, alternate forms, split half, and internal consistency. Despite the method used, in each case, the goal is to obtain two administrations or versions of the test that perfectly correlate. Mathematically stated, a perfect correlation is equal to 1.

The correlation of the test with itself provides a direct measure of variance; that is, the reliability coefficient derived from the correlation analysis can be interpreted as a percentage of true score variance when multiplied by 100. This is not the case for a normal correlation coefficient, in which it must be squared first (coefficient of determination) before being multiplied by 100 to indicate variance. Further, two administrations of the test should correlate perfectly because the same people took the test and, except for error, they should provide the same results for each administration. Any deviation from a perfect correlation is considered error.

■ Methods of Estimating Reliability

There are several methods used to estimate reliability. Each method has its strengths and weaknesses, and these should be considered when evaluating the reliability coefficients. Methods of estimating reliability include test–retest, alternate forms, split half, and internal consistency.

Test–Retest Reliability

- The test–retest method involves administering a test to a group of people and then readministering the same test to the same group of people at a later time. The correlation of the test results from both administrations provides a measure of reliability for the instrument.
- This method is limited by the practice effect (people may score better on the second administration because of taking the test before) or fatigue (people may lose interest in the test if it is given too soon after the first administration).

Alternative Forms Reliability

- The alternate forms method involves giving two equal (e.g., in difficulty, kinds of items, etc.) but different versions of the same instrument with limited time between administrations and then computing a correlation of the two tests.
- Shortcomings of this method are that it is costly and time consuming to produce two versions of the same test, and it is difficult to establish equivalence between two forms of the test for some constructs.

The split-half method of computing reliability mitigates some of the problems with the alternate forms method and yields about the same results. This procedure is described next.

Odd–Even Split-Half Reliability

- The odd–even split-half method uses an odd–even split of items to create two composite scores for a test that can be correlated.
- By applying the odd–even split approach, an equal number of items from the beginning, middle, and end of the test are represented in each form of resulting tests.
- A limitation of this method is that by decreasing the number of items on the test by half, the reliability also is reduced because, generally, reliability increases when the number of items on a test is increased and decreases when the number of test items is reduced.

To correct for the shortcoming of the split-half method that arises from splitting the test, researchers use the Spearman–Brown formula. After correlating the odd items of the test with the even items of the test, the Spearman–Brown formula is used to increase the value of the reliability coefficient and to find out what the reliability coefficient would have been if the number of items were doubled.

Internal Consistency

- The internal consistency method of calculating reliability provides an estimate of the consistency with which the test items measure their purported construct and the correlations among all of the test items.
- Internal consistency is computed by using the number of items on the test and the mean intercorrelation of these items.
- The results of the test are a standardized estimate of reliability known as **Cronbach's alpha,** which is a method of establishing internal consistency for test items that are not scored dichotomously, such as questionnaires (Abrami et al., 2001).

Standard Error of Measurement

Once the reliability coefficient is derived, the degree of consistency in the test is known. However, it is also important to know how the level of reliability affects the accuracy of an individual measured score. To determine this, the statistic known as the standard error of measurement (*SEM*) is used.

> **Standard error of measurement:** An estimate of how accurate the observed scores are at approximating the true score.

More specifically, *SEM* is an indication of the variability of all possible true scores around the observed score due to error. If a test produces reliable scores, then the *SEM* should be relatively small, indicating less variability around the score. However, if the test does not produce reliable scores, *SEM* is larger, indicating more variability around the observed score and less certitude that the score is an accurate reflection of an individual's true score. The *SEM* can be explained using the normal distribution. The individual's observed score forms the center of a normal distribution of all possible true scores. The *SEM* works just like a standard deviation with 68% of possible true scores for an individual falling within 1 standard deviation. The observed score is only one point on the distribution of all possible true scores. There is no way of knowing the individual's true score; however, using the *SEM* deviation of the score, one can estimate the range of scores that likely includes the individual's true score. *SEM* is calculated using the formula $SD\,1 - r_{xx}$, where *SD* is the standard deviation of the measured score and r_{xx} is reliability.

The Confidence Interval

SEM can be applied in practice through the use of the confidence interval (CI).

> **Confidence interval:** the range of scores that represents some percentage of confidence of including a person's true score.

The CI can be demonstrated using the normal distribution of all possible true scores where the center of the distribution is the observed score. One then determines the level of confidence that is acceptable for the current use of the test. The level of confidence is described as percentage of area under the normal distribution around the observed score. Common percentages that are used include 68%, 90%, 95%, and 99%. The CI is derived by multiplying a number (z score) representing the percentage of confidence by the *SEM* and then adding and subtracting the resultant value from the observed score to form a lower and upper limit. So the equations for common confidence intervals are 68% CI = ± 1 * *SEM*, 90% CI = ± 1.65 * *SEM*, 95% CI = ± 1.96 * *SEM*, and 99% CI = ± 2.58 * *SEM*. If the CI was set at 95%, one would be 95% confident that the true score lies within a range ± 1.96 * *SEM* of the observed score.

E X A M P L E

Calculating the Confidence Interval

Observed score = 85, *SEM* = 2.6, 95% CI = ± 1.96 * *SEM*

Observed score ± 1.96 * *SEM*

85 ± 1.96 * 2.6 =

85 ± 5.1 =

CI = 79.9 – 90.1 or about 80–90.

One is 95% confident that the true score lies between 80 and 90.

VALIDITY

Validity is a term used colloquially to refer to something that is well grounded or evidenced. For example, a journalist who supports a newspaper column with relevant, factual evidence provides valid information. In the realm of psychological assessment, validity is the most important factor of consideration when evaluating the construction of a good instrument. Tests that measure what they claim to measure are said to have strong validity (Abrami et al., 2001; Sprinthall, 2003).

Validity: Evidence that the psychological test measures the attribute or ability it purports to measure in the test manual.

From a practical standpoint, a test is considered valid when it provides useful information for the decision that will be made based, in part, on the test results. Ultimately, psychological tests should provide helpful information for making sound decisions about the person taking the test. Therefore, a test selected to assist in decision making for a client must provide a valid measurement of the attribute or ability that has bearing on the decision. Finally, one can say that validity is a property of both the test and the context in which the test is used.

Just as there are numerous approaches to determining test reliability, there are also several ways of verifying test validity, namely, content validity, face validity, construct validity, and criterion-related validity. Each of these types of validity yields a particular type of evidence that, when aggregated, indicates whether the test confidently provides valid information.

■ Content Validity

Content validity of a psychological test is established by showing that the test items on an instrument are representative of the attribute being measured (Abrami et al., 2001). Assessing the content validity of a test does not require sophisticated statistics, but rather, is established through a review of the test's content by a content expert. A test with high content validity covers not only a breadth of material, but also sufficient depth in each identified subject area.

EXAMPLE

Establishing Content Validity

Imagine that a professor who teaches an introduction to psychology course wants to give a cumulative final examination at the end of the semester. To establish content validity for the exam, the professor must ensure that any and all of the subject matter that was covered during the semester potentially can appear on the final exam. This is known as the universe of content. Because the professor is testing for comprehension with regard to psychological concepts, the professor would restrict the items on the exam to those that deal directly with the subject matter at hand and would not, for example, ask questions related to other fields of study such as mathematics, sociology, or business.

■ Face Validity

Face validity is similar to content validity in that both involve judgments concerning the content of a test. However, **face validity** generally is determined from the point of view of the person being tested and is a less formal assessment of what the test appears to measure (Sprinthall, 2003). Judgments made based on face validity often have implications on a test's perceived effectiveness or an individual's willingness to participate in testing. Ultimately, face validity represents a testing instrument's apparent validity and should be used only as an initial indicator of the test's content validity.

■ Construct Validity

Establishing construct validity begins with a clear understanding of the construct that the instrument is intended to measure. Construct can be defined broadly this way:

Construct: An abstraction or concept inferred from the observation of regularly occurring patterns of behavior.

Constructs define naturally occurring mental phenomenon and include such examples as extraversion, intelligence, depression, awareness, or self-esteem. A common feature of psychological constructs is that they are either directly or indirectly related to a behavior or experience. For example, intelligence is a construct associated with one's verbal behavior. Those with sophisticated vocabularies and the ability to reason well with language are considered to have high intelligence. Of course, one can never see or touch intelligence because it is an abstraction, but one can infer the existence of intelligence from a person's regular behavior patterns such as vocabulary and reasoning behaviors.

Construct validation is a determination of how well test scores are indicative of the characteristics of the construct being measured (Abrami et al., 2001). Construct validity is demonstrated when test scores evidence, through correlation analysis, patterns indicative of the construct. There are several ways to assess and obtain evidence for construct validity, namely, factor analysis and the multitrait–multimethod approach.

Procedures for Determining Construct Validity

- *Factor analysis* involves a sophisticated correlation analysis designed to identify interrelations between measured variables that emerge as *factors*. The factors are not directly measured but are inferred based on the relation among the observed variables. In this way, the factor represents the construct, and the variables represent the observed behaviors.
- The *multitrait–multimethod approach* involves a number of different methods of measuring several different constructs, also known as traits. The chosen constructs should be theoretically unrelated to emphasize the correlations among different measures of the same construct.

EXAMPLE

Using Factor Analysis

A test developer is attempting to validate the construct validity of an instrument purported to measure mathematics ability. Using factor analytic techniques, the developer tries to ensure that all of the individual items that measure mathematics skills, such as addition and subtraction problems, are correlated and "load" on a single factor labeled mathematics. Through factor analysis, questions about world history, for example, that may have been included on the test would not correlate well with the mathematics questions and, therefore, would be identified as not supporting the construct of interest.

■ Criterion-Related Validity

Criterion-related validity is demonstrated when there is a high association or correlation between the test score and some other measure of interest (Abrami et al., 2001). This measure of interest is called the *criterion*. In psychological assessment, a criterion can include such things as behavior, speed, or ability. For example, decisions made using college placement examinations are based on a predicted correlation between the test score and the future success with the subject. There are two types of validation strategies contained under the category of criterion-related validity: *concurrent* and *predictive validity.* The basic difference between the two has to do with the time frame in which the criterion is measured relative to the administration of the test. Concurrent means the test and the criterion are measured at about the same time and predictive means the criterion is measured after the test and typically after a decision, such as hiring, was made about the person.

Aspects of Concurrent Validity

- Concurrent validity is a measure of the relation between the criterion measure of a test and test scores that are obtained at the same time.
- Concurrent validity is useful in determining how test scores may be used to estimate an individual's present performance on the selected criterion (e.g., when scores obtained on a depression inventory are validated against established diagnostic criteria for depression, there is strong concurrent validity).
- Concurrent validity also can be used when comparing one test with another. When prior research supports the validity of one test, we can use that test as the validating criterion and compare other tests to it to establish their concurrent validity.
- Conducting a concurrent validity study in this way also provides evidence of the construct validity of a test (i.e., if there is a high correlation between the test of de-

pression described earlier and the outcomes of a rigorous diagnostic process, the test is said to be a valid measure of the construct of depression).

Aspects of Predictive Validity

- Predictive validity involves making decisions based on correlations between previously obtained test scores, and yet-to-be-obtained criterion scores.
- Predictive validity allows for prediction of the criterion based on how well an individual's score on a test will correlate with a criterion established after the test has been administered.

EXAMPLE

SAT and Predictive Validity

A modern example of predictive validity is the use of standardized tests, such as the SAT, for admission to college. The notion behind using such tests is that they predict a student's academic performance in college. In this case, predictive validity is established by examining the correlation between a student's scores on the SAT and their grade-point average as a freshman, the criterion. A strong, positive correlation indicates that the SAT has strong predictive validity.

TEST CONSTRUCTION

Test construction is a process that must be done carefully and correctly to ensure that a test is a reliable, valid, and nonbiased psychometric measure. The steps that should be taken to ensure a test meets these requirements include the following:

- Determine the method of test development.
- Write the items.
- Select items through the item try-out process.
- Norm the test on a representative sample.
- Write the test manual.

■ Methods of Test Development

The first step of test construction is to choose from among several systems of test development, including the rational-theoretical approach, the empirical approach, and the internal consistency approach. Each method considers validity from a different perspective, which, therefore, results in various processes of test question development.

Approaches to Test Question Development

1. The *rational-theoretical approach* assumes that the items created for the test are indicative of a specific theory of the construct being measured and primarily focuses on content validity of the test items.
2. The *empirical or empirically keyed approach* focuses on criterion-related validity and assumes that good test questions are correlated with a criterion.
3. The *internal consistency approach* uses factor analysis to determine if items load together to support the construct being measured by the test and, thus, construct validity. Items that load on the factor indicative of the construct of interest are included in the test.

In modern test construction, a combination of all three approaches often is invoked for developing the test items. Establishing the internal consistency of the item set through factor analysis as well as concurrent or predictive validity, is achieved through the comparison of the test results to external criteria.

EXAMPLE

Empirical Approach to Test Construction

If people with schizophrenia tend to endorse a particular item as true and those without schizophrenia tend to endorse the item as false, the item would be included on a test of schizophrenia because the item is correlated with external criterion of being diagnosed with schizophrenia.

■ Writing the Items

After a method of test development is chosen, the next step in test construction is writing the items for the test. Several guidelines characterize this part of the test development process. First, all test items need to be written clearly so they are only associated with the construct of interest. Second, developers always want to write more items than are necessary because some items may be thrown out during the item try-out phase of test construction. Finally, when writing questions for a test, the test developers have many choices in the types of items for the test and must decide which types of items are most suitable to the instrument and construct being tested. A few of the test item formats are mentioned next.

Common Types of Items Used by Test Developers

- True–false.
- Multiple choice.
- Short answer, completion, or closed.
- Essay.
- Rating or Likert scales.

Item Try-Out

After the test items are written, they need to be examined for bias, reliability, and validity through a process known as item try-out. The item try-out process is both rigorous and complex. The main steps in this process are summarized only briefly here.

Steps in the Item Try-Out Process

- Administer the test to a representative sample population.
- Conduct a bias analysis to see if systematic errors in measurement or prediction were made. Bias can be detected by using statistical procedures, such as factor analysis and regression techniques. Additionally, expert reviewers can detect bias in test language, content, and format.
- Select the best items by the process of item analysis, which includes examinations of item difficulty and item discrimination. Analysis of item difficulty yields a value that describes the proportion of individuals that got an item right or endorsed an item in a particular way. Analysis of item discrimination allows test developers to determine how closely an item tests for the construct of interest.
- Examine the test's reliability and validity.

Normative Sample

An important aspect of test construction is developing a normative sample that is representative of the target population for the test. To obtain a representative sample, the sample must be standardized on a number of factors. Sample factors on which tests commonly are normed include geographic location, gender, income, ethnicity, age, and level of education. After the sample is chosen, there are a number of steps that need to take place, namely, administering the test to the sample, computing standard scores based on the sample's results, creating percentiles through area transformations to determine what percentages of individuals in the sample population obtain certain scores, and setting the standard error of measurement to provide confidence intervals around the measured scores.

■ Writing the Manual

The last step of the test construction process is writing the manual. The manual provides an overall summary of the test construction and recommended procedures to the test administrator. The test manual provides information regarding the quality of the test, the sample intended, and administration and scoring procedures.

Chapter 20: Key Terms

- ▶ Analysis of covariance (ANCOVA)
- ▶ Anonymity
- ▶ Chi-square statistic
- ▶ Confidence interval
- ▶ Construct
- ▶ Construct validation
- ▶ Content validity
- ▶ Correlations
- ▶ Covariate
- ▶ Criterion-related validity
- ▶ Cronbach's alpha
- ▶ Descriptive statistics
- ▶ Face validity
- ▶ Factor analysis
- ▶ Inferential statistics
- ▶ Informed consent
- ▶ Interval scales
- ▶ Kurtosis
- ▶ Mean
- ▶ Median
- ▶ Mode
- ▶ Negatively skewed data
- ▶ Nominal scales
- ▶ One-way analysis of variance (ANOVA)
- ▶ Ordinal scales
- ▶ Percentiles
- ▶ Positively skewed data
- ▶ Probability
- ▶ Range
- ▶ Ratio scales
- ▶ Reliability
- ▶ Repeated measures ANOVA
- ▶ Risk of harm
- ▶ Standard deviation (SD)
- ▶ Standard error of measurement
- ▶ Tests of linear regression
- ▶ t test
- ▶ Validity
- ▶ Variance
- ▶ Voluntary participation
- ▶ z score

Testing and Assessment in Counseling Practice

Jeffrey A. Miller
Tara Greene
Nate E. Kegal
Julie Williams
Duquesne University

In This Chapter

▶ *Overview of Assessment*
  ■ Uses of Assessments
  ■ Professional Organizations Supporting Assessment

▶ *Assessment Process*
  ■ Review Referral Information
  ■ Decide Whether to Take the Case
  ■ Obtain Background Information
  ■ Consider Systematic Influences
  ■ Observe the Client in Several Settings
  ■ Select and Administer an Appropriate Test Battery
  ■ Interpret Results
  ■ Develop Intervention Strategies
  ■ Document the Assessment
  ■ Meet With Concerned Individuals
  ■ Follow Up on Recommendations

▶ *Cognitive Assessment*
  ■ Nature of Intelligence
  ■ Stanford–Binet Intelligence Test
  ■ Wechsler Scales
  ■ Woodcock–Johnson Scales

▶ *Educational Assessment*
  ■ Achievement Tests
  ■ Aptitude Tests
  ■ Psychoeducational Test Batteries

▶ *Personality Assessment*
  ■ Rorschach Psychodiagnostic Test
  ■ Thematic Apperception Test
  ■ Minnesota Multiphasic Personality Inventory
  ■ MMPI–A
  ■ NEO Personality Inventory–Revised

▶ *Behavioral Assessment*
  ■ Self-Report
  ■ Direct Observation
  ■ Behavior Rating Scales

▶ *Neuropsychological Assessment*
  ■ The Mini Mental State Examination
  ■ The Wechsler Memory Scale–Third Edition
  ■ The Halstead–Reitan Neuropsychological Battery

▶ *NEPSY*

In This Chapter (*continued*)

▶ *Interest in Employment*
  ▪ Strong Interest Inventory
  ▪ Armed Services Vocational Aptitude Battery
  ▪ General Aptitude Test Battery
  ▪ Myers–Briggs Type Indicator

▶ *Assessment of Organizational Culture*
  ▪ Discussion of Organizational Culture
  ▪ Job Descriptive Index
  ▪ Minnesota Satisfaction Questionnaire
  ▪ Organizational Commitment Questionnaire

OVERVIEW OF ASSESSMENT

Assessments provide information about clients' strengths and weaknesses to help counselors and helping professionals decide on a course of treatment. Specifically, **assessment** refers to the process of collecting and integrating data from interviews, case studies, observations, and psychometric tools for the purposes of guiding treatment.

■ Uses of Assessments

Assessment is useful for psychologists and counselors because it provides a standard method to obtain information about a client. Not only is assessment beneficial for counselors, but it is also beneficial for clients as it improves the chances of successful treatment and increased quality of life.

■ Professional Organizations Supporting Assessment

There are several professional organizations that support and promote assessment in counseling. These professional bodies work to enhance and ensure the quality of the work of teachers, researchers, and practitioners in the area of assessment, as the integrity and quality of assessment is vital to treatment success. Some of the professional organizations of interest to counselors are provided next.

Professional Associations for Assessment

- Association for Assessment in Counseling and Education (AACE).
- American Education Research Association (AERA).
- National Center for Research on Evaluation Standards, and Student Testing (CRESST).
- Joint Committee on Standards for Educational Evaluations (JCSEE).
- Joint Committee on Testing Practices (JCTP).
- National Council on Measurement in Education (NCME).

 The AACE is a division of ACA. Check out the Web site of AACE for more information on testing:

▶ http://aac.ncat.edu/

ASSESSMENT PROCESS

To treat clients effectively, counselors need to make accurate assessments of clients' core issues. Sattler (2001) described 11 steps to conducting a good assessment. Each step within the assessment process is essential to understanding the client and the referral question. The **referral question** is a statement given by the client or other parties close to the client about the area of concern. The referral question guides counselors in making informed decisions to ensure proper treatment. All of the information that is gathered in interviews, observations, and tests should be considered when making interpretations on which the treatment will be based. The 11 steps to a comprehensive assessment are as follows:

1. Review referral information.
2. Decide whether to take the case.
3. Obtain background information.
4. Consider systematic influences.
5. Observe the client in several settings.
6. Select and administer an appropriate test battery.
7. Interpret results.
8. Develop intervention strategies.
9. Document the assessment.
10. Meet with concerned individuals.
11. Follow up on recommendations.

■ Review Referral Information

The referral should be carefully considered to help the client clearly communicate the concern. Vague and incomplete referral information should be clarified. Based on the client's report of referral and subsequent clarifications, the refined referral question guides subsequent assessment-related decisions.

■ Decide Whether to Take the Case

The case should be accepted only if the assessment professional has the necessary training and experience to answer the referral question and provide useful information for decision making.

■ Obtain Background Information

Counselors should ask for relevant information that pertains to the problem and its treatment. Medical, educational, and developmental histories should be recorded and used.

Consider Systematic Influences

Each person who is related to the client may view the problem differently. It is important to keep in mind that the client's problem may be activated only in certain situations. By interviewing multiple people, counselors and psychologists become more certain about what situations trigger the problem, what the consequences are, and what maintains the occurrences. Others also may provide information about how they attempt to alleviate the problem. The treatment then can be based on successful past techniques.

See Chapter 26 for more information on using multiple people or key informant interviews in the assessment of addictions.

Observe the Client in Several Settings

By observing the client, professionals may notice antecedents and consequences to behaviors that are overlooked by others. These predictors or triggers to behavior can be situation specific and, as such, provide valuable information to clinicians.

Select and Administer an Appropriate Test Battery

Many tests are available for use, and counselors must decide which ones are appropriate to administer. Published literature, conference presentations, and colleagues can provide information about appropriate tests. The chosen tests should measure the nature of the referral question and possess high reliability and validity. Before administering the tests, psychologists and counselors should carefully read the testing manuals. The administration and scoring directions in the manuals must be followed completely and correctly for the score to be properly calculated.

Interpret Results

The referral information, interviews, observations, and test scores are all necessary to make an interpretation. The interpretation should not be based on any one factor alone.

All of the information from the previous steps is integrated to find reoccurring patterns and to view the person as a whole. If the information is conflicting or unclear, more interviews, observations, and tests are needed.

Develop Intervention Strategies

The interventions should take into account the strengths and weaknesses of the client. Interventions should be directly linked to the assessment data and include only resources that are reasonably available to the client.

■ Document the Assessment

The report should be written immediately after the evaluation. It should clearly and concisely discuss the findings, interpretations, and recommendations.

■ Meet With Concerned Individuals

When discussing the conclusions of the assessment, professionals should avoid jargon and confusing language. The concerned individuals should be encouraged to ask questions about the process.

■ Follow Up on Recommendations

Both short-term and long-term follow-ups are necessary to monitor the treatment integrity and effectiveness. Follow-up is crucial to providing ethical services and a continuum of care to clients.

COGNITIVE ASSESSMENT

As is evidenced in Sattler's (2001) description of the assessment process, a client evaluation is a comprehensive look at a person's life—the process involves much more than simply administering an appropriate test. However, knowing which assessment instrument to administer and how to administer, score, and interpret the test is a crucial part of the assessment process. One type of assessment that counselors may employ is the cognitive assessment.

> **Cognitive assessment:** The gathering of information about an individual's overall cognitive ability and functioning.

Intelligence tests make up the better part of cognitive assessment. These evaluative tools have been developed largely from the original Binet scales, published beginning in 1905. Central to all intelligence scales is the construct *intelligence,* which the tests purport to measure. Therefore, in this section we provide a cursory understanding of what is meant by intelligence. Additionally, there are three families of cognitive scales that frequently are used today that are discussed:

1. Stanford–Binet scales.
2. Wechsler scales.
3. Woodcock–Johnson scales.

■ Nature of Intelligence

Creating tests that measure cognitive abilities, and specifically intelligence, requires a clearly defined understanding of the construct called intelligence. One definition that can be adopted is as follows:

General intelligence: A construct used in the field of psychology that measures what is common to the scores of all cognitive intelligence tests (abbreviated g).

To further define intelligence, Cattell and Horn (Catell, 1963; Horn, 1968) described two characteristics of intelligence, called fluid intelligence and crystallized intelligence.

Fluid intelligence: Abilities such as reasoning and concept formation that are related to mental operations and processes that decline over time.

Crystallized intelligence: Acquired skills and knowledge such as verbal abilities and general information that increase over time.

Carroll (1993) proposed an update of Cattell and Horn's work called the three-stratum theory of cognitive abilities. Each of the three components of Carroll's theory is briefly summarized.

Carroll's Three-Stratum Theory of Cognitive Abilities

1. The first stratum consists of narrow, more specific abilities like perceptual speed, spatial relations, and lexical knowledge.
2. The second stratum consists of broad factors like fluid and crystallized intelligence, as well as visual processing, auditory processing, and processing speed.
3. The third stratum is represented by a single factor of general intelligence (often referred to as g).

Cattell, Horn, and Carroll's work represents several ways of characterizing intelligence. Modern theories of cognitive assessment also are supported with further evidence obtained using factor analytic techniques that identify different types of intelligence or facets of intelligence.

Additional factor analytic work led those interested in psychoeducational assessment to integrate the Cattell–Horn theory with Carroll's theory in what is known as the Cattell–Horn–Carroll (CHC) model of cognitive abilities, consisting only of a narrow stratum and a broad stratum. These models, along with other recent multiple factor models such as Gardner's (1999) theory of multiple intelligences, have had a considerable impact on the current direction of cognitive assessment.

■ Stanford–Binet Intelligence Test

At the end of the 19th century, Binet, Henri, and Simon developed methods of cognitive assessment in France. In 1905, their efforts resulted in the development of the first intelligence test, known as the Binet–Simon Scales.

Uses of the Binet–Simon Scales

- Identifying school-aged children with mental retardation.
- Determining if a child is performing at an average level for children of the same age.

In 1916, the Binet–Simon Scales were revised as part of a collaborative effort led by Terman at Stanford University and became known as the Stanford–Binet. This test was the first to use the IQ, or intelligence quotient. The Stanford–Binet Intelligence Scales (5th edition [SB5]; Roid, 2003) is the most current version of the test and is substantially different from previous editions of the test. It is appropriate for examinees aged 2 to 85 years and older.

Components of the SB5 Scales

- The test yields a Full-Scale IQ based on all 10 subtests, and Verbal and Nonverbal IQ scores based on 5 subtests each.
- There are two *routing* subtests (Object Series/Matrices and Vocabulary) that can be used to determine the starting point for the examinee on the Verbal and Nonverbal subtests and serve as a subtest for the Verbal (Vocabulary) and Nonverbal (Object Series/Matrices) scales.
- The five Verbal and Nonverbal subtests are based on the five cognitive factors measured by the SB5.
- The cognitive factors measured by the SB5 are fluid reasoning, knowledge, quantitative reasoning, visual-spatial processing, and working memory.

■ Wechsler Scales

Binet and his colleagues were not the only individuals to develop tests of cognitive ability. The most frequently used tests of cognitive ability and general intelligence are the Wechsler scales. Originally developed by David Wechsler, the Wechsler scales have gone through revisions since his death, but still bear his name. The first versions of Wechsler's intelligence tests were developed on the premise that intelligence is both a global construct and an entity comprised of unique abilities. The most current versions of the Wechsler scales apply modern theories of cognitive ability and psychometrics. Psychometrics can be understood as follows:

> **Psychometrics:** Any form of mental testing or the branch of counseling and psychology that deals with testing.

There are several Wechsler tests of intelligence that have been created and adapted for various populations.

Wechsler Tests of Intelligence

- The Wechsler–Bellevue Intelligence Scale was developed in the 1930s and had 11 subtests believed to accurately comprise general intellectual ability.
- The Wechsler Adult Intelligence Scale (WAIS; Wechsler, 1955) was developed in the 1950s.
- The Wechsler Intelligence Scale for Children (WISC; Wechsler, 1949) incorporated many of the original subtests in the measurement of intelligence.

The Wechsler Adult Intelligence Scale (Wechsler, 1955) is perhaps the most widely used tool for assessing intellectual functioning; its current version is the Wechsler Adult Intelligence Scale–Third Edition (WAIS–III; Wechsler, 1997b).

Key Characteristics of the WAIS–III

- Measures cognitive ability of individuals aged 16 to 74 years.
- Contains 11 core subtests and 3 supplementary subtests.
- Provides a Verbal IQ score (range = 48–155), a Performance IQ score (range = 47–155), and a Full-Scale IQ score (range = 45–155) based on the 11 core subtests.
- Provides a set of index scores based on the supplementary subtests.

There are six components of the verbal tests and five components of the performance tests on the WAIS–III; additionally, there are three supplementary scales. The areas measured are listed next.

Components of the Verbal IQ Score on the WAIS–III

- Vocabulary.
- Similarities.
- Arithmetic.
- Digit Span.
- Information.
- Comprehension.

Components of the Performance IQ Score on the WAIS–III

- Picture Completion.
- Digit-Symbol Coding.
- Block Design.

- Matrix Reasoning.
- Picture Arrangement.

Supplementary Subtests of the WAIS–III

- Symbol Search.
- Letter–Number Sequencing.
- Object Assembly.

The Wechsler Intelligence Scale for Children–Fourth Edition (WISC–IV; Wechsler, 2003) is the most current version of this popular test of cognitive ability for children ages 6 to 16 years. The WISC–IV is similar to the WAIS–III in many ways, particularly in its use of subtests, many of which are identical to the WAIS–III. However, there are several areas in which the two tests differ.

Points of Difference Between the WISC–IV and the WAIS–III

- The subtests on the WISC–IV contribute to a Full-Scale IQ score and four index scores (Verbal Comprehension, Perceptual Reasoning, Working Memory, and Processing Speed).
- The WISC–IV does not provide for the calculation of a Verbal or Performance IQ score.
- The WISC–IV is made up of 10 core subtests and 5 supplemental subtests.

■ Woodcock–Johnson Scales

The Woodcock–Johnson III Tests of Cognitive Abilities (WJ III COG; Woodcock, McGrew, & Mather, 2001) is another individually administered battery of tests of cognitive abilities.

Key Characteristics of the WJ III COG

- Used with individuals ages 2 to 90 years and older.
- Incorporates many aspects of the CHC model of cognitive functioning, including its division of tests into seven CHC clusters (Comprehension-Knowledge, Long-Term Retrieval, Visual-Spatial Thinking, Auditory Processing, Fluid Reasoning, Processing Speed, and Short-Term Memory).
- Contains 10 tests in the Standard Battery and 10 tests in the Extended Battery.
- Yields an overall score known as the General Intellectual Ability (GIA).

The WJ III COG can be scored only by computer and the test scores that comprise the GIA are differentially weighted based on the age of the examinee. Various empirically and theoretically derived composite scores also can be computed.

EDUCATIONAL ASSESSMENT

Another testing area that may offer important information to counselors besides cognitive ability is educational assessment, which can be defined this way:

Educational assessment: Methods for obtaining information relating to a student's overall academic progress and informal and formal learning.

There are a number of contexts and situations when the use of educational assessment is deemed appropriate.

General Uses of Educational Assessments

- Results from educational assessments allow counselors and others who work in schools to make decisions regarding a student's academic advancement to higher grades.
- Educational assessments play a role in identifying learning disabilities.
- With adult populations, educational assessments can be used to recommend remedial education to allay employment stress related to academic underachievement.

The major areas of educational assessment include achievement, aptitude, and psychoeducational testing. Each of these areas are addressed individually in the following sections; examples of tests of achievement, aptitude, and psychoeducation also are described.

■ Achievement Tests

Achievement batteries measure accomplishment related both to specific and general academic areas. Achievement tests can be understood as follows:

Achievement tests: Measures of the effects of learning from specific, controlled experiences such as academic courses or programs of instruction.

These tests allow for the identification of learning difficulties and the monitoring of achievement levels. In addition, the achievement batteries measure the amount of learning that takes place at certain academic-based or age-based levels. Two examples of achievement measures are the Wechsler Individual Achievement Test–Second Edition (WIAT–II; Wechsler, 2001) and the Wide Range Achievement Test–3 (WRAT–3; Wilkenson, 1993).

Key Characteristics of the WIAT–II

- Provides a measure of general ability.
- Able to be administered to individuals ages 4 to adult.
- Yields information that is helpful in developing individualized academic intervention plans.

The WIAT–II is composed of nine subtests that measure the areas of specific learning disabilities described in the Individuals With Disabilities Educational Act (IDEA, 1997).

Subtests of the WIAT–II

- Oral Expression.
- Listening Comprehension.
- Written Expression.
- Spelling.
- Word reading.
- Pseudoword Decoding.
- Reading Comprehension.
- Numerical Operations.
- Mathematics Reasoning.

Scoring of the WIAT–II can be done using either age-based or grade-based normative comparisons, and computer scoring software also is available.

Another measure of general achievement is the WRAT–3 (Wilkenson, 1993). Some important elements of the WRAT–3 are provided next.

Key Components of the WRAT–3

- Able to be administered individually or in groups.
- Used appropriately with individuals between the ages of 5 and 75 years old.
- Provides a rapid screening of academic skills.

There are three main subtests that comprise the WRAT–3, listed here.

Subtests of the WRAT–3

- Reading.
- Spelling.
- Arithmetic Subtests.

Administration typically takes 15 to 30 minutes, and scoring takes approximately 5 minutes. Scoring is done using age-based norms, and grade-equivalent scores are available.

■ Aptitude Tests

Aptitude tests generally are distinguished from achievement tests. An understanding of aptitude testing that counselors can adopt is as follows:

> **Aptitude tests:** Measure informal learning from a variety of uncontrolled experiences and are said to measure innate potential, as well as predict future academic performance.

Unlike the individually administered cognitive tests described earlier (e.g., Wechsler scales), aptitude tests tend to be group administered and are associated with readiness testing and entrance into academic programs.

There are several aptitude tests that are designed for different age levels. The Metropolitan Readiness Test (MRT) frequently is used at the elementary level. The test was normed on 30,000 children throughout the United States and was standardized on the following factors: geographic regions, socioeconomic factors, prior school experience, and ethnic background. The MRT was tested for reliability and validity measures.

Key Elements of the MRT

- Contains two divisions: Level I for beginning and middle kindergarteners, and Level II for end of kindergarten to first grade.
- Represents a group-administered battery.
- Assesses the beginning reading and math skills of early learners.
- Administration typically takes 90 minutes.

An aptitude measure that commonly is used for secondary students entering college is the SAT. The SAT is a psychometrically sound instrument and has been reported as a very reliable and valid measure of aptitude.

Key Elements of the SAT

- Contains three main sections: critical reading, writing, and math.
- Includes additional subtests that measure the subject areas of English, math, history, science, and languages that may be requested by college or universities on admittance.
- Provides scores for each main section on a scale of 200 to 800, with the average score being 500.
- Administration usually takes 3 hours and 45 minutes.

■ Psychoeducational Test Batteries

Along with aptitude and achievement tests, psychoeducational batteries are another arm of educational assessments. Psychoeducatonal instruments can be understood this way:

Psychoeducational tests: Take information from both cognitive and achievement measures to provide an overall picture of a student's abilities related to academic success and to measure academic achievement related to reading, math, and writing.

Two commonly used psychoeducational test batteries are the Differential Ability Scales (DAS; Elliott, 1990a, 1990b) and the Woodcock–Johnson III (WJ III; Woodcock et al., 2001).

The DAS are an adaptation of the British Ability Scales for use in the United States. This psychometrically reliable and valid measure was standardized on 3,475 individuals for the following factors: sex, race and ethnicity, parent education, geographic region, and preschool enrollment.

Key Characteristics of the DAS

- Uses the general conceptual ability or *g* theory of intelligence.
- Emphasizes conceptual and reasoning abilities.
- Measures both ability and achievement for individuals ages 2.5 years to 17 years, 11 months.
- Comprises 17 cognitive subtests divided into two overlapping age levels.
- Includes three achievement subtests (similar to the WRAT–3).
- Provides scores based on preschool age or school age standard scores.
- Provides a Special Nonverbal Composite score that is useful for the assessment of those for whom English is not the primary language.
- Administration takes approximately 30 to 90 minutes depending on age.

The WJ III (Woodcock et al., 2001) is a psychoeducational measure that includes numerous tests of ability (WJ III Tests of Cognitive Abilities) and achievement (WJ III Tests of Achievement). The WJ III is a psychometrically valid and reliable test battery designed for individuals ages 2 to 90 and older and is based on the CHC theory of cognitive abilities.

Tests of Cognitive Abilities Measured by the WJ III

- General intelligence.
- Achievement.
- Scholastic aptitude.
- Oral language.

The Tests of Achievement contain parallel forms, A and B, that are divided into a standard test battery of 12 subtests and an extended battery of 10 subtests. Scoring only can be done by computer and may be done using either age- and grade-based norms.

Some Areas Measured by the WJ III Tests of Achievement

- Reading.
- Oral language.
- Mathematics.
- Written language.
- Knowledge supplemental.

PERSONALITY ASSESSMENT

Counselors are often very interested in personality assessment, which can be defined as follows:

Personality assessment: A method that counselors use to measure a variety of components of personality, including traits, states, identity, cognitive and behavioral styles, and other individual characteristics.

Personality can be assessed using numerous theoretical approaches that include psychoanalytic, cognitive-learning, behavioral, dispositional, humanistic and existential, and multicultural approaches. Common forms of personality assessment include projective and objective measures. Projective and objective assessments can be defined this way:

Projective measures: Allow for inferences about an individual's personality through responses to ambiguous or unstructured stimuli and often are used for educational, forensic, and therapeutic assessment.

Objective measures: Tools that evaluate personality through the use of forced choice responses to questions.

Two projective measures include the Rorschach Psychodiagnostic Test (Rorschach, 1921/1975) and the Thematic Apperception Test (TAT; Morgan & Murray, 1935).

■ Rorschach Psychodiagnostic Test

The Rorschach (Rorschach, 1921/1975), traditionally used for psychodiagnosis, is commonly known as the inkblot technique of assessment. The test consists of 10 bilaterally symmetrical (mirror images if folded) inkblot images. Five images are black and white; two are black, white, and red; and three are multicolored. The test comes with the cards only, and no test manual or administration score are provided. However, Exner (2002) developed the most common system of test administration, scoring, and interpretation. In his system, scores are organized into a Structural Summary by comparing a person's responses to a set of norms (Exner, 2002).

Administration of the Rorschach

- Administration begins with a free association phase during which the individual generates a list of descriptions of what he or she sees in each image.
- The inquiry phase of assessment follows free association and is the period during which the therapist examines the list of client responses one by one in an attempt to interpret the individual's responses.

■ Thematic Apperception Test

The TAT (Morgan & Murray, 1935) originally was developed for use in psychoanalytic therapy to identify drives, emotions, sentiments, conflicts, and complexes. It is widely used now to examine aspects of interpersonal functioning, including mate selection, interpersonal conflicts, and factors that motive behavior. The TAT relies on pictorial techniques and consists of one blank card and 30 cards with black-and-white pictorial scenes designed to present the test taker with classic human situations. The target population for the TAT is individuals 10 years of age and older.

Administration of the TAT

- The examinee tells a story about what is happening in the picture.
- The examinee describes what happened before and after the scene of the picture.
- The examinee describes what the people are thinking and feeling.
- The examinee imagines a scene on the blank card and tell a story about that imagined scene.

Interpretation of storytelling techniques such as the TAT requires extensive study and tends to focus on cognition, emotion, object relations, and motivation (Teglasi, 2001).

Although the Rorschach and the TAT represent projective measures of personality, the same construct also can be assessed using objective measures. Two common examples are the Minnesota Multiphasic Personality Inventory (MMPI; Butcher, Dahlstrom, Graham, Tellegen, & Kaemmer, 1989b) and the NEO Personality Inventory–Revised (NEO–PI–R; Costa & McCrae, 1993).

■ Minnesota Multiphasic Personality Inventory

The MMPI, first developed by Hathaway and McKinley in 1943, is the most widely researched and used test to assess personality and psychopathology in adults 18 and older (Hathaway & McKinley, 1983). The most updated version of the test is the MMPI–2, which was standardized on a sample of 2,600 individuals matched to the 1980 U.S. Census data on the variables of age, gender, minority status, social class, and education. The test contains 567 true–false items (Butcher et al., 1989b) on

TABLE 21.1 Interpretation of High MMPI–2 Scale Scores	
Scale	*Interpretation*
1. Hypochondriasis (*Hs*)	Concern with physical complaints
2. Depression (*D*)	Depression and pessimism
3. Hysteria (*Hy*)	Hysterical reaction to severe psychological stress
4. Psychopathic deviate (*Pd*)	Social deviation, disregard for law, rights of others, and morality
5. Masculinity–Femininity (*Mf*)	Marked interest in the opposite sex role
6. Paranoia (*Pa*)	Paranoid thoughts and feelings
7. Psychasthenia (*Pt*)	Anxiety, obsessive thoughts, and compulsive behaviors
8. Schizophrenia (*Sc*)	Bizarre thoughts, social withdrawal, experience distortions of reality
9. Hypomania (*Ma*)	Elevated mood and activity level, outgoing, and impulsive
10. Social introversion–extroversion (*Si*)	Withdrawn from social contact, socially inhibited, and shy

10 clinical scales. There are a variety of reasons that counselors may use the MMPI–2, including those listed here.

Uses of the MMPI–2

- Examine social and personal maladjustment.
- Develop treatment plans.
- Inform career, marriage, and family counseling.

Table 21.1 lists the basic interpretation of high scores. However, MMPI–2 interpretation typically is done by interpreting frequently observed profiles of scores.

■ MMPI–A

The MMPI also has a version for adolescents, better known as the MMPI–A (Williams, Butcher, Ben-Porath, & Graham, 1992) which commonly is used in clinical and school settings. Because adolescents tended to score higher on the original version of the test, the MMPI–A was developed for the population of teens between 14 and 18 years old. The instrument consists of 478 true–false items and was normed on a sample of 1,620 individuals.

Uses of the MMPI–A

- Assess psychopathology.
- Aid in identifying personal, social, behavioral, school, and familial problems.

■ NEO Personality Inventory–Revised

Another objective measure used to assess personality is the NEO–PI–R (Costa & McCrae, 1993). This battery is used to describe and measure normal personality based on a five-dimension model of personality, better known as the Big Five (Costa & McCrae, 1985).

Five Domains of Personality Measured by the NEO–PI–R

- *Neuroticism* is related to hostility, depression, and anxiety.
- *Extraversion* measures the extent to which individuals prefer to be alone or with others.
- *Openness* to experience measures one's artistic sense, originality, and knowledge.
- *Agreeableness* measures the extent to which individuals are liked by others.
- *Conscientiousness* is the extent one is hard working, careful, neat, and organized.

The test is made up of 243 items, 240 facet and domain items rated on a 5-point scale, and 3 validity items. It takes approximately 40 minutes to administer. The target population for the NEO–PI–R is people over 17 years of age.

BEHAVIORAL ASSESSMENT

Behavioral assessments increasingly are used in clinical and school settings. The following is a basic understanding of behavioral assessment that can be adopted:

> **Behavioral assessment:** A process of systematically gathering observations of a set of target behaviors, examining the relations between these observations and possible causes of the behavior, and applying the information to treatment planning and progress monitoring.

There are several ways of assessing behavior, and counselors choose among these approaches depending on the environment in which the behavior is assessed and the goals of the observation. These approaches include behavioral analysis, applied behavioral analysis, and functional analysis.

Ways to Assess Behavior

- Behavior analysis includes systematic observations of behavior within experimental conditions.
- Applied behavioral analysis is used to describe behavioral analysis in applied settings.
- Functional analysis is concerned with the relation between the causes of a behavior and the behavior.

Regardless of which method counselors pursue for the behavioral assessment, there are two basic procedures that are used to gather information; these are known as the self-report and direct observation methods.

■ Self-Report

One way of gathering data for behavioral assessments is self-report. This method can be understood as follows:

Self-report: Information gathering that relies on the client's input about behaviors of interest.

There are a number of ways that a self-report can be conducted, including those listed next.

Ways to Conduct Self-Report Behavioral Assessment

- Clinical interviews by a counselor.
- Self-monitoring records of behaviors of interest.
- Checklists and inventories.

■ Direct Observation

Direct observation is another way of gathering data for behavioral assessments and can be defined as follows:

Direct observation: Systematic observation of a person in a naturalistic setting in which the observer simultaneously considers the person's behavior and the environmental context.

Expected and deviant behaviors are recorded and tallied on an appropriate form. Typical approaches to making systematic observations are time-sampling, frequency coding, duration coding, and latency coding.

Methods of Recording Direct Observations

- Time-sampling observations are made every 30 seconds to allow for examination of the setting and context.
- Frequency coding observations require the tallying of each instance of the behavior throughout the observation interval.
- Duration coding observations focus on the length of time the behavior spans; the behavior is timed from start to finish.
- Latency coding observations are used to determine the time between a cue and the beginning of the behavior such as observing the time it takes a person to act following a request.

■ Behavior Rating Scales

Behavior rating scales represent an application of both self-report and direct observation methods for making determinations about behavior. Behavior rating scales have structured questions and typically have **forced choice response** options, or a scale with an even number of responses and no middle, neutral, or undecided responses so that the responder is forced to choose from the options given, such as *never, sometimes,* and *always.* Responses are summed and compared to a normative sample for interpretation. Behavior rating scales are useful because they give a rapid assessment of a variety of behaviors.

A popular behavior rating scale is the Behavioral Assessment System for Children–Second Edition (BASC–2; Reynolds & Kamphaus, 2004). The BASC–2 is a parent, teacher, and self-report instrument used to sample the behaviors and emotions of children ages 2 to 21. It can be used to assess a variety of positive and problematic behaviors.

Behaviors Assessed by the BASC–2

- Aggression.
- Depression.
- Social skills.
- Anxiety.
- Attention problems.
- Hyperactivity.
- Leadership.
- Study skills.
- Somatization.
- Assorted other domains.

The BASC–2 allows for input from teachers, parents, and the children being assessed; there is a corresponding scale for each of these sources of information.

Scales on the BASC–2

- Teacher Rating Scales (TRS).
- Parent Rating Scales (PRS).
- Self-Report of Personality (SRP).
- Student Observation System (SOS).
- Structured Developmental History (SDH).

The administration of the rating scales take approximately 10 to 20 minutes for the TRS and PRS, and 30 minutes for the SRP. Computer scoring is available.

NEUROPSYCHOLOGICAL ASSESSMENT

The assessments described thus far focus on psychosocial constructs such as intelligence, personality traits, and behavior. Neuropsychological assessments look for biological factors that influence behavior. This type of assessment can be described as follows:

Neuropsychological assessment: Used to draw inferences about brain functioning based on behaviors exhibited by the person under structured conditions.

Process of Conducting Neuropsychological Examinations

- Gather a thorough history of the examinee, including individual and family histories, psychosocial history, and any past disturbances in sensorimotor functioning.
- Evaluate the examinee's physical appearance, including involuntary movements, muscle tone and strength, and reflexes.
- Use the information gathered in the initial mental status and physical examination to administer either a flexible or fixed battery of neuropsychological tests.

A **flexible battery** consists of specific tests tailored to the examinee's apparent presenting problem, whereas a **fixed battery** is an instrument consisting of a number of standardized subtests administered in a determined fashion. Some of the instruments described here are common examples of fixed batteries.

■ The Mini Mental State Examination

The Mini Mental State Examination (MMSE; Folstein, Folstein, & McHugh, 1975) is a widely used method for assessing cognitive mental status in adults that typically takes about 5 to 10 minutes to administer. The MMSE can be used to detect impairment, follow the course of treatment, and monitor response to treatment.

Assessments of the MMSE

- Orientation.
- Attention.
- Immediate short-term recall language.
- Ability to follow simple verbal and written commands.

The exam itself consists of a series of questions and tasks grouped into 11 categories, for which a maximum of 30 points can be obtained if all items are answered correctly. The authors of the test recommend that the four classifications are distinguished based on score.

Scoring and Results of the MMSE

- Normal (27–30).
- Mild cognitive impairment (21–26).
- Moderate cognitive impairment (11–20).
- Severe cognitive impairment (0–10).

The Wechsler Memory Scale–Third Edition

The Wechsler Memory Scale–Third Edition (WMS–III; Wechsler, 1997a) provides a detailed assessment of clinically relevant aspects of memory functioning in adults using auditory and visual stimuli. The test consists of eight primary indexes (Auditory Immediate, Auditory Delayed, Visual Immediate, Visual Delayed, Immediate Memory, Auditory Recognition Delayed, General Memory, and Working Memory), and four supplementary indexes (Single-Trial Learning, Learning Slope, Retention, and Retrieval). Subtests in each of the index categories are used to determine index scores.

The Halstead–Reitan Neuropsychological Battery

The Halstead–Reitan Neuropsychological Test Battery (HRB; Reitan & Wolfson, 1993) is a comprehensive, fixed assessment battery used to evaluate brain behavior functioning of individuals. The HRB can be used to identify neuropsychological impairments in cognitive, perceptual, and motor functioning, as well as deficits associated with learning disabilities. The test can be administered to three different age groups (5–8, 9–14, and 15 and over), and requires up to a full day to administer. There are seven major subtests of the HRB.

Subtests of the HRB

1. The Category test requires the examinee to identify characteristics in common between two stimulus pictures flashed on a screen.
2. The Tactual Performance test requires examinees to complete a form board blindfolded then draw the form board from memory.
3. The Rhythm test involves the examinee discriminating between like and unlike pairs of musical beats.
4. The Speech Sounds Perception test refers to the playing of nonsense words via audiotape from which the examinee must discriminate a spoken syllable.
5. The Finger-Tapping test involves the measurement of the tapping speed of the index finger on each hand of the examinee.
6. The Strength-of-Grip test uses standard hand dynamometer that measures the strength of both dominant and nondominant hands.
7. The Trial Making test requires the examinee to connect numbered and lettered circles.

NEPSY

The NEPSY (Korkman, Kirk, & Kemp, 1997) is a relatively modern neuropsychological assessment battery appropriate for ages 3 to 12 years. NEPSY assessment is based on five functional domains.

Domains Assessed by the NEPSY

- Attention and executive functioning.
- Language.
- Sensorimotor functioning.
- Visuospatial processing.
- Memory and learning.

Each domain is composed of subtests (the battery includes 27 tests) that assess possible neurobehavioral factors of a primary deficit. It is not necessary to administer all subtests to every examinee. Specific subtests may be given based on the child's age, needs, time constraints, and setting. Due to the large number of subtests, it is critical that the clinician be very familiar with the subtests prior to using the instrument.

General Uses of the NEPSY

- Allow clinicians to examine relative strengths of the child across domains.
- Aid in developing treatment interventions based on strengths and weaknesses of the child.

INTEREST IN EMPLOYMENT

Counselors commonly are approached with employment issues by their clients. Problems or concerns associated with employment may be related to two areas: interest in employment and organizational culture. Issues of interests or ability need to be addressed with an employment battery, whereas issues concerned with the organizational culture and relation to the clients require different forms of assessment. Although these two areas may address different issues, they both derive from employment and knowing which assessment tool to use in each situation is important. The section focuses on employment batteries, while the next section addresses assessments related to organizational culture.

Career counseling competence requires counselors to know how to address and measure clients' career-related questions. Counselors often help their clients address employment issues by assessing clients' skills and interests. Career assessment includes the use of interest inventories as well as tests discussed earlier, including ability, personality, and achievement tests.

Measures commonly used to assess job interests or the skills related to particular jobs include the following:

- Strong Interest Inventory (SII; Harmon, Hansen, Borgen, & Hammer, 1994).
- The Armed Services Vocational Aptitude Battery (ASVAB).
- The General Aptitude Test Battery (GATB).
- The Myers–Briggs Type Indicator (MBTI; Myers & McCaulley, 1985).

■ Strong Interest Inventory

The SII (Harmon et al., 1994) is the most widely used career planning instrument designed to measure human interests as it relates to occupation.

Key Elements of the SII

- Assesses the fit between a person's interests and a desired career choice.
- Helps develop possible career options based on personality.
- Includes four scales—the General Occupational Themes scale, the Basic Interest scales, the Personal Styles scales, and Occupational scales—that relate to more than 120 careers.
- Used appropriately for high school and college career counseling, one-on-one management coaching, and staff development programs.

See Chapter 15 for more information on the SII.

■ Armed Services Vocational Aptitude Battery

The ASVAB and corresponding program originally was used to predict future academic and occupational success in military occupations. Today, the ASVAB Career Exploration Program is used for the purposes of predicting academic success and occupational success in many different areas.

Main Components of the ASVAB

- The ASVAB program includes a multiple aptitude test battery, an interest inventory, and career planning tools.
- The ASVAB is intended for use with 10th-, 11th-, and 12th-grade students, as well as postsecondary students to help with career exploration and planning.
- The ASVAB test battery is a norm-referenced test that allows clinicians to measure a person's ability and compare the scores with others in the same peer group.

General Aptitude Test Battery

Another ability and aptitude measure that can be used in career assessment is the GATB developed by the U.S. Employment Services. The GATB is composed of 12 timed tests that measure nine aptitudes in occupations.

Areas Measured by the GATB

- General learning ability.
- Verbal aptitude.
- Numerical aptitude.
- Spatial aptitude.
- Form perception.
- Clerical perception.
- Motor coordination.
- Finger dexterity.
- Manual dexterity.

The battery takes approximately 3 hours to administer and is divided into psychomotor tasks and paper-and-pencil tasks. The results are provided in three composite scores of cognitive, perceptual, and psychomotor aptitudes.

Myers–Briggs Type Indicator

Finally, the MBTI (Myers & McCaulley, 1985) is a personality measure that commonly is used by employers. The aim of the MBTI is to identify individuals' psychological type and to understand how people take in information and make decisions.

Key Characteristics of the MBTI

- Relies on Jung's theory of psychological types to classify people into four personality categories: extraversion–introversion (EI), sensing–intuition (SN), thinking–feeling (TF), and judging–perceiving (JP).
- Combines the four personality categories into 16 different personality types.
- Describes each personality type by the letter code for each side of the dichotomy (e.g., INTP stands for introversion, intuition, thinking, and perceiving).
- Uses personality types to match careers with individuals' personality types.

See Chapter 15 for more information on the MBTI.

ASSESSMENT OF ORGANIZATIONAL CULTURE

Every organization has its own culture and develops traditions around how the organization is to be run and how people are to act within that organization. Organizational culture is defined as follows:

> **Organizational culture:** The "socially transmitted behavior patterns characteristic of a particular organization or company" (Cohen & Swerdlik, 2004, p. 552).

The behaviors inherent in an organizational culture include the structure and roles of the organization, leadership style, dominant values, norms, sanctions, support mechanisms, past traditions, and characteristic ways of interacting with people and institutions outside of the culture (Cohen & Swerdlik). Understanding how an organization functions and creates a culture around itself is important because, ultimately, the organizational structure can affect various aspects of the organization, including health of employees, job satisfaction, and other measures.

There are a number of assessment instruments that are useful in responding to needs related to organizational culture:

- Discussion of Organizational Culture (DOC).
- Job Description Index (JDI).
- Minnesota Satisfaction Questionnaire (MSQ).

■ Discussion of Organizational Culture

One scale used to measure organizational culture is the DOC (Cohen, 2001). It was devised with the intent of self-examination and self-improvement of a job environment.

Key Traits of the DOC Instrument

- Identifies the strengths and weaknesses of a culture to allow organizations to utilize their strengths and improve their weaknesses.
- Uses the form of an interview and discussion format to cover 10 topics, such as first impression, physical space, and prevailing values that bring understanding of pivotal aspects of an organization.

■ Job Descriptive Index

The JDI (Balzer et al., 1997) is one of the most widely used measures of job satisfaction. A key concept in organizations and employment needs, job satisfaction can be described this way:

> **Job satisfaction:** The pleasure that relates to one's occupational experience.

Key Characteristics of the JDI

- Uses 72 items to measure work on present job, present pay, opportunities for promotion, supervision, and coworkers.
- Allows for testing in several different languages and dialects.
- Provides a valid and reliable measure of job satisfaction (Johnson, Smith, & Tucker, 1982; Kinicki, Mckee-Ryan, Schriesheim, & Carson, 2002).

■ Minnesota Satisfaction Questionnaire

The MSQ (Weiss, Dawis, England, & Lofquist, 1967) not only measures job satisfaction, but also can be used to examine client vocational needs and to generate information about a particular job's reinforcers. The MSQ was normed on 25 representative occupations, plus employed disabled and employed nondisabled workers.

The MSQ is available in two different forms. The long version takes 15 to 20 minutes to administer, and the short version takes 5 minutes to administer. The longer version measures 20 different areas of job satisfaction and gives a global job satisfaction score. The shorter version consists of 20 items that represent the 20 different areas examined in the longer version.

■ Organizational Commitment Questionnaire

The Organizational Commitment Questionnaire (OCQ; Porter, Steers, Mowday, & Boulian, 1974) is a useful tool for measuring another employment and organizational culture concept known as organizational commitment, defined as follows:

Organizational commitment: The degree to which one identifies with a particular organization.

The OCQ is comprised of 15 items measured on a Likert scale that provides a measure of the amount of commitment both in the individual employee and the overall organization. Questions on the organizational level address the areas of absenteeism, tardiness, turnover, and quality of work, whereas belongingness, security, and opportunity for advancement and personal growth are measured by the individual level.

Chapter 21: **Key Terms**

- ▶ Assessment
- ▶ Referral question
- ▶ Cognitive assessment
- ▶ General intelligence
- ▶ Fluid intelligence
- ▶ Crystallized intelligence
- ▶ Psychometrics
- ▶ Educational assessment
- ▶ Achievement tests

- ▶ Aptitude tests
- ▶ Psychoeducational tests
- ▶ Personality assessment
- ▶ Projective measures
- ▶ Objective measures
- ▶ Behavioral assessment

- ▶ Self-report
- ▶ Direct observation
- ▶ Forced choice response
- ▶ Neuropsychological assessment
- ▶ Flexible battery

- ▶ Fixed battery
- ▶ Organizational culture
- ▶ Job satisfaction
- ▶ Organizational commitment

Quantitative Research Designs

Launcelot I. Brown
Duquesne University

In This Chapter

▶ *Foundations of Research Design*
  - The Hypothesis
  - Types of Research Hypotheses
  - The Null Hypothesis
  - Decision to Reject or Accept the Null
  - Alpha or Significance Level
  - Point Estimates and Confidence Intervals
  - Hypothesis Testing

▶ *Experimental Research*
  - Manipulation
  - Random Assignment
  - Controlling for Confounds
  - Treatment Integrity
  - Manipulation Check
  - Settings for Conducting Experiments

▶ *Experimental Validity*
  - Internal Validity
  - External Validity

▶ *Basic Experimental Design*
  - One Group Posttest Only Design
  - Treatment–Control Posttest Only
  - One Group Pretest–Posttest Design

  - Pretest–Posttest Control Group Design
  - Posttest Only Design
  - Treatments and Concomitant Variables
  - Factorial Designs
  - Solomon Four-Group Design

▶ *Quasi-Experimental Designs*
  - The Nonequivalent Control Group Design
  - Interrupted Time-Series Design
  - Counterbalanced Designs
  - Single Case Experimental Designs
  - Multiple-Baseline Designs
  - Alternating Treatments Design and Changing Criterion Design

▶ *Nonexperimental Research Designs*
  - Classifications of Independent Variable
  - Purposes of Nonexperimental Research Design
  - Types of Nonexperimental Designs
  - Combining Experimental and Nonexperimental Designs
  - Interpretation of Nonexperimental Research
  - Longitudinal Research

FOUNDATIONS OF RESEARCH DESIGN

There are many texts written on quantitative research designs, some more technical than others. This chapter does not attempt to serve as a replacement for these texts; the sheer brevity of the chapter does not make that possible. Rather, information contained herein is presented in a simple, concise manner and uses scenarios of interest from the counseling field to frame the discussion around the various topics.

■ The Hypothesis

Research studies usually are born out of a researcher's interest in a particular phenomenon or topic. When engaging in serious study of the area of interest, one of a researcher's first tasks is to become familiar with the literature already written about the chosen area and to use that literature search to narrow and clarify the specific question(s) he or she will decide to investigate. Ultimately, through careful consideration of the literature, researchers formulate a research hypothesis, which not only underlies the selection of the research design, but, more important, guides and frames the research (Heppner & Heppner, 2004). There are some essential elements that are often addressed in the research hypothesis.

Components of the Research Hypothesis

- The researcher's intentions with regard to what will be observed.
- The expected relationship between variables that are being observed.
- The sample representing the population of interest.
- The measuring instruments.
- The design of the study.
- The data analytic procedures.
- The tentative prediction of the findings.

The hypothesis is never an educated guess. The researcher's prediction is the **alternative** or **scientific hypothesis** (H_1) and is based on theory or studious observations.

■ Types of Research Hypotheses

The research hypothesis can be directional or nondirectional.

Directional hypothesis: Specific statement about which group will exhibit more or less of a treatment effect.

Nondirectional hypothesis: Statement that there is simply a relationship between variables or that groups differ on the variable of interest.

> # EXAMPLE
>
> ### Writing Research Hypotheses
>
> A school counselor in an urban high school wants to test the effectiveness of two counseling techniques on increasing the self-concept of students in her school. She makes the following nondirectional hypotheses:
>
> There is a significant difference in the mean self-concept of urban high school students in the cognitive therapy group and those in the behavioral counseling group.
>
> $$H_1 : \mu_1 \neq \mu_2$$
>
> On sharing her hypothesis with one of her colleagues she learns about two recent studies that looked at the effectiveness of cognitive and behavioral counseling and concluded that cognitive approaches have longer lasting residual effects. After reading the two articles, she changes her hypothesis to one or the other of the following directional hypotheses:
>
> Cognitive therapy will be significantly more effective than behavioral counseling in increasing the self-concept of urban high school students.
>
> $$H_1 : \mu_1 > \mu_2$$
>
> Urban high school students in the behavioral counseling group will show significantly lower levels of self-concept than those in the cognitive therapy group.
>
> $$H_1 : \mu_1 < \mu_2$$
>
> Both the directional and nondirectional hypotheses are tested against the null hypothesis (H_0), which states that both counseling methods are equally effective. In other words, there is no significant difference between the two counseling methods with regard to the self-concept of urban high school students. Any differences found are due to chance or sampling error.
>
> $$H_0 : \mu_1 = \mu_2 \text{ or } H_0 : \mu_1 - \mu_2 = 0$$

■ The Null Hypothesis

Generally, the null hypothesis is a statement about the population parameter and can be understood as follows:

Null hypothesis: States that in the population, there is no change, no effect, no difference, and no relationship due to the effect of the treatment or condition.

Stated differently, the null hypothesis says that with regard to the independent variable (in the preceding example, the manipulated or independent variable is the counseling technique) there is no effect on the dependent or outcome variable (self-concept). That is, the null is true. The alternative hypothesis says that there is an effect and the null is false.

■ Decision to Reject or Accept the Null

Most often, the researcher hopes that the evidence collected is sufficiently incompatible with the null if the null was true. If the evidence supports the research hypothesis, the null is said to be false and is rejected. If there is not sufficient evidence to support the research hypothesis, the null is accepted, or as is more commonly stated, the researcher fails to reject the null.

It is important to remember that failing to reject the null does not mean that the null is true. It simply says that the evidence is not sufficient to support rejection of the null. It is analogous to the concept of innocent until proven guilty. However, there is the caveat; before a researcher rejects the condition of innocence, the evidence must indicate guilt beyond a reasonable doubt.

■ Alpha or Significance Level

Keeping with the analogy of innocent until proven guilty, the alpha (α) or **level of significance** is the criterion beyond which one determines there is reasonable doubt. Alpha can be defined as follows:

Alpha: The predetermined probability value selected by the researcher to make a decision about the null hypothesis.

In the behavioral sciences, that probability value (p value) is usually 5 in 100 ($p = .05$) or 1 in 100 ($p = .01$). An alpha equal to or less than .05 or .01 indicates that there is a 5% or 1% probability that the findings are due to chance or sampling error. Alternatively, we can say there is 95% or 99% probability that the findings are due to the effect of the independent variable on the dependent variable. Both statements convey the same information that the findings, when considering the probability that they might be due to sampling error, are inconsistent with the null if the null were true.

The researcher selects the alpha level depending on how serious the consequences are of rejecting the null when it is true. Errors can occur in drawing conclusions about the null hypothesis, and these are known as Type I and Type II errors.

Type I error: Occurs when a researcher finds a significant difference or relationship when there is none.

Type II error: Occurs when the researcher fails to reject a false null when a significant difference exists.

Stated differently, Type I errors occur when the researcher rejects the null hypothesis when there is no difference, and Type II errors occur when the researcher fails to reject the null when actual differences exist.

■ Point Estimates and Confidence Intervals

Important to the interpretation of significance is an understanding of the difference between the point estimate (calculated sample statistic) and the confidence interval (CI).

Point estimate: One statistic in the range of possible statistics within the confidence interval that estimates the population parameter.

Confidence interval: Range of values within which the true value of the population parameter is found.

Of critical importance is the width of the CI that supposedly captures the parameter. The wider the CI, the more imprecise the point estimate calculated from the sample, and accordingly, the less confidence one can have in the calculated statistic. The level of confidence one has in the CI depends on the alpha level selected by the researcher prior to conducting the research. Therefore a 95% CI (CI_{95}) means that in drawing an infinite number of CIs from the population of interest, 95% of the time the population parameter will fall or be captured within the CI.

Although the CI does not give a single estimate of the population parameter, it gives more information on the possible value of the parameter. This knowledge becomes important when comparing studies on the same topic. By examining the overlap of CIs across studies (Thompson, 2002), one can get a clearer picture of the values that can be attributed to the population parameter.

■ Hypothesis Testing

The information presented thus far provides an outline of some of the basic terms and ideas necessary to conduct research. Putting this information together in the actual process of testing hypotheses is the next step. Following is a listing of some of the procedures that happen while testing the hypotheses.

Steps in Hypothesis Testing

- State the null and alternative hypotheses.
- Select the alpha level.
- Select the appropriate test statistic.
- Collect and summarize the sample data.
- Run the test and make a statistical decision to reject or retain the null.
- Draw conclusions.

EXPERIMENTAL RESEARCH

The experiment is the most structured and thorough of all quantitative research methods for testing hypotheses to determine whether the relationship between two or more variables is due to cause and effect. A meticulously conducted experiment is the only quantitative method for establishing cause-and-effect relationships. For research to be considered truly experimental, two occurrences must take place:

- Manipulation of at least one variable.
- Random assignment of participants to treatment and control groups.

■ Manipulation

For research to be experimental, the independent variable must be manipulated while all other variables, particularly the dependent variable, are held constant. The independent and dependent variables can be understood in the following way:

Independent variable: Variable that is hypothesized to be responsible for the effect and also is called the treatment or experimental variable.

Dependent variable: Variable that is considered the consequence of the independent variable to the extent that it is predicted by the independent variable.

Manipulation requires that the researcher create levels of the treatment, then assign individuals to different levels. This might mean that the **treatment group** receives the treatment and a **control group** receives no treatment or that groups are assigned to different levels of the treatment.

E X A M P L E

Manipulation of Intensity of Treatment Versus Type of Treatment

Imagine that a researcher wants to discover the most effective approach to tutoring. The researcher may decide that one group receives 1 hour of tutoring 1 day per week, another group receives 1 hour 2 days per week, and yet another group gets 1 hour of tutoring 3 days per week, while a control group receives no tutoring. In this example, the researcher controls the amount or intensity of the treatment. The same researcher may later decide she is more interested in what type of tutoring is most effective. One group receives tutoring from peers, another receives online tutoring, and yet another group is assigned to instructor-led tutoring sessions. In this instance, the researcher is manipulating the type of treatment.

■ Random Assignment

Also important to experimental design is the concept of random assignment or randomization.

Random assignment: Individuals are assigned to either the experimental group or the control group, or some level of the treatment on the basis of chance.

Randomization is the most effective method for ensuring group equivalence by controlling for extraneous or confounding variables that could bias the outcome of the study. There are always extraneous variables in research studies in the behavioral sciences. However, these variables are only of concern when they influence the independent variable, and as a result, the dependent or outcome variable. If the extraneous variables influence the independent variable, the results of the study can be confounded.

How Random Assignment Accounts for Extraneous Variables

- Randomization capitalizes on chance assignment to the treatment condition and, therefore, each participant has an equal chance of being assigned to any of the treatment conditions.
- Randomization as a control procedure does not remove the influence of extraneous variables, but eliminates **differential influence** or influence that differs for different groups in the study.
- Random distribution of individuals to treatment levels also distributes in no particular order (by chance) the extraneous variables.
- Random assignment equates groups by diffusing the influence of the extraneous variables across all groups (i.e., the extraneous variables are held constant across all groups).

■ Controlling for Confounds

In addition to randomization, there are a number of other methods researchers can use to control for extraneous or confounding variables that can have an impact on the research outcomes. Confound can be defined this way:

Confound: Variable not considered in the study (extraneous variable) that influences the outcome of the study and consequently does not allow for valid interpretation of the results.

Methods of Controlling Extraneous Variables

- Manipulation allows the researcher to control the characteristics of the independent variable by creating of levels of the independent variable, controlling the amount or intensity of the treatment, or controlling the nature of the treatment.

- Elimination refers to the researcher's decision to control for extraneous variables by holding them constant.
- Inclusion allows the researcher to control for extraneous variables by including them in the study so their effects can be taken into account.
- Statistical control allows the researcher to control for the effects of extraneous variables through statistical analyses.

EXAMPLE

Finding Ways to Control for Confounds

There are several ways researchers can control for confounding variables. If a researcher believes that gender, for example, can make a difference in outcome, the researcher can include both sexes in the analysis. On the other hand, the researcher may want to hold constant confounding variables by eliminating them from the study. A researcher may, therefore, choose to involve only girls, only children from single-parent families, or only children with learning disabilities in the study. Finally, researchers also can use statistics to their benefit when trying to control for confounds. The analysis of covariance (ANCOVA) is a statistical procedure that measures the extraneous variable as a covariate and, therefore, allows the researcher to draw conclusions about the impact of that variable on the results.

■ Treatment Integrity

In preparation for beginning a research study, it is the responsibility of the researcher to ensure that the treatment is administered as intended and consistently across treatment conditions.

Treatment integrity: The extent to which the treatment is the same for all groups across all contexts.

There are a number of precautions researchers can take to ensure treatment integrity.

Ways to Maximize Treatment Integrity

- Train research assistants in carrying out their functions and keeping records.
- Adopt standardized procedures.
- Use standardized instruments.
- Create clear, well-defined instructions.

By maintaining treatment integrity, researchers can ensure (as much as possible) congruence in understanding among all participants as to their roles and responsibilities and decrease the chances of dissimilar interpretations of the instructions and procedures.

■ Manipulation Check

In addition to ensuring treatment integrity prior to launching a study, the researcher also must do a manipulation check to consider what variables besides the treatment variable might influence the dependent variable.

> **Manipulation check:** Process of examining the impact of the treatment to determine whether the outcome was expected or whether the outcome had unintended effects.

A thorough literature review and piloting of the instruments helps researchers identify some of the variables that potentially could have unintended effects on the dependent variable. Just as important is determining whether the treatment works the same for all subgroups in the experiment.

EXAMPLE

Using the Manipulation Check

A researcher decides to give an exam for which everyone is required to do an Internet search. In this case, computer anxiety could become an artifact that has an impact on exam scores. Therefore, anxiety must be a consideration in the a priori planning for the study. Additionally, if boys did better than girls on the test, the researcher needs to know whether the difference in performance was due to the boys' greater understanding of the content or to their being less computer anxious. If the latter is true, then the testing format is working in favor of the boys.

■ Settings for Conducting Experiments

The laboratory and the field are two primary settings in which research can take place. Laboratories are set up specifically for the study, whereas field research uses a naturally occurring setting. There are advantages to each venue.

Advantages of the Laboratory Setting

- Supports the purpose of the study by affording greater control over potentially extraneous variables that can confound the results of the study.
- Allows for greater internal validity.

The limitation of a laboratory setting, however, is that it is artificial and, therefore, generally has lower external validity.

Advantages of Field Work

- Accounts for the reality of the environment.
- Allows for higher external validity.

The drawback of field experiments is that in allowing for less control over extraneous variables, the study is generally less internally valid.

There is always a trade-off when choosing the setting for a study. The basis for choosing one setting over the other depends on the purpose of the study and the importance attached to internal versus external validity.

EXPERIMENTAL VALIDITY

Experimental validity refers to the internal and external validity of the experiment. This section outlines some of the major concerns related to experimental validity of which researchers must be aware and able to address to the extent possible when conducting an investigation.

■ Internal Validity

When an experiment has high **internal validity,** the results of the experiment are attributable to the manipulated independent variable and cannot be explained by other factors (extraneous variables) that have affected the outcome. There are a number of threats to internal validity of which researchers must be aware. These are outlined and defined next.

Threats to Internal Validity

- **History** refers to any event that is not part of the experimental treatment but occurs during the study and influences responses on the dependent variable.
- **Maturation** is a threat in studies that occurs over time that increases the chances that participants undergo changes during the life of the study.
- **Instrumentation** or data collection devices must be reliable and must be consistent across measuring occasions to avoid internal threats to validity.
- **Testing** or **pretest sensitization** occurs when participants' performance on a test is improved because of having taken a pretest. The threat to internal validity is more likely to occur when the time between the pretest and the posttest is short, or when the test is based on factual information that can be recalled.
- **Mortality** or **attrition** is a threat that occurs when participants drop out of the study in different numbers and for different reasons and, in turn, affect the sample size and the composition of the treatment and control groups. The threat becomes even greater when the dropout rate is proportionally different between groups (differential attrition).

- **Selection** refers to inherent differences between groups at the outset of the study and is more likely to happen with intact groups. One cannot say that the participants are representatives of the population. There is the possibility of sample bias.
- **Regression toward the mean** occurs when participants scoring at the extremes on the pretest tend to move toward the middle or mean on the posttest. This concept has to do with the effects of random errors. Therefore, the correlation between two variables, or between scores on the same variables measured on different occasions, are not perfect. (See Pedhazur & Schmelkin, 1991, for a more in-depth treatment of the topic.)
- **Diffusion or imitation of treatments** occurs when the treatment or control group becomes aware of the experimental treatment and, because of the awareness, does not respond as they normally would on the dependent variable.
- **Compensatory rivalry** or the **John Henry effect** is a threat related to diffusion that occurs when the effects of the treatment are negated because one group sees the other group as competitors and consequently works harder than usual.
- **Resentful demoralization** occurs when the responses of the participants do not reflect their natural behaviors.

EXAMPLE

Threats to Internal Validity: Studies Prior to and Post 9/11

A good example of the threat of history can be seen in any study about the perception of immigrants before and after September 11, 2001. Media coverage on terrorists and government action to scrutinize immigrants more carefully certainly can have an impact on the way the public views immigrants, which may, therefore, pose a threat to validity.

■ External Validity

High **external validity** refers to the generalizability of the results or the extent to which results are replicable to other groups and contexts beyond the experimental setting. For individuals to benefit from the results of research studies, the investigations must have high external validity. Just as there are a number of threats to internal validity, there are also threats to external validity of which researchers must be aware (Gay & Airasian, 2003).

Threats to External Validity

- Treatment by attributes interaction is a threat to the effectiveness of treatment that emerges because of certain attributes or characteristics (e.g., gender, race, age, educational level) of the participants.

- The **Hawthorne effect** refers to the fact that participants behave differently simply because they know they are being studied.
- Treatment by setting interaction suggests that results can fluctuate depending on the setting of the study.
- Pretest sensitization suggests that the preset itself triggers a change in results.

BASIC EXPERIMENTAL DESIGN

The research design is the plan for conducting the research, and there are many research designs from which researchers can choose. Some are more effective than others for controlling threats to the validity of the study, and some are more sophisticated than others, thus requiring additional resources and skill. Selection of a research design is based on its appropriateness to test the hypothesis and answer the identified research questions. This section outlines some of the various designs that commonly are used in experimental research.

One Group Posttest Only Design

One of the simplest of all research designs, the one group posttest only design, involves one group that is exposed to a treatment (X) and then tested (O_2). A major limitation of this design is that one cannot say that the measure on the outcome variable was due to the effects of the treatment. Thus, most researchers recognize the inadequacy of this design, and it rarely is used.

Treatment–Control Posttest Only

The treatment–control posttest only design is a variant of the one group posttest design. In this design, one group receives a treatment, while another group is used as a control and, therefore, does not receive any treatment. A test is given to both groups only after the treatment is administered.

EXAMPLE

Treatment–Control Posttest Only Design

Let us consider a study that is intended to measure the effectiveness of a special teaching approach on students' grades in math. In this design, the control group of students receives the traditional teaching approach, whereas the experimental group gets the treatment, which is a special approach to teaching math. At the end of the treatment administration, the students take a test and differences in scores are analyzed. Another example can be found in medical research. One group is given medication, and the control group receives a placebo (i.e., no treatment). In this design, the conditions before the test are not known.

The design can be depicted this way:

$$X_1 \quad O_1$$
$$O_2$$

■ One Group Pretest–Posttest Design

The one group pretest–posttest design is an improvement on the one group posttest only design. In this approach, the research participants first are measured on the dependent variable via a pretest (O_1). The participants then are exposed to the treatment (X) and tested again on the dependent variable via a posttest (O_2). The effectiveness of the treatment is determined by the difference between the pretest and posttest scores. It is tempting to believe that whatever success is observed is due to the treatment. However, other sources of influence cannot be ruled out as explanations for the differences between the pretest and posttest scores.

EXAMPLE

One Group Pretest–Posttest Design: Limitations

Consider a hypothetical study. The high school in one school district has been merged with the middle and high school of an adjacent school district. A school counselor is concerned that the anxiety caused by the transition to the new setting affects students' participation in school activities and their academic performance. To test her hypothesis, she introduces a program aimed at addressing student anxiety. On the first day of the new term, she administers an anxiety test (pretest) to the new arrivals. The students participate in the 3-week program designated as the treatment. At the end of the program she again administers the test (the posttest) and observes a significant decline in their levels of anxiety. The counselor is pleased with the outcome of the program.

The question is: Can the decrease in anxiety level be attributed to the program? Other factors must be considered. For instance, the students were singled out for special treatment, and the teacher might consider what impact being singled out might have on their test scores. Also, the students were in school 3 weeks between testing times, and their initial anxiety naturally may have diminished. Additionally, they may have realized that their present school setting was not much different from their former school setting and may have started to make friends. All these are possible reasons (extraneous variables or confounds) that can explain the decrease in levels of anxiety. Therefore, if this design is used, extreme caution must be applied to any interpretation of the results.

■ Pretest–Posttest Control Group Design

The pretest–posttest control group design does an excellent job of controlling for alternative hypotheses that might explain the changes in the dependent variable. In this design, individuals are randomly assigned to at least two groups and pretested on the outcome variable. One group is exposed to the treatment and the other continues with the existing conditions. Both groups are posttested on the dependent variable. Although randomization is the most effective procedure for equating groups, it does not guarantee group equivalence. A general weakness of all designs that use a pretest is the possibility of sensitizing participants to the posttest and the possible interaction of the pretest with the treatment. In this design, however, the control group controls for the effects of testing.

In all the previous designs, if the groups are equivalent on the pretest, the posttest scores of the groups can be compared using the *t* test, or the analysis of variance (ANOVA). If groups differ on the pretest, the ANCOVA is the appropriate analysis to adopt.

EXAMPLE

Pretest–Posttest Control Group Design

In this design, there are three randomly assigned groups: two to different levels of the treatment and one to the control. Pictorially, the design looks like this:

$$O \quad X_1 \quad O$$
$$O \quad X_2 \quad O$$
$$O \qquad\quad O$$

There are many variations to the pretest–posttest control group design. In the following diagram, the treatment effects (O) are tested immediately after treatment and again at a later date. This variation on the original design looks like this:

$$O \quad X_1 \quad O \quad O$$
$$O \quad X_2 \quad O \quad O$$

■ Posttest Only Design

In the posttest only design, at least one group of participants receives a treatment and is compared to a control group that was not exposed to the experimental treatment. Both groups are posttested. The weakness of this design is that there is no pretest to determine prior individual level of performance on the dependent variable. Despite this weakness, this design controls for pretest sensitization and is useful especially when it is unethical to withhold treatment from individuals.

E X A M P L E

Posttest Only Design

The design can be extended to include any number of groups. For example, a design that includes three groups is displayed this way:

$$X_1 \quad O_1$$

$$X_2 \quad O_2$$

$$X_3 \quad O_3$$

Groups can be compared on three different counseling strategies, such as behavioral, cognitive, and Gestalt therapies. Or, as in medical research, two groups are given the treatment—medication and a placebo—and another receives no treatment. Participants are randomly assigned to each group, and groups are compared one to the other or against a control group.

■ Treatments and Concomitant Variables

Concomitant variables are subject attributes that can influence the effects of the treatment on the dependent variable. This design is essentially the same as the pretest–posttest control group design, however, instead of the pretest, the concomitant variable C is measured.

E X A M P L E

Treatments and Concomitant Variables

A research design that accounts for concomitant variables looks like this:

$$C \quad X_1 \quad O$$

$$C \quad X_2 \quad O$$

$$C \qquad\quad O$$

A study of the effects of different counseling methods on peer relationships would have to take into consideration the concomitant variable social skills. The concomitant variable is measured before the application of the treatment and serves as the covariate in the ANCOVA.

■ Factorial Designs

Factorial design allows for the simultaneous study of more than one independent variable to determine both the effects of the independent variables and the interaction on the dependent variable. In fact, a factorial design can consist of any number of factors, and factors can have any number of categories. A $2 \times 2 \times 3$ design (see Figure 22.1) consists of three factors: two of two categories each and one of three categories.

E X A M P L E

Factorial Design

In the factorial design, the letters refer to the independent variables or factors. The design can be displayed like this:

$$A1 \quad B_1 \quad O_1$$

$$A_1 \quad B_2 \quad O_2$$

$$A_2 \quad B_1 \quad O_3$$

$$A_2 \quad B_2 \quad O_4$$

Let us say A is divided into two age groups, younger and older, and B refers to two counseling methods. The factorial design allows researchers to estimate main effects. That is, researchers are able to determine whether the difference observed is due to (a) age A_1 and A_2, (b) the difference in counseling methods B_1 and B_2, or (c) the result of an interaction between age and method, where one method works better than the other for one age group but not the other.

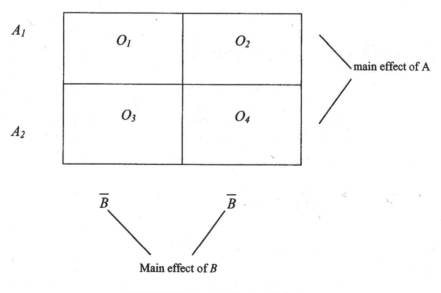

FIGURE 22.1 2×2 factorial design.

■ Solomon Four-Group Design

The Solomon four-group design combines the pretest–posttest control group design and the treatment control posttest only design. As the name implies, the design consists of four groups, two of which are pretested and two of which are not pretested. Individuals are randomly assigned to one of the four groups. The treatment is given to one of the pretested groups and one of the groups that did not receive the pretest. All groups are then posttested.

EXAMPLE

Solomon Four-Group Design

The Solomon four-group design is depicted this way:

$$O_1 \quad X \quad O_2$$
$$O_3 \quad O_4$$
$$X \quad O_5$$
$$O_6$$

This design allows researchers to determine whether the pretest sensitizes individuals to the posttest. It also determines whether the effects of the treatment are consistent when measured in more than one way. The appropriate analysis for this design is a 2 × 2 factorial design with treatment–control and pretest–no pretest as the independent variables.

QUASI-EXPERIMENTAL DESIGNS

Quasi-experimental design includes at least one manipulated independent variable and does not use random assignment to treatment groups. A quasi-experimental design is used instead of an experimental design when it is not possible to randomly assign individuals to groups, or it is unethical to do so. There are two types of quasi-experimental designs:

1. Nonequivalent control group.
2. Interrupted time-series.

■ The Nonequivalent Control Group Design

This design is exactly like the pretest–posttest control group design except that instead of randomly assigning individuals to the treatment, intact groups are assigned. The more similar the intact groups are, the stronger the study. In an effort to equate groups, it is sometimes necessary to match individuals on the variable of interest. For example, highly anxious clients are paired with other highly anxious clients. As with the experimental designs, similar variations and extensions to the base design can be applied; similar statistical analytic procedures also are conducted in quasi-experimental designs. The major drawback to the nonequivalent control group is that the results must be interpreted with great caution because the absence of random assignment makes it impossible to consider and control all possible extraneous variables, particularly those related to group membership.

■ Interrupted Time-Series Design

It is not always possible to have more than one group available for conducting a study. In such instances, the group is pretested a number of times until the pretest scores are stable and a baseline is established. The group then is exposed to the treatment and posttested a number of times. If, following the treatment, there is evidence of consistent improvement, the researcher is more confident in asserting that the improvement was due to the effects of the treatment (see Figure 22.2).

Researchers must be aware that the absence of random assignment always increases the possibility of rival hypotheses explaining the observed change. A variation of this design can be created by including a nonequivalent control group. The first group is exposed to the treatment condition and the second group serves as the control. This design is useful when the researcher wishes to determine whether the effects of treatment or intervention persist when the treatment is terminated. A graphical representation of an interrupted time series design is found in the following example.

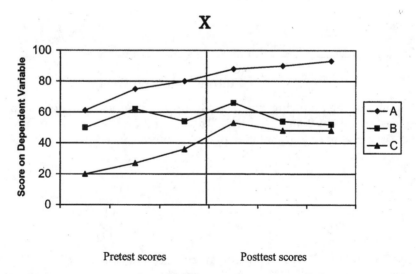

FIGURE 22.2 Possible patterns of behaviors on a study based on a time-series design. X shows the introduction of the treatment.

EXAMPLE

Interrupted Time-Series Design

The interrupted time-series design looks like this:

Multiple pretest   Treatment   Multiple posttest

$$O_1\,O_2\,O_3\,O_4 \qquad\qquad X \qquad\qquad O_5\,O_6\,O_7\,O_8$$

The interrupted time-series design also can include a control group.

$$O_1\,O_2\,O_3\,O_4 \quad X \quad O_5\,O_6\,O_7\,O_8$$

$$\overline{O_1\,O_2\,O_3\,O_4 \qquad\quad O_5\,O_6\,O_7\,O_8}$$

■ Counterbalanced Designs

The counterbalanced design is applicable to medical and pharmaceutical research, but also should be of interest to counselors. In this design all groups receive all treatment but in a different order. This design most often is used when it is not possible to administer a pretest and it is unethical to deprive any individual of the treatment. The order in which the treatment is given randomly is determined to control for the potential effects from the order of testing. The following example provides a diagram of the counterbalanced design.

EXAMPLE

Counterbalanced Design

As shown in the following diagram, Group A receives Treatment 1 and is posttested, then receives Treatment 2 and a posttest, Treatment 3 and a posttest, finally Treatment 4 and a posttest. A pictorial representation of the counterbalanced design is as follows:

A	X_1O	X_2O	X_3O	X_4O
B	X_2O	X_3O	X_4O	X_1O
C	X_3O	X_4O	X_1O	X_2O
D	X_4O	X_1O	X_2O	X_3O

A gets Treatment 1, B receives Treatment 2, C receives Treatment 3, and D receives Treatment 4; all groups are posttested. The effectiveness of the treatment is determined by comparing the mean posttest score of each group on each treatment.

■ Single Case Experimental Designs

Of interest to counselors is the single case, or single subject designs. These designs are applicable when one individual or one homogenous group comprises the participants of the study. Similar to the interrupted time-series design, this design entails repeated measure of the dependent variable pre- and postexposure to the treatment condition. The pretreatment responses constitute the baseline that is compared to the posttreatment responses to determine the effect of the independent variable on the dependent variable. Having pretreatment and posttreatment multiple measures on the dependent variable helps to control for history and maturation that could confound the results.

EXAMPLE

Single Case Designs

There are two basic types of single case designs: A-B-A and A-B-A-B designs.

The A-B-A designs have a pretreatment baseline, treatment phase, and posttreatment baseline. The A-B-A-B design simply adds a second treatment phase to the end of the process. The A-B-A-B design is displayed this way:

Baseline A1	Treatment B1	Baseline A2	Treatment B2
O O O O O	X O X O X O X O	O O O O O	X O X O X O X O

The addition of treatment phases and the subsequent calculation of new baselines can provide convincing evidence that the observed effects are due to the treatment and not extraneous variables.

■ Multiple-Baseline Designs

There are three basic types of multiple-baseline designs.

Categories of Multiple-Baseline Designs

1. Across behaviors design that focuses on two or more behaviors in the same individual.
2. Across participants design that focuses on two or more individuals exhibiting the same behaviors.
3. Across settings design that focuses on a specific behavior exhibited by the same individual in different settings.

In all three designs, baseline behavior is calculated (O) and the treatment (X) is applied to successive individuals, settings, or behaviors. A desired change in each behavior or each individual that appears only after the application of the treatment provides convincing evidence as to the effectiveness of the treatment.

EXAMPLE

Multiple-Baseline Design

The multiple-baseline design graphically is represented this way:

1st individual: O O O O O XO XO XO XO XO XO XO XO XO XO XO

2nd individual: O O O O O O O O O O XO XO XO XO XO XO XO XO

3rd individual: O O O O O O O O O O O O O O O XO XO XO XO XO XO

A variation of this design is the inclusion of an additional baseline phase and treatment phase using the same successive approach to the application of the phases.

■ Alternating Treatments Design and Changing Criterion Design

The alternating treatments and changing criterion designs are useful to counselors. The alternating treatments design is used in a single case context to assess the relative effectiveness of two or more treatments.

Characteristics of Alternating Treatments Design

- The design requires that the researcher, on a random basis, alternate types of treatment methods throughout the experiment.
- The main weakness with this design is the potential for carryover effects (multiple-treatment interference) from one treatment to another.

The changing criterion design is useful when it is necessary to set new baselines of increasing complexity, or baselines that demand more of the behavior.

Characteristics of Changing Criterion Design

- An initial baseline measure is calculated, and then the individual is exposed to the treatment condition until the criterion is achieved.
- This new level of performance becomes the new baseline, and the criterion is increased.

■ Successful achievement of the increased criterion leads to the establishment of new minimum performance levels until the desired level of performance is achieved.

NONEXPERIMENTAL RESEARCH DESIGNS

Nonexperimental research begins with a dependent variable (i.e., the phenomenon of interest) and attempts to discern factors that will explain or predict it. Unlike in experimental designs, in nonexperimental designs, the independent variable is neither manipulated nor randomly assigned to treatment. Because of certain features of the independent variable, the researcher has no control over the independent variable.

Features of the Independent Variable in Nonexperimental Research

■ Independent variables are fixed and nonmanipulable (e.g., sex).
■ Independent variables reflect a state of being (e.g., marital status).
■ Independent variables may not be ethically manipulated (e.g., drug usage).
■ The relation among variables is not known and needs to be discovered by research (e.g., factors that motivate substance abusers to seek intervention, or peer support and reduction in bullying in schools).

■ Classifications of Independent Variable

In nonexperimental design, independent variables can be described as categorical or continuous, defined as follows:

Categorical independent variables: Participants are classified into discrete groups (e.g., gender, race, marital status, religious affiliation, level of education).

Continuous independent variables: Participants are placed or fall along some continuum (e.g., age, IQ, self-esteem, persistence, goal orientation).

In most cases in which the independent variable is categorical, the researcher hypothesizes that groups differ on some dependent variable. Therefore, the questions of interest are whether or not groups differ, the extent to which groups differ, or the direction of the difference on some dependent variable. In research in which the primary independent variable is continuous, researchers are interested in the strength or nature of the relationship between the independent and dependent variables. For example, the researcher hypothesizes that there is a relationship between causal attribution and academic achievement in high school.

■ Purposes of Nonexperimental Research Design

There are two major purposes of nonexperimental designs: (a) to explain some phenomenon of interest on the basis of one or more variables, and (b) to predict some phenomenon of interest on the basis of one or more variables.

EXAMPLE

Using Nonexperimental Design to Answer Research Questions

In trying to explain a phenomenon of interest, researchers might ask questions such as these:

To what extent does level of test anxiety explain differences in achievement?
Is there a relation between gender and attitude toward sex orientation?
Are there sex differences in student willingness to seek help from counselors?

When researchers are interested in trying to identify factors that predict a phenomenon of interest, the research questions may look like this:

How well does the GRE predict success in graduate school?
To what extent does level of education predict willingness to seek help from counselors?
Does professional certification predict subsequent performance on the job?

■ Types of Nonexperimental Designs

Nonexperimental designs can be divided into three broad types, the causal-comparative study, correlational study, and longitudinal study. These are defined here:

Causal-comparative study: Designs that use categorical independent variables.

Correlational study: Designs that use continuous independent variables.

Longitudinal study: Research design in which data are collected more than once over a period of time.

In reality, most published research is a cross between causal-comparative and correlational; in fact, the distinction between the two is artificial. By simply creating categories of the continuous variable (e.g., above average, average, below average intelligence) one can change a correlational study to a causal-comparative study. Often, researchers examine the effects of categorical variables (gender and ethnicity) in combination with continuous variables (self-perception and perception of others) on the dependent variable (school climate).

■ Combining Experimental and Nonexperimental Designs

Many designs are combinations of experimental and nonexperimental. Researchers may manipulate one variable (e.g., sex of the counselor) but include another variable that is not manipulated (e.g., attitude toward persons of the opposite sex) as part of the study.

■ Interpretation of Nonexperimental Research

Even when there is statistical evidence of group differences or strong relations between independent and dependent variables, it is necessary to be cautious in interpreting the results of nonexperimental research. The major limitation to nonexperimental research is its inability to rule out extraneous and confounding variables as alternative hypotheses for explaining the results; thus, the possibility of other plausible explanations for the results always exist. The evidence must be overwhelming before one can imply cause.

■ Longitudinal Research

Longitudinal research refers to research in which data are collected more than once over a period of time. Two types of longitudinal research are trend studies and panel studies.

> **Trend study:** Type of study in which the researcher takes a new sample of persons from the population of interest each year. All samples are asked the same questions or administered the same treatment.

> **Panel study:** A study in which the same individuals are tested at successive points in time over the period of the study.

Like trend studies, panel studies focus primarily on questions related to change or developmental level across time. However, panel studies are more powerful than trend studies because in measuring the same individuals at successive time points, sampling error is reduced. A researcher might be interested in the factors that explain the changes, or may examine present factors that predict an outcome. Panel studies are the most effective nonexperimental design for establishing causality. Drawbacks to panel studies include high expenses, lengthy amounts of time to complete the study, and high levels of attrition. Additionally, analytic procedures are usually complex for longitudinal data. Among the simplest are the repeated measures ANOVA and variants of this analytic procedure.

EXAMPLE

Trend and Panel Studies

A researcher wants to conduct a trend study examining counselor opinions on rehabilitation of sex offenders. Each year for 5 years the researcher takes a sample of students entering the graduate counseling programs and canvases their opinions on a number of variables related to the rehabilitation of sex offenders. The research is particularly interested in the generational change in perception and compares the perception of one cohort to a previous cohort to track changes across time.

Panel studies have been used extensively in medical research, and these have been effective in establishing causation. Immediate examples of such studies are those that establish a causal relation between smoking and lung cancer and between air pollution and a variety of illnesses.

Chapter 22: Key Terms

- Alternative hypothesis
- Scientific hypothesis
- Directional hypothesis
- Nondirectional hypothesis
- Null hypothesis
- Alpha
- Level of significance
- Type I error
- Type II error
- Point estimate
- Confidence interval
- Independent variable
- Dependent variable
- Treatment group
- Control group
- Random assignment

- Differential influence
- Confound
- Treatment integrity
- Manipulation check
- Internal validity
- History
- Maturation
- Instrumentation
- Testing or pretest sensitization
- Mortality
- Attrition
- Selection
- Regression toward the mean
- Diffusion or imitation of treatments

- Compensatory rivalry
- John Henry effect
- Resentful demoralization
- External validity
- Hawthorne effect
- Categorical independent variables
- Continuous independent variables
- Causal-comparative study
- Correlational study
- Longitudinal study
- Trend study
- Panel study

Fundamentals of Qualitative Research

Gary Shank
Duquesne University

In This Chapter

▶ *Roots of Qualitative Research*
  ▪ Cultural Anthropology
  ▪ Sociology
  ▪ Education

▶ *Meaning in Qualitative Research*
  ▪ The World Is Meaningful
  ▪ Some Things Are Only Meaningful
  ▪ Knowledge Depends on Understanding

▶ *How to Recognize Qualitative Research*
  ▪ Natural Setting
  ▪ Holistic Approach
  ▪ Researcher Involvement
  ▪ Role of Qualitative Researcher

▶ *Basic Techniques of Qualitative Research*
  ▪ Observation
  ▪ Interviews
  ▪ Participation
  ▪ Interpretation

▶ *Basic Products of Qualitative Research*
  ▪ Ethnography
  ▪ Case Study
  ▪ Portraiture
  ▪ Grounded Theory
  ▪ The Glaser Approach
  ▪ Material Analysis

▶ *The Role and Future of Qualitative Research in Counseling*
  ▪ Qualitative Research Tackles Complex Questions and Issues
  ▪ Counselors and Qualitative Researchers Share Similarities
  ▪ Qualitative Research Provides Possibility and Freedom

ROOTS OF QUALITATIVE RESEARCH

The goal of this chapter is to introduce a counseling audience to the fundamentals of qualitative research in the social sciences. In one sense, qualitative research has only been around for a few decades. In a deeper sense, however, it has an extensive track record. That record is best understood by looking at its history within the main content domains of its development—cultural anthropology, sociology, and education.

■ Cultural Anthropology

Cultural anthropology is that branch of anthropology that seeks to study cultures in their native habitats. At the turn of the 20th century, cultural anthropologists began developing a specialized form of field work known as ethnography. A key concept in **ethnography** is that field work should be conducted with as few presuppositions and as few predetermined goals as possible.

■ Sociology

Like anthropology, sociology has a rich tradition within the qualitative domain (Lancy, 1993). Three key developments in sociology have helped shape the nature of contemporary qualitative research:

1. The Chicago School of Sociology introduced the concept of applied field work to the discipline (Bogdan & Bicklen, 1998), which served as a basis for all future qualitative research—including efforts such as action research and emancipatory research—that focused not just on finding out truth, but on improving people's lives.
2. Within the field of medical sociology, Glaser and Strauss (1967) introduced the basic procedures of grounded theory, which provided a middle ground between experimental design on one hand and armchair theorizing on the other hand.
3. Schutz (1932) and Berger and Luckmann (1966) advocated for field research that did not just look at the strange, far off, and exotic, but for field work in the study of everyday social settings and everyday lives.

Berger and Luckmann (1966) took the notion of research in the everyday realm a step further, by suggesting that social settings were palettes for creating complex and involved sorts of lives that nonetheless feel routine and natural to those of us who live within, and embrace, these complex settings. They called this notion the *social construction of reality*.

■ Education

A final key field in qualitative research in the social sciences is that of education. At first, educators explored the potential of qualitative research in the conduct of evaluation. Guba (Guba & Lincoln, 1994; Lincoln & Guba, 1985, 2000) was the pioneer of this approach. Other key figures in qualitative approaches to education include Patton (2002) and Fetterman (Fetterman, Kaftarian, & Wandersman, 1996). Over the years, qualitative research has gained more and more of a foothold in educational research. A good sampling of the various areas can be found in Denzin and Lincoln (2005).

MEANING IN QUALITATIVE RESEARCH

At its core, **qualitative research** can be described as an empirical inquiry into meaning (Shank, 2002). Meaning is the key dynamic and the key area of concentration for all forms of qualitative research. There are a number of important things we need to understand about meaning to grasp its role in qualitative research.

> At its core, qualitative research can be described as an empirical inquiry into meaning (Shank, 2002). Meaning is the key dynamic and the key area of concentration for all forms of qualitative research.

■ The World Is Meaningful

Too often, we have been led to believe that meaning is something that we create to understand the world and navigate within it. Although it is true that we can and do craft meaning for these purposes, the concept of meaning goes far beyond the notion of a psychological tool.

Assumptions About Meaning in Qualitative Research

- ■ Meaning seems to be part of the very fabric of reality.
- ■ Although meaning is often subtle and hidden, it is invariably present.
- ■ More often than not, we do not have to create or construct meaning; instead, we need to be able to discern meaning.

These awarenesses lead to two very important "corrections" about meaning that qualitative researchers often have to make in their research efforts. First, qualitative

researchers have to abandon the notion that there is no meaning in situations unless we put that meaning there ourselves. Second, researchers have to challenge the
assumption that the world is relatively meaning poor.

■ Some Things Are Only Meaningful

Many times, the inquiry into meaning is the start of a path that leads to making and
testing truth claims. Hypotheses, for instance, are really nothing more than meaning claims. At the same time, however, there are some things in the world that are
only meaningful. It does not matter if they are true or not. They point us toward a
deeper and richer understanding of the world as it really is.

EXAMPLE

Children's Stories: A Way to Suggest Meaning

Think about the familiar bedtime story of the wolf and the three little pigs. Is this story true?
Was there really a wolf and were there really three little pigs? Can wolves and pigs talk, build
houses, and blow down buildings? At the level of truth, this story is nonsensical. At the level
of meaning, however, it teaches children important lessons from our culture.

■ Knowledge Depends on Understanding

The philosopher Peirce (1992, 1998) knew that meaning is not a game. Instead, we
are governed by a compulsion to know what things mean. The lack of this sort of
understanding is what Pierce called *genuine doubt,* a painful and unnerving state of
being. Based on Peirce's suggestions, some generalizations about the relation between knowledge and meaning or understanding can be made.

Relation Between Knowledge and Understanding

- Basic understanding is a standard on which knowledge can be efficiently built.
- Unlike the common perception that knowledge drives understanding, it is actually the other way around.
- Unless we already have some basic realm of understanding, then we do not
  know where to even look for knowledge in the first place.

HOW TO RECOGNIZE QUALITATIVE RESEARCH

Qualitative research is a markedly different approach to understanding than is quantitative research. Over the years, the following criteria have been used to identify qualitative studies:

- Qualitative research studies take place in natural settings.
- Qualitative research seeks to understand things in a holistic manner.
- Qualitative research often goes beyond merely studying things.

■ Natural Setting

Only by seeing things in the natural contexts can we really come to understand their true natures and the impact they have on the world. Therefore qualitative research recognizes the need to examine things ecologically—that is, in their natural settings. Also, whereas quantitative research seeks to generalize its effects, qualitative research considers it necessary to ground its findings in the context of discovery.

■ Holistic Approach

Many forms of quantitative research employ the strategies of controlling and isolating key aspects of the phenomenon under investigation. Qualitative research takes a much different approach. In addition to studying a phenomenon in its natural environment, qualitative researchers resist the temptation to break down a phenomenon into component parts and investigate how the various aspects of a phenomenon work together in their natural settings.

EXAMPLE

Studying Context in Qualitative Research

Recent nutritional research seems to suggest that vitamin C works better when ingested in natural foods, like oranges, than it does when delivered as a supplement. What is it about foods, such as oranges, that allow vitamin C to be more beneficial for us? Is it the case that the whole is greater than the sum of the parts? Are there subtle dynamics and interactions that are lost when the vitamin is produced in a lab and delivered in a pill?

Qualitative researchers in the social sciences are not so much interested in aspirins or vitamins, but they study complex phenomena in complex settings every day. Preserving the ecological nature of these phenomena within these settings is a key process in many qualitative research efforts.

■ Researcher Involvement

Separation is a basic activity within traditional quantitative research. Researchers must learn to stand apart from those things that they study. They attempt to be as objective as possible; they are there to discover, test, and report findings. How they might feel about those tests or findings is not important. The research and its findings need to stand on their own. Because of the holistic, contextual approach of qualitative research and because separation from the phenomenon being study is not valued in qualitative research as it is in quantitative research, the role of the researcher is substantially different from that of the quantitative researcher.

Role of the Qualitative Researcher

- Qualitative researchers accept that their work often involves some degree of involvement.
- Researchers often find themselves to be participants in the research process itself, engaging in routine activities with other participants or even acting as advocates for others in the field.
- Qualitative researchers are in the field to discover and illuminate our understandings, and sometimes that requires setting aside the "ideal" of separation and jumping right into the mix.

BASIC TECHNIQUES OF QUALITATIVE RESEARCH

The most interesting thing about qualitative research is the fact that its basic tools are nothing more than the ordinary skills we use every day to interact with our fellow human beings (Shank, 2006). In this way, qualitative research resembles counseling to some degree. Like counseling, as well, these skills are refined and sharpened when they are used to do actual research. In all, there are four basic human skills that qualitative researchers identify and refine in their endeavors:

1. Observation.
2. Interviews.
3. Participation.
4. Interpretation.

■ Observation

Observation is one of the cornerstones to qualitative research. We are all born observers, but research observation is a particularly intense and demanding skill

(Adler & Adler, 1994). Over the years, qualitative researchers have refined and re-thought the dynamics of observation (Angrosino & de Perez, 2000).

EXAMPLE

Observation at Work

To help students learn the technique of observation, they can be asked to observe a quiet and empty setting. The setting should be isolated, but safe, and one in which they can observe for at least 30 minutes. Although newcomers to qualitative research and the technique of observation may be tempted to observe busy and interesting settings, the drawback is a feeling of being overwhelmed by the sheer volume of data. Therefore, it makes sense to keep things simple, at least at first. In fact, this is good advice for all qualitative researchers, as they begin the observational process for any given project.

■ Interviews

Qualitative researchers talk and listen to people in the field. Proper interviewing skills are difficult to learn. Too often, the novice interviewer employs ordinary conversational techniques, such as mutual disclosure, that actually can impede the data gathering process. Fortunately, most counselors are well versed in interview techniques via their therapeutic training and experience. Within the qualitative research tradition, both Seidman (1991) and Kvale (1996) are excellent resources for qualitative research interviewing techniques.

Variations in Interviewing Techniques

- Informal conversational interview.
- General interview guide approach.
- Standardized open-ended interview.
- Semistructured interview guide.

■ Participation

Observation, in its purest form, is the passive extreme of qualitative research. Its counterpoint on the active side is participation. Participation can range from just standing around to becoming an actual member and advocate of the community under study. Most qualitative researchers opt for a middle position known as participant observation (Bogdevic, 1999; Spradley, 1980).

Participant observation: Individuals make it clear to the community that they are researchers, but then try to partake, as much as possible and as much as allowed, in the daily and ordinary activities within that community.

Whyte (1955) provided an early and very famous example of such participant observation when he managed to integrate himself within the everyday life of his target community.

 Tips for conducting interviews and using direct observation techniques can be found at the USAID Web site:

  ▶ www.dec.org/partners/evalweb/resources/tipsseries.cfm

■ Interpretation

Interpretation in qualitative research is a rich and complex area. Qualitative researchers need to learn the ins and outs, the fine details, and the subtle touches of the art of interpretation.

Aspects of Interpretation in Qualitative Research

■ All interpretation starts with careful observation and a particular form of description known as *thick description,* which was first defined and employed by Geertz (1973).

■ To help understand data and findings, researchers use an interpretive framework that very often is grounded in such systems of thought as feminism, race theory, economic theory, and the like; collectively, these theories are known as critical theories (Geuss, 1981).

■ In addition to critical theories, a number of other interpretive frameworks that often are used to incorporate and understand qualitative data include phenomenology (see, e.g., Moustakas, 1994) and semiotics, which is grounded in looking for codes and patterns of meaning (see, e.g., Eco, 1990).

■ Interpretation involves the reporting and "telling" of the findings and results of any qualitative study (see Van Maanen, 1988, for valuable guides on conceptualizing the task of writing up these "tales from the field").

 For more on the role of semiotics in qualitative research, see an article written by Shank (1995):

  ▶ http://www.nova.edu/ssss/QR/QR2-3/shank.html

BASIC PRODUCTS OF QUALITATIVE RESEARCH

There are many different types of products that qualitative researchers generate as they do their research. Four of the key types of products that might have broad appeal and utility for counselors doing research are described next.

■ Ethnography

Spradley (1979, 1980) is perhaps the best guide for traditional ethnographic technique. His reflections on interviewing and participant observation are still fresh and useful. In general, though, traditional ethnography can be characterized as having had very few rules.

Aspects of Traditional Ethnography

- The ethnographer was literally deposited into a culture with very little training in the ways and means of that culture.
- The ethnographer often did not speak the language of the people.
- The ethnographer had no training in ethnographic technique.
- Observation typically lasted for a year, and another year was used to gather, sort, and report the resulting data.

The lack of cultural training and preparation prevented the ethnographer from making presuppositions about the group of interest, thus allowing the ethnographer to view the setting with fresh eyes and ears. Also, because the ethnographer had no formal training in research technique, he or she came into the setting with a heightened sense of awareness. Finally, because the researcher did not know what was important beforehand, everything was potentially important.

For a variety of reasons, the scope and nature of ethnography has changed over the years (LeCompte, 2002). Four of the most important directions of change in ethnography are identified here.

Changes in Ethnographic Research

1. Whereas traditional ethnographic accounts are very objective in nature and even a bit dry, an expansion and experimentation with ethnographic writing style has resulted in writing that has become more literary in nature (Clifford & Marcus, 1986, were important early trendsetters).
2. Ethnography has moved from the exploration of exotic, isolated locales to the exploration of everyday settings (Pratt, 1986), which are a rich source of ethnographic exploration and complement the new forms of writing.
3. Given the proliferation of chat rooms, blogs, and other communicative communities online, ethnographic efforts are being extended to the Internet as an exciting site for ethnographic exploration (see Eichhorn, 2001, and Gatson &

Zweerink, 2002, for a discussion about the techniques and implications of on-line research).

4. Through the approach of autoethnography, researchers are beginning to turn the ethnographic lens on themselves, combining ethnographic precision with reflexive autobiographical insights to yield a rich picture (see, e.g., Ellis & Bochner, 2000).

■ Case Study

The case study is at the heart of many qualitative research projects. In its simplest form, the case study is an examination of a single person in a natural setting, or a single setting in terms of its basic interpersonal dynamics. There are a variety of manifestations and permutations on this basic model. Five of the most popular and useful varieties are presented.

Clinical Case Study

- The first case studies in the social sciences were performed as clinical exercises within the medical and mental health fields and, to this day, comprise an important dimension of medical and mental health inquiry.
- The clinical case study is almost always a detailed report on some puzzling or intractable patient or situation.
- Sacks (1990) is a popular and highly readable example of this form of case study.

Case Study Proper

- The case study proper is the most common form found in qualitative research.
- One person or a small group of people are selected carefully to explore or illustrate some specific point or issue.
- The goal of the case study is depth, not breadth.
- Stake (1995) and Merriam (1998) are two of the best introductions to the art and science of conducting case studies in qualitative research.

Extended Case Study

- The extended case study is preferred over the ordinary case study to deal with particularly complex issues.
- The extended case study has a much wider scope than the case study proper, both in terms of participants and in terms of time and effort.
- Heath (1983) is probably the most familiar example of an extended case study in the qualitative research literature.

Portraiture

- Portraiture is intended not only to gather information and insights about the persons involved, but also to give a picture of who they are (Lawrence-Lightfoot & Davis, 1997).
- Portraiture is very useful when we seek to understand the people involved as living and breathing persons.
- The use of biographical detail, and the artistic use of words and images, combines to yield a rich picture of the topic in question.
- Portraiture is the best resource when it is hard to separate the people from what they do.

Focus Group

- A focus group consists of a group of individuals (usually 4–8 in number) who meet together with a moderator to answer questions and discuss a given topic.
- Focus groups were first modeled after group therapy when therapists realized that a group of clients might address a topic in greater depth than any given individual.
- This propensity for depth via group participation is at the heart of the concept of focus groups.
- The use of focus groups is evolving to include computer-mediated and online settings (Franklin & Lowry, 2001).
- Morgan (1998) has been one of the pioneers in the use of focus groups in qualitative research, and his work is an excellent starting place.

Each of these five case study products provides context-rich information about a person, group of persons, or setting. Consider the example of Heath's (1983) research in which an extended case study was chosen over the case study proper to deal with the complex issues related to race, communication patterns, and children's behavioral problems.

EXAMPLE

Extended Case Study

In her study, Heath (1983) was concerned about the inability of White teachers and minority children to interact properly in a rural Southern town. The children were passively aggressive and uncommunicative. To get to the root of the problem, Heath launched an in-depth study. She spent time within the minority community, learning and understanding communication patterns. As a result, she found that White teachers and minority students were operating under two independent and conflicting communication models. In fact, the children were trying their hardest to be respectful and polite with teachers who were unintentionally insulting their intelligence and abilities. These findings would not have been found had the case study not become as extensive as it was.

For tips on running focus groups, look for the link from the USAID Web site:

▶ www.dec.org/partners/evalweb/resources/tipsseries.cfm

■ Grounded Theory

Grounded theory is perhaps the most technical form of qualitative research. In its original form (Glaser & Strauss, 1967), grounded theory was designed as a way to generate theory from the bottom up, so to speak. A number of steps highlight the process of grounded theory research.

Process of Conducting Grounded Theory

1. Set aside any assumptions or presuppositions about the area of study.
2. Collect observational data.
3. Compare data as they begin to accumulate and as the rudiments of a conceptual framework began to take shape.
4. Place new data where theoretically appropriate.
5. Stop creating or modifying conceptual categories when it becomes apparent that all new data can be easily placed and saturation has been reached.
6. Articulate the theory in its final form.

Grounded theory has continued to evolve and develop as a method (see Charmaz, 2000, for a general discussion on this matter). At the same time, there has been a parting of ways between the original two founders of the method. Characteristics of the Glaser and Strauss approaches are described next.

The Glaser Approach (Glaser, 1978)

- Glaser created a theoretical and more flexible approach to grounded theory.
- Grounded theory was a skill that a person developed over long years of practice, and the acquisition of said skills and insights could not be rushed or encapsulated in any sort of algorithmic manner.
- Glaser emphasized the art of grounded theory.

The Strauss Approach (Strauss, 1995)

- Strauss (1995) was concerned with the development of grounded theory as a practical tool.

- Along with Corbin (Strauss & Corbin, 1998), Strauss created a handbook of clear and precise steps that the grounded theory researcher could follow.
- Although this approach has been attacked as being too mechanical, it nonetheless has served as the basis for an enormous amount of work in grounded theory.

■ Material Analysis

Qualitative researchers do not get their data just from interviews and observations. Sometimes, they study the material products that people and cultures create. Material sources can be classified as formal or informal. Formal sources tend to be archived and usually are official documents. Informal sources typically come from the wealth and depth of documents and artifacts that make up popular culture. Some of the possibilities are listed here.

Formal Sources of Qualitative Data

- Birth announcements.
- Death announcements.
- Marriage licenses.
- Real estate transactions.
- Court proceedings.

Informal Sources of Qualitative Data

- TV.
- Comic books.
- Movie posters.
- Blogs.

Hill (1993) is an excellent starting place for qualitative researchers interested in accessing and using archival data in their work, and Hodder (2000) is a good introduction to the exploration and study of our reservoir of material culture.

THE ROLE AND FUTURE OF QUALITATIVE RESEARCH IN COUNSELING

The role and future of qualitative research ultimately must be decided by counseling researchers. It is up to these researchers to examine the field and apply these methods to their areas of concern and questions of interest. In the meantime, however, here are three thoughts on how the discipline of counseling and qualitative research will continue to be intertwined.

■ Qualitative Research Tackles Complex Questions and Issues

Counselors deal with human beings, and human beings are complex creatures. Therefore, it makes sense that research in counseling might often lean in the direction of exploring issues in depth. The ability to conduct research at such depth is one of the main strengths of qualitative research.

■ Counselors and Qualitative Researchers Share Similarities

Counseling, as a field, has always been concerned with issues of meaning. Therefore, it seems natural that a mode of inquiry that foregrounds meaning is a natural fit with counselors seeking to do research.

■ Qualitative Research Provides Possibility and Freedom

Traditional research in the social sciences has been concerned with finding and isolating the effects of characteristics that can be applied to a broad spectrum of persons. Although this endeavor is certainly valuable, it does not address all research needs in a field as rich and complex as counseling. Counselor researchers need to be able to tackle not only the typical, but also the possible. They need to be able to look at individuals as individuals and study them in real depth. It is this ability to seek and use depth that makes qualitative research methods so potentially valuable to counselor researchers.

Chapter 23: Key Term

► Participant observation
► Ethnography
► Qualitative research

What Are the Special Topics and Important Trends That Counselors Might Encounter?

A Look at Consultation

Jocelyn Gregoire
Leslie Slagel
Duquesne University

In This Chapter

▶ *Historical Evolution of Consultation*
- Clinical or Expert Approach
- Organizational Consultation
- Client-Centered Consultation
- Total Quality Management Approach
- Social Work Perspective
- Definition of Consultation
- The Counselor as Consultant
- Stages in Consultation

▶ *Theories of Consultation*
- Person-Centered Theory of Consultation
- Learning Theory of Consultation
- Gestalt Theory of Consultation
- Psychoanalytic Theory of Consultation
- Chaos Theory of Consultation

▶ *The Consultation Relationship*
- Consultant-Centered Orientation
- System-Centered Orientation

▶ *Mental Health Consultation*
- Definition of Mental Health Consultation
- Basic Characteristics of Mental Health Consultation

- Psychodynamic Orientation of Mental Health Counseling
- Types of Mental Health Consultation

▶ *Behavioral Consultation*
- Definition of Behavioral Consultation
- Characteristics of Behavioral Consultation
- Bergan and Kratochwill's Model of Behavioral Consultation

▶ *Organizational Consultation*
- Definition of Organizational Consultation
- Use of Systems Theory
- Diagnosing Organizational Problems
- Content and Process Consultation
- Organizational Paradigm
- Paradigm Shift

▶ *School-Based Consultation*
- Collaboration
- Types of School Consultation
- Theoretical Approach to School Consultation

▶ *Chapter Summary*

HISTORICAL EVOLUTION OF CONSULTATION

At its beginnings in the 1940s, consultation was a direct helping approach that occurred within the dyadic consultant–consultee relationship. Although the aim of consultation remains the same today, the process has evolved to include a triadic interaction among the consultant, consultee, and client or client system. Recent trends in consultation reflect the transformation of the practice. The systemic perspective, for example, assumes that the consultant must examine the interrelations among all components of the client system, make suggestions for change, and assist the consultee in viewing the system contextually to solidify interventions for change. Our aims in this chapter are to provide a short historical review of the development of consultation, address the consultation relationship, and discuss major theories and models of consultation.

■ Clinical or Expert Approach

Some scholars trace the emergence of consultation to the period between 1940 and 1950 (Kurpius & Robinson, 1978), others, however, locate its earliest beginnings in the 13th-century doctor–patient relationship (Gallessich, 1982). This early model of consultation, which has been widely practiced in the medical community from the mid-19th century to the present, is characterized by a hierarchical relationship in which the consultant controls the intervention by managing the nature of the interview and systematically reinforcing behaviors that support his or her goals (Brown, Pryzwansky, & Schulte, 2006). However, the advent of newer approaches to consultation, coupled with the aversion of many professionals toward the authoritarian philosophy germane to this model, gradually brought about a decline in the popularity of the clinical-expert approach (Schulte & Osborne, 2003).

■ Organizational Consultation

Representing an evolution of consultation from a dyadic to a triadic process, the organizational model can be linked to Lewin's (1951) field theory and to the system theory of Bertalanffy (1968). In the organizational model, the consultation process rests on the humanistic assumption that to achieve success, a relationship must promote coequality during the change process (Brown et al., 2006).

■ Client-Centered Consultation

In his book *The Theory and Practice of Mental Health Consultation,* which now has become a classic in the field of consultation, Caplan (1970) coined the term *client-centered consultation.* He believed that the consultant–consultee relationship should be nonhierarchical and coequal in nature. However, Caplan did not totally distance himself from the authoritarian model because of his belief that, at times, consultants might have to bypass consultees' wishes to make sure that the consultant's views are reflected in the intervention (Schulte & Osborne, 2003).

■ Total Quality Management Approach

Championed by Deming (1993), the total quality management approach has tremendously influenced management and leadership theory, as well as ideas about organizational business and education. This approach rests on four basic principles.

Principles of Total Quality Management Consultation

1. Setting long-term goals.
2. Eliminating fear, jealousy, revenge, and anger from management and the change process.
3. Eliminating practices that hinder self-confidence.
4. Promoting every chance that will enhance people's pride in their work and the improvements that take place.

■ Social Work Perspective

Social work is another tradition that has had an impact on the evolution of consultation. One of the unique contributions that social work has offered is a systemic, collaborative perspective to the practice of consultation. Working from this perspective, Homan (2004) suggested that situations of interest are examined within a larger context, and it is through collaborative interventions that consultation takes shape and instigates needed changes. Similar views also have been expressed by Steffy and Lindle (1994), who emphasized the importance of a systemic approach involving the community.

■ Definition of Consultation

As the brief historical review has shown, the notion of consultation differs according to the perspective from which it is viewed. Moreover, among the body of literature addressing consultation, an authoritative definition of the practice of consultation is lacking (Kurpius & Robinson, 1978). Most definitions of consultation, however, generally concur that (a) the goal of consultation is to solve problems; (b) consultation is tripartite in nature; (c) consultation involves a consultant, a consultee, and a client system; and (d) consultation is aimed at improving both the client system and the consultee. Dougherty (2005) expressed this concise, widely accepted definition of consultation:

> **Consultation:** "[A] process in which a human service professional assists a consultee with a work-related (or caretaking-related) problem with a client system, with the goal of helping both the consultee and the client system in some specified way" (p. 11).

■ The Counselor as Consultant

Due to their professional responsibilities, counselors provide an array of counseling services (Randolph & Graun, 1988). However, it was not until the late 1960s and early 1970s that textbooks and journal articles began to foster the notion of consultation activities as a function of counselors' work-related activities (Caplan, 1970; Dinkmeyer, 1973; Faust, 1968). In 1973, Congress passed the Community Mental Center Act, which encouraged helping professionals gradually to substitute their approach from individual and small group remediation activity to the adoption of a more developmental and preventive one (Jackson & Hayes, 1993).

■ Stages in Consultation

Literature about consultation commonly portrays it as a problem-solving process that involves a series of stages (Bergan & Kratochwill, 1990; Hansen, Himes, & Meier, 1990, Kurpius, 1978). Brown et al. (2006) proposed an eight-stage process that includes the following steps.

Brown et al.'s Stages of Consultation

1. Entry into the organization.
2. Initiation of the consultation relationship.
3. Assessment.
4. Problem definition and goal setting.
5. Strategy selection.
6. Strategy implementation.
7. Evaluation.
8. Termination.

Block (1981) presented five phases of the consultation process. These are described briefly here.

Block's Five Phases of the Consultation Process

1. *Entry and contracting* includes an initial contact between the consultant and client when the consultant's skills are assessed, goals are set, the client's strengths are evaluated, and areas of improvement are identified.
2. *Data collection and diagnosis* occurs when the consultant attempts to make sense of the problems and determines who will be participating in this phase of the project, what information is vital, and how information will be collected.
3. *Feedback and decision to act* refers to the period when the consultant pays close attention to the concerns and feedback of the consultee and mutually agrees on the areas of change.
4. *Implementation* occurs when the consultant proceeds with the appropriate intervention model that will foster change in the mutually agreed areas.
5. *Extension, recycle, or termination* follows the initial implementation of the intervention, and a reevaluation is done to assess its effectiveness. The results will determine whether a new contract should be discussed or appropriate steps toward termination should be initiated.

Block's model is one conceptualization of the stages of consultation. In an effort to explain how a consultant enters a system, facilitates change, and leaves, Kurpius, Fuqua, and Rozecki (1993) proposed another six-stage model of the consultation process.

Kurpius et al.'s Stages of Consultation

1. *Preentry* is the first stage during which the consultant conceptualizes and articulates to self and to others what he or she has been asked to do.
2. *Entry, problem exploration, and contracting* takes place when the consultant makes contact with the consulting system, explores the problem, and defines the contract between the consultant and the consulting system.
3. *Information gathering, problem confirmation, and goal setting* is the period during which the consultant collects reliable and valid data that are analyzed, synthesized, and interpreted to be able to confirm, deny, or revise the initial identification of the problem. Outcomes of this stage allow the consultant to set achievable goals for the organization and to begin to examine methods for change.
4. *Solution searching and intervention selection* refers to the period when the consultant begins to determine strategies that will push the system to make deep changes and prevent future problems.
5. *Evaluation* allows the consultant to know what worked, what did not work, and what his or her strengths and weaknesses are. Evaluation can be summative (e.g., statistical analysis of the behaviors that were to be changed), formative (e.g., ongoing evaluations by the members involved in the consultation process as it is happening), or both.
6. *Termination* occurs when the consultation relationship comes to an end either because success is pending or because the goals were not met. In either case, the ending of any relationship involves loss, and individuals should be given the opportunity to share feelings about ending the consulting relationship.

THEORIES OF CONSULTATION

Theories of consultation provide a conceptual framework from which the consultant practices. They vary depending on whether the emphasis is on the types of interventions; the organizational context; the needs of the client; the relationship among the consultant, consultee, and client; and the attribution of the solution or problem. Over the past 60 years, not only has the consultative process evolved, but the theoretical underpinnings of the practice have been developed, researched, and tested. In this section we look at five theoretical approaches to consultation:

- Person-centered theory.
- Learning theory.
- Gestalt theory.
- Psychoanalytic theory.
- Chaos theory.

■ Person-Centered Theory of Consultation

The purpose of person-centered theory is to facilitate the change process in a nondirective fashion while implementing the core conditions of empathy, genuineness, and positive regard. Interventions include running groups whose aim is to encourage individuals to more effectively hear one another's points of view and an underlying belief of this approach is that the natural process of the group will assist the system in healing itself.

■ Learning Theory of Consultation

Learning-oriented consultation is grounded in behavioral, cognitive-behavioral, and social learning theories. Consultants may be oriented toward one learning theory more than another, which affects conceptualization of the problem and intervention. Behaviorally oriented learning consultants focus on concretely defining the problem and developing specific strategies to reduce incidence of the problem, whereas cognitively oriented consultants look for problematic beliefs that can be addressed through reeducation, self-observation, and cognitive restructuring. Social learning consultants define the consultee's issues in terms of behavioral, interpersonal, and environmental factors and then identify resources that consultees can use to manage future problems. Basic counseling skills are crucial to the beginning of the process. Resistance by the consultee is believed to be a natural part of the process and may require the consultant to adjust the goals to better meet the consultee's needs.

Gestalt Theory of Consultation

The main goal of the Gestalt theory of consultation is to enhance the experience of the consultee and others involved in the consultative process in an effort to decrease defenses and reduce neurotic behaviors. Introducing the consultant into the system disrupts established boundaries and is, in itself, transformative. The consultant enters the system to encourage the expression of feelings and the loosening of boundaries in an effort to promote increased awareness and true encounter with self and others. The consultant is responsible for helping the consultee embrace fears present in various aspects of the experience. Termination is a naturally occurring process that begins when fears subside, awareness is increased, and resistance to the initial problem has been transformed into positive solutions.

Psychoanalytic Theory of Consultation

Implicit and unconscious aspects of a client or client system's behavior support manifest problems. Confrontation is not believed to be the most effective method of intervention because consultees may not be aware of the unconscious roots of the problem. The main goal of the psychoanalytic approach is to make sense of the unconscious processes that underlie the problems. Exposing unconscious processes may be accomplished through direct or triadic interventions. Direct interventions involve the consultant giving feedback to an individual or a group as a whole; triadic interventions imply that members of the system interact with one another as well as the consultant about the problem. Problems are seen as the projections of the individual's unconscious processes. Resistance is an important defense that protects the individual or the system from unnecessary stress. Termination occurs when the consultant is assured that the changes made to the system are stable.

Chaos Theory of Consultation

Chaos theory is based on the belief that the world is largely unpredictable; error in systems is perhaps the only predictable component. Understanding the system-specific chaos as it exists at all levels is the first task of the consultant. Chaotic variables present at one level may directly affect variables at another level of the system. Consultants help consultees expect and value change. A primary goal of consultation within the chaos theory approach is helping consultees use the unpredictable nature of the system to risk new approaches to solutions. Termination occurs when consultees can consistently develop positive ways of dealing with chaos rather than resisting it.

THE CONSULTATION RELATIONSHIP

Styles of consultation refer to the ways the consultant operates in the consulting relationship. Depending on his or her style, the consultant may choose either a consultant-centered orientation or a system-centered orientation to enter into the consultation process (Neukrug, 2003).

■ Consultant-Centered Orientation

In this orientation, the emphasis is on the consultant offering suggestions and advice for system change. Thus, the consultant is identified by the following characteristics.

Roles of the Consultant in the Consultant-Centered Orientation

- *Expert consultant* takes the responsibility to come into the system for the purpose of finding a cure (Schein, 1969).
- *Prescriptive consultant* gathers relevant data, makes a diagnosis of the problem, and proposes solutions to the consultee (Kurpius, 1978).
- *Trainer or educator* teaches or trains the staff of the system into which he or she has been hired.

■ System-Centered Orientation

In the system-centered orientation, the consultant assists others to use their resources for system change. The following characteristics can be observed in consultants who espouse this orientation.

Roles of the Consultant in the System-Centered Orientation

- *Consultant as negotiator* facilitates communication and understanding among individuals within the system and helps them resolve conflicts among themselves.
- *Consultant as collaborator* uses his or her expertise and, relying on the individuals in the system, works collaboratively with the consultee to offer input into the problems and solutions to facilitate the change process (Kurpius, 1978).
- *Process-oriented consultant* functions on the convictions that he or she is not in possession of all the answers, and that at times it is necessary to withhold expertise so that the consultees' self-esteem and developed sense of ownership of the problem can help individuals in the system find their own solution (Schein, 1969).

For more information on the consultative relationship, refer to the *Journal of Educational and Psychological Consultation* at

▶ http://www.leaonline.com/loi/jepc

MENTAL HEALTH CONSULTATION

There are four major models of consultation (i.e., mental health consultation, behavioral consultation, organizational consultation, and school consultation), and among them, mental health consultation is one of the most popular models of consultation. This model, which is also known as psychological consultation, attempts to promote the mental health of the community through consultants in a preventative way (Dougherty, 1990). Rooted in psychiatry, the most influential figure in the field of psychological consultation has been Caplan, whose ideas are still pervasive and reflect an environmental and psychodynamic perspective (Brown et al., 2006). Main goals of a mental health model of consultation are to focus on the performance of the client and to expand consultees' knowledge, skill, and objectivity as related to the remediation and prevention of the problem at hand (Gelso & Fretz, 2001).

■ Definition of Mental Health Consultation

According to Caplan (1970), mental health consultation can be defined this way:

Mental health consultation: "[A] process of interaction between two professional persons—the consultant, who is a specialist, and the consultee, who invokes the consultant's help in regard to a current work problem with which he is having some difficulty and which he has decided is within the other's area of specialized competence" (p. 19).

■ Basic Characteristics of Mental Health Consultation

Mental health consultation occurs among professionals to assist in the mental health aspects of work-related problems that concern a client or an organization. According to Caplan, there are some basic characteristics inherent to mental health consultation, some of which are listed here (Dougherty, 2005).

Characteristics of the Mental Health Consultation Relationship

- Two professionals enter into a consultative relationship to deal with a mental-health-related problem of a lay client or a program for such clients.
- The basic relationship between the two professionals is collaborative, nonauthoritarian, and nonhierarchical.
- Personal and private material is not permitted in the consultation relationship.

Characteristics of the Mental Health Consultation Process

- Consultation usually is arranged in a series of two or three sessions; dependence is not fostered with continuing contact beyond the current concern.
- Consultation is expected to continue indefinitely as the consultees become more competent and sophisticated.
- The twin goals of consultation are to help consultees handle the current work difficulty and prepare them to master similar, potential problems.
- Successful consultation may have a therapeutic effect by increasing consultees' feelings of self-worth because of successful job performance.
- Consultation does not require that the consultant have specialized knowledge about the topic for which the consultee needs help.

In the collaborative, nonhierarchical approach espoused by the mental health consultation approach, there are a number of implications for both the consultee and the consultant. A few of these are mentioned next.

Responsibilities of the Consultee in Mental Health Consultation

- Define the work problem as being mental-health-related.
- Accept or reject the consultant's ideas or suggestions.

Responsibilities of the Consultant in Mental Health Consultation

- Accepts neither professional nor administrative responsibility for the consultee's work or for the outcome of the client's case.
- Does not enter the consultation process with predetermined body of information that he or she intends to impart to a particular consultee.
- Discusses personal problems only as they relate to the client's case and work setting.
- Reverts to the role of psychiatrist, psychologist, or social worker and gives advice or takes action when consultee's actions are endangering the welfare of the client.

Psychodynamic Orientation of Mental Health Counseling

Based on the belief that behavior is a product of unconscious motivation and that most childhood experiences create issues that result in inner conflicts that affect behavior, Caplan assumed a psychodynamic orientation for his mental health model of consultation. The consultant is expected to use an indirect approach to deal with these issues. Transfer of effect and one-downmanship are key terms pertaining to the psychodynamic orientation and are defined as follows (Dougherty, 2005):

Transfer of effect: What is learned in one situation should be transferred and used in future similar situations.

One-downmanship: The relationship between the consultant and the consultee is one of equals or peers.

Types of Mental Health Consultation

Caplan (1970) identified four categories of consultation utilized in mental health settings: client-centered case consultation, consultee-centered case consultation, program-centered administrative consultation, and consultee-centered administrative consultation (Mendoza, 1993). The focus, the identifiable goals, and the roles and responsibilities of the consultant of each type are listed next.

Client-Centered Case Consultation

- The focus is on developing plans and strategies that will help a specific client.
- The primary goal is to help solve the client's difficulties and subsequently to help the consultee gain skills to handle similar future cases.
- The consultee experiences the consultant as a coequal peer and collaborator and is free to accept, adapt, or reject the consultant's recommendations.
- The consultant is viewed as a responsible expert to assess and diagnose the problems and prescribe a course of actions for the consultee's client.

Consultee-Centered Case Consultation

- The focus is on specific attributes of the consultee, such as lack of knowledge, lack of skill, lack of confidence, and lack of objectivity that are hindering his or her functioning with the client (Brown et al., 2006; Dougherty 2005).
- The primary goal is to help the consultee remediate weaknesses in his or her performance that are contributing to the difficulties with the client.
- The consultee is responsible for the case while seeking to improve and enrich his or her understanding and emotional mastery of the case.
- The consultant plays the role of an expert detective who, through active listening, investigates the cognitive and emotional problem of the consultee, and who

also educates and trains the consultee on how to solve current and future similar problems (Dougherty, 2005).

Program-Centered Administrative Consultation

- The focus is on helping the consultee deal with a current problem of program development or organizational functioning.
- The goal is to facilitate the creation of new programs or policies that will improve on the existing ones.
- The consultee initiates the consultation process and is the primary person to whom the consultant provides recommendations and submits the written report.
- The consultant acts as a data collector and an action planner who provides recommendations to the organization in the form of a written report.

Consultee-Centered Administration Consultation

- The focus is on improving the professional performance of the organization's administrative staff as it relates to a specific program or policy.
- The goal is to help the administration develop professional competency and problem-solving skills that will enable it to deal with current difficulties in organizational planning, program development, management, and policy implementation.
- The consultee, or the administrator who hired the consultant, receives the recommendations of the consultant and applies, alters, or implements them as they fit.
- The consultant enters the organization; promotes relationship building; examines the social climate of the institution; develops an intervention for individuals, groups, or the entire organization; and assesses the outcomes (Dougherty, 2005).

 Check out this site for a Microsoft PowerPoint presentation on mental health consultation, theory, cases, and ethics:

▶ http://edtech.tennessee.edu/itc/grants/twt2000/modules/wconwill/ mental_health.ppt

---

BEHAVIORAL CONSULTATION

Behavioral consultation was founded on social learning theory and focuses on the overt behaviors of the consultee and the client (Parsons & Kahn, 2005). The primary focus of behavioral consultation is to change specific behaviors in clients or client systems and consultees. The method involves clearly defined steps geared toward problem identification, analysis, plan implementation, and plan evaluation (Brigman, Mullis, Webb, & White, 2005). The goals of consultation may include but are not limited to the following.

Goals of Behavioral Consultation

- Enhance the consultee's professional functioning.
- Help the consultee make positive changes in the client's environment.
- Change the environment to promote behavioral changes (Conoley & Conoley, 1992).

■ Definition of Behavioral Consultation

Combining ideas from Keller (1981), Dougherty (2005) offered the following definition of behavioral consultation:

> **Behavioral consultation:** "[A] relationship whereby services consistent with a behavioral orientation are provided either indirectly to a client or a system (through the mediation of important others in the client's environment or of those charged with the system's well-being) or directly by training consultees to enhance their skills with clients or systems" (p. 222).

■ Characteristics of Behavioral Consultation

Broadly speaking, behavioral consultation is a problem-solving process grounded in the scientific view of human behavior that integrates philosophies of behavioral psychology and learning theories. Although approaches to behavioral consultation vary according to the consultant's preferences (Wallace & Hall, 1996), there are some basic tenets that characterize this model of consultation. The following list identifies those key tenets (Harrison, 2004).

Tenets of Behavioral Consultation Interventions

- They are indirect services specially geared toward cases and clients even when they take place in organizational settings.
- They are most often used to solve problems as well as improve competency in the consultee.
- Interventions are aimed at altering the client's or the consultee's behaviors and bringing about changes in organizations.
- The length of the consulting relationship varies from minutes to months.

- The consultant–consultee relationship ranges from collegial to hierarchical, with the consultant having some control in the relationship.
- The consultant should have a degree of expert knowledge in learning principles, social learning theory, and behavioral technology to design, implement, and assess interventions.
- The consultant's major role ranges from a facilitator to an expert who imparts psychological information and principles to consultees.
- Primary tasks of the consultant include helping the consultee problem solve and enhancing the probability that the consultee will accept the consultant's recommendations.
- The client and the consultee goals need to be defined in behavioral terms.
- Most approaches emphasize direct observation techniques and focus on present influences on overt behavior.
- Interventions and evaluations lend themselves to empirical testing.

Bergan and Kratochwill's Model of Behavioral Consultation

Bergan (1977) developed the behavioral consultation model that was later revised and extended by Bergan and Kratochwill (1990). They observed that three elements interact with each other during the consultation process: the consultant's role, the consultee's role, and the client's role.

The Consultant's Role

- Assess the client's problematic behavior and its effects.
- Set up and help clients walk through the various stages of the consultation process.
- Develop intervention strategies and make sure that they are implemented.
- Use the authority of an expert to encourage the consultee to comply with the goals of the consultation.

The Consultee's Role

- Explain the client's problem that demands the consultation request.
- Judge the legitimacy of suggested behavioral plans and assess their value.
- Evaluate the client's behavior or performance and execute behavioral plans designed to positively alter behavior.
- Monitor the client's behavioral changes following consultation.

The Client's Role

- Cooperate and commit to the goals of the consultation.
- Receive and respond to the behavioral conditions set up through the consultation process.

Bergan's problem-solving consultation model proceeds through a series of four major stages that provide the framework and orientation for the consultation process. Each of these stages has its own specific objectives and tasks. The stages are the problem identification stage, the problem analysis stage, the plan implementation stage, and the problem evaluation stage (Bergan, 1977).

 For more information on behavioral consultation, visit the Web site of the *International Journal of Behavioral Consultation and Therapy* at

► http://www.ijbct.com/

ORGANIZATIONAL CONSULTATION

An organization is constituted when a group of people decide to work together to achieve a common goal (Hanna, 1988). There are various forces, both internal and external, that are at work in every organization to influence its growth. Consequently, most organizations are involved in an endless process of adaptation, problem solving, and planning that compels them to constantly seek the expertise of organizational consultants who embrace a variety of discipline and approaches.

■ Definition of Organizational Consultation

Viewing organizational consultation as a comprehensive process, Dougherty (1990) proposed the following definition:

> **Organizational consultation:** "[T]he process in which a professional, functioning either internally or externally to an organization, provides assistance of a technical, diagnostic/perspective, or facilitative nature to an individual or group from the organization in order to enhance the organization's ability to deal with change and maintain or enhance its effectiveness in some designated way" (p. 187).

■ Use of Systems Theory

Embedded within every organization is the philosophical principle of systems theory that views "the whole organization as one large entity or system composed of smaller, interconnected divisions" (Wallace & Hall, 1996, p. 62). Those smaller units have been described by Brown, Pryzwansky, and Schulte (2006) as subsystems, and together they form part of an **organizational structure,** or "a strategic configuration of organizational functions, jobs, and policies in a pattern that best serves organizational goals" (Wallace & Hall, p. 63). Consequently, organizational consultants are well advised to take into account the systems implications of the consultation problems.

Diagnosing Organizational Problems

Organizational diagnosis is the process through which both the consultants and the consultees seek to grasp the dynamic, problematic, organizational situations. The more accurate the diagnosis of the processes is the greater is the assurance of the success of the organizational interventions (Kurpius et al., 1993). Although consultants are not limited to the use of only one specific diagnostic framework and corresponding techniques, they do need to follow some steps or guidelines for diagnosing organizational problems.

Steps for Diagnosing Organizational Problems

- *Problem recognition* is an acknowledgment of the existence of a problem that needs to be addressed.
- *Selecting consultants* refers to the hiring of an internal or external consultant for identification, assessment, and conceptualization of the organizational problems.
- *Data gathering* entails initiating the collection of information about the problems and separating casual factors.
- *Analyzing valid information* is an exploration, synthesis, and analysis of valid data to determine the relation between organizational problems and diagnostic discoveries.
- *Diagnostic feedback* involves analyzing and synthesizing the findings and presenting them in meaningful formulations to the consultee, so that conceptual frameworks for corrective actions can be developed and implemented.

Content and Process Consultation

According to Schein (1987), organizational consultation can be either content oriented or process oriented. These two can be described as follows:

Content-oriented consultation: Implies that the consultee lacks understanding and awareness and, therefore, needs the consultant to provide expertise to successfully solve the problems.

Process-oriented consultation: "[A] set of activities on the part of the consultant that help the client (consultee) to perceive, understand, and act upon the process events that occur in the client's (consultee's) environment" (p. 34).

Schein proposed two types of content-oriented consultation in the organizational model: (a) the purchase of expertise model, and (b) the doctor–patient model. Characteristics of these two types of approach are mentioned next.

Aspects of the Content-Oriented Consultation

- The consultee knows what the problem is, how to solve it, and who can be of help.
- The conslutee is given information and taught skills through an education or training approach.
- The consultee knows that there is a problem, but is unable to identify it.
- The consultant diagnoses the problem and prescribes a cure.

Schein's process-oreinted model involves both consultant and consultee working as a team to identify, assess, and define the problem; collaboratively, they also explore solutions to the problem. Several factors need to be considered when engaging in process-oriented consultation.

Factors to Be Considered in Process-Oriented Consultation

- Consultee must own the problem and commit to actively participating in the problem-solving process.
- Consultee's insights and judgment must be reflected in all decisions and solutions.
- Consultee must be cognitively and behaviorally competent to perform consultation tasks and propose solutions.
- Consultee should be able to achieve necessary skills to solve future organization problems.

■ Organizational Paradigm

Most organizations function on rules and policies, operating structures and production methods, and beliefs and values that are passed on from one generation to another, especially when they lead to success. Sometimes, these organizational elements evolve into unchallenged rules or an organizational paradigm, which Baker (1992) defined as follows:

> **Paradigm:** "[A] set of rules and regulations (written or unwritten) that does two things: (1) it establishes or defines boundaries; and (2) it tells you how to behave inside the boundaries in order to be successful" (p. 32).

■ Paradigm Shift

When their products fail to satisfy their environments, organizations need to resort to a paradigm shift if they wish to survive. A paradigm shift signifies a modification in the way people used to think when they try to give meaning to their situations (Fuqua & Kurpius, 1993). Although it is not always easy for consultants to identify obsolete paradigms and replace them with better practices, some guidelines can be followed to facilitate the process (Wallace & Hall, 1996).

Guidelines for Creating a Paradigm Shift

- Organizational members must acknowledge outdated beliefs and be open to an alteration of their paradigm.
- Consultants and organizational members work collaboratively to identify and analyze repetitive patterns of behavior that are inconsistent with environmental demands.
- Consultants must remember that a paradigm shift responds to predictable events, trends, and conditions, and, therefore, must anticipate the organization's future.
- Consultants must expect and deal with strong resistance to the paradigm shift.
- Consultants must help organizations get rid of their unrealistic or fearful beliefs that paradigm shifts are highly risky change strategies.
- Consultants must help organizational members handle and integrate effectively into the organizational infrastructure the changes brought about by the paradigm shift.

✓ See the following site for a listing of process consultation information resources:

▶ http://www.headstartinfo.org/infocenter/guides/processconsultation.htm

SCHOOL-BASED CONSULTATION

In the school systems, counselors commonly take on the dual roles of counselor and consultant. As counselors, they help the individual student function in the school environment, and as consultants, they work with a broader range of people, including families, teachers, administrators, and community agencies to help change the environment. Most consultees' (e.g., parents, teachers, or administrators) issues involve a person, system, or both (Dinkmeyer & Carlson, 2001). Through the process of consultation, the consultant provides parents and teachers the knowledge and skills to become more objective and self-confident when working with students to achieve academic success as well as personal and social development (Harrison, 2004). Dinkmeyer and Carlson provided four characteristics that are inherent to school consultation.

Characteristics of School Consultation

- Information, observations, and concerns about a problem are shared between the consultant and the consultee.
- Tentative hypotheses are developed to change the situation.
- Joint planning and collaboration occurs between consultant and consultee.
- Hypotheses or recommendations reflect and respect the uniqueness of the child, the teacher, and the setting.

School-based consultation can be conceptualized in stages or as a process. Harrison offered a generic blueprint of the phases of school consultation.

Generic School Consultation Stages

- A request for help from the consultee to the consultant occurs and expectations of the relationship are established.
- Boundaries are determined.
- The consultant determines who owns the problem.
- The consultant gathers information to understand the problem.
- Goals are established to meet the desired change.
- Strategies must be chosen, applied, assessed, and customized as needed.
- Termination occurs when all parties are in agreement.

■ Collaboration

According to Brown et al. (2006) there is a movement to make the consultation process more collaborative in all stages with the exception of the intervention phase. Collaboration parallels consultation in terms of process issues such as entry, developing relationships, and obtaining permission. In consultation, the responsibility of the outcomes lies with the consultee. Similarly, in collaboration, consultees assume primary responsibility except that accountability for the outcome is shared between the collaborating partners (Brown et al.). In a collaborative relationship, there is more than one person involved in the diagnosis and treatment plan. Each participant may not share in equal parts of the decision making and roles within the organization. However, it is imperative to have a successful working relationship to produce a positive outcome (Harrison, 2004).

See Chapter 3 for more on the importance of collaboration for school counselors.

■ Types of School Consultation

School-based consultation can be conceptualized as involving direct service, indirect service, or both (Dougherty, 2005). According to Dougherty, consultation is an indirect service to a student and attempts to help others work successfully with the student. Collaboration combines indirect and direct services to students. Parsons and Meyers (1984) defined these four categories of school consultation.

Categories of School Consultation

- *Direct service to the client* suggests that consultants seek to adjust the behavior, attitudes, or feelings of a particular client or clients who present a problem or problems. Information is gathered by the consultant using behavioral observation, individual testing, and interviewing.
- *Indirect service to the client* suggests that consultants seek to adjust the behavior, attitudes, or feelings of a particular client or clients who present a problem or problems. The information needed to address the client's issues is gathered by the consultee to be shared with the consultant.
- *Service to the consultee* suggests that the consultant's goal is to change the behavior, attitude, or feelings of the consultee.
- *Service to the system* suggests that service by the consultant is to target and improve the functioning of the system as a whole, resulting in improved mental health for both client and individual consultee in the organization.

■ Theoretical Approach to School Consultation

Consultants within the school system often take a behavioral, cognitive, or humanistic approach to consultation. Conoley and Conoley (1992) suggested that the consultant chooses an intervention that corresponds with the theoretical beliefs of the consultee. When choosing an intervention that closely matches the theoretical orientation of the consultee, the acceptability of the intervention is increased.

 See the following Web site for a handout outlining major approaches to school-based consultation:

▶ http://www.education.uiowa.edu/schpsych/handouts/school%20consultation.pdf

CHAPTER SUMMARY

Consultation continues to be an evolving discipline, and it is an increasingly popular career avenue that trained counselors in a variety of settings pursue. Understanding the various systems of consultation, including mental health, behavioral, organizational, and school based, as well as the roles of the consultant, consultee, and client, can aid counselors who wish to expand the uses of their professional training.

Chapter 24: Key Terms

- ▶ Consultation
- ▶ Transfer of effect
- ▶ One-downmanship
- ▶ Mental health consultation
- ▶ Behavioral consultation

- ▶ Organizational consultation
- ▶ Organizational structure
- ▶ Organizational diagnosis
- ▶ Content-oriented consultation

- ▶ Process-oriented consultation
- ▶ Paradigm

Crisis Intervention in Counseling

Rick A. Myer
Duquesne University

Pam Cogdal
University of Memphis

In This Chapter

▶ *Understanding Crisis and Crisis Intervention*
  - Definition of Crisis
  - Types of Crisis
  - Crisis in Culture
  - Characteristics of an Effective Crisis Counselor

▶ *Differences Among Psychological Emergency, Crisis, and Trauma*
  - Psychological Emergency
  - Crisis
  - Trauma

▶ *Crisis Response: The Six-Step Model of Intervention*
  - Step 1: Define the Problem
  - Step 2: Ensure Safety
  - Step 3: Provide Support
  - Step 4: Examine Alternatives
  - Step 5: Make Plans
  - Step 6: Obtain Commitment

▶ *Crisis Assessment: Using the Triage Assessment Form*
  - Assessment of Crisis Reactions
  - Severity Scales

▶ *Trends in Crisis Intervention*
  - Contextual Models
  - Strength-Based Approach
  - Systemic Approach

UNDERSTANDING CRISIS AND CRISIS INTERVENTION

The catastrophic 1942 fire at Cocoanut Grove Melody Lounge in Boston that killed 492 people gave birth to the field of crisis intervention. In helping survivors cope with the loss, Lindemann (1944) developed a model for bereavement that has served as a practical foundation for crisis intervention. Since that time, various factors have contributed to the exponential growth of literature in the field of crisis intervention. Some of these factors are noted here.

Public Events

- Columbine school massacre—April 20, 1999.
- Terrorist attacks on World Trade Center and Pentagon—September 11, 2001.
- Washington, DC sniper shootings—October 2–24, 2002.
- Red Lake school shootings—March 21, 2005.

Individual Incidents (Rudd, Joiner, Jobes, & King, 1999; Sanchez, 2001)

- Domestic violence.
- Sexual assault.
- Climbing suicide rates (Eisler, 1995; Kreidler & England, 1990; Salter, 1988; Walker, 1989).

Related Factors in the Mental Health Profession

- Changes in the way managed health care delivers mental health services (Kolski, Avriette, & Jongsma, 2001).
- Shifting treatment approach toward specialized crisis treatment for the prevention of serious psychological problems (Raphael & Wilson, 2000; Ursano, Grieger, & McCarroll, 1996).
- Expansion of community mental health services.
- Advent of crisis hotlines (Kleespies & Blackburn, 1998; Seely, 1997).

■ Definition of Crisis

James and Gilliland (2005) defined crisis this way:

> **Crisis:** "[T]he perception or experiencing of an event or situation as an intolerable difficulty that exceeds the resources and coping mechanisms of the person, and unless the person gains relief the crisis has the potential to cause severe affective, cognitive, and behavioral malfunctioning" (p. 3).

■ Types of Crisis

There are a variety of contexts and precipitating events that may give rise to crises. Four commonly recognized classifications of crises are (a) developmental, (b) situational, (c) existential, and (d) systemic (James & Gilliland, 2005). The defining aspects of each type of crisis are explained here.

> **Developmental crisis:** Occurs when events in the normal flow of human growth are disrupted by a dramatic shift that precipitates a change in the way people function (Brammer, 1985; Myer & James, 2005).
>
> **Situational crisis:** Emerges with the advent of unexpected events that lie outside the realm of normal functioning; individuals neither anticipate nor have a way of controlling situational crises (Brammer, 1985; Myer & James, 2005).
>
> **Existential crisis:** Occurs when individuals become aware that an important intrapersonal aspect of their lives may never be fulfilled. This, in turn, has an impact on self-purpose and self-worth (Brammer, 1985).
>
> **Systemic crisis:** Occurs when an identifiable event ripples out into large segments of the population and the environment and has a psychological impact not only on the immediate victims, but on people throughout the world (James & Gilliland).

The events leading to a crisis can vary, as described in the four categories of crisis. To clarify the distinction among developmental, situational, existential, and systemic crises, consider the following examples.

Developmental Crises

- Birth of a child.
- Retirement.
- College graduation.
- Career changes.

Situational Crises

- Automobile accidents.
- Sexual assault.
- Sudden illness.
- Job loss.

Existential Crises

- Failure to fulfill a lifelong dream.
- Intrapersonal conflicts about a lack of meaning in one's life.
- Realization that one has not formed significant relationships.

Systemic Crises

- Natural disasters.
- Hurricanes.
- Droughts.
- Wildfires.
- Terrorist attacks.
- School shootings.

 The four types of crises can also occur in a variety of settings. Check out the National Association for School Psychologists Web site for useful resources for responding to crises in schools.

▶ http://www.nasponline.org/NEAT/crisismain.html

■ Crisis and Culture

Crisis intervention can be identified as a specialty area in counseling; like other branches of the profession, crisis intervention often is influenced by cultural elements. The four types of crisis outlined earlier can serve as a context for examining the impact of culture on crisis situations. Developmental crises frequently involve a cultural issue (Myer, 2001). For example, pregnancy out of wedlock may precipitate a crisis in cultures where pregnancy outside of marriage is unacceptable or immoral according to religious belief; however, the same situation may be tolerated or even widely accepted in other cultures. Unlike developmental crises, situational crises are less likely to be tied to culture (Myer, 2001). There are few cultures in which sexual assault, mugging, or automobile accidents are not considered crises. Similar to developmental crises, existential crises may vary across cultures. Death is a prime example because the meaning and occurrence of death varies according to culture and religious belief. Finally, systemic crises—like situational crises— tend to be universal. Large-scale disasters such as hurricanes, tsunamis, or earthquakes, as examples, are almost always considered crisis events regardless of locale.

■ Characteristics of an Effective Crisis Counselor

Wanting to help and being able to help are two different things in crisis intervention. Not all counselors are able to work with clients in crisis. Counselors who regularly assist clients in crisis must flourish in the fast pace of crisis intervention, tolerate the lack of follow-up and long-term therapeutic relationships, and appreciate the patience needed to work with clients who are at the end of their ropes. Although crisis intervention techniques and strategies can be learned, certain personal characteristics are needed to move beyond simply using appropriate skills. The most effective crisis intervention counselors will have some combination of the characteristics.

Poise

- Counselors remain calm in the face of clients who are overwhelmed.
- Counselors create an island of stability to help restore clients' sense of equilibrium and activate problem-solving skills (James & Gilliland, 2005).
- Counselors practice good self-care and relaxation techniques to enhance their composure when helping clients.

Flexibility

- Counselors adapt to clients' needs.
- Counselors have a repertoire of strategies that address affective, behavioral, and cognitive reactions.
- Counselors can navigate smoothly among a variety of techniques to determine which are appropriate to clients' reactions.

Creativity (James & Gilliland, 2005)

- Counselors are willing to take risks in responding in new ways to crisis situations.
- Counselors practice divergent thinking that allows them to conceptualize crises from alternate perspectives.

Resilience (Collins & Collins, 2005)

- Counselors have the ability to bounce back after helping clients through such rough times as suicide or homicide.
- Counselors make regular use of continuing education seminars and peer supervision.
- Counselors monitor their energy levels, get enough rest, and maintain a healthy diet.

In addition to possessing certain personal qualities, effective crisis counselors also are adept at making appropriate referrals. Counselors are cognizant of local agencies that provide a wide range of services and keep an updated phone list for ease of use. Although technical skill is required for identifying instances when referral is the best option, personal awareness also plays an important part in the referral process. Counselors must recognize and accept the limitations of their own or their agency's ability to assist and must value the referral process as inherently important to supporting clients' variety of needs.

EXAMPLE

Bolstering Creativity Through Role Play

Crisis workers have to be able to think outside of the box to respond to people in crisis. Counselors can develop creativity through the use of role-played scenarios. One such role play involves a mother whose son was just diagnosed with leukemia. To save her child from the pain and discomfort of treatment, the mother is contemplating killing her son and then committing suicide. In this situation counselors are called on to make many decisions quickly and muster all the creativity they can to help the mother, who is struggling to deal with devastating news. Role play gives counselors the opportunity to stretch the possibility of response within the safety of an enactment and to receive feedback from peers and supervisors about their handling of the situation.

DIFFERENCES AMONG PSYCHOLOGICAL EMERGENCY, CRISIS, AND TRAUMA

James and Gilliland's (2005) understanding of crisis is succinct and comprehensive; however, their definition does not account for the confusing terminology often used to describe crises (Callahan, 1994). Three terms—psychological emergency, crisis, and trauma—are used routinely to refer to crisis, which leads to misconceptions about the crisis experience. One such misconception is that the crisis experience unfolds in a linear progression that begins with an emergency, leads to a crisis, and culminates in a trauma. However, individuals may experience an emergency and not be in crisis, or have a traumatic experience without the presence of a crisis. Figure 25.1 depicts the relation of psychological emergency, crisis, and trauma. Characteristics salient to each of the three experiences overlap; yet, the experiences described as psychological emergency, crisis, and trauma have unique features that distinguish them from one another.

Being able to sort through the maze of similarities and differences in these terms is important for practitioners so that they will be able to form a clear understanding of people's experience of catastrophic events (Silove, 2000), provide the appropriate level and type of intervention (Callahan, 1994), and improve communication among the many professionals (e.g., psychiatrists, psychologists, mental health counselors, nurses, social workers; Callahan, 1998) and settings (e.g., hospital emergency room, domestic violent shelters, rape trauma centers) involved in the treatment process.

■ Psychological Emergency

The defining characteristic of a **psychological emergency** is the presence of immediate danger. Permanent damage—psychological or physical—is always a possi-

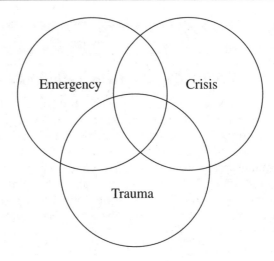

FIGURE 25.1   Relation of crisis, emergency, and trauma.

bility for people experiencing a psychological emergency. An important but less central feature of psychological emergencies is the suddenness of onset (Callahan, 1998). According to Callahan, many psychological emergencies surface with little or no forewarning. Typically, warning signs or symptoms either were not recognized or ignored (Myer & James, 2005).

Traits of People in Psychological Emergency (Baldwin, 1978; Callahan, 1998)

- Inability to function in a culturally acceptable manner.
- Evidence of incompetence.
- Inability to assume personal responsibility.
- Defenselessness.
- Incapacity to care for self or others.

Because psychological emergencies are dramatic and generally involve imminent risk of psychological or physical harm, intervention needs to occur as quickly as possible to prevent irreversible physical or psychological damage. Thus, treatment is intentionally protective in nature. Voluntary or involuntary hospitalization frequently is required to assure the safety of self or others (Myer, 2001).

Context of Treatment for Psychological Emergencies

- Immediate and swift.
- Straightforward.
- Protective of everyone involved.

- Open to involuntary commitment as a means of intervention.
- Open to the use of agencies as a means of protecting children and the elderly.

The following instances highlight the features of eminent danger or immediate onset characteristic of psychological emergencies.

Potential Psychological Emergencies

- An individual threatens suicide or is in the process of committing suicide.
- A substance abuser loses consciousness and leaves young children to care for themselves.
- A person in the midst of a psychotic episode walks along a busy highway oblivious to the perilous situation.
- A person unexpectedly overdoses on drugs.
- An individual has a psychotic break or undergoes a significant personality change and enters a dissociative state.

■ Crisis

The defining characteristic of crisis is a sense of disequilibrium (Myer & James, 2005). As in a psychological emergency, people in crisis are vulnerable to varying degrees. However, the critical distinction between an emergency and a crisis is that the vulnerability inherent in a crisis does not involve an immediate risk of harm. Generally, people in crisis reestablish a sense of equilibrium or stability about 6 weeks after the onset of a crisis (Callahan, 1998).

Traits of People in Crisis

- Likely to be overwhelmed.
- Impaired in their ability to use typical coping strategies to resolve the problem.
- Susceptible to long-term emotional, behavioral, and cognitive problems.
- Capable of bouncing back when inner resiliencies are sought out and support from family, friends, or professionals is received.

Treatment for people in crisis varies according to the severity of the reaction. More severe crisis reactions may warrant very directive interventions, whereas less serious responses may allow for more client autonomy, as in traditional counseling. In both instances, however, the intervention is focused on resolving the crisis state, not on remediation of a problem (James & Gilliland, 2005). If other issues surface during the intervention process, they may be acknowledged but should not become a focus of intervention unless they prevent a resolution of the crisis. After crisis intervention is complete, counselors can recommend assistance for peripheral issues.

Goals of Crisis Treatment

- Reestablish precrisis level of functioning (Cournoyer, 1996).
- Respond to immediate needs rather than assist people in making major life or personality changes.
- Recognize that not all issues will be resolved (James & Gilliland).

The following examples highlight the sense of disequilibrium that is a key characteristic of crisis situations. In both instances, the level of extreme vulnerability probably is not severe enough to cause immediate danger to those involved.

Potential Crises

- A woman diagnosed with breast cancer who is overwhelmed at the news of her threatened health.
- A man who discovers his teenage daughter is pregnant does not know how to respond to the news.

■ Trauma

A **trauma** occurs when an individual experiences or perceives an enormous sense of helplessness and physical threat that leads to the interruption of normal development (van der Kolk & McFarlane, 1996). People also experience psychological trauma due to episodic events that occur over extended periods of time (Pynoos, Steinberg, & Goenjian, 1996). Van der Kolk and McFarlane (1996) speculated that the memory of a trauma is not integrated into victims' life experience and leads to a disruption in development. The authors hypothesized that the memory of the traumatic event develops its own existence independent of coping abilities. Indeed, people who have traumatic experiences tend to fixate on the event (Myer & James, 2005) such that it continues to intrude into their lives well beyond the 6-week restabilization period seen in crisis (McFarlane & Yehuda, 1996).

Traits of People in Trauma

- Demonstrate evidence of permanent changes in beliefs about the world (Echterling, Presbury, & McKee, 2005).
- Exhibit inability to form healthy relationships (Pynoos et al.).
- Manifest a decreased ability to understand complex emotions (van der Kolk).
- Exhibit changes in neurological functioning (van der Kolk).
- Testify to the presence of nightmares, flashbacks, and intense emotions (e.g., rage, panic).
- Fixate on and reenact the trauma, causing the trauma to remain rooted in the contemporary experience of peoples' lives (van der Kolk & McFarlane).

The general treatment goal for people who have been traumatized is overcoming the trauma by coping with the memories in a way that does not force clients to repeatedly reexperience the trauma (van der Kolk & McFarlane, 1996). Because there is a wide range of symptoms associated with trauma, treatment greatly varies . Care and caution in selecting interventions is advocated prior to agreeing to provide treatment for people who have been traumatized (Lohr, Montgomery, Lilienfeld, & Tolin, 1999). These authors believe that not all interventions are helpful and some may cause further traumatization.

The following instances have the potential to be traumatic for individuals who experience them.

Potential Traumas

- A person witnesses a murder.
- An individual gets caught in a natural disaster such as a tornado.
- An individual sees a family member being killed in an automobile accident.
- A person witnesses or is a victim of prolonged domestic violence.

CRISIS RESPONSE: THE SIX-STEP MODEL OF INTERVENTION

Crisis intervention focuses treatment on a single issue (Cournoyer, 1996) by targeting affective, behavioral, and cognitive reactions that result from an experience that overwhelms people's ability to cope. A key element of crisis intervention is a quick focusing on the problem (Kleespies, Deleppo, Mori, & Niles, 1998). Taking a few sessions to develop treatment goals and allow a therapeutic relationship to build is a luxury not afforded to crisis intervention. Spending too much time developing rapport leaves people feeling as if they have not been helped. Often, treatment must begin within minutes. An action-oriented approach that rapidly engages clients is therefore essential.

> Crisis intervention focuses treatment on a single issue (Cournoyer, 1996) by targeting affective, behavioral, and cognitive reactions that result from an experience that overwhelms people's ability to cope. A key element of crisis intervention is a quick focusing on the problem.

The six-step model used by James and Gilliland (2005) is a guide counselors can follow in crisis intervention. What makes this model attractive is that it is neither static nor does it need to be followed mechanically; rather, the model allows the counselor to move back and forth through the steps to meet clients' immediate needs. In the first three steps, the emphasis is on listening. Skills needed for the first three steps are attending, observing, understanding, empathizing, and accepting; being nonjudgmental, caring, respectful, and genuine is also important. The second three steps emphasize acting. Counselors become involved in the intervention at a nondirective, collaborative, or directive level according to the assessed needs of the client and the availability of environmental supports and coping mechanisms (Myer & James, 2005).

Specifically, the six-step model promotes the following actions by the counselor:

1. Define the problem.
2. Ensure safety.
3. Provide support.
4. Examine alternatives.
5. Make plans.
6. Obtain commitment.

■ Step 1: Define the Problem

Although time limits may compress a counselor's ability to define the problem, a crucial aspect of providing help is gaining as clear an understanding as possible about what is going on with the client (James & Gilliland, 2005). Care must be taken not to confuse a "presenting" event with the actual crisis. Take for example, a father whose 15-year-old daughter just announced that she is pregnant. The father is active in church, owns a business, and volunteers in the community. At first glance, the crisis may seem to be the pregnancy, but the father also may be embarrassed about his daughter with church acquaintances. He might be concerned about decreased business if his customers discover his daughter is pregnant or fear losing his standing in the community.

Goals of Step 1

- Understand the meaning given to the event by the client.
- Query the client as to the source of the crisis.
- Inquire about the events that have moved the client into a crisis mode.
- Determine the ways in which the events have altered the client's affect, behavior, and cognitions from the precrisis state.

■ Step 2: Ensure Safety

The high potential for violence to self or others in a crisis situation suggests that safety be assessed (Myer & James, 2005). It is absolutely paramount that crisis workers be aware of safety considerations for their clients, others, and most important, for themselves (Hendricks, McKean, & Hendricks, 2003). This step cuts across all other steps of crisis intervention.

Goals of Step 2

- Assess safety needs from the beginning to the end of the crisis intervention.
- Determine immediacy of the threat to self or others by checking for evidence of a definite plan, means to enact the plan, and commitment to act within 4 days.

■ Step 3: Provide Support

Unlike traditional individual counseling where counselors guard against being too directive for fear of breeding client dependency, in crisis intervention therapists must communicate to clients that they are prized, accepted, and valued (Hoff, 1995).

Goals of Step 3

- Assess client vulnerability as determined by defenselessness against being taken advantage of, inability to locate and access resources to help in the crisis, and exceeding unfamiliarity with problems associated with the crisis.
- Facilitate dependency when clients are too vulnerable to care for themselves.
- Help clients regain their sense of equilibrium as well as their independence once immediate client care has been provided.

■ Step 4: Examine Alternatives

Clients in crisis often believe they have no options left—the crisis has left them so immobilized that they cannot resume control of their lives (Myer & James, 2005). Examining alternatives empowers clients to overcome the sense of helplessness that often accompanies a crisis and take steps to regain control.

Goals of Step 4

- Search for situational supports.
- Generate coping mechanisms.
- Engage in positive thinking.
- Attempt to restore control by finding past behaviors and helpful environmental resources that the client may have forgotten or dismissed as ineffective.

■ Step 5: Make Plans

Most counseling approaches use action plans as a means of taking what is learned in therapy into clients' everyday lives. Crisis intervention is no different; planning is considered a major component of returning the client to a state of precrisis equilibrium (Myer & James, 2005). Crisis intervention planning is unique, however, in that planning is time sensitive. As opposed to weekly, monthly, or even lifetime plans that are part of a traditional therapeutic regimen, crisis intervention plans are immediate and short term, written in terms of days, hours, and sometimes even minutes.

Goals of Step 5

- Determine whether the client's mental clarity and physical resources allow him or her to establish a plan of action.
- Work collaboratively with clients—even to the point of taking initiative—to decide which supportive persons and services are needed.
- Create a plan of action that responds to immediate needs with goals and outcomes that are short term rather than long term.
- As much as possible, attempt to return control to clients so they may reclaim their autonomy.

■ Step 6: Obtain Commitment

Obtaining a commitment is a particularly important way of moving clients into action (James & Gilliland, 2005). The issues of client autonomy and control are extremely relevant to the commitment stage because it does little good for the crisis worker to force clients to commit to actions they lack the resources to carry out. Thus, gaining a commitment should be done as empathically and collaboratively as possible so the clients do not attempt actions that are forced on them by the crisis worker. If planning has been effective, the commitment step should be short, concise, and easily accomplished.

CRISIS ASSESSMENT: USING THE TRIAGE ASSESSMENT FORM

Assessment is a vital aspect of the six-step model that serves as an umbrella process conducted continuously throughout treatment. Continuous assessment allows counselors to monitor clients' needs and modify their intervention approach where necessary. The Triage Assessment Form: Crisis Intervention (TAF; Myer, 2001) is particularly suited for use in the six-step model. The TAF, first introduced by Myer, Williams, Ottens, and Schmidt (1992), is an excellent visual and verbal assessment device for determining the seriousness of a client's safety needs. The TAF offers a dynamic way to understand clients' needs by dividing the impact of a crisis into affective, behavioral, and cognitive reactions. Each response is further divided into three categories. The interaction and severity of these reactions provides the information needed for helping clients.

■ Assessment of Crisis Reactions

Three affective, behavioral, and cognitive responses to crises are assessed by the TAF.

Affective Response

- Anger/hostility.
- Anxiety/fear.
- Sadness/despair.

Affective response is a natural, almost instinctive reaction to crisis. The TAF evaluates the most commonly identified emotional reactions (James & Gilliland, 2005).

Behavioral Response

- Immobility.
- Avoidance.
- Approach.

Behavioral reactions can be either constructive or destructive. Constructive reactions are those that help to resolve the situation, whereas destructive reactions negatively heighten the crisis situation. For example, sometimes it might better serve a specific client to avoid a situation rather than approach it. Approaching can be potentially destructive if the client is not emotionally prepared.

Cognitive Response

- Transgression.
- Threat.
- Loss.

Cognitive reactions are best understood through the framework of time. When the client believes the crisis is occurring in the present moment, the cognitive reaction is labeled transgression. If a client perceives the crisis as future oriented, it is considered a threat. When a client understands the crisis situation as located in the past, the cognitive response is identified as loss.

■ Severity Scales

The Severity scales used in the TAF rate clients numerically on affective, behavioral, and cognitive dimensions of functioning by comparing written scale definitions against the observations a crisis worker makes of the client's words and actions. The key to assessing severity is to observe the client's ability to control the reaction, the intensity of the reaction, and the stability of the reaction. The more severe the reaction, the less control clients have; the more intense their experience of the reaction, the less stable the reaction.

Scoring

- Each of the three scales can be scored from a range of 1 to 10, for a total possible score of 30.
- Scores ranging from 3 to 14 indicate minimum impairment, those ranging from 15 to 23 indicate moderate impairment, and scores from 24 to 30 indicate severe impairment.
- The higher end scores indicate that the client needs to be placed in a setting where he or she will be secure and safe.
- A score on a single scale of 10 also indicates that the client should be placed in a protective setting.

Suffice it to say that few clients who are in crisis will be in the low impairment range, and many may be angrily acting out against others or attempting to harm themselves.

TRENDS IN CRISIS INTERVENTION

The field of crisis intervention continues to evolve. Three notable and emerging trends include the development of contextual models, strength-based approaches, and systemic perspectives.

■ Contextual Models

A recent trend in crisis intervention is toward recognizing the usefulness of contextual issues to theory development in crisis work (McNally, Bryant, & Ehlers, 2003). The contextual or ecological perspective is based on the belief that crises do not occur in a vacuum and are shaped by the social and cultural contexts in which they occur (Deiter & Pearlman, 1998; van der Kolk & McFarlane, 1996). Promptings in the direction of theory development are related to several factors.

Factors Related to Contextual Theory Development

- Issues related to the provision of aid and support, the nature of crises, and intervention models that can be used to manage postcrisis reactions (Paton, Violanti, & Dunning, 2000) have been the primary focus of crisis literature, while little attention has been paid to theory development (Slaikeu, 1990).
- Existing crisis theories resemble a cluster of assumptions or collection of clinical observations more than a set of data-based principles able to explain or predict the effect of crises (Ursano et al., 1996).
- Ecological models have emerged that are suitable to theory development and make sense of the impact of crises on individuals as well as systems (Collins & Collins, 2005; James & Gilliland, 2005; Myer & Moore, 2006; Stuhlmiller & Dunning, 2000a).

■ Strength-Based Approach

Another important movement in the field of crisis intervention is the shift from a pathological to a strength-based treatment approach (Stuhlmiller & Dunning, 2000b). Although more research is needed about the factors that make some people more resilient than others, some statements about the underlying beliefs and assumptions of this approach can be made.

Assumptions of Strength-Based Approach

- Diagnostic labels tend to be reductionistic and of limited usefulness to explain reactions to crises (Myer, Moore, & Hughes, 2003; Silove, 2000; Stuhlmiller & Dunning, 2000b).
- Diagnostic labels are ineffective for understanding and assisting people in crisis (Myer et al., 2003; Shalev, 1996; Silove, 2000) because most individuals do not develop debilitating psychological problems after a crisis (Bonanno, 2004; Echterling et al., 2005).
- Categorizing normal or typical reactions to a crisis as pathological is not appropriate (Tucker, Pfefferbaum, Nixon, & Dickson, 2000).
- Use of a pathological approach ignores the psychological growth that takes place for many people who have experienced a crisis (Stuhlmiller & Dunning, 2000a).
- Ingenuity, strengths, and resourcefulness are important for understanding how people in overwhelming experiences bounce back in spite of the odds.

See Chapter 19 for further information on a critique of traditional approaches to assessment and diagnosis.

■ Systemic Approach

Another area of crisis intervention that is beginning to flourish, particularly in the wake of the terrorist attacks of September 11, 2001, is planned intervention at the organizational level (Myer & Moore, 2006). Literature in the area of crisis management for businesses long has recognized the need to prepare for crises and disasters (Mitroff, 2004); however, the impact of crises on employees either has been neglected or addressed through recommendations to refer employees to outside professionals.

Features of Systemic Perspective

- Crisis intervention within organizations must shift from a clinical to a consultative model that focuses on working with organizations to make decisions in the best interest of their employees (Braverman, 1999).
- A consultation model focuses on providing support at the managerial level and with crisis response teams.

Additional research in this area is needed to provide assessment tools that can guide the intervention process (Myer, Conte, & Peterson, in press).

Crisis intervention is here to stay. The one constant all counselors have is that they can count on working with clients who are in crisis. Training either through formal course work or continuing education is needed if counselors are to be prepared to provide the assistance needed to individuals in crisis. Although the approach and techniques used in traditional individual and group counseling are helpful, counselors must apply them differently. Clinical errors in crisis intervention can result in disastrous outcomes.

Chapter 25: Key Terms

- ▶ Crisis
- ▶ Developmental crisis
- ▶ Situational crisis
- ▶ Existential crisis
- ▶ Systemic crisis
- ▶ Psychological emergency
- ▶ Trauma

Addictions Counseling

David L. Delmonico
Duquesne University

Elizabeth J. Griffin
Internet Behavior Consulting

In This Chapter

▶ *Fundamentals of the Addictive Process*
  ▪ The Use–Dependence Continuum
  ▪ Classifications of Dependence
  ▪ Progression
  ▪ Hallmarks of Addictive Behavior
  ▪ Tolerance and Withdrawal

▶ *Models of Addiction*
  ▪ Moral
  ▪ Medical and Disease
  ▪ Spirituality
  ▪ Impulse Control
  ▪ Genetic
  ▪ Social Learning
  ▪ Bio-Psycho-Social
  ▪ Cultural Implications for Addiction
    Models

▶ *Screening and Assessment*
  ▪ Physiological and Behavioral Assessment
  ▪ Clinical Interviewing
  ▪ Psychometric Instruments
  ▪ Diagnosis and Co-Occurring Disorders
  ▪ Intervention Level Assessment

▶ *Intervention and Treatment Considerations*
  ▪ Crisis Management
  ▪ Behavioral Change
  ▪ Treatment Modalities
  ▪ Beyond Addiction Management
  ▪ Dual Diagnosis
  ▪ Pharmacological Interventions
  ▪ Special Populations
  ▪ Defining Successful Treatment
  ▪ Legal, Ethical, and Professional Issues

FUNDAMENTALS OF THE ADDICTIVE PROCESS

Our purpose in this chapter is to introduce underlying concepts and tenets that mental health professionals need to provide even the most basic level of care to individuals struggling with addictive behaviors. We present theoretical concepts, followed by information on basic assessment and treatment procedures. This chapter is not focused on chemical dependency, but rather takes a broad approach by presenting ideas about the process of addiction, regardless of the drug or behavior the individual chooses to satisfy the addictive cycle. Reading this chapter will not make you an adept addiction counselor, but you will have an understanding of many of the concepts from which addiction counselors operate.

■ The Use–Dependence Continuum

Addiction is an umbrella word that encompasses many forms of behavior and a myriad of other terms. For example, the *Diagnostic and Statistical Manual of Mental Disorders* (4th ed., text revision [*DSM–IV–TR*]; American Psychiatric Association, 2000) outlines several types of problematic use of substances. Combined with the recreational ways individuals use a substance, a continuum is formed ranging from health to increasing pathology.

The initial job of the clinician is often to help the client identify where on the continuum their behavior falls. Therefore, understanding the fundamental concepts of addiction is critical to the assessment and treatment process for those who present with substance and behavioral concerns.

Points on the Use–Dependence Continuum

1. *Use* is the idea that the person using the substance or behavior does not experience any difficulties as a result of that use.
2. *Misuse* refers to individuals using the substance or behavior in ways that, if continued, could develop into more problematic issues. These individuals can manage their behavior and use except under limited times and circumstances.
3. *Abuse* occurs when people are experiencing difficulties as a result of the use of a substance or behavior. They may be suffering consequences in their life as a result of the substance or behavior. This is the first point along the continuum where we may use the word addiction.
4. *Dependence* is the polar opposite of use; individuals are considered dependent if they abuse a substance or behavior and also develop tolerance and withdrawal associated with the substance or behavior.

■ Classifications of Dependence

The use–dependence continuum can be used to address both substance and process or behavioral addictions. These two types of addictive behaviors can be described this way:

Substance addiction: An addiction that requires the ingestion of a mood-altering substance (e.g., alcohol, drugs, etc.).

Process or behavioral addiction: An addiction that does not require a substance to be ingested, but often presents similar problems as a substance-related addiction (e.g., shopping, sex, workaholism, etc.).

Although process addictions are not addressed specifically in the *DSM–IV–TR*, many clinicians consider them equally problematic as substance addictions.

■ Progression

There are many models through which to view addictions; however, most clinicians subscribe to the idea that addiction is a process, not an event. It is often assumed individuals progress through a series of stages in both their addiction and treatment. Progression can be defined this way:

Progression: The process whereby individuals experience an ever-increasing feeling of being out of control, increased consequences, and obsessive thinking related to their behavior.

The disease model subscribers believe this progression leads to one of two outcomes: death or recovery. In many ways, it is the process of moving from use toward dependence.

Although there are many theories of how individuals start and continue through addiction and its recovery, they often follow a similar pattern. Moving through the stages is more complex than it may first appear. Addicts may pass through a stage, only to revisit it later in their addiction or recovery. It may be better to consider these phases rather than stages, as the term *phase* suggests addicts do not necessarily move in a consistent direction, nor does one stage need to be completed before moving to the next.

EXAMPLE

Individual Differences in Progression

Individuals may experience progression at unpredictable and varied paces. One individual may spend his or her entire lifetime going through the stages, whereas others may never fully progress to addiction or dependence. Additionally, individuals spend varying amounts of time at points along the continuum. One individual may spend 6 months at one point and 6 years at another point; another person may spend his or her entire lifetime at a single point.

■ Hallmarks of Addictive Behavior

In considering the continuum concept, professionals often struggle with knowing when an individual crosses over from the use and misuse side to the abuse and dependence side. Schneider (1994) provided three hallmark criteria useful in making this decision.

Three Essential Criteria of Addictive Behaviors

1. Loss of ability to freely choose whether to stop or continue a behavior.
2. Continuation of a behavior despite adverse consequences such as loss of health, job, marriage, or freedom.
3. Obsession with the activity.

First, the loss of ability to freely choose has been widely debated, and depending on the model from which you conceptualize addictive behaviors (discussed later), the belief that someone truly loses his or her ability to choose, or simply has the feeling that he or she has lost the ability to choose, will vary. Second, the consequences may or may not be identifiable by the addict. This is one reason it is important not just to assess the addict, but also to gather information from other sources as well. Finally, obsession is a subjective judgment, but addicts often will spend inordinate amounts of time either preparing for their addictive behavior (ritualizations) or thinking about their addiction even when not engaged in the behavior itself. Although there is no magic number of hours that constitute obsession, if the thoughts are having an impact on other areas of the individual's life, it is likely this criteria is met.

■ Tolerance and Withdrawal

Tolerance and withdrawal are two additional concepts critical to consider in distinguishing addictive process from use or misuse. The American Psychiatric Association (2000) made this distinction:

Tolerance: Refers to either needing more of a substance to achieve intoxication or the desired effect, or a significant decrease in the effect of the substance when the same amount is used.

Withdrawal: Physiological symptoms associated with a physical withdrawal (differs by substance), or the substance as used to relieve or avoid the withdrawal symptoms.

According to the *DSM–IV–TR*, an individual can be substance dependent either with or without tolerance and withdrawal; however, an individual only can be considered physiologically dependent if tolerance and withdrawal are present. One of the issues the *DSM–IV–TR* does not discuss directly is the concept of psychological dependence. The differentiation in these terms can be understood this way:

Physiological dependence: Occurs when individuals experience tolerance and withdrawal in relation to a substance.

Psychological dependence: Refers to individuals who remain dependent on a substance or behavior for reasons other than physiological ones.

There has been growing acknowledgment, especially in the behavioral addiction field, that tolerance and withdrawal do occur in cases of psychological dependence. Consider the following example of the psychological dependence related to a gambling addiction.

EXAMPLE

Gambling: Making the Case for Psychological Dependence

If one examines the criteria for pathological gambling in the *DSM–IV–TR*, it is clear there are references to psychological and behavioral symptoms of tolerance and withdrawal. Consider an addiction to gambling. The criteria state an individual becomes "restless or irritable when attempting to cut down or stop gambling," or "needs to gamble with increasing amounts of money in order to achieve the desired excitement" (American Psychiatric Association, 2000). Facets of these criteria reflect similar terminology and understanding of physiological dependence.

MODELS OF ADDICTION

There are many models to conceptualize why individuals engage in problematic use of behavior and substances. There are also a variety of ways to explain how individuals develop, continue, and recover from an addiction. All the models would be too numerous to cover in this chapter, but listed here are some common models for thinking about addictive behavior, along with a very brief description of each (Coombs, 2005).

■ Moral

The moral model suggests addiction is a form of moral weakness, and if the addict would develop healthy and culturally acceptable morals, the addiction would dissipate.

■ Medical and Disease

This model suggests addiction is a disease that if left untreated will continue to progress and worsen and eventually result in the death of the patient. This model is commonly subscribed to in 12-step circles (e.g., Alcoholics Anonymous, Narcotics Anonymous, Gamblers Anonymous, etc.), but is greatly debated by medical and mental health professionals. Critics believe it dismisses the personal responsibility an individual must assume for his or her behaviors. Some believe addictions, especially behavioral addictions, are not diseases.

■ Spirituality

Although similar to the moral model, this model asserts the individual lacks spirituality, and if he or she would become more spiritual, the addiction would be healed. Although most clinicians believe spirituality is an important component of addiction recovery, this model does not see spirituality as one component, but rather the only issue that needs to be addressed.

■ Impulse Control

This model asserts addictive behavior is due to a lack of internal "stops," leading to poor impulse control. Pathological gambling is one of the few behavioral addictions that merited inclusion in the *DSM–IV–TR*, and it is included under impulse control disorders. Treatment methods in this model include strong emphasis on teaching individuals how to identify, manage, and control impulses. Most clinicians believe addicts demonstrate poor impulse control, but not all would agree that addiction and impulse control disorders are one and the same.

■ Genetic

The genetic model focuses on understanding the etiology (cause of) addictive behaviors. The genetic model asserts addictive behaviors are genetically encoded and individuals with addiction encoding have genetic predispositions to developing addictive behavior. This model does not indicate that simply because one has an "addiction" gene, he or she will automatically become an addict, but rather that these people are vulnerable to developing addictions given the right environmental circumstances. The model has yet to explain why individuals choose one substance or behavior over another, even if an addiction gene can be identified.

■ Social Learning

This model suggests addiction is a learned behavior. The process of behavioral and emotional reinforcement has encouraged the behavior to be repeated with increased frequency and impact. For example, feelings of pleasure associated with chemical use can reinforce the repeated use of the substance. Addicts also may experience relief from their emotional distress as a result of a behavior and use the behavior in the future to medicate their stress, another form of reinforcement.

Bio-Psycho-Social

This model encompasses many of the previously described models. It suggests that addictions are complex issues involving a myriad of variables—biological and genetic, psychological, and social and environmental. It also asserts treatment methods must be holistic in their approach and include all aspects (biological, psychological, and social) to be effective.

Cultural Implications for Addiction Models

It is important to recognize there are a number of researchers, writers, and clinicians who believe addiction is a culturally derived term, and the addiction diagnosis is widely overutilized and damaging to individuals struggling with behavioral and chemical issues (Peele, 1992). Some would argue behavioral addictions are simply bad behavioral habits, and the term *addiction* or *dependence* should be reserved for the physiological dependence one develops to a particular ingested substance (e.g., alcohol, heroin, etc.).

SCREENING AND ASSESSMENT

There are numerous approaches to screening for addictions and each of these approaches offers the clinician valuable information in making an accurate diagnosis. We outline a number of these in this section along with important considerations to screening and assessment.

Physiological and Behavioral Assessment

Assessing for the presence of an addiction is often a lengthy and complex process. The clinician turns detective and looks for clues suggesting the individual has endured a sustained pattern of out of control behavior for an extended period of time, typically 12 months or more. A number of factors can hinder the counselor in making an accurate physiological and behavioral assessment.

Barriers in Physiological and Behavioral Assessments

- Addicts often are not forthcoming or honest about their current or past behaviors.
- The addict often has perfected strategies to hide his or her addiction from others—including clinicians.
- Secrecy about the addiction is valued because it has allowed the addict to sustain maladaptive patterns.
- Addiction has become an organizing principle in an addict's life and a way to escape and medicate his or her negative thoughts and feelings.

In part because of these barriers to making an accurate assessment, if possible, it is important to interview not only the addict about his or her behavior, but also those known as collateral informants.

> **Collateral informants:** Individuals who are close to the situation (e.g., partner, family, employer, etc.) and who are most likely to know about the addiction.

The intent of engaging in collateral interviews is not to catch or punish the addict; rather, there are a number of positive aims of this strategy, some of which are listed here.

Goals of Using Collateral Informants

- The perception of others is often enlightening not only to the clinician, but also to the addict himself or herself.
- Collateral interviews make apparent that the behavior the addict believed he or she was concealing so well was known to others.
- Collateral interviews illuminate the breadth and depth of issues with which the addict is struggling.

Interviewing a significant other can create some professional dilemmas and be detrimental to the addict if not done with sensitivity and caution. It is suggested close supervision or consultation be used should a clinician decide to conduct collateral interviews.

■ Clinical Interviewing

A clinical interview is an important step in the assessment and treatment planning process. There are a number of benefits to the interview process.

Advantages of the Clinical Interview

- The clinical interview can help the client clarify the problem and its history, the first step in solution development.
- It can provide a wealth of information to be incorporated into the treatment planning process, both short term and longer term.
- The clinical interview is extremely useful in establishing a strong rapport with the addict—disclosing a secret life in a safe, healthy way can create a strong, trusting bond between a clinician and client.

A clinical interview is not a one-time event, but best occurs over a series of meetings where both the client and clinician have an opportunity to process the questions and responses. There are a number of standardized clinical interview protocols published to help assess addicts, especially those who are chemically dependent. These standardized interviews can be useful, but clinicians should not rely on them solely. Good addiction clinicians use their intuition and help direct the client in the moment, rather than ask a series of seemingly unrelated questions. There are a number of areas that the clinical interview should address.

Key Components of a Clinical Interview

- Complete family (past and present) history.
- Educational history.
- Work history.
- Legal history.
- Psychosocial background.
- Medical history.
- Drug and alcohol use history.

One interviewing method that has grown in popularity over the past several years is called motivational interviewing (MI; Miller & Rollnick, 2002).

> **Motivational interviewing:** An interview method in the addictions field that is founded on a high-quality clinical interview, incorporates many basic counseling skills (e.g., active listening, reflection of feeling and content, paraphrasing, etc.), and has a focus on an addict's motivation to engage in the change process.

MI not only helps gather important information about the addict's story, but helps clarify the addict's strengths and abilities, which in turn aids the addict in becoming more motivated for change. The stages of change are addressed later in this chapter, but suffice it to say that MI assesses motivation and helps the addict move from thinking about change into becoming motivated to take action for change.

For more on MI and the role and place of motivation in the change process, see Chapter 27.

■ Psychometric Instruments

There are hundreds of screening and assessment instruments available to assess for the presence and extent of addictive behavior. Most of these instruments are structured to assess for chemical or substance use. Few assess for behavioral addictions, and those that do exist have limited validity and reliability. In cases where behavioral addictions are suspected, general addiction instruments may be used, but should be interpreted cautiously.

When deciding to use a psychometric instrument, the clinician should keep in mind the following suggestions for interpreting results.

Recommendations for Using Psychometric Test Results

- Test results should always be used in conjunction with other methods of assessment, including clinical interviewing and history taking.
- The results of testing should always be interpreted in the context of other information such as demographic characteristics of the client (e.g., reading level, cultural differences, age, etc.), results of clinical interviews, diagnostic criteria, collateral informants, and so on.

For a comprehensive list of tests for both substance-related addictions and behavioral addictions, please refer to the Coombs and Howatt (2005) text called *The Addiction Counselor's Desk Reference*.

■ Diagnosis and Co-Occurring Disorders

The official diagnosis of substance dependence or other addictive type behavior requires clinicians to review multiple areas of the *DSM–IV–TR* to assess addicts for co-occurring conditions that may be present with addictive disorders, substance use and otherwise. For example, pathological gambling is included under impulse control disorders. Impulse control disorders also may apply to other addictive behaviors (e.g., work, shopping, etc.), but only if they meet the basic criteria for an impulse control disorder.

Although it is important to screen for major personality issues with addicts, it is also important to look for common co-occurring factors such as depression, anxiety, attention deficits, obsessive-compulsive features, and so on. Addicts who stop their addictive behavior or substance use are likely to relapse if these other issues are not assessed and addressed.

Although it is important to screen for major personality issues with addicts, it is also important to look for common co-occurring factors such as depression, anxiety, attention deficits, obsessive-compulsive features, and so on. Addicts who stop their addictive behavior or substance use are likely to relapse if these other issues are not assessed and addressed. A full psychological evaluation, including common psychological testing (e.g., Minnesota Multiphasic Personality Inventory–II) is imperative to effective treatment planning for any type of addict.

■ Intervention Level Assessment

One goal of the assessment process is to determine the intervention level to best fit the needs of the addict. Listed next is the American Society for Addiction Medicine's (ASAM, 2001) Patient Placement Criteria levels used to place patients at the appropriate level of treatment.

Intervention Levels (ASAM, 2001)

- *Level .5: Early interventions* include psychoeducational tasks that teach individuals about addictive behavior and attempt to get change to occur with little intervention or treatment.
- *Level I: Outpatient* represents a standard outpatient setting where the individual participates in various modalities of treatment (individual, group, family, etc.) throughout the week, but continues all other areas of his or her life as normal.
- *Level II: Intensive outpatient/partial* is one step above an outpatient setting and allows for more intensive time with the addict. Typically the individual spends several hours each day, 5 days per week, meeting with therapists, participating in groups, and so on. The addict typically maintains his or her schooling or employment and participates in the intensive program in the evening or on weekends.
- *Level III: Residential/inpatient* requires an admission to a treatment facility for anywhere between 14 and 30 days in length. During this time the individual stays at the treatment center. He or she participates in many individual, group, and family sessions, while eating, sleeping, and living with other addicts struggling to manage their own addictions.
- *Level IV: Medically managed intensive inpatient* requires admission to a medical facility. This level of management typically is required when substance withdrawal occurs that could place the addict into medical danger if not monitored by a medical staff.

A well-performed, comprehensive assessment is critical in planning appropriately staged interventions. Although there is no exact science to determining these levels, some basic guidelines for assessment are suggested.

Some Guides for Determining Level of Treatment

- Begin with the least intrusive method and increase the intensity of treatment if necessary.
- Remember that the more significant the history, current crisis, and pace of progression the greater the warrant for a more intense intervention level.
- Keep in mind that one goal of treatment is to help addicts function in a less restrictive environment.

EXAMPLE

Making Adjustments in Assessment

Initially it may appear an addict is best suited for outpatient treatment; however, if once treatment begins the addict shows increased problematic signs, or it is discovered the problem is more significant than initially believed, the treatment may be raised to a higher level. Making necessary adjustments is important because addicts who are placed at the wrong level and remain there for too long actually may decline in overall health and wellness and have less chance of long-term recovery.

INTERVENTION AND TREATMENT CONSIDERATIONS

Addiction treatment and recovery is complex and often is an individualized process. Some of the more salient features of the intervention and treatment process are mentioned here.

■ Crisis Management

Addicts often present in treatment in a state of crisis. The crisis may be precipitated by a family discovery, legal consequences, medical issue, or the internal sense they have "hit their bottom." It is for this reason that good crisis management skills are necessary in addictions counseling. Some suggestions for handling crises are provided next.

Recommendations for Responding to Crises

- Triage the situation and determine a priority of interventions.
- Manage immediate crises in a swift and direct manner, so other forms of treatment will be successful once the crisis situation dissipates.
- Adhere to a crisis assessment model to make decisions regarding crisis intervention.

One model that helps triage the level of crisis is the triage assessment model (Myer, 2000), and although space limits its inclusion in this chapter, it is strongly suggested that clinicians use this or a similar model.

See Chapter 25 for more on crisis and the triage assessment model.

■ Behavioral Change

One of the most helpful concepts in understanding addiction treatment is the stages of behavior change (Prochaska, Norcross, & DiClemente, 1995). These stages apply to any significant change an individual makes in his or her life. Therefore, although they are useful in addiction work, these stages also are very useful in other forms of treatment. The stages are listed next, along with a brief explanation of each.

Stages of Behavior Change

1. *Precontemplation* occurs when individuals are not aware of any problems or issues and are not even considering that change may be necessary.
2. *Contemplation* begins when individuals explore the possibility that change may be forthcoming. They tend to be ambivalent about whether or not change is necessary, but they are at least considering the possibility of change.
3. *Preparation* begins when individuals try small changes just to see how they respond to the changes. This is the time when they are testing the waters just to see what might happen if change should occur.
4. *Action* is noticeable when individuals have determined that change is necessary and actually are making the changes in their life. To consider someone to be in the action stage, that person has to be making behavioral changes for more than 3 months.
5. *Maintenance* refers to individuals who remain in the action phase for more than 6 months and have made a commitment to sustaining the changed behavior.
6. *Relapse* is a normal part of the change process. As individuals learn about the new behavior and experiment with the differences they feel as a result of the behavior change, it is not unusual to encounter relapse. The relapse itself is often not the issue, but how the individual responds to the relapse can determine whether he or she returns to the contemplation or the action phase.
7. *Termination* occurs when individuals are certain their behavior has been successfully changed and resolved. They believe the behavior will not return, and they need to do little to prevent any form of relapse. Most addiction professionals believe that this stage is not realistic in the treatment of addicts, as it is often viewed as a lifelong issue.

■ Treatment Modalities

There are many ways to intervene with an addiction, and much of the process is dependent on the model from which one conceptualizes addictive behavior. However, the modalities of treatments are fairly universal. A list of common treatment strategies is provided here.

Common Treatment Strategies

- Individual treatment often is useful in early treatment to allow for a full assessment and help the individual more fully understand his or her addiction.
- Group therapy is another highly useful modality of treatment for addicts because other addicts can help confront and support one another under the guidance of a trained group leader.
- Twelve-step recovery groups often serve as an adjunct to individual and group treatment. These groups are extremely useful in helping addicts get clarity on their issue and develop intimate friendships with others struggling with similar issues.
- Couples or family therapy is also useful, because addictive behavior typically impacts the entire family, and everyone in the family can work together to heal the relationships that may have been affected by the addiction.

Each modality of treatment has advantages and disadvantages, but all should be considered in the treatment planning process.

■ Beyond Addiction Management

The slang term "dry drunk" is used to describe an addict who has become abstinent from his or her addictive drug or behavior, but continues to exhibit traits that often accompany an addiction. For this reason, treatment of addicts goes far beyond simply getting them to stop their behavior.

Ways to Address Periphery Issues in Addictions

- Recognize traits such as poor social skills, inability to develop intimate relationships, narcissistic features, and lack of self-care as accompaniments to addiction.
- Address underlying issues that led to the addiction in the first place.
- Address new issues (e.g., intimacy, sexuality, spirituality, grief and loss, family of origin, trauma or abuse) that rise to the surface as the addiction is being managed.

■ Dual Diagnosis

Dual diagnosis is not uncommon in work with addicted clients because addictive disorders can develop due to other disorders, and vice versa; however, it is often overlooked and complex to treat. The term dual diagnosis can be understood this way:

> **Dual diagnosis:** Refers to individuals who have some form of addiction, typically a chemical addiction, and an additional Axis I diagnosis.

Often the nonaddiction diagnosis requires medications carefully balanced not to create new problems or other forms of dependence (i.e., switching addictions). Additionally, both diagnoses must be addressed and managed to avoid creating an environment for an addictive relapse or other mental health difficulties. Some of the more frequently seen co-occurring diagnoses are listed here.

Common Co-Occurring Disorders With Addictions

- Mood disorders (e.g., depression, anxiety, etc.).
- Adjustment disorders.
- Impulse control disorders.
- Obsessive-compulsive disorders.
- Attention deficit disorder.

An individual might not meet the full criteria for a secondary mental health disorder (e.g., obsessive-compulsive disorder) but may have many of the characteristics of the disorder. Clinicians often report addicts have "features" of a disorder, rather than meeting the full criteria for a disorder. Although this technically is not a dually diagnosed individual, the features of the other disorders must be addressed for addiction treatment to have a long-lasting impact.

■ Pharmacological Interventions

As we learn more about the brain and addictive disorders, and the relation between various neurochemicals, the use of medications in the treatment of addictions is playing a more critical role. As previously mentioned, the addiction may be one symptom in a myriad of issues needing to be addressed with all forms of treatment, including medications. Everything from alcohol-sensitivity medications (Antabuse) to medications for depression, anxiety, and obsessive-compulsive disorders has been used.

Recommendations for Clinicians Regarding Psychopharmacological Interventions

- Recognize that the use of prescription medications to treat some addictive behaviors often is warranted.
- Use caution when discussing medications with clients.
- Ensure that addicts are under the care of a qualified physician.
- Remain current on the types of treatments employed by the medical profession in treating addictive disorders.

■ Special Populations

There are standardized ways of approaching the treatment of addiction, often depending on the addiction model being used (see addiction models). However, there are special populations that may require additional consideration. These groups include addicted women; adolescents; and gay, bisexual, and lesbian individuals, just to name a few. These groups may have some unique issues to consider in the treatment of their addiction. Given space limitations, it is not possible to discuss the unique characteristics of these and other groups, but clinicians should know they exist and not ignore them when conducting assessments and preparing for treatment.

■ Defining Successful Treatment

Success is often a subjective, not objective measure. There are objective variables one could measure—relapse, attendance at meetings or group therapy, improvement on measures of addiction, lower depression and anxiety scores, and so on—but these measures do not necessarily measure success. For example, an individual who has a relapse objectively may be considered a treatment failure, when in fact, the relapse is naturally occurring part of recovery that helps the individual become even more committed to a program of recovery, thereby, making it a subjective success rather than an objective failure.

Another point to consider when defining success is the concept of abstinence versus controlled (or moderated) use. Two important terms in controlled use are moderated management and spontaneous recovery, defined as follows:

Moderated management: Models of addiction treatment that see the goal of recovery as moderation rather than complete abstinence from the behavior or substance.

Spontaneous recovery: The premise on which moderated management is built; refers to the assumption that many individuals learn to manage their "bad habit" without any type of professional intervention—it just simply happens. Therefore, many addicts do not require lifelong abstinence, but rather other forms of treatment that help them to not misuse a substance or behavior.

Most chemical dependency professionals believe in the abstinence model, which is another perspective used in assessing successful treatment.

Abstinence model: Individuals only can be considered healthy and recovering if they are not using any of the substance to which they are addicted.

In this model, abstinence is seen as a lifelong goal where individuals must forfeit their use of a substance or unhealthy behavior for the remainder of their life. This model may work well for substance addictions that are not a necessary part of survival, but it is difficult to translate these ideas into behavioral addictions such as food and sex, where abstinence is not the goal, but rather healthy, moderated use. This is not to say that the food addict or sex addict may have certain behaviors or foods that are "off limits," but it is unhealthy to assume individuals would be abstinent from all food or sexual behavior.

The other concept worth mentioning at this point is switching addictions.

> **Switching addictions:** The phenomenon often seen when individuals stop or reduce one addiction and trade it for another.

Until the addiction process is addressed, many times individuals simply bounce from one substance or behavior to another. Outlined next are typical points in the addiction process.

Points on the Addiction Cycle

- An individual uses a substance or a behavior to experience pleasure or medicate negative feelings.
- After the effect of the behavior or substance subsides, feelings of guilt and remorse associated with the choice to use generate more negative thoughts and feelings.
- Unsure of how to cope with these thoughts and feelings, addicts often turn to their drug of choice to feel better again.
- The cycle feeds itself and in a well-established pattern, may repeat hundreds or thousands of times in an addict's life.

There is no simple way to measure an addict's success, other than to know it is a very individualized definition. Perhaps some chemically dependent individuals can learn to moderate their alcohol intake, but others cannot. Perhaps one sex addict can learn to incorporate healthy masturbation into his or her life, but for another, masturbation is a trigger sending him or her into an out-of-control downward spiral of negative thoughts, feelings, and behaviors. Success is individually defined, but should be done with the help of a knowledgeable, objective, and honest outside person, such as a qualified addiction clinician.

EXAMPLE

Being Aware of Addiction Switching

It is not uncommon for an alcohol-dependent individual to switch to nicotine when he or she becomes "sober" from alcohol. Or, an individual might switch his or her gambling addiction to compulsive shopping or spending. This is one reason it is important for helping professionals to understand the process of addiction rather than focus on the specific behavior or chemical in question.

■ Legal, Ethical, and Professional Issues

Many times when working with addicted individuals, the legal system will be involved. Sometimes addicts have difficulty controlling their behaviors in other areas of their lives as well, and issues such as domestic violence, assault, and abuse or neglect of children are not uncommon among addicted individuals. When the legal system is involved, cases are often very complex and clinicians can easily encounter ethical and professional dilemmas.

Additionally, issues of confidentiality differ for addiction treatment agencies and may vary by state. The professional issues that arise are complicated enough to warrant mentioning, but too complicated to delineate in this chapter. When working with the addicted population, it is important to have good supervision, consulting relationships with other medical and mental health providers, and a well-versed attorney regarding professional issues in treating addictions in your state.

Chapter 26: Key Terms

- ▶ Substance addiction
- ▶ Process or behavioral addiction
- ▶ Progression
- ▶ Tolerance

- ▶ Withdrawal
- ▶ Physiological dependence
- ▶ Psychological dependence
- ▶ Collateral informants
- ▶ Motivational interviewing

- ▶ Dual diagnosis
- ▶ Moderated management
- ▶ Spontaneous recovery
- ▶ Abstinence model
- ▶ Switching addictions

Ecological-Transactional and Motivational Perspectives in Counseling

Martin F. Lynch
University of South Florida

Lisa Lopez Levers
Duquesne University

In This Chapter

▶ *Background to the Ecological-Transactional Model*
  ▪ Best Practices in Counselor Education: Emphasis on Context and Culture
  ▪ Deficits of Traditional Theories in Counselor Education

▶ *An Ecological-Transactional Developmental Framework*
  ▪ Learning Theory: Vygotsky
  ▪ Attachment Theory: Bowlby
  ▪ Bioecological Human Development: Bronfenbrenner

▶ *The Ecological-Transactional Model and Professional Counseling*
  ▪ Developmental Psychopathology
  ▪ Resilience
  ▪ Assessing Risks and Protective Factors

▶ *Self-Determination Theory*
  ▪ Organismic and Dialectical Underpinnings of Self-Determination Theory
  ▪ Basic Psychological Needs and the Social Context
  ▪ Reasons for Nonintrinsic Actions
  ▪ Motivation

▶ *Relating Self-Determination Theory to the Helping Professions*
  ▪ Blocks to Clients' Motivation Toward Change
  ▪ How Can Counselors Help Motivate Clients for Change?
  ▪ Empirical Evidence for Self-Determination Theory and Autonomy Support
  ▪ Recommendations for Providing an Autonomy Supportive Context

▶ *Conclusion*

BACKGROUND TO THE ECOLOGICAL-TRANSACTIONAL MODEL

In this chapter, we provide a brief discussion of the ecological-transactional approach, followed by a more extensive discussion of a contemporary motivational approach known as self-determination theory (SDT). These two perspectives share a view of the individual-within-larger-multiple contexts, and together suggest a useful model for understanding the process of change within counseling. Throughout, we offer theory-based examples of counseling interventions that are compatible with these perspectives.

■ Best Practices in Counselor Education: Emphasis on Context and Culture

Widely accepted best practices in counselor education typically promote course work that emphasizes the importance of mediating counseling endeavors through appropriate cultural lenses and in consideration of social contexts. A number of areas that are endorsed in these best practices include the following:

Best Practice Areas Emphasized in Counselor Education Curriculum

- Diversity counseling.
- Psychosocial interventions.
- Systems approaches.
- Developmental and integrative theoretical perspectives.

The theoretical tone that underlies these best practice areas encourages a shift from thinking exclusively in terms of the largely decontextualized psychological perspective on which counselor education curricula often are based. Rather, counseling professionals are encouraged to embrace a broader paradigmatic perspective that reflects a more interdisciplinary, and hence, psychosocial and culture-inclusive view (see Cottone, 1992, for excellent analyses of multiple paradigms of counseling).

■ Deficits of Traditional Theories in Counselor Education

Some traditionally accepted psychological theories (e.g., Freud's psychoanalytic approach, Erikson's psychosocial perspective, etc.) that are taught in counselor education programs might be critiqued as being generally necessary but not sufficient. These models tend to focus necessarily on the individual, but do not account sufficiently for important social, cultural, and contextual influences that individuals continually must negotiate within their environments. A few earlier psychological models account for environmental and transactional dimensions of human existence; the term *transactional* implies that person and environment mutually and reciprocally influence each other. These earlier models, however, historically have not been emphasized in counselor education programs, beyond rudimentary mention in the one "womb-to-tomb" human development overview course that counselor trainees are required to take within the larger counselor education curriculum. These earlier models as well as two newer models are mentioned here as examples of approaches that account for the social and cultural deficits of traditional psychological theories.

Models That Account for Contextual Influences

- Bowlby's (1973, 1980, 1982, 1988) attachment theory.
- Bronfenbrenner's bioecological model of human development (Bronfenbrenner, 1979, 2001, 2004; Bronfenbrenner & Ceci, 1994).
- Developmental psychopathology (e.g., Belsky, 1993; Cicchetti & Aber, 1998; Cicchetti & Lynch, 1993, 1995; Cicchetti & Toth, 1995; Garmezy 1993).
- An ecological-transactional approach (e.g., Cicchetti & Lynch, 1993; Cicchetti & Toth, 1995).

Both the developmental psychopathology perspective and ecological-transactional models are theoretical approaches not typically emphasized in counselor education programs. However, these models are of enormous utility for professional counselors working, for example, with maltreated children, and by extension, for working with adults who exhibit the characteristics of psychopathology often associated with early childhood trauma.

AN ECOLOGICAL-TRANSACTIONAL DEVELOPMENTAL FRAMEWORK

This section provides a brief background on three theoretical perspectives that form the ecological-transactional developmental framework suggested to be of importance to counselors. Summaries of the ideas posed by three key theoreticians—Vygotsky, Bowlby, and Bronfenbrenner—are presented; applications of this framework along with several salient concepts are offered.

■ Learning Theory: Vygotsky

Although Vygotsky originally developed his models in relation to learning theory and child development, these theories have been incorporated usefully into adult learning and development theory. Two of the most helpful concepts that Vygotsky (1978, 1986, 1997) introduced are the zone of proximal development and scaffolding, understood this way:

Zone of proximal development: The dynamic and interactive process between what a child is capable of doing by himself or herself and what a child can do with the assistance of a parent, teacher, or mentor.

Scaffolding: The fluidity of children's competencies on which further development can hinge.

See Chapter 8 for more on Vygotsky and these key concepts.

■ Attachment Theory: Bowlby

Some developmental theorists point to the primacy of the mother–infant relationship, especially early attachment (e.g., Bowlby, 1973, 1980, 1982, 1988) and infant competency and its interactive dimensions (e.g., Belsky, Rovine, & Taylor, 1984; Belsky, Spritz, & Crnic, 1996; Isabella, Belsky, & von Eye, 1989; Lebovici, 1995; Osofsky, Wewers, Hann, & Fick, 1993; Vygotsky, 1978). Accordingly, development does not result simply from how the parent acts on the child, but rather, is viewed as evolving from the reciprocal interaction of caregiver and child. Attachment theory (e.g., Bowlby) has provided a framework for understanding the human need for security and safety and the effects on individuals of separation, loss, and trauma.

■ Bioecological Human Development: Bronfenbrenner

Within the context of his bioecological model, Bronfenbrenner (2004) defined development this way:

Human development: The "phenomenon of continuity and change in the biopsychological characteristics of human beings both as individuals and as groups. The phenomenon extends over the life course across successive generations and through historical time, both past and present" (p. 3).

Bronfenbrenner's (1979) theory of human development views the individual, with all his or her personal attributes, as affected by and interactive with multiple environmental systems. These systems are interactive with one another and with the individual, postulating reciprocal influences between the individual and the environment. The ecological systems of influence that Bronfenbrenner identified are noted here.

Ecological Spheres of Human Development

- Ontogenic (individual).
- Microsystemic (immediate family environment).
- Exosystemic (community and neighborhood).
- Macrosystemic (broad cultural values and beliefs).

From proximal to distal influences, environmental factors have an impact on the person in stage-salient ways; and continual transactions within the environment, or ecology, determine the risk or protective factors present in the individual's ecology. Risk and protective factors can be defined this way:

Risk factors: Those that have the potential to interrupt the individual's normal developmental pathway or trajectory, such as exposure to violence.

Protective factors: Those that can serve to buffer the individual from the influence of risk factors, such as the presence of a caring and nurturing adult.

Bronfenbrenner also identified 10 propositions that can be viewed as intrinsic to the model, as well as to the continuing evolution of, assessment of, and research from the perspective of the model. Elements from a number of these propositions are mentioned here.

Some Key Elements of Bronfenbrenner's Model of Development

- The importance of subjective experience, along with the objective perspective is stressed.
- **Proximal processes** (those more immediate to the person within the larger ecological system), or enduring forms of interaction over extended periods of time, are emphasized.
- Involvement in progressively more complex processes is recognized.
- Mutual attachments that endure over time are highlighted.
- Continuity and change are integral properties of the model.

Finally, an essential characteristic of Bronfenbrenner's model is the rich framework it provides for clinicians in assessing risks and protective factors in the lives of clients and in constructing interventions that can minimize or eliminate risks, mediate risks, or foster or enhance protective factors. This provides a vast horizon for creative applications, both theoretically and clinically.

EXAMPLE

Bronfenbrenner's Bioecological Theory in Clinical Practice

Using Bronfenbrenner's model, the clinician can conduct an assessment of the risk and protective factors present within the various levels of the client's ecological system. The clinician might discover, for example, that a child client lives in a neighborhood where a risk factor such as exposure to violence is common. The clinician might, however, be in a position to facilitate access to resources, such as a university-sponsored after-school program, that could help to offset the risk of that exposure, even though the violence itself may continue. As this example suggests, taking an ecological perspective can sometimes mean stepping outside the confines of the counseling office, figuratively and perhaps at times literally.

THE ECOLOGICAL-TRANSACTIONAL MODEL AND PROFESSIONAL COUNSELING

A significant aspect of the theoretical models discussed here is the possibility for constructing interventions that resonate at the individual, environmental, and systemic levels. An important application of ecological and transactional models can be seen in the rich and growing areas of developmental psychopathology (e.g., Cicchetti & Lynch, 1993, 1995; Cicchetti & Toth, 1995) and resiliency.

■ Developmental Psychopathology

Traditional educational and psychological theories regarding child and adolescent development in normative populations, and psychiatric theories regarding psychopathology in clinical populations, have fallen short of providing the much needed ecological perspective from which to view the contextual experiences of children coping with abuse or other types of maltreatment. Developmental psychopathology has evolved in response to the need for more effective ways to help people recover from traumatic experiences and provides a theoretical basis for considering environmental risks and protective factors. This approach can be defined this way:

> **Developmental psychopathology:** A combination of ecological and transactional theories that studies the contributions of the person and the environment to both adaptive and maladaptive developmental outcomes. Such an approach, for example, might identify maltreated, or at-risk children, as being deleteriously affected by abnormal events, or risk factors, that alter what would be their otherwise relatively normal developmental pathways.

In developmental psychopathology, it is this disrupted or alternative developmental trajectory that is viewed as deviant, not the child. Without intervention, the affected children eventually may develop characteristics associated with and perhaps leading to psychopathology, but the emphasis of the neoecological theories is on the need for identifying protective factors to mediate environmental risks.

Developmental psychopathology (Belsky, 1993; Cicchetti & Lynch, 1993, 1995; Cicchetti & Toth, 1995) provides a framework that accounts for some of the shortcomings of traditional approaches.

How Developmental Psychopathology Accounts for Shortcomings in Traditional Theory

- The theory understands the interplay between normal development and abnormal events.
- The theory provides essential clues for beginning to comprehend the effects of chronic violence on children, especially in terms of risk factors.

- Developmental psychopathology accounts for distal and proximal influences across nested systemic levels that affect children in stage-salient ways.

Importantly, in the face of multiple and interactive risk factors, some children have emerged from "high-risk" situations exhibiting compensatory or protective factors (Garmezy, 1993). Cicchetti and Lynch (1993) detailed an ecological-transactional model, offering an avenue for comprehensively understanding the influence of multiple factors, at multiple levels, on children's development. Continual transactions within the environment, or ecology, determine what constitutes risk or protective factors.

EXAMPLE

Implications of Developmental Psychopathology for Treatment of Traumatized Adults

The transactional nature of development offered in this model is imperative to understanding the complex, sometimes paradoxical, effects of maltreatment on children at multiple systemic levels and then intervening effectively. Although developmental psychopathology focuses on the developmental issues of maltreated children, as well as the possibility for mediating the risks associated with maltreatment, there are definite implications for the development of adults who have survived early childhood trauma. Many professional counselors are assisting clients, across the life span, in dealing with issues of trauma. Any traumatic incident can pose multiple risks for the individual, but by accounting for protective factors that can mediate (or ameliorate) more intrusive risk factors, the model also allows for a productive consideration of facilitating resiliency in the face of trauma.

■ Resilience

Following this developmental-ecological theoretical discourse, Garbarino (1993) presented a "framework for understanding the developmental significance of violence-related trauma in the lives of young children" (p. 103). He posited that there are significant developmental differences between acute trauma and chronic trauma, as well as differing phenomenological constructions for responses and adaptations to perceived danger versus responses and adaptations to actual trauma. Interaction and competence become key factors in situations of trauma, because the child's competency-based development depends on having access to reliable adults who can help interpret meaning in a protective, or at least self-efficacious, way.

Garbarino (1995) linked the child's "reservoirs of resiliency" to the ability of parents (or other responsible caregivers) not only to "buffer" the consequences of trauma, but beyond that, to interpret events in ways that enable children to derive a sense of personal meaning reflective of self-preservation; this ability to engage in personal meaning making (Bruner, 1990; Carlsen, 1988) can be considered a resiliency factor, one that contributes to a restoration or construction of a personal sense of safety or equilibrium, as appropriate to the situation. Broadly speaking, resilience can be defined this way:

> **Resilience:** Positive or adaptive developmental outcomes, despite the presence of risk factors or adversity.

For example, a child who has been exposed to multiple or chronic risk factors, but whose adjustment in major life domains (e.g., interpersonal relationships, school success, and self-concept) is on the whole positive, could be said to demonstrate a degree of resilience. Boyce et al. (1998) stated that such "contexts have multiple dimensions that add to, moderate, and mediate one another in influencing children's behavioral and emotional development" (p. 147). Although Luthar, Cicchetti, and Becker (2000) cautioned that research in the area of resilience must attend to the serious conceptual and methodological problems that have been present in a number of studies to date, they emphasized legitimate avenues of resiliency research that can enhance current understandings of at-risk children.

■ Assessing Risks and Protective Factors

The bioecological model offers a theoretical framework for assessing the risks that may be present across multiple systemic environments in the life of an individual. By better understanding a person's risk factors, a counselor may be positioned better to identify protective factors and inner resources that also may be present, thus opening the possibility for successful intervention and mediation. However, important questions emerge about client motivation. In other words, when people are experiencing the negative effects of multiple environmental or interpersonal risks, professional counselors need to consider how to motivate them to tap into their own existing resiliencies or to use what protection is available from the environment. One theory of motivation that is compatible with ecological and transactional theories is self-determination theory (SDT).

SELF-DETERMINATION THEORY

Self-Determination Theory (SDT) is a theory of personality development and self-motivated behavior change that uses traditional empirical methods while emphasizing the application of research findings in a number of practical domains such as education, sports, work, religion, and, importantly, counseling and psychotherapy (Deci & Ryan, 1985; Ryan & Deci, 2000). Deci and Ryan's (1985) elegant theory of self-determination accounts for individual, as well as environmental, motivational aspects of persons' experiences. Their theory is congruent with other ecological and transactional theories. In this introduction to SDT, three core tenets of the theory are described:

1. Organismic and dialectical perspectives from which SDT developed.
2. The role of basic psychological needs and the environment in SDT.
3. Internal and external motivation.

■ Organismic and Dialectical Underpinnings of Self-Determination Theory

In its study of personality growth and development, SDT embraces a perspective that is both organismic and dialectical. Organismic theories have roots that extend back as far as Aristotle, and find more contemporary expression in the work of thinkers such as Piaget, Dewey, and the humanistic psychologists. A basic assumption of the organismic viewpoint is that living things are different from nonliving things in some pretty fundamental respects (see Overton, 1976; Ryan & Deci, 2002; Sheldon, Williams, & Joyner, 2003). Three other assumptions that are an outgrowth of this fundamental belief and that are central to SDT are noted next.

Organismic Assumptions of SDT

1. There is a natural tendency toward growth and integration that characterizes things that are alive, including human beings. Living things naturally tend to integrate and organize their experience, attaining greater and greater complexity over their life course.
2. Humans are by nature more active than reactive. Although we are never entirely free of environmental influences, we are proactive, guided by inner motives and needs that subserve the first principle, that of growth, organization, and integration.
3. The tendency toward growth and integration, and the tendency to be proactive rather than reactive, are not taken for granted.

Particularly in regard to the third assumption, SDT concerns itself with the social-contextual circumstances that can either support these natural, organismic tendencies, or can forestall and undermine them.

SDT thus provides an account for a wide range of developmental outcomes, suggesting that growth and positive development are promoted in contexts that foster these natural tendencies, whereas less favorable outcomes can be expected in contexts that prevent or inhibit them. In other words, SDT posits a kind of dialectical tension between an active, integrating human person on the one hand, and the social environment, on the other. The classic formula or dialectic process that underlies SDT is summarized here.

Dialectical Formula

- Life in the physical and social world presents challenges (*theses*).
- The person must respond to the world's challenges (*antitheses*).
- Responses to *theses*, or life challenges, optimally lead to new levels of complexity and integration (*syntheses*).

The organismic tendency, in other words, unfolds in a physical-social context in a dialectical fashion. Its organismic-dialectical perspective thus situates SDT within the ecological-transactional framework outlined by Bronfenbrenner (1979) and by Cicchetti and Lynch (1993).

■ Basic Psychological Needs and the Social Context

Drawing on the organismic perspective, early SDT theorists recognized that living things clearly have biological needs for things like hydration, nourishment, and warmth (Deci & Ryan, 1985). When these needs are satisfied, the living organism survives and thrives; when these needs fail to be satisfied, the organism suffers and, if the deprivation is sufficiently severe or prolonged, eventually dies. These theorists reasoned that humans, as highly social, complex, living organisms with a prolonged period of dependency during infancy and childhood, also have evolved basic psychological needs (Ryan, Kuhl, & Deci, 1997). Ryan and Deci (2002) defined basic psychological needs this way:

> **Basic psychological needs:** Inner resources with important survival value that are held to be universal and that include the needs for relatedness, competence, and autonomy.

Each of the needs serves as a source of the energy and direction characteristic of motivated human behavior (Deci & Ryan, 1985; Reeve, 2005), in that people strive to satisfy them in their daily lives, although the way in which needs are satisfied may vary from person to person, situation to situation, and culture to culture.

Three Basic Psychological Needs Identified in SDT

1. *Relatedness* refers to a sense of belongingness with others and with one's community; it includes the presence of relationships that are characterized by mutual caring (Baumeister & Leary, 1995; Bowlby, 1979; Harlow, 1958). As such, it is more akin to emotional intimacy than to sex, strictly speaking. People are inherently motivated to seek meaningful, mutual, and lasting relationships.
2. *Competence* reflects the capacity to feel, and indeed, to be effective in one's interactions with the physical and social environment. It includes having opportunities to exercise and expand one's capabilities. People are motivated to seek optimal challenges that will afford them such opportunities.

3. *Autonomy* refers to the experience of being the initiator of one's own behavior. It refers to feeling that one is an origin or source, rather than a "pawn" pushed around by external forces (deCharms, 1968; Deci & Ryan, 1985). It includes the experience of having voice and choice in one's activities.

SDT distinguishes between autonomy and independence, which is characterized by a freedom from other people and lack of reliance on them. Research in the SDT tradition has demonstrated that autonomy and independence are different and distinct constructs: Adolescents who experience a high degree of autonomy, for example, are also characterized by a willingness to rely on (depend on) their parents for emotional support (Ryan, 1993; Ryan & Lynch, 1989). Conceptualizing autonomy as a basic need, SDT suggests that people are generally motivated to exercise choice and to take initiative in their daily lives.

SDT further suggests that social contexts that afford opportunities to meet these three basic psychological needs for relatedness, competence, and autonomy promote the organizing and integrating tendencies that are associated with optimal development and well-being (Ryan & Connell, 1989; Ryan & Deci, 2000, 2002). Social contexts can accordingly either promote or disrupt development, as noted here.

Impact of Social Context on Development (Ryan & Deci, 2000)

1. Social contexts that are responsive to basic psychological needs provide a developmental network within which people can naturally ascend.
2. Social contexts characterized by excessive control, nonoptimal challenges, and lack of connectedness disturb the natural actualizing tendencies, inhibit initiative and responsibility, and can result in distress and psychopathology.

Attention to basic psychological needs and the contexts that either support or thwart them is thus a central aspect of the SDT approach to counseling and psychotherapy.

■ Reasons for Nonintrinsic Actions

Human beings, from birth on, are embedded in social contexts. As such, not all of our motives and initiatives are self-generated or intrinsic. SDT recognizes a number of reasons not all actions are motivated toward meeting the basic psychological needs.

Explanations for Nonintrinsic or Externally Motivated Actions

■ We constantly are adapting and adjusting to the wishes, demands, expectations, and hopes of others.

- Not all external influences are in accord with our inner psychological needs, which otherwise would serve as the primary guides for our actions.
- Because of outside influences, we frequently find ourselves carrying out actions that did not originate from within ourselves.

■ Motivation

Given that, because of outside influence, people are not always capable of acting on their need for relatedness, competence, and autonomy, SDT suggests that the motivation to carry out any action can be either more internally or more externally motivated.

Internal motivation: Initiatives that are characterized by a sense of autonomy and choice.

External motivation: Initiatives that are characterized by a sense of pressure, coercion, and control.

Humans are embedded within a physical and social context, and so many of the things we do are prompted, initially, by forces outside ourselves. SDT suggests that the quality of our motivation for such actions is what matters most. Because initiatives that come from outside ourselves can be either willingly consented to or enacted grudgingly, and in this respect can feel more or less autonomous or controlled, SDT proposes a continuum of motivation.

The Motivation Continuum in SDT

- The continuum ranges from external motivation at one end to integrated or internal motivation at the other end.
- Social contexts that satisfy the basic psychological needs have been shown to promote more internal motivation, whereas contexts that thwart satisfaction of those needs have been associated with more controlled or external forms of motivation (Ryan & Connell, 1989).
- The motivation continuum is not static, but rather dynamic: Motivation for any activity can change, becoming either more or less autonomous, in response to environmental circumstances that are experienced as either more need-satisfying or more need-thwarting, respectively.

This continuum is used to describe the (dialectical) process of internalization, which can be understood as follows:

Internalization: An aspect of socialization in which external values, norms, and regulations are taken in by the active, organismic self, and are experienced by that self as either endorsed and congruent or alien and incongruent.

According to SDT, satisfaction of the basic needs, and of the need for autonomy, in particular, leads to greater endorsement or congruence (greater internalization) of the value or behavior in question, and this in turn is associated with more optimal psychological and developmental outcomes. In short, the process of internalization is promoted by support for the basic needs.

RELATING SELF-DETERMINATION THEORY TO THE HELPING PROFESSIONS

As noted, SDT provides a framework, based on its organismic and dialectical propositions, for conceptualizing the presenting problems that clients bring with them to counseling. If it is indeed true that satisfying the needs for relatedness, competence, and autonomy is vital for growth and development, indeed for well-being, then it stands to reason that the experience of serious, possibly chronic, deprivation in any of these three areas may underlie many forms of human distress. Certainly, such a position is consistent with the perspectives and experience of clinicians from the humanistic (Rogers, 1959) and object relations (Basch, 1995; Miller, 1997) traditions. Accordingly, the theoretical perspective offered by SDT may serve to guide interventions targeted to address chronic deprivation (whether historical or current) of any of the three basic needs posited by the theory. Work in this area has thus far been limited. Much more work has been done, however, on applying SDT's body of findings on human motivation to the helping process itself.

■ Blocks to Clients' Motivation Toward Change

Identifying and facilitating clients' motivation for change is a central issue faced by counselors and other helping professionals. Any number of hindrances can stand in the way of a client's ability to change; a few barriers to clients' motivation to change that counselors may encounter are noted here.

Hindrances to the Change Process

- Change can be painful and difficult.
- Certain quality of motivation is required both to initiate and maintain any serious program of change.
- Clients frequently come to counseling not entirely of their own will (e.g., the spouse who is pressured to seek help by a well-meaning but exasperated partner, or the child who is compelled to "get fixed" by the school authorities or by parents).
- Clients who come to counseling willingly, on their own initiative, may experience some ambivalence over the prospect of change when they are faced with the reality of what such change may actually entail.

SDT acknowledges the central role of motivation in the counseling process, recognizing that, as in any endeavor, the quality of motivation for counseling—whether more internal, or more external—will have an important impact on the quality of experience and the nature of the outcomes. When clients are more internally motivated, their experience of and attitude toward counseling are expected to be more positive, and their outcomes more favorable.

■ How Can Counselors Help Motivate Clients for Change?

SDT proposes a process model of change that has been tested empirically in a number of clinical settings. The main components of this change model are provided briefly as follows.

Assumptions of the SDT Process Model of Change

- Clients bring to the task of counseling a certain quality of motivation, which to some extent may represent an individual difference in the form of a tendency to act more autonomously or more heteronomously (i.e., with a sense of being pressured and controlled by external forces).
- The social context represented by the counseling relationship (or even the institutional setting in which counseling occurs) can foster movement of the client's motivation along the motivation continuum in the direction of either greater autonomy or greater control.
- Movement takes place according to whether the social context is experienced by the client as providing either more or less opportunity to satisfy the basic psychological needs.
- Under conditions of greater need satisfaction, motivation for a given domain of activity tends to become more autonomous. Specifically, the model suggests that when clients experience their care providers as more supportive of clients' need for autonomy, the clients will gradually adopt a more autonomous motivational orientation toward the process of counseling, and will also experience greater felt competence to participate in that process.

The experience of having an autonomy supportive care provider, in other words, leads to more autonomous motivation and to greater perceived competence for engaging in counseling. Greater autonomy and greater competence, in turn, lead to greater actual engagement in counseling, to greater willingness to extend oneself beyond one's comfort zone (or perhaps to extend oneself within one's zone of proximal development, to borrow Vygotsky's concept) and take risks by trying new behaviors, and indeed to measurable improvement on target outcomes and maintained behavioral change over time. By facilitating client choice, the model hypothesizes that counselors can help their clients to identify and embrace their own reasons for change; that is, whatever clients' initial reasons for coming to counseling, for participating or not participating, their motivation will become more internal than external, and they will accordingly experience the more positive outcomes associated with internal motivation, when they experience their counselors as autonomy supportive.

EXAMPLE

Applying the SDT Process Model of Change to Addictions

Many clients in addictions rehabilitation centers are mandated to treatment, often by the court system. A constant struggle for counselors in these settings is how to "reach" clients who have not chosen treatment so that positive change (e.g., eradication of the addictive behaviors) can occur. SDT suggests that a key to breaking through barriers to change is using the counseling relationship as a place where the client can make autonomous or self-motivated decisions in treatment. SDT implies that counselors who help clients make their own decisions about kinds of involvement in treatment will be more effective in supporting clients' change process than if they force clients into interventions. For further discussion, see Markland, Ryan, Tobin, and Rollnick (2005).

■ Empirical Evidence for Self-Determination Theory and Autonomy Support

To date, the general SDT process model has been tested in several areas.

Settings Studied for the Effectiveness of SDT

- Alcohol treatment (Ryan, Plant, & O'Malley, 1995).
- Weight loss (Williams, Grow, Freedman, Ryan, & Deci, 1996).
- Medication adherence (Williams, Rodin, Ryan, Grolnick, & Deci, 1998).
- Diabetes management (Williams, Freedman, & Deci, 1998).
- Smoking cessation (Williams, Gagne, Ryan, & Deci, 2002).
- Eating disorders (Vansteenkiste, Soenens, & Vandereycken, 2005).

This body of research shows a number of results linked to clients' experiences of their counselors and health care providers as providing autonomy support. Some of the positive implications of autonomy support are provided here.

Impact of Autonomy Support on Client Development

- Clients are more likely to endorse internal reasons for participating in the change process.
- Clients are more likely to feel competent about their internal motivation to change.
- Clients are more likely to attend sessions and to participate in the process.
- Clients are more likely to initiate and to maintain targeted behavioral changes.

Notably, not only counselors and health care providers, but also important others (spouse, family members, friends) have been shown to play a role in the SDT model: When clients experience autonomy support from their important others, aside from the support they may experience from their professional care provider, they are more likely to endorse an autonomous motivation for change, and to experience competence to engage in the change process (Williams et al., 2006). Importantly, many of the studies cited have consisted of longitudinal, clinical trials. Although most of them have been in the area of health psychology, at least one study has demonstrated the utility of conceptualizing clients' motivation for therapy in SDT terms (Pelletier, Tuson, & Haddad, 1997). Indeed, the general model of how social contexts shape the motivation of the people within them has been demonstrated in various settings, including an inpatient psychiatric hospital for youth (Lynch, Plant, & Ryan, 2005), a nursing home (Kasser & Ryan, 1999), educational contexts (Reeve, 2002; Williams & Deci, 1996), and parenting (Grolnick & Apostoleris, 2002; Niemic et al., 2006), to name a few.

Recommendations for Providing an Autonomy Supportive Context

A number of recommendations can be drawn from the SDT literature on how counselors and other helping professionals can apply the SDT process model to facilitate greater internal motivation among their clients. A laboratory experiment (Deci, Eghrari, Patrick, & Leone, 1994), for example, identified specific elements of the social context that constitute autonomy support. Other research in settings such as education (see Reeve, 2002, for a summary) confirms the findings of that experiment. Adapting the results of this body of research to the counseling setting leads to the following recommendations for supporting clients' autonomy and thus facilitating internalization, autonomous motivation for change, and perceived competence.

Suggestions for Counselors in Promoting Autonomous Changes in Clients

1. Provide a meaningful rationale for why a particular course of action is being recommended, especially when a client is unsure of the need for counseling at all. Presumably, understanding the rationale for an action for which the client is not initially internally motivated can help to foster the experience of choice, which is a key element in satisfying the need for autonomy.
2. Acknowledge clients' feelings and perspectives to help them to feel understood and to help to reduce defensiveness and resistance. This can be especially important when their feelings about coming to counseling in the first place, or about undertaking a proposed change, may not be very positive. Having the opportunity to express one's feelings, feeling understood, and experiencing that one's feelings and opinions matter, are important aspects of the experience of autonomy.
3. Use an interpersonal style that promotes choice and that minimizes control to help to remove some of the sense of pressure or coercion that clients can some-

times experience, whether that pressure comes from sources that are external (e.g., a pressuring partner or parent; the offer of reward for success or punishment for failure) or internal (e.g., feelings of "should," "ought," or shame avoidance).

Counselors, as parents, teachers, managers, and other authority figures, can present themselves as experts who hold the reins of power, implicitly imposing their will and demanding compliance of those under their care; or, alternatively, they can empower clients to see that many of the choices entailed in the counseling process are in fact theirs to make. Notably, all three of the "mini-interventions" just listed as aspects of the counselor's therapeutic style, are aimed at fostering the client's experience of autonomy and, hence, at promoting internalization of the reasons for change as well as engagement in the process of counseling. This follows from the SDT proposition that autonomy is a basic psychological need.

Other specific interventions that are compatible with this approach may be drawn from motivational interviewing, which Miller and Rollnick (2002) defined as follows:

Motivational interviewing: A directive, client-centered counseling style for eliciting behavior change by helping clients explore and resolve ambivalence.

Motivational interviewing has been shown to provide many of the social facilitating techniques that promote the organismic growth tendency that SDT theoretically articulates (Markland et al., 2005). The body of SDT research suggests that motivational interventions that are undertaken in the dialectical context of the counseling relationship, and that are aimed at supporting clients' experience of satisfaction for their organismic needs for autonomy, competence, and relatedness, are likely to be the most successful in helping clients to initiate and maintain meaningful change in their lives.

EXAMPLE

Using Recommended SDT Approaches With Adolescents

Imagine that an adolescent male, is brought to counseling by his mother, who is concerned about her son's behaviors that include being verbally disrespectful to teachers, instigating fights with peers at school, listening to "loud and angry" music, and wearing inappropriate clothing. Because the client was "brought" to counseling by his mother, his level of interest in the therapeutic process is minimal and his behavior can be characterized as resistant as he often listens to his music while in session with the counselor and at times refuses to speak. In approaching the client, a counselor who tries to apply SDT recommendations might first try to create a reasonable rationale for why his mother referred him for treatment and for any interventions in which they jointly engage. The counselor also may spend one or more sessions validating the client's feelings about being "brought" to therapy. Already, these approaches can help the client to know that the counselor is interested in his experiences and wants his input in the therapeutic process. Throughout the counseling relationship, the therapist who uses an SDT approach also may find it effective to help the client gain a sense of ownership—and promote internal motivation—over his goals for change and not necessarily those of his mother or the counselor.

See Chapter 26 for more on motivational interviewing as applied to addictions counseling.

 Check out this site for more information on motivational interviewing:

▶ http://www.motivationalinterview.org/

CONCLUSION

Ecological-transactional and motivational theories serve to inform clinical practice in profound ways. The organismic, bioecological, dialectical viewpoint implicit in the approaches outlined herein suggests an active human person who is in constant interaction with the surrounding environment. To each situation, at each moment throughout the day, the person brings a set of basic psychological needs that he or she is striving to fulfill within the given social and physical context, all in the service of organismic growth, integration, and development.

This perspective provides a model for understanding how many forms of psychopathology emerge. As previously noted, need satisfaction is a dialectical process involving the individual in a multilayered social context. When basic needs are thwarted or deprived within a person's interpersonal world, ill-being results. When they are consistently, chronically, or traumatically thwarted, more serious forms of pathology and suffering are to be expected. The converse, however, is also true: When opportunities to satisfy basic needs are consistently available and accessible within the environment, it is expected that the natural propensities for growth and development will unfold, and well-being will ensue. The model thus looks at both deficits and resources, within the person and within the environment. By shedding light on both the positive and negative aspects of living, by providing an avenue for understanding both pathology as well as optimal development, and by shedding light on the contributions of both the person and the environment, these insights can inform the processes of assessment (understanding how the client got that way) and intervention (providing a guide for therapeutic action) in counseling.

> The model thus looks at both deficits and resources, within the person and within the environment. By shedding light on both the positive and negative aspects of living, by providing an avenue for understanding both pathology as well as optimal development, and by shedding light on the contributions of both the person and the environment, these insights can inform the processes of assessment (understanding how the client got that way) and intervention (providing a guide for therapeutic action) in counseling.

Importantly, the organismic, bioecological viewpoint also suggests a model for the counseling relationship itself. The counseling dyad, or the group, if the setting is one of group counseling, is itself an environment, an interpersonal context. As such, the counselor can act in such a way as to support the client's basic needs for autonomy, competence, and relatedness, by promoting choice, efficacy, and genuine interpersonal contact, or the counselor can subtly or not so subtly act to undermine the client's psychological needs by withholding these important resources. The goal is not for the counselor to become a surrogate need provider. Rather, by helping clients learn how to identify and begin to satisfy their basic needs, and by facilitating autonomously motivated action on the clients' part, first in the context of counseling, and then in their daily lives, they are likely to see clients who are able to initiate and to maintain healthy change in their lives, experiencing greater competence and interpersonal satisfaction in the process. This may be especially important for clients whose prior life experience may not have provided them with many opportunities to experience need satisfaction at developmentally critical periods, as in the case of early childhood neglect, or whose life experience may even have traumatically undermined or interrupted the organismic process of integration and development that otherwise would have naturally unfolded.

Although we have emphasized the importance of need satisfaction in this dialectical model, it is essential for counselors and their clients to realize that this organismic process is not an inherently selfish or one-sided one. Indeed, recent research demonstrates that, within interpersonal relationships, need satisfaction involves a give and take, and that providing for another's needs is at least as important to one's own well-being as receiving need satisfaction from the other person (Deci, La Guardia, Moller, Scheiner, & Ryan, 2006). In the end, and in line with the bioecological model, that indeed is the nature of the dialectical process, which implies the reciprocal influence and interconnectedness of the members in any ecological unit.

Chapter 27: Key Terms

- Zone of proximal development
- Scaffolding
- Human development
- Risk factors

- Protective factors
- Proximal processes
- Developmental psychopathology
- Resilience

- Basic psychological needs
- Internal motivation
- External motivation
- Internalization
- Motivational interviewing

Neuroscience in Psychotherapeutic Practices

28

Stacie Leffard
Duquesne University

In This Chapter

▶ *Neuroscience and Psychotherapeutic Practices*
- Neuroscience and Psychotherapy: Early Connections
- What Is Neuroscience and Why Is It Important to Therapists?

▶ *The Nervous System*
- Systems Within the Nervous System
- Neurons
- Action Potential

▶ *The Brain*
- The Cerebral Cortex
- The Forebrain
- Midbrain
- Hindbrain

▶ *Facilitating Neural Change*
- How Does Neural Change Occur?
- Principles for Brain-Based Psychotherapy
- Understanding Schemas
- Dealing With Problematic Schemas
- Changing View About Incoming Stimuli
- Impact of Stress on Neural Change
- Utilizing the Hemispheres

▶ *Ensuring Lasting Neural Change*
- Automization of Internalized Processes
- Monitoring Change in Client Thinking
- Monitoring Change in Clients' Executive State
- Techniques for Engaging Emotional States

▶ *Clients With Processing Deficits*
- Effectiveness of Cognitive Remediation Therapy
- Cautions When Using Cognitive Rehabilitation

▶ *Attention-Related Processing Deficits*
- Individualizing the Length of Therapy Sessions
- Use of Cues

▶ *Memory-Related Processing Deficits*
- Rehearsal
- Mnemonic Strategies
- Labels, Notebooks, and Calendars
- Spaced Retrieval

▶ *Executive Functions Deficits*
- Goal Management Training
- Other Approaches to Helping Clients With Executive Functioning Deficits

▶ *Summary*

NEUROSCIENCE AND PSYCHOTHERAPEUTIC PRACTICES

The purpose of this chapter is first to provide the reader with a basic understanding of the brain and its functions and, second, to relate the basic principles of brain function to the practice of psychotherapy. Neuroscience-based techniques for helping individuals who have processing deficits also are described. The relation between neuroscience and psychotherapy is not based in any specific theoretical orientation, and therefore, can be used by any therapist to improve the effectiveness of psychotherapy.

■ Neuroscience and Psychotherapy: Early Connections

Examinations of the relation between neuroscience and psychotherapy are not a recent development in the field of psychology. Freud, in the late 19th century, began to investigate the relation between the brain and the mind. Freud observed symptoms in his practice of neurology that could not be explained or treated based solely on the available understanding of the brain. Consequently, he developed psychotherapeutic methods to treat symptoms that, at that time, could not be explained by neuroscience (Cozolino, 2002). Scientific advances in the area of neuroscience now provide the opportunity not only to explain the symptoms that Freud could not explain neurologically, but also to describe the neuroscientific underpinnings of psychotherapy.

■ What Is Neuroscience and Why Is It Important to Therapists?

Neuroscience is the study of the nervous system. Therapists are trained to understand, and in some cases, modify human behavior to improve the functioning of their clients. Each of the behaviors or cognitions therapists strive to understand and assist their clients in understanding is the result of nervous system functioning. In addition to understanding the external motivations or influences on human behavior, gaining knowledge about the internal neural underpinnings of behavior adds an additional lens through which to understand behavior and facilitate change.

THE NERVOUS SYSTEM

This goal of this section and the next, which is focused on the brain, is to provide a basic structure for understanding neurological functioning. Therefore, it is necessary to briefly leave the world of psychology and enter the realm of biology. Hopefully, this thumbnail sketch of neurology will create a frame of reference for readers to more fully grasp the applications of neuroscience to psychotherapy. Turning now to the section at hand, the nervous system is described through the following topics:

- Systems within the nervous system.
- Neurons.
- Action potential reaction.
- Autonomic nervous system.

■ Systems Within the Nervous System

The nervous system is made up of two systems, namely, the central nervous system and the peripheral nervous system. The **central nervous system (CNS)**, responsible for control of all major systems of the body, contains the brain and the spinal cord. The peripheral nervous system (PNS) is comprised of nerves extending from the spinal cord to the rest of the body (e.g., organs and muscles).

Part of the PNS, the system of nerves that connects the rest of the body to the spinal cord or the CNS, also affects behavior and is known as the autonomic nervous system. The *autonomic nervous system* (ANS) controls breathing, heart rate, and sweating. The ANS is composed of two systems: the sympathetic and parasympathetic nervous systems.

Systems in the ANS (Blumenfeld, 2002)

1. The *sympathetic nervous system* is related to the fight or flight response in that it increases heart rate, blood pressure, and rate of breathing.
2. The *parasympathetic nervous system* slows heart rate, blood pressure, and breathing rate.

■ Neurons

The brain, and the rest of the nervous system, is composed of cells called neurons, which are responsible for communication within the nervous system. There are two types of neurons, afferent and efferent neurons, defined as follows:

Afferent neurons: Sensory neurons that carry signals toward the CNS.

Efferent neurons: Motor neurons that carry signals away from the CNS.

Neurons are complex cells. It is important to have a general knowledge of the composition of the neuron to understand how neurons communicate by passing information to one another.

Components of the Neuron

- The **cell body** contains the nucleus of the neuron and makes up gray matter in the brain such as the cerebral cortex.
- **Dendrites** are branches that extend from the cell body and receive signals from other neurons.
- The **axon** extends from the cell body and carries output signals to other neurons.
- The **synapse** is the area between neurons, and because neurons do not touch, chemicals pass between neurons across the synapse (Balbernie, 2001). In the synapse, information is passed from the terminal buttons at the end of one neuron's axon to the dendrites of another neuron.
- **Neurotransmitters** are chemicals released by terminal buttons at the end of one neuron and received at receptor sites on the dendrites of other neurons. Common neurotransmitters include glutamate, GABA, acetylcholine, norepinephrine, dopamine, serotonin, histamine, glycine, and peptides (Blumenfeld, 2002).
- Axons are insulated by a **myelin sheath,** a covering that increases the speed at which signals travel. Axons insulated with myelin make up white matter in the brain. White matter areas are responsible for communication in the brain (Blumenfeld, 2002).
- A **neural pathway** or pattern is formed when a series of neurons fire or release electrical impulses in the form of neurotransmitters. If repeated enough, the series of firing forms a permanent circuit (Balbernie, 2001; Gevarter, 1982).

■ Action Potential

When a neuron receives enough input signals from other neurons and must send the signal to another neuron, a chemical reaction called an action potential occurs, traveling from the cell body down the axon and resulting in the release of an output signal at the terminal buttons. This reaction occurs in approximately 1 millisecond and can travel down the axon at speeds of 60 meters per second (Blumenfeld, 2002). The amount of stimulation it takes for an action potential to occur is affected by stress, diet, drug use, fatigue, and emotionality (Gevarter, 1982). Neurotransmitters can affect action potentials by speeding them up or slowing them down.

THE BRAIN

The brain, part of the CNS, is divided into two halves, the right and left hemispheres. In general, the left hemisphere processes verbal and detail information, whereas the right hemisphere processes spatial and perceptual information (Robbins, 1985). These hemispheres are connected by the corpus collosum, a wide band of neural fibers (Blumenfeld, 2002; Lezak, Howieson, & Loring, 2004). The various parts of the brain discussed in this section include the following:

- The cerebral cortex.
- The forebrain.
- The midbrain.
- The hindbrain.

The Cerebral Cortex

The outermost part of the brain is known as the **cerebral cortex.** The surface of the cortex is composed of folds, the tops of which are called gyri, and the crevices of which are called sulci. The cortex is divided into four areas, or lobes.

Four Lobes of the Cerebral Cortex

1. The **frontal lobe,** the front-most and largest area of the cortex, contains the motor cortex and sensory cortex. The prefrontal cortex, the frontmost part of the frontal cortex, is related to inhibition, motivation, and sequencing. It also contains working memory functions, processes for new learning, set shifting, and selective attention (Blumenfeld, 2002). The prefrontal cortex is necessary for self-reflection, self-evaluation, evaluation of social situations, and perspective taking (Seltzer, 2005). Broca's area in the left frontal lobe is responsible for language production.
2. The **temporal lobes,** located on the right and left sides of the cortex in the area around the ear, are important for language processing. Wernicke's area in the left temporal lobe is responsible for language comprehension.
3. The **occipital lobe,** at the back of the head, is responsible for visual processing. There are two pathways of information through which information reaches the visual cortex. The ventral pathway processes "what" information, whereas the dorsal pathway processes "where" information (Blumenfeld).
4. The **parietal lobe,** found at the top of the head between the frontal lobe and the occipital lobe, contains motor and sensory processing areas (Blumenfeld).

The Forebrain

Below the cortex is the **forebrain,** which is comprised of the limbic system, the thalamus, the hypothalamus, and the basal ganglia. The forebrain contains communication, motor control, memory, and emotional processing centers of the brain.

The primary functions of the limbic system are olfaction, memory, emotions, and homeostatic functions (Blumenfeld, 2002). Martin and colleagues (2001) found that interpersonal psychotherapy resulted in activation, or increased blood flow of the limbic system in clients with Major Depressive Disorder. Clients with medication treatment did not have changes in activation in this area of the brain. Components of the limbic system include the amygdala, the cingulate gyrus, and the hippocampus.

Components of the Limbic System: Amygdala, Cingulate Gyrus, and Hippocampus

- The **amygdala** is responsible largely for emotional control, and especially fear and aggression.
- The amygdala is related to ANS responses through connections with the hypothalamus (Blumenfeld, 2002) such as the fight or flight response (Seltzer, 2005).
- The amygdala evaluates information in terms of both survival and emotional needs, and labels it with a degree of importance. Through this process, emotional information is programmed to override intellectual information (Atkinson, 2005; Tootle, 2003), serving as a protective measure so survival needs are met before all others (Seltzer).
- The **cingulate gyrus** is involved with attention, response selection, error detection, and emotional behavior (Lezak et al., 2004).
- The **hippocampus** is responsible for memory function (Blumenfeld) through involvement in the creation of new memories and recall of old memories.
- The hippocampus processes the context in which a new memory is created; it also relays information between short- and long-term memory and between the limbic system and cortical areas. This transfer of information is, however, interrupted when the amygdala evaluates stimuli as threatening (Seltzer).

Besides the limbic system, other parts of the forebrain include the thalamus, hypothalamus, and basal ganglia, each of which are described next.

Features of the Thalamus and Hypothalamus

- The **thalamus** is a relay center in the brain. It facilitates connections between the cortex and limbic system (Lezak et al., 2004). Most neural pathways that connect to the cerebral cortex pass through the thalamus (Blumenfeld, 2002).
- The **hypothalamus,** located beneath the thalamus, is important for control of ANS responses. It is the link between the neural and endocrine systems.
- The hypothalamus uses hormone release of the pituitary gland to maintain homeostasis in the body by regulating hunger, thirst, sleep–wake cycles, heart rate, and other body functions.
- The hypothalamus is also connected to the limbic system, which explains the link between ANS responses to emotion, such as sweating when nervous (Blumenfeld).

- The hypothalamus manages internal sensory information and processes information flowing from the body to the higher brain (Tootle, 2003). The parasympathetic and sympathetic systems are controlled by the hypothalamus and limbic system.

Features of the Basal Ganglia

- The **basal ganglia** are related to movement and disorders such as Huntington's disease and Parkinson's disease characterized by involuntary or slowed muscle movements.
- It is also related to emotional control, eye movement (Blumenfeld, 2002), turning cognition into action, and motor control (Lezak et al., 2004).

■ Midbrain

The **midbrain** is a small section of the brain between the forebrain and the hindbrain. The primary function of this section of the brain is sensorimotor integration (Lezak et al., 2004). Part of the midbrain, the reticular activating system (RAS), extends from the thalamus into the hindbrain. The RAS is involved with waking and alerting mechanisms. It is linked to cognition by arousing the cerebral cortex. It also is involved with reflexes (Lezak et al.).

■ Hindbrain

The **hindbrain,** found at the base of the brain between the cortex and the spinal cord, is the pathway between the brain and the rest of the body (Blumenfeld, 2002). Major sensory and motor information passes through the brain stem to the spinal cord and the rest of the body. The brain stem itself also is involved with level of consciousness, muscle tone, posture and nonvoluntary body functions such as breathing (Lezak et al., 2004). The hindbrain is comprised of the medulla oblongata, reticular formation, pons, and cerebellum.

Components of the Hindbrain

- The **medulla oblongata,** located at the base of the brain near the spinal cord, is the control center for essential bodily functions such as breathing, blood pressure, heart rate, the gag reflex, and swallowing (Lezak et al.).
- The **reticular formation** is important for regulating consciousness, which is a combination of alertness, attention, and awareness (Blumenfeld). The RAS that begins in the midbrain is also part of the reticular formation and runs through the length of the brain stem. It controls awareness levels such as deep sleep and alertness (Gevarter, 1982), and also is involved with posture, smoothness of muscle movements, and maintenance of muscle tone (Lezak et al.).

- The **pons** is involved in posture, muscle movements, and coordination (Lezak et al.).
- The **cerebellum** receives sensory inputs from the brain and spinal cord that are used to coordinate movement (Blumenfeld). The cerebellum also is involved with higher cognition through connections with the cortex (Lezak et al.).

FACILITATING NEURAL CHANGE

Psychotherapy is based on the assumption that the client can learn from the therapist and others in the client's environment. In the brain, new learning is linked to plasticity, which Cozolino (2002) defined as follows:

Plasticity: The ability of neurons and neural networks to change.

Although the brain is more plastic in young children than adults, intervention can result in change at any age (Tootle, 2003). Changes in behavior and cognitive processes may lead to changes in the brain, and changes in the structure or function of the brain may lead to changes in cognitive processes or behavior (Ilardi, 2002). The reciprocal relation between behavior and cognition and the brain allows for effective intervention in the form of psychotherapy.

> Changes in behavior and cognitive processes may lead to changes in the brain, and changes in the structure or function of the brain may lead to changes in cognitive processes or behavior. The reciprocal relation between behavior and cognition and the brain allows for effective intervention in the form of psychotherapy.

■ How Does Neural Change Occur?

Neuroscience research indicates that neural change occurs when dendrites branch out, thereby extending the reach and connectivity of neurons. When neurons connect with new neurons, or end connections with other neurons, a change occurs in the neural network and learning takes place (Cozolino, 2002). Psychotherapy can change neural networks based on information that environmental factors, such as degree of stimulation, can affect the organization of neurons in the brain (Cozolino).

■ Principles for Brain-Based Psychotherapy

Cappas, Andres-Hyman, and Davidson (2005) suggested several principles for brain-based psychotherapy:

- Experience transforms the brain by strengthening or weakening neural connections. In psychotherapy, the therapist can provide experiences for the client that strengthen neural connections of adaptive behaviors and cognitions and weaken neural connections associated with maladaptive behaviors and cognitions.
- Cognitive and emotional processes work together, and by understanding this relation, therapists can modify behavior patterns that negatively are affecting the client's functioning.
- Imagery can induce change in the same way actual experience can. This means that the therapist can use imagery in the same way as actual experience to facilitate neural change.
- The brain processes nonverbal and unconscious information, so therapists should be aware of their nonverbal behavior, such as facial expressions, at all times.

■ Understanding Schemas

The brain is composed of neural systems that process information automatically (Atkinson, 2005). Shallice (2002) described these automatic processes as **schemas,** or ways of processing information for specific activities. Every time a particular activity is completed (Shallice), the schema for that activity is activated through a process called the contingency scheduler. When a situation arises for which the brain does not have a process in place, another system called the supervisory attention system takes over processing and guides creation of a new schema.

■ Dealing With Problematic Schemas

Therapists can use information about schemas to help clients identify problematic schemas that are triggered by a client's contingency scheduler. Then, the therapist can engage the supervisory attention system by presenting the client with situations in which his or her schema is not accurate or effective. By aiding the client in constructing new schemas and helping with repeated implementation of these new schemas, the therapist may help to ensure that change that occurs in therapy sessions will last.

■ Changing View About Incoming Stimuli

In addition to changing schemas, another major goal of psychotherapy is to change the view or label placed on incoming stimuli. Gevarter (1982) suggested multiple ways of changing these labels.

Ways to Reframe Incoming Stimuli

- Break up the client's existing response patterns to stimuli.
- Reshape the client's existing response pattern to stimuli.
- Permanently modify brain circuitry to eliminate existing response patterns.

Several models of psychotherapy including Rogers's client-centered therapy, Ellis's rational emotive therapy, and Glasser's reality therapy are based on the principles of reshaping how information is processed (Gevarter).

■ Impact of Stress on Neural Change

Besides reframing, stressful situations also can stimulate the process of neural change, or new learning, in the brain. Extreme stress, however, has been found to inhibit new learning (Cozolino, 2002). Based on this information, Cozolino suggested that stress can play a role in the success or failure of psychotherapy. He went as far as to suggest that by inducing low levels of stress in the therapy session, the therapist can induce new learning to improve the client's mental health. By provoking low levels of stress, neural change processes are activated, and the therapist can use this change to promote successful psychotherapy and lasting learning. Cozolino (2002) suggested some ways to augment neural change that are mentioned here.

Ways to Enhance Learning Through Stress Induction

- Establish trust with the client.
- Alternate between low to moderate levels of stress and calm or safety in the session.
- Induce stress in a controlled way with very specific goals in mind.
- Combine conceptual understanding with emotional processing of new information through narratives constructed with the therapist.
- Teach the client to process information in this way outside of therapy to promote further positive change

■ Utilizing the Hemispheres

Considering differences in processing between the two hemispheres also can facilitate successful psychotherapy. Therapists who find a client to be resistant can attempt to tap into the right hemisphere through metaphor and symbolic language. This helps bypass the resistance to change associated with left-hemisphere processing (Robbins, 1985).

ENSURING LASTING NEURAL CHANGE

Psychotherapy is considered successful when the processes used in psychotherapy are internalized by clients, and they are able to use them on their own (Cozolino, 2002). Psychotherapists often underestimate the importance of repeated practice to the generalization of learning and the maintenance of change after the therapeutic relationship has ended (Atkinson et al., 2005). The only therapies that will result in enduring change are those that result in neural change (Gevarter, 1982).

■ Automization of Internalized Processes

Gevarter (1982) suggested that creating automatic, desired behaviors happens through rehearsal and applied practice. Luria (1981), however, conceptualized automatization as the gradual transition from the reliance on external support to the emergence of autonomous, internalized processing. The movement from external to internal processing has been used in neuropsychological intervention (Cicerone & Giacino, 1992). The application of these ideas occurs in psychotherapy in the context described here.

Context for Promoting Internal Processing

- The therapist initially acts as the external agent of change who structures new ways of thinking for the client.
- As the client becomes comfortable with these new ways of thinking, the therapist slowly allows the client to guide his or her own thinking by withdrawing structure.
- When the client is able to use the new ways of thinking independently by talking through the steps, the techniques are beginning to be internalized.
- Eventually, the client no longer needs to vocalize the steps and the new ways of thinking become completely internalized.

■ Monitoring Change in Client Thinking

Therapists should consider the movement from external support to internal processing when introducing techniques to their clients. Moreover, the therapist should evaluate where the client is in the process of internalization throughout the therapeutic relationship. Once the therapist sees that the client's thinking has changed, the therapist has evidence that neural change has occurred and that changes observed in the therapy session will be both lasting and generalized to the client's functioning outside of therapy sessions.

Monitoring Change in Clients' Executive State

In addition to monitoring the changes in clients' thinking, Atkinson and colleagues (2005) recommended monitoring the executive state of the client. Seven states or executive processes that can be used in various situations have been suggested in the literature (Atkinson, 2002; Atkinson et al., 2005; Panksepp, 1998).

Executive Processes That Require Evaluation

1. Aggressive instinct.
2. Avoidance of danger instinct.
3. Desire for emotional contact or closeness.
4. Tenderness or care for others.
5. Spontaneous or playful social contact.
6. Sexual desire.
7. Curiosity or anticipation of learning.

Atkinson and colleagues (2005) indicated that it is imperative for the therapist to understand the state or executive process from which a client is operating during the session. Therapists often find that their clients have difficulty generalizing learning in therapy sessions to other environments. Part of the difficulty may be attributed to differences in the state of the client in these different environments (Atkinson et al.).

EXAMPLE

Executive States in Therapy and at Home

A client who is in an anticipation of learning state in the therapeutic session is able both to learn and practice techniques to diffuse frustration with a spouse; however, when the client is at home and interacting with the spouse, any of the emotional states may be engaged. The client is unable to engage new techniques for diffusing frustration at home because he or she is in an emotional state rather than the anticipation of learning state. If the client practices the new techniques in an emotional state during the therapy session, such as the moderate stress suggested by Cozolino (2002), then the techniques will be practiced more easily in external settings such as the client's home.

Techniques for Engaging Emotional States

Atkinson and colleagues (2005) provided techniques for engaging the emotional states in the therapy session and disengaging them in other environments.

Recommendations for Creating Emotional States in Therapy

- Make recordings of the client's spouse repeating phrases that are typically a source of frustration and shift the client into an emotional executive state.
- Use the tape in the therapy session to practice techniques when the client is in an emotional executive state. The opposite technique is used to diffuse emotional states.
- Provide the client with a tape on which the therapist's voice is recorded prompting the client to use techniques from the therapy session.
- Encourage the client to use this tape to change his or her executive state so that situations can be handled with the techniques taught in therapy sessions. These tapes, in addition to inducing a specific executive state, allow for further practice of techniques in multiple settings.

CLIENTS WITH PROCESSING DEFICITS

If a client has a processing deficit, such as in the areas of attention, memory, or executive functioning, it may be difficult for the therapist to be effective. Therapists who suspect that a client has a processing deficit that has not been documented should refer the client to a neuropsychologist for assessment to ensure that processing deficits are accurately identified and appropriate interventions are recommended. Processing deficits can occur in many client populations.

EXAMPLE

Identifying Some Processing Deficits

Psychiatric disorders such as depression, anxiety, mania, and schizophrenia all can cause impaired attention (Blumenfeld, 2002). A client with attention difficulties may find it difficult to focus for the duration of the therapeutic session. A client with memory deficits may have difficulty retaining techniques learned across sessions. A client with executive functions deficits may have difficulty initiating new thinking strategies, inhibiting old behavior patterns, or monitoring his or her own behavior or thoughts for change.

■ Effectiveness of Cognitive Remediation Therapy

Fortunately, developments in the rehabilitation literature have provided interventions for persons with processing deficits that improve the effectiveness of the psychotherapy. Wykes and colleagues (2002) found that cognitive remediation therapy in schizophrenic clients improved memory performance. In addition to increased memory performance, clients that had cognitive remediation therapy also showed differences in frontal lobe activation, indicating that neural change occurred. Laatsch, Pavel, Jobe, Lin, and Quintana (1999) also found increases in cerebral blood flow along with improvement in neuropsychological test performance after cognitive rehabilitation therapy. These results indicate that interventions for cognitive processing deficits can be effective. Glisky and Glisky (2002) discussed four approaches to intervention for cognitive processes.

Interventions for Persons With Cognitive Processing Deficits

1. Restoration of damaged function through practice and drills.
2. Optimization of residual functions or retraining normal processes by teaching strategies.
3. Compensation of lost function by using external aids and environmental supports to bypass deficits.
4. Substitution of intact functions for damaged functions by teaching new strategies for task completion.

■ Cautions When Using Cognitive Rehabilitation

In the context of facilitating effective psychotherapy, the therapist should determine what processing deficit is inhibiting progress in therapy and determine what empirically supported intervention can be added to the therapy session to bypass that processing deficit. Only therapists trained in cognitive rehabilitation should try to rebuild lost processes. Therapists not trained in cognitive rehabilitation should focus on bypassing the processing deficit so that psychotherapy in any context can be successful.

ATTENTION-RELATED PROCESSING DEFICITS

As previously noted, a client with a processing deficit in attention may have difficulty maintaining his or her focus throughout a full therapy session. There are, however, some useful approaches to helping these individuals.

■ Individualizing the Length of Therapy Sessions

Wilson and Robertson (1992) implemented an intervention for a client who had difficulty reading for extended periods because of a sustained attention deficit. The intervention consisted of the client reading for short periods of time during which he was able to attend consistently to the material. After three successful short periods of reading, the length of each reading period was increased. This basic framework can be applied to a therapeutic session.

Process of Creating a Session of Appropriate Length

- Determine how long the client is able to focus successfully on the session.
- Break each session into shorter periods of therapy with breaks between based on the amount of time the client can focus.
- If the client consistently is able to focus for this set amount of time, an increase in the amount of time for each therapy period may be attempted.
- Monitor the ability of the client to maintain focus to ensure that an appropriate length of session is in place for productive therapy time.

■ Use of Cues

Another environmental support for a client with attention difficulties is suggested by Manly, Ward, and Robertson (2002). They presented a tone to clients at random times while asking the client to complete a goal. The tone served as a reminder for the client to stay on task. In the context of therapy, the processes described next can be implemented.

How to Use Cues for Therapeutic Success

- Determine what cues can be used to facilitate staying on task while not disrupting the flow of the therapy session.
- Provide the client with some kind of cue for staying on task, such as playing a recording with tones at random times to remind the client to stay on task.

MEMORY-RELATED PROCESSING DEFICITS

Clients who have a processing deficit in any area of memory may have difficulty retaining new techniques or insights from one therapy session to the next. Several types of intervention have been suggested to improve retention in clients with memory deficits. Interventions discussed in this section include the following:

- Rehearsal.
- Mnemonic strategies.
- Labels, notebooks, and calendars.
- Space retrieval.

■ Rehearsal

Repeated practice and rehearsal to learn specific pieces of information can be useful (Glisky & Glisky, 2002). Therapists should practice techniques with clients multiple times before attempting implementation in other environments. The therapist also may summarize what information was gained in each session at the end of each session and the beginning of the next session to facilitate retention.

■ Mnemonic Strategies

Mnemonic strategies such as visual imagery, association, or acronyms (Glisky & Glisky, 2002) can provide additional context to facilitate retrieval for the client. The therapist can use the same image or acronym as a retrieval cue for the client.

■ Labels, Notebooks, and Calendars

Environmental supports such as labels, notebooks, or calendars (Glisky & Glisky, 2002; Sohlberg & Mateer, 1989) can remind clients of techniques or homework assignments. The therapist must take the time to teach the client how to use these external supports and monitor their effectiveness (Sohlberg & Mateer).

■ Spaced Retrieval

Spaced retrieval is a technique in which the interval between the presentation of information and the retrieval of that information gradually is increased (Landauer & Bjork, 1978). For example, the therapist can ask the client to retrieve strategies immediately after they are presented. Once the information is retained, the therapist can ask the client to retrieve the information several minutes later. Retention intervals gradually are extended until the client is able to retain information across sessions.

EXECUTIVE FUNCTIONS DEFICITS

Executive functioning is a difficult domain of cognitive processing to define; however, it typically is understood to include processes such as problem solving, planning, and self-monitoring (Cicerone, 2002). Clients with executive functioning deficits may have difficulty in therapy because of their impaired ability to monitor and alter their own behavior based on changes in the environment.

■ Goal Management Training

Interventions in this area involve breaking problems or tasks into small steps and learning cues to remember the steps (Alderman, Fry, & Youngson, 1995; Cicerone,

2002; Levine et al., 2000). If the client has difficulty solving a problem or learning a new task, the steps outlined by Levine and colleagues in goal management training can be implemented to structure activities. The therapist should act as a facilitator by prompting and providing structure at each step.

Steps of Goal Management Training

- The client is first told to orient himself or herself to the task by identifying the task.
- The client defines the goal for the task.
- The client breaks the task into smaller steps.
- The client learns the steps.
- The client completes the task using the steps identified.
- The client confirms that the completed task matches the initial goal that was set.

■ Other Approaches to Helping Clients With Executive Functioning Deficits

If a client is having difficulty with self-monitoring, other behavioral steps have been suggested to improve the client's accuracy (Alderman et al., 1995).

Alternate Behavioral Steps for Aiding Clients

- The therapist records an initial baseline of the behavior to be monitored.
- The client monitors the behavior by using some form of recording technique such as a counter. The client's count is compared with the therapist's count of the behavior.
- Next, the therapist monitors the client's recording of the behavior and prompts him or her to record any occurrences that are missed.
- The client records the behaviors independently and is rewarded for accuracy.
- When the client is able to successfully monitor the identified behavior, goals for modifying the problematic behavior can be set and hopefully change can occur.

SUMMARY

By understanding the components of the nervous system and how they influence behaviors, psychotherapists can gain insight as to why their clients behave as they do and why change in these behaviors can be difficult. For behavior change to be lasting, neural change must occur through repetition of techniques (Gevarter, 1982), low levels of stress to induce learning (Cozolino, 2002), practice in the appropriate executive state (Atkinson et al., 2005), or engagement of the supervisory attention system (Shallice, 2002) to change existing or build new schemas. An understanding of the brain also can assist in facilitating effective therapy for clients with processing deficits. Therapists can utilize empirically supported interventions such as breaking the session into shorter time periods for clients with attention difficulties (Wilson & Robertson, 1992), providing environmental supports for clients with memory deficits (Glisky & Glisky, 2002; Sohlberg & Mateer, 1989), and building structure around problem-solving tasks for patients with executive functions deficits (Levine et al., 2000). Considering the role of neural functioning in each client's behavior and therapeutic progress can clarify a therapist's understanding of the patient and help ensure that gains made in therapeutic sessions will be retained across sessions and across the client's future experiences.

Chapter 28: Key Terms

- ► Cenervous system
- ► Peripheral nervous system
- ► Afferent neurons
- ► Efferent neurons
- ► Cell body
- ► Dendrites
- ► Axon
- ► Synapse
- ► Neurotransmitters
- ► Myelin sheath
- ► Neural pathway

- ► Frontal lobe
- ► Temporal lobes
- ► Occipital lobe
- ► Parietal lobe
- ► Medulla oblongata
- ► Reticular formation
- ► Pons
- ► Cerebellum
- ► Plasticity
- ► Schemas
- ► Cerebral cortex

- ► Forebrain
- ► Amygdala
- ► Cingulate gyrus
- ► Hippocampus
- ► Thalamus
- ► Hypothalamus
- ► Basal ganglia
- ► Midbrain
- ► Hindbrain

Developmental Counseling and Therapy

Jane Myers
University of Connecticut

Thomas Sweeney
Ohio University

Sandra Rigazio-DiGilio
University of Connecticut

Allen Ivey
University of South Florida

In This Chapter

▶ *Historical Context of Developmental Counseling and Therapy*
- Influences of Piagetian Cognitive-Emotional Developmental Theory
- Influences of Life-Span Developmental Theory
- Influences of Postmodern Theory
- Influences of Wellness Theory and Research
- Impact of Traditional Theories of Counseling and Psychotherapy
- Influence of Multicultural Counseling

▶ *Underlying Philosophy of Developmental Counseling and Therapy*
- Developmental Nature of Being
- Multidimensionality in Developmental Counseling and Therapy
- Cultural Relevancy of Developmental Counseling and Therapy

▶ *Modes of Consciousness in Developmental Counseling and Therapy*
- Sensorimotor-Elemental Style
- Concrete-Situational Style
- Formal-Operational Style
- Dialectic-Systemic Style

▶ *Developmental Counseling and Therapy Approach to Wellness*
- The Indivisible Self: Evidence-Based Model of Wellness
- Core Factors of the Indivisible Self

▶ *Fundamentals of Systemic Cognitive Developmental Therapy*
- Defining Disorder from the Systemic Cognitive Developmental Therapy Perspective
- Assessment in Systemic Cognitive Developmental Therapy
- Treatment in Systemic Cognitive Developmental Therapy

▶ *Developmental Counseling and Therapy Techniques: Developmental Strategies Questioning Sequence*
- Questioning Strategies in the Opening Presentation of Issue
- Questioning Strategies in the Sensorimotor-Elemental Style
- Questioning Strategies in the Concrete-Situational Style
- Questioning Strategies in the Formal-Pattern Style
- Questioning Strategies in the Dialectic-Systemic-Integrative Style

▶ *Role of the Therapist in Developmental Counseling and Therapy*
- Precision Matching
- Active Engagement of the Therapist

▶ *Evaluation of Developmental Counseling and Therapy*

HISTORICAL CONTEXT OF DEVELOPMENTAL COUNSELING AND THERAPY

Developmental counseling and therapy (DCT) is an integrative theory that was developed within a counseling, wellness, developmental, and coconstructive framework (Ivey, 1986; Ivey, Ivey, Myers, & Sweeney, 2005; Rigazio-DiGilio, Ivey, & Ivey, 1997). It is unique in that it is not only integrative, but also a well-tested counseling model, and it is the only theory that brings all types of developmental theory into the interview itself. It has proven effective in individual, group, family, and network practice.

■ Influences of Piagetian Cognitive-Emotional Developmental Theory

DCT is the first theory to show how major Piagetian constructs can be used actively in the session. There are very practical ways to use an adaptation of Piagetian constructs in the here and now of the interview and in treatment planning.

■ Influences of Life-Span Developmental Theory

An axiom of the counseling field is that helpers are "developmentalists," but relatively little attention has been given as to how counselors can integrate life-span theory into direct practice. The basic cognitive-developmental framework of DCT integrates well with life-span theory. By utilizing a specific set of strategies to help clients examine their life patterns, DCT directly links developmental theories to practice in ways that can be particularly useful in guiding developmentally tailored and culturally responsive assessment and treatment.

■ Influences of Postmodern Theory

The coconstructivist philosophy undergirding DCT suggests that culture and context permeate development and shape our worldview (Rigazio-DiGilio & Ivey, 1995). DCT emphasizes the importance of person–environment interaction and shows how counseling can be understood through this transactional lens. Extensions of DCT to families and networks provide specific guidelines for assessing and intervening in the client's broader life space.

■ Influences of Wellness Theory and Research

Drawing on the work of Myers and Sweeney (2005b), DCT rejects concepts of pathology and takes a positive and holistic approach to human change that provides a solid base of strengths on which to facilitate client positive movement.

■ Impact of Traditional Theories of Counseling and Psychotherapy

DCT includes the key systems of helping under its concepts and practices, keeping developmental, wellness, coconstructive, and multicultural variables in the foreground of assessment and treatment planning.

■ Influence of Multicultural Counseling

DCT recognizes the centrality and importance of culture and context. The theory provides practical ways to understand how clients view their world within a cultural context and to construct multiculturally sensitive treatment plans tailored to these views and cultural contexts. It holds that all counseling is multicultural in nature.

UNDERLYING PHILOSOPHY OF DEVELOPMENTAL COUNSELING AND THERAPY

DCT is simultaneously a theory of helping within itself. A series of questions and treatment strategies exist to facilitate client development, even clients with severe issues. As indicated in the brief historical evolution, DCT integrates a wide variety of perspectives into this approach. Perhaps most striking is the developmental foundation.

■ Developmental Nature of Being

The philosophy of continuous development over time is foundational to DCT, and the evolution of consciousness is central. DCT is a counseling approach that enables a client to progress to new ways of thinking, feeling, and behaving. Expansion of alternatives is basic. The specific questioning sequences of DCT, coupled with appropriate treatment strategies, help expand the potential for human development.

■ Multidimensionality in Developmental Counseling and Therapy

Traditional theories of counseling tend to focus on the concrete and formal aspects of human development. DCT is unique in that it gives special attention to the body, including nutrition and exercise. In addition, special attention is given to strategies such as meditation, guided imagery, and other interventions designed to bring clients to the here and now.

■ Cultural Relevancy of Developmental Counseling and Therapy

DCT, along with feminist therapy, ecosystemic therapy, and multicultural counseling and therapy, gives special attention to the cultural, contextual, and environmental aspects of clients. While attending to individual issues, DCT includes a social action dimension as well. Ellis (2000) commented on this aspect of DCT as follows:

> To be sure, REBT has not emphasized dialectic/systemic counseling as much as it is heavily encouraged in DCT and SCDT. Quite possibly, it—and most other popular therapies—are relatively lax in this respect. The unique element of both DCT and SCDT is the way Ivey and Rigazio-DiGilio stress this fourth process; and REBT had better seriously consider emphasizing it more than it sometimes has done in the past, and thereby learn from DCT and SCDT. But, as also noted above, much can be said on the hazards as well as the advantages of stressing this aspect of therapy. It is nonetheless accurate, as Rigazio-DiGilio, Ivey, and Locke (1997, p. 241) note, "Theories of counseling and practice that perpetuate the notion of individual and family dysfunction without giving equal attention to societal dysfunction and to the dysfunctional interactions that can occur between individuals, families, and societies (e.g., intentional and unintentional power differentials) may unwittingly reinforce the oppressive paradigm." All systems of counseling had better give serious thought to this hypothesis—as, in fact, few of them have to date done. (pp. 101–102)

Another vital part of DCT's cultural component is its integration with multicultural counseling and therapy's concept of cultural identity development. DCT points out that the four styles of consciousness closely relate to the four levels of cultural identity development. See Table 29.1 as an illustration.

In addition, DCT has proven useful in bibliotherapy, spirituality, and counseling, with early recollections in Adlerian theory, and in supervision.

TABLE 29.1
Cognitive-Emotional Developmental Change: Two Theoretical Perspectives

Cultural Identity Theory	Developmental Counseling and Therapy	Actions for Change
Preencounter (Naiveté with acceptance of status quo)	Sensorimotor-elemental	Ask for clients to describe life experiences through stories of oppression
Encounter (Naming and resistance with anger a common emotion)	Concrete-situational	Name and confront contractions between self and contextual systems
Immersion-emersion (Redefinition and reflection)	Formal-reflective	Support pattern recognition and self-in-system reflections
Internalization (Multiperspectival integration)	Dialectic-systemic	Continue emphasis on dialogic thought and coinvestigation of reality; joint action to transform reality

For more information on cultural identity development and multicultural counseling and therapy, see Chapter 4. See Chapter 27 for an example of an ecological, transactional theory of counseling.

MODES OF CONSCIOUSNESS IN DEVELOPMENTAL COUNSELING AND THERAPY

Four styles of consciousness are identified within the DCT model that parallel Piagetian cognitive-emotional concepts. Each style has value. Practically speaking, counselors who use DCT start by identifying the client's underlying style(s) of communication, match their style to that of the client, and develop thinking, feeling, and behavior strengths in the originally presented style(s). Later, encouraging the client to expand consciousness via other styles is important in DCT. In the following segments, the four styles of consciousness briefly are described:

1. Sensorimotor-elemental.
2. Concrete-situational.
3. Formal-operational.
4. Dialectic-systemic.

■ Sensorimotor-Elemental Style

The client whose style is sensorimotor-elemental is able to experience emotions and cognitions holistically in the here and now and be in the moment. There is no separation of self from experience. Counselors often will find a random expression of thoughts and feelings in clients who exhibit the sensorimotor-elemental style. Counselors should look for the ability to be in touch with the body, but expect a short attention span. With the sensorimotor style, some magical or irrational thinking may appear. On an affective level, there are a number of characteristics related to the sensorimotor style.

Emotional Aspects of the Sensorimotor Style

- Feelings are experienced in the here and now rather than described or reflected on.
- There is an emphasis on bodily experience.
- Crying, laughing, and catharsis of deep emotion represents this style.

In the sensorimotor style, clients are susceptible to a number of barriers in their development. Some of the more salient blocks to development are mentioned here.

Potential Developmental Blocks in the Sensorimotor Style

- Clients may have difficulty in telling a clear, linear story of what happened.
- Clients will have real difficulty in reflecting on themselves and the situation.
- Behavior may tend to follow the same pattern—namely, short attention span and frequent body movement.
- There may be an inappropriate impulsive expression with tears, anger, or other emotions.

In response to the developmental blocks present in this style, counselors have a number of treatment options at their disposal.

Treatment Recommendations for the Sensorimotor Style

- Body-oriented work.
- Acupuncture.
- Massage.
- Yoga.
- Imagery.
- Relaxation training.
- Medication.
- Psychodynamic free association.
- Gestalt exercises.
- Metaphor.
- Hypnosis.

■ Concrete-Situational Style

The client whose style reflects a concrete-situational stage gives concrete, linear descriptions and stories about what happened, often with a fair amount of detail. Nonverbal clients, however, may give short "yes" and "no" responses. At the late concrete style, the client will display some causal reasoning, which is exemplified by if–then thinking. Moving to behavioral action is easy. The manifestation of emotions in this style reflects some of the following characteristics.

Emotional Manifestations in the Concrete-Situational Style

- Specific feelings will be named and described but not reflected on.
- Clients typically will verbalize emotions in this way: "I feel X because … "
- Some clients will have difficulty in naming emotion, but naming is basic to concrete emotional experiencing. This is an important step, but nonetheless, a move away from direct here-and-now emotional experiencing.

Clients who operate from the concrete-situational mode tend to exhibit some common blocks in growth. A few are presented here.

Potential Developmental Blocks in the Concrete-Situational Style

- Clients repeatedly may tell detailed stories of their problems and share many examples of the same patterned behavior, but be unable to see patterns in their behavior.
- Clients will have difficulty in generalizing learning with one problem discussed in the session to another that is obviously parallel to the interviewer.
- Clients often have difficulty in seeing a perspective other than their own.

Treatment options for clients in the concrete-situational stage include some of the following suggestions.

Treatment Recommendations for the Concrete-Situational Style

- Concrete narrative storytelling.
- Assertiveness training and many cognitive and behavioral techniques.
- Social skills training.
- Decision and problem-solving counseling.
- Rational-emotive behavior therapy and A-B-C analysis.
- Reality therapy.
- Crisis intervention.
- Desensitization.
- Psychoeducation.
- Adlerian therapy with if–then problem analysis.

■ Formal-Operational Style

There are a number of strengths that people in the formal-operational mode of relating exhibit. These people can talk about themselves and their feelings—sometimes even from the perspectives of others. Their conversations tend to be abstract. At the late formal style, these clients can recognize commonalities in repeating patterns of behaviors or thoughts. This is the type of client many counselors feel most comfortable with, as they are often into analyzing themselves and their own identity. The emotional manifestations of clients who operate from this style include the following characteristics.

Emotional Experiences in the Formal-Operational Style

- Feelings are reflected on and discussed rather than experienced.
- Patterns of emotional experience may be discussed.

Clients who prefer the formal-operational mode benefit from being able to analyze and actively reflect on their experiences. However, they are also prone to some blocks in development, a number of which are mentioned here.

Potential Developmental Blocks in the Formal-Operational Style

- Clients who present at the formal style may be good at pattern recognition, but have difficulty in giving concrete examples.
- They may reflect on themselves and situations, but they may fail to see the assumptions on which their thinking is based.
- They may be overly abstract and have difficulty in moving experiencing emotion at the sensorimotor style.

To counter the developmental barriers in the formal-operational style, counselors have a number of tools at their disposal; some of these are provided here.

Treatment Options for the Formal-Operational Style

- Reflection on narratives and stories.
- Most Rogerian person-centered work.
- Analysis of a Beck automatic thoughts chart or REBT thought patterns.
- Psychodynamic dream analysis.
- Adlerian strategies.
- Cognitive therapy.
- Logotherapy.
- Family genograms.

■ Dialectic-Systemic Style

Most people ordinarily do not make sense of their worlds from this perspective. A woman who realizes that sexism is the cause of her depression is using systemic thought. A Native American Indian or a Canadian Dene who realizes that systemic oppression leads to individual feelings or hurt and even depression is using dialectic thought. Multiple perspective-taking and many alternatives are to be expected. The client is aware of systems of knowledge and is aware of how he or she is affected by the environment. Also, the client will be able to challenge and reflect deeply on his or her own or others' style of thought and feeling.

Emotions Frequently Present in the Dialectic-Systemic Style

- The client may be highly effective at analyzing and thinking about emotions.
- Emotions are often contextualized.

- A client may say "I'm sad about the loss of my parents in this accident, but proud of the life they led. In some ways I miss them terribly, but in my heart they are still there."
- The emotions change with the perspective taken.

The dialectic-systemic style lends itself to a number of barriers to development. Some examples are presented next.

Potential Developmental Blocks in the Dialectic–Systemic Style

- The clients can "analyze it to death."
- Their ability to think constantly in new ways may result in intellectualization and distancing from the real problems.
- Some clients would rather think about the problem than do anything about it.
- There may be real difficulty in experiencing emotion at the sensorimotor style or even being able to name what they are feeling accurately.

For clients who operate out of the dialectic-systemic mode, counselors may employ a number of treatment options.

Treatment Strategies for the Dialectic-Systemic Style

- Advocacy for social justice.
- Community or neighborhood action.
- Community genogram.
- Family dream analysis.
- Multicultural counseling and therapy.

DEVELOPMENTAL COUNSELING AND THERAPY APPROACH TO WELLNESS

Wellness theory and research are central to DCT and provide a holistic, positive conceptual framework that emphasizes client strengths as the basis for change and growth. Consistent with a developmental view of pathology, the wellness perspective fosters an understanding of clients in terms of prevention and optimization of human development rather than merely diagnosis and remediation of dysfunction. Clients respond readily to interventions that begin with a positive wellness base.

■ The Indivisible Self: Evidence-Based Model of Wellness

Myers and Sweeney (2005b) presented the indivisible self, an evidence-based model of wellness grounded in more than a dozen years of research, that may be used to better understand healthy or well behavior. This model is an alterative to the theoretical wheel of wellness model, which was based in multidisciplinary literature (Myers, Sweeney, & Witmer, 2000; Witmer & Sweeney, 1992) and proposed spirituality as the core characteristic of healthy persons. In contrast, structural equation modeling revealed that no characteristic of wellness is predominant; rather, as proposed earlier by Adler (1954), the self is truly indivisible. All components of wellness are important and necessary for healthy functioning.

See Chapter 9 for more on Adler's conceptualization of human nature.

■ Core Factors of the Indivisible Self

The indivisible self model includes a superordinate holistic wellness factor—the self—that cannot be divided into its component parts. From a holistic vantage point, people move toward wellness through the way they live their life, in general, or move away from wellness through their lifestyle choices. To be optimally well, attention to all components of one's functioning is necessary. Such a global perspective is useful in understanding the impact of lifestyle choices but less useful to clinicians in knowing where to start to help clients become more well. As a consequence, a second-order factor structure depicts the self in terms of five areas that are both independent and interactive, in that change in one area will cause or contribute to changes in each of the other areas. Significantly, change can be for better or for worse.

The five factors of the indivisible self include the creative, coping, social, essential, and physical self. Each "self" includes additional wellness factors that provide a specific focus for wellness-enhancing interventions.

Five Factors of the Indivisible Self

1. The *creative self* is defined as the unique combination of individual attributes that each of us forms that allows us to define and manage ourselves in a proactive manner in our social interactions.
2. The *coping self* helps us regulate our responses to life events and when negative circumstances occur, helps us transcend their negative affects.
3. The *social self* is comprised of our relationships with others on a continuum extending from friendships through love, including both family and intimate relationships.
4. The *essential self* is the core of our beliefs and values through which we interpret the events of our lives.
5. The *physical self* includes the manner in which we care for our bodies through nutrition and activity.

Although all of the factors of wellness are salient for each individual, the importance of any one factor may vary over the life span as a function of life circumstances and transitions. In addition, the indivisible self model is ecological, in that contextual variables, such as schools, neighborhoods, government, and the media, are recognized as influencing and being influenced by the wellness of individuals. An important context, chronometrical, speaks to the life-span nature of wellness. DCT, which emphasizes positive growth and development over the life span, thus incorporates wellness as both a process and goal.

See Chapter 30 for more information about wellness and the indivisible self model.

FUNDAMENTALS OF SYSTEMIC COGNITIVE DEVELOPMENTAL THERAPY

Systemic cognitive developmental therapy (SCDT; Rigazio-DiGilio, 2000) adapts DCT constructs for work with families and wider networks. SCDT examines the internal meaning making of individuals, families, and institutional systems and the factors that influence exchanges across these systems. Imbalances within or across individual, family, and community environments can trigger developmental impasses. This system–environment transaction must be accounted for in relational diagnostic procedures, and should attend to how factors such as culture, ethnic heritage, contemporary social issues, family values, spiritual beliefs, community experiences, and developmental history directly influence the current intellectual, emotional, and behavioral lives of individuals and systems.

See Chapter 18 for other perspectives on family therapy.

■ Defining Disorder From the Systemic Cognitive Developmental Therapy Perspective

Regardless of where problems are situated, they are expressed within the relationships among individuals, families, and wider systems and the broader illness narratives that evolve and are maintained by these interactions. Treatment often is initiated when these exchanges lead to unifying and constraining interpretations of problems, or to predominant interpretations that elicit dissonant or oppressive transactions involving issues of superiority, blame, and responsibility. The goal is to facilitate a sense of shared responsibility, mutual understanding, resource utilization, and positive problem solving. Starting with the family and working internally with its members and externally with personnel from community institutions and agencies, the counselor creates counseling and consulting environments that are solution focused and aimed at loosening constraints and accessing underutilized resources.

■ Assessment in Systemic Cognitive Developmental Therapy

Relational assessment explores the worldviews of relational units, participating systems, and cultural and societal norms, all of which are evident in the behaviors, goals, and emotional bonds expressed by those contributing to and defining the problem. By applying SCDT assessment strategies, counselors can identify the information processing styles held by each family member, the family as a relational unit, and other participating groups and agency personnel. Issues of how family members are connected to one another and the wider systems also can be classified in terms of power.

Assessing Power in Relational Units and Systems

- Issues of social and economic oppression can negatively influence the development of individual and family resources.
- Environmental demands for interactions that are outside of the family's physical, psychological, cultural, moral, or spiritual sense of self or self-in-relationship can cause dissonance.
- Oppression that is created when the environment labels a family's familiar ways of perceiving and acting as substandard or deviant is particularly insidious.

Knowing who has the real or imagined means to wield the most power and influence is critical to determining the options for change. Understanding family and systemic relatedness also can be classified in terms of embeddedness, which can be assessed by determining the types of unanimity and conformity existing in how problems are defined and managed.

Advantages of Accounting for Embeddedness in Assessment

- Accounting for embeddedness allows the counselor to be a firsthand participant in those systems relevant to the presenting problem and to determine where they can intervene most flexibly to relieve unproductive meanings and exchanges.
- The wider narrative becomes the point of departure to advance multiple perspectives regarding the presenting problem.
- Embeddedness opens alternative ways for all participants to understand one another and work together toward the management or dissolution of the problem.

■ Treatment in Systemic Cognitive Developmental Therapy

As with DCT, treatment occurs within counseling and consulting environments that correspond with the processing styles being explored at different times and during different encounters. Expanding on the DCT model, counselors use SCDT questioning strategies and draw from systemic and ecosystemic approaches—organized within a developmental, coconstructive metaframework—to tailor treatment to these processing styles, and to evaluate the impact of any intervention, either inside or outside the family.[1]

> SCDT treatment is geared toward ensuring that families take an empowered position within the interactive system. Although the clinician works from several intervention points, a central focus is for the family to become an active and equal participant in constructing and acting on solutions.

SCDT treatment is geared toward ensuring that families take an empowered position within the interactive system. Although the clinician works from several intervention points, a central focus is for the family to become an active and equal participant in constructing and acting on solutions. SCDT treatment planning focuses on three levels, which are described next.

Aims of Treatment Planning in SCDT

1. To help relational units strengthen and master resources that had not been effectively utilized within the current worldview.
2. To assist relational units to explore new perspectives and new options associated with other styles.
3. To assist all members of the interactive system to work together on common goals within a coherent worldview that links all members.

Using SCDT helps clinicians realize internal and external contexts and permits the wide use of various interventions for treatment, which results in an expansion of the possibilities of relational counseling.

DEVELOPMENTAL COUNSELING AND THERAPY TECHNIQUES: DEVELOPMENTAL STRATEGIES QUESTIONING SEQUENCE

DCT uses a number of strategies to help clients. It is possible to identify the cognitive-emotional developmental style of a client by listening to and observing language used in the interview. After observing the cognitive-emotional level of the client, the counselor matches the counseling or therapeutic intervention so that the client can understand and act on what he or she has said. Mismatching interven-

---

[1]Research indicates that collective information processing styles can be identified and help guide the treatment process (Speirs, 2006).

tions may be equally helpful. An overly abstract client, for example, may benefit from an approach that focuses on concrete specifics. Similarly, a concrete client may be helped toward an understanding of self and situations by facilitating more abstract conversation. This generic approach can be used across individual, group, and family work. It is helpful to use this system in all theories of counseling and therapy as it enables the counselor to reach clients where they are conceptually, emotionally, and behaviorally.

DCT offers some specific questioning strategies to facilitate expansion of consciousness within and between the various styles. If a counselor works through these questions carefully with a client, cognitive and emotional change is very likely to occur. If one adds some behavioral methods to the mix, the change is very likely to generalize to the client's daily life. The questioning process also can be used to facilitate individual understanding of herself or himself as a multicultural being. The dialectic-systemic questions help put clients in touch with how environmental and contextual issues have shaped them. Following is an abbreviated version of the questioning strategies used for each developmental style that clients present (Ivey, Rigazio-DiGilio, & Ivey, 2005).

■ Questioning Strategies in the Opening Presentation of Issue

When a client first presents the issues of concern, counselors can ask two questions that help guide the session:

1. Could you tell me what you'd like to talk about today?
2. What happens for you when you focus on your family?

In an attempt to be brief and to the point, the counselor obtains a story of 50 to 100 words. Strategies for doing so are listed next.

Ways to Obtain a Story of 50 to 100 Words

- Assess client cognitive-emotional style.
- Use questions, encouragers, paraphrasing, and reflection of feeling to bring out data, but try to influence the client's story minimally.
- Get the story as he or she constructs it.
- Summarize key facts and feelings about what the client has said before moving on.

■ Questioning Strategies in the Sensorimotor-Elemental Style

If the assessment of the client suggests a sensorimotor-elemental style, the counselor can ask either of these questions that correspond to the style:

1. Could you think of one visual image that occurs to you in that situation?
2. What are you seeing? Hearing? Feeling? Where do you locate the feeling in your body?

In obtaining some minimal information, the counselor elicits an example from the client and asks what was seen, heard, or felt.

Strategies for Eliciting Examples and Sensory Experiences

- Aim for here-and-now experiencing.
- Accept randomness.
- Summarize at the end of the segment.
- Counselors may want to ask: "What one thing stands out for you from this?"

■ Questioning Strategies in the Concrete-Situational Style

For clients who operate from the concrete-situation style, counselors can ask two questions such as these:

1. Could you give me a specific example of the situation, issue, or problem?
2. Can you describe your feelings in the situation?

The goal of the counselor who is working with concrete-situational clients is to obtain a clear or logical description of the event. Some ways to achieve this goal are as follows.

Ways to Obtain a Linear Description of the Event

- Look for if–then causal reasoning.
- Ask: "What did he or she do? Say? What happened before? What happened next? What happened after?"
- Possibly pose the question "If he or she did X, then what happened?"
- Summarize before moving on.
- For affective development, ask: "What did you feel?"
- The statement: "You felt X because … " helps integrate cognition with affect at this level.

■ Questioning Strategies in the Formal-Pattern Style

When working with clients in the formal-pattern style, counselors may ask either of these sets of questions:

1. Does this happen in other situations? Is this a pattern for you?
2. Do you feel that way in other situations? Are those feelings a pattern for you?

Counselors aim to help clients elucidate patterns or typical ways of feeling or behaving. Some recommendations for achieving this goal are provided.

Suggestions for Highlighting Repeating Patterns and Situations

- Ask: "What were you saying to yourself when that happened? Have you felt like that in other situations?"
- Reflect feelings and paraphrase as appropriate.
- Summarize key facts and feelings carefully before moving on.

■ Questioning Strategies in the Dialectic-Systemic-Integrative Style

Working in the dialectic or systemic style, counselors begin by summarizing all that has been said. Two key approaches for guiding the summary are these:

1. How do you put together/organize all that you told me? What one thing stands out for you most?
2. How many different ways could you describe your feelings and how they change?

Some specific approaches or tasks that aid the counselor in getting to the client's summation of experience are suggested next.

Process of Obtaining an Integrated Summary of the Dialogue

- Enable the client to see how reality is coconstructed, not developed from a single view.
- Obtain different perspectives on the same situation and be aware that each is just one perspective.
- Note flaws in the present construction, coconstruction, or perspective.
- Move to action.

ROLE OF THE THERAPIST IN DEVELOPMENTAL COUNSELING AND THERAPY

DCT recasts the traditional superior and separate role of clinicians to that of equal partners engaged in the coconstruction of client worldviews that are solution focused rather than problem saturated.

■ Precision Matching

The counselor's role is based on understanding and being with the client. Much like person-centered therapy, DCT counselors enter the client's world. However, DCT favors what it terms **precision matching**, in which it is crucial that the therapist meet the client where he or she is. Rapport needs to be based far more on the style and worldview of the client.

■ Active Engagement of the Therapist

The counselor is quite active within the DCT model. Questions are generally unwelcome in the person-centered model, but are foundational to DCT. At issue is the educational concept of drawing out what is already in the client. Strategies used depend on the client and may include a wide array of theories. Illustrations of varying treatment examples drawn from multiple theories are listed under each of the information processing styles identified earlier.

EVALUATION OF DEVELOPMENTAL COUNSELING AND THERAPY

DCT's greatest strengths are simultaneously its greatest weaknesses. They can be summarized as shown in Table 29.2. DCT offers a developmental, coconstructive, and wellness-oriented integrative therapy model that can be used with individuals, partners, families, and wider networks. DCT and its ecosystemic extension are models considered easy to learn, apply, and research (Borders, 1994), and they ad-

TABLE 29.2
Strengths and Weaknesses of Developmental Counseling and Therapy

Strengths	Limitations
Theoretically dense, accounting for many dimensions of the helping process	Requires more study, thought, and practice than most other theoretical orientations
Multicultural issues are central	There are those who resist multiculturalism
Effective with children, adolescents, and adults as well as families and networks	Requires fundamental understanding of counseling and is at an advanced level of practice
Makes possible systematic integration of multiple theories of helping and encourages knowledge of many approaches	This may be challenging to those who wish to work within a single theory
Wellness emphasis with accompanying rejection of psychopathology	The dominant pathological and problem-centered point of view disagrees with this orientation.

dress the comprehensive importance of culture, family systems, and partner and family worldviews (Arciniega & Newlon, 1994). As a true integrative theoretical model, DCT brings together a combination of theories and approaches and forms a new theory and treatment system that builds and improves on each of the individual approaches to form a better product. Treatment is therefore theory focused rather than technique driven (Seligman, 2006).

Chapter 29: Key Terms

- ▶ Developmental Counseling and Therapy
- ▶ Precision Matching
- ▶ Systemic Cognitive Developmental Counseling

Counseling for Wellness

30

Thomas J. Sweeney
Ohio University

Jane E. Myers
University of North Carolina

In This Chapter

▶ *Historical Context of the Wellness Movement*
- Philosophical Groundwork of Wellness
- Counseling-Based Approach to Wellness

▶ *Modern Definitions of Wellness*
- Differentiation Between Health and Wellness
- Multiple Understandings of Wellness
- Wellness Defined From a Counseling Perspective

▶ *Wellness Models*
- Wheel of Wellness Model
- Indivisible Self (IS-WEL): Evidence-Based Model of Wellness

▶ *Assessment Tools for Examining Wellness*
- The Wellness Evaluation of Lifestyle
- The Five Factor Wellness Inventory

▶ *Counseling for Wellness*
- Step 1: Introduction of the Wellness Model
- Step 2: Assessment of the Components of the Wellness Models
- Step 3: Intentional Interventions to Enhance Wellness
- Step 4: Evaluation and Follow-Up

HISTORICAL CONTEXT OF THE WELLNESS MOVEMENT

In this chapter, we review modern definitions of wellness and briefly describe models of wellness arising from these definitions. Most of the early models evolved from the health sciences professions are holistic in concept; in application the focus has remained on physical aspects of functioning and how physical change affects other components of well-being. New models of wellness are being developed with the aim of assessing equally all aspects of physical, emotional, cognitive, and spiritual functioning.

■ Philosophical Groundwork of Wellness

The Greek philosopher Aristotle, writing in the 5th century BC, is credited with being the first to write about wellness. His scientific attempts to explain health and illness resulted in a model of good health as one in which we avoid the extremes of excess and deficiency. Stated succinctly, this philosophy is expressed as "nothing in excess." The son of a physician, Aristotle identified *eudaemonia*, a state of happiness or flourishing, as the ultimate expression of a person's ability to live and fare well.

The health of body and mind were linked until some centuries later when Descartes (1596–1650), credited as being the father of modern philosophy, explained human functioning based on scientific reasoning. He believed that the mind and body were two separate entities that worked together in a mechanistic manner. This philosophy resulted in a reductionistic and fragmented approach to human functioning, with illness viewed as being only in the mind. Fortunately, solid research in medicine as well as health-related professions is rapidly creating a new paradigm wherein not only are the mind and body viewed as inseparable, but the spirit is also seen as integral to understanding health and illness (Larson, 1999).

■ Counseling-Based Approach to Wellness

Counseling-based models of wellness that emerged over the past two decades are holistic in nature and have a strong foundation in psychological theory as an organizing and integrative focus. The recent emergence of positive psychology, with emotion as the central and perhaps sole focus of efforts to understand well-being, is yet another attempt to determine how people can live in an optimal manner. So far, such models such as positive psychology are not truly holistic in nature, however, and have not incorporated other equally important components of health and wellness (e.g., culture).

MODERN DEFINITIONS OF WELLNESS

Understanding wellness requires an understanding of health and how the two concepts differ.

■ Differentiation Between Health and Wellness

The World Health Organization (WHO) as early as 1947 defined health as "physical, mental, and social well-being, not merely the absence of disease" (WHO, 1958, p. 1) and later provided the following definition of optimal health: "a state of complete physical, mental, and social well-being and not merely the absence of disease or infirmity" (WHO, 1964, p. 1). *The American Heritage Dictionary of the English Language* (2000) defined wellness as "the condition of good physical and mental health, especially when maintained by proper diet, exercise, and habits." Both of these definitions imply a static state of existence.

■ Multiple Understandings of Wellness

In the modern wellness movement, wellness is viewed as a dynamic process and not a static state. Indeed, high-level wellness is a deliberate state in which the process of making choices toward greater wellness becomes self-perpetuating. From the perspective of multiple authors, wellness can be described as both an outcome and a process, at once an overarching goal for living and a day-by-day, minute-by-minute way of being. This global concept is multifaceted and hence has given rise to a variety of models that purport to explain both the process and goal of optimum human functioning that is called wellness.

> In the modern wellness movement, wellness is viewed as a dynamic process and not a static state. Indeed, high-level wellness is a deliberate state in which the process of making choices toward greater wellness becomes self-perpetuating.

Key Figures Who Define Wellness

- Dr. Halbert Dunn (1961, 1977), architect of the modern wellness movement, defined wellness as "an integrated method of functioning which is oriented toward maximizing the potential of which the individual is capable, [provided] that the individual maintain a continuum of balance and purposeful direction within the environment where he is functioning" (Dunn, 1961, p. 4).
- Dr. Bill Hettler, a public health physician, and father of wellness as we now know it, defined wellness as "an active process through which people become aware of, and make choices toward a more successful existence," (http://www.hettler.com/).
- Don Ardell authored 15 books about wellness and his continually evolving definitions of the concept include self-responsibility and global healing.

- Dr. John Travis saw health as a neutral point on a continuum that ranges from illness on one end to wellness at the other (Travis & Ryan, 1988). He described high-level wellness as involving "giving good care to your physical self, using your mind constructively, expressing your emotions effectively, being creatively involved with those around you, and being concerned about your physical, psychological and spiritual environments" (Wellness Associates, nd).
- Psychologists Archer, Probert, and Gage (1987) conducted an extensive literature review on wellness and concluded that wellness is "the process and state of a quest for maximum human functioning that involves the body, mind, and spirit" (p. 311).

From the perspective of multiple authors, we can conclude that wellness is both an outcome and a process, at once an overarching goal for living and a day-by-day, minute-by-minute way of being. This global concept is multifaceted and hence has given rise to a variety of models that purport to explain both the process and goal of optimum human functioning that we call wellness.

 For more information on health and wellness visit:

▶ http://thewellspring.com/pubs/iw_cont.html

Wellness Defined From a Counseling Perspective

Wellness also has been defined from a counseling perspective. Myers et al. (2000), after reviewing literature from multiple disciplines, concluded that wellness can be conceptualized in this way:

> **Wellness:** "[A] way of life oriented toward optimal health and well-being, in which body, mind, and spirit are integrated by the individual to live life more fully within the human and natural community. Ideally, it is the optimum state of health and well-being that each individual is capable of achieving" (p. 252).

WELLNESS MODELS

Early models of wellness, as noted earlier, evolved from physical health sciences and medicine. Notable among these are Dunn's model of high-level wellness, Hettler's hexagon model, and Travis and Ryan's illness–wellness continuum. Ardell developed a series of three models to describe wellness. Early writings by authors such as and Ryff and Keyes (1995) led to the emergence of the positive psychology movement, which does not claim an emphasis on holistic wellness, but rather is considered to be the "scientific study of ordinary human strengths and virtues" (Sheldon & King, 2001, p. 216). More recently, two models of wellness emerged in the counseling field: the wheel of wellness model and the indivisible self model.

■ Wheel of Wellness Model

Wellness models in counseling, notably the early model by Sweeney and Witmer (1991) and Witmer and Sweeney (1992a) and the revision of this model by Myers et al. (2000), were the first models to emerge in the mental health professions. Sweeney and Witmer (1991) and Witmer and Sweeney (1992a) conducted cross-disciplinary studies to identify correlates of health, quality of life, and longevity. The development of the wheel of wellness was the outcome of this early thought and research.

Characteristics of the Wheel of Wellness

■ With Adlerian individual psychology (Adler, 1927/1954; Ansbacher & Ansbacher, 1967; Sweeney, 1998) as an organizing system, the model highlights relations among 12 components of wellness depicted graphically in a wheel (see Figure 30.1).

The Wheel of Wellness

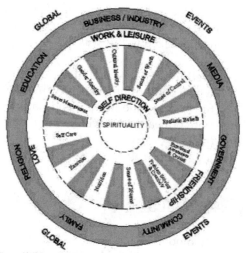

Copyright J.W. Witmer, T.J. Sweeney, & J.E. Myers, 1996

FIGURE 30.1   Wheel of wellness. From Witmer, Sweeney, & Myers (1996). Reprinted by permission.

- After early research, this model was expanded and refined to include 17 components (Myers et al., 2000) that interact with contextual and global forces to impact holistic well-being.
- Spirituality is depicted as the center of the wheel and the most important characteristic of well-being by relating the self to meaning and purpose in life.
- Surrounding the center is a series of 12 spokes in the life task of self-direction that helps to regulate or direct the self as we respond to the Adlerian life tasks of work (and leisure), friendship, love, self, and spirit.

12 Life Tasks in the Wheel of Wellness

- Sense of worth.
- Sense of control.
- Realistic beliefs.
- Emotional responsiveness and management.
- Intellectual stimulation, problem solving, and creativity.
- Sense of humor.
- Exercise.
- Nutrition.
- Self-care.
- Stress management.
- Gender identity.
- Cultural identity.

This model is the basis of an assessment instrument for wellness, the Wellness Evaluation of Lifestyle (WEL; Myers, Sweeney, & Witmer, 1998), and has been used widely in workshops, seminars, and empirical research.

■ Indivisible Self (IS–WEL): Evidence-Based Model of Wellness

Use of the wheel model and the WEL over a decade led to the development of a large empirical database from which a manual and norms were developed (see Myers & Sweeney, 2005c). Subsequently, these data were analyzed using structural equation modeling (Hattie, Myers, & Sweeney, 2004). The outcome of exploratory and confirmatory factor analyses resulted in a clearly defined structural model, and led to a new, evidence-based model of wellness called the indivisible self (IS–WEL; see Figure 30.2).

Traits of the Indivisible Self Model of Wellness

- Consistent with Adlerian principles, the self is the central and indivisible core of wellness, represented by a single, higher order factor called wellness.

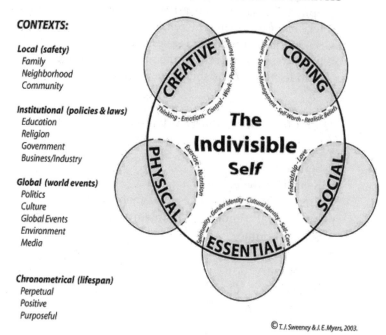

FIGURE 30.2 The indivisible self: An evidence-based model of wellness. From Sweeney & Myers (2003). Reprinted by permission.

- Within this core are five second-rder factors: creative self, coping self, social self, essential self, and physical self.
- Although the circumplex structure hypothesized in the theoretical wheel model was not supported by factor analysis, each of the original 17 components of wellness was confirmed as distinct third-order factors.
- In the IS–WEL model, these factors are grouped within the five second-order factors of the self.
- Contextual variables comprise an important part of this model and include local, institutional, global, and chronometrical variables.

ASSESSMENT TOOLS FOR EXAMINING WELLNESS

To help all people work toward high-level wellness, formal assessment methods that inform self-understanding and contribute to an emerging knowledge base of well functioning were developed.

■ The Wellness Evaluation of Lifestyle

The need for assessment was met initially through development and validation of the Wellness Evaluation of Lifestyle (WEL). After 15 years of research involving more than three dozen studies, five separate and increasingly more useful versions of the WEL resulted in the Five Factor Wellness Inventory (5F–WEL, discussed at length in the next section).

Elements of the WEL

- The initial version (WEL–O; Witmer, Sweeney, & Myers, 1993) included 114 items designed to assess the 17 components in the wheel of wellness.
- Items were statements (e.g., "I usually achieve the goals I set for myself") that respondents rated using a 5-point Likert-type scale with choices including (5) strongly agree, (4) agree, (3) neutral or undecided, (2) disagree, and (1) strongly disagree.
- Over a period of 10 years, the instrument was field tested with a variety of adult populations.
- Extensive item and scale analyses resulted in several revisions, the most recent being the WEL–S (Myers et al., 2000), which includes 131 items.
- Convergent and divergent validity were investigated by comparing scores on the various WEL scales to similar scales on other instruments.
- As reported in the *WEL Manual,* Myers (1998) found that scores measuring conceptually similar constructs had high correlations (convergent validity) and scores measuring different constructs had lower correlations (divergent validity).

Both scale and item scores can be examined and may be helpful in targeting specific areas of wellness for intentional change. The lack of factor analytic studies limits the usefulness of the WEL for research.

■ The Five Factor Wellness Inventory

The Five Factor Wellness Inventory (5F–WEL) grew out of factor analytic studies of the original WEL database and measures the factors included in the indivisible self model of wellness. Multiple versions of the 5F–WEL, including cross-cultural translations and versions for children and adolescents as well as adults have made this a useful instrument for clinical and research purposes.

Elements of the 5F–WEL

- The paper-and-pencil instrument includes 73 items measuring the single higher order wellness factor (total wellness), the five second-order factors (creative, coping, social, essential, and physical selves), and the original 17 discrete scales measured in the WEL.

- Most of the scales include four to six items.
- An additional 19 items measure the four contexts included in the IS–WEL model (local, institutional, global, and chronometrical).

Use of the 5F–WEL in multiple dissertation and other studies provides evidence of both convergent and divergent validity of the scales relative to constructs such as ethnic identity, acculturation, body image, self-esteem, and gender role conflict (Myers & Sweeney, 2005a).

Available Forms of the 5F–WEL

- The ninth-grade reading level version (for use with high school students or adults).
- The maximum sixth-grade reading level version.
- The third-grade reading level version (for use with middle and elementary school students).

In addition to its applicability to a variety of age groups, the 5F–WEL is also adjusted for use with clients of differing cultural backgrounds for whom English is not a first language.

Cultural Adaptations of the 5F–WEL

- The adult version has been translated into Korean (translation by C. Chang, 1998), Turkish (translation by T. Dogan, 2005), and Spanish (in progress; translation by N. Ivers and J. Myers, 2006).
- The sixth-grade version has been translated into Hebrew (translation by M. Tatar; See Tatar & Myers, in press).
- The third-grade version translation into Spanish is in progress.
- A Chinese language adaptation currently is being explored.

COUNSELING FOR WELLNESS

Suggestions for using wellness in counseling incorporate four steps that are highlighted in this section:

1. Introduction of one of the wellness models, including a life-span, choice-based focus.
2. Formal assessment, informal assessment, or both, based on the model.
3. Intentional interventions to enhance wellness in selected areas of wellness.
4. Evaluation and follow-up.

■ Step 1: Introduction of the Wellness Model

The first step in the process of wellness counseling is typically to introduce the counselee to a different paradigm than simply symptom relief. Most counselees want and deserve help with their presenting issues. As is often the case, the presenting issues are an expression of lifestyle behaviors, attitudes, and expectations that the counselees are not fully aware contribute to their presenting issues. No more time is required to include an expectation that more good can be accomplished than symptom relief or a solution to an immediate issue. Having empathized and shown interest in the presenting issues, the counselor may introduce the idea of wellness near the end of the first session.

There are a number of ways that counselors can approach the topic of wellness, including talking about wellness, conceptualizing wellness as a personal choice, emphasizing the multidimensional nature of wellness, introducing wellness as part of life-span development, and reviewing the personal meaning of wellness to the client.

Talk About Wellness

- Express a desire to encourage higher level wellness as an ultimate goal.
- Provide a short definition of wellness.
- Introduce one of the models (IS–WEL or wheel of wellness).
- Explain how a focus on healthy living can contribute to overall well-being.
- Share a copy of the model with the counselee in which each characteristic in the model is briefly described.
- Ensure clients that these characteristics are derived from across disciplines through multiple studies over several decades.

The interaction of the indivisible components of the model is an important concept when presenting the wellness model.

Conceptualize Wellness as a Personal Choice

- Explain that change in any one area can contribute to or create changes in other areas, and these changes can be for better or worse.
- Define wellness as a choice.
- Remind clients that each choice made toward wellness leads to greater happiness and life satisfaction through enhanced well-being in the areas that contribute to wellness.

After introducing the topic of wellness and underscoring the choice clients have to incorporate wellness into their therapeutic goals, it is helpful, when presenting the wellness models, to emphasize the three- or even four-dimensional nature of wellness.

Emphasize the Multidimensional Nature of Wellness

- Encourage counselees to view the wheel of wellness model as a sphere or globe, the center of which is round and full when the central component is personally satisfying. If the central component is unsatisfying, the rest of the sphere cannot be firm and round.
- Help clients visualize the tasks of self-direction as spokes in a wheel that allow the wheel to roll along solidly through time and space when strong, but that hinder the wheel's movement when they are defective.
- Describe the human experience of stress holistically—from physical, spiritual, and emotional perspectives.
- Educate clients that strengthening one component of well-being has positive effects on all the others.

The wheel represents the components of wellness over the life span, and attention to each component has consequences that multiply over the course of the life span.

Introduce Wellness as Part of Life-Span Development

- Describe wellness choices as having a cumulative effect over the life span by increasing wellness in all dimensions, thereby contributing to quality of life and longevity.
- Encourage counselees to take a life-span perspective on their total wellness by reviewing the impact of prior choices in each dimension of wellness and projecting the future impact of choices made at this time.

Finally, counselees are asked to review the model and reflect on the personal meaning of wellness.

Review the Personal Meaning of Wellness to the Client

- Ask clients if they would like to learn how to solve the presenting issue, and additionally, enjoy their life more.
- Encourage clients to define wellness in their own words. They likely will need help reflecting on wellness as a process rather than an outcome.
- Encourage clients to study the components of the model such as the wheel and reflect on the personal meaning of each concept.

■ Step 2: Assessment of the Components of the Wellness Models

Although models of wellness are useful for conceptualizing human functioning, it is even more important that these models be used as a basis for self-understanding and intentional decision making to enhance wellness in a positive direction. To do so most effectively requires some means of assessing how one is doing in each of the areas of well-being. Assessment may be conducted in a variety of ways and either informally or formally. Informal assessment methods usually rely on the use of two simple scaling questions for which clients make ratings.

Scaling Questions

1. How well do you feel?
2. How satisfied are you with your level of wellness in this area?

A sample rating scale for spiritual wellness would look something like Table 30.1.

A global self-report assessment of a counselee's functioning in each of the components of the wheel similarly can be obtained in an informal assessment.

Process of Obtaining a Global Self-Report

■ Ask the counselee to rate his or her overall wellness in each dimension on a scale of 1 (*very low*) to 10 (*very high*).
■ Honor counselees' scores—even mid- to low levels of wellness in an area—if they are content with their score at a particular point in time and have no desire for change.
■ Encourage clients to reflect on the scores to determine themes and patterns.
■ Ask counselees to confirm that these ratings are accurate in terms of how they see their wellness at this point in time.

In addition to or in place of an informal assessment, wellness in each dimension may be assessed using the WEL (Myers et al., 1998), which is based on the wheels of wellness model or the 5F-WEL (Myers & Sweeney, 2004), which is based on the IS–WEL. There are a number of advantages to using formal assessment methods. First, the WEL and the 5F–WEL provide systematic ways to evaluate the components of the wheel of wellness or IS–WEL, respectively. Second, these tools allow for a measurement of one's wellness on a continuum from not well to high-level wellness. Finally, formal assessment provides a basis for developing a personal wellness plan that contributes to greater total wellness.

There are some guiding principles that counselors can follow when using the WEL or 5F–WEL assessment tools.

TABLE 30.1
Sample Spiritual Wellness Rating Scale

Spirituality	Circle the Number That Best Reflects Your Overall Spiritual Wellness and Your Satisfaction With Your Spiritual Wellness.									
Overall Wellness	1	2	3	4	5	6	7	8	9	10
Satisfaction	1	2	3	4	5	6	7	8	9	10

Guidelines for Using the WEL or the 5F–WEL Inventories

- Encourage counselees to reflect on their scores, determine how well the scores reflect their perceptions of their total wellness, and reflect on the pattern of their high and low scores.
- Select one or more of the low scores as areas for which the client would like to develop a personal wellness plan.
- Help clients choose an area in which they received a high score, and yet would like to enhance that area of personal wellness.
- Attempt to build on assets to overcome perceived weaknesses. If humor is one of an individual's strengths, for example, the counselor may help the counselee find the paradox in some well-intended but self-defeating behaviors.

■ Step 3: Intentional Interventions to Enhance Wellness

Once wellness in each dimension has been assessed, either informally or formally, counselees can be asked to choose one or more areas of wellness that they would like to change and improve. It is not recommended that counselees try to affect change in all areas simultaneously for two reasons. First, choosing to change in more than two to three areas likely will represent an overwhelming array of tasks for anyone. Second, because change in one area will cause changes in other areas, awareness of wellness needs combined with change in any one area is likely to increase overall wellness and wellness in specific additional areas of the model.

The two main tasks of the third step in counseling for wellness are coconstructing a personal wellness plan and developing a written behavioral plan. Once the counselee identifies those dimensions that he or she would like to change in the direction of greater wellness, the counselor and counselee work to coconstruct a personal wellness plan in each targeted area.

Tasks of Coconstructing a Personal Plan

- Restate the definition of wellness for the identified dimension followed by a rating scale consisting of the numbers 1 through 10.
- Direct the counselee to circle the number reflecting his or her wellness in this area. (For generic worksheets that can be used, see *Wellness and Habit Change Workbook* [Myers & Sweeney, 2004]).
- Instruct the counselee to write comments on the worksheet concerning his or her satisfaction with the self-rating. (For some counselees with limited sight or other impairments, the counselor records their remarks.)
- Discuss concerns related to the counselee's level of satisfaction.
- Ask the counselee to complete an informal self-assessment of personal strengths and limitations related to the wellness area targeted for change.

After the counselor and counselee create the personal wellness plan, they develop a written behavioral plan that supports the personalized plan.

Components of the Written Behavioral Wellness Plan

- Objectives for change.
- Methods to be used to effect change.
- Resources that will be employed as the plan is implemented.
- Involvement of key persons in the implementation of the wellness plan.

Step 4: Evaluation and Follow-Up

Finally, a discussion of evaluation procedures and timelines is an important part of the behavioral plan.

Ways to Individualize Evaluation and Follow-Up Procedures

- Encourage the counselee to use an ongoing plan for regular and systematic evaluation, with identified markers that signify progress in making change.
- Use feedback from friends and family when possible as an indicator that efforts to enhance wellness are being made.
- Help counselees develop both short- and long-range plans to improve their wellness.
- Respond to the counselees' level of self-directed change by allowing highly motivated individuals to develop and implement their own wellness plans with some guidelines, or by engaging in a more focused, step-by-step process with others.
- Capitalize on the areas of wellness that are popular in the media today, such as nutrition and exercise, for which little outside intervention may be required to help a counselee experience positive change in these dimensions.
- Provide traditional counseling intervention for other areas, such as emotional awareness and coping and realistic beliefs to facilitate change.

Use the counseling process to introduce counselees to wellness; teach techniques for self-assessment, planning, evaluation, and follow-up; and encourage them to develop a view of wellness as a lifelong process through which many changes will occur.

Strengths and Limitations

This is a strength-based approach to helping. It is based on development over the life span, taking into account contextual factors and influences. Dynamic in nature, just as is human growth, the approach addresses factors of importance to all persons, cultures, genders, and people of diverse races.

The chief limitation of this approach is that greater empirical support and application across generations and cultures geographically is needed. There is promising evidence from persons in this country, Korea, India, Africa, Israel, and Turkey, but there is great need for others, including those who are of Spanish cultures and language.

Chapter 30: **Key Term**

▶ Wellness

Spirituality and Pastoral Counseling Practices*

Grafton T. Eliason
California University of Pennsylvania

Colleen Triffanoff
Thomas Jefferson High School

Maria Leventis
Pace University

In This Chapter

▶ *The Importance of Spirituality in Counseling*
- Spirituality in Professional Counseling and Psychology Organizations
- Spirituality in American Society

▶ *Pastoral Counseling and Related Ideology*
- Religion and Spirituality
- Spirituality and Counseling
- Evolution of Pastoral Counseling

▶ *Ethics, Spirituality, and Counseling*
- Ethical Decision-Making Criteria
- Purpose of Ethical Codes
- Counselor Competence
- Supervision

▶ *Psychodynamic Theories and Spirituality*
- Freud and Psychoanalysis
- Jungian Psychology

▶ *Existential and Phenomenological Theories and Spirituality*
- Frankl and Logotherapy
- May and Existentialism
- Rogers and Client-Centered Theory
- Perls and Gestalt Therapy

▶ *Behavioral Theories and Spirituality*
- Watson and Behaviorism
- Skinner and Behavioral Conditioning
- Lazarus and Multimodal Therapy

▶ *Cognitive and Cognitive Behavioral Theories and Spirituality*
- Glasser and Choice Theory
- Ellis and REBT

▶ *Conclusion*

*Sincere thanks to Springer Publishing Company and to Routledge/Taylor & Francis Group for granting permission to reprint and update two previous publications:

Copyright © 2001. From by G. Eliason, C. Hanley, & M. Leventis, The role of spirituality: Four theoretical orientations. *Pastoral Psychology, 50*(2), 77–91. Reproduced by permission of Spring Publishing.

Copyright © 2000. From G. Eliason, Spirituality and counseling of the older adult. In A. Tomer (Ed.), *Death attitudes and the older adult*. Reproduced by permission of Routledge/Taylor & Francis Group, LLC.

THE IMPORTANCE OF SPIRITUALITY IN COUNSELING

The integration of spirituality in counseling and psychotherapy is needed to treat the individual from a holistic framework. In this chapter, we provide a basic overview of spirituality and counseling. Although most of the chapter can be applied to a broad range of religious faiths, we look specifically at pastoral counseling in the Judeo-Christian tradition. Finally, we discuss the role of spirituality in the field from the perspective of four primary psychological schools of thought: psychodynamic, existential or phenomenological, behavioral, and cognitive.

■ Spirituality in Professional Counseling and Psychology Organizations

Both the American Psychological Association (APA) and the American Counseling Association (ACA) have professional divisions related to spirituality and religion.

Professional Associations for Spirituality and Counseling

- The APA division is the Psychology of Religion.
- The ACA division is the Association for Spiritual, Ethical, and Religious Values in Counseling (ASERVIC).

 For more information on ACA and spirituality and the APA division on psychology and religion:

▶ www.aservic.org
▶ www.apa.org/divisions/div36/homepage.html

Each of these divisions is growing in membership. In addition, the Council for Accreditation of Counseling and Related Educational Programs (CACREP) included spirituality as a component in its 2001 standards. This speaks, on a professional level, to the importance of spirituality in the field (ACA, 2005a; APA, 2005; Miller, 2003).

■ Spirituality in American Society

From its inception, the United States has been a nation steeped in religious beliefs, spirituality, and freedom. This is no different for our contemporary society. Miller (2003) cited a number of statistics that support this reality:

- 95% of Americans believe in God (Baker, 1997, as cited in Miller, 2003).
- 85% believe that prayer has healing power (Wallis, 1996, as cited in Miller, 2003).

- 62% belong to religious organizations.
- 60% believe that religion is a very important part of their lives.
- A large percentage worship close to once a week (*The Harvard Mental Health Letter*, 2001, as cited in Miller, 2003).

Matthews and Clark (1998) pointed to extensive studies showing a positive correlation between faith and good health, both physical and mental. Many studies also show a correlation between a lack of faith and poor health or recovery.

In 1992, Gallup was commissioned by the Samaritan Institute and the American Association of Pastoral Counselors (AAPC) to survey Americans' attitudes toward pastoral counseling, the importance of spirituality, and its perceived impact on their mental health. This was followed by a second survey in 2000 conducted by Greenburg Quinlan Research. The results showed that a large percentage of Americans acknowledge a relation among spirituality, faith, religious values, and mental health. They also would prefer to seek counseling from a provider who integrates spirituality into treatment (AAPC, 2000, as cited in AAPC, 2005). A number of findings were presented by AAPC.

Attitudes Toward Pastoral Counseling, Spirituality, and Mental Health

- 83% of respondents feel their spiritual faith and religious beliefs are closely tied to their state of mental and emotional health.
- 75% of respondents say it is important to see a professional counselor who integrates their values and beliefs into the counseling process.
- 69% believe it is important to see a professional counselor who represents spiritual values and beliefs if they had a serious problem that required counseling.
- 77% say it would be important for an elderly parent or relative who was in need of treatment to get assistance from a mental health professional who knew and understood their spiritual beliefs and values.
- More people mention pastoral counselors and others with religious training than any other professionals (29%; AAPC, 2000, as cited in AAPC, 2005).

Practitioners with specific training in spirituality, religion, and counseling can offer a valuable service to the mental health and religious communities by providing specific skills and training that may better meet the spiritual and psychoemotional needs of the public (AAPC, 2000, as cited in AAPC, 2005).

PASTORAL COUNSELING AND RELATED IDEOLOGY

To truly comprehend any concept, it is important to understand the context in which that concept is situated. Differentiating religion and spirituality is important to the field of pastoral counseling.

■ Religion and Spirituality

Religion differs from spirituality in that religion refers to the organized practice of worship and ritual. Etymologically, religion stems from the Latin root *religio*, meaning "religious scruple, conscientiousness, sense of right; religion, sect, cult, mode of worship; object of veneration, sacred object, sacred place; divine service, worship, religious observation" (Traupman, 1966, p. 265). The word *religion* also comes from *religare*, meaning "to bind back, to bind together, to tie up, or to moor (a ship)" (Traupman, 1966, p. 463). A definition of religion that can be adopted is as follows:

> **Religion:** The belief system and ritual practices of a sect or denomination of individuals that binds them together in worship, practice, and community.

The etymological origin of the word *spirit* is from the Latin *spiritus*, meaning "breath, inspiration, character," or the soul (Traupman, 1966, pp. 292–293, 497). Spirit was literally the breath of life in Hebrew, Greek, and Roman cultures. Western belief systems see the spirit, in one sense, as that which gives life, self-awareness, personality, and animation. In another sense, it is that which is other than our corporeal body (Eliason, 2000). Spirituality can be understood in this way:

> **Spirituality:** That which allows humans to transcend the corporeal body and to connect on many levels with that which is other.

During the 1996 Summit on Spirituality, ASERVIC, the branch of ACA that specializes in spirituality and counseling, expanded the definition of spirituality. The association proposed an understanding of spirituality that included a variety of components.

Defining Components of Spirituality (ASERVIC, 2006; Miller, 2003)

- Spirituality is the drawing out and infusion of spirit in one's life and is experienced as an active and passive process.
- Spirituality is a capacity and tendency that is innate and unique to all persons.
- The spiritual tendency moves individuals toward knowledge, love, meaning, peace, hope, transcendence, connectedness, compassion, wellness, and wholeness.
- Spirituality includes one's capacity for creativity, growth, and the development of a value system.
- Spirituality encompasses a variety of phenomena, including experiences, beliefs, and practices.
- Spirituality is approached from a variety of perspectives, including psycho-spiritual, religious, and transpersonal.

■ Spirituality and Counseling

From a counseling perspective, spirituality can become the unifying factor in Buber's (1923/1970) concept of the *I and Thou* experience. Humans experience relationships with self, with other, and with a higher power. Each of us maintains an internal dialogue and a perception of self. We have the ability to gain greater self-awareness. We experience empathic encounters with other humans, both in our personal relationships and in professional counseling relationships. Humans also can have a personal experience with a higher power. It is the dynamic of spirituality and the I–thou relationship that facilitates growth in pastoral counseling. "The role of spirituality in counseling is multidimensional. On one level, the client explores her or his own spirituality and calls upon faith and the spiritual I/Thou relationship to act dynamically in the healing process. On another level, the counselor draws upon her or his spiritual faith to enhance the interaction and the I/Thou experience between counselor, client, and God" (Buber, 1923/1970; Eliason, 2000, p. 244).

■ Evolution of Pastoral Counseling

Although pastoral counseling is becoming recognized as a unique field, it always will be influenced by its shared history of religion, psychology, and counseling. The AAPC (2005) defined pastoral counseling this way:

> **Pastoral counseling:** "[A] process in which a pastoral counselor utilizes insights and principles derived from the disciplines of theology and the behavioral sciences in working with individuals, couples, families, groups and social systems toward the achievement of wholeness and health" (http://www.acpe.edu).

Kelly (1995) and Strunk (1993) viewed the academic study of the psychology of religion as the precursor to pastoral counseling. They pointed to James, Allport, Pruyser, Johnson, and Boisen as founders of that movement and, in turn, the field of pastoral counseling, beginning with the publication of James's (1902/1961) *The Varieties of Religious Experience.*

Two specific movements had an impact on the training of clergy and paved the way for the development of pastoral counseling (Strunk, 1993): the Emmanuel movement and the clinical pastoral education (CPE) movement. The efforts to bring together the fields of medicine, psychology, and religion and the eventual formation of the AAPC, which today regulates pastoral counseling, is highlighted by these events.

Historical Development of Pastoral Counseling

- ■ Elwood Worchester, rector of the Emmanuel Worchester Church, and several physicians in Boston established a clinic for spiritual healing.

- By 1940, due to a lack of training, growth, and a breakdown of relationships between the religious and medical communities, the Emmanuel movement ended.
- In 1925, W. S. Keller, R. C. Cabot, and A. T. Boisen started the CPE movement that continues to be successful today.
- In 1963, the first conference of pastoral counselors was held in New York City.
- The AAPC held its first formal conference in 1964.
- The Association for Clinical Pastoral Education (ACPE) was formed in 1967 as a merger of four CPE organizations and has partnerships with 23 faith groups and agencies (ACPE, 2005; Strunk, 1993).

Today, CPE offers training to help clergy effectively respond to individuals experiencing crisis and to achieve overall professional competence in pastoral ministry, and the AAPC maintains an active role in the development of pastoral counseling. As the field of pastoral counseling continues to evolve and grow, one must consider a wide realm of concerns involving both religious and secular issues. It is important to understand the history of this field in relation to spirituality, religion, psychology, and counseling, so that the most appropriate decisions can be made for the future (Strunk, 1993).

ETHICS, SPIRITUALITY, AND COUNSELING

The focus of counseling is on individuals, couples, or families and their specific psychological issues. Psychotherapeutic theories and interventions can enhance our understanding of the issue while facilitating growth through awareness and positive action. Out of respect for the client's autonomy, it is not the counselor's role to evangelize the client or to subject the client to specific values or belief systems. Rather, the counselor assists the client on her or his own spiritual journey (Browning, 1987, 1993; Capps, 1995; Eliason, 2000). Indeed, all professional counselors are charged with upholding the highest ethical standards that protect a client's right to beneficence, nonmaleficence, autonomy, justice, and fidelity.

■ Ethical Decision-Making Criteria

Mental health and pastoral counselors can rely on four criteria in making appropriate ethical decisions.

Considerations for Making Ethical Decisions

1. The current legal system, including federal law, state law, and court precedents.
2. Membership in professional organizations and abidance to codes and standards of ethics.

3. Education, including degrees, certifications, licensure, and continued training.
4. Ongoing supervision in the field (Corey, 2004a; Eliason, 2000).

■ Purpose of Ethical Codes

Herlihy and Corey (1996) maintained that codes of ethics serve a number of purposes:

- To educate the counselors and public about professional responsibilities.
- To provide a measure for accountability to protect the public and counselors.
- To provide a basis for reflection so that counselors might improve the quality of practice.

See Chapter 2 for more on ethics in counseling.

■ Counselor Competence

Degrees, certifications, licenses, and training standards are established to maintain a level of competency in a profession that relates to the quality of care due to clients. Counselors also must be aware of their own beliefs, values, biases, and limitations. Butman (1997) maintained that, "The assumption is usually made that a client's welfare is directly affected by whether or not the mental health professional knows her or his limitations and weaknesses, as well as her or his strengths and skills" (p. 57). Butman succinctly defined competence this way:

> **Competence:** A "combination of clinical expertise, high levels of self-awareness and interpersonal effectiveness" (p. 57).

Secular organizations such as the APA and the ACA evaluate their professional membership and maintain accrediting bodies such as APA accreditation or CACREP. Other organizations such as the National Board for Certified Counselors (NBCC) also provide standards and testing for the national certification of counselors. Licensure regulates the practice by setting standards of due care, training qualifications, and designating the legal use of titles (ACA, 2005c; APA, 2005; Bullis & Mazur, 1993; NBCC, 2005a).

Pastoral counselors, like mental health counselors, are held to a high level of professionalism. To ensure competence, the AAPC accredits training programs based on its standards of practice; additionally, many recognized organizations including the AAPC require graduate-level training in both theology and pastoral counseling to obtain certification as a pastoral counselor.

Certification Requirements of AAPC

- Master of divinity or doctoral degree in theological, spiritual, or biblical studies or a master or doctoral degree in pastoral counseling.

- Religious body endorsement.
- Active relationship to a local religious community.
- Three years of ministry.
- 375 hours of pastoral counseling plus 125 supervision hours, one third of which must be provided by an approved AAPC supervisor.

In the counseling field where the place of spirituality in the therapeutic relationship increasingly is recognized, pastoral counselors have a special opportunity to integrate traditional therapeutic approaches with their awareness of the spiritual dimension (AAPC, 1998).

 Check out the AACP Web site for more information on the AAPC and its certification process:

▶ www.aapc.org

■ Supervision

In addition to initial degrees, certifications, licensure, and training, it is important for practicing mental health and pastoral counselors to continue their education and to maintain clinical supervision through consultation with other professionals concerning cases, ethics, and self-awareness. The process of personal growth continues throughout one's professional career and directly affects the quality of care provided to clients, as well as one's personal satisfaction and level of competence (Butman, 1997; Corey, 2004a).

See Chapters 5 and 6 for more on clinical supervision.

PSYCHODYNAMIC THEORIES AND SPIRITUALITY

Psychodynamic theories include a number of well-recognized approaches and theorists. Freud is perhaps one of the most recognized theorists due to the originality and longevity of psychoanalysis. Jung and Adler worked closely with Freud (1943, 1969), but eventually left to pursue their own theoretical orientations. Erikson (1963), Berne, and many other theorists have built on the basic premises of Freud and continue to use his theory as a benchmark (Corey, 2004a). In this section, the place of religion and spirituality in Freud and Jung's lives and theories is highlighted.

■ Freud and Psychoanalysis

Freud (1913, 1927) struggled with religious belief throughout his life, which is readily observed in his work. A number of authors (Bakan, 1958, as cited in Merkur, 1997; Meier, Minirth, Wichern, & Ratcliff, 1997; Vitz, 1988/1993) noted that Freud was raised in a Hasidic Jewish household with an affectionate, but strict father. However, his Roman Catholic nanny may have had a profound influence on him in early childhood. Freud was taken to Roman Catholic church services and taught rudimentary concepts of Christianity. Vitz maintained that this early focus on Christianity may have been the impetus for Freud's interest in it throughout his life. It is also theorized that Freud may have resorted to atheism to resolve the internal conflict between the two faiths, secularizing much of his religious tradition. Nonetheless, as Capps (2001) shows in *Freud and Freudians on Religion,* Freud wrote about religion throughout his career, from *Obsessive Actions and Religious Practices* in 1907, to *Moses and Monotheism: Three Essays* in 1939.

In spite of Freud's noted atheism, aspects of his religious heritage and spirituality can be noticed in psychoanalytic theory.

Aspects of Religion in Psychoanalysis

- Bakan (1958, as cited in Merkur, 1997) noted that there may be similarities between the practice of Jewish mysticism known as Kabbalah and Freud's theory of psychoanalysis.
- Kabbalah places a great emphasis on dream interpretation and human sexuality, and Freud depicted religion as a guilt-centered neurosis and discussed the unconscious symbolism of dreams and human sexuality (Jacobs & Capps, 1997; Meier et al., 1997).
- Freud's hypothesis that God and Satan represent two divergent aspects of a primal father figure shows the limitations of a static God image, an understanding that can, in fact, expand our personal and religious construct of hope and the ever changing *I am.*

Counselors may continue to glean effective theoretical applications—even spiritual applications—from Freud's model. Capps applied Freud's (1962) idea of religious projection to the Judeo-Christian concept of God, future, and hope. Capps (1995) concluded, first, that Freud's understanding of God as an "enormously exalted father" suggests that religion may at times serve to limit our image of God and, second, that when God is viewed only as an enormously exalted father, the development of religion is stunted in a childlike stage.

Psychoanalytic theory can help to explain our human and religious experiences, and how these experiences are expressed symbolically through our unconscious (Jacobs & Capps, 1997). Freud's contribution of defense mechanisms in relation to the unconscious mind can be used on a more functional level in the field of counseling. Although Freud's view of human nature is thought to be deterministic, the client can initiate positive change through self-awareness. Psychoanalytic techniques can be used in a counseling setting and do not have to be limited to strict psychoanalysis.

For more on psychoanalytic goals, techniques, and role of the counselor, see Chapter 9.

■ Jungian Psychology

Jung was born in Switzerland in 1875 as the only surviving son of a Swiss Reformed church pastor; his sister was born when he was 9 years old (Engler, 1984; Vitz, 1977/1994). Disenchanted with the experience of communion as a young boy, Jung spent much of his life in search of religious and spiritual answers. This search led him to his studies and theories in psychology, religion, myth, and the occult (Jung, 1965). Although Jung did not possess a traditional view of religion, his understanding of spirituality was able to cross many religious boundaries, including Judaism, Christianity, and Buddhism. Jung eventually moved away from Freud's theory; some of the core ideas of Jung's orientation reflect spiritual undertones.

Facets of Spirituality in Jungian Psychology

- The unconscious has two parts, the personal unconscious and the collective unconscious, which refer to experiences throughout human history.
- Each person receives unconscious memories of these experiences that are brought to light as symbols, or archetypes.
- The concept of archetypes is used to help people gain deeper understanding of life subjects and images such as God and the divine, which although seemingly inaccessible, are nonetheless real.
- Sexuality is viewed as a symbol and a creative mystery unto itself (Engler, 1984).

Jung's use of myth, metaphor, and archetype has had a significant influence on theology, psychology, counseling, sociology, and cultural anthropology, having been originally applied to dream work and ritual theory. The theological bent is quite evident in his writings, such as in *An Answer to Job*. However, Jung's ideas are also now widely used in counseling and have been applied to human spirituality and biblical criticism by Ricoeur (1976, 1980), Frye (1957, 1982), and other contemporary authors (Meier et al., 1997). Jung's insight into myth, metaphor, archetype, and ritual has provided an opportunity for spiritual growth and psychic healing in the contemporary counseling setting.

See Chapter 9 for more information on Jungian psychology.

EXISTENTIAL AND PHENOMENOLOGICAL THEORIES AND SPIRITUALITY

Unlike other theoretical orientations, existentialism and phenomenology are rooted in a philosophical context (Kierkegaard, Sartre, Nietzsche, Tillich), providing a framework from which one can view the world and life (Engler, 1984). At the heart of this framework is humanity's search for meaning. The process of living in the shadow of our finitude becomes the focus, rather than the end product of our existence (Frankl, 1946/1984). In contemplating our own death, we can begin to live more fully in the present. Existentialism refutes the psychoanalytic concept of determinism and maintains that humans have the freedom of choice. As such, existential counseling rejects the medical model and the ability to cure. Rather, the goal is to facilitate self-reflection and to help the client identify options that might provide meaning in her or his life. Self-reflection is not self-absorption; rather, it points outside of the self. Needless to say, this journey is often a spiritual one. The word *existentialism* is derived from the Latin *exsistere*, meaning to "exist," "stand out," or to "emerge," referring to the growth of an individual (Engler, 1984).

■ Frankl and Logotherapy

One of the most noted existential theorists, Frankl drew from his own past to express his theory and spirituality. Frankl's experience as a prisoner in the Nazi death camps of Auschwitz and Dachau profoundly shaped his existential philosophy of life, resulting in the theory of logotherapy. Of Greek origin, *logos* refers to "meaning," "word," or in a theological sense, "the Word." As a prisoner, Frankl lost his entire family except for one sister. He noticed that some individuals in the camps lost hope and the will to survive, whereas others struggled to live. Those who survived carried a notion of something that gave their life meaning. Humanity's will to meaning is our guiding motivational force (Frankl, 1946/1984).

The search for meaning—a deeply spiritual endeavor—is a pillar of Frankl's approach to life and therapy; indeed, the therapy in general suggests an integration between spirituality and logotherapy (Meier et al., 1997).

Connection Between Spirituality and Logotherapy

- Society generally is characterized by noogenic neurosis, or a search for meaning.
- Clients are given the freedom to choose, and then are held responsible for the choices they make.
- The counselee is encouraged to deemphasize the self in favor of more ultimate tasks in life.
- Love allows people to deeply understand one another, at the innermost core of their beings.

Frankl's concept of love transcends the physical and sexual motivations of Freud's theory. It becomes the basis for our therapeutic relationship, as well as our relationship with others in this world. Frankl saw love as one of the most meaningful aspirations of humanity, and his search for meaning led him to apply his personal spiritual awareness to existential theory.

■ May and Existentialism

May grew up in a sensitive middle-American family, where, unfortunately, intellectual pursuits were not appreciated. In his own search for meaning, May traveled to Greece and later studied theology at Union Theological Seminary in New York City and psychotherapy with Adler in Vienna. In his 30s, May contracted tuberculosis. During this illness, he read Freud, Kierkegaard, and Tillich. May began to focus on humanity's experience of existential crisis and anxiety, as well as the contrasting experiences of meaningfulness, hope, and joy (Engler, 1984; Vitz, 1977/1994). May has contributed to our understanding of love and violence and has been a critic of contemporary society.

Reflections of Spirituality in May's Approach to Counseling

- May pointed to our spiritual impotence in a technological age of narcissism and postulated that our Western concept of love has moved inward, mutating into forms of apathy or power.
- The concept of meaning suggests that "the future lies with the man or woman who can live as an individual, conscious *within* the solidarity of the human race. He then uses the tension between individuality and solidarity as the source of his ethical creativity" (May, 1972, p. 254).
- "For every act of love and will—and in the long run they are both present in each genuine act—we mold ourselves and our world simultaneously. This is what it means to embrace the future" (May, 1969, p. 322).

■ Rogers and Client-Centered Theory

Rogers' client-centered theory expands on aspects of existential philosophy, and more specifically, draws its primary emphasis from phenomenological humanism. Rogers grew up in an atmosphere of strict religious standards. Although his family was close, his mother could be judgmental. Rogers studied agriculture at the University of Wisconsin and later began religious studies at Union Theological Seminary in New York City. However, he could not ascribe to a single set of beliefs and transferred to Columbia Teachers College where he studied philosophy and clinical psychology (Corey, 2004a; Engler, 1984).

The etymology of phenomenology comes from the Greek, *phainomenon*, referring to a "phenomenon," or "that which appears or shows itself." Rogers followed a constructivist viewpoint focusing on the client's individual experience and her or his subjective interpretation of that phenomenon. The attempt to truly understand the other—to connect with clients on a spiritual, rather than corporeal level—lies at the heart of this theory. Spirituality is evident in these broad assumptions of client-centered therapy (Rogers, 1951, 1961).

Assumptions of Client-Centered Therapy

- Significant, trusting relationships lie at the heart of powerful therapy.
- A trusting therapeutic relationship is established through congruence or genuineness, unconditional positive regard, and accurate empathic understanding.
- Counselors are urged to seek the inherent worth in clients.
- Clients must be allowed the freedom to explore all frightening, undesirable aspects of their personhood within the therapeutic relationship without fear of judgment.

When counselors and clients are able to connect with one another, a client's defenses are lowered, and she or he becomes open to the therapist's response. Techniques at this point include drawing attention to the client's subjective reality through active listening, reflection, summarization, clarification, and gentle confrontation. Ultimately, the client moves from a static point of fixity to a life experience of the present, process, change, and flow (Vitz, 1977/1994). Rogers' theory continues to be applicable today, stressing the importance of the counselor's attitude toward the worth of the client.

See Chapter 9 for more about Rogerian therapy.

■ Perls and Gestalt Therapy

As the originator of Gestalt therapy, Perls (1969) also built on the existential and phenomenological approaches of philosophy and psychology. He was born to a Jewish family in Berlin and had trouble with the authorities as a youth. Through perseverance, he completed his medical degree and served as a medic in the German army. He later worked with brain-damaged soldiers after the war. *Gestalt* is of German origin, meaning "a unified whole." Perls emphasized integration of the person as a whole individual and strove for awareness as a therapeutic goal. His theory is existential in that through awareness individuals can choose, change, and become responsible for their actions. Gestalt therapy is phenomenological, in that it considers an individual's subjective reality (Meier et al., 1997).

Spirituality and Gestalt therapy come together most apparently in the link between Perls' vision of the therapeutic relationship and the I/thou concept proposed by Buber. In his book *I and Thou*, Buber (1923/1970) synthesized the spiritual idea of self, human relationship, and divine relationship, stating, "The basic word I-You can be spoken only with one's whole being. The concentration and fusion into a whole being can never be accomplished by me, can never be accomplished without me. I require a You to become; becoming I, I say You" (p. 62).

Aspects of Spirituality in Gestalt Therapy

- The I/thou relationship between the therapist and the client, or between one client and another client, is of utmost importance.

- The therapist must be wholly present for the client and open to both the client's subjective experience and the present therapeutic experience.
- The goal of therapy is to help clients, through awareness, to become a gestalt or a whole.
- The therapist challenges the client to become aware of her or his layers of neurosis so that unfinished business might be dealt with and attached anxiety might be expressed through feelings (Meier et al., 1997).

Just as in Buber's theological understanding of the I/thou relationship one cannot exist without the other, Perls underscored the importance of the relationship, and the challenges offered by the therapist are crucial—required, even—for the client's awareness and ultimately, wholeness.

See Chapter 9 for more information about Gestalt therapy.

BEHAVIORAL THEORIES AND SPIRITUALITY

One might easily question the role of spirituality and religion in behavioral psychology. Behavioral psychology originally arose as the antithesis to previous psychological theories and to the concepts of religion, soul, and human freedom. Watson and Skinner were two pioneers in behavioral psychology, contributing to classical and operant conditioning (Watson, 1925; Wood & Wood, 1993).

■ Watson and Behaviorism

Watson was born on a farm in South Carolina to a very religious mother and an alcoholic father who was unfaithful to his wife and abandoned the family. Watson applied the methods of observable science to the field of psychology. Rejecting the concepts of consciousness and spirit, Watson relied on measurable actions and observable behaviors. His most famous study examined the conditioned fear response of little Albert. Ironically, Watson later wrote the book *Psychological Care of the Infant and Child*. He later left academia and incorporated his theory to become a success in advertising (Watson, 1925; Wolpe, 1990; Wood & Wood, 1993). Watson made these statements about behaviorism.

Polarity Between Spirituality and Behaviorism (Watson, 1925, p. 3)

- "All schools of psychology except that of behaviorism claim that *'consciousness' is the subject matter of psychology.* Behaviorism, on the contrary, holds that the subject matter of human psychology is the *behavior or activities of the human being.*"
- "Behaviorism claims that 'consciousness' is neither a definable nor a usable concept; that it is merely another word for the 'soul' of more ancient times."
- [In contrast to behaviorism], "the old psychology is ... dominated by a kind of subtle religious philosophy."

■ Skinner and Behavioral Conditioning

Skinner was born in Susquehanna, Pennsylvania and enjoyed school. It is interesting that he resented many of his college's attempts to control his behavior, particularly mandatory chapel attendance. In rebellion, Skinner was known for playing practical jokes. As a behaviorist, he expanded on classical and operant conditioning and emphasized the role of reinforcement (Wood & Wood, 1993).

The role of spirituality in the behavioral approach is purposely less pronounced. Whereas spirituality is understood as that which allows people to connect with one another or with the divine apart from a corporeal level, behaviorism focuses primarily on bodily interactions and casts doubt on free choice and self-determination.

Perhaps the most positive contribution of behaviorism to the field of psychology was the concepts of behavior modification and positive reinforcement. As contemporary theorists move away from the radical concepts of classical behaviorism, the emphasis moves toward individual learning theory and cognitive psychology. In understanding how behavior is learned and unlearned, therapists can focus on empowering clients rather than controlling them.

■ Lazarus and Multimodal Therapy

Lazarus grew up in Johannesburg, South Africa, and later moved to the United States to head the Behavior Therapy Institute. There has been a movement toward cognitive behaviorism since Bandura's social learning theory combined classical and operant conditioning with observational learning, thus making a case for the acceptance of cognition in the behavioral science.

The current view of human nature in behavior theory falls somewhere between that of humanistic theorists and classical behaviorists, which broadens the context of the theory and allows counselors to maintain a spiritual and humanistic framework, at the same time applying behavioral learning theory and modification techniques in the therapeutic setting.

Expansions of Behaviorism in Multimodal Therapy

- Humans are viewed as both the producers and the products of their own environments (Bandura, 1974, 1977, 1986; as cited in Corey, 1996, p. 285).
- Cognitive techniques expanded traditional, determinist behavioral methods to allow for greater follow-up with clients after the end of therapy (Lazarus, 1981).

Lazarus' (1981) work in multimodal therapy and Wolpe's (1990) work in behavior therapy are prime examples of the beneficial techniques that can be drawn from behavioral studies and applied to the counseling setting. There has been much success in the treatment of depression, anxiety, phobias, and behavior disorders (Wolpe, 1990).

COGNITIVE AND COGNITIVE BEHAVIORAL THEORIES AND SPIRITUALITY

Two of the main proponents of cognitive and cognitive behavioral therapy are Glasser and Ellis. Although they might not have addressed spirituality directly, their philosophies and assumptions of therapy reveal spiritual undertones.

■ Glasser and Choice Theory

In his training at the Veterans Administration Center in West Los Angeles and as a consulting psychiatrist at the Ventura School for Girls, Glasser became frustrated between his psychoanalytic education and what seemed to work best in therapy. Glasser brought together many aspects of cognitive, behavioral, existential, person-centered, and Gestalt theories and incorporated them in his theory of reality therapy or choice theory. Although Glasser rarely made reference to the nature of religion or spirituality, his theory parallels much of what has been said in humanistic psychology (Meier et al., 1997).

Glasser maintained that individuals encounter problems when basic needs are not fulfilled and irrational thoughts are manifested. These basic needs echo much of the I/thou experience in that Glasser (1965) stressed our need for healthy human relationships.

Features of Spirituality in Choice Therapy

- An individual person must be involved with (i.e., care about and be cared for) by at least one other person in life.
- Only through relationships are the basic human needs fulfilled.
- The goal of reality therapy is to help people fulfill the need to love and be loved and to feel self-worth and a sense of being of worth to others.
- People have the freedom of choice over thoughts, feelings, and actions and are held responsible for the choices they make.

Like Rogers, Glasser stressed the relationship between therapist and client. Corey (1996) summarized these basic beliefs, "which are that we are all responsible for what we choose to do with our lives and that in a warm, accepting, non-punitive therapeutic environment we are willing to learn more effective choices, or more responsible ways to live our lives" (p. 258). Glasser's reality therapy is very appropriate for counseling when combined with an individual's spiritual framework. Other benefits of the theory include Glasser's use of brief therapy and the model's applications to the school setting.

■ Ellis and REBT

Ellis often is referred to as the grandfather of cognitive-behavior therapy. After several years of psychoanalytic training and therapy, he began to look for more effective therapies. Similar to Glasser, he drew from many different theories including Adler's individual psychology, and incorporated what seemed to work in his theory of rational-emotive behavior therapy. Many of his techniques were a result of his struggle to overcome poor health and personal anxieties. Ellis believed that humans are capable of both rational and irrational beliefs. The belief about an experience is more important for the individual than the actual reality of the phenomena. Ellis credited Greek philosophers for their impact on his theoretical orientation and referred to Epictetus as saying, "Men are disturbed not by things, but by the view which they take of them" (Ellis, 1973, p. 166).

Although Ellis did not concentrate on the role of spirituality, he did challenge the irrational idea that others must approve of us, and support the rational idea of self-acceptance and the acceptance of others. Ellis's (1973) fundamental ideas about therapy and human personality are listed next.

Evidence of Spirituality in REBT

- People can come to enjoy their life in the present through challenging irrational belief systems.
- REBT helps individuals to foster positive, natural human tendencies toward individuality, freedom of choice, and enjoyment and to minimize defeating tendencies to be comforting, suggestible, and unenjoying.
- People can learn how to enhance the positive side their humanness and be at peace with—not squelch or repress—the side that still requires development and change.

CONCLUSION

What is the role of spirituality in our own therapeutic practices? The therapist needs to explore her or his own spiritual belief system and develop a congruent personal theory of counseling. The therapist then can enter into a genuine relationship from a centered perspective. The therapist also must acknowledge the many ways religious and spiritual beliefs are part of a larger multicultural context. In the continuous process of spiritual development, the therapist must attend to the common threads echoed throughout philosophy, theology, and the human sciences. The goal of incorporating spirituality in counseling is to facilitate the client's spiritual and psychological growth as we continue to grow ourselves (Eliason, 2000).

Chapter 31: **Key Terms**

- ▶ Religion
- ▶ Spirituality
- ▶ Pastoral counseling
- ▶ Competence

Preparing for the National Counselor Exam: What You Need to Know

As we stated in the preface, *The Counselor's Companion* is a tool for those thinking of taking a licensure or certification examination, and more specifically, the National Counselor Examination (NCE). To help you practice for the exam, we have compiled a 200-item test based on the eight content areas warranted by the Council for Accreditation of Counseling and Related Educational Programs (CACREP) and tested on the NCE. The questions all are drawn from information presented in the chapters that comprise this book. Hence, the key concepts you need to know to complete the sample exam successfully, as well as review for the actual exam created by the National Board of Certified Counselors, are at your fingertips.

CLASSIFICATION OF MULTIPLE-CHOICE ITEMS

Similar to most examinations using multiple-choice items, including the NCE, the questions on the sample examination are written to address three cognition levels:

1. *Recall.* Your best ally here is your memory, from which you will retrieve information, facts, concepts, theories, or procedures to tackle these items.

EXAMPLE OF A RECALL ITEM

The acronym CACREP stands for the _____.

   a. Counseling Association for Cultural Representation and Equity in Practice.
   b. Council for Accreditation of Counseling and Related Educational Programs.
   c. Corporation of All Counseling and Related Education Programs.
   d. Company for the Allocation to Counselors of Resources and Equitable Parity.

2. *Application.* If you are able to apply low-level problem skills, you need not worry too much about these items, which call for interpretation and application of data.

EXAMPLE OF AN APPLICATION ITEM

A brief solutions-focused family therapist views resistance as:

a. The family's conviction that their situation is the best available.
b. A result of social disorganization.
c. A sign that the suggestions of the therapist were not optimal ones.
d. A form of protection from threatening emotions.

3. *Analysis.* Once you combine your good judgment with your problem-solving skills, doing well on these test items is easy as you evaluate data, resolve problems, and draw on the information presented in this text as a review.

EXAMPLE OF AN ANALYSIS ITEM

John has been participating in a person-centered group for 4 months and continually engages in confrontational behaviors with several other group members. He has not achieved any of the original goals he has set for himself. John:

a. Has not been part of the group process long enough for change to begin to occur.
b. Is in the "insight and reorientation phase" of the group, and his behavior is appropriate.
c. Is not progressing through the stages of counseling appropriately.
d. None of the above.

TYPES OF ITEMS

The multiple-choice items in the sample NCE exam mirror the format commonly used by most credentialing examinations in that you are asked to choose the single best response for three forms of items.

■ Direct Question

EXAMPLE OF DIRECT QUESTION

The Stanford–Binet and the Wechsler Adult Intelligence Scale measure which of the following constructs?

a. Cognition.
b. Occupation.
c. Personality.
d. Behavior.

■ Incomplete Statement

EXAMPLE OF INCOMPLETE STATEMENT

According to Jean Piaget's cognitive development theory, children alter their schemas or organized psychological structures through the processes of assimilation and _____.

a. Organization.
b. Symbolic substitution.
c. Accommodation.
d. Equilibration.

■ Calculation

EXAMPLE OF CALCULATION

Discovering a personality test on the Internet, a counselor decides to perform a reliability test before using it with his clients. He discovers that the test has a reliability coefficient of .55. The counselor knows that the reliability coefficient indicates that:

a. 45% of the people who are tested will score accurately.
b. 55% of the score is accurate and 45% is not.
c. 55% of the people tested will score accurately.
d. 45% of the score is accurate and 55% is not.

GIVE IT YOUR BEST SHOT

As we mentioned earlier, the items on this sample examination are drawn from the eight core curriculum areas sanctioned by CACREP. You will be allotted 4 hours to complete the 200-item examination when you sit for the NCE. For those who intend to sit for a credentialing examination or a licensure examination, we recommend that you set some time aside and give the sample exam your best shot. Find a quiet and comfortable place where you will not be disturbed and have time for yourself as you start to take the test. Answer all questions. On the actual NCE exam you will be evaluated on only 160 of the 200 items, and you will not be penalized for guessing, which means that for items for which you are uncertain, just mark your best guess as the answer.

We have provided an answer key that you can use to check your responses and see how well you have done on the test. Because this book is broken down into chapters (see the Table of Contents) we have also provided a table of the chapters as they relate to the corresponding question numbers. If you have trouble with Question 1, for example, you can use Table A.2 at the end of the test to find that this question relates to information in Chapters 7 and 8 (human growth and development). Using Table A.2 will help you to easily locate the areas where you might need to fine-tune your knowledge based on the items with which you had difficulty. We hope that this simple tool will help foster your professional development and wish you good luck!

TESTING AREAS AND CORRESPONDING CHAPTERS

Table A.1 provides a list of the chapters in which you will find information relating to each testing area covered in the sample exam.

TABLE A.1
Testing Areas and Corresponding Chapters

Area of Testing	Chapters
Human growth and development	7, 8
Social and cultural foundations	4, 11
Helping relationships	9, 10, 18, 26, 27
Group work	12, 13, 14
Career counseling	15 , 16
Appraisal	20 , 21
Research	22 , 23
Professional orientation	1, 2, 3, 5

SAMPLE CREDENTIALING EXAMINATION

Set some time aside and answer all questions. Time yourself as you start. When taking the NCE you usually will be allotted 4 hours for the completion of all 200 items. An answer key is provided so that you will be able to evaluate your progress after you finish. Guessing is permitted, so make sure you answer all the questions. Table A.2, which provides the question numbers associated to their relevant chapters is also available to you for revision purposes. Good luck.

1. A counselor explained to her pregnant client that some of the behaviors in which she is currently involved are placing her unborn child at high risk for developmental disruptions known as teratogens. The counselor was able to make such an assumption based on the fact that her pregnant client was:

   a. Sleeping only 6 hours a day instead of 9 hours.
   b. Working 8 hours a day without proper protection at a processing plant that disposes of toxic waste.
   c. Listening to too much loud music when alone.
   d. Spending 10 hours a week working out at the gym.

2. During a supervision session a trainee counselor expressed his frustrations about one of his client's apparent resistance: "He tends to evade my every attempt to get him to address issues regarding his family. He does not want to disclose anything about his mom and dad or even his siblings. I am convinced the source of his problems is rooted in the family, but he is so resistant to talk about it. Moreover, it is so hard to get him to maintain eye contact with me, in spite of my constant invitation for him to do so." The trainee's client is most likely:

   a. An Arab American.
   b. A Latino American.
   c. An African American.
   d. A Native American.

3. A counselor trainee told her supervisor, "I am so inadequate." After a discussion about her "inadequacy," the counselor trainee was able to restate the same experience in the following terms: "I asked a client today whether or not our therapy sessions are helping and he replied no. I wish I could help him solve his problem with his family, but I do not how to do that." The supervisor has helped the trainee to be more:

   a. Empathic and warm.
   b. Confronting and challenging.
   c. Concrete and specific.
   d. Fluent and outspoken.

4. During a group therapy session, the leader keeps reminding the members of the following principle: People have no power over others' behaviors, but they do have control over their own behavior, for which they are responsible. The group is operating from the perspective of:

   a. Psychoanalytic group therapy.
   b. Reality group therapy.
   c. Person-centered group therapy.
   d. Rational Emotive Behavioral Therapy (REBT) group.

5. As he nears graduation from college, Stan is still very confused about his career choices. He seeks the help of a guidance counselor who, after talking to him and reviewing the results of a battery of personality tests that he took, told him that he will be excellent as a teacher or in sales. The guidance counselor was able to come to this conclusion because:

   a. Stan is person-oriented as suggested by Anne Roe's needs theory.
   b. Stan is still in the anticipation stage as suggested by Tiedeman, Miller-Tiedeman, and O'Hara's individualistic theory.
   c. She has made use of Gottfredson's theory of circumscription and compromise.
   d. She has utilized John Krumboltz's social learning career theory.

6. Discovering a personality test on the Internet, a counselor decides to perform a reliability test before using it with his clients. He discovers that the test has a reliability coefficient of .55. This indicates that:

   a. 5% of the people who are tested will score accurately.
   b. 55% of the score is accurate and 45% is not.
   c. 55% of the people tested will score accurately.
   d. 45% of the score is accurate and 55% is not.

7. A group of clients is being observed in a research study, and the researcher notes improvement in the clients even though they are not receiving counseling. She hypothesizes that their improvement is a consequence of the attention she has given them and explained it as:

   a. The halo effect.
   b. The side effect.
   c. The placebo effect.
   d. The Hawthorne effect.

8. To promote his practice, a counselor decides to start his own personal Web site where he will advertise his services. Not being an expert in computer technology, he asks one of his clients, who is a software programmer with a huge com-

puter company, to set up his Web site in exchange for free counseling. Such a practice is known as_____ and is _____.

    a. Bartering; unethical.
    b. Bargaining, ethical.
    c. Reciprocity, highly recommended for clients with limited income.
    d. Dual-relationship, unethical.

9. A researcher is interested in finding out the role of social interaction in predicting well-being among residents of nursing homes. The research design that is most appropriate to the researcher's aims is:

    a. Longitudinal study.
    b. Pretest–posttest design.
    c. Correlation.
    d. Quasi-experimental design.

10. Having developed an achievement test that yielded a high reliability coefficient, a counselor started to use it with her clients. After receiving complaints from several clients that the test was too long, she decided to shorten it. To measure the impact that the shortening of the test will have on its reliability, the counselor will most likely use:

    a. The Spearman Brown formula.
    b. The Kuder–Richardson coefficients of equivalence.
    c. The Cronbach's alpha.
    d. The odd–even split-half method.

11. A counselor is working with a client who wants to conduct her career search primarily through online sources. Aware of this, the counselor recommends that the client access _____, which is a widely used description of job titles.

    a. The Strong Interest Inventory.
    b. O*Net.
    c. The Life Career Rainbow.
    d. MBTI.

12. Groups often are co-led; that is, they have two facilitators. Coleading groups places certain demands on leaders. Good coleaders will:

    a. Have competing leadership styles to introduce diversity to the group.
    b. Be close personal friends.
    c. Discuss their relationship, perceptions, and experiences of each other.
    d. Share similar theoretical approaches to group work.

13. Life scripts are intended to:

   a. Allow clients to let go of harmful critical parent messages.
   b. Give permission to clients to behave against the direction of their parent ego.
   c. Allow clients to rewrite their programmed scripts into more productive interactions.
   d. Act as a contract between the client and the therapist about the nature of the therapeutic relationship.

14. Culturally sensitive research in the field of career counseling should include the following:

   a. Attention to adequate sample size.
   b. Longitudinal studies involving a variety of cultural groups.
   c. Examinations of new and adjusted career models.
   d. All of the above.

15. A counselor meets with a client for career counseling. Until this point in her career, the client has focused primarily on "getting ahead" and increasing her wealth. She willingly admits that she has shown little regard for the welfare of others in her work endeavors and confesses that at times she even knowingly engaged in behaviors that denigrated her coworkers because she was trying to impress her boss. Evaluating the client in terms of Kohlberg's theory of moral development, the counselor would most appropriately classify the client in which stage?

   a. Postconventional morality stage.
   b. Preoperational stage.
   c. Preconventional morality stage.
   d. Conventional morality stage.

16. Mores can be defined as:

   a. The impact of culture on human development.
   b. The moral rightness or wrongness of behavior.
   c. A combination of learned thoughts, behaviors, and beliefs.
   d. Overlapping cultural dimensions that have an impact on one another.

17. In a structural family therapy session, the father is talking about how he is always blamed for the family problems. The therapist would best:

   a. Teach the family about why scapegoating occurs.
   b. Exaggerate blaming the father for everything to illustrate the way in which he is not responsible for all of the family's problems.
   c. Ask the father what it would look like if the family stopped blaming him for problems.
   d. Ally with the father and support him in expressing his feelings.

18. During a psychodramatic group session, Dan declares, "I am so short tempered that I sometimes experience it as curse that has been cast on me. I wish I could relate with my family and friends with more empathic understanding." Using the _____ technique, the leader encourages Dan to barter his ill temper for some more active listening skills with the other members.

    a. Magic shop.
    b. Role reversal.
    c. Mirror.
    d. Sculpting.

19. In her sophomore year in college, Lori, 26 years old, has not yet selected a major. She has been in different unsatisfying jobs and has decided to go to college to be able to find a more fulfilling job in the future. For now, though, she cannot identify a career she really wants to pursue or a major that will help her prepare for her choice. After meeting the guidance counselor on campus, she was given a copy of one of Holland's inventories that will help her identify her interests and skills. The inventory that Lori most probably took home was the:

    a. Career Assessment Inventory.
    b. Self-Directed Search.
    c. Position Classification Inventory.
    d. O*Net Interest Profiler.

20. Coming out from a visit to his therapist, Andy told a friend that the therapist made him take a test where he had to (a) describe what came to his mind when he was asked to look at an inkblot, (b) complete several sentences with real feelings, and (c) draw a person. The friend concluded that Andy had been given:

    a. An IQ test.
    b. A projective personality test.
    c. A standardized personality test.
    d. The Myers–Briggs Type Indicator.

21. For his doctoral dissertation, John chose to compare men grieving their fathers' deaths according to birth order. After some preliminary work with a population of 60 men, the chair of his committee advised John to increase the sample size. This will:

    a. Increase the construct validity.
    b. Reduce Type I and Type II errors.
    c. Not impact Type I and Type II errors.
    d. Produce a placebo effect.

22. Privileged communication can be most accurately defined as:

    a. A legal concept that guards against required disclosure in legal proceedings that breaks a promise of privacy.

    b. An ethical term that safeguards clients from unauthorized disclosures of information.

    c. The constitutional right of people to decide when and where they will share themselves with others.

    d. The counselor's right to disclose clients' information in court proceedings.

23. Which of the following properties are often *not* found in qualitative research?

    a. Use of naturalistic settings.

    b. Researcher involvement in the process.

    c. Laboratory settings.

    d. A holistic approach.

24. Concurrent validity provides the most appropriate type of validation for a test designed to:

    a. Select high-level job applications.

    b. Screen out untrainable industrial workers.

    c. Diagnose a psychiatric condition.

    d. Examine applications for admissions to graduate school.

25. When engaging in career counseling with an Asian American client, a counselor may need to keep the following ideas in mind:

    a. Asian Americans typically adopt a collectivist and interdependent worldview that influences their career choice.

    b. A career counseling approach that capitalizes on autonomy will be useful.

    c. Direct interventions may be most effective with Asian American clients.

    d. Asian American clients probably will be very open to discussing their career-related issues.

26. Group members' ability to connect with one another through similar experiences, behaviors, thoughts, and feelings is known as:

    a. Universality.

    b. Cohesion.

    c. Group dynamics.

    d. Processing.

27. A counselor who subscribes to logotherapy would likely make the following statement to a client:

    a. Tell me about your family dynamics—are you the first born, last born, or middle child?
    b. What meaning does this experience hold for you?
    c. What is present for you now, in this moment?
    d. What are you thinking as you tell me about that experience?

28. Culture can best be defined as:

    a. Learned behaviors, thoughts, and beliefs that are promoted by and shared among members of a particular society.
    b. Racial and ethnic factors that influence development.
    c. Ideas about the rightness or wrongness of behavior.
    d. Social and political beliefs held by a dominant group.

29. In Freud's personality theory, the id is guided by:

    a. The reality principle.
    b. Parental and social values.
    c. The pleasure principle.
    d. The imaginary audience.

30. During a class discussion on multiculturalism a student made the following remarks: "Immigrants who come to our country have chosen to do so freely. They must, therefore, forgo their language and culture and learn our own in order to get along with us. Since they decided to come here and we are hospitable to them, it is normal that they espouse our values and not the other way around." The student's remarks reveal him to be someone who is:

    a. Culturally encapsulated.
    b. Xenophobic.
    c. Very altruistic.
    d. Operating out of an emic viewpoint.

31. Invited to assess the problems of an organization, the consultant was able to help his client discover that the organization has been working with obsolete beliefs and visions, and was repeating patterns of behavior that were inconsistent with the current environmental demands. The consultant will most likely push for:

    a. An organizational diagnosis.
    b. A transfer of effect.
    c. A paradigm shift.
    d. A total quality management approach.

32. After his first group meeting, a counselor trainee told his supervisor, "I felt very ill at ease during the group session. There were too many moments of silence that seemed to last eternally. Members were just being nice to each other, no one wanted to disclose as if they were afraid of each other. The resistance was so thick that it could be sliced with a knife." After reviewing the stages of group with the trainee and helping him realize that the group is still at the forming stage, the supervisor encouraged the trainee to work at promoting the following therapeutic factors during the next group session:

    a. Imparting information and altruism.
    b. Imitative behavior and development of socializing skills.
    c. Instillation of hope and universality.
    d. Catharsis and interpersonal learning.

33. After completing Holland's General Occupational Themes (GOT), a counselor helped Andy summarize his interests using the three-letter RIASEC type code. Andy was found to be the kind of person who is (a) persuasive, likes leadership role, sees himself as stable, adventurous, bold, and self-confident; (b) concerned about others, nurturer, introspective, responsible, likes social situations, verbally skilled; (c) artistic, creative and imaginative, sensitive, introspective, and independent. Andy's code therefore is:

    a. ESA.
    b. REA.
    c. SEA.
    d. IEA.

34. After testing a new IQ test, a researcher found out that it has a standard error of measurement (*SEM*) of 3. A client took the test and scored 123 on the new IQ test. If the client took the test over and over at a 68% confidence interval, the researcher can predict that about 68% of the time:

    a. The client will score between 100 and 126.
    b. The client will score between 100 and 120.
    c. The client will score between 120 and 126.
    d. The client will score between 68 and 100.

35. A nondirectional hypothesis contends that:

    a. There are no differences between groups.
    b. There are differences between groups.
    c. One research treatment will be more effective than another treatment.
    d. Any differences that are found are due to chance.

36. A counselor spent a great deal of time in the gym growing up and considers herself to be an expert on nutrition. She does not, however, hold any degree or certifications in nutrition. When her overweight client discusses his weight is-

sues, the counselor immediately writes out a detailed nutrition plan for her client. This is an example of:

   a. Ethical behavior.
   b. Practicing outside of one's competency.
   c. Beneficence.
   d. A culturally insensitive intervention.

37. A brief solutions-focused family therapist views resistance as:

   a. The family's conviction that their situation is the best available.
   b. A result of social disorganization.
   c. A sign that the suggestions of the therapist were not optimal ones.
   d. A form of protection from threatening emotions.

38. A mother was expressing her concerns about her 3-year-old son's linguistic development to a counselor, stating that he communicates mostly with two-word sentences. Based on the information gathered from the mother, the counselor concludes that:

   a. The child was communicating within a holophrastic pattern.
   b. The child was using telegraphic expressions to communicate.
   c. The child is evolving normally in his linguistic development.
   d. The child is able to underextend and overextend words of meaning.

39. Joe is a very devout Christian who has been diagnosed with lung cancer caused by heavy smoking. Despite his illness, he has never quit using tobacco. Speaking to his counselor, Joe expresses that his deep faith in God and intensive prayer life will help him go through this illness and come out victorious. When advised to quit smoking, he is very reluctant. The counselor can apply _____ as a motivator for change with Joe by helping him become aware of inconsistencies in his thoughts and behaviors.

   a. Heider's balance theory.
   b. Congruity theory.
   c. Attribution theory.
   d. Dissonance theory.

40. As a clinician you are explaining to a client the reason you believe he has developed an addiction. You mention that throughout his life he has learned to medicate negative thoughts and feelings with the addiction, and that this reinforcement has led to a repeated pattern of using the behavior. Which model of addiction are you explaining?

   a. Social learning model.
   b. Disease model.
   c. Genetic model.
   d. Impulse control model.

41. A counselor decides to start a counseling group in his high school. While planning for the group, the counselor must decide which students should participate in the group. The counselor should remember which of the following when selecting participants?

    a. It is important to choose members whose needs and goals are compatible with those of the group.
    b. It is important to find members who will have enough self-esteem to endure negative feedback.
    c. It is important to select members with a narrow range of personality styles.
    d. It is important to encourage diversity by having a broad range of depressed and anxious clients.

42. All of the following are key components of Super's theory of career development except:

    a. Life span.
    b. Life space.
    c. Self-concept.
    d. Circumscription.

43. Achievement tools measure accomplishment related to a specific academic area, whereas aptitude tests measure:

    a. IQ.
    b. The total academic needs of a child.
    c. Potential of an individual.
    d. Academic personality of a child.

44. A 13-year-old girl threatens to commit suicide, and her counselor fails to inform her parents. The counselor's behavior can best be described as:

    a. An example of informed consent.
    b. An example of negligence.
    c. An appropriate use of beneficence in the therapeutic relationship.
    d. The desire to maintain the confidentiality of the therapy relationship.

45. A teacher was complaining to a school counselor that she was not being successful with a number of students in her language class. After listening to the narrative of the teacher, the counselor explained to the teacher that the core of the problem is that those students with whom she was unsuccessful were in fact skipping the fast mapping process. In other words, those students were:

    a. Not able to build vocabularies very quickly by learning to connect new words with their underlying concepts after only brief encounter.
    b. Were too knowledgeable of their metacognitions.
    c. Relying on word meanings to learn grammatical rules.
    d. Discovering the meaning of words by observing how the words are used in syntax.

46. The statistical test known as ANOVA is most frequently used:

    a. To examine the differences between two or more means.
    b. To determine the correlation between two factors.
    c. To determine the predictive ability of one factor in relation to another.
    d. To examine the differences between two or more means while also accounting for confounding variables.

47. A form of assessment that relies primarily on direct observation is:

    a. Cognitive assessment.
    b. Behavioral assessment.
    c. Occupational assessment.
    d. Personality assessment.

48. Which of the following is *not* a division of the American Counseling Association?

    a. Association for Play.
    b. Association for Counselor Education and Supervision.
    c. American Mental Health Counselors Association.
    d. National Career Development Association.

49. After being happily married for 25 years and having been a housewife whose major career so far has been to take care of the home and the children, Suzan suddenly found herself a widow after losing her husband to a massive heart attack. From her primary responsibility of taking care of the home and the children, Suzan is now forced to look for outside paid job. People like Suzan are referred to as _____ and would benefit more from _____ prior to career counseling.

    a. Downshifting; moving sideways.
    b. Enriching the status quo; moving up.
    c. Displaced homemakers; personal counseling.
    d. Midlife career changers; dual-career considerations.

50. A client told to his therapist during an individual counseling session that he would like to join a therapy group where he will be able to reexperience with other members relationships that are similar to his own family relationships, and develop greater insight into his defenses and resistances. The therapist is more likely to orient her client toward a:

    a. Psychodramatic therapy group.
    b. Gestalt therapy group.
    c. Psychoanalytic therapy group.
    d. Rational emotive therapy group.

51. During a counseling session with his therapist, a client routinely replies to the therapist with compliance. Operating from a transactional analysis approach, the therapist might say that the client is responding from:

    a. The free or natural child ego state.
    b. The adult ego state.
    c. The parent ego state.
    d. The adapted child ego state.

52. Which of the following therapeutic techniques is most closely aligned with Skinnerian behavioral therapy?

    a. Extinction.
    b. Free association.
    c. Social modeling.
    d. Thought interrupting.

53. The viewpoint that suggests that older Americans are less capable than their younger counterparts is known as:

    a. Ableism.
    b. Ageism.
    c. Sexism.
    d. Bias.

54. A conjoint family therapist is primarily interested in how families:

    a. Negotiate power.
    b. Long for love and acceptance of each other.
    c. Communicate with one another.
    d. Prioritize their time so the family can spend time together.

55. Margie has been participating in a Gestalt group for several months. She recently has been asked to head her preschooler's parent–teacher organization, but politely refused by stating that she currently has several other commitments. Margie has demonstrated the ability to:

    a. Translate her insights into action.
    b. Define her boundaries with clarity.
    c. Have awareness of what she is feeling, sensing, or thinking in the present.
    d. Use self-support instead of looking to others for confirmation.

56. _____ is often considered the father of vocational guidance or career counseling.

    a. Frank Parsons.
    b. Donald Super.
    c. John Holland.
    d. John Krumboltz.

57. An IQ score of 75 falls within the:

    a. Genius range.
    b. Below-average range.
    c. Average range.
    d. Above-average range.

58. A researcher believes that students who play golf are more likely to do very well in mathematics. Dividing the students into three groups, one experimental group plays golf three times a week, another one plays once a week, and the third group does not play at all. The statistic that the researcher will most likely choose to analyze her results will be:

    a. The t test.
    b. The MANCOVA.
    c. The ANOVA.
    d. The chi-square.

59. In the case of *Tarasoff v. Board of Regents of the University of California,* the counselor of record was cited primarily for:

    a. Failure to accurately evaluate his client's psychological state.
    b. Failure to warn and protect a threatened person from potential harm.
    c. Failure to properly document a threat against another person that was disclosed by the client.
    d. Failure to uphold the client's right to confidentiality.

60. During a family therapy session, a counselor commented to the parents, "Based on my observations of your children, I must say that you use an authoritative style of parenting." The counselor made this remark because:

    a. He had noticed some maladaptive antisocial behaviors in the children.
    b. The children were overly sensitive and angry.
    c. The children were socially well-behaved and emphatic with one another.
    d. The children were emotionally dry and uncaring toward one another.

61. Sandy complains to her therapist that after 23 years of working for a huge insurance company, she has never been promoted beyond the status of a sales representative. She assumes that her boss does not care for the employees in the sales department, and favors only young male recruits from the accounting department. In helping Sandy discover what reasons could be driving her boss's decisions, the therapist is using _____.

    a. The law of reciprocity.
    b. Attribution theory.
    c. Newcomb's A-B-X model of interpersonal attraction.
    d. Symbolic interaction theory.

62. A counselor declares to his client, "My goal is to help you achieve a greater degree of independence and integration, and not to solve your problem." This counselor is operating from a:

    a. Person-centered theoretical perspective.
    b. Psychoanalytic theoretical perspective.
    c. Cognitive-behavior theoretical perspective.
    d. Solution-focused theoretical perspective.

63. John has been participating in a person-centered group for 4 months and continually engages in confrontational behaviors with several other group members. He has not achieved any of the original goals he has set for himself. John:

    a. Has not been part of the group process long enough for change to begin to occur.
    b. Is in the "insight and reorientation phase" of the group, and his behavior is appropriate.
    c. Is not progressing through the stages of counseling appropriately.
    d. None of the above.

64. What is the main criticism of the current career theories and models as they are applied within a multicultural context or with diverse clients?

    a. There is currently only one model of multicultural career counseling.
    b. Most career theories are not comprehensive enough.
    c. Most career theories were developed years ago and are outdated.
    d. Most career theories were tested with White undergraduate students and therefore are not necessarily valid across cultural groups.

65. The _____ is a job-related personality measure that is based on Jung's theory of personality.

    a. General Aptitude Test Battery.
    b. Myers–Briggs Type Indicator.
    c. MMPI.
    d. Armed Services Vocational Aptitude Battery.

66. A researcher concludes that there is a significant difference or relation between the treatment and control groups when in actuality there is none. This is known as:

    a. John Henry effect.
    b. Confidence interval.
    c. Type II error.
    d. Type I error.

67. The acronym CACREP stands for the ____.

    a. Counseling Association for Cultural Representation and Equity in Practice.
    b. Council for Accreditation of Counseling and Related Educational Programs.
    c. Corporation of All Counseling and Related Education Programs.
    d. Company for the Allocation to Counselors of Resources and Equitable Parity.

68. A 10th-grade student shared with her counselor: "I have some money saved so that after graduating from high school, I can go to college and hopefully graduate with an MBA. Then I would like to open my own insurance company. I know it is still a dream, but I will do everything in my power to fulfill it, even though some people think I am crazy." The student's disclosure indicates her psychological well-being and a healthy search for a sense of self, which prompted the counselor to conclude that her attitude reflects both _____ and _____.

    a. Identity achievement and identity foreclosure.
    b. Identity moratorium and identity foreclosure.
    c. Identity diffusion and identity achievement.
    d. Identity achievement and identity moratorium.

69. _____ is considered to be the primary figure in existential family therapy.

    a. Virginia Satir.
    b. Viktor Frankl.
    c. Salvador Minuchin.
    d. Carl Whitaker.

70. Sue Lin has not been her normal self for a while. She hinted to one of her close colleagues that she was having marital problems. The colleague advised her to seek the help of a counselor and referred her to the best therapist in town. Even though Sue Lin was very grateful to her colleague and accepted the referral, she never went into therapy. The most probable reason for Sue Lin's behavior is:

    a. The therapist is a White man.
    b. Doing so will bring shame on her family.
    c. Her religious values advocate against it.
    d. She did not want to say no to her friend for fear of hurting her feelings.

71. A counselor is conducting a study about how engineers decided to make their career choice. The counselor accounts for educational opportunity, socioeconomic status, and mentoring received by professionals in the field. However,

the counselor failed to account for the impact of gender socialization on career choice. In this case, gender socialization can be considered a:

    a. Hawthorne effect.
    b. John Henry effect.
    c. Independent variable.
    d. Confound.

72. Before using a standard score for a test, researchers first must transform raw score data into z scores. If a researcher has a raw test score of 25, a raw mean score of 10, and a raw score standard deviation of 3, what is the z score?

    a. 15.
    b. 5.
    c. 12.
    d. 20.

73. The principle function of item analysis is to:

    a. Identify test items that may be faulty.
    b. Determine the discrimination index for a test.
    c. Shorten a test.
    d. Calculate the validity of items on a test.

74. In psychodramatic therapy, the protagontist is encouraged to expand his or her emotional response pattern by trying out different responses to a situation, relationship, or other concern at the direction of the leader. This exercise takes place during which phase?

    a. The warm-up phase.
    b. The action phase.
    c. The discussion phase.
    d. The sharing phase.

75. A client was asked to complete a personality test by his guidance counselor. He was very resistant to the proposal and declared that he hated personality tests in general because they might reveal something about him that he does not like. "It is best for me to be ignorant about my shadows," said the client. "Take this one," the counselor responded, "it is based on the premise that all personality preferences are equally valuable." Satisfied with the counselor's response, the client took the _____ and completed it with much trepidation.

    a. Sixteen Personality Factor (16PF).
    b. Vocational Preference Inventory.
    c. Myers–Briggs Type Inventory (MBTI).
    d. Minnesota Multiphasic Personality Inventory–2 (MMPI–2).

76. In experimental research, the control group receives _____ and the treatment group receives _____.

     a. Treatment; a more intense treatment.
     b. No treatment; no treatment.
     c. Randomly assigned participants; nonrandomly assigned participants.
     d. No treatment; treatment.

77. The founding association that eventually became the American Counseling Association began in _____.

     a. 1992.
     b. 1983.
     c. 1952.
     d. 1947.

78. The use of assessment tools in career counseling was initiated through which theoretical approach?

     a. Needs theory.
     b. Social learning theory.
     c. Life-span, life-space theory.
     d. Trait and factor theory.

79. A researcher created a 15-item achievement instrument, and the reliability test for the instrument yielded a coefficient of .80. Based on feedback from other colleagues, she decided to lengthen the test with 10 more items, logically assuming that reliability coefficient would now:

     a. Be approximately .89.
     b. Remain unchanged.
     c. Be at least 10 points higher or lower.
     d. Be higher than .80.

80. Which of the following is one of the four stages of a typical Adlerian group?

     a. Confrontation of group members.
     b. Establishment of openness and sharing in the group.
     c. Promotion of individual insight and self-awareness.
     d. Action exercises.

81. The Life Career Rainbow is most closely associated with the work of:

     a. Anne Roe.
     b. John Holland.
     c. Gottfredson.
     d. Donald Super.

82. Which theorist is most associated with the bioecological model of human development?

    a. B. F. Skinner.
    b. Uri Bronfenbrenner.
    c. Carl Rogers.
    d. Sigmund Freud.

83. A group whose goal is to teach new parenting skills to teenage mothers could best be characterized as which type of group?

    a. Counseling.
    b. Task.
    c. Psychoeducational.
    d. Psychotherapeutic.

84. The American Counseling Association promotes multicultural competence among all helpers. Adhering to multicultural competencies means that counselors recognize their need to do all of the following *except*:

    a. Be aware of personal values, beliefs, and worldviews.
    b. Rely on mainstream understandings of or stereotypes about diverse groups.
    c. Engage in research about diverse groups with whom they are working.
    d. Create culturally sensitive interventions for diverse populations.

85. Meeting with his supervisor after attending a weekend seminar, a counselor trainee made the following statement, which he says he had learned from the seminar: "I have the capacity to 'self-regulate' in my environment for I am fully aware of what is happening around me." The supervisor deducts that he has attended a seminar on _____ and is simply stating one of the basic principles of that therapy.

    a. Reality therapy.
    b. Neurolinguistic programming (NLP).
    c. Thought field therapy (TFT).
    d. Gestalt therapy.

86. Which of the following memory processes appears to show the least decline with age?

    a. Fluid intelligence.
    b. Semantic memory.
    c. Episodic memory.
    d. Working memory.

87. Rajeev, a 17-year-old youth, is finding it hard to adapt to his newly found home and shares his grief about having to leave his home in India to follow his family

to the United States. The counselor advises him that it will be best for him to let go of his past, to make new American friends, go to see Hollywood movies, and listen to rap and hip-hop music. In other words, it is in his best interest to change so that he can "fit into" American society. The counselor is working from an:

a. Autocratic perspective.
b. Autoplastic perspective.
c. Authoritarian perspective.
d. Alloplastic perspective.

88. Gestalt therapy promotes all of the following except:

a. Increasing awareness.
b. Dealing with unfinished experiences and feelings.
c. Examining childhood traumas.
d. Acknowledging and dealing with the most pressing needs first.

89. One of the members in a counseling group repeatedly criticizes another member's way of sharing. This is likely happening during which stage of the group?

a. Storming.
b. Performing.
c. Norming.
d. Adjourning.

90. More than other career theories, Gottfredson's theory of career development focuses on:

a. The role of childhood experiences in career choice.
b. The role of gender in career choice.
c. The role of personality factors in career choice.
d. The role of economic factors in career choice.

91. The Minnesota Multiphasic Personality Inventory and the NEO–Personality Inventory–Revised both are:

a. Measures of personality.
b. Objective measures.
c. Tools that measure the Big Five.
d. Both a and b.

92. Which form of ethnography looks at the observations and reflections of a single person?

a. Standard ethnography.
b. Autoethnography.
c. Online ethnography.
d. Protraiture.

93. Based on the ethical precept of _____, a counselor has an obligation to explain the purpose of using a paradoxical technique.

    a. Nonmaleficence.
    b. Justice.
    c. Utilitarianism.
    d. Fidelity.

94. State licensure typically requires which of the following?

    a. A graduate degree that includes supervised practicum and internship experiences.
    b. Two to three postdegree years of supervised clinical experience.
    c. Successful completion of an examination.
    d. All of the above.

95. Levinson's season's of life theory focused on adult development. The main thrust of development in later life, according to Levinson is:

    a. Disengagement, or withdrawal from social activities.
    b. Overcoming social and physical barriers to active involvement in later life.
    c. The search for intimacy during which the focus is on relationships with significant others.
    d. Reaching out and giving to the next generation.

96. The emic perspective to counseling is characterized by all of the following *except*:

    a. Universal definitions of health and wellness.
    b. Application of therapeutic techniques similarly across cultures.
    c. Counselors using their own cultural realities as a measure for understanding clients' experiences.
    d. Unique definitions of normal and abnormal or healthy and unhealthy behavior.

97. A client has been court mandated to enter drug and alcohol rehabilitation. Besides being arrested for drunken driving more than once, the client also spends all of her income on liquor, spends hours in a bar each evening, and has developed a high tolerance for alcohol. When confronted with these factors in therapy, the client innocently says that she does not have a problem with drinking. The client's response can be characterized as:

    a. Repression.
    b. Sublimation.
    c. Displacement.
    d. Denial.

98. According to the Association for Specialists in Group Work, groups can be divided into which of the following four areas?

    a. Beginning, transition, working, and concluding.
    b. Task, psychoeduational, counseling, and psychotherapeutic.
    c. Interpersonal, intrapersonal, leadership, and conflict resolution.
    d. None of the above.

99. When questioned about his views on individual development, a student responded, "I don't believe that my individual development is dictated by my inherent genetic make-up, but rather, it is my interactions with the environment that influence my development and even impact all of my behaviors." This student is purporting a(n) _____ viewpoint.

    a. Ecologist.
    b. Naturist.
    c. Nurturist.
    d. Biologist.

100. Bordin's psychoanalytic model relates career choice to Freud's psychosexual stages and places importance on the role of _____ in adult work.

    a. Id.
    b. Superego.
    c. Repressed drives.
    d. Play.

101. Which discipline area has not played a key role in the development of qualitative research?

    a. Statistics.
    b. Anthropology.
    c. Education.
    d. Sociology.

102. A sexual relationship between client and therapist is:

    a. Ethical if the client initiates the relationship.
    b. Ethical if both the client and the counselor consent to the relationship.
    c. Never ethical.
    d. Ethical if the counselor uses the relationship toward a therapeutic goal.

103. The career theory based on the idea of self-efficacy is tied to the work of:

    a. Hoyt.
    b. Krumboltz.
    c. Super.
    d. Bandura.

104. The Stanford–Binet and the Wechsler Adult Intelligence Scale measure which of the following constructs?
    a. Cognition.
    b. Occupation.
    c. Personality.
    d. Behavior.

105. Carkuff developed a training model for helpers and added three concepts to Rogers's essential characteristics of counselors. Carkuff's model is known as:
    a. Microskills.
    b. Human resources development model.
    c. Relationship enhancement therapy.
    d. Interpersonal process recall.

106. The classical theoretical formulation of group developmental stage theories was formulated by:
    a. Gerald Corey.
    b. Irvin Yalom.
    c. George Gazda.
    d. Bruce Tuckman.

107. According to Jean Piaget's cognitive development theory, children alter their schemas or organized psychological structures through the processes of assimilation and _____.
    a. Organization.
    b. Symbolic substitution.
    c. Accommodation.
    d. Equilibration.

108. A counselor who advises her minority client to make adjustments in her traditions and worldview to find economic success can be said to be promoting the following viewpoint:
    a. Accommodation.
    b. Ethnocentrism.
    c. Autoplastic.
    d. Cultural encapsulation.

109. In the nature versus nurture controversy, naturists subscribe to the belief that:
    a. Human development is primarily determined by genetics, yet is influenced by environmental interactions.
    b. Human development is the primary result of environmental interactions, yet influenced to some degree by genetic predisposition.
    c. Human development is equally the result of both hereditary and environmental forces.
    d. Human development is the result of genetic predisposition and is not significantly affected by environmental experiences.

110. When working with an African American client, a common mistake that a non-Black counselor may make is:

    a. Using a socioecological approach that accounts for environmental factors.

    b. Assuming an active and directive stance.

    c. Avoiding a medical model approach.

    d. Ignoring the issue of race and maintaining a stance of color-blindness.

111. A therapy group that is led by a facilitator whose style can be characterized largely as laissez faire would likely:

    a. Invite members to begin on time during each session, but have minimal interventions throughout the group.

    b. Use directive interventions.

    c. Model appropriate behavior to members.

    d. Be very active at the beginning of the group experience and slowly taper off her interventions as the process proceeded.

112. Using Betz and Hackett's career theory for women, a counselor who is working with a female client around career and vocational issues might do the following:

    a. Encourage the client to self-reflect on her interests.

    b. Use an assessment tool to determine how well the client's current job fits with her personality.

    c. Direct the client to observe female role models in the career area in which she is interested but doubts the chances of her potential success.

    d. Help the client understand if she prefers working with other individuals or alone.

113. The best definition of reliability is:

    a. Consistency.

    b. Exactness of measurement.

    c. Correlation coefficient.

    d. Ability to measure what an instrument purports to measure.

114. After receiving several complaints from a group of parents about the results of research conducted among 12th graders, a panel of investigators found out that the researcher had unconsciously rated blond athletic males as more socially skilled than others. This is an example of:

    a. The halo effect.

    b. The side effect.

    c. The placebo effect.

    d. John Henry effect.

115. HIPAA, enacted in 1996, requires health care providers to protect client health care information. HIPAA stands for:

  a. Health Insurance Privacy and Accountability Act.
  b. Health Insurance Portability and Accountability Act.
  c. Health Information Protection and Authorization Act.
  d. Health Information Privacy and Authorization Act.

116. A career can be described as:

  a. A conscious effort aimed primarily at producing benefits for oneself and others.
  b. The constellation of work and leisure experiences one has in a lifetime.
  c. Relatively self-determined activities one has because of discretionary time, money, and resources.
  d. The understanding one has of his or her interests and skills.

117. When conducting an assessment, a counselor needs to engage in all of the following actions, apart from which exception?

  a. Obtaining background information.
  b. Considering systemic influences.
  c. Observing the client in a natural setting when possible.
  d. Prescribing medication based on the assessment.

118. Acculturation can be described as:

  a. The degree to which an individual understands race as affecting workplace opportunities.
  b. The process by which minority groups overcome institutionalized racism.
  c. The degree of identification an individual from an incoming cultural group makes with a dominant culture.
  d. The degree to which a dominant culture adjusts to incoming minority groups.

119. For a cognitive-behavioral therapist, _____ is more important than _____.

  a. Assessment; evaluation.
  b. Insight; action.
  c. Change; understanding the genesis of a problem.
  d. Thought stopping; exposure.

120. Which theorist is credited with discovering the concept of imprinting?

  a. Bowlby.
  b. Freud.
  c. Piaget.
  d. Lorenz.

121. A feminist therapist would be less likely to approach a family therapy session from the perspective of the _____ than a _____ therapist.

   a. Teacher; psychodynamic.
   b. Model; conjoint.
   c. Expert; strategic.
   d. Negotiator; brief solution-focused.

122. McIntosh suggested that dominant groups carry an invisible knapsack that affords them advantages over other minority groups. The idea of the invisible knapsack is commonly used to refer to:

   a. White privilege.
   b. Racial identity development.
   c. Discrimination.
   d. Prejudice.

123. Random assignment has which of the following benefits to experimental research?

   a. It removes all of the influences from extraneous variables.
   b. It decreases error by equating groups and diffusing the influence of extraneous variables across groups.
   c. It statistically controls for the effects of variables through analysis procedures.
   d. It makes sure that groups are gender diverse.

124. Rogers characterized the effective helper as having three essential qualities. They are:

   a. Openness, respect, concreteness.
   b. Empathy, unconditional positive regard, congruency.
   c. Congruency, intentionality, warmth.
   d. Unconditional positive regard, communication competence, respect.

125. The assessment instrument known as the self-directed search was developed by:

   a. Ginzberg.
   b. Roe.
   c. Crites.
   d. Holland.

126. Each week during participation in an REBT group, a group member makes statements such as "I should have spent more time on my school work," and "Only students who spend hours on studying can succeed." To respond to the client, the group leader would:

   a. Help the group member dispute her irrational thoughts.
   b. Give the member suggestions on how to become a better student.
   c. Ask the member to act out her emotions to gain further insight.
   d. Invite the member to work on repressed childhood memories.

127. The one-group posttest-only design is particularly vulnerable to which of the following threats to internal validity?

    a. History.
    b. Diffusion of the treatment.
    c. Testing.
    d. Regression toward the mean.

128. The professionalization of counselors has included all of the following *except*:

    a. State licensure.
    b. National professional credentialing.
    c. Accreditation of counselor education programs.
    d. Third-party reimbursement.

129. The branch of ACA that deals with career development is known as the National Career Development Association. It is formerly known as:

    a. The American Career Association.
    b. The National Vocational Guidance Association.
    c. The Professional Association for Career and Guidance.
    d. The American Vocational Association.

130. Which of the following *least* describes the normal distribution curve?

    a. A majority of scores are either high or low.
    b. The mean is in the middle at the highest elevation of the curve.
    c. One standard deviation in either direction from the mean is an inflection point.
    d. The curve is asymptotic.

131. The theory of the BASIC ID is most closely associated with the work of which theorist?

    a. Bandura.
    b. Beck.
    c. Lazarus.
    d. Adler.

132. During a group session of a psychoanalytic group, members report their feelings or impressions as they arise. This process relates to which therapeutic technique?

    a. Interpretation.
    b. Dream analysis.
    c. Transference.
    d. Free association.

133. Pavlov is best known for his theory of:

    a. Classical conditioning.
    b. Operant conditioning.
    c. Higher order conditioning.
    d. Reverse conditioning.

134. The experience known as loss of face is associated most with which cultural group?

    a. African Americans.
    b. Asian Americans.
    c. Native Americans.
    d. Gay and lesbian Americans.

135. A counselor is helping her client to stop interpreting events and actions as if they were directly related to the client, even when they are not. This counselor can best be described as operating from which perspective?

    a. Cognitive.
    b. Cognitive-behavioral.
    c. Rational emotive.
    d. Existential.

136. The _____ consists of the words that are shared between individuals in a group while the _____ is the relationship between the members.

    a. Topics; cohesion.
    b. Content; process.
    c. Feedback; universality.
    d. Conflict; structure.

137. In a session, a client tells the counselor that she is considering going back to work because her family is struggling financially. Although being supportive of the client's desires, the counselor also would like to help the client form realistic expectations about how her going to work can have an impact on the family. The counselor may suggest that the client consider which of the following?

    a. The impact of dual working parents on child–parent relationships.
    b. The adjustments that may have to occur in household duties.
    c. The impact of dual working partners on time spent together.
    d. All of the above.

138. The _____ method of estimating reliability involves only one test administration.

    a. Test–retest.
    b. Alternate forms.
    c. Split-half.
    d. Internal consistency.

139. The 1974 Family Education Rights and Privacy Act (FERPA) is most appropriately defined as:

    a. Federal legislation that governs educational records and dictates how all written information on a student will be handled and disseminated for the protection of the student and his or her family.

    b. Federal legislation that allows school counselors to disclose information on student and family records to any agency or school without requiring written consent from the child or family.

    c. Federal legislation that prohibits eligible students, those who reach the age of 18 while in secondary schools, from having access to their records without parent or guardian written consent.

    d. Federal legislation that governs how counselors in agencies will handle and disseminate client records.

140. A counselor is working with a client who was recently laid off of his job. The counselor might expect the client to display which of the following reactions as a result of the job loss?

    a. Withdrawal.

    b. Loss of positive self-image.

    c. Confusion.

    d. Both a and b.

141. A counselor who is conducting research on test anxiety decides to plot her data and finds that most of the students scored in a below-average range of anxiety, whereas only a few scored in an average or above-average range. The counselor can best describe her data as:

    a. Positively skewed.

    b. Normally distributed.

    c. Negatively skewed.

    d. None of the above.

142. An addict has recently stopped using heroin and now has started using cocaine for the first time. This is an example of:

    a. A new addiction.

    b. Switching addictions.

    c. A passing phase.

    d. A process addiction.

143. Jose is a member of a behavioral therapy group. He recently stated in a group that he is very afraid of public speaking and becomes so anxious at the thought of talking in front of large groups that his heart races, his palms get sweaty, and he begins to tremble. Utilizing behavioral therapy, a group leader may suggest that Jose:

    a. Participate in assertion training so he is better able to deal with his fears.

    b. Be given homework assignments that address his fears.

c. Rehearse a short presentation to himself when he is alone, then make several short presentations to his group members, and finally give the same presentation to his group members and 5 to 10 other family members and friends who are invited to hear his presentation.

d. Focus on his ability to choose whether or not to be anxious when he is asked to speak publicly.

144. The theorist Thorndike came to the conclusion that behavior is learned via trial and error with the resulting behavior having a higher propensity to reoccur if the consequence of that behavior is positively reinforcing. Thorndike's proposition is called:

   a. Adverse stimuli.
   b. Law of effect.
   c. Law of exercise.
   d. Positive reinforcement.

145. Racial and cultural identity development models examine the process through which minority groups form their personal and cultural identities. The process through which minorities progress, as described by the racial and cultural identity development model includes all of the following except:

   a. Conformity to the dominant culture.
   b. Resistance to the dominant culture.
   c. Overt negativity and prejudice against the dominant culture.
   d. Acceptance of the minority culture to which one belongs.

146. The key premise of rational emotive behavioral therapy is that:

   a. Interpretation is used to help group members gain insight into their behaviors.
   b. All anyone can control is their own present life.
   c. If people are successful at controlling their irrational thoughts, they will feel happy.
   d. Unconditional positive regard and genuineness of a therapist leads to positive changes in the client.

147. Multicultural group work can be understood as:

   a. Group work inclusive of need for an expansion of personal and group consciousness of self in relation by providing intentional, competent, and ethical helping behaviors that promote the mental health of group members.
   b. Group work inclusive of race and ethnicity.
   c. Group work inclusive of race, ethnicity, sexual orientation, and gender.
   d. Group work that focuses only on issues of diversity among members.

148. One of the most frequently used personality inventories in career counseling is the Myers–Briggs, which counselors use to assess clients in four areas of personality. These personality types include all of the following except:

    a. Investigative-Introversion.
    b. Introversion-Extroversion.
    c. Thinking-Feeling.
    d. Sensing-Intuiting.

149. In statistics, $p = .05$ means:

    a. There is a 5% chance that results are due to chance factors.
    b. In 95% of the cases, the results are not due to chance factors.
    c. Every 5 out of 100 scores is due to chance factors.
    d. The test is not highly reliable.

150. The most important advantage of the Solomon Four-Group design with respect to internal validity is that _____ is controlled.

    a. Instrumentation.
    b. Selection.
    c. Resentful demoralization.
    d. Testing.

151. When complex ethical dilemmas arise, counselors are best advised to:

    a. Consult with friends who have dealt with similar ethical dilemmas.
    b. Trust their "gut" response in deciding how to proceed.
    c. Seek supervision with other professionals.
    d. Ask the client how she or he wants to deal with the dilemma.

152. A counselor using Holland's theory of career development would be interested in knowing the personality traits of the client. All of the following are among the six classifications of personality described by Holland except:

    a. Realistic.
    b. Artistic.
    c. Social.
    d. Extrovert.

153. A counselor is trying to decide on a test to measure depression. The manual for the test reports that the instrument has a reliability coefficient of $r = .5$. Based on what he knows about reliability coefficients, the counselor should:

    a. Decide not to use the test.
    b. Use the test with great assurance that the results will be reliable.
    c. Use the test and then consult with colleagues about the results.
    d. Contact the publisher of the instrument for further information.

154. Adler emphasized all of the following concepts in his approach to psychology, *except*:

    a. Family constellation.
    b. Birth order.
    c. Social interest.
    d. Automatic thoughts.

155. Core competencies for multicultural group work include:

    a. Group workers' awareness of their personal values, beliefs, stereotypes, and biases.
    b. Group workers' knowledge of diverse members' values, life experiences, and worldviews.
    c. Group workers ability to lead diversity-sensitive interventions with group members.
    d. All of the above.

156. When asked about his career choice, an adolescent experiencing identity foreclosure is most likely to say:

    a. My Mom says I should be a pediatrician like her.
    b. I don't know, I haven't thought about it.
    c. I don't know, I'm still considering what I might like as a career.
    d. I've decided that I want to be an astronaut.

157. A client recently has complained to her counselor that she is involved in a carpool for her children. Among the three families in the carpool, one family is only driving once a week, whereas she and the third family drive three times each. The counselor understands that the client is operating from:

    a. Law of effect.
    b. Law of exercise.
    c. Attribution theory.
    d. Law of reciprocity.

158. Longitudinal studies investigate:

    a. Differences in the same subjects over time.
    b. Trends in sample populations over time.
    c. Differences in the same group of people at one point in time.
    d. Both a and b.

159. Professional counselors are obligated to do all of the following *except*:

    a. Attend to the welfare of clients and students.
    b. Belong to professional organizations.
    c. Recruit others to join their professional field.
    d. Adhere to the standards of competency set by the professionals in the field.

160. Tiedeman, Miller-Tiedeman, and O'Hara described two stages of career development: anticipation and implementation. The anticipation stage is comprised of four phases known as:

    a. Exploration, crystallization, choice, and clarification.
    b. Orientation to size and power, orientation to sex roles, orientation to social valuation, orientation to unique, internal self.
    c. Dealing with change, developing career focus, exploring options, preparing for the job search.
    d. Fantasy stage, tentative stage, realistic stage, and choice stage.

161. There are a number of different types of validity. Researchers should put the *least* amount of confidence in which type of validity?

    a. Concurrent validity.
    b. Content validity.
    c. Construct validity.
    d. Face validity.

162. Archetypes can be described as primordial images that contain psychic energy and assign meaning to experience. Which of the following theorists is the originator of this concept?

    a. Freud.
    b. Bandler.
    c. Jung.
    d. Beck.

163. According to Maslow's needs hierarchy, there is one need that must be met before a person can move toward higher development. This need is:

    a. Biological needs.
    b. Self-actualization.
    c. Love and belongingness.
    d. Safety needs.

164. A counselor is interested in knowing the effect of a 12-week cognitive treatment program on the self-concepts of girls with eating disorders. The counselor has read several articles about the subject and is getting ready to begin her research project. Prior to testing, she states the null hypothesis this way:

    a. Cognitive therapy will be significantly more effective than no cognitive therapy.
    b. Girls with eating disorders who participate in a cognitive treatment group will have significantly higher self-concepts than girls who do not participate in the cognitive treatment program.
    c. There will be no significant differences in the self-concepts of girls who participate in the treatment program and girls who do not.
    d. Girls with eating disorders who participate in a cognitive treatment group will have significantly lower self-concepts than girls who do not participate in the cognitive treatment program.

165. Balance theory purports that:

    a. People will tend to agree on interests and ideas to increase the stability of their relationships.
    b. People tend to look for internal reasons for their motivations.
    c. Relationships are strongest when people both give and take.
    d. Behavior is influenced by socially imposed roles.

166. Egan's problem management training model entails three stages, each of which is characterized by three steps. The first stage is guided by the question, "What's going on?" A goal of this stage includes the following:

    a. Helping clients tell their stories.
    b. Creating goals for the client.
    c. Assessing action strategies.
    d. Helping clients find incentives for change.

167. When group leaders are not culturally sensitive, there may be a number of negative implications for group members. Which of the following is not a repercussion of a leader's lack of multicultural competence?

    a. The group worker may unconsciously impose personal or theoretical values, beliefs, and attitudes on members.
    b. Group members holding a different worldview and value system may not be empowered to live life more fully.
    c. Group members will feel understood and appreciated for their cultural heritages.
    d. The group member(s) holding a different worldview and value system may physically or psychologically leave the group or get little to nothing from the group experience.

168. If a client is taking a test with forced choice responses, this means that the client:

    a. Will most likely be answering questions on a Likert scale.
    b. Must answer all questions to give a valid and reliable score.
    c. Will have the opportunity to write in personal responses to questions.
    d. Will use free association techniques in responding to pictures or inkblots.

169. The emic perspective suggests that:

    a. Cultural values, worldview, and contexts are important to understanding behavior.
    b. Action inputs must equal action outputs.
    c. Behavior is universal and can be understood similarly across cultures.
    d. People should adjust to the dominant culture rather than having the dominant culture adjust to minority groups.

170. The life events such as marriage, a first job, a first child, and so on, that follow age-graded patterns based on societal and cultural expectations are referred to as:

    a. The biological clock.
    b. The social clock.
    c. The family life cycle.
    d. The social convoy.

171. The most widely used and researched personality measure is:

    a. TAT.
    b. Rorschach.
    c. MMPI–2.
    d. BASC–2.

172. Quasi-experimental designs are used when:

    a. The researcher wants to control for extraneous variables with random assignment.
    b. There are no manipulated independent variables.
    c. It is not possible or ethical to use randomization.
    d. The researcher wants to examine the correlations between an independent and dependent variable.

173. The ACA Code of Ethics as well as the ASCA Code of Ethics serve all of the following purposes *except*:

    a. Protect counselors from issues of liability and malpractice.
    b. Offer guidelines and standards with which counselors must be familiar before beginning their practices.
    c. Reflect changes in the practice of ethical conduct with which counselors must remain current and to which counselors can turn in times of uncertainty.
    d. Provide the community with a sense of security essential to a profession.

174. Eight-year-old Julia has just transferred to a new school and has been identified by several teachers as a student who may benefit from talking to the school counselor. Julia reported to the counselor that a group of girls at her new school tease her and tell her that she can't play with them at recess. The counselor understands that the girls are engaging in which of the following?

    a. Overt aggression.
    b. Associative play.
    c. Instrumental aggression.
    d. Relational aggression.

175. Culture can be understood as including the following dimension(s):

     a. Race.
     b. Gender.
     c. Religion.
     d. All of the above.

176. A client shares with the counselor that her daughter has recently died in a car accident. The counselor responds, "That must be a terrible loss for you. Surely, your heart is breaking." The counselor's response is an example of:

     a. Restating.
     b. Summarization.
     c. Interpreting.
     d. Empathizing.

177. Which of Piaget's cognitive development stages involves monumental advances in mental representations of objects and events, as well as animistic thought?

     a. Sensorimotor.
     b. Concrete operational.
     c. Preoperational.
     d. Formal operational.

178. A school counselor decides to start a lunchtime counseling group for elementary-age students who are being bullied. Before she begins to meet with the students, the counselor is obligated to:

     a. Advertise the group in the school.
     b. Obtain permission from the school principal.
     c. Reserve an appropriate space for the group to take place.
     d. Secure informed consent from the parents of group participants.

179. Active listening skills such as _____, summarization, and restatement are three Adlerian therapeutic techniques utilized in group therapy.

     a. Integration.
     b. Reflection.
     c. Ulterior transactions.
     d. Genuineness.

180. Projective measures such as the TAT and Rorschach use unstructured stimuli to infer:

     a. Attitudes.
     b. Personality traits.
     c. Feelings.
     d. All of the above.

181. An independent variable is one that the researcher:

    a. Manipulates.
    b. Holds constant.
    c. Correlates with other variables.
    d. None of the above.

182. Irvin Yalom is a premier figure in describing therapeutic factors in group counseling. These factors are elements that increase clients' ability to change as a result of participation in group therapy. Which of the following are therapeutic factors described by Yalom?

    a. Forming, storming, norming, and performing.
    b. Instillation of hope, universality, interpersonal learning, group cohesiveness.
    c. Catharsis, venting, relief, sharing.
    d. Insight, awareness, risk-taking, and cohesiveness.

183. A dependent variable can best be described as:

    a. The variable that is held constant and that the researcher is interested in measuring.
    b. The treatment a researcher applies to an experimental group.
    c. The variable that the researcher manipulates.
    d. The variable that the researcher hypothesizes to be responsible for a treatment effect.

184. The field of counseling is increasingly recognizing the place of supervision in the careers of professional counselors. Which of the following is most true about supervision?

    a. Clinical supervision is most beneficial during graduate school training.
    b. Clinical supervision is only called for during crisis moments or during ethical dilemmas.
    c. Clinical supervision is most effective when it is applied throughout the expanse of a professional counselor's career.
    d. Clinical supervision is used only when trying to obtain counselor licensure.

185. According to Freud's psychosexual theory of human development, each child passes through a series of psychosexual stages. These stages are:

    a. Concrete, phallic, oral, anal, and genital.
    b. Phallic, latency, oral, and anal.
    c. Oral, anal, phallic, and latency.
    d. Oral, anal, phallic, latency, and genital.

186. In group therapy, a counselor continues to shun a particular member because he reminds her of her abusive father. The counselor's behavior is an example of:

    a. Countertransference.
    b. Transference.
    c. Repression.
    d. Denial.

187. Alpha level can best be described as which of the following?

    a. A predetermined probability value.
    b. Equal to $p \leq .05$ or $p \leq .001$ in behavioral sciences.
    c. Both a and b.
    d. None of the above.

188. The mother of an infant who displays the ambivalent-resistant pattern of attachment is most likely to behave in which of the following ways when interacting with her infant?

    a. Abusive.
    b. Permissive.
    c. Overcontrolling.
    d. Inconsistent.

189. A counselor who is operating from an ethnocentric viewpoint:

    a. Tends to use his or her cultural standards to evaluate and understand clients' issues.
    b. Disregards his or her own cultural views and assumes the views of the client.
    c. Recommends that dominant cultures should accommodate to minority groups.
    d. None of the above.

190. A counselor practices in a rural area that has few mental health resources apart from her own private practice. In trying to serve the needs of the community, the counselor works 6 days a week and often works 10-hour days. Although the counselor strongly desires to serve the people in her community, she is noticing that lately she is fatigued, not listening empathically to her clients, and her mind wanders while in session. This counselor may be said to be:

    a. Negligent.
    b. Suffering from burnout.
    c. Extremely incompetent.
    d. Acting in her own best self-interest.

191. During which of Erikson's stages does an individual develop trust for others through warm responses with from people in his or her environment?

   a. Autonomy versus shame and guilt.
   b. Initiative versus guilt.
   c. Identity versus identity diffusion.
   d. Basic trust versus distrust.

192. A counselor learns that his client has recently been involved in a high-profile affair, and chooses to spread slanderous information about the client to other professionals in the agency. This counselor could be accused of:

   a. Nonmaleficence.
   b. Defamation.
   c. Fidelity.
   d. Boundary violation.

193. A counselor is working with a client who is in his 70s. All of the following potentially can be issues that a counselor will decide to explore first with the client, *except*:

   a. Spousal death.
   b. Financial concerns.
   c. Relocation to a health care institution.
   d. Career change.

194. A counselor has just completed a 2-hour continuing education seminar on infusing hypnotherapy into treatment of clients who suffer from trauma. Ethically, the counselor can now advertise herself as:

   a. A certified hypnotherapist.
   b. A licensed hypnotherapist.
   c. A professional hypnotherapist.
   d. None of the above.

195. When alpha is changed from .01 to .05:

   a. The probability of incurring a Type II error increases.
   b. The probability of incurring a Type I error increases.
   c. There is a lower chance that the results will occur only by chance.
   d. The probability of failing to reject the null hypothesis increases.

196. A supervisor listens to a supervisee's comments and watches counseling videotapes, and notices that the supervisee is not demonstrating many basic intervention skills. Moreover, the supervisee seems insecure about the counseling process. The supervision model that may best assist this supervisee is:

   a. Developmental supervision.
   b. Supervision from an REBT theoretical framework.
   c. Supervision using microskills training.
   d. An eclectic approach to supervision.

197. In his social-learning theory, Bandura proposed that learning occurs not only by way of classical and operant conditioning but also as a result of a process called _____ or _____.

    a. Observational learning; imitation.
    b. Observational learning; attention.
    c. Attention; vicarious reinforcement.
    d. Retention; attention.

198. Social exchange theory postulates that:

    a. People strive to make their thoughts and behaviors consistent with one another.
    b. People with similar interests are more likely to be attracted to one another than people with dissimilar interests.
    c. People unconsciously account for the costs and benefits in relationships and value relationships with the greatest benefits.
    d. People have a higher degree of commitment to activities that are immediately reinforced.

199. A researcher is interested in knowing the effect of assertiveness training on assertiveness levels in a group of high school seniors who are looking for their first jobs. In this example, the dependent variable is:

    a. The training that students receive.
    b. The group of students.
    c. The students' level of assertiveness.
    d. The instrument the researcher uses to measure assertiveness.

200. A counselor's caseload is full, so she provides referral numbers of other counselors in the area to a person she cannot take on as a new client. This counselor is adhering to:

    a. Mandatory ethics.
    b. Aspirational ethics.
    c. Ethical principle of beneficence.
    d. The ethical principle of justice.

SAMPLE TEST ANSWER KEY

1. B	44. B	87. B	130. A
2. C	45. A	88. C	131. C
3. C	46. A	89. A	132. D
4. B	47. B	90. B	133. A
5. A	48. A	91. D	134. B
6. B	49. C	92. B	135. A
7. D	50. C	93. A	136. B
8. A	51. D	94. D	137. D
9. C	52. A	95. C	138. C
10. A	53. B	96. *	139. A
11. B	54. C	97. D	140. D
12. C	55. B	98. B	141. A
13. C	56. A	99. C	142. B
14. D	57. B	100. D	143. C
15. C	58. C	101. A	144. B
16. B	59. B	102. C	145. C
17. D	60. C	103. D	146. C
18. A	61. B	104. A	147. A
19. B	62. A	105. B	148. A
20. B	63. C	106. D	149. B
21. B	64. D	107. C	150. D
22. A	65. B	108. C	151. C
23. C	66. D	109. D	152. D
24. C	67. B	110. D	153. A
25. A	68. D	111. A	154. D
26. A	69. D	112. C	155. D
27. B	70. B	113. A	156. A
28. A	71. D	114. A	157. D
29. C	72. B	115. B	158. D
30. A	73. A	116. B	159. C
31. C	74. B	117. D	160. A
32. C	75. C	118. C	161. D
33. A	76. D	119. C	162. C
34. C	77. C	120. D	163. D
35. B	78. D	121. C	164. C
36. B	79. D	122. A	165. A
37. A	80. B	123. B	166. A
38. B	81. D	124. B	167. C
39. D	82. B	125. D	168. A
40. A	83. C	126. A	169. A
41. A	84. B	127. A	170. B
42. D	85. D	128. D	171. C
43. C	86. B	129. B	172. C

38/50   63/81   36/45 = 4/5
76%   80%

157/199 = 79%

173. A	180. D	187. C	194. D
174. D	181. A	188. D	195. B
175. D	182. B	189. A	196. C
176. D	183. A	190. B	197. A
177. C	184. C	191. D	198. C
178. D	185. D	192. B	199. C
179. B	186. A	193. D	200. B

* Discard # 96

REVISING THE SAMPLE TEST QUESTIONS

If you missed any of the questions in the sample exam, you may want to review the content area that corresponds to the question(s) missed.

Table A.2 provides a list of the question numbers that correspond to each of the content areas. Additionally, the chapters in which you will find information relating to each testing area are indicated.

TABLE A.2
Questions Corresponding to Area of Testing

Area of Testing	Question Numbers
Human growth and development ++++ ||| (Chapters 7, 8)	1, 15, 29, 38, 45, 52, 60, 68, 86, 95, 99, 107, 109, 120, 133, 144, 156, 163, 170, 174, 177, 185, 188, 191, 197
Social and cultural foundations |||| (Chapters 4, 11)	2, 14, 16, 28, 30, 39, 53, 70, 84, 87, 96, 108, 110, 118, 122, 134, 145, 157, 165, 169, 175, 189, 193, 198
Helping relationships ++++ || (Chapters 9, 10, 18, 26, 27)	3, 13, 17, 27, 31, 37, 40, 51, 54, 62, 69, 72, 82, 85, 88, 97, 105, 119, 121, 124, 131, 135, 142, 146, 154, 162, 166, 176, 186, 196
Group work ++++ | (Chapters 12, 13, 14)	4, 12, 18, 26, 32, 41, 50, 55, 63, 74, 80, 83, 89, 98, 106, 111, 126, 132, 136, 143, 147, 155, 167, 179, 182
Career Counseling |||| (Chapters 15, 16)	5, 11, 19, 25, 33, 42, 49, 56, 61, 64, 75, 81, 90, 100, 103, 112, 116, 125, 129, 137, 140, 148, 152, 160
Appraisal ++++ | (Chapters 20, 21)	6, 10, 20, 24, 34, 43, 47, 57, 65, 73, 79, 91, 104, 113, 117, 130, 138, 141, 149, 153, 161, 168, 171, 180
Research |||| (Chapters 22, 23)	7, 9, 21, 23, 35, 46, 58, 66, 71, 76, 78, 92, 101, 114, 123, 127, 150, 158, 164, 172, 181, 183, 187, 195, 199
Professional orientation ||| (Chapters 1, 2, 3, 5)	8, 22, 36, 44, 48, 59, 67, 77, 93, 94, 102, 115, 128, 139, 151, 159, 173, 178, 184, 190, 192, 194, 200

Your Online Companion
in Electronic Case Management:
An Introduction to Penelope Software

Another remarkable tool included in this book is a 120-day subscription to a student version of Penelope software (at a minimal $7.95 charge). Penelope is an innovative software package developed by Athena Software that is sure to revolutionize your counseling practice. An excellent example of the type of case management software that often is utilized in mental health agencies, Penelope is a wonderful tool that will give you a chance to learn about the important tasks of case management. Whether you are a counselor trainee doing your practicum or internship or a professional clinician who has worked in the helping field for many years, you will find that Penelope has been conceived to make your tasks such as record keeping, assessment and intake, case and progress note taking, supervisory logging, billing, and many other paper nightmares easy—and, why not—an enjoyable process! To learn more, please visit www.AthenaSoftware.net/ Counselors_Companion.html.

WHAT IS PENELOPE?

Penelope is a multiversion case management software solution for social and human service organizations. It is a comprehensive and user-friendly Web-based program that integrates client information, scheduling, and a full range of service delivery tracking, including treatment planning and progress monitoring, billing, outcome evaluation, reporting, and more. The version of the software known as Penelope Light comes in a variety of "flavors," so that users can pick and choose which software package works best for them. The various package offerings of Penelope are specifically designed for solo practitioners and small clinical settings. For information about the software packages that Athena offers, please visit their Web site at http://www.athenasoftware.net/penelope_light-get- started.html.

Directions on how to access your subscription to the student version of Penelope are included at the end of this appendix.

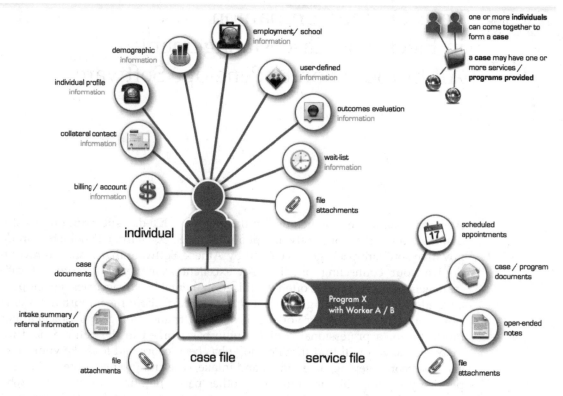

FIGURE B.1 Penelope uses a client-centric model of service delivery. Case files are composed of one or more individuals that may receive services together or independently.

INDIVIDUALS AND CASES

Files can be created for individuals who interact in some manner with you or your organization. Individuals represent anyone who has participated in education or community-building programs, workers at other agencies, clinical clients (case members), including group members, and so on. Cases can be created for clients receiving clinical services, and it is in these case files that confidential clinical information is stored, workers are assigned to deliver service within a program, and activities are scheduled and documented.

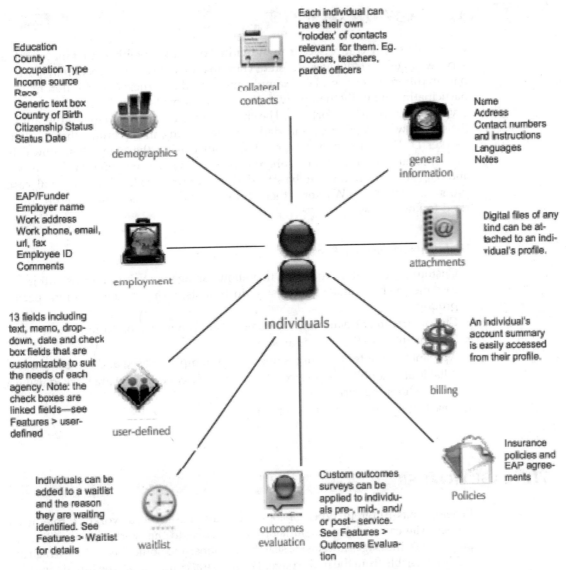

Education
County
Occupation Type
Income source
Race
Generic text box
Country of Birth
Citizenship Status
Status Date

demographics

Each individual can
have their own
'rolodex' of contacts
relevant for them. Eg.
Doctors, teachers,
parole officers

collateral
contacts

Name
Address
Contact numbers
and instructions
Languages
Notes

general
information

EAP/Funder
Employer name
Work address
Work phone, email,
url, fax
Employee ID
Comments

employment

Digital files of any
kind can be at-
tached to an indi-
vidual's profile.

attachments

13 fields including
text, memo, drop-
down, date and check
box fields that are
customizable to suit
the needs of each
agency. Note: the
check boxes are
linked fields—see
Features > user-
defined

user-defined

individuals

An individual's
account summary
is easily accessed
from their profile.

billing

Insurance
policies and
EAP agree-
ments

Policies

Individuals can be
added to a waitlist
and the reason
they are waiting
identified. See
Features > Waitlist
for details

waitlist

outcomes
evaluation

Custom outcomes
surveys can be
applied to individu-
als pre-, mid-, and/
or post- service.
See Features >
Outcomes Evalua-
tion

FIGURE B.2 In this image, you see the multifaceted options for keeping track of information about each individual client. A wealth of information can be recorded at the individual, case, program, and activity levels of the case file. Penelope also contains an outcomes evaluation survey tool that allows agencies to build outcomes tools into the system and monitor outcomes throughout or following service for each client.

GETTING TO KNOW THE CASE FILE

Cases are usually comprised of an individual or family members that may receive services together. However, different combinations of case members may participate in different services. For example, mom, dad and their two children may be participating in family therapy with Worker A. Mom also may be coming in for individual therapy with Worker B. The children may be coming in for art therapy on their own with Worker C, and dad may be coming in for group therapy with Worker D. Programs may be closed without closing the case. This allows the agency to have a complete and coherent record of what is happening with the case, and relevant information can be stored at the appropriate levels (individual, case, program, activity). Workers then have access to case information on a need-to-know basis.

Highlights of the Case File

- Custom document creation tool that allows an agency to build forms within the case file, such as intake and closing documents, forms, or logs used in specific programs.
- Custom treatment planning, assessment, and progress monitoring tools.
- Multimedia case file with attachments.
- Appointment notes tool that is free form or template based and can be locked.
- Billable and nonbillable services, including service codes that are tracked using a simple shopping cart model.
- Case history and a wealth of other reports.

THE CASE WORKER

Penelope has different types of login accounts based on a worker's role at an agency. The case worker account provides access to the worker's case files, appointments, messages and tasks, search functions, and some links, all of which are easily accessible from the home page. The intake account has all the functions of the case worker account plus the ability to create a case file, assign clients to a program and worker, and access the schedule of the whole agency.

LOGGING INTO PENELOPE

Every case worker has access to a personalized home page in Athena. After logging in, each screen in Penelope has a title that appears at the top left, and, on the top

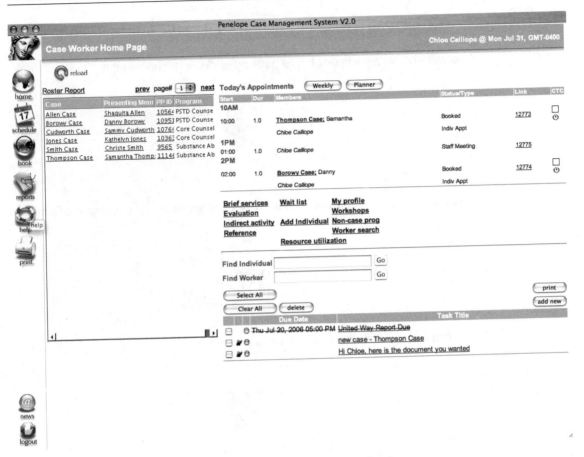

FIGURE B.3 A screen shot of the case worker home page.

right, the name of the worker, along with the date appear. In addition, the case worker can always access the home page by clicking the Home icon at the top left of all Athena screens.

Every home page also displays the currently assigned clients and programs. To access the service file, click the Program Provided ID (PP ID; see column with numbers such as 1007, 5675, 1018, etc.). To access information on the program participant, click the name of the program member you want to see.

WHAT ARE SOME OF THE USEFUL TOOLS ON MY HOME PAGE?

You can always get to your home page by clicking the home icon.

You can access the color-coded master agency schedule by clicking the Schedule icon.

You can book a case appointment or find a case by clicking the Book Appt icon.

A wealth of help resources can be accessed by clicking the Help icon.

You can print any page you are on by clicking the Print icon. (Note: All reports may be printed from within the report, without using this Print button.)

Additionally, there are tools that will help with the following functions:

- You can navigate back to the last screen visited by clicking the *Back* button, and you can refresh the information on the page by clicking the *Reload* button.
- You can access the *Case Information* page by clicking any of the case links in the case applet.
- You can access the *Individual Profile* page of the primary client by clicking their name.
- You can refer to the *Reference Page,* which contains links to Web sites, documents, and other information.
- You can access your own worker information—to change your availability or password, for example—by clicking the *My Profile* link.
- You can access each of your *Appts. for the Day* by clicking its link.
- You can access your Appts. for the Week by clicking the *Weekly View* button.
- You can access the schedule of the entire agency by clicking the *Today's Agency Appts.* link (intake account required).
- You can leave messages for yourself or other workers by using the *Tasks* feature displayed underneath the case applet.
- You can view or create news items by clicking the *News* icon.
- You can check the status of each case by looking at the *CTC* check box, which indicates Call to Confirm the activity.

WHAT ARE SOME OTHER COOL FEATURES OF PENELOPE?

In addition to the basic features described as useful tools in the Penelope software, there are many other features that make Penelope the online resource of choice for counselors and agencies. Some of these features include the following:

- Secure/encrypted Web-based application.
- Centralized or individualized scheduling—including group appointments.
- Internal messaging, tasks, and alerts.
- Wait-list, community-based service, and brief service tracking (e.g., crisis calls, referrals, seminar presentations, outreach contacts, etc.).
- Indirect activity tracking (meetings, nonclinical appointments, etc.).
- Extensive reports and data export capabilities.
- Extensive billing and accounts receivable features enable sliding scale self-pay and copay, EAP, and Medicaid billing.
- User-customizable.

Adding one or more individuals and creating a case file: from your homepage:

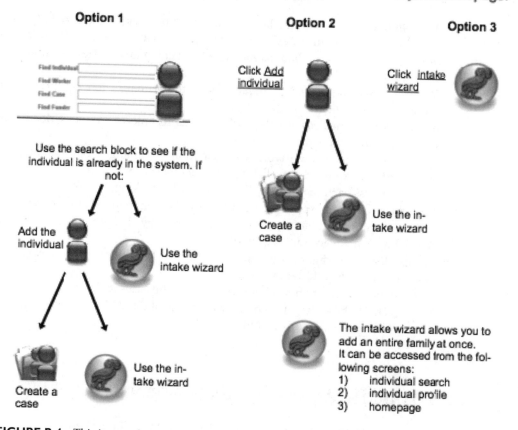

FIGURE B.4 This image shows some of the various options for adding individuals and creating case files.

SAMPLE PROCESS: HOW DO I ADD AN INDIVIDUAL?

You can add individuals either one at a time—through the Add Individual link on the home page—or more than one at a time—through the Intake Wizard (which adds them as case members in their newly created case).

SAMPLE PROCESS: HOW DO I BOOK AN APPOINTMENT?

Another great tool in the Penelope software is its ability to let you keep your appointment calendar online. When you have finished with each session, just log in and update your appointment book to keep track of your schedule.

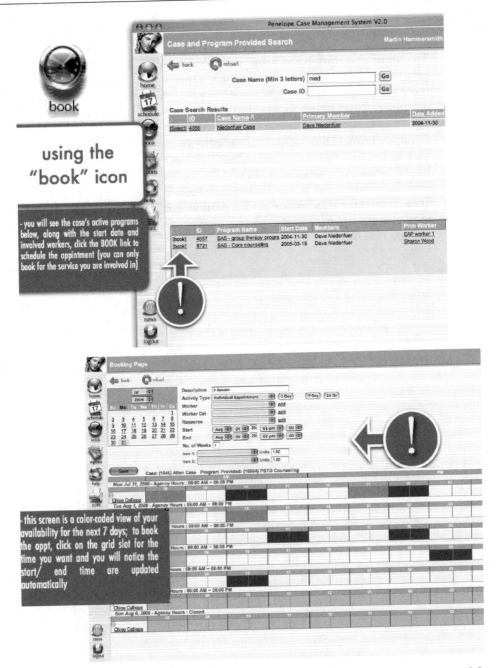

FIGURE B.5 This screen shot indicates how to use the appointment calendar that is part of the software.

CONCLUSION

This short description has provided just a glimpse of what this powerful software program is all about. There are a lot of other things to discover and tons of other mechanisms available to you as you explore the student version of Penelope. We encourage you to explore, use it to its full potential, and enjoy!

For more information, visit Athena Software at:

http://www.AthenaSoftware.net

To access your Counselor's Companion subscription to the student version of Penelope for just $7.95, please visit www.AthenaSoftware.net/Counselors_Companion.html

Hints, Helps, and FAQs About Working in a Managed Care Environment

The managed care revolution has brought dramatic transformations in the provision and financing of mental health treatments in the private sector. With the advent of managed mental health care (MMHC), "the familiar fee-for-service system is being replaced by a system in which costs are controlled by placing limits on the amount and type of services, by monitoring services intensively, and by changing the nature of services" (Foos, Ottens, & Hill, 1991, p. 332). These changes have required mental health counselors to develop new knowledge and skills to establish and maintain economically viable practices. As managers in businesses and industries became aware of the fast escalation of their employees' mental health care benefits over the costs of other medical benefits, they realized that such benefits needed to be restrained. Consequently, any method that is developed to bring containment to the costs of employees' mental health benefits inevitably affects all mental health providers, as well as professional counselors.

THE BOURGEONING OF HEALTH MAINTENANCE ORGANIZATIONS

To control costs, insurance companies, corporate businesses, and the health care providers are appealing more and more to health maintenance organizations (HMOs) and other managed care systems. The methods that are utilized to ensure cost control and clinical effectiveness can include the following:

- Submitting every proposed treatment plan for peer review.
- Ensuring early detection and treatment of mental health issues.
- Ensuring that treatment modality matches presenting problem.
- Giving preauthorization for hospital admission.
- Paying close attention to case management.

THE STRUCTURE OF MANAGED MENTAL HEALTH CARE

As corporations, insurance companies, and business organizations placed caps on the financing and delivery of mental health services, new models of managed care have emerged. According to Foos et al. (1991), the four most common models are:

1. *Employee assistance programs (EAPs).* These began as programs to treat alcoholism in the workforce, and they have now evolved and are utilized by businesses "to provide services such as wellness in the workplace, stress reduction, smoking cessation seminars, alcohol and drug interventions, and referral" (p. 333).
2. *Utilization and concurrent review (UR).* This requires practitioners to justify and submit in writing a comprehensive treatment plan that is then analyzed by a utilization reviewer for appropriateness.
3. *Preferred provider organizations (PPOs).* These are "a network of providers that collectively offer comprehensive services or specialty care" (MacCluskie & Ingersoll, 2001, p. 252), under certain guidelines such as submission to UR and acceptance of reduced fees from insurance companies or businesses.
4. *Staff model HMOs.* Subscribers covered under this model are eligible for reimbursed services only if the services are obtained from a provider employed by the mental health HMO.

ADVANTAGES OF MANAGED MENTAL HEALTH CARE

The managed care revolution brought along in its trail a plethora of advantages and disadvantages for clients, counselors, and the counseling profession as a whole (Lawless, Ginter, & Kelly, 1999). Listed next are some of these advantages and disadvantages.

Advantages of MMHC

- The spiraling costs of health care services are kept under control.
- Clients have better access to mental health care.
- Referrals for some practitioners are on the rise.
- Quality control and standards of practice become the norm.

Disadvantages of MMHC

- There is a reduction in some types of usually available services.
- Pharmacological interventions are overused.
- The duration for treating some disorders is inadequate.
- Outpatient services are overly relied on.

IMPACT OF MANAGED MENTAL HEALTH CARE ON COUNSELING

Johnson and Combs (2001) reported that there is a good cluster of evidence from the counseling literature that indicates "that brief, time-limited therapies which emphasize primarily cognitive-behavioral or brief therapies appear, in and of themselves, effective in treating some disorders" (p. 88). They further postulated that the importance given by managed care companies to these interventions has contributed to the rise in popularity of these approaches. The following are some of the implications that the advent of MMHC has for counselors and the counseling field.

Implications for Counselors

- Counseling is taking a more holistic orientation, embracing interventions that produce positive change in the health of clients and is moving counselors to offer premium and highly effective prevention programs.
- The use of medical services by employees is reducing the benefit of counseling, based on the fact that a great percentage of physical symptoms have emotional rather than organic causes, which are sometimes resolved through brief counseling (Cummings, 1977).
- Effectiveness of treatment offered on outpatient basis as opposed to inpatient basis is becoming the treatment of choice, attracting employers and third-party payers who are finding it hard to absorb the spiraling costs of residential treatment.
- Due to parameters set on time and caps placed on costs for counseling services, counselors will need to develop proficiency in brief or time-limited therapies, rapid formulation of treatment plans, and familiarity with counseling interventions that focus on crisis interventions and active problem solving (Austad, DeStafano, & Kisch, 1988).
- Individual practice in counseling is greatly reduced, clearing the way for group practice to become the standard, at the same time transforming the field of counseling into a competitive market.

SURVIVING THE MANAGED CARE ENVIRONMENT

Based on the recommendations of Lawless et al. (1999), MacCluskie and Ingersoll (2001) proposed the following skills that counselors need to master to effectively work in a managed care environment.

Counselors' Skills

- Business know-how and aptitude.
- Ability to utilize the *Diagnostic and Statistical Manual of Mental Disorders* (4th ed. [*DSM–IV*]; American Psychiatric Association, 2000) effectively.
- Ability to design and write effective treatment plans.

- Ability to keep records and manage billing.
- Ability to function with brief and solution-focused therapy.
- Ability to develop research skills.
- Ability to provide clear treatment philosophy to both clients and managed care organizations.
- Ability to work as a team with other service providers and utilization reviewers.
- Ability to develop awareness of standards of practice for various clinical problems.
- Ability to master managed care jargon.

MAKING IT WORK PROFITABLY: HINTS FOR COUNSELORS

Anderson (2000) offered some practical suggestions on how to deal constructively with managed care organizations. A former mental health counselor and managed care case manager, Anderson provided some hints on how mental health counselors can:

- Develop working relationships with case managers.
- Do treatment planning.
- Submit claim forms.
- Resolve disputes.

How Can Counselors Develop Working Relationships With Case Managers?

- Mental health counselors need to provide the case manager with clear and specific clinical information about the clients' treatment that include current symptoms, past interventions, success or failure of these interventions, and goals and objectives for treatment.
- Mental health counselors need to adhere to the managed care company's guidelines as a network provider.
- Mental health counselors need to avoid taking the managed care process personally and see case managers' questions not as a concern about their clinical expertise, but rather as a genuine attempt to secure accurate information about how clients can be helped.
- Mental health counselors need to develop a familiarity with managed care procedures, and consult with the case manager whenever there is a doubt about the procedures.
- Mental health counselors need to get to know their clients' benefits, the amount used, the amount that remains, as well as the referral procedures, the criteria for medical necessity, and the emergency procedures.

- Mental health counselors need to treat the case manager as they wish to be treated themselves, which involves not delaying to return phone calls and to respond to the case manager's requests.
- Mental health counselors need to use the case manager as a resource for guidance when needed.

What Are Skills Counselors Need to Do Treatment Planning?

- Mental health counselors need to develop clear individualized treatment plans for the clients.
- Mental health counselors need to be well informed and conscientious in their clinical duties, which involve being able to state clearly the symptoms of the clients, and articulate specific plans and outcomes that make clinical sense.
- Mental health counselors need to provide to the case manager a good treatment plan that includes the following elements: a clear statement of the client's problem, specific goals with measurable criteria and time frames for completion of the goals, and a clear statement of the means to be used to achieve these goals.
- Mental health counselors need to communicate progress of clients to case managers when performing clinical reviews of treatment plans, so that continued sessions can be certified when benefits are available.

How Do Counselors Go About Submitting Claim Forms?

- Mental health counselors need to accurately use service codes on claim forms that reflect exactly what counseling services have been certified to avoid denial of claim by the case manager.
- Mental health counselors need to clarify with the case manager what services have been certified when clinical review is being done by phone.
- Mental health counselors need to keep copies of certification forms that outline exactly what has been certified.
- Mental health counselors need to advise the case manager of any deviation from what has been certified so that adjustment could be made to the certification form to reflect what exactly took place.
- Mental health counselors need to know that certifications are often time limited and that claims for the services provided prior to the beginning date and past the ending date will be rejected.
- Mental health counselors need to be aware that reimbursement for services is in accordance with the rate negotiated in the original contract with the managed care provider, and that the contract will need to be renegotiated if the rate should be changed.
- Mental health counselors need to know that case managers can help when problems with claims arise.

What Can Counselors Do for Resolving Disputes?

- In cases where clients' benefits are not covered by an individual insurance plan, counselors and case managers can team up to devise strategies that will help clients make the best use of their existing benefits, or identify other sources of funding.

- In cases where benefits have been exhausted it is imperative that counselors work together with the case manager right at the beginning of treatment to grasp the scope and amount of benefits available to clients.

- In cases where disagreements arise over medical necessity, mental health counselors can do the following to bring about a resolution: Provide clear therapeutic reasons for the medical necessity, explain the rationale and intended outcomes behind the request, provide clear information that matches the specific criteria used by the case manager to determine medical necessity, be knowledgeable of pragmatic references that support the treatment request, keep the relationship with the case manager nonadversarial, and initiate the appeal process in the last resort.

FREQUENTLY ASKED QUESTIONS ABOUT MANAGED CARE

✓ This section of frequently asked questions is based on the series of bulletins offered by Walsh and Dasenbrook on the American Counseling Association's Web site at:

► http://www.counseling.org/Counseling/PrivatePracticePointers.aspx

■ 1. How Easy Is It to Become a Managed Care Provider?

Because of the bureaucracy and paperwork involved in managed care, becoming a provider can be very difficult, but not impossible.

■ 2. Are Mental Health Counselors Accepted as Third-Party Payers?

Some 40 national and regional managed care and insurance companies accept licensed mental health professionals as third-party payers. Although this figure varies from state to state, 80% of the top insurance companies like Blue Cross/Blue Shield will pay third-party reimbursement in most states.

■ 3. What Does One Do if One Is Not on the Client's Panel or if a Panel Is Closed in One's Area?

Not a problem! There is always the option of entering through the "back door" and attempting to become an ad hoc provider, which means you are accepted for one client. You will then be included in the system and will be given provider status with a provider number.

■ 4. What Are the Steps That Need to Be Followed if One Chooses to Use the Back Door System?

1. The client writes a clear, polite letter to the employer requesting that the managed care company consider paying you as his or her chosen mental health clinician. The letter must speak about your credentials and experience as a therapist, and indicate that you meet all the necessary requirements of your state for licensed professional counselors. The letter goes to the benefits manager of the company and a copy is sent to the managed care company provider relations director.
2. A second letter is sent to the managed care company by you, the licensed mental health professional, requesting to be considered for reimbursement for service delivery. A copy of the letter that includes your credentials and explains the benefits of the mental health professional services for the employee and the company in general is also sent to the client's employer.
3. Secure a letter from the state counselors association of which you are a member to be sent to the managed care company on your behalf. The letter will advocate your case for accepting licensed mental health counselors into a mental health option package.

■ 5. Should Counselors Be HIPAA Compliant?

The Health Insurance Portability and Accountability Act of 1996 (HIPPA) regulations are in force, and any professional counselor considered as a covered entity is legally obliged to comply.

■ 6. What Is Meant by "Covered Entity?"

Any provider that uses electronic forms to transmit information is a "covered entity." It is advisable that counselors become HIPAA compliant on account of credibility of professionalism vis-à-vis their clients. Moreover, whether you are a covered entity or not, or elect not to comply, the HIPAA still impacts release of information, record keeping, and confidentiality.

KEY TERMS FOR MANAGED CARE PROVIDERS

Counselors working in a managed care environment need to develop a familiarity with terms and language commonly used in that setting.

Capitation: A form of payment in which a fixed amount of money is paid in advance to a provider for the delivery of health care services on a per-patient, per-unit-of-time basis.

Case management: A process that uses clinical protocols as a guide to assign the least expensive appropriate treatment for special populations who are expected to generate large expenditures, such as people with severe persistent mental illness and children with severe emotional disturbances.

Case manager: A nurse, doctor, or social worker who works with patients, providers, and insurers to coordinate all services deemed necessary to provide the patient with a plan of medically necessary and appropriate health care.

Case rate: A previously agreed-on fee paid to a provider for the entire course of treatment for one case.

Cost-containment case management: A model that allows case managers to develop treatment plans that take into account the client's social and medical needs. This may include authorizing services beyond the coverage of the plan, particularly if such treatment proves less costly.

Employee assistance programs (EAPs): Worksite-based programs designed to assist in the identification and resolution of productivity problems associated with employees impaired by personal concerns including, but not limited to health, marital, family, financial, alcohol, drug, legal, emotional, stress, or other personal concerns that may adversely affect employee job performance.

Gatekeeper: Under some health insurance arrangements a primary care provider serves as the patient's agent, and arranges for and coordinates appropriate medical services, laboratory studies, hospitalizations, and other necessary and appropriate referrals.

Health maintenance organization (HMO): A type of health care plan usually associated with specific geographical areas where members pay a flat monthly rate in return for health care services delivered by a group of mental health and medical professionals.

HMO group practice: An HMO that contracts with a single multispecialty medical group partnership to provide services to its members on preagreed per-capita rate, which the group distributes among its physicians.

HMO staff: A type of closed-panel HMO in which medical professionals are employed by the HMO to provide care to members in the HMO's own facilities.

Indemnity health insurance: Through this type of plan, the patient or the provider receives reimbursement for services as expenses are incurred.

Independent practice associations (IPAs): Groups of independent medical practitioners who band together for the purpose of contracting their services to HMOs, preferred provider organizations (PPOs), and insurance companies, to provide services to both HMO and non-HMO plan participants on an agreed, prepaid, capitated rate.

Management services organization: An organization whose task is to provide business-related services, such as marketing and data collection, to individual groups of providers.

Medical staff organization: A group of physicians who have teamed together to contract with others for provision of services.

Mixed model: A prepaid system that combines features of more than one HMO model, without one particular model dominating another.

Network: An HMO model that contracts with two or more independent group practices to provide services to HMO members, and may involve large single and multispecialty groups.

Open-ended or open panel HMO: An HMO that allows its members to utilize health care services from providers outside their own network of providers without referral authorization.

Preferred provider organization (PPO): A health care delivery system that contracts with providers of medical care to provide services at discounted fees to members. Members may seek care from nonparticipating providers but generally are financially penalized for doing so by the loss of the discount and subjection to copayments and deductibles.

Third-party administrators (TPAs): Individuals or firms that an employer hires to handle claims processing, reimburse providers, and deal with all other health-insurance-related matters.

Utilization management: The process of evaluating the necessity, appropriateness, and efficiency of health care services against established guidelines and criteria.

Utilization review (UR): A formal process for reviewing the appropriateness and quality of health care services delivered to clients before, during, or after the delivery of the services.

References

Abrami, P. C., Cholmsky, P., Gordon, R. (2001). *Statistical analysis for the social sciences: An interactive approach*. Boston: Allyn & Bacon.

Achinstein, B., & Meyer, T. (1997, March). *The uneasy marriage between friendship and critique: Dilemmas of fostering critical friendship in a novice teacher learning community*. Paper presented at the Annual Meeting of the American Educational Research Association, Chicago. (ERIC Document Reproduction Service No. ED 412188)

Ackerman, N. W. (1967). Prejudice and scapegoating in the family. In G. Zuk & I. Boszormenyi-Nagy (Eds.), *Family therapy and disturbed families* (pp. 48–58). Palo Alto, CA: Science and Behavior Books.

Ackerman, N. W. (1982). The family approach to marital disorders. In D. Bloch & R. Simon (Eds.), *The strength of family therapy: Selected papers of Nathan W. Ackerman* (pp. 364–371). New York: Brunner/Mazel.

Adkins, W. R. (1984). Life skills education: A video-based counseling/learning delivery system. In D. Larson (Ed.), *Teaching psychological skills: Models for giving psychology away* (pp. 44–68). Monterey, CA: Brooks/Cole.

Adler, A. (1954). *Understanding human nature* (W. B. Wolf, Trans.) New York: Fawcett. (Original work published, 1927)

Adler, A. (1963). *The practice and theory of individual psychology*. Paterson, NJ: Littlefield, Adams.

Adler, P. A., & Adler, P. (1994). Observational techniques. In N. K. Denzin & Y. S. Lincoln (Eds.), *Handbook of qualitative research* (pp. 377–392). Thousand Oaks, CA: Sage.

Ainsworth, M. D. S. (1979). Infant–mother attachment. *American Psychologist, 34,* 932–937.

Alderman, N., Fry, R. K., & Youngson, H. A. (1995). Improvement of self monitoring skills, reduction of behavior disturbance, and the dysexecutive syndrome. *Neuropsychological Rehabilitation, 5,* 193–222.

Alexander, K., & Alexander, M. D. (2005). *American public school law* (6th ed.). Belmont, CA: Thomson West.

Allstetter-Neufeldt, S. (1999). *Supervision strategies for the first practicum* (2nd ed.). Boston: Allyn & Bacon.

Alonso, A. (1983). A developmental theory of psychodynamic supervision. *Clinical Supervisor, 1*(3), 23–26.

American-Arab Anti-Discrimination Committee. (1993). *Educational outreach and action guide: Working with school systems*. Washington, DC: Author.

American Association of Pastoral Counselors. (1998). *The pastoral counselor in an era of managed care*. Retrieved November 15, 1998, from www.metanoia.org/aapc/

American Association of Pastoral Counselors. (2005). American Association of Pastoral Counselors. Retrieved April 29, 2005, from http://www.aapc.org/

American Counseling Association. (1997). *Resources*. Retrieved August 12, 2005, from http://www.counseling.org/Content/NavigationMenu/RESOURCES/PROFESSIONAL COUNSELORSSERVINGALLPEOPLE/Professional_Counse.htm

American Counseling Association. (2001). *U.S. student to counselor ratios* (Briefing paper). Alexandria, VA: Author.

American Counseling Association. (2002). *Resources*. Retrieved August 12, 2005, from http://www.counseling.org/Content/NavigationMenu/RESOURCES/FAQSABOUT COUNSELING/Answers_to_common_q.htm

American Counseling Association. (2005). *ACA code of ethics and standards of practice*. Alexandria, VA: Author.

American Counseling Association. (2006). *Licensure requirements for professional counselors*. Alexandria, VA: Author.

***American Heritage Dictionary of the English Language*. (2000).

American Psychiatric Association. (2000, June). *Diagnostic and statistical manual of mental disorders* (4th ed., text revision). Washington, DC: Author.

American Psychological Association. (2005). *American Psychological Association*. Retrieved April 29, 2005, from www.apa.org

American School Counselor Association. (1997). *Definition of school counseling*. Alexandria, VA: Author.

American School Counselor Association. (2003). *ASCA national model: A framework for school counseling programs*. Alexandria, VA: Author.

American School Counselor Association. (2004a). *ASCA national standards for students*. Alexandria, VA: Author.

American School Counselor Association. (2004b). *Ethical standards for school counselors*. Alexandria, VA: Author.

American School Counselor Association. (2005). *The ASCA national model: A framework for school counseling programs* (2nd ed.). Alexandria, VA: Author.

American School Counselor Association. (2006). *Public elementary and secondary students, staff, schools, and school districts: School year 2003–04*. Retrieved June 24, 2006, from http://www.schoolcounselor.org/content.asp?contentid=459

American Society for Addiction Medicine. (2001). *Patient placement criteria* (2nd ed., revised). Chevy Chase, MD: Author.

***Americans with Disabilities Act. (1990). The U.S. Equal Employment Opportunity Commission.

Amundson, N., Harris-Bowlsbey, J., & Niles, S. (2004). *Essential elements of career counseling*. Columbus, OH: Prentice-Hall.

Anderson, B. S. (1996). *The counselor and the law* (4th ed.). Alexandria, VA: American Counseling Association.

Anderson, C. E. (2000). Dealing constructively with managed care: Suggestions from an insider. *Journal of Mental Health Counseling, 22,* 4.

Anderson, T. (1987). The reflecting team: Dialogue and meta-dialogue in clinical work. *Family Process, 26,* 415–428.

Angrosino, M. V., & de Perez, K. A. M. (2000). Rethinking observation: From method to context. In N. K. Denzin & Y. S. Lincoln (Eds.), *Handbook of qualitative research* (2nd ed., pp. 673–702). Thousand Oaks, CA: Sage.

Ansbacher, H. L. (1974). Goal-oriented individual psychology: Alfred Adler's theory. In A. Burton (Ed.), *Operational theories of personality* (pp. 99–142). New York: Brunner/Mazel.

Ansbacher, H. L., & Ansbacher, R. R. (Eds.). (1967). *The individual psychology of Alfred Adler*. New York: Harper & Row.

Arbona, C. (1995). Theory and research on racial and ethnic minorities: Hispanic Americans. In F. T. L. Leong (Ed.), *Career development and vocational behavior of racial and ethnic minorities* (pp. 37–66). Mahwah, NJ: Lawrence Erlbaum Associates, Inc.

Arab American Institute. (2006a). *Arab Americans.* Retrieved July 5, 2006, from http://www.aaiusa.org/arab-americans

Arab American Institute. (2006b). *Demographics.* Retrieved July 5, 2006, from http://www.aaiusa.org/arab-americans/22/demographics

Arbona, C. (1996). Career theory and practice in a multicultural context. In M. L. W. Savickas & W. Bruce (Ed.), *Handbook of career counseling theory and practice* (pp. 45–54). Palo Alto, CA: Davies-Black.

Archer, J., Probert, B. S., & Gage, L. (1987). College students' attitudes toward wellness. *Journal of College Student Personnel, 2,* 311–317.

Arciniega, G. M., & Newlon, B. J. (1994). Counseling and psychotherapy: Multicultural considerations. In D. Capuzzi & D. Gross (Eds.), *Counseling and psychotherapy: Theories and interventions* (pp. 557–587). Columbus, OH: Macmillan/Merrill.

Arredondo, P. (1999). Multicultural counseling competencies as tools to address oppression and racism. *Journal of Counseling and Development, 77,* 102–108.

Association for Advanced Training (1991).

Association for Clinical Pastoral Education. (2005). *Association for Clinical Pastoral Education, Inc.* Retrieved April 29, 2005, from http://www.acpe.edu/

Association for Counselor Education and Supervision. (1993). ACES ethical guidelines for counseling supervisors. *ACES Spectrum, 53*(4), 5–8.

Association for Specialists in Group Work. (1999). Principles for diversity-competent group workers. *Journal for Specialists in Group Work, 24,* 7–14.

Association for Specialists in Group Work. (2000). *Association for Specialists in Group Work Professional Standards for the Training of Group Workers.* Retrieved October 25, 2005 from http://www.asgw.org/training_standards.htm

Association for Spiritual, Ethical, and Religious Values in Counseling (ASERVIC). (2006). *Association for Spiritual, Ethical, and Religious Values in Counseling.* Retrieved October 30, 2006, from www.aservic.org/index.htm

Atkinson, B. (2002). Brain to brain: New ways to help couples avoid relapse. *Psychotherapy Networker, 26,* 38–45.

Atkinson, B. (2005). *Emotional intelligence in couples therapy: Advances from neurobiology and the science of intimate relationships.* New York: Norton.

Atkinson, B., Atkinson, L., Kutz, P., Lata, J., Lata, K. W., Szekely, J., et al. (2005). Rewiring neural states in couples therapy: Advances from affective neuroscience. *Journal of Systemic Therapies, 24,* 3–16.

Atkinson, D. R., Morton, G., & Sue, D. W. (1998). *Counseling American minorities: A cross-cultural perspective* (5th ed.). Boston: McGraw-Hill.

Austad, C. S, DeStafano, L., & Kisch, J. (1988). The health maintenance organisation: II. Implications for psychotherapy. *Psychotherapy, 25,* 449–454.

Austin, L. (1999). *The counseling primer.* Philadelphia: Taylor & Francis.

Avers, N., & Myers, J. E. (2006). *The five factor wellness inventory, elementary, Spanish version.* Greensboro, NC: Authors.

Baker, J. (1992). *Paradigms: The business of discovering the future.* New York: HarperCollins.

Baker, S. B., & Daniels, T. (1989). Integrating research on the microcounselling program: A meta-analysis. *Journal of Counseling Psychology, 36,* 213–222.

Baker, S. B., & Gerler, E. R. (2004). *School counseling for the twenty-first century* (4th ed.). Upper Saddle River, NJ: Merrill/Prentice-Hall.

Balbernie, R. (2001). Circuits and circumstances: The neurobiological consequences of early relationship experiences and how they shape later behavior. *Journal of Child Psychotherapy, 27,* 237–255.

Baldwin, B. A. (1978). A paradigm for the classification of emotional crises: Implications for crisis intervention. *American Journal of Orthopsychiatry, 48,* 538–551.

Balzer, W. K., Kihm, J. A., Smith, P. C., Irwin, J. L., Bachiochi, P. D., Robie, C., et al. (1997). *Users' manual for the Job Descriptive Index (JDI; 1997 Revision) and the Job In General scales.* Bowling Green, OH: Bowling Green State University.

Bambino, D. (2002). Critical friends. *Educational Leadership, 59*(6), 25–27.

Bandler, R., Grinder, J., & Satir, V. (1976). *Changing with families.* Palo Alto, CA: Science & Behavior Books.

Bandura, A. (1969). *Principles of behavior modification.* New York: Holt, Rinehart & Winston.

Bandura, A. (Ed.). (1971). *Psychological modeling: Conflicting theories.* Chicago: Aldine-Atherton.

Bandura, A. (1977). Self-efficacy: Toward a unifying theory of behavioral change. *Psychological Review, 84,* 191–215.

Bandura, A. (1986). *Social foundations of thought and action: A social cognitive theory.* Englewood Cliffs, NJ: Prentice-Hall.

Barlow, S. H., Fuhriman, A. J., & Burlingame, G. M. (2004). The history of group counseling and psychotherapy. In J. L. DeLucia-Waack, D. A. Gerrity, C. R. Kalodner, & M. T. Riva (Eds.), *Handbook of group counseling and psychotherapy* (pp. 3–22). Thousand Oaks, CA: Sage.

Basch, M. F. (1995). *Doing brief psychotherapy.* New York: Basic Books.

Baumeister, R., & Leary, M. R. (1995). The need to belong: Desire for interpersonal attachments as a fundamental human motivation. *Psychological Bulletin, 117,* 497–529.

Baumrind, D. (1971). Harmonious parents and their preschool children. *Developmental Psychology, 41,* 92–102.

Beck, A. T. (1976). *Cognitive therapy and emotional disorders.* New York: International Universities Press.

Beck, A. T., Steer, R. A., & Brown, G. K. (1996). *BDI–II manual.* San Antonio, TX: Psychological Corporation.

Bednar, R. L., & Kaul, T. J. (1978). Experiential group research: Current perspectives. In A. Bergin & S. Garfield (Eds.), *Handbook of psychotherapy and behavior change* (2nd ed., pp. 631–663). New York: Wiley.

Bednar, R. L., & Kaul, T. J. (1994). Experiential group research: Can the cannon fire? In A. E. Bergin & S. L. Garfield (Eds.), *Handbook of psychotherapy and behavior change* (4th ed., pp. 631–663). New York: Wiley.

Bednar, R. L., Melnick, J., & Kaul, T. J. (1974). Risk, responsibility, and structure: A conceptual framework for initiating group counseling and psychotherapy. *Journal of Counseling Psychology, 21,* 31–37.

Belsky, J. (1993). Etiology of child maltreatment: A developmental-ecological analysis. *Psychological Bulletin, 114,* 413–434.

Belsky, J., Rovine, M., & Taylor, D. G. (1984). The development of reciprocal interaction in the mother–infant dyad. *Child Development, 55,* 706–717.

Belsky, J., Spritz, B., & Crnic, K. (1996). Infant attachment security and affective-cognitive information processing at age 3. *Psychological Science, 7,* 111–114.

Bemmels, B. (1991). Attribution theory and discipline arbitration. *Industrial and Labor Relations Review, 44,* 548–562.

Berg, I. K., & DeJong, P. (1996). Solution-building conversations: Co-constructing a sense of competence with clients. *Families in Society, 77,* 376–391.

Bergan, J. R. (1977). *Behavioral consultation.* Columbus, OH: Merrill.

Bergan, J. R., & Kratochwill, T. R. (1990). *Behavioral consultation and therapy.* New York: Plenum.

Berger, P. L., & Luckmann, T. (1966). *The social construction of reality: A treatise in the sociology of knowledge.* Garden City, NY: Doubleday.

Berk, L. E. (1997). *Child development* (3rd ed.). Needham Heights, MA: Allyn & Bacon.

Berk, L. E. (2004). *Development through the lifespan* (3rd ed.). Boston: Pearson.

Berkowitz, S. (1982). Behavior therapy. In L. E. Abt & I. R. Stuart (Eds.), *The newer therapies: A sourcebook* (pp. 19–31). New York: Von Nostrand Reinhold.

Bernal, M. E., & Knight, G. P. (1993). *Ethnic identity: formulation and transmission among Hispanics and other minorities.* Albany: State University of New York Press.

Bernard, J. M. (1979). Supervisor training: A discrimination model. *Counselor Education and Supervision, 19,* 60–68.

Bernard, J. M. (1997). The discrimination model. In C. E. Watkins (Ed.), *Handbook of psychotherapy supervision* (pp. 310–327). New York: Wiley.

Bernard, J. M., & Goodyear, R. K. (1998). *Fundamentals of clinical supervision* (2nd ed.). Needham Heights, MA: Allyn & Bacon.

Bernard, J. M., & Goodyear, R. K. (2004). *Fundamentals of clinical supervision* (3rd ed.). Boston: Pearson/Allyn & Bacon.

Berne, E. (1964). *Games people play.* New York: Grove.

Berne, E. (1966). *Principles of group treatment.* New York: Oxford University Press.

Berry, J. W., Poortinga, Y. H., Segall, M. H., & Dasen, P. R. (1992). *Cross-cultural psychology: Research and applications.* New York: Cambridge University Press.

Bertalanffy, L. V. (1968). *General system theory: Foundations, development, applications* (rev. ed.). New York: George Braziller.

Bingham, R. P., & Ward, C. M. (1996). Practical applications of career counseling with ethnic minority women. In M. L. Savickas & W. B. Walsh (Eds.), *Handbook of career counseling theory and practice* (pp. 291–314). Palo Alto, CA: Davies-Black.

Bingham, R. P., & Ward, C. M. (1997). Theory into assessment: A model for women of color. *Journal of Career Assessment, 5,* 403–418.

Bloch, S., & Crouch, E. (1985). *Therapeutic factors in group psychotherapy.* Oxford, UK: Oxford University Press.

Block, C. B. (1981). Black Americans and cross-cultural counseling and psychotherapy experience. In A. Marsella & P. Pedersen (Eds.), *Cross-cultural counseling psychotherapy* (pp. 177–194). New York: Pergamon.

Block, P. (1981). *Flawless consulting.* Austin, TX: Learning Concepts.

Blumenfeld, H. (2002). *Neuroanatomy through clinical cases.* Sunderland, MA: Sinauer.

Blustein, D. L. (1997). A context rich perspective of career exploration and cross life roles. *Career Development Quarterly, 45,* 260–275.

Bogdan, R. C., & Biklen, S. K. (1998). *Qualitative research for education: An introduction to theory and methods* (3rd ed.). Boston: Allyn & Bacon.

Bogdevic, S. R. (1999). Participant observation. In B. F. Crabtree & W. L. Miller (Eds.), *Doing qualitative research* (2nd ed., pp. 47–70). Thousand Oaks, CA: Sage.

Bolton-Brownlee, A. (1987). Issues in multicultural counseling. *Highlights: An ERIC/CAPS Digest.* Retrieved April 5, 2006, from http://www.ed.gov/databases/ERIC_Digests/ed279995.html

Bonanno, G. A. (2004). Loss, trauma, and human resilience: Have we underestimated the human capacity to thrive after extremely aversive events. *American Psychologist, 59,* 20–28.

Borders, L. (1994). Potential for DCT/SCDT in addressing two elusive themes of mental health counseling. *Journal of Mental Health Counseling, 16,* 75–78.

Borders, L. D., Bernard, J. M., Dye, H. A., Fong, M. L., & Nance, D. W. (1991). Curriculum guide for training counseling supervisors: Rationale, development, and implementation. *Counselor Education and Supervision, 31,* 58–80.

Borders, L. D., & Brown, L. L. (2005). *The new handbook of counseling supervision*. Mahwah, NJ: Lawrence Erlbaum Associates, Inc.

Borders, L. D., & Leddick, G. R. (1998). A nationwide survey of supervisory training. *Counseling Education and Supervision, 27,* 271–283.

Bordin, E. S. (1983). A working alliance model for supervision. *Counseling Psychologist, 11,* 35–42.

Bordin, E. S. (1994). Theory and research on the therapeutic working alliance: New directions. In A. O. Horvath & L. S. Greenberg (Eds.), *The working alliance: Theory, research, and practice* (pp. 13–37). New York: Wiley.

Bordin, E. S., Nachmann, B., & Segal, S. J. (1963). An articulated framework for vocational development. *Journal of Counseling Psychology, 10,* 107–116.

Borgatta, E. F., & Bales, R. F. (1953). Interaction of individuals in reconstituted groups. *Sociometry, 16,* 302–320.

Boszormenyi-Nagy, I. (1970). Critical incidents in the context of family therapy. In N. Ackerman, J. Lieb, & J. K. Pearce (Eds.), *International psychiatry clinics* (Vol. 7, No. 4: Family therapy in transition, pp. 251–260). Boston: Little, Brown.

Boszormenyi-Nagy, I. (1986). Transgenerational solidarity: The expanding context of therapy and prevention. *The American Journal of Family Therapy, 14,* 195–212.

Boszormenyi-Nagy, I., & Spark, G. M. (Eds.). (1973). *Invisible loyalties: Reciprocity in intergenerational family therapy*. New York: Harper & Row.

Botwinick, J. (1977). *Aging and behavior: A comprehensive integration of research findings* (2nd ed.). New York: Springer.

Boulding, K. E. (1962). Conflict and defense: A general theory. New York: Harper & Row.

Bowen, M. (1976a). Principles and techniques of multiple family therapy. In P. J. Guerin (Ed.), *Family therapy: Theory and practice* (pp. 388–404). New York: Gardner.

Bowen, M. (1976b). Theory in the practice of psychotherapy. In P. J. Guerin (Ed.), *Family therapy: Theory and practice* (pp. 42–90). New York: Gardner.

Bowen, M. (1985). *Family therapy in clinical practice* (3rd ed.). Northvale, NJ: Aronson.

Bowers, J., Hatch, T., & Schwallie-Giddis, P. (2001). *The brain storm*. Retrieved June 21, 2006 from http://www.schoolcounselor.org/files/brainstorm.pdf

Bowlby, J. (1973). *Attachment and loss: Vol. 2. Separation, anxiety and anger*. New York: Basic Books.

Bowlby, J. (1979). *The making and breaking of affectional bonds*. London: Tavistock.

Bowlby, J. (1980). *Attachment and loss: Vol. 3. Loss*. New York: Basic Books.

Bowlby, J. (1982). *Attachment and loss: Vol. 1. Attachment* (2nd ed.). New York: Basic Books.

Bowlby, J. (1988). *A secure base*. New York: Basic Books.

Boyce, W. T., Frank, E., Jensen, P. S., Kessler, R. C., Nelson, C. A., Steinberg, L., et al. (1998). Social context in developmental psychopathology: Recommendations for future research from the MacArthur Network on Psychopathology and Development. *Development and Psychopathology, 10,* 143–164.

Bozarth, J. D. (1981). The person-centered approach in the large community group. In G. Gazda (Ed.), *Innovations to group psychotherapy* (2nd ed.). Pacific Grove, CA: Brooks/Cole.

Bradley, A. (1990). *Counseling midlife career changers*. Garrett Park, MD: Garrett Park Press.

Bradley, L. J., & Ladany, N. (Eds.). (2001). *Counselor supervision: Principles, process, and practice* (3rd ed.). Philadelphia: Brunner-Routledge.

Brammer, L. M. (1985). *The helping relationship: Process and skills* (3rd ed.). Englewood Cliffs, NJ: Prentice-Hall.

Brammer, L., & Abrego, P. (1981). Intervention strategies for coping with transitions. *The Counseling Psychologist, 9,* 19–36.

Brammer, L. M., & Macdonald, G. (1999). *The helping relationship: Process and skills* (7th ed.) Needham Heights, MA: Allyn & Bacon.

Braverman, L. (1986). Beyond families: Strategic family therapy and the female client. *Family Therapy, 13,* 143–152.

Braverman, M. (1999). *Preventing workplace violence: A guide for employers and practitioners.* Thousand Oaks, CA: Sage.

Brief, A. P., Dietz, J., Cohen, R. R., Pugh, S. D., & Vaslow, J. B. (2000). Just doing business: Modern racism and obedience to authority as explanations for employment discrimination. *Organizational Behavior and Human Decision Processes, 81,* 72–97.

Brigman, G., Mullis, F., Webb, L., & White, J. (2005). *School counselor consultation: Skills for working effectively with parents, teachers, and other school personnel.* Hoboken, NJ: Wiley.

Bronfenbrenner, U. (1979). *The ecology of human development: Experiments by nature and design.* Cambridge, MA: Harvard University Press.

Bronfenbrenner, U. (2001). The bioecological theory of human development. In N. J. Smelser & P. B. Baltes (Eds.), *International encyclopedia of the social and behavioral sciences* (Vol. 10, pp. 6963–6970). New York: Elsevier.

Bronfenbrenner, U. (Ed.). (2004). The bioecological theory of human development. In U. Bronfenbrenner (Ed.), *Making human beings human: Bioecological perspectives on human development* (pp. 3–15). Thousand Oaks, CA: Sage.

Bronfenbrenner, U., & Ceci, S. J. (1994). Nature–nurture reconceptualized in developmental perspective: A bioecological model. *Psychological Review, 101,* 568–586.

Brown, D., Pryzwansky, W. B., & Schulte, A. C. (2006). *Psychological consultation and laboration: Introduction to theory and practice* (6th ed.). Boston: Pearson/Allyn & Bacon.

Brown, M. T. (1995). The career development of African Americans: Theoretical and empirical issues In F. T. L. Leong (Ed.), *Career development and vocational behavior of racial and ethnic minorities* (pp. 7–36). Mahwah, NJ: Lawrence Erlbaum Associates, Inc.

Browning, D. S. (1987). *Religious thought and the modern psychologies: A critical conversation in the theology of culture.* Philadelphia: Fortress.

Browning, D. S. (1993). Introduction to pastoral counseling. In R. J. Wicks, R. D. Parsons, & D. Capps (Eds.), *Clinical handbook of pastoral counseling* (Vol. 1, expanded ed., pp. 5–13). New York: Paulist Press.

Bruner, J. S. (1990). *Acts of meaning.* Cambridge, MA: Harvard University Press.

Buber, M. (1970). *I and thou.* New York: Scribner's. (Original work published 1923)

Bullis, R. K. (1993). *Law and management of a counseling agency or private practice* (Vol. 3, ACA Legal Series). Alexandria, VA: American Counseling Association.

Bullis, R. K., & Mazur, C. S. (1993). *Legal issues and religious counseling.* Louisville, KY: Westminster/John Knox.

Bureau of Labor Statistics, U.S. Department of Labor. (2004). *Occupational outlook.* Retrieved February 23, 2006, from http://www.bls.gov/oco/ocos067.htm

Burlingame, G. M., Fuhriman, A., & Johnson, J. E. (2001). Cohesion in group psychotherapy. *Psychotherapy, 38,* 373–379.

Burr, V. (1995). *An introduction to social constructionism.* London: Routledge.

Butcher, J. N., Dahlstrom, W. G., Graham, J. R., Tellegen, A., & Kaemmer, B. (1989a). *Manual for administration and scoring: MMPI–2.* Minneapolis: University of Minnesota Press.

Butcher, J. N., Dahlstrom, W. G., Graham, J. R., Tellegen, A., & Kaemmer, B. (1989b). *Manual for the restandardized MMPI: MMPI–2: An administrative and interpretive guide.* Minneapolis: University of Minnesota Press.

Butman, R. E. (1997). Qualifications of the Christian mental health professional. In R. K. Sanders (Ed.), *Christian counseling ethics: A handbook for therapists, pastors and counselors* (pp. 43–56). Downers Grove, IL: InterVarsity.

Byars, A. M., & Hackett, G. (1998). Applications of social cognitive theory to the career development of women of color. *Applied and Preventive Psychology, 7*, 255–267.

Cade, B., & O'Hanlon, W. (1993). *A brief guide to brief therapy.* New York: Norton.

Call, K. T., Finch, M. A., Huck, S. M., & Kane, R. A. (1999). Caregiver burden from a social exchange perspective: Caring for older people after hospital discharge. *Journal of Marriage and the Family, 61*, 688–700.

Callahan, J. (1994). Defining crisis and emergency. *Crisis, 15*, 164–171.

Callahan, J. (1998). Crisis theory and crisis intervention in emergencies. In P. M. Kleespies (Ed.), *Emergencies in mental health practice: Evaluation and management* (pp. 22–40). New York: Guilford.

Campbell, C. A., & Dahir, C. A. (1997). *Sharing the vision: The national standards for school counseling programs.* Alexandria, VA: American School Counseling Association.

Campbell, D., & Draper, R. (1985). Creating a context for change: An overview. In A. Bentovim, G. G. Barnes, & A. Cooklin (Series Eds.) & D. Campbell & R. Draper (Vol. Eds.), *Complementary frameworks of theory and practice: Vol. 3. Applications of systemic family therapy: The Milan approach* (pp. 1–10). London: Grune & Stratton.

Campbell, D., Strong, E. K., & Hansen, J. (1991). *The Strong Interest Inventory.* Palo Alto, CA: Consulting Psychologists Press.

Campbell, J. M. (2000). *Becoming an effective supervisor: A workbook for counselors and psychotherapists.* Ann Arbor, MI: Sheridan Books.

Caplan, G. (1970). *The theory and practice of mental health consultation.* New York: Basic Books.

Cappas, N. M., Andres-Hyman, R., & Davidson, L. (2005). What psychotherapists can begin to learn from neuroscience: Seven principles of brain-based psychotherapy. *Psychotherapy: Theory, Research, Practice, Training, 42*, 374–383.

Capps, D. (1995). *Hope: A pastoral psychology.* Minneapolis, MN: Fortress Press.

Capps, D. (Ed.). (2001). *Freud and freudians on religion: A reader.* New Haven, CT: Yale University Press.

Capuzzi, D., & Gross, D. R. (1992). *Introduction to group counseling.* Denver, CO: Love.

Carkhuff, R. (1968). Differential functioning of lay and professional helpers. *Journal of Counseling Psychology, 15*, 117–126.

Carkhuff, R., & Berenson, B. (1967). *Beyond counseling and psychotherapy.* New York: Holt, Reinhart & Winston.

Carlsen, M. B. (1988). *Meaning-making: Therapeutic processes in adult development.* New York: Norton.

Carmichael, K. D. (2004). *Culturally sensitive issues in play therapy with Islamic Arab Americans.* Retrieved July 9, 2006, from http://www.gapt.org/pdf_files/ARTICLES%20VOL%201–9/09-03%20CULTURALLY%20SENSATIVE%20ISSUES%20IN%20PT%20WITH%20ARABS-CARMICHAEL.pdf#search='www.Carmichaelcounseling.com'

Carroll, J. B. (1993). *Human cognitive abilities: A survey of factor-analytical studies.* New York: Cambridge University Press.

Carta-Falsa, J., & Anderson, L. (2001). A model of clinical/counseling supervision. *The California Therapist, 13*(2), 47–51.

Carter, B. (1992, January–February). Stonewalling feminism. *Networker,* pp. 64–69.

Carter, R. T., & Cook, D. A. (1992). A culturally relevant perspective for understanding the career paths of visible racial/ethnic group people. In H. D. Lea & Z. B. Leibowitz (Eds.), *Adult career development: Concepts, issues, and practices* (pp. 192–217). Alexandria, VA: National Career Development Association.

Casile, W. J., & Davison, R. (1998). Collaborative leadership and partnership management. In V. Williams (Ed.), *New directions for school leadership: Conceptual and practical issues in school leadership* (pp. 35–48). San Francisco: Jossey-Bass.

Cattell, R. B. (1963). Theory of fluid and crystallized intelligence: A critical experiment. *Journal of Educational Psychology, 54*, 1–22.

Cecchin, G., Lane, G., & Ray, W. A. (1993). From strategizing to nonintervention: Toward irreverence in systemic practice. *Journal of Marital and Family Therapy, 19*, 125–136.

Center for Credentialing and Education. (2001). *Approved clinical supervisors certificate.* Retrieved July 3, 2006, from http://www.cce-global.org/credentials-offered/acs

Chang, C. Y. (1998). *The role of distinctiveness in acculturation, ethnic identity, and wellness in Korean-American adolescents and young adults.* Unpublished doctoral dissertation. Greensboro, NC:University of North Carolina at Greensboro. Unpublished doctoral dissertation. Ankara, Turkey, NC: Hachette University.

Charmaz, K. (2000). Grounded theory: Objectivist and constructivist methods. In N. K. Denzin & Y. S. Lincoln (Eds.), *Handbook of qualitative research* (2nd ed., pp. 509–536). Thousand Oaks, CA: Sage.

Cheatham, H. E. (1990). Africentricity and career development of African Americans. *Career Development Quarterly, 38*, 334–346.

Cicchetti, D., & Aber, J. L. (1998). Contextualism and developmental psychopathology. *Development and Psychopathology, 10*, 137–141.

Cicchetti, D., & Lynch, M. (1993). Toward an ecological/transactional model of community violence and child maltreatment: Consequences for children's development. *Psychiatry: Interpersonal and Biological Processes, 56*, 96–118.

Cicchetti, D., & Lynch, M. (1995). Failures in the expectable environment and their impact on individual development: The case of child maltreatment. In D. Cicchetti & D. J. Cohen (Eds.), *Developmental psychopathology* (pp. 32–71). New York: Wiley.

Cicchetti, D., & Toth, S. L. (1995). A developmental psychopathology perspective on child abuse and neglect. *Journal of the American Academy of Child and Adolescent Psychiatry, 34*, 541–565.

Cicerone, K. D. (2002). The enigma of executive functioning: Theoretical contributions to therapeutic interventions. In P. J. Eslinger (Ed.), *Neuropsychological interventions: Clinical research and practice* (pp. 246–265). New York: Guilford.

Cicerone, K. D., & Giacino, J. T. (1992). Remediation of executive function deficits after traumatic brain injury. *NeuroRehabilitation, 68*, 111–115.

Clark, M., & Stone, C. (2000). The developmental school counselor as educational leader. In J. Wittmer (Ed.), *Managing your school counseling program: K–12 developmental strategies* (2nd ed., pp. 75–81). Minneapolis, MN: Educational Media.

Clifford, J., & Marcus, G. F. (Eds.). (1986). *Writing culture: The poetics and politics of ethnography.* Berkeley: University of California Press.

Clifton, D., Doan, R., & Mitchell, D. (1990). The reauthoring of therapist's stories: Taking doses of our own medicine. *Journal of Strategic and Systemic Therapies, 9*, 61–66.

Cohen, R. J. (2001). *Discussion of organizational culture (DOC).* Jamaica, NY: Author.

Cohen, R. J., & Swerdlik, M. E. (2002). *Psychological testing and assessment: An introduction to tests and measurements* (5th ed.). Boston: McGraw-Hill.

Cohen, R. J., & Swerdlik, M. E. (2004). *Psychological testing and assessment: An introduction to tests and measurements* (6th ed.). Boston: McGraw-Hill.

Collins, B. G., & Collins, T. M. (2005). *Crisis and trauma: Developmental-ecological intervention.* Boston: Lahaska.

Combs, A. (1982). *A personal approach to teaching: Beliefs that make a difference.* Boston: Allyn & Bacon.

Comer, R. J. (2001). *Abnormal psychology* (4th ed.). New York: Worth.

Comer, R. J. (2004). *Abnormal psychology* (5th ed.). New York: Worth.

Commission on Rehabilitation Counselor Certification. (2002). Retrieved September 15, 2005, from http://www.crccertification.com/pdf/code_ethics_2002.pdf

Connolly, J., & Goldberg, A. (1999). Romantic relationships in adolescence: The role of friends and peers in their emergence and development. In W. Furman, B. B. Brown, & C. Feiring (Eds.), *The development of romantic relationships in adolescence* (pp. 266–290). New York: Cambridge University Press.

Conoley, J. C., & Conoley, C., W. (1992). *School consultation: Practice and training.* Boston: Allyn & Bacon.

Coombs, R. H., & Howatt, W. A. (2005). *The addiction counselor's desk reference.* Hoboken, NJ: Wiley.

Corey, G. (1995). *Student manual for theory and group counseling.* (4th ed.). Pacific Grove, CA: Brooks/Cole.

Corey, G. (1996). *Theory and practice of counseling and psychotherapy* (5th ed.). New York: Brooks/Cole.

Corey, G. (2001). *Theory and practice of counseling and psychotherapy* (6th ed.). Belmont, CA: Wadsworth/Brooks/Cole.

Corey, G. (2004a). *Theory and practice of counseling and psychotherapy* (7th ed.). Pacific Grove, CA: Brooks/Cole.

Corey, G. (2004b). *Theory and practice of group counseling* (6th ed.). Pacific Grove, CA: Brooks/Cole.

Corey, G. (2005). *Theory and practice of counseling and psychotherapy* (7th ed.). Belmont, CA: Brooks/Cole.

Corey, G., Corey, M. S., & Callanan, P. (2003). *Issues and ethics in the helping profession* (5th ed.). Pacific Grove, CA: Brooks/Cole.

Corey, M. S., & Corey, G. (2001). *Groups: Process and practice* (5th ed.). Pacific Grove, CA: Wadsworth.

Corey, M. S., & Corey, G. (2006). *Groups: Process and practice* (7th ed.). Belmont, CA: Thompson/Brooks/Cole.

Cormier, S., & Hackney, H. (2005). *Counseling strategies and interventions* (6th ed.). Boston: Allyn & Bacon.

Cornell, S., & Hartmann, D. (1997). *Ethnicity and race: Making identities in a changing world.* Thousand Oaks, CA: Pine Forge Press.

Costa, P. T., Jr., & McCrae, R. R. (1985). *The NEO Personality Inventory manual.* Odessa, FL: Psychological Assessment Resources.

Costa, P. T., Jr., & McCrae, R. R. (1993). *Revised NEO–Personality Inventory: NEO–PI–R and NEO Five-Factor Inventory (NEO–FFI) manual.* Odessa, FL: Psychological Assessment Resources.

Costa, S. R., & Kallick, B. (1993). Through the lens of a critical friend. *Educational Leadership, 51,* 49–51.

Cottone, R. R. (1992). *Theories and paradigms of counseling and psychotherapy.* Boston: Allyn & Bacon.

Council for Accreditation of Counseling and Related Educational Programs. (2001). *2001 Standards.* Retrieved July 5, 2006, from http://www.cacrep.org/2001Standards.html

Cournoyer, B. R. (1996). Converging themes in crisis intervention, task-centered and brief treatment approaches. In A. R. Roberts (Ed.), *Crisis management and brief treatment* (pp. 3–15). Chicago: Nelson-Hall.

Coyne, J., & Biglan, A. (1984). Paradoxical techniques in strategic family therapy: A behavioral analysis. *Journal of Behavior Therapy and Experimental Psychiatry, 15,* 221–227.

Cozolino, L. J. (2002). *The neuroscience of psychotherapy: Building and rebuilding the human brain.* New York: Norton.

Crace, R. K., & Brown, D. (1996). *Life Values Inventory.* Chapel Hill, NC: Life Values Resources.

Crawford, R. L. (1994). *Avoiding counselor malpractice* (Vol. 12, ACA Legal Series). Alexandria, VA: American Counseling Association.

Cristofalo, V. J., Tresini, M., Francis, M. K., & Volker, C. (1999). Biological theories of senescence. In V. L. Bengtson & K. W. Schaie (Eds.), *Handbook of theories of aging* (pp. 98–112). New York: Springer.

Cross, W. E. (1972). The negro-to-black conversion experience. *Black World, 20,* 13–27.

Cross, W. E. (1995). The psychology of Nigrescence: Revising the Cross model. In J. G. Ponterotto, J. M. Casas, L. A. Suzuki, & C. M. Alexander (Eds.), *Handbook of multicultural counseling* (pp. 93–122). Thousand Oaks, CA: Sage.

Crouch, E. C., Bloch, S., & Wanlass, J. (1994). Therapeutic factors: Interpersonal and intrapersonal mechanisms. In A. Fuhriman & G. M. Burlingame (Eds.), *Handbook of group psychotherapy* (pp. 269–316). New York: Wiley.

Cumming, E., & Henry, W. E. (1961). *Growing old: The process of disengagement.* New York: Basic Books.

Cummings, N. A. (1977). The anatomy of psychotherapy under national health insurance. *American Psychologist, 32,* 711–718.

Dandeneau, C. J., & Guth, L. J. (2005, June). From analog to digital supervision. *Counseling Today,* p. 27.

Daniels, T. (2003). Microcounselling research: What over 450 data-based studies reveal. In A. Ivey & M. Ivey (Eds.), *Intentional interviewing and counselling* [CD-ROM]. CA: Brooks/Cole

Dattilio, F. M., Epstein, N. B., & Baucom, D. H. (1998). An introduction to cognitive-behavioral therapy with couples and families. In F. M. Dattilio (Ed.), *Case studies in couple and family therapy: Systemic and cognitive perspectives* (pp. 1–36). New York: Guilford.

Davis, T., & Ritchie, M. (1993). Confidentiality and the school counselor: A challenge for the 1990s. *The School Counselor, 41*(1), 23–30.

Dawkins, M. P. (1981). Mobility aspirations of Black adolescents: A comparison of males and females. *Adolescence, 16,* 701–710.

Day, S. X., & Rounds, J. (1998). Universality of vocational interest structure among racial and ethnic minorities. *American Psychologist, 53,* 728–736.

Day, S. X., Rounds, J., & Swaney, K. (1998). The structure of vocational interests for diverse racial-ethnic groups. *Psychological Science, 9,* 40–44.

deCharms, R. (1968). *Personal causation: The internal affective determinants of behavior.* New York: Academic.

Deci, E. L., Eghrari, H., Patrick, B. C., & Leone, D. R. (1994). Facilitating internalization: The self-determination theory perspective. *Journal of Personality, 62,* 119–142.

Deci, E. L., La Guardia, J. G., Moller, A. C., Scheiner, M. J., & Ryan, R. M. (2006). On the benefits of giving as well as receiving autonomy support: Mutuality in close friendships. *Personality and Social Psychology Bulletin, 32,* 313–327.

Deci, E. L., & Ryan, R. M. (1985). *Intrinsic motivation and self-determination in human behavior.* New York: Plenum.

Deiter, P. J., & Pearlman, L. A. (1998). Responding to self-injurious behavior. In P. M. Kleespies (Ed.), *Emergencies in mental health practice: Evaluation and management* (pp. 235–257). New York: Guilford.

DeLucia-Waack, J. L., & Donigian, J. (2004). *The practice of multicultural group work: Visions and perspectives from the field.* Belmont, CA: Thompson/Brooks/Cole.

DeLucia-Waack, J. L., Gerrity, D. A., Kalodner, C. R., & Riva, M. T. (Eds.). (2004). *Handbook of group counseling and psychotherapy.* Thousand Oaks, CA: Sage.

Deming, W. E. (1993). *The new economics for industry, government, and education.* Cambridge, MA: Center for Advanced Engineering Study.

Denzin, N. K., & Lincoln, Y. S. (2005). *Handbook of qualitative research* (3rd ed.). Thousand Oaks, CA: Sage.

deShazer, S. (1984). The death of resistance. *Family Process, 23*(11), 11–17.

deShazer, S. (1985). *Keys to solution in brief therapy.* New York: Norton.

deShazer, S., & Molnar, A. (1984). Four useful interventions in brief family therapy. *Journal of Marital and Family Therapy, 10,* 297–304.

Deurzen-Smith, E. van. (1990). *Existential therapy.* London: Society for Existential Analysis Publications.

Dies, R. R. (1983). Clinical implications of research on leadership in short-term group psychotherapy. In R. R. Dies & K. R. MacKenzie (Eds.), *Advances in group psychotherapy: Integrating research and practice* (pp. 27–78). New York: International Universities Press.

Dinkmeyer, D. C. (1973). Consulting: A strategy for change. *The School Counselor, 21,* 52–55.

Dinkmeyer, D. C., & Carlson, J. (2001). *Consultation: Creating school-based interventions* (2nd ed.). Philadelphia: Brunner-Routledge.

Disney, M. J., & Stephens, A. M. (1994). *Legal issues in supervision* (Vol. 10, The ACA Legal Series). Alexandria, VA: American Counseling Association.

Doehrmann, M. (1976). Parallel processes in supervision and psychotherapy. *Bulletin of The Menninger Clinic, 40,* 3–104.

Dogan, T. (2003). *Adaptation of the wellness evaluation of lifestyle scale to Turkish.*

Dougherty, M. A. (1990). *Consultation: Practice and perspectives.* Belmont, CA: Brooks/Cole.

Dougherty, M. A. (2005). *Psychological consultation and collaboration in school and community settings* (4th ed.). Pacific Grove, CA: Brooks/Cole.

Dreikurs, R. (1950). *Fundamentals of Adlerian psychology.* New York: Greenberg.

Drummond, R. (2004). *Appraisal procedures for counselors and helping professionals* (5th ed.). Upper Saddle River, NJ: Pearson.

Dryden, W. (2000). Rational emotive behavior therapy. In C. Feltham & I. Horton (Eds.), *Handbook of counseling and psychotherapy* (pp. 314–320). London: Sage.

Duffy, M. (2007a). Conflict of interest, boundaries, and the use of power. In L. Sperry (Ed.), *The ethical and professional practice of counseling and psychotherapy* (pp. 126–144). Boston: Pearson Education.

Duffy, M. (2007b). Informed consent. In L. Sperry (Ed.), *The ethical and professional practice of counseling and psychotherapy* (pp. 109–125). Boston: Pearson Education.

Duhl, B. (1995). Virginia Satir: The use of self in therapy. *Journal of Marital and Family Therapy, 21,* 99–100.

Duncan, B. L. (1992). Strategic therapy, eclecticism, and the therapeutic relationship. *Journal of Marital and Family Therapy, 18,* 17–24.

Duncan, B., & Solovey, A. (1989). Strategic brief therapy: An insight-oriented approach? *Journal of Marital and Family Therapy, 15,* 1–9.

Dunn, H. L. (1961). *High-level wellness.* Arlington, VA: R.W. Beatty.

Dunn, H. L. (1977). What high-level wellness means. *Health Values: Achieving High Level Wellness, 1,* 9–16.

Echterling, L. G., Presbury, J. H., & McKee, J. E. (2005). *Crisis intervention: Promoting resilience and resolution in troubled times.* Upper Saddle River, NJ: Pearson.

Eco, U. (1990). *The limits of interpretation.* Bloomington: Indiana University Press.

Education Trust. (1997). *Working definition of school counseling.* Washington, DC: Author.

Edwards, A., & Polite, C. (1992). *Children of the dream: The psychology of Black success.* New York: Bantam.

Egan, G. (1998). *The skilled helper: A problem management approach to helping* (6th ed.). Pacific Grove, CA: Brooks/Cole.

Egan, G. (2002). *The skilled helper: A problem-management approach to helping* (7th ed.). Pacific Grove, CA: Brooks/Cole.

Egan, G., & Cowan, M. (1979). *People in systems: A model for development in the human-services professions and education.* Monterey, CA: Brooks/Cole.

Eichhorn, K. (2001). Sites unseen: Ethnographic research in a textual community. *Qualitative Studies in Education, 14,* 565–578.

Eisenberg, N., Fabes, R. A., Guthrie, I. K., & Reiser, M. (2002). The role of emotionality and regulation in children's social competence and adjustment. In L. Pulkkinen & A. Caspi (Eds.), *Paths to successful development: Personality in the life course* (pp. 46–70). New York: Cambridge University Press.

Eisler, R. (1995). *Sacred pleasure: Sex, myth, and the politics of the body.* San Francisco: HarperCollins.

Elbert, S., Rosman, B., Minuchin, S., & Guerney, B. (1964). A method for the clinical study of family interaction. *American Journal of Orthopsychiatry, 34,* 885–894.

Eliason, G. (2000). Spirituality and counseling of the older adult. In A. Tomer (Ed.), *Death attitudes and the older adult* (pp. 241–256). Washington, DC: Taylor & Francis.

Eliason, G., Hanley, C., & Leventis, M. (2001). The role of spirituality: Four theoretical orientations. *Pastoral Psychology, 50,* 77–91.

Elkind, D., & Bowen, R. (1979). Imaginary audience behavior in children and adolescents. *Developmental Psychology, 15,* 33–44.

Elliot, C. N. (1990a). *Differential Ability Scales.* San Antonio, TX: Psychological Corporation.

Elliot, C. N. (1990b). *Technical handbook: Differential Ability Scales.* San Antonio, TX: Psychological Corporation.

Ellis, A. (1973). Rational emotive therapy. In R. Corsini (Ed.), *Current psychotherapies* (pp. 167–206). Itasca, IL: Peacock.

Ellis, A. (1989). Thoughts on supervising counselors and therapists. *Psychology: A Journal of Human Behavior, 26,* 3–5.

Ellis, A. (1999). Early theories and practices of rational emotive behavior therapy and how they have been augmented and revised during the last three decades. *Journal of Rational-Emotive and Cognitive Behavior Therapy, 17,* 69–93.

Ellis, A. (2000). A continuation of the dialogue on issues in counseling in the postmodern era. *Journal of Mental Health Counseling, 22,* 97–106.

Ellis, A., & Dryden, W. (1987). *The practice of rational-emotive therapy.* New York: Springer.

Ellis, C., & Bochner, A. P. (2000). Autoethnography, personal narrative, reflexivity: Researcher as subject. In N. K. Denzin & Y. S. Lincoln (Eds.), *Handbook of qualitative research* (2nd ed., pp. 733–768). Thousand Oaks, CA: Sage.

Engler, B. (1984). *Personality theories* (3rd ed.). Boston: Houghton-Mifflin.

Enns, C. Z. (1997). *Feminist theories and feminist psychotherapies: Origins, themes, and variations.* New York: Haworth.

Erikson, E. (1963). *Childhood and society.* New York: Norton.

Etaugh, C., & Bridges, J. (2001). *The psychology of women: A lifespan perspective.* Needham Heights, MA: Allyn & Bacon.

Exner, J. E., Jr. (2002). *The Rorschach* (4th ed.). Hoboken, NJ: Wiley.

Falendar, C., & Shafranske, E. (2004). *Clinical supervision: A competency-based approach.* Washington, DC: American Psychological Association.

Falicov, C. J. (1998). *Latino families in therapy: A guide to multicultural practice.* New York: Guilford.

Fall, K. A., & Holder, J. M. (2003). *Theoretical models of counseling and psychotherapy.* New York: Brunner-Routledge.

Falvey, J. E. (2002). *Managing clinical supervision: Ethical practice and legal risk management.* Pacific Grove, CA: Brooks/Cole.

Falvey, J. E., Caldwell, C. F., & Cohen, C. R. (2002). *Documentation in supervision: The focused risk management supervision system.* Pacific Grove, CA: Brooks/Cole.

Family Educational Rights and Privacy Act, 20 U.S.C 1232g. (1974). Retrieved October 18, 2005, from http://dictionary.lp.findlaw.com/scripts/results.plco=dictionary.findlaw.com&topic=31/31of117c83da70f2987351c8893ce99d

Faust, N. (1968). *The counselor-consultant in the elementary school.* Boston: Houghton-Mifflin.

Feller, R., & Walz, G. (Ed.). (1997). *Career transitions in turbulent times: Exploring work, learning and careers.* Greensboro, NC: ERIC Counseling and Student Services Clearinghouse.

Fetterman, D., Kaftarian, S., & Wandersman, A. (Eds.). (1996). *Empowerment evaluation: Knowledge and tools for self-assessment and accountability.* Thousand Oaks, CA: Sage.

Fischer, L., & Sorenson, G. P. (1996). *School law for counselors, psychologists, and social workers* (3rd ed.). White Plains, NY: Longman.

Fitzgerald, L. F., & Betz, N. E. (1994). Career development in cultural context: The role of gender, race, class and sexual orientation. In M. L. Savickas & R. W. Lent (Eds.), *Convergence in career development theories: Implications for science and practice* (pp. 103–117). Palo Alto, CA: Consulting Psychologists Press.

Flores, L. Y., & O'Brien, K. M. (2002). The career development of Mexican American adolescent women: A test of social cognitive career theory. *Journal of Counseling Psychology, 49,* 14–27.

Folstein, M. F., Folstein, S. E., & McHugh, P. R. (1975). Mini-Mental State: A practical method for grading the cognitive state of patients for the clinician. *Journal of Psychiatric Research, 12,* 189–198.

Foos, J. A., Ottens, A. J., & Hill, L. K., (1991). Managed mental health: A primer for counselors. *Journal of Counseling and Development, 69,* 332–336.

Forester-Miller, H., & Davis, T. (1996). *A practitioner's guide to ethical decision making.* Retrieved September 13, 2005, from http://www.counseling.org/AM/PrinterTemplate.cfm?Section=A_Practitioner_s_Guide_to_Ethical_Decision_Making&Template=/CM/HTMLDisplay.cfm&ContentID=2935&FuseFlag=1

Forsyth, D. (1987). *Social psychology.* Monterey, CA: Brooks/Cole.

Forsyth, D. R. (1998). Methodological advances in the study of group dynamics. *Group Dynamics: Theory, Research, and Practice, 2,* 211–212.

Fosnot, C. (1996). *Constructivism: Theory, perspectives, and practice.* New York: Teachers College Press.

Fouad, N. A. (1995). Career behavior of Hispanics: Assessment and career intervention. In F. T. L. Leong (Ed.), *Career development and vocational behavior of racial and ethnic minorities* (pp. 165–191). Mahwah, NJ: Lawrence Erlbaum Associates, Inc.

Fouad, N. A., & Arbona, C. (1994). Careers in a cultural context. *Career Development Quarterly, 43,* 96–104.

Fouad, N. A., & Bingham, R. P. (1995). Career counseling with racial and ethnic minorities. In W. B. Walsh & S. H. Osipow (Eds.), *Handbook of vocational psychology: Theory, research and practice* (2nd ed., pp. 331–365). Mahwah, NJ: Lawrence Erlbaum Associates, Inc.

Foulkes, S. H., & Anthony, E. J. (1965). *Group psychotherapy: The psychoanalytic approach* (2nd ed.). Baltimore: Penguin.

Framo, J. L. (1965). Rationale and techniques of intensive family therapy. In N. W. Ackerman & J. L. Framo (Eds.), *Intensive family therapy: Theoretical and practical aspects* (pp. 142–212). New York: Harper & Row.

Framo, J. L. (1970). Symptoms from a family transactional viewpoint. In N. Ackerman, J. Lieb, & J. K. Pearce (Eds.), *Family therapy in transition* (pp. 125–171). Boston: Little, Brown.

Framo, J. L. (1994). The family life cycle: Impressions. *Contemporary Family Therapy, 16,* 87–117.

Framo, J. (1996). A personal retrospective of the family therapy field: Then and now. *Journal of Marital and Family Therapy, 22,* 289–316.

Frankl, V. E. (1984). *Man's search for meaning.* New York: Pocket Books. (Original work published 1946)

Franklin, K. K., & Lowry, C. (2001). Computer-mediated focus group sessions: Naturalistic inquiry in a networked environment. *Qualitative Research, 1,* 169–184.

Frawley-O'Dea, M. G., & Sarnat, M. J. (2001). *The supervisory relationship: A contemporary psychodynamic approach.* New York: Guilford.

Frederickson, J. (1999). *Psychodynamic psychotherapy: Learning to listen from multiple perspectives.* Philadelphia: Brunner/Mazel.

Freeman, M. (1999). Gender matters in the Satir growth model. *American Journal of Family Therapy, 27,* 345–363.

Freire, P. (1988). *Pedagogy of the oppressed.* New York: Continuum.

Freud, S. (1913). *Totem and taboo.* London: Hogarth.

Freud, S. (1927). *The future of an illusion.* New York: Norton.

Freud, S. (1943). *Introductory lectures on psychoanalysis.* London: Allen & Unwin.

Freud, S. (1959). *Group psychotherapy and the analysis of the ego.* New York: Liveright.

Freud, S. (1962). *Civilization and its discontents.* New York: Norton.

Freud, S. (1969). *A general introduction to psychoanalysis.* New York: Pocket Books.

Frye, N. (1957). *Anatomy of criticism: Four essays.* Princeton, NJ: Princeton University Press.

Frye, N. (1982). *The great code: The Bible and literature.* New York: Harcourt Brace Jovanovich.

Fuqua, D., & Kurpius, D. (1993). Conceptual models in organizational consultation. *Journal of Counseling and Development, 71,* 607–618.

Gale, A. U., & Austin, B. D. (2003). Professionalism's challenges to professional counselors' collective identity. *Journal of Counseling and Development, 81,* 3–10.

Gallessish, J. (1982). *The profession and practice of consultation: A handbook for consultants, trainers of consultants, and consumers of consultation services.* San Francisco: Jossey-Bass.

Garbarino, J. (1993). Children's response to community violence: What do we know? *Infant Mental Health Journal, 14,* 103–115.

Garbarino, J. (1995). *Raising children in a socially toxic environment.* San Francisco: Jossey-Bass.

Gardner, H. (1999). *Intelligence reframed: Multiple intelligences for the 21st century.* New York: Basic Books.

Garmezy, N. (1993). Children in poverty: Resilience despite risk. *Psychiatry, 56,* 127–136.

Gatson, S. N., & Zweerink, A. (2002). Ethnography online: "Natives" practising and inscribing community. *Qualitative Research, 2,* 179–200.

Gay, L. R., & Airasian, P. (2003). *Educational research: Competencies for analysis and application* (7th ed.). Upper Saddle River, NJ: Merrill.

Gazda, G. M., Ginter, E. J., & Horne, A. M. (2001). *Group counseling and group psychotherapy.* Needham Heights, MA: Allyn & Bacon.

Geertz, C. (1973). *The interpretation of cultures.* New York: Basic Books.

Gelso, C., & Fretz, B. (2001). *Counseling psychology* (2nd ed.). Belmont, CA: Wadsworth/Thomson Learning.

Geuss, R. (1981). *The idea of a critical theory: Habermas and the Frankfurt school.* Cambridge, UK: Cambridge University Press.

Gevarter, W. B. (1982). Psychotherapy and the brain. *Man–Environment Systems, 12,* 73–88.

Gibson, R. L., & Mitchell, M. H. (2003). *Introduction to counseling and guidance* (6th ed.). Upper Saddle River, NJ: Merrill Prentice-Hall.

Gill, S. (Ed.). (2001). *The supervisory alliance: Facilitating the psychotherapist's learning experience*. Northvale, NJ: Aronson.

Ginzberg, E., Ginsburg, S. W., Axlerad, S., & Herma, J. (1951). *Occupational choice: An approach to a general theory*. New York: Columbia University Press.

Gladding, S. T. (1992). *Counseling: A comprehensive profession* (2nd ed.). New York: Macmillan.

Gladding, S. T. (2000). *Counseling: A comprehensive profession*. Englewood Cliffs, NJ: Prentice-Hall.

Gladding, S. (2002a). *Family therapy: History, theory and practice* (3rd ed.). Upper Saddle River, NJ: Merrill Prentice-Hall.

Gladding, S. T. (2002b). *Group work: A counseling specialty*. Upper Saddle River, NJ: Prentice-Hall.

Gladding, S. (2005). Ethical and legal issues in family therapy. In R. H. Coombs (Ed.), *Family therapy review: Preparing for comprehensive and licensing exams* (pp. 531–547). Mahwah, NJ: Lawrence Erlbaum Associates, Inc.

Glaser, B. G. (1978). *Theoretical sensitivity*. Mill Valley, CA: Sociology Press.

Glaser, B. G., & Strauss, A. L. (1967). *The discovery of grounded theory: Strategies for qualitative research*. Chicago: Aldine.

Glasser, W. (1965). *Reality therapy: A new approach to psychiatry*. New York: Harper & Row.

Glasser, W. (1984). Reality therapy. In R. J. Corsini (Ed.), *Current psychotherapies* (3rd ed., pp. 320–353). Itasca, IL: Peacock.

Glasser, W. (1985). *Control theory: A new explanation of how we control our lives*. New York: Harper & Row.

Glasser, W. (1998). *Choice theory: A new psychology of personal freedom*. New York: HarperCollins.

Glasser, W. (2000). *Counseling with choice theory: The new reality therapy*. New York: HarperCollins.

Glasser, W., & Zunin, L. M. (1973). Reality therapy. In R. Corsini (Ed.), *Current psychotherapies* (pp. 293–321). Itasca, IL: Peacock.

Gleitman, L. R. (1990). The structural sources of verb meanings. *Language Acquisition, 1,* 3–55.

Glisky, E. L., & Glisky, M. L. (2002). Learning and memory impairments. In P. J. Eslinger (Ed.), *Neuropsychological interventions: Clinical research and practice* (pp. 137–162). New York: Guilford.

Goals 2000. (1994). *Goals 2000: Educate America Act*. Retrieved June 4, 2006, from http://www.ed.gov/legislation/GOALS2000/TheAct

Goh, M. (2005). Cultural competence and master therapists: An inextricable relationship. *Journal of Mental Health Counseling, 27,* 71–81.

Goldner, V. (1985). Feminism and family therapy. *Family Process, 24,* 31–47.

Goldstein, A. P. (1973). *Structured learning therapy: Toward a psychotherapy for the poor*. New York: Academic.

Gordon, T. (1951). Group-centered leadership and administration. In C. R. Rogers (Ed.), *Client-centered therapy* (pp. 320–383). Boston: Houghton-Mifflin.

Gottesman, I. I. (1963). Genetic aspects of intelligent behavior. In N. Ellis (Ed.), *Handbook of mental deficiency* (pp. 253–296). New York: McGraw-Hill.

Gottfredson, L. S. (1981). Circumscription and compromise: A developmental theory of occupational aspirations. *Journal of Counseling Psychology, 28,* 545–579.

Gottfredson, L. S. (2002). Gottfredson's theory of circumscription, compromise and self-creation. In D. Brown & Associates (Eds.), *Career choice and development* (4th ed., pp. 85–148). San Francisco: Jossey-Bass.

Gray-Little, B., & Hafdahl, A. R. (2000). Factors influencing racial comparisons of self-esteem: A quantitative review. *Psychological Bulletin, 126,* 26–54.

Green, M., & Piel, J. A. (2002). *Theories of human development: A comparative approach.* Boston: Allyn & Bacon.

Greenberg, K. R. (2003). *Group counseling in K–12 schools: A handbook for school counselors.* Boston: Allyn & Bacon.

Grolnick, W. S., & Apostoleris, N. H. (2002). What makes parents controlling? In E. L. Deci & R. M. Ryan (Eds.), *Handbook of self-determination research* (pp. 161–181). Rochester, NY: University of Rochester Press.

Groth-Marnat, G. (2003). *Handbook of psychological assessment* (4th ed.). Hoboken, NJ: Wiley.

Guba, E. G., & Lincoln, Y. S. (1994). Competing paradigms in qualitative research. In N. K. Denzin & Y. S. Lincoln (Eds.), *Handbook of qualitative research* (pp. 105–117). Thousand Oaks, CA: Sage.

Guerney, B. (1977). *Relationship enhancement.* San Francisco: Jossey-Bass.

Gysbers, N. C., & Henderson, P. (2000). *Developing and managing your school guidance program* (3rd ed.). Alexandria, VA: American Counseling Association.

Gysbers, N. C., & Moore, E. J. (1981). *Improving guidance programs.* Englewood Cliffs, NJ: Prentice-Hall.

Gyspbers, N. C., Heppner, M. J., & Johnston, J. A. (2003). *Career counseling: Process, issues, and techniques* (2nd ed.). Boston: Allyn & Bacon.

Hackett, G., & Betz, N. E. (1981). A self-efficacy approach to the career development of women. *Journal of Vocational Behavior, 18,* 326–339.

Hackett, G., Betz, N. E., Casas, J. M., & Rocha-Singh, I. A. (1992). Gender, ethnicity, and social cognitive factors predicting the academic achievement of students in engineering. *Journal of Counseling Psychology, 39,* 527–538.

Hackney, H. L., & Goodyear, R. K. (1984). Carl Rogers' client-centered supervision. In R. F. Levant & J. M. Schlep (Eds.), *Client-centered therapy and the person-centered approach* (pp. 278–297). New York: Praeger.

Hadden, S. B. (1955). Historic background of group psychotherapy. *International Journal of Group Psychotherapy, 5,* 162–168.

Haley, J. (1973). Approaches to family therapy. In J. Haley (Ed.), *Changing families: A family therapy reader* (pp. 227–236). New York: Grune & Stratton.

Haley, J. (1980). *Leaving home.* New York: McGraw-Hill.

Haley, J. (1987). *Problem solving therapy* (2nd ed.). New York: Harper Colophon.

Haley, T. (2002). The fit between reflecting teams and a social constructionist approach. *Journal of Systemic Therapies, 21,* 20–40.

Hall, C. S., & Lindzey, G. (1978). *Theories of personality* (3rd ed.). New York: Wiley.

Hanna, D. (1988). *Designing Organizations for high performance.* Reading, MA: Addison-Wesley.

Hanna, F. J., & Bemak, F. (1997). The quest for identity in the counseling profession. *Counselor Education and Supervision, 36,* 194–206.

Hansen, J. C., Himes, B. S., & Meier, S. (1990). *Consultation: Concepts and practice.* Englewood Cliffs, NJ: Prentice-Hall.

Hansen, J. C., Warner, R. W., & Smith, E. J. (1980). *Group counseling: Theory and process* (2nd ed.). Chicago: Rand McNally.

Hardin, E. E., Leong, F. T. L., & Osipow, S. H. (2001). Cultural relativity in the conceptualization of career maturity. *Journal of Vocational Behavior, 58,* 36–52.

Hare, P., & Naveh, D. (1984). Group development at the Camp David Summit. *Small Group Behavior, 15,* 299–318.

Hare-Mustin, R. T. (1978). A feminist approach to family therapy. *Family Process, 17,* 181–194.

Hare-Mustin, R. (1986). The problem of gender in family therapy theory. *Family Process, 26,* 15–27.

Hare-Mustin, R. T. (1994). Discourses in the mirrored room: A postmodern analysis of therapy. *Family Process, 33,* 19–35.

Harlow, H. F. (1958). The nature of love. *American Psychologist, 13,* 673–685.

Harmon, L. W., Hansen, J. C., Borgen, F. H., & Hammer, A. I. (1994). *Strong Interest Inventory: Applications and technical guide.* Palo Alto, CA: Consulting Psychologists Press.

Harper, F. D., & McFadden, J. (2003). *Culture and counseling: New approaches.* Boston: Pearson Education.

Harrington, T., & O'Shea, A. (1992). *Harrington–O'Shea career decision making system.* Circle Pines, MN: American Guidance Service.

Harrison, T. C. (2004). *Consultation for contemporary helping professionals.* Boston: Pearson/Allyn & Bacon.

Hart, G., Borders, L. D., Nance, D., & Paradise, L. (1995). Ethical guidelines for counseling supervisors. *Counselor Education and Supervision, 34,* 270–276.

Harter, S. (1999). *The construction of self: A developmental perspective.* New York: Guilford.

Hartung, P. J., Vandiver, B. J., Leong, F. T. L., Pope, M., Niles, S. G., & Farrow, B. (1998). Appraising cultural identity in career-development assessment and counseling. *Career Development Quarterly, 46,* 276–293.

Haskell, M. R. (1975). *Socioanalysis: Self-direction via sociometry and psychodrama.* Long Beach, CA: Role Training Associates.

Hathaway, S. R., & McKinley, J. C. (1983). *The Minnesota Multiphasic Personality Inventory manual.* New York: Psychological Corporation.

Hattie, J. A., Myers, J. E., & Sweeney, T. J. (2004). A factor structure of wellness: Theory, assessment, analysis, and practice. *Journal of Counseling & Development, 82,* 354–364.

Hawkins, P., & Shohet, R. (1989). *Supervision in the helping professions.* Milton Keynes, UK: Open University Press.

Hawkins, P., & Shohet, R. (2000). *Supervision in the helping professions* (2nd ed.). Philadelphia: Open University Press.

Haynes, R., Corey, G., & Moulton, P. (2003). *Clinical supervision in the helping professions: A practical guide.* Pacific Grove, CA: Brooks/Cole.

Heath, S. B. (1983). *Ways with words.* Cambridge, UK: Cambridge University Press.

Heider, F. (1958). *The psychology of interpersonal relations.* New York: Wiley.

Held, B. S. (1990). What's in a name? Some confusions and concerns about constructivism. *Journal of Marital and Family Therapy, 16,* 179–186.

Helms, J. E. (1984). Toward a theoretical explanation of the effects of race on counseling: A Black and White model. *Counseling Psychologist, 12,* 153–165.

Helms, J. E. (1992). Why is there no study of cultural equivalence in standardized cognitive ability testing? *American Psychologist, 47,* 1083–1101.

Helms, J. E. (1993). *Black and White racial identity: Theory, research and practice.* Westport, CT: Praeger.

Helms, J. E. (1995). An update of Helms' White and people of color racial identity models. In J. G. Ponterotto, J. M. Casas, L. A. Suzuki, & C. M. Alexander (Eds.), *Handbook of multicultural counseling* (pp. 181–198). Thousand Oaks, CA: Sage.

Helms, J. E., & Cook, D. A. (1999). *Using race and culture in counseling and psychotherapy: Theory and process.* Needham Heights, MA: Allyn & Bacon.

Helms, J. E., & Piper, R. E. (1994). Implications of racial identity theory for vocational psychology. *Journal of Vocational Behavior, 44,* 124–138.

Hendricks, J. E., McKean, J., & Hendricks, C. G. (2003). *Crisis intervention: Contemporary issues for on-site interveners.* Springfield, IL: Thomas.

Heppner, P. P., & Heppner, M. J. (2004). *Writing and publishing your thesis, dissertation, and research: A guide for students in the helping professions.* Toronto: Brooks/Cole.

Herlihy, B., & Corey, G. (1996). *ACA ethical standards casebook* (5th ed.). Alexandria, VA: American Counseling Association.

Herlihy, B., & Sheeley, V. L. (1988). Counselor liability and the duty to warn: Selected cases, statutory trends, and implications for practice. *Counselor Education and Supervision, 27,* 203–215.

Herr, E. L. (2003). Historical roots and future issues. In B. T. Erford (Ed.), *Transforming the school counseling profession* (pp. 21–38). Upper Saddle River, NJ: Pearson Education.

Hess, A. K. (1986). Growth in supervision: Stages of supervisee and supervisor development. *Clinical Supervisor, 4,* 51–67.

Hettler, W. (2006). *Hettler.com.* Retrieved October 27, 2006 from http://www/hettler.com

Hill, C. E., & O'Brien, K. M. (1999). *Helping skills: Facilitating exploration, insight, and action.* Washington, DC: American Psychological Association.

Hill, G. W. (2002). *Critical friendship.* Australia: Mottram d'Hill & Associates.

Hill, M. R. (1993). *Archival strategies and techniques.* Newbury Park, CA: Sage.

Hobbs, N. (1951). Group-centered psychotherapy. In C. R. Rogers (Ed.), *Client-centered therapy* (pp. 278–319). Boston: Houghton-Mifflin.

Hodder, I. (2000). The interpretation of documents and material culture. In N. K. Denzin & Y. S. Lincoln (Eds.), *Handbook of qualitative research* (2nd ed., pp. 703–716). Thousand Oaks, CA: Sage.

Hoff, L. A. (1995). *People in crisis: Understanding and helping* (4th ed.). San Francisco: Jossey-Bass.

Holland, J. L. (1959). A theory of vocational choice. *Journal of Counseling Psychology, 6,* 35–45.

Holland, J. L. (1985a). *Making vocational choices: A theory of vocational personalities and work environments* (2nd ed.). Englewood Cliffs, NJ: Prentice-Hall.

Holland, J. L. (1985b). *Vocational preference inventory.* Odessa, FL: Psychological Assessment Resources.

Holland, J. L. (1994). *Self-directed search.* Odessa, FL: Psychological Assessment Resources.

Hollander, M., & Kazaoka, K. (1988). Behavior therapy groups. In S. Long (Ed.), *Six group therapies* (pp. 257–326). New York: Plenum.

Holloway, E. L. (1995). *Clinical supervision: A systems approach.* Thousand Oaks, CA: Sage.

Holloway, E. L. (1997). Structures for the analysis and teaching of psychotherapy. In C. E. Watkins, Jr. (Ed.), *Handbook of psychotherapy supervision* (pp. 249–276). New York: Wiley.

Holloway, E., & Carrol, M. (Eds.). (1999). *Training counselling supervisors: Strategies, methods and techniques.* London: Sage.

Homan, M. S. (2004). *Promoting community change: Making it happen in the real world* (3rd ed.). Pacific Grove, CA: Brooks/Cole.

Hooker, E. (1957). The adjustment of the male overt homosexual. *Journal of Projective Techniques, 21,* 18–31.

Horn, J. L. (1968). Organization of abilities and the development of intelligence. *Psychological Review, 75,* 242–259.

Hoyt, M. F. (1994). Competency-based, future-oriented therapy. In M. F. Hoyt (Ed.), *Constructive therapies* (Vol. 1, pp. 1–10). New York: Guilford.

Ibrahim, F. A. (1985). Effective cross-cultural counseling and psychotherapy: A framework. *The Counseling Psychologist, 13,* 625–638.

Ibrahim, F. A. (1991). Contribution of cultural worldview to generic counseling and development. *Journal of Counseling and Development, 70,* 13–18.

Idol, L., Nevin, A., & Paolucci-Whitcomb, P. (2000). *Collaborative consultation* (3rd ed.). Austin, TX: PRO-ED.

Ilardi, S. S. (2002). The cognitive neuroscience framework and its implications for behavior therapy: Clarifying some important misconceptions. *The Behavior Therapist, 25,* 87–90.

Imber, M., & Van Geel, T. (2004). *Education law* (3rd ed.). Mahwah, NJ: Lawrence Erlbaum Associates, Inc.

Individuals with Disabilities Education Act, 20, U.S.C, & Sect. 1400, et. seq. I.D.E.A. (1997).

Inhelder, B., & Piaget, J. (1958). *The growth of logical thinking from childhood to adolescence: An essay on the construction of formal operational structures.* New York: Basic Books.

Isaacson, L. E., & Brown, D. (2000). *Career information, career counseling, and career development.* Needham Heights, MA: Allyn & Bacon.

Isabella, R. A., Belsky, J., & von Eye, A. (1989). Origins of infant–mother attachment: An examination of interactional synchrony during the infant's first year. *Developmental Psychology, 25,* 12–21.

Ivey, A. E. (1986). *Developmental therapy: Theory into practice.* San Francisco: Jossey-Bass

Ivey, A. E., D'Andrea, M., Ivey, M. B., & Simek-Morgan, L. (2002). *Theories of counseling and psychotherapy: A multicultural perspective* (5th ed.). Boston: Allyn & Bacon.

Ivey, A. E., & Ivey, M. B. (1998). Reframing *DSM–IV*: Positive strategies from developmental counseling and therapy. *Journal of Counseling and Development, 76,* 334–350.

Ivey, A. E., & Ivey, M. B. (2003). *Intentional interviewing and counseling: Facilitating client development in a multicultural society* (5th ed.). Pacific Grove, CA: Brooks/Cole.

Ivey, A., & Ivey, M. (2007). *Intentional interviewing and counseling* (6th ed.). Belmont, CA: Thomson/Brooks/Cole.

Ivey, A. E., Ivey, M., Myers, P., & Sweeney, T., (2005). *Developmental counseling and therapy.* Boston: Lahaska Press.

Ivey, A. E., Normington, C. J., Miller, C., Morrill, W., & Hause, R. (1968). Microcounseling and attending behavior: An approach to prepracticum counselor training. *Journal of Counseling Psychology, 15*(5), 1–12.

Ivey, A. E., Rigazio-DiGilio, S. A., & Ivey, M. B. (2005). The standard cognitive developmental interview. In A. Ivey, M. B. Ivey, J. Myers, & T. Sweeney (Eds.), *Developmental counseling and therapy: Promoting wellness over the lifespan* (pp. 201–213). Boston: Lahaska Press.

Jackson, B. (1975). Black identity development. *MEFORM: Journal of Educational Diversity & Innovation, 2,* 19–25.

Jackson, D. N. (1991). *Jackson Vocational Interest Survey.* Port Huron, MI: Sigma Assessment Systems.

Jackson, D. N., & Hayes, D. H. (1993). Multicultural issues in consultation. *Journal of Counseling and Development, 72,* 144–147.

Jackson, J. S., & Sellers, S. L. (1997). Psychological, social, and cultural perspectives on minority health in adolescence: A life-course framework. In D. K. Wilson, J. R. Rodriguez, & W. C. Taylor (Eds.), *Health-promoting and health-compromising behaviors among minority adolescents* (pp. 29–54). Washington, DC: American Psychological Association.

Jacobs, E. E., Masson, R. L., & Harvill, R. L. (2002). *Group counseling: Strategies and skills* (4th ed.). Pacific Grove, CA: Wadsworth.

Jacobs, J. L., & Capps, D. (Eds.). (1997). *Religion, society, and psychoanalysis.* Boulder, CO: Westview.

James, R. K., & Gilliland, B. E. (2005). *Crisis intervention strategies* (5th ed.). Pacific Grove, CA: Brooks/Cole.

James, W. (1961). *The varieties of religious experience.* New York: Macmillan Collier. (Original work published 1902)

Jaschik, S. (2005). Different kinds of diversity. *Inside Higher Ed.* Retrieved July 9, 2006, from http://www.insidehighered.com/news/2005/08/22/counseling

Jennings, L., & Skovholt, T. M. (1999). The cognitive, emotional, and relational characteristics of master therapists. *Journal of Counseling Psychology, 46,* 3–11.

Johnson, M. J., Swartz, J. L., & Martin, W. E., Jr. (1995). Applications of psychological theories of career development with Native Americans. In F. T. L. Leong (Ed.), *Career development and vocational behavior of racial and ethnic minorities* (pp. 103–133). Mahwah, NJ: Lawrence Erlbaum Associates, Inc.

Johnson, S. M., Smith, P. C., & Tucker, S. M. (1982). Response format of the Job Descriptive Index: Assessment of reliability and validity by the multitrait–multimethod matrix. *Journal of Applied Psychology, 67,* 500–505.

Johnson, S. W., & Combs, D. C. (2001). Factors associated with the inclusion of managed care concepts in the curricula of master's level counselor preparation. *TCA Journal, 29*(1), 88–96.

Jones, E. (1993). *Family systems therapy: Developments in the Milan-systemic therapies.* New York: Wiley.

Jung, C. G. (1928). *Contributions to analytic psychology.* New York: Harcourt.

Jung, C. G. (1957). *The undiscovered self.* New York: Penguin.

Jung, C. G. (1958/1973). *Answer to job* (R. F. C. Hull, Trans.) Princeton, NJ: Bolligen Series, Princeton University Press.

Jung, C. G. (1965). *Memories, dreams, reflections.* New York: Vintage Books.

Juntunen, C. L., Atkinson, D. R., & Tierney, G. (2003). School counselors and school psychologists as school–home–community liaisons in ethnically diverse schools. In P. B. Pedersen & J. C. Carey (Eds.), *Multicultural counseling in schools: A practical handbook* (pp. 149–168). Boston: Pearson Education.

Kadushin, A. (1992). *Supervision in social work* (3rd ed.). New York: Columbia University Press.

Kagan, N. (1976). *Influencing human interaction.* Mason, MI: Mason Media.

Kagan, N. (1980). Influencing human interaction—Eighteen years with IPR. In A. K. Hess (Ed.), *Psychotherapy supervision: Theory, research and practice* (pp. 262–286). New York: Wiley.

Kalodner, C. R. (1995). Cognitive-behavioral theories. In D. Capuzzi & D. R. Gross (Eds.), *Counseling and psychotherapy: Theories and interventions* (pp. 353–384). Columbus, OH: Prentice-Hall.

Kasser, V. M., & Ryan, R. M. (1999). The relation of psychological needs for autonomy and relatedness to health, vitality, well-being and mortality in a nursing home. *Journal of Applied Social Psychology, 29,* 935–954.

Kell, B. L., & Mueller, W. J. (1966). *Impact and change: A study of counseling relationships.* Englewood Cliffs, NJ: Prentice-Hall.

Keller, H. R. (1988). Behavioral consultation. In J. Conoley (Ed.), *Consultation in schools* (pp. 59–100). New York: Academic Press.

Kelley, H. H. (1967). Attribution in social psychology. *Nebraska Symposium on Motivation, 15,* 192–238.

Kelly, E. W., Jr. (1995). *Spirituality and religion in counseling and psychotherapy: Diversity in theory and practice.* Alexandria, VA: American Counseling Association.

Kenyon, B. L. (2001). Current research in children's conceptions of death: A critical review. *Omega, 43,* 63–91.

Kern, C. W. (1999). Professional school counselors: Inservice providers who can change the school environment. *NASSP Bulletin,* 603–10–18.

Kerr, M. E. (1985). Obstacles to differentiation of self. In A. D. Gurman (Ed.), *Casebook of marital therapy* (pp. 111–154). New York: Guilford.

Kerwin, C., Ponterotto, J. G., Jackson, B. L., & Harris, A. (1993). Racial identity in biracial children: A qualitative investigation. *Journal of Counseling Psychology, 40,* 221–231.

Kinicki, A. J., Mckee-Ryan, F. M., Schriesheim, C. A., & Carson, K. P. (2002) Assessing the construct validity of the Job Descriptive Index: A review and meta-analysis. *Journal of Applied Psychology, 87,* 14–32.

Kitchener, K. S. (1984). Intuition, critical evaluation and ethical principles: The foundation for ethical decisions in counseling psychology. *Counseling Psychologist, 12,* 43–55.

Kivlighan, D. M., Coleman, M. N., & Anderson, D. C. (2000). Process, outcomes and methodology in group counseling research. In S. D. Brown & R. Lent (Eds.), *Handbook of counseling psychology* (3rd ed.). New York: Wiley.

Kivlighan, D. M., Coleman, M. N., & Anderson, D. C. (2000). Process, outcomes and methodology in group counseling research. In S. D. Brown & R. Lent (Eds.), *Handbook of counseling psychology* (3rd ed.). New York: John Wiley.

Kivlighan, D. M., & Holmes, S. E. (2004) The importance of therapeutic factors: A typology of therapeutic factors studies. In J. L. DeLucia-Waack, D. A. Gerrity, C. R. Kalodner, & M. T. Riva (Eds.), *Handbook of group counseling and psychotherapy* (pp. 23–36). Thousand Oaks, CA: Sage.

Kivlighan, D. M., Jr., & Mullison, D. (1988). Participants' perceptions of therapeutic factors in group counseling: The role of interpersonal style and stage of group development. *Small Group Behavior, 19,* 452–468.

Kleckner, T., Frank, L., Bland, C., Amendt, J., & Bryant, R. (1992). The myth of the unfeeling strategic therapist. *Journal of Marital and Family Therapy, 18,* 41–51.

Kleespies, P. M., & Blackburn, E. J. (1998). The emergency telephone call. In P. M. Kleespies (Ed.), *Emergencies in mental health practices: Evaluation and management* (pp. 174–195). New York: Guilford.

Kleespies, P. M., Deleppo, J. D., Mori, D. L., & Niles, B. L. (1998). The emergency interview. In P. M. Kleespies (Ed.), *Emergencies in mental health practices: Evaluation and management* (pp. 41–74). New York: Guilford.

Kluckhohn, F. R., & Strodtbeck, F. L. (1961). *Variations in value orientations.* Evanston, IL: Row, Patterson.

Knapp, R. R., & Knapp, L. (1992). *Career occupational preference survey.* San Diego: CA. EDITS.

Knudson-Martin, C. (1994). The female voice: Applications to Bowen's family systems theory. *Journal of Marital and Family Therapy, 20,* 35–46.

Knudson-Martin, C. (2002). Expanding Bowen's legacy to family therapy: A response to Horne and Hicks. *Journal of Marital and Family Therapy, 28,* 115–118.

Kolski, T. D., Avriette, M., & Jongsma, A. E., Jr. (2001). *The crisis counseling and traumatic events treatment planner.* New York: Wiley.

Koper, R. J., & Jaasma, M. A. (2001). Interpersonal style: Are human social orientations guided by generalized interpersonal needs? *Communication Reports, 14,* 117–130.

Korkman, M., Kirk, U., & Kemp, S. (1997). *NEPSY.* San Antonio, TX: Psychological Corporation.

Kottler, J. A. (2000). *Nuts and bolts of helping.* Needham Heights, MA: Allyn & Bacon.

Kreidler, M. C., & England, D. B. (1990). Empowerment through group support: Adult women who are survivors of incest. *Journal of Family Violence, 5,* 35–41.

Krumboltz, J. D. (1996). A learning theory of career counseling. In M. L. W. Savickas & W. Bruce (Ed.), *Handbook of career counseling theory and practice* (pp. 55–80). Palo Alto, CA: Davies-Black.

Krumboltz, J. D., & Thoresen, C. E. (1969). *Behavioral counseling: Cases and techniques.* New York: Holt, Rinehart & Winston.

Krushinski, M. F. (2005). A comparison of the perceptions of the importance of formal supervision training between formally trained counselor supervisors and non-formally trained counselor supervisors. *Dissertation Abstracts International,* 65(10), 12142004–132220.

Kübler-Ross, E. (1969). *On death and dying.* New York: Macmillan.

Kuhn, D. (1999). Metacognitive development. *Current Directions in Psychological Science, 9,* 178–181.

Kurpius, D. J. (1978). Consultation theory and process: An integrated model. *Personal and Guidance Journal, 56,* 335–338.

Kurpius, D., Fuqua, D., & Rozecki, T. (1993). The consulting process: A multidimensional approach. *Journal of Counseling and Development, 71,* 601–606.

Kurpius, D. J., & Robinson, S. E. (1978). An overview of consultation. *Personal and Guidance Journal, 56,* 321–323.

Kvale, S. (1996). *InterViews: An introduction to qualitative research interviewing.* Thousand Oaks, CA: Sage.

Laatsch, L., Pavel, D., Jobe, T., Lin, Q., & Quintana, J. C. (1999). Incorporation of SPECT imaging in a longitudinal cognitive rehabilitation therapy programme. *Brain Injury, 13,* 555–570.

Ladany, N., Brittan-Powell, C. S., & Pannau, R. K. (1997). The influence of supervisory racial identity interaction and racial matching on the supervisory working alliance and supervisee multicultural competence. *Counselor Education and Supervision, 36,* 284–304.

Ladany, N., Constantine, M. G., Miller, K., Erickson, C. D., & Muse-Burke, J. L. (2000). Supervisor countertransference: A qualitative investigation into its identification and description. *Journal of Counseling Psychology, 47,* 102–115.

Ladany, N., Inman, A. G., Constantine, M. G., & Nutt, E. A. (1997). Supervisee multicultural case conceptualization ability and self-reported multicultural competence as functions of supervisee racial identity and supervisor focus. *Journal of Counseling Psychology, 44,* 284–293.

Lafreniere, P. J. (2000). *Emotional development: A biosocial perspective.* Belmont, CA: Wadsworth.

Lambers, E. (2000). Supervision in person-centered therapy: Facilitating congruence. In E. Mearns & B. Thorne (Eds.), *Person-centered therapy today: New frontiers in theory and practice* (pp. 196–211). London: Sage.

Lancy, D. F. (1993). *Qualitative research in education: An introduction to the major traditions.* New York: Longman.

Landauer, T. K., & Bjork, R. A. (1978). Optimum rehearsal patterns and name learning. In M. M. Gruneberg, P. E. Morris, & R. N. Sykes (Eds.), *Practical aspects of memory* (pp. 625–632). London: Academic.

Lang, F. R., Staudinger, U. M., & Carstensen, L. L. (1998). Perspectives on socioemotional selectivity in late life: How personality and social context do (and do not) make a difference. *Journal of Gerontology, 53,* 21–30.

Larson, D. (1984). *Teaching psychological skills: Models for giving psychology away.* Belmont, CA: Brooks/Cole.

Larson, D. D. (1999). The conceptualization of health. *Medical Care Research and Review, 56,* 123–136.

Latner, J. (1973). *The Gestalt therapy book.* New York: Julian Press.

Lawless, L. L., Ginter, E. J., & Kelly, K. R., (1999). Managed care: What mental health counselors need to know. *Journal of Mental Health Counseling, 21,* 50–65.

Lawrence-Lightfoot, S., & Davis, J. H. (1997). *The art and science of portraiture.* San Francisco: Jossey-Bass.

Lazarus, A. A. (1981). *The practice of multi-modal therapy.* New York: McGraw-Hill.

Lazarus, A. A. (1989). *The practice of multi-modal therapy.* Baltimore: Johns Hopkins University Press.

Lazarus, R. S., & Lazarus, B. N. (1994). *Passion and reason.* New York: Oxford University Press.

Lebovici, S. (1995). Creativity and the infant's competence. *Infant Mental Health Journal, 16,* 10–15.

LeCompte, M. (2002). The transformation of ethnographic practice: Past and current challenges. *Qualitative Research, 2,* 283–299.

Lent, R. W., Brown, S. D., & Hackett, G. (1994). Toward a unifying social cognitive theory of career and academic interest, choice and performance. *Journal of Vocational Behavior, 45,* 79–122.

Lent, R. W., Brown, S. D., & Hackett, G. (2000). Contextual supports and barriers to career choice: A social cognitive analysis. *Journal of Counseling Psychology, 47,* 36–49.

Leong, F. T. L. (1993). The career counseling process with racial/ethnic minorities: The case of Asian Americans. *Career Development Quarterly, 42,* 26–40.

Leong, F. T. L. (1995). *Career development and vocational behavior of racial and ethnic minorities.* Mahwah, NJ: Lawrence Erlbaum Associates, Inc.

Leong, F. T. L. (1996). Toward an integrative model for cross-cultural counseling and psychotherapy. *Applied and Preventative Psychology, 5,* 189–209.

Leong, F. T. L. (1998). Career development and vocational behaviors. In L. Lee & N. Zane (Eds.), *Asian American psychology handbook* (pp. 359–398). Thousand Oaks, CA: Sage.

Leong, F. T. L., & Brown, M. T. (1995). Theoretical issues in cross cultural career development: Cultural validity and cultural specificity. In W. B. Walsh & S. H. Osipow (Eds.), *Handbook of vocational psychology: Theory, research and practice* (2nd ed., pp. 143–180). Mahwah, NJ: Lawrence Erlbaum Associates, Inc.

Leong, F. T. L., & Chou, E. L. (1994). The role of ethnic identity and acculturation in the vocational behavior of Asian Americans: An integrative review. *Journal of Vocational Behavior, 44,* 155–172.

Leong, F., & Hardin, E. (2002). Career psychology and Asian Americans: Cultural validity and cultural specificity. In G. C. Nagayama Hall &S. Okazaki (Eds.), *Asian American psychology: The science of lives in context* (pp. 131–152). Washington, DC: American Psychological Association.

Leong, F. T. L., & Hartung, P. J. (1997). Career assessment with culturally different clients: Proposing an integrative-sequential conceptual framework for cross-cultural career counseling research and practice. *Journal of Career Assessment, 5,* 183–202.

Leong, F. T. L., & Hartung, P. J. (2003). Cross-cultural career counseling. In G. Bernal, J. E. Trimble, A. K. Burlew, & F. T. L. Leong (Eds.), *Handbook of racial and ethnic minority psychology* (pp. 504–520). Thousand Oaks, CA: Sage.

Leong, F. T. L., & Serafica, F. C. (1995). Career development of Asian Americans: A research area in need of a good theory. In F. T. L. Leong (Ed.), *Career development and vocational of racial and ethnic minorities* (pp. 67–102). Mahwah, NJ: Lawrence Erlbaum Associates, Inc.

Leong, F. T. L., & Tata, S. P. (1990). Sex and acculturation differences in occupational values among Chinese American children. *Journal of Counseling Psychology, 37,* 208–212.

Leung, S. A. (1993). Circumscription and compromise: A replication study with Asian Americans. *Journal of Counseling Psychology, 40,* 188–193.

Leung, S. A., Ivey, D., & Suzuki, L. (1994). Factors affecting the career aspirations of Asian Americans. *Journal of Counseling & Development, 72,* 404–410.

Levers, L. L. (1997). Counseling as a recursive dynamic: Relationship and process, meaning-making and empowerment. In T. F. Riggar & D. R. Maki (Eds.), *Rehabilitation counseling: Profession and practice* (2nd ed., pp. 170–182). New York: Springer.

Levine, B., Robertson, I. A., Clare, L., Carter, G., Hong, J., Wilson, B. A., et al. (2000). Rehabilitation of executive functioning: An experimental-clinical validation of goal management training. *Journal of the International Neuropsychological Society, 6,* 299–312.

Levinson, D. J. (1978). *The seasons of a man's life*. New York: Knopf.

Lewin, K. (1951). *Field theory in social science*. New York: Harper.

Lewin, K., Lippitt, R., & White, R. K. (1939). Patterns of aggressive behavior in experimentally created social climates. *Journal of Social Psychology, 10*, 271–299.

Lewis, J., Lewis, M., Daniels, J., & D'Andrea, M. (2003). *Community counseling: Empowerment strategies for a diverse society* (3rd ed.). Pacific Grove, CA: Brooks/Cole.

Lezak, M. D., Howieson, D. B., & Loring, D. W. (2004). *Neuropsychological assessment*. New York: Oxford University Press.

Libow, J., Raskin, P., & Caust, B. (1982). Feminist and family systems theory: Are they irreconcilable? *American Journal of Family Therapy, 10*(3), 3–12.

Liddle, H. A., Becker, D., & Diamond, G. M. (1997). Family therapy supervision. In C. E. Watkins, Jr. (Ed.), *Handbook of psychotherapy supervision* (pp. 400–421). New York: Wiley.

Lieberman, M. A., Yalom, I. D., & Miles, M. B. (1973). *Encounter groups: First facts*. New York: Basic Books.

Liese, B. S., & Beck, J. S. (1997). Cognitive therapy supervision. In C. E. Watkins (Ed.), *Handbook of psychotherapy supervision* (pp. 114–133). New York: Wiley.

Lincoln, Y. S., & Guba, E. G. (1985). *Naturalistic inquiry*. Newbury Park, CA: Sage.

Lincoln, Y. S., & Guba, E. G. (2000). Paradigmatic controversies, contradictions, and emerging confluences. In N. K. Denzin & Y. S. Lincoln (Eds.), *Handbook of qualitative research* (2nd ed., pp. 163–188). Thousand Oaks, CA: Sage.

Lindemann, E. (1944). Symptomatology and management of acute grief. *American Journal of Psychiatry, 101*, 141–148.

Littrell, J. M., Lee-Borden, N., & Lorenz, J. A. (1979). A developmental framework for counseling supervision. *Counselor Education and Supervision, 19*, 119–136.

Locke, E. A., & Latham, G. P. (1990). *A theory of goal setting and task performance*. Englewood Cliffs, NJ: Prentice-Hall.

Loganbill, C., Hardy, E., & Delworth, U. (1982). Supervision: A conceptual model. *Counseling Psychologist, 10*, 3–42.

Lohr, J. M., Montgomery, R. W., Lilienfeld, S. O., & Tolin, D. F. (1999). Pseudoscience and the commercial promotion of trauma treatments. In R. Gist & B. Lubin (Eds.), *Response to disaster: Psychosocial, community, and ecological approaches* (pp. 291–326). Philadelphia: Brunner/Mazel.

Lovell, K. (2000). Behavioural psychotherapy. In C. Feltham & I. Horton (Eds.), *Handbook of counseling and psychotherapy* (pp. 314–320). London: Sage.

Luria, A. R. (1981). *Language and cognition*. Washington, DC: Winston.

Luthar, S. S., Cicchetti, D., & Becker, B. (2000). The construct of resilience: A critical evaluation and guidelines for future work. *Child Development, 71*, 543–562.

Lynch, M. F., Plant, R. W., & Ryan, R. M. (2005). Psychological needs and threat to safety: Implications for staff and patients in a psychiatric hospital for youth. *Professional Psychology: Research and Practice, 36*, 415–425.

MacCluskie, K. C., & Ingersoll, R. E. (2001). *Becoming a 21st century agency counselor: Personal and professional explorations*. Belmont, CA: Brooks/Cole.

Maccoby, E. E., & Martin, J. A. (1983). Socialization in the context of the family: Parent–child interaction. In E. M. Hetherington (Ed.), *Handbook of child psychology: Vol. 4. Socialization, personality, and social development* (4th ed., pp 1–101). New York: Wiley.

MacKenzie, K. R. (1987). Therapeutic factors in group psychotherapy: A contemporary view. *Group, 11*, 26–34.

MacKenzie, K. R. (1994). Group development. In A. Fuhriman & G. M. Burlingame (Eds.), *Handbook of group psychotherapy: An empirical and clinical synthesis* (pp. 559–562). New York: Wiley.

Madanes, C. (1981). *Strategic family therapy*. San Francisco: Jossey-Bass.

Maddox, G. L. (1963). Activity and morale: A longitudinal study of selected elderly subjects. *Social Forces, 42*, 195–204.

Main, M., & Solomon, J. (1986). Discovery of an insecure, disorganized/disoriented attachment pattern: Procedures, findings, and implications for the classification of behavior. In M. Yogman & T. B. Brazelton (Eds.), *Affective development in infancy* (pp. 95–124). Norwood, NJ: Ablex.

Manaster, G. G., & Corsini, R. J. (1982). *Individual psychology: Theory and practice*. Itasca, IL: Peacock.

Manly, T., Ward, S., & Robertson, I. (2002). The rehabilitation of attention. In P. J. Eslinger (Ed.), *Neuropsychological interventions: Clinical research and practice* (pp. 105–136). New York: Guilford.

Marcia, J. E. (1980). Identity in adolescence. In J. Adelson (Ed.), *Handbook of adolescent psychology* (pp. 159–187). New York: Wiley.

Marcus, D. K. (1998). Studying group dynamics with the social relations model. *Group Dynamics: Theory, Research, and Practice, 2*, 230–240.

Marek, L. I., Sandifer, D. M., Beach, A., Coward, R. L., & Protinsky, H. O. (1994). Supervision without the problem: A model of solution-focused supervision. *Journal of Family Psychotherapy, 5*, 57–64.

Markland, D., Ryan, R. M., Tobin, V. J., & Rollnick, S. (2005). Motivational interviewing and self-determination theory. *Journal of Social and Clinical Psychology, 24*, 811–831.

Martin, F. (1985). The development of systemic family therapy and its place in the field. In A. Bentovim, G. G. Barnes, & A. Cooklin (Series Eds.) & D. Campbell & R. Draper (Vol. Eds.), *Complementary frameworks of theory and practice: Vol. 3. Applications of systemic family therapy: The Milan approach* (pp. 11–22). London: Grune & Stratton.

Martin, P. (1998). *Transforming school counseling*. Unpublished manuscript. Washington, DC: The Education Trust.

Martin, S. D., Martin, E., Rai, S. S., Richardson, M. A., Royall, R., & Eng, C. (2001). Brain blood flow changes in depressed clients treated with interpersonal psychotherapy or velafaxine hydrochloride: Preliminary findings. *Archives of General Psychiatry, 58*, 641–648.

Maslow, A. (1962). *Toward a psychology of being*. New York: Van Nostrand.

Maslow, A. H. (1943). A theory of human motivation. *Psychological Review, 50*, 370–396.

Matthews, D. A., & Clark, C. (1998). *The faith factor: Proof of the healing power of prayer*. New York: Viking.

May, K. (1998). A feminist and multicultural perspective in family therapy. *The Family Journal: Counseling and Therapy for Couples and Families, 6*, 123–124.

May, R. (1969). *Love and will*. New York: Dell.

May, R. (1972). *Power and innocence: A search for the sources of violence*. New York: Dell.

May, R. (1981). *Freedom and destiny*. New York: Norton.

Mazur, J. E. (2002). *Learning and behavior* (5th ed.). Upper Saddle River, NJ: Prentice-Hall.

McAuliffe, G. J., Eriksen, K. P., & Associates. (2000). *Preparing counselors and therapists: Creating constructivist and developmental programs*. Alexandria, VA: Association for Counselor Education and Supervision.

McDermott, J. F. (1989). Book forum: Family evaluation. *The American Journal of Psychiatry, 146*, 1503–1504.

McFarlane, A. C. (2000). Can debriefing work? Critical appraisal of theories of intervention and outcomes, with directions for future research. In B. Raphael & J. P. Wilson (Eds.), *Psychological debriefing: Theory, practice, and evidence* (pp. 327–336). Cambridge, UK: Cambridge University Press.

McGinn, L. (1998). Interview: Otto F. Kernberg. *American Journal of Psychotherapy, 52,* 191–201.

McGoldrick, M., Giordano, J., & Pearce, J. K. (Eds.). (1996). *Ethnicity and family therapy.* New York: Guilford.

McGoldrick, M., Heiman, M., & Carter, B. (1993). The changing family life cycle: A perspective in normalcy. In F. Walsh (Ed.), *Normal family processes* (pp. 405–443). New York: Guilford.

McIntosh, P. (1988). *White privilege: Unpacking the invisible knapsack* (Working Paper No. 189). Wellesley, MA: Wellesley College Center for Research on Women.

McIntosh, P. (1992). White privilege and male privilege: A personal account of coming to see correspondences through work in women's studies. In M. L. Andersen & P. H. Collins (Eds.), *Race, class, and gender: An anthology* (pp. 70–81). Belmont, CA: Wadsworth.

McNally, R. J., Bryant, R. A., & Ehlers, A. (2003). Does early psychological intervention promote recovery from posttraumatic stress? *Psychological Science in the Public Interest, 4,* 45–79.

McWhinney, M., Haskins-Herkenham, D., & Hare, I. (1992). *The school social worker and confidentiality* (Position Statement of the National Association of Social Workers, Commission on Education). Washington, DC: National Association of Social Workers.

McWilliams, N. (1999). *Psychoanalytic case formulation.* New York: Guilford.

Meier, P. D., Minirth, F. B., Wichern, F. B., & Ratcliff, D. E. (1997). *Introduction to psychology and counseling: Christian perspectives and applications* (2nd ed.). Grand Rapids, MI: Baker Books.

Mendoza, D. W. (1993). A review of Gerald Caplan's theory and practice of mental health consultation. *Journal of Counseling and Development, 71,* 629–635.

Mento, A. J., Steele, R. P., & Karren, R. J. (1987). A meta-analytic study of the effects of goal setting on task performance. *Organizational Behavior and Human Decision Processes, 39,* 52–83.

Merkur, D. (1997). Freud and Hasidism. In J. L. Jacobs & D. Capps (Eds.), *Religion, society, and psychoanalysis* (pp. 11–22). Boulder, CO: Westview.

Merriam, S. B. (1998). *Qualitative research and case study applications in education.* San Francisco: Jossey-Bass.

Miller, A. (1997). *The drama of the gifted child: The search for the true self* (R. Ward, Trans.). New York: Basic Books.

Miller, G. (2003). *Incorporating spirituality in counseling and psychotherapy: Theory and technique.* Hoboken, NJ: Wiley.

Miller, R. B., Anderson, S., & Keala, D. K. (2004). Is Bowen theory valid? A review of basic research. *Journal of Marital and Family Therapy, 30,* 453–466.

Miller, W. R., & Rollnick, S. (2002). *Motivational interviewing: Preparing people for change* (2nd ed.). New York: Guilford.

Minuchin, P., Colapinto, J., & Minuchin, S. (1998). *Working with families of the poor.* New York: Guilford.

Minuchin, S. (1974). *Families and family therapy.* Cambridge, MA: Harvard University Press.

Minuchin, S. (1998). Where is the family in narrative family therapy? *Journal of Marital and Family Therapy, 24,* 397–403.

Minuchin, S., & Fishman, H. C. (1981). *Family therapy techniques.* Cambridge, MA: Harvard University Press.

Minuchin, S., & Montalvo, B. (1967). Techniques for working with disorganized low socioeconomic families. *American Journal of Orthopsychiatry, 37,* 880–887.

Mitroff, I. I. (2004). *Crisis leadership: Planning for the unthinkable.* Hoboken, NJ: Wiley.

Moleski, S. M., & Kiselica, M. S. (2005). Dual relationships: A continuum ranging from destructive to therapeutic. *Journal of Counseling & Development, 83*(1), 3–12.

Montgomery, M. L., Hendricks, C. B., & Bradley, L. J. (2001). Using systems perspective in supervision. *Family Journal: Counseling and Therapy for Couples and Families, 9,* 305–313.

Moreno, J. L. (1964). *Psychodrama: Vol. 1* (3rd ed.). Beacon, NY: Beacon House.

Morgan, C. D., & Murray, H. A. (1935). A method for investigating fantasies: The Thematic Apperception Test. *Archives of Neurology and Psychiatry, 34,* 289–306.

Morgan, D. L. (1998). *The focus group guidebook.* Thousand Oaks, CA: Sage.

Morran, D. K. (1992). An interview with Rex Stockton. *The Journal for Specialists in Group Work, 17,* 4–9.

Morran, D. K., Stockton, R., Cline, R. J., & Teed, C. (1998). Facilitating feedback exchange in groups: Leader interventions. *The Journal for Specialists in Group Work, 23,* 257–268.

Morran, D. K., Stockton, R., & Whittingham, M. H. (2004). Effective leadership in group counseling and psychotherapy: Research and practice. In J. L. DeLucia-Waack, D. A. Gerrity, C. R. Kalodner, & M. T. Riva (Eds.), *Handbook of group counseling and psychotherapy* (pp. 91–103). Thousand Oaks, CA: Sage.

Morris, J. R., & Robinson, D. T. (1996). A review of multicultural counseling. *Journal of Humanistic Education and Development, 35,* 50–60.

Moustakas, C. (1994). *Phenomenological research methods.* Thousand Oaks, CA: Sage.

Myer, R. A. (2000). *Assessment for crisis intervention: A triage assessment model.* Belmont, CA: Wadsworth.

Myer, R. A. (2001). *Assessment for crisis intervention: Triage assessment model.* Pacific Grove, CA: Brooks/Cole.

Myer, R. A., Conte, C., & Peterson, S. E. (in press). *Human impact issues for crisis management in organizations.* In press.

Myer, R. A., & James, R. K. (2005). *Workbook for crisis intervention and CD-ROM.* Pacific Grove, CA: Brooks/Cole.

Myer, R. A., & Moore, H. (2006). Crisis in context: An ecological model. *Journal of Counseling and Development, 84,* 139–147.

Myer, R. A., Moore, H., & Hughes, T. (2003). September 11th survivors and the refugee model. *Journal of Mental Health Counseling, 25,* 245–258.

Myer, R. A., Williams, R. C., Ottens, A. J., & Schmidt, A. E. (1992). Crisis assessment: A three dimensional model for triage. *Journal of Mental Health Counseling, 14,* 137–148.

Myers, I., & Briggs, K. (1993). *The Myers–Briggs Type Indicator.* Palo Alto, CA: Consulting Psychologists Press.

Myers, I. B., & McCaulley, M. H. (1985). *Manual: A guide to the development and use of the Myers–Briggs Type Indicator.* Palo Alto, CA: Consulting Psychologists Press.

Myers, J. E. (1998). *Manual for the Wellness Evaluation of Lifestyle.* Greensboro, NC: Author.

Myers, J. E., & Sweeney, T. J. (2004). Advocacy for the counseling profession: Results of a national survey. *Journal of Counseling and Development, 82,* 466–471.

Myers, J. E., & Sweeney, T. J. (2005a). *Counseling for wellness: Theory, research, and practice.* Alexandria, VA: American Counseling Association.

Myers, J. E., & Sweeney, T. J. (2005b). The indivisible self: An evidence-based model of wellness. *Journal of Individual Psychology, 61,* 269–279.

Myers, J. E., & Sweeney, T. J. (2005c). *Manual for the Five Factor Wellness Inventory.* Palo Alto, CA: Mindgarden.

Myers, J. E., Sweeney, T. J., & White, V. E. (2002). Advocacy for counseling and counselors: A professional imperative. *Journal of Counseling and Development, 78,* 251–266.

Myers, J. E., Sweeney, T. J., & Witmer, J. M. (1998). *The Wellness Evaluation of Lifestyle.* Palo Alto, CA: Mindgarden.

Myers, J. E., Sweeney, T. J., & Witmer, J. M. (2000). The wheel of wellness counseling for wellness: A holistic model for treatment planning. *Journal of Counseling and Development, 78,* 251–266.

Mytton, J. (2000). Cognitive therapy. In C. Feltham & I. Horton (Eds.), *Handbook of counseling and psychotherapy* (pp. 314–320). London: Sage.

Napier, A., & Whitaker, C. (1978). *The family crucible.* New York: Harper & Row.

Napier, R. W., & Gershenfeld, M. K. (1993). *Groups: Theory and experience* (5th ed.). Boston: Houghton-Mifflin.

National Board for Certified Counselors. (1999). *Standards for the ethical practice of clinical supervision.* Washington, DC: Author.

National Board for Certified Counselors. (2005a). *National Board for Certified Counselors.* Retrieved September 5, 2005, from www.nbcc.org/.

National Board for Certified Counselors. (2005b). *NBCC code of ethics.* Washington, DC: Author.

Neufeldt, S. A. (1997). A social constructivist approach to counseling supervision. In T. Sexton & B. Grifin (Eds.), *Constructivist thinking in counseling practice, research, and thinking* (pp. 191–210). New York: Teachers College Press.

Neufeldt, S. A. (1999). *Supervision strategies for the first practicum.* Alexandria, VA: American Counseling Association.

Neugarten, B. L. (1968). The awareness of middle aging. In B. L. Neugarten (Ed.), *Middle age and aging* (pp. 93–98). Chicago: University of Chicago Press.

Neugarten, B. L. (1979). Time, age, and the life cycle. *American Journal of Psychiatry, 136,* 887–894.

Neukrug, E. (2003). *The world of the counselor: An introduction to the counseling profession* (2nd ed.). Pacific Grove, CA: Brooks/Cole.

Neukrug, E. S., & Schwitzer, A. M. (2006). *Skills and tools for today's counselors and psychotherapists: From natural helping to professional counseling.* Belmont, CA: Brooks/Cole.

Newcomb, T. M. (1953). An approach to the study of communicative acts. *Psychological Review, 60,* 393–404.

Nichols, M. P., & Schwartz, R. C. (2004). *Family therapy: Concepts and methods* (6th ed.). New York: Pearson.

Nichols, W. C., & Everett, C. A. (1986). *Systemic family therapy: An integrative approach.* New York: Guilford.

Niemic, C. P., Lynch, M. F., Vansteenkiste, M., Bernstein, J., Deci, E. L., & Ryan, R. M. (2006). The antecedents and consequences of autonomous self-regulation for college: A self-determination theory perspective on socialization. *Journal of Adolescence, 29,* 761–775.

Norcross, J. C., & Halgin, R. P. (1997). Integrative approaches to psychotherapy supervision. In J. C. E. Watkins (Ed.), *Handbook of psychotherapy supervision* (pp. 203–222). New York: Wiley.

Nugent, F. (1990). *An introduction to the profession of counseling.* Columbus, OH: Merrill.

Nykodym, N., Ruud, W., & Liverpool, P. (1986). Quality circles: Will transaction analysis improve their effectiveness? *Transactional Analysis Journal, 16,* 182–187.

Nylund, D., & Corsiglia, V. (1994). Becoming solution-focused forced in brief therapy: Remembering something important we already knew. *Journal of Systemic Therapies, 13*(1), 5–12.

Nystul, M. S. (2003). *Introduction to counseling: An art and science perspective.* Boston: Allyn & Bacon.

O'Connell, B. (2003). Introduction to the solution-focused approach. In B. O'Connell & S. Palmer (Eds.), *Handbook of solution-focused therapy* (pp. 1–105). London: Sage.

O'Hanlon, B., & Weiner-Davis, M. (1989). *In search of solutions: A new direction in psychotherapy.* New York: Norton.

O'Hanlon, B., & Wilk, J. (1987). *Shifting contexts: The generation of effective psychotherapy.* New York: Guilford.

Ohlsen, M. M., Horne, A. M., & Lawe, C. F. (1988). *Group counseling* (3rd ed.). New York: Holt, Rinehart, & Winston.

Okech, J. E. A., & Kline, W. B. (2005). A qualitative exploration of group co-leader relationships. *The Journal for Specialists in Group Work, 30,* 173–190.

Okun, B. F. (2001). *Effective helping: Interviewing and counseling techniques* (5th ed.). Boston: Wadsworth.

Omer, H. (1996). Three styles of constructive therapy. In M. F. Hoyt (Ed.), *Constructive therapies* (Vol. 2, pp. 319–333). New York: Guilford.

Osgood, C., & Tannenbaum, P. (1955). The principle of congruity in the prediction of attitude change. *Psychology Review, 62,* 42–55.

Osofsky, J. D., Wewers, S., Hann, D. M., & Fick, A. C. (1993). Chronic community violence: What is happening to our children? *Psychiatry, 56,* 36–45.

Overton, W. F. (1976). The active organism in structuralism. *Human Development, 19,* 71–86.

Pack-Brown, S. P., & Fleming, A. (2004). Group counseling with African Americans. In J. Delucia-Waack (Ed.), *Handbook of group counseling and therapy* (pp. 183–199). Thousand Oaks, CA: Sage.

Pack-Brown, S. P., & Whittington-Clark, L. E. (2002). *"I am because we are!" Afrocentric approaches to group work (A diversity-competent model).* Farmingham, MA: Microtraining Associates.

Pack-Brown, S. P., Whittington-Clark, L. E., & Parker, W. M. (2002). *Images of me: A guide to group work with African American women.* Framington, MA: Mictrotraining Associates.

Padilla, A. M. (1980). *Acculturation: Theory, models, and some new findings.* Boulder, CO: Westview.

Palmer, P. J. (1998). *The courage to teach: Exploring the inner landscape of a teacher's life.* San Francisco: Jossey-Bass.

Panksepp, J. (1988). *Affective neuroscience: The foundations of human and animal emotions.* New York: Oxford University Press.

Parham, T. A., & Austin, N. L. (1994). Career development and African Americans: A contextual reappraisal using the Nigrescence construct. *Journal of Vocational Behavior, 44,* 139–154.

Parsons, F. (1909). *Choosing a vocation.* Boston: Houghton-Mifflin.

Parsons, R. D. (2004). *Fundamentals of the helping process.* Long Grove, IL: Waveland.

Parsons, R. D., & Kahn, W. J. (2005). *The school counselor as consultant: An integrated model for school-based consultation.* Belmont, CA: Brooks/Cole.

Parsons, R. D., & Meyers, J. (1984). *Developing consultation skills: Theory and practice.* New York: Brunner/Mazel.

Parten, M. (1932). Social participation among preschool children. *Journal of Abnormal and Social Psychology, 27,* 243–269.

Pate, R. H., Jr. (1992). Are you liable? *American Counselor, 1*(3), 15–19.

Paton, D., Violanti, J. M., & Dunning, C. (2000). Posttraumatic stress intervention: Challenges, issues, and perspectives. In J. M. Violanti, D. Paton, & C. Dunning (Eds.), *Posttraumatic stress intervention: Challenges, issues, and perspectives* (pp. 3–9). Springfield, IL: Thomas.

Patterson, C. H. (1997). Client-centered supervision. In C. E. Watkins, Jr. (Ed.), *Handbook of psychotherapy supervision* (pp. 134–146). New York: Wiley.

Patton, M. Q. (2002). *Qualitative research and evaluation methods* (3rd ed.). Thousand Oaks, CA: Sage.

Pedersen, P. B. (1976). The field of intercultural counseling. In P. B. Pedersen, W. J. Lonner, & J. G. Draguns (Eds.), *Counseling across cultures* (pp. 17–41). Honolulu: University of Hawaii Press.

Pedersen, P. (1987). Ten frequent assumptions of cultural bias in counseling. *Journal of Multicultural Counseling and Development, 15*(1), 16–24.

Pedersen, P. B. (1991). Multiculturalism as the forth force in counseling. *Journal of Counseling and Development, 70*(1), 6–12.

Pedersen, P. B., Draguns, J. G., Lonner, W. J., & Trimble, J. E. (Eds.). (2002). *Counseling across cultures.* Thousand Oaks, CA: Sage.

Pedhazur, E. J., & Schmelkin, L. (1991). *Measurement, design, and analysis: An integrated approach.* Hillsdale, NJ: Lawrence Erlbaum Associates, Inc.

Peele, S. (1992). *The truth about addiction and recovery.* New York: Fireside Press/Simon & Schuster.

Peirce, C. S. (1992). *The essential Peirce: Volume 1. 1867–1893* (N. Houser & C. Kloesel, Eds.). Bloomington: Indiana University Press.

Peirce, C. S. (1998). *The essential Peirce: Volume 2. 1893–1913* (The Peirce Edition Project, Eds.). Bloomington: Indiana University Press.

Pelletier, L. G., Tuson, K. M., & Haddad, N. K. (1997). Client Motivation for Therapy Scale: A measure of intrinsic motivation, extrinsic motivation, and amotivation for therapy. *Journal of Personality Assessment, 68,* 414–435.

Perls, F. S. (1969a). *Ego, hunger, and aggression: The Gestalt therapy of sensory awakening through spontaneous personal encounter, fantasy and contemplation.* New York: Vintage Books.

Perls, F. (1969b). *Gestalt therapy verbatim.* Moab: UT: Real People Press.

Perls, F. (1969c). *In and out of the garbage pail.* Moab: UT: Real People Press.

Perls, F. S. (1973). *The Gestalt approach.* Palo Alto, CA: Science & Behavior Books.

Perls, F., Hefferline, R. F., & Goodman, P. (1951). *Gestalt therapy.* New York: Dell.

Ponterotto, J. G., & Casas, J. M. (1991). *Handbook of racial/ethnic minority counseling research.* Springfield, IL: Thomas.

Pope, M. (1999). Backup of applications of group career counseling techniques in Asian cultures. *Journal of Multicultural Counseling and Development, 27,* pp. 18–31.

Pope-Davis, D. B., & Coleman, H. L. K. (Eds.). (1997). *Multicultural counseling competencies: Assessment, education and training, and supervision.* Thousand Oaks, CA: Sage.

Porter, L. W., Steers, R. M., Mowday, R. T., & Boulian, P. V. (1974). Organizational commitment, job satisfaction, and turnover among psychiatric technicians. *Journal of Applied Psychology, 59,* 603–609.

Post, P., Stewart, M. A., & Smith, P. L. (1991). Self-efficacy, interest, and consideration of math/science and non-math/science occupations among Black freshmen. *Journal of Vocational Behavior, 38,* 179–186.

Post-Kammer, P., & Smith, P. L. (1986). Sex differences in math and science career self-efficacy among disadvantaged students. *Journal of Vocational Behavior, 29,* 89–101.

Pratt, M. L. (1986). Fieldwork in common places. In J. Clifford & G. F. Marcus (Eds.), *Writing culture: The poetics and politics of ethnography* (pp. 27–50). Berkeley: University of California Press.

Prochaska, J. O., & Norcross, J. C. (2003). *Systems of psychotherapy: A trantheoretical analysis* (5th ed.). Pacific Grove, CA: Thomson/Brooks/Cole.

Prochaska, J., Norcross, J. C., & DiClemente, C. C. (1995). *Changing for good*. New York: HarperCollins.

Prouty, A. M., Thomas, V., Johnson, S., & Long, J. K. (2001). Methods of feminist family therapy supervision. *Journal of Marital and Family Therapy, 27*, 85–97.

Psychology 200. (2005). Retrieved April 5, 2005, from http://www.insidehighered.com/news/2005/08/22/counseling

Pynoos, R. S., Steinburg, A. M., & Goenjian, A. (1996). Traumatic stress in childhood and adolescence: Recent developments and current controversies. In B. A. van der Kolk, A. C. McFarlane, & L. Weisaeth (Eds.), *Traumatic stress: The effects of overwhelming experience on mind, body, and society* (pp. 331–358). New York: Guilford.

Randolph, D. L., & Graun, K. (1988). Resistance to consultation: A synthesis for counselor-consultants. *Journal of Counseling and Development, 67*, 182–184.

Raphael, B., & Wilson, J. P. (2000). Introduction and overview: Key issues in the conceptualization of debriefing. In B. Raphael & J. P. Wilson (Eds.), *Psychological debriefing: Theory, practice, and evidence* (pp. 1–16). Cambridge, UK: Cambridge Press.

Rapin, L. S. (2004). Guidelines for ethical and legal practice in counseling and psychotherapy groups. In J. L. DeLucia-Waack, D. A. Gerrity, C. R. Kalodner, & M. T. Riva (Eds.), *Handbook of group counseling and psychotherapy* (pp. 151–168). Thousand Oaks, CA: Sage.

Raskin, N. J. (1986). Client-centered group psychotherapy, Part 1: Development of client-centered groups. *Person-Centered Review, 1*, 272–290.

Redding, S. G., & Ng, M. (1982). The role of "face" in the organizational perceptions of Chinese managers. *Organization-Studies, 3*, 201–219.

Reeve, J. (2002). Self-determination theory applied to educational settings. In E. L. Deci & R. M. Ryan (Eds.), *Handbook of self-determination research* (pp. 193–204). Rochester, NY: University of Rochester Press.

Reeve, J. (2005). *Understanding motivation and emotion* (4th ed.). Hoboken, NJ: Wiley.

Reitan, R. M., & Wolfson, D. (1993). *The Halstead–Reitan Neuropsychological Test Battery: Theory and clinical interpretation* (2nd ed.). Tucson, AZ: Neuropsychology Press.

Remley, T., Jr., & Herlihy, B. (2001). *Ethical, legal, and professional issues in counseling*. Upper Saddle River, NJ: Merrill/Prentice-Hall.

Reynolds, C. R., & Kamphaus, R. W. (2004). *Behavior Assessment System for Children manual* (2nd ed.). Circle Pines, MN: AGS.

Richeport-Haley, M. (1998). Ethnicity in family therapy: A comparison of brief strategic therapy and culture-focused therapy. *American Journal of Family Therapy, 26*, 77–90.

Ricoeur, P. (1976). *Interpretation theory: Discourse and the surplus of meaning*. Fort Worth: Texas Christian University Press.

Ricoeur, P. (1980). *Essays on biblical interpretation*. Philadelphia: Fortress Press.

Ridley, C. R. (1989). Racism in counseling as an aversive behavioral process. In P. Pedersen, J. Draguns, W. Lormer, & J. Trimble (Eds.), *Counseling across cultures* (3rd ed., pp. 55–77). Honolulu: University of Hawaii Press.

Rigazio-DiGilio, S. A. (2000). Reconstructing psychological distress and disorder from a relational perspective: A systemic coconstructive-developmental framework. In R. Neimeyer & J. Raskin (Eds.), *Constructions of disorder* (pp. 309–332). Washington, DC: American Psychological Association.

Rigazio-DiGilio, S. A., & Ivey, A. E. (1995). Individual and family issues in intercultural counselling and therapy: A culturally-centered perspective. *Canadian Journal of Counseling, 29*, 244–261.

Rigazio-DiGilio, S. A., Ivey, A. E., & Ivey, M. B. (1997). Developmental counseling and therapy: Individual and family therapy. In A. Ivey, M. Ivey, & L. Simek-Morgan (Eds.), *Coun-

seling and psychotherapy: A multicultural perspective (4th ed., pp. 89–129). Needham Heights, MA: Allyn & Bacon.

Rigazio-DiGilio, S. A., Ivey, A. E., & Locke, D. C. (1997). Continuing the post-modern dialogue: Enhancing and contextualizing multiple voices. *Journal of Mental Health Counseling, 19,* 233–255.

Rita, E. S. (1998). Solution-focused supervision. *Clinical Supervisor, 17,* 125–139.

Ritchie, M. H. (1990). Counseling is not a profession—yet. *Counselor Education and Supervision, 37,* 166–178.

Riva, M. T., Wachtel, M., & Lasky, G. B. (2004). Effective leadership in group counseling and psychotherapy: Research and practice. In J. L. DeLucia-Waack, D. A. Gerrity, C. R. Kalodner, & M. T. Riva (Eds.), *Handbook of group counseling and psychotherapy* (pp. 37–48). Thousand Oaks, CA: Sage.

Robbins, S. B. (1985). Left–right brain research and its premature generalization to the counseling setting. *Journal of Counseling and Development, 65,* 235–239.

Robinson, T. L. (2005). *The convergence of race, ethnicity and gender: Multiple identities in counseling.* Upper Saddle River, NJ: Pearson Education.

Robinson, T. L., & Howard-Hamilton, M. F. (2000). *The convergence of race, ethnicity, and gender: Multiple identities in counseling.* Upper Saddle River, NJ: Merrill/Prentice-Hall.

Roe, A. (1956). *The psychology of occupations.* New York: Wiley.

Roe, A., & Klos, D. (1972). Classification of occupations. In J. M. Whiteley & A. Resnikoff (Eds.), *Perspectives on vocational development* (pp. 199–221). Washington, DC: American Personnel and Guidance Association.

Roe, A., & Lunneborg, P. W. (1990). Personality development and career choice. In D. Brown, L. Brooks, & Associates (Eds.), *Career choice and development: Applying theories to practice* (2nd ed., pp. 68–101). San Francisco: Jossey-Bass.

Rogers, C. R. (1951). *Client-centered therapy: Its current practice, implications, and theory.* Boston: Houghton-Mifflin.

Rogers, C. R. (1959). A theory of therapy, personality, and interpersonal relationships as developed in the client-centered framework. In S. Koch (Ed.), *Psychology: The study of a science: Vol. 3. Formulations of the person and the social context* (pp. 184–256). New York: McGraw-Hill.

Rogers, C. R. (1961). *On becoming a person: A therapist's view of psychotherapy.* Boston: Houghton-Mifflin.

Rogers, C. R. (1967). The process of the basic encounter group. In J. F. T. Bugenthal (Ed.), *Challenges of humanistic psychology* (pp. 261–278). New York: McGraw-Hill.

Rogers, C. R. (1970). *Carl Rogers on encounter groups.* New York: Harper & Row.

Rogers, C. R. (1980). *A way of being.* Boston: Houghton-Mifflin.

Roid, G. H. (2003). *Stanford–Binet Intelligence Scales* (5th ed.). Itasca, IL: Riverside.

Rønnestad, M. H., & Skovholt, T. M. (1993). Supervision of beginning and advanced graduate students of counseling and psychotherapy. *Journal of Counseling and Development, 71,* 396–405.

Rorschach, H. (1975). *Psychodiagnostics: A diagnostic test based on perception.* New York: Grune & Stratton. (Original work published 1921)

Rose, S. D. (1977). *Group therapy: A behavioral approach.* Englewood Cliffs, NJ: Prentice-Hall.

Rose, S. D. (1980). *A casebook in group therapy: A behavioral-cognitive approach.* Englewood Cliffs, NJ: Prentice-Hall.

Rose, S. D. (1983). Behavior therapy in groups. In H. I. Kaplan & B. J. Sadock (Eds.), *Comprehensive group psychotherapy* (2nd ed., pp. 292–327). Baltimore: Williams & Wilkins.

Rosenbaum, M., & Ronen, T. (1998). Clinical supervision from the standpoint of cognitive-behavioral therapy. *Psychotherapy, 35,* 220–230.

Rounds, J. B., Henly, G. A., Dawis, R. V., Loftquist, L. H., & Weiss, D. (1981). *Manual for the Minnesota Importance Questionnaire.* Minneapolis: University of Minnesota, Department of Psychology.

Rowntree, D. (2004). *Statistics without tears: A primer for non-mathematicians.* Boston: Allyn & Bacon.

Roysircar-Sodowsy, G., & Maestas, M. V. (2000). Acculturation, ethnic identity, and acculturative stress: Evidence and measurement. In R. H. Dana (Ed.), *Handbook of cross-cultural and multicultural personality assessment* (pp. 131–172). Mahwah, NJ: Lawrence Erlbaum Associates, Inc.

Rudd, M. D., Joiner, T. E., Jr., Jobes, D. A., & King, C. A. (1999). The outpatient treatment of suicidality: An integration of science and recognition of its limitations. *Professional Psychology: Research and Practice, 30,* 437–446.

Russell-Chapin, L., & Ivey, A. (2004a). Microcounselling supervision model: An innovative approach to supervision. *Canadian Journal for Counselling, 7,* 165–176.

Russell-Chapin, L., & Ivey, A. (2004b). *Your supervised practicum and internship: Field resources for turning theory into action.* Pacific Grove, CA: Thomson/Brooks/Cole.

Russell-Chapin, L. A., & Sherman, N. E. (2000). The counselling interview rating form: A teaching and evaluation tool for counselor education. *British Journal of Guidance and Counselling, 28,* 115–124.

Ryan, R. M. (1993). Agency and organization: Intrinsic motivation, autonomy and the self in psychological development. In J. Jacobs (Ed.), *Nebraska symposium on motivation: Developmental perspectives on motivation* (Vol. 40, pp. 1–56). Lincoln: University of Nebraska Press.

Ryan, R. M., & Connell, J. P. (1989). Perceived locus of causality and internalization: Examining reasons for acting in two domains. *Journal of Personality and Social Psychology, 57,* 749–761.

Ryan, R. M., & Deci, E. L. (2000). Self-determination theory and the facilitation of intrinsic motivation, social development, and well-being. *American Psychologist, 55,* 68–78.

Ryan, R. M., & Deci, E. L. (2002). An overview of self-determination theory: An organismic-dialectical perspective. In E. L. Deci & R. M. Ryan (Eds.), *Handbook of self-determination research* (pp. 3–33). Rochester, NY: University of Rochester Press.

Ryan, R. M., Kuhl, J., & Deci, E. L. (1997). Nature and autonomy: An organizational view of social and neurobiological aspects of self-regulation in behavior and development. *Development and Psychopathology, 9,* 701–728.

Ryan, R. M., & Lynch, J. H. (1989). Emotional autonomy versus detachment: Revisiting the vicissitudes of adolescence and young adulthood. *Child Development, 60,* 340–356.

Ryan, R. M., Plant, R. W., & O'Malley, S. (1995). Initial motivations for alcohol treatment: Relations with patient characteristics, treatment involvement, and dropout. *Addictive Behaviors, 20,* 279–297.

Ryff, C. D., & Keyes, C. L. (1995). The structure of psychological well-being revisited. *Journal of Personality and Social Psychology, 69,* 719–727.

Sacks, O. (1990). *The man who mistook his wife for a hat, and other clinical tales.* New York: Quality Paperback Book Club.

Salter, A. C. (1988). *Treating child sex offenders and victims: A practical guide.* Newbury Park, CA: Sage.

Sanchez, H. G. (2001). Risk factor for model suicide assessment and intervention. *Professional Psychology: Research and Practice, 32,* 351–358.

Santrock, J. W. (1999). *Life-span development* (7th ed.). Boston: McGraw-Hill.

Satir, V. (1983). *Conjoint family therapy* (3rd ed.). Palo Alto, CA: Science & Behavior Books.

Satir, V., Stachowiak, J., & Taschman, H. (1975). *Helping families to change*. New York: Aronson.

Sattler, J. M. (2001). *Assessment of children: Cognitive applications* (4th ed.). San Diego, CA: Author.

Savickas, M. L. (1995a). Constructivist counseling for career indecision. *Career Development Quarterly, 43*, 363–373.

Savickas, M. L. (1995b). Current theoretical issues in vocational psychology: Convergence, divergence, and schism. In W. B. Walsh & S. H. Osipow (Eds.), *Handbook of vocational psychology: Theory, research and practice* (2nd ed., pp. 1–34). Mahwah, NJ: Lawrence Erlbaum Associates, Inc.

Scarr, S. (1984). What's a parent to do? *Psychology Today, 18*, 58–63.

Schaie, K. W. (1996). *Intellectual development in adulthood: The Seattle Longitudinal Study*. New York: Cambridge University Press.

Schein, E. (1969). *Process consultation: Its role in organizational consultation*. Reading, MA: Addison-Wesley.

Schein, E. (1987). *Process consultation: Lessons for managers and consultants* (Vol. 2). Reading, MA: Addison-Wesley.

Schmidt, J. J. (2006). *Social and cultural foundations of counseling and human services: Multiple influences on self-concept development*. Boston: Pearson Education.

Schneider, J. P. (1994). Sex addiction: Controversy within mainstream addiction medicine, diagnosis based on the *DSM–III–R* and physician case histories. *Sexual Addiction and Compulsivity: The Journal of Treatment and Prevention, 1*, 19–44.

Schön, B. (1987). *Educating the reflective practitioner*. San Francisco: Jossey-Bass.

Schulte, E. H., & Osborne, S. S. (2003). Why assumptive worlds collide: A review of definitions of collaboration in consultation. *Journal of Educational and Psychological Consultation, 14*, 109–138.

Schutz, A. (1932). *The phenomenology of the social world*. Evanston, IL: Northwestern University Press.

Schwartz, B. (1989). *Psychology of learning and behavior* (3rd ed.). New York: Norton.

Seely, M. F. (1997). The discreet role of the hotline. *Crisis, 18*(2), 53–54.

Segal, J. (2000). Psychodynamic theory. In C. Feltham & I. Horton (Eds.), *Handbook of counseling and psychotherapy* (pp. 303–308). London: Sage.

Seidman, I. E. (1991). *Interviewing as qualitative research*. New York: Teacher's College Press.

Seligman, L. (1994). *Developmental career counseling and assessment*. Thousand Oaks, CA: Sage.

Seligman, L. (2001). *Systems, strategies, and skills of counseling and psychotherapy*. Upper Saddle River, NJ: Merrill/Prentice-Hall.

Seligman, L. (2004). *Technical and conceptual skills for mental health professionals*. Upper Saddle River, NJ: Merrill/Prentice-Hall.

Seligman, L. (2006). *Theories of counseling and psychotherapy: Systems, strategies, and skills*. Upper Saddle River, NJ: Merrill/ Prentice-Hall.

Seligman, M. E. (1995). The effectiveness of psychotherapy: The Consumer Reports study. *American Psychologist, 50*, 965–974.

Seltzer, W. J. (2005). Pre-cognitive therapy: A way to integrate neuroscience and psychotherapy. *Journal of Systemic Therapies, 24*, 32–48.

Selvini Palazzoli, M., Boscolo, L., Cecchin, G., & Prata, G. (1980). Hypothesizing, circularity, neutrality: Three guidelines for the conductor of the session. *Family Process, 19*(1), 3–12.

Sexton, T. (1997). Constructivist thinking within the history of idea: The challenge of a new paradigm. In T. Sexton & B. Grifin (Eds.), *Constructivist thinking in counseling practice, research, and thinking* (pp. 3–18). New York: Teachers College Press.

Shalev, A. Y. (1996). Stress versus traumatic stress: From acute homeostatic reactions to chronic psychopathology. In B. A. van der Kolk, A. C. MacFarlane, & L. Weisaeth (Eds.), *Traumatic stress* (pp. 77–101). New York: Guilford.

Shallice, T. (2002). Fractionation of the supervisory system. In D. T. Stuss & R. T. Knight (Eds.), *Principles of frontal lobe function* (pp. 261–277). New York: Oxford University Press.

Shank, G. (1995). Semiotics and qualitative research in education: The third crossroad. *The Qualitative Report, 2*(3). Retrieved October 18, 2006, from http://www.nova.edu/ssss/QR/QR2-3/shank.html

Shank, G. D. (2006). *Qualitative research: A personal skills approach* (2nd ed.). Englewood Cliffs, NJ: Prentice-Hall.

Sharf, R. S. (1996). *Theories of psychotherapy and counseling: Concepts and cases.* Pacific Grove, CA: Brooks/Cole.

Sharf, R. (1997). *Applying career development theory to counseling.* Pacific Grove, CA: Brooks/Cole.

Shatz, M., & Gelman, R. (1973). The development of communication skills: Modifications in the speech of young children as a function of the listener. *Monographs of the Society for Research in Child Development, 38*(5, Serial No. 152).

Shaver, P., Furman, W., & Buhrmester, D. (1985). Transition to college: Network changes, social skills, and loneliness. In S. Duck & D. Perlman (Eds.), *Understanding personal relationships: An interdisciplinary approach* (pp. 193–219). London: Sage.

Sheldon, K. M., & King, L. (2001). Why positive psychology is necessary. *American Psychologist, 56,* 216–217.

Sheldon, K. M., Williams, G., & Joiner, T. (2003). *Self-determination theory in the clinic: Motivating physical and mental health.* New Haven, CT: Yale University Press.

Shirk, S., & Russell, R. (1996). *Change processes in child psychotherapy.* New York: Guilford.

Silove, D. (2000). A conceptual framework for mass trauma: Implication for adaptation, intervention, and debriefing. In B. Raphael & J. P. Wilson (Eds.), *Psychological debriefing: Theory, practice and evidence* (pp. 337–350). New York: Cambridge University Press.

Sink, C. (Ed.). (2005). *Contemporary school counseling: Theory, research, and practice.* Boston: Lahaska Press.

Skinner, B. F. (1953). *Science and human behavior.* New York: Thre Free Press.

Skinner, B. F. (1959). *Cumulative record.* New York: Appleton-Century-Crofts.

Skinner, B. F. (1971). *Beyond freedom and dignity.* New York: Bantam/Vintage.

Skinner, B. F. (1974). *About behaviorism.* New York: Knopf.

Skovholt, T. M., & Rivers, D. A. (2004). *Skills and strategies for the helping professions.* Denver, CO: Love.

Skovholt, T. M., & Rønnestad, M. H. (1992). *The evolving professional self: Stages and themes in therapist and counselor development.* Chichester, UK: Wiley.

Skovholt, T. M., Rønnestad, M. H., & Jennings, L. (1997). Searching for expertise in counseling, psychotherapy, and professional psychology. *Educational Psychology Review, 9,* 361–369.

Skowron, E. A. (2000). The role of differentiation of self in marital adjustment. *Journal of Counseling Psychology, 47,* 229–237.

Skowron, E. A. (2004). Differentiation of self, personal adjustment, problem solving, and ethnic group belonging among persons of color. *Journal of Counseling and Development, 82,* 447–456.

Skynner, R. (1976). *Systems of family and marital psychotherapy.* New York: Brunner/Mazel.

Slaikeu, K. A. (1990). *Crisis intervention: A handbook for practice and research* (2nd ed.). Needham Heights, MA: Allyn & Bacon.

Slawski, C. (1981). *Social psychological theories: A comparative handbook for students.* Glenview, IL: Scott, Foresman.

Smart, D. W., & Smart, J. F. (2006). Models of disability: Implications for the counseling profession. *Journal of Counseling and Development, 84,* 29–40.

Smedley, A., & Smedley, B. D. (2005). Race as biology is fiction, racism as a social problem is real: Anthropological and historical perspectives on the social construction of race. *American Psychologist, 60,* 16–26.

Sohlberg, M. M., & Mateer, C. A. (1989). Training use of compensatory memory books: A three stage behavioral approach. *Journal of Clinical and Experimental Neuropsychology, 11,* 871–887.

Sonstegard, M. A., & Bitter, J. R. (1998). Adlerian group counseling: Step-by-step. *Individual Psychology, 54,* 217–250.

Speirs, K. (2006). *Reliability and predictive validity of the SCDT questioning strategies and classification system.* Unpublished thesis, University of Connecticut, Storrs, CT.

Sperry, L., Carlson, J., & Kjos, D. (2003). *Becoming an effective therapist.* Boston: Allyn & Bacon.

Spradley, J. P. (1979). *The ethnographic interview.* New York: Holt, Rinehart & Winston.

Spradley, J. P. (1980). *Participant observation.* New York: Holt, Rinehart & Winston.

Sprinthall, R. C. (2003). *Basic statistical analysis.* Boston: Allyn & Bacon.

Stake, R. E. (1995). *The art of case study research.* Thousand Oaks, CA: Sage.

Stalker, C., Levene, J., & Coady, N. (1999). Solution-focused brief therapy—One model fits all? *Families in Society, 80,* 468–477.

Steffy, B. E., & Lindle, S. (1994). *Building coalitions: How to link TQE schools with government, business, and community.* Thousand Oaks, CA: Corwin.

Sternberg, R. J. (1987). Liking versus loving: A comparative evaluation of theories. *Psychological Bulletin, 102,* 331–345.

Sternberg, R. J. (1988). Triangulating love. In R. J. Sternberg & M. L. Barnes (Eds.), *The psychology of love* (pp. 119–138). New Haven, CT: Yale University Press.

Stewart, S., & Anderson, C. A. (1984). Resistance revisited: Tales of my death have been greatly exaggerated (Mark Twain). *Family Process, 23*(11), 17–21.

Stockton, R., Morran, D. K., & Nitza, A. G. (2000). Processing group events: A conceptual map for leaders. *The Journal for Specialists in Group Work, 25,* 343–355.

Stockton, R., Rohde, R. I., & Haughey, J. (1992). The effects of structured group exercises on cohesion, engagement, avoidance, and conflict. *Small Group Research, 23,* 155–168.

Stockton, R., & Toth, P. (2000). Small group counseling in school settings: K–12 developmental strategies. In J. Wittmer (Ed.), *Managing your school counseling program* (2nd ed., pp. 111–122). Minneapolis, MN: Educational Media.

Stoltenberg, C. D. (1981). Approaching supervision from a developmental perspective: The counselor-complexity model. *Journal of Counseling Psychologist, 28,* 59–65.

Stoltenberg, C. D., & Delworth, U. (1987). *Supervising counselors and therapists.* San Francisco: Jossey-Bass.

Stoltenberg, C. D., & Delworth, U. (1988). Developmental models of supervision: It is development—Response to Holloway. *Professional Psychology: Research and Practice, 19,* 134–137.

Stoltenberg, C. D., McNeill, B. W., & Delworth, U. (1998). *IDM supervision: An integrated developmental model for supervising counselors and therapists.* San Francisco: Jossey-Bass.

Stone, C. (2001). *Legal and ethical issues in working with minors in schools* [Film]. Alexandria, VA: American Counseling Association.

Stone, C. (2005). *School counseling principles: Ethics and law.* Alexandria, VA: American School Counselor Association.

Stone, C., & Dahir, C. (2006a). *School counselor accountability: A measure of student success* (2nd ed.). Upper Saddle River, NJ: Pearson Education.

Stone, C., & Dahir, C. (2006b). *The transformed school counselor.* Boston: Lahaska Press.

Stone, G., & Peeks, B. (1986). The use of strategic family therapy in the school setting: A case study. *Journal of Counseling and Development, 65,* 200–203.

Strauss, A. (1995). Notes on the nature and development of general theories. *Qualitative Inquiry, 1,* 7–18.

Strauss, A., & Corbin, J. (1998). *Basics of qualitative research: Techniques and procedures for developing grounded theory.* Thousand Oaks, CA: Sage.

Strunk, O., Jr. (1993). A prolegomenon to a history of pastoral counseling. In R. J. Wicks, R. D. Parsons, & D. Capps (Eds.), *Clinical handbook of pastoral counseling: Vol. 1* (expanded ed., pp. 14–25). New York: Paulist Press.

Stuhlmiller, C., & Dunning, C. (2000a). Challenging the mainstream: From pathogenic to salutogenic models of posttrauma intervention. In J. M. Violanti, D. Paton, & C. Dunning (Eds.), *Posttraumatic stress intervention: Challenges, issues, and perspectives* (pp. 10–42). Springfield, IL: Thomas.

Stuhlmiller, C., & Dunning, C. (2000b). Concerns about debriefing: Challenging the mainstream. In B. Raphael & J. P. Wilson (Eds.), *Psychological debriefing: Theory, evidence, and practice* (pp. 305–320). Cambridge, UK: Cambridge University Press.

Sue, D. (1995). Toward a theory of multicultural counseling and therapy. In J. A. Banks & C. A. McGee Banks (Eds.), *Handbook of research on multicultural education* (pp. 647–659). New York: Macmillan.

Sue, D., & Sue, D. W. (1990). *Counseling the culturally different.* New York: Wiley.

Sue, D. W., Arredondo, P., & McDavis, R. J. (1992). Multicultural competencies and standards: A call to the profession. *Journal of Counseling and Development, 70,* 477–486.

Sue, D. W., Ivey, A., & Pedersen, P. B. (Eds.). (1996). *A theory of multicultural counseling and therapy.* Pacific Grove, CA: Brooks/Cole.

Sue, D. W., & Sue, D. (1999). *Counseling the culturally different: Theory and practice* (3rd ed.). New York: Wiley.

Sue, D. W., & Sue, S. (1990). *Counseling the culturally different: Theory and practice* (2nd ed.). New York: Wiley.

Sue, D. W., & Sue, S. (2003). *Counseling the culturally diverse: Theory and practice* (4th ed.). New York: Wiley.

Super, D. E. (1953). A theory of vocational development *American Psychologist, 8,* 185–190.

Super, D. E. (1964). *Work Values Inventory.* Boston: Houghton-Mifflin.

Super, D. E. (1983). Assessment in career guidance: Toward truly developmental counseling. *Personnel and Guidance Journal, 61,* 555–562.

Super, D. E. (1990). A life-span, life-space approach to career development. In D. Brown, L. Brooks, & Associates (Eds.), *Career choice and development: Applying theories to practice* (2nd ed., pp. 197–261). San Francisco: Jossey-Bass.

Super, D. E. (1992). Toward a comprehensive theory of career development. In D. H. Montross & C. J. Shinkman (Eds.), *Career development: Theory and practice* (pp. 35–64). Springfield, IL: Thomas.

Super, D. E. (1994). A life span, life space perspective on convergence. In M. L. Savickas & R. W. Lent (Eds.), *Convergence in career theory: Implications for science and practice* (pp. 63–74). Palo Alto, CA: Consulting Psychologists Press.

Swanson J. L. (1995). The process and outcomes of career counseling. In W. B. Walsh & S. H. Osipow (Eds.), *Handbook of vocational psychology: Theory, research and practice* (pp. 217–259). Hillsdale, NJ: Lawrence Erlbaum Associates, Inc.

Sweeney, T. J. (1998). *Adlerian counseling: A practitioners approach* (4th ed.). Philadelphia: Taylor & Francis.

Sweeney, T. J., & Myers, J. E. (2003). *The indivisible self: An evidence-based model of wellness.* Greensboro, NC: Authors.

Sweeney, T. J., & Witmer, J. M. (1991). Beyond social interest: Striving toward optimum health and wellness. *Individual Psychology, 47,* 527–540.

Tang, M., Fouad, N. A., & Smith, P. L. (1999). Asian Americans' career choices: A path model to examine factors influencing their career choices. *Journal of Vocational Behavior, 54,* 142–157.

Tatar, M., & Myers, J. E. (in press). Wellness of children in Israel and the United States: A preliminary examination of culture and well-being. *Counseling Psychology Quarterly, 19*(2).

Teglasi, H. (2001). *Essentials of TAT and other storytelling techniques assessment.* New York: Wiley.

Terner, J., & Pew, W. L. (1978). *The courage to be imperfect: The life and work of Rudolf Dreikurs.* New York: Hawthorn.

Thomas, R. M. (1992). *Comparing theories of child development* (3rd ed.). Belmont, CA: Wadsworth.

Thompson, B. (2002). What future quantitative social science research could look like: Confidence intervals for effect sizes. *Educational Researcher, 31*(3), 24–31.

Thompson, C. L., Rudolph, L. B., & Henderson, D. (2004). *Counseling children* (6th ed.). Pacific Grove, CA: Brooks/Cole.

Tiedeman, D. V., & O'Hara, R. P. (1963). *Career development: Choice and adjustment.* New York: College Entrance Examination Board.

Tootle, A. (2003). Neuroscience applications in marital and family therapy. *The Family Journal: Counseling and Therapy for Couples and Families, 11,* 185–190.

Traupman, J. C. (1966). *The new college Latin & English dictionary.* New York: Bantam.

Travis, J. W., & Ryan, R. (1988). *The wellness workbook* (2nd ed.). Berkeley, CA: Ten Speed Press.

Trochim, W. (2002). *Research methods knowledge base.* Retrieved June 22, 2006, from: http://www.socialresearchmethods.net/kb/

Truax, C., & Carkhuff, R. (1967). *Toward effective counseling and psychotherapy: Training and practice.* Chicago: Aldine.

Tucker, P., Pfefferbaum, B., Nixon, S. J., & Dickson, W. (2000). Predictors of post-traumatic stress symptoms in Oklahoma City: Exposure, social support, and peri-traumatic responses. *The Journal of Behavioral Health Services and Research, 24,* 406–416.

Tuckman, B. W. (1965). Developmental sequences in small groups. *Psychological Bulletin, 63,* 384–399.

Tuckman, B. W., & Jensen, M. A. (1977). Stages of group development revisited. *Group and Organizational Studies, 2,* 419–427.

United States Census. (2000). Washington, DC: U.S. Department of Commerce, Economics and Statistics Administration.

United States Employment Service. (2002). *O*Net interest profiler.* Washington, DC: Author.

University of Notre Dame Counseling Center. (2003). *Counseling services.* Retrieved February 23, 2006, from http://www.nd.ed/~ucc

Ursano, R. J., Grieger, T. A., & McCarroll, J. E. (1996). Prevention of posttraumatic stress: Consultation, training, and early treatment. In B. A. van der Kolk, A. C. McFarlane, & L.

Weisaeth (Eds.), *Traumatic stress: The effects of overwhelming experience on mind, body, and society* (pp. 441–462). New York: Guilford.

Valliant, G. E. (1977). *Adaptation to life.* Boston: Little, Brown.

van der Kolk, B. S. (1996). The body keeps score: Approaches to the psychobiology of posttraumatic stress disorder. In B. A. van der Kolk, A. C. McFarlane, & L. Weisaeth (Eds.), *Traumatic stress: The effects of overwhelming experience on mind, body, and society* (pp. 214–241). New York: Guilford.

van der Kolk, B. S., & McFarlane, A. C. (1996). The black whole of trauma. In B. A. van der Kolk, A. C. McFarlane, & L. Weisaeth (Eds.), *Traumatic stress: The effects of overwhelming experience on mind, body, and society* (pp. 3–23). New York: Guilford.

Vandiver, B. J., & Bowman, S. L. (1996). A schematic reconceptualization and application of Gottfredson's model. In M. L. W. Savickas & W. B. Walsh (Eds.), *Handbook of career counseling theory and practice* (pp. 155–168). Palo Alto, CA: Davies-Black.

Van Hesteren, F., & Ivey, A. E. (1990). Counseling and development: Toward a new identity for a profession in transition. *Journal of Counseling and Development, 68,* 524–528.

Van Maanen, J. (1988). *Tales of the field: On writing ethnography.* Chicago: University of Chicago Press.

Vansteenkiste, M., Soenens, B., & Vandereycken, W. (2005). Motivation to change in eating disorder patients: A conceptual clarification on the basis of self-determination theory. *International Journal of Eating Disorders, 37,* 207–219.

Vernon, A. (2004). *Counseling children and adolescents* (3rd ed.). Denver, CO: Love.

Vitz, P. C. (1994). *Psychology as religion: The cult of self worship* (2nd ed.). Grand Rapids, MI: Eerdmans. (Original work published 1977)

Vitz, P. C. (1993). *Sigmund Freud's Christian unconscious.* New York: Guilford. (Original work published 1988)

Vontress, C. E., & Jackson, M. L. (2004). Reactions to the multicultural counseling competencies debate. *Journal of Mental Health Counseling, 26,* 74–80.

Vygotsky, L. S. (1978). *Mind in society: The development of higher psychological processes.* Cambridge, MA: Harvard University Press.

Vygotsky, L. S. (1986). *Thought and language* (A. Kozulin, Ed. & Trans.). Cambridge, MA: MIT Press.

Vygotsky, L. S. (1997). *Educational psychology.* Boca Raton, FL: St. Lucie Press.

Waddington, C. H. (1957). *The strategy of the genes.* London: Allen & Unwin.

Walker, L. E. (1989). *Terrifying love: Why women kill and how society responds.* New York: Harper & Row.

Wallace, W. A., & Hall, D. L. (1996). *Psychological consultation: Perspectives and applications.* Pacific Grove, CA: Brooks/Cole.

Ward, C. M., & Bingham, R. P. (1993). Career assessment of ethnic minority women. *Journal of Career Assessment, 1,* 246–257.

Ward, D. E., & Litchy, M. (2004). The effective use of processing in groups. In J. L. DeLucia-Waack, D. A. Gerrity, C. R. Kalodner, & M. T. Riva (Eds.), *Handbook of group counseling and psychotherapy* (pp. 3–22). Thousand Oaks, CA: Sage.

Watkins, C. E., Jr. (1995). Psychotherapy supervisor and supervisee: Developmental models and research nine years later. *Clinical Psychology Review, 15,* 647–680.

Watson, J. B. (1913). Psychology as a behaviorist views it. *Psychological Review, 20,* 158–177.

Watson, J. B. (1925). *Behaviorism.* New York: The People's Institute.

Watzlawick, P., Weakland, J. H., & Fisch, R. (1974). *Change: Principles of problem formation and problem resolution.* New York: Norton.

Wechsler, D. (1949). *Wechsler Intelligence Scale for Children.* New York: Psychological Corporation.

Wechsler, D. (1955). *Manual for the Wechsler Adult Intelligence Scale.* New York: Psychological Corporation.

Wechsler, D. (1997a). *Administration and scoring manual for the Wechsler Memory Scale–Third edition.* San Antonio, TX: Psychological Corporation.

Wechsler, D. (1997b). *Wechsler Adult Intelligence Scale–Third edition.* San Antonio, TX: Psychological Corporation.

Wechsler, D. (2001). *Wechsler Individual Achievement Test–Second edition.* San Antonio, TX: Psychological Corporation.

Wechsler, D. (2003). *Wechsler Intelligence Scale for Children—Third edition: Administration and scoring manual.* San Antonio, TX: Psychological Corporation.

Weinrach, S. G. (1996). The psychological and vocational interests patterns of Donald Super and John Holland. *Journal of Counseling and Development, 75,* 5–19.

Weiss, D., Dawis, R., England, G., & Lofquist, L. (1967). *Manual for the Minnesota Satisfaction Questionnaire.* Minneapolis: University of Minnesota, Industrial Relations Center.

Weiss, R. L., & Perry, B. A. (2002). Behavioral couples therapy. In F. W. Kaslow (Series Ed.) & T. Patterson (Vol. Ed.), *Comprehensive handbook of psychotherapy: Vol. 4. Cognitive-behavioral approaches* (pp. 373–394). New York: Wiley.

Welfel, E. R. (2002). *Ethics in counseling and psychotherapy: Standards, research, and emerging issues.* Pacific Grove, CA: Brooks/Cole.

Wellness Associates,. (ND). *Illness/wellness continuum.* Retrieved October 27, 2006 from http://thewellspring.com/Pubs/iw_cont.html

Wessler, R. L., & Hankin, S. (1988). Rational-emotive and other cognitively oriented therapies. In S. Long (Ed.), *Six group therapies* (pp. 159–215). New York: Plenum.

West, C. (1993). *Race matters.* Boston: Beacon Press.

West, J. F., & Idol, L.(1987). School consultation: An interdisciplinary perspective on theory, models, and research. *Journal of Learning Disabilities, 20,* 388–407.

Whisman, M. A., & Weinstock, L. M. (2002). Cognitive therapy with couples. In F. W. Kaslow (Series Ed.), & T. Patterson (Vol. Ed.), *Comprehensive handbook of psychotherapy: Vol. 4. Cognitive-behavioral approaches* (pp. 373–394). New York: Wiley.

Whitaker, C., & Keith, D. (1981). Symbolic-experiential family therapy. In A. Gurman & D. Krisken (Eds.), *Handbook of family therapy* (pp. 187–225). New York: Brunner/Mazel.

Whitaker, D. S., & Lieberman, M. A. (1964). *Psychotherapy through the group process.* New York: Atherton.

Whitaker, D. S., & Lieberman, M. A. (1965). *Psychotherapy through the group process.* New York: Atherton.

White, J. L., & Parham, T. A. (1990). *The psychology of Blacks.* Englewood Cliffs, NJ: Prentice-Hall.

Whyte, W. F. (1955). *Street corner society: The social structure of an Italian slum.* Chicago: University of Chicago Press

Widiger, T. (2005). A dimensional model of psychopathology. *Psychopathology, 38,* 211–214.

Widiger, T., & Samuel, D. (2005). Diagnostic categories or dimensions? A question for the Diagnostic and Statistical Manual of Mental Disorders–Fifth edition. *Journal of Abnormal Psychology, 114,* 494–504.

Wilkenson, G. S. (1993). *Wide Range Achievement Test—Revision 3.* Wilmington, DE: Jastak Associates.

Williams, C. L., Butcher, J. N., Ben-Porath, Y. S., & Graham, J. R. (1992). *MMPI–A content scales: Assessing psychopathology in adolescents.* Minneapolis: University of Minnesota Press.

Williams, G. C., & Deci, E. L. (1996). Internalization of biopsychosocial values by medical students: A test of self-determination theory. *Journal of Personality and Social Psychology, 70,* 767–779.

Williams, G. C., Freedman, Z., & Deci, E. L. (1998). Supporting autonomy to motivate patients with diabetes for glucose control. *Diabetes Care, 21*, 1644–1651.

Williams, G. C., Gagne, M., Ryan, R. M., & Deci, E. L. (2002). Facilitating autonomous motivation for smoking cessation. *Health Psychology, 21*, 40–50.

Williams, G. C., Grow, V. M., Freedman, Z. R., Ryan, R. M., & Deci, E. L. (1996). Motivational predictors of weight loss and weight-loss maintenance. *Journal of Personality and Social Psychology, 70*, 115–126.

Williams, G. C., Lynch, M. F., McGregor, H. A., Ryan, R. M., Sharp, D., & Deci, E. L. (2006). Validation of the important other climate questionnaire: Assessing autonomy support for health-related change. *Families, Systems, & Health, 24*, 179–194.

Williams, G. C., Rodin, G. C., Ryan, R. M., Grolnick, W. S., & Deci, E. L. (1998). Autonomous regulation and long-term medication adherence in adult outpatients. *Health Psychology, 17*, 269–276.

Wilson, C., & Robertson, I. H. (1992). A home-based intervention for attentional slips during reading following head injury: A single case study. *Neuropsychological Rehabilitation, 2*, 193–205.

Wilson, G. T. (1989). Behavior therapy. In R. J. Corsini & D. Wedding (Eds.), *Current psychotherapies* (4th ed., pp. 241–282). Itasca, IL: Peacock.

Witmer, J. M., & Sweeney, T. J. (1992a). A holistic model for wellness and prevention over the lifespan. *Journal of Counseling and Development, 71*, 140–148.

Witmer, J. M., & Sweeney, T. J. (1992b). Wellness throughout the life span. *Journal of Counseling and Development, 71*, 140–148.

Witmer, J. M., Sweeney, T. J., & Myers, J. E. (1993). *The wellness evaluation of lifestyle.* Greensboro, NC: Author.

Witmer, J. M., Sweeney, T. J., & Myers, J. E. (1993). *The wheel of wellness.* Greensboro, NC: Authors.

Wolf, A., & Schwarz, E. K. (1962). *Psychoanalysis in groups.* New York: Grune & Stratton.

Wolpe, J. (1990). *The practice of behavior therapy.* New York: Pergamon.

Wood, E. R. G., & Wood, S. E. (1993). *The world of psychology.* Needham Heights, MA: Allyn & Bacon.

Woodcock, R. W., McGrew, K. S., & Mather, N. (2001). *Woodcock–Johnson Psychoeducational Battery–Third edition.* Chicago: Riverside.

Woods, P. J., & Ellis, A. (1996). Supervision in rational emotive behavior therapy. *Journal of Rational-Emotive and Cognitive Behavior Therapy, 14*, 135–152.

Woollams, S., & Brown M. (1979). *TA: The total handbook of transactional analysis.* Englewood Cliffs, NJ: Prentice-Hall.

Work Importance Locator. (2001). United States Department of Labor, Employment, and Training Administration. Washington, DC: Author.

Work Importance Profiler. (2002). United States Department of Labor, Employment, and Training Administration. Washington, DC: Author.

World Health Organization. (1958). *Constitution of the World Health Organization, Annex.* Geneva, Switzerland: Author.

World Health Organization. (1964). *Basic documents* (15th ed.). Geneva, Switzerland: Author.

World Health Organization. (1992). *The IDC–10 classification system of mental and behavioral disorder: Clinical descriptions and diagnostic guidelines.* Geneva, Switzerland: Author.

Wrenn, C. G. (1962). The culturally encapsulated counselor. *Harvard Educational Review, 32*, 444–449.

Wrenn, C. G. (1985). Afterward: The culturally encapsulated counselor revisited. In P. Pedersen (Ed.), *Handbook of cross-cultural counseling and therapy* (pp. 323–329). Westport, CT: Greenwood.

Wykes, T., Brammer, M., Mellers, J., Bray, P., Reeder, C., Williams, C., et al. (2002). Effects on the brain of a psychological treatment: Cognitive remediation therapy. *British Journal of Psychiatry, 181,* 144–152.

Wynne, L., Ryckoff, I. M., Day, J., & Hirsch, S. I. (1958). Pseudo-mutuality in the family relations of schizophrenics. *Psychiatry, 21,* 205–220.

Yalom, I. D. (1975). *The theory and practice of group psychotherapy* (2nd ed.). New York: Basic Books.

Yalom, I. D. (1985). *The theory and practice of group psychotherapy* (3rd ed.). New York: Basic Books.

Yalom, I. D. (1995). *The theory and practice of group psychotherapy* (4th ed.). New York: Basic Books.

Young, M. E. (2001). *Learning the art of helping: Building blocks and techniques* (2nd ed.). Upper Saddle River, NJ: Merrill/Prentice-Hall.

Zeran, F. N., Lallas, J. E., & Wegner, K. W. (1964). *Guidance: Theory and practice.* New York: American Book Company.

Zimbardo, P. G., Weber, A. L., & Johnson, R. L. (2000). *Psychology* (3rd ed.). Needham Heights, MA: Allyn & Bacon.

Zimmerman, J. L., & Dickerson, V. C. (1994). Tales of the body thief: Externalizing and deconstructing eating problems. In M. F. Hoyt (Ed.), *Constructive therapies* (Vol. 1, pp. 295–318). New York: Guilford.

Zimpher, D. G. (1996). Five-year follow-up of doctoral graduates in counseling. *Journal of Counseling and Development, 69,* 51–56.

Zimpher, D. G., & DeTrude, J. C. (1990). Follow-up of doctoral graduates in counseling. *Counselor Education and Supervision, 35,* 218–229.

Zinker, J. (1978). *Creative process in Gestalt therapy.* New York: Random House.

Zuckerman, M. (1990). Some dubious premises in research and theory on racial differences. *American Psychologist, 45,* 1297–1303.

Zunker, V. G. (1998). *Career counseling: Applied concepts of life planning.* Pacific Grove CA: Brooks/Cole.

Zytowski, D. G., & Kuder, F. (1999). *Kuder career search with person match.* Adel, IA: National Career Assessment Services.

Index

A

A–B–C model of personality: In REBT, this model suggests that A (the activating event) does not cause C (the emotional consequence). Instead, B, which is the person's belief about A, largely causes C, the emotional reaction. 176

Aber, J. L., 588

Ableism: A pervasive system of discrimination and exclusion that oppresses people who have mental, emotional, and physical disabilities. 63, 65–66, 241–242

Abrami, P. C., 440, 441, 445, 448, 449, 450, 451, 452

Abrego, P., 333

Abstinence model: Individuals can only be considered healthy and recovering if they are not using any of the substance to which they are addicted. 583

Academic development: Strategies and activities implemented to support and maximize student learning and help students understand the significance of education to their future economic success and their quality of life. 364–365

Accommodation: In Piaget's theory of cognitive development, the process of altering current ways of thinking or creating new ways of thinking to understand new knowledge. In structural family therapy, the process through which the therapist adapts to enter the family system, and the process that the family undergoes to make changes. 147, 398

Accreditation, 8

Acculturation: Suggests that minority groups adapt to the culture, values, and norms of the dominant group rather than the dominant group adjusting to the presence of the minority group. 59

Achievement tests: Measures of the effects of learning from specific, controlled experiences such as academic courses or programs of instruction. 468, 470

Achinstein, B., 98

Ackerman, J., 389

Ackerman, N. W., 390, 391

Active mastery: In the microskills approach, the ability to produce specific and intentional results from the chosen counseling skill. 81–82

Adaptability: In Bowenian family therapy, the degree to which a person is able to manage life stress is de-

pendent on the degree to which a person is emotionally dependent on others. 380

Addiction, 568
    assessment, 574–579
    models, 572–574
    process, 569–572
    treatment, 579–585

Adjourning: The termination stage in a counseling group when members may feel a sense of loss and a need to make sense of what has happened in the group. 289, 295

Adkins, W. R., 204, 205

Adler, A., 161, 162, 163, 249, 633, 646

Adler, P. A., 518

Adler, P., 518

Adult ego state: The ego state in transactional analysis that acts much like a computer, taking in and regulating information from the parent, the child, and the environment. This ego state is the logical and realistic part of a person and makes the best possible decision in a given situation. 165, 252

Adultism: Prejudice and accompanying systematic discrimination against young people. 63, 65

Advocacy, 13–14

Affectional orientation: The type of person with whom a given individual is predisposed to bond emotionally and share personal affection. 55, 62, 65

Affectional prejudice: Subsumes homophobia as it incorporates negative attitudes and biases based on affectional orientation, including homosexuality, bisexuality, or heterosexuality. 65

Affective assessment tools: Tools measuring affective variables by asking for ideas, preferences, self-descriptors, and opinions. 328

Afferent neurons: Sensory neurons that carry signals toward the central nervous system. 608

Ageism: Systematic and stereotypic prejudice against people simply because they are old. 63, 65, 239

Ainsworth, M. D. S., 116

Airasian, P., 496

Alderian approach, 249–251

Alderman, N., 621, 622

Alexander, K., 42, 43

Alexander, M. D., 42, 43

Alloplastic perspective: Suggests that people focus primarily on working to adjust society to better fit their needs and preferences. 59–60

Allstetter-Neufeldt, S., 90, 96

Alonso, A., 109

Alpha level: The predetermined probability value selected by the researcher to make a decision about the null hypothesis. 489–490

American Association of Pastoral Counselors, 660

American Counseling Association, 3, 20, 73, 659

American Psychiatric Association, 212, 243, 408, 569, 571, 572

American School Counselor Association, 11, 12, 361

American Society for Addiction Medicine, 578

American-Arab Anti-Discrimination Committee, 238

Americans with Disabilities Act: The act passed by Congress to end discrimination against people with disabilities in the employment sector. 241, 316, 335

Amundson, N., 316

Amygdala: Part of the limbic system that is responsible largely for emotional control, and especially fear and aggression. 611

Analysis of covariance(ANCOVA): Used to test for statistically significant differences in same means of three or more groups; however, by combining the ANOVA with a correlation, it also statistically removes the effects of identified covariates or confounding variables that potentially can influence the dependent variable. 444, 493, 500

Anderson, B. S., 36, 37, 41

Anderson, C. E., 94

Anderson, S., 382

Anderson, T., 395

Andres-Hyman, R., 614

Androcentrism: The practice, conscious or otherwise, of placing male human beings or the masculine point of view at the center of one's view of the world and its culture and history. 61

Androgynous: A person who has both feminine and masculine qualities and who may assume female and male roles. 61

Angrosino, M. V., 518

Animism: Attributing live characteristics to inanimate objects. 118

Anonymity: A facet of protecting participants from risk of harm in which participants are ensured that their identities or any identifying information will not be revealed or used in the study. 435

Ansbacher, H. L., 164, 646

Anthony, E. J., 248

Anti-Semitism: The systematic discrimination against, hatred of, denigration of, or oppression of Judaism, Jews, and the cultural, religious, and intellectual heritage of Jewish people. 63, 65

Apostoleris, N. H., 601

Apply: Stage in the FERA inquiry learning model that involves monitoring the implementation of new learning as it is used in the practice of counseling and supervision. 100, 103, 106, 108

Aptitude tests: Measure informal learning from a variety of uncontrolled experiences and are said to measure innate potential, as well as predict future academic performance. 470

Arab American Institute, 236

Arbitrary interferences: The conclusions that people make about situations without due cause. 173

Arbona, C., 341, 345, 349, 357

Archer, J., 645

Archetypes: Described in Jungian psychology, these are a priori structures in the psyche that form the building blocks of psychological reality; they are primordial images that contain psychic energy and assign meaning to experience. 160, 667

Arciniega, G. M., 641

Arredondo, P., 54, 203

Arrestment: In psychoanalytic theory, the inability to move to a higher level of development because of inadequate gratification. 140–141

ASCA Ethical Guidelines on Educational Records, 43–44

ASCA National Model: A model that integrates the three widely accepted and respected approaches to program development—comprehensive, developmental, and results-based approaches—that were created to assist school districts in designing school counseling programs that support the academic success of every student. 367–368

ASCA National Standards: National standards for the school counseling profession that define what students should know and be able to do in academic, career, personal, and social realms as a result of participating in a comprehensive, developmental K–12 school counseling program. 364

Aspirational ethics: The highest standards of conduct to which counselors aim to meet ethical standards. 21–22

Assertion training: Training that increases individuals' behavioral repertoire so they are better able to choose whether or not to behave assertively in a given situation. 169, 259

Assessment: The process of collecting and integrating data from interviews, case studies, observations, and psychometric tools for the purposes of informing clinical decisions. 460–463

    behavioral, 475–477

    cognitive, 463–467

    educational, 468–472

    employment interest, 480–482

    neuropsychological, 478–480

    personality, 472–475

Assimilation: In Piaget's theory of cognitive development, the process of using preexisting knowledge to make sense of new experiences. Also refers to adaptations that are made by the minority group to the norms, values, and culture of the dominant group as well as structural adaptations made by the dominant group to include portions of the culture, values, and norms of the minority group. 59

Association for Advanced Training, 221

Association for Clinical Pastoral Education, 663

Association for Specialists in Group Work, 12, 275

Associations, 11–12

Atkinson, B., 224, 611, 614, 616, 617, 622

Atkinson, D. R., 68, 69

Attachment: The bond between a child and the primary caregiver. 151

Attrition: A threat to internal validity that occurs when participants drop out of the study in different numbers and for different reasons, which in turn affects the sample size and the composition of the treatment and control groups. 495, 509

Audience: In psychodramatic group therapy, the remaining group members who witness an enactment and hopefully experience a release of feelings and increased insight into their own struggles while observing a performance. 126, 255

Austin, B. D., 6, 8

Austin, L., 264, 272

Austin, N. L., 350

Automatic thoughts: Deep-seated personal beliefs that are triggered by the environment and typically result in maladaptive feelings and behaviors. 174, 631

Autonomy: The ethical precept that counselors respect clients' right to be self-governed. 25–26, 166, 557, 562, 596, 598, 600–601

Autoplastic perspective: Suggests that people focus on adapting to the regulations of the dominant social structure and setting. 59–60

Auxiliary ego: In psychodramatic group therapy, the group members selected by the protagonist to represent inanimate objects, pets, or persons who are dead, alive, real, or imagined. 255–256

Aversive conditioning: An undesirable stimulus is presented after a target behavior to decrease the probability that such behavior will happen again. 145

Axlerad, S., 315

Axon: Extends from the cell body and carries output signals to other neurons. 608–609

B

Baker, J., 47, 80

Baker, S. B., 544, 659

Balbernie, R., 608, 609

Baldwin, B. A., 556

Bales, R. F., 288

Balzer, W. K., 483

Bambino, D., 98

Bandler, R., 393–394

Bandura, A., 170, 172

Barlow, S. H., 257, 324, 672

Basal ganglia: Part of the forebrain related to emotional control, eye movement, turning cognition into action, and motor control. 610–612

Basch, M. F., 598

Basic mastery: In the Microskills counseling approach, the ability to demonstrate chosen counseling skills during the counseling interview. 80, 82

Basic psychological needs: In self-determination theory, the inner resources with important survival value that are held to be universal and include the needs for relatedness, competence, and autonomy. 595–599

Baucom, D. H., 379

Baumeister, R., 595

Baumrind, D., 121

Beach, A., 94

Beck, A. T., 173, 378, 409

Beck, J. S., 94

Becker, B., 593

Becker, D., 94

Bednar, R. L., 288, 290

Behavioral approach, 257–260

Behavioral assessment: A process of systematically gathering observations of a set of target behaviors, examining the relations between these observations and possible causes of the behavior, and applying the information to treatment planning and progress monitoring. 475–477, 574

Behavioral consultation: A relationship whereby services consistent with a behavioral orientation are provided either indirectly to a client or a system (through the mediation of important others in the client's environment or of those charged with the system's well-being) or directly by training consultees to enhance their skills with clients or systems. 539–542

Belsky, J., 588, 589, 591

Bemak, F., 6, 8

Bemmels, B., 217

Beneficence: The ethical precept that counselors should attempt to perform some good for their clients (as opposed to merely avoiding harm). 24–25

Ben-Porath, Y. S., 474

Berenson, B., 199

Berg, I. K., 394, 395

Bergan, J. R., 531, 541, 542

Berger, P. L., 513

Berk, L. E., 126, 140, 141, 142, 148, 150

Berkowitz, S., 258

Bernal, M. E., 68

Bernard, J. M., 74, 77, 78, 83, 87, 88, 93, 94, 95, 100, 106
Berne, E., 165, 167, 251, 253, 254, 665
Bernstein, J., 164
Berry, J. W., 58, 341
Bertalanffy, L. V., 529
Betz, N. E., 324, 342, 347, 348
Bias: A preference, tendency, or inclination toward particular ideas, values, people, or groups. 64–65, 158, 306, 388, 455
Biglan, A., 397
Bingham, R. P., 341, 354, 355
Birth order: A child's chronological or psychological birth position that influences the child's behavior and eventual perception of his or her world. 162, 164, 237, 249, 381
Blaming: In conjoint family therapy, a communication style in which a person declares himself or herself to be in control and more powerful than others. 392
Bloch, S., 280
Block, C. B., 230
Block, P., 230, 531
Blocking: A specific type of protection that is used to stop a group member from storytelling, rambling, or otherwise talking in a manner that runs counter to the purposes of the group. 294
Blumenfeld, H., 609, 610, 611, 612, 613
Blustein, D. L., 320
Bochner, A. P., 521
Bogdan, R. C., 513
Bogdevic, S. R., 518
Bonanno, G. A., 565
Borders, L. D., 82, 87, 95, 106, 641
Bordin, E. S., 101, 321
Borgatta, E. F., 288
Borgen, F. H., 481
Boscolo, L., 401
Boszormenyi-Nagy, I., 389, 390
Botwinick, J., 130
Boulding, K. E., 279
Boulian, P. V., 484
Boundaries: The physical and psychological limits that frame a professional counseling relationship. 29, 268, 399, 544
Bowen, M., 380, 381, 382
Bowen, R., 126
Bowers, J., 364
Bowlby, J., 150, 151, 588, 589, 595
Bowman, S. L., 346
Boyce, W. T., 593
Bozarth, J. D., 266
Bradley, A., 335
Bradley, L. J., 88, 94
Brammer, L. M., 197, 199, 201, 552
Brammer, L., 333
Braverman, L., 396, 397, 398, 566

Bridges, J., 388, 389
Brief, A. P., 62
Briggs, K., 330
Brigman, G., 540
Broadband tools: Tools that simultaneously measure a wide range of characteristics, behaviors, and symptoms that can be used to diagnose one or several disorders. 409
Bronfenbrenner, U., 588, 589, 595
Brown, D., 317, 318, 323
Brown, G. K., 409
Brown, L. L., 95, 106
Brown, M. T., 252, 341, 342, 349, 350, 357
Brown, S. D., 343
Browning, D. S., 663
Bruner, J. S., 593
Bryant, R. A., 397, 564
Buber, M., 662, 670
Buhrmester, D., 130
Bullis, R. K., 36, 664
Bureau of Labor Statistics, 10, 362
Burlingame, G. M., 275, 280, 288
Burnout: Occurs when professional counselors do not take care of their physical, emotional, spiritual, and existential needs and continually encounter high levels of stress. 16–17
Burr, V., 383
Butcher, J. N., 409, 473, 474
Butman, R. E., 664, 665
Byars, A. M., 347, 348

C

Cade, B., 394
Call, K. T., 213
Callahan, J., 555, 556, 557
Callanan, P., 46
Campbell, C. A., 364, 365, 366, 372, 374
Campbell, D., 330, 401
Campbell, J. M., 87, 96
Canalization: Situations in which the environment has little impact on inherited characteristics. 113
Capitation: A form of payment in which a fixed amount of money is paid in advance to a provider for the delivery of health care services on a per-patient, per-unit-of-time basis. 738
Caplan, G., 529, 530, 531, 536, 538
Cappas, N. M., 614
Capps, D., 663, 666
Capuzzi, D., 300
Career: The totality of work and leisure one does in a lifetime. 317
Career counseling, 315–317
    assessment tools, 328–332

multicultural issues, 341–357

process, 325

special issues, 332–336

technological competencies, 336–338

theory, 317–325

Career development: Strategies and activities implemented to help students acquire attitudes, knowledge, and skills to successfully transition from grade level to grade level, from school to postsecondary education, and ultimately to the world of work. 317

Career maturity: In Super's life-span, life-space career theory, the ability to perform the developmental tasks of life stages. 344

Career self-efficacy expectations: Beliefs about one's own ability to perform occupationally relevant behaviors successfully; these expectations determine one's actions, effort, and persistence in regard to career behaviors. 347

Carkhuff, R., 199, 210

Carlsen, M. B., 593

Carlson, J., 195, 545, 546

Carmichael, K. D., 237, 238

Carroll, J. B., 464

Carta-Falsa, J., 94

Carter, B., 133, 387

Carter, R. T., 345

Casas, J. M., 53, 347

Case management: A process that uses clinical protocols as guides to assign the least expensive appropriate treatment for special populations who are expected to generate large expenditures, such as people with severe persistent mental illness and children with severe emotional disturbances. 738

Case manager: A nurse, doctor, or social worker who works with patients, providers, and insurers to coordinate all services deemed necessary to provide the patient with a plan of medically necessary and appropriate health care. 738

Case rate: A previously agreed on fee paid to a provider for the entire course of treatment for one case. 738

Casile, W. J., 97

Categorical independent variables: In a nonexperimental design, participants are classified into discrete groups (e.g., gender, race, marital status, religious affiliation, level of education). 507, 508

Causal-comparative study: Designs that use categorical independent variables. 508

Caust, B., 387

Cecchin, G., 401, 402

Ceci, S. J., 588

Cell body: Contains the nucleus of the neuron and makes up gray matter in the brain such as the cerebral cortex. 609

Center for Credentialing and Education, 73, 88

Central nervous system (CNS): Responsible for control of all major systems of the body; contains the brain and the spinal cord. 420, 608

Centration: A narrow topical focus. 121, 148

Cephalocaudal: The sequence of growth that occurs first in the head and progresses downward. 114, 115, 127

Cerebellum: Part of the hindbrain that receives sensory inputs from the brain and spinal cord that are used to coordinate movement, and also to support higher cognition through connections with the cortex. 612, 613

Cerebral cortex: The outermost part of the brain that is comprised of the frontal, temporal, occipital, and parietal lobes. 610

Certification, 10–11

Charmaz, K., 523

Cheatham, H. E., 342

Child ego state: An ego state described in transactional analysis that consists of the adapted child and the free child (or natural child). The adapted child conforms to the rules and wishes of the parent ego state and is basically compliant. The free child is spontaneous, fun, creative, and curious, caring for its needs without regard for others. 165

Chi-square statistic: Statistical test that provides a measure of goodness of fit or independence. It allows researchers to infer if two nominal variables are independent of one another or are related. 445

Cholmsky, P., 440

Chou, E. L., 348, 350

Cicchetti, D., 588, 591, 592, 593, 595

Cicerone, K. D., 616, 621

Cingulate gyrus: Part of the limbic system that is involved with attention, response selection, error detection, and emotional behavior. 611

Circular interviewing: In constructivist family therapy, a technique in which family members are questioned about how others in the family connect to a problematic issue to illuminate a variety of perspectives and highlight the systemic nature of problems. 384

Circumscription: In Gottfredson's career counseling theory, the process by which individuals gradually restrict the occupations they consider acceptable, based on their developing self-concept. 322, 346

Cisgender: Describes people who possess a gender identity or perform a gender role society considers appropriate for one's sex. 61

Civil law: Includes everything that does not fall under the category of criminal law and is exemplified by lawsuits resulting in sanctions (generally monetary awards). 36

Clark, C., 660

Clark, L. E., 310, 311

Clark, M., 375

Classical conditioning, 143

Clifford, J., 520

Clifton, D., 94

Cline, R. J., 292

Cliques: Small groups of five to seven members who tend to resemble one another in family background, interests, and social status. 130

Cognitive assessment tools: Measure cognitive variables, such as aptitude or skill tests, which typically pose questions that have correct or incorrect answers. 465

Cognitive assessment: The gathering of information about an individual's overall cognitive ability and functioning. 463

Cognitive–behavioral approaches, 167
  behaviorism, 167–169
  cognitive therapy, 172–175
  multimodal therapy, 182–184
  neo-behaviorism, 169–172
  rational emotive therapy, 176–179
  reality therapy, 179–181

Cognitive development: Involves changes of inherent intellectual and linguistic abilities through stimulating interactions with the surrounding environment. 146

Cognitive maps: Mental representations of large-scale spaces. 148

Cohen, R. J., 439, 483

Cohen, R. R., 62

Colapinto, J., 398

Collateral informants: Individuals who are close to a situation of addiction (e.g., partner, family, employer, etc.) and who are most likely to know about the addiction. 575

Collective unconscious: The unconscious memories and common images, such as mother, earth, or death shared by all of humanity that are inherited from the ancestral past. 160

Collins, B. G., 554, 565

Collins, T. M., 554, 565

Combs, A., 199, 200, 732

Comer, R. J., 406, 423, 424, 426

Coming out: Individuals have accepted and announced their homosexuality. 243

Commission on Rehabilitation Counselor Certification, 15

Compensatory rivalry: A threat to internal validity that occurs when the effects of the treatment are negated because one group sees the other group as competitors and consequently works harder than usual. 496

Competence: A combination of clinical expertise, high levels of self-awareness, and interpersonal effectiveness. 40–41

Comprehensive school counseling program: Counseling program that is intended to deliver counseling to all students; it has an organizational structure that includes standards and competencies, as well as a management and delivery system. 367, 369

Compromise: In Gottfredson's career counseling theory, the process by which individuals choose among available, but imperfect occupational alternatives by compromising some needs for others. 322

Conditioned response (CR): The response that is elicited in the presence of the conditioned stimulus. 143

Conditioned stimulus (CS): Stimulus that is paired with the unconditional stimulus with the goal of evoking the same response as the unconditional stimulus. 143

Confidence interval (CI): The range of scores that represents some percentage of confidence of including a person's true score. 448

Confidentiality: An ethical standard that safeguards clients from unauthorized disclosures of information given in a counseling relationship. 28, 46
  in schools, 47–48

Conformity prescription: Seeks to make clients fit the therapy by trying to enhance in them a positive appreciation for the therapeutic relationship. 205

Confound: Variable not considered in the study (extraneous variables) that influences the outcome of the study and consequently does not allow for valid interpretation of the results. 492

Congruence: In Holland's career theory, the match between personal interest and work environment. 199

Congruent: In conjoint family therapy, the pattern of communication reflects the reality of the self and the other in that moment. Looks, feelings, tone of voice, and body language are all reflecting the same message. 392

Congruity, 215–216

Connell, J. P., 596, 597

Connolly, J., 129

Conoley, C. W., 540, 547

Conoley, J. C., 540, 547

Conscious: The smallest piece of the mind that contains the thoughts and feelings of which a person is aware. 157

Conservation: The ability to recognize that an object's physical properties remain constant despite alteration to the object's appearance. 124

Consistency: In Holland's career theory, the similarity between an individual's top few interests. 214, 217

Consonance: Exists when two cognitions are aligned or consistent with one another. 214

Construct validation: A determination of how well test scores are indicative of the characteristics of the construct being measured. 451

Construct: An abstraction or concept inferred from the observation of regularly occurring patterns of behavior. 451

Consultation: A process in which a human service professional assists a consultee with a work-related (or caretaking-related) problem with a client system,

with the goal of helping both the consultee and the client system in some specified way. 40–41, 528
  behavioral, 539–542
  Block's model, 532
  historical evolution, 529–532
  mental health, 536–539
  organizational, 542–545
  orientation, 535–536
  school-based, 545–547
  theories, 533–534
Conte, C., 566
Content validity: The test items on an instrument are representative of the attribute being measured. 450
Content-oriented consultation: Implies that the consultee lacks understanding and awareness and, therefore, needs the consultant to provide expertise to successfully solve the problems. 543
Continuous development: Development that occurs gradually over the life span in a fashion that may be thought of as cumulative or quantitative in nature. 138
Continuous independent variable: In nonexperimental designs, participants are placed or fall along some continuum such as age, IQ, self-esteem, persistence, or goal orientation. 507
Control group: In an experimental design, the group that receives no treatment or the groups that are assigned to different levels of the treatment. 499
Conventional morality: The second level of Kohlberg's moral development stages in which ethical decision making is based on societal expectations and necessities for the purpose of maintaining societal normality. 148
Convergence: The phenomenon of overlapping cultural dimensions affecting experience and identity. 55
Cook, D. A., 62, 345
Coombs, R. H., 572, 577
Coping skills development, 203–205
Corbin, J., 524
Corey, C., 82
Corey, G., 157, 158, 162, 164, 167, 170, 172, 173, 174, 176, 177, 181, 185, 186, 188, 189, 190, 202, 248, 251, 257, 259, 271, 272, 387, 396, 664, 669, 676, 673
Corey, M. S., 282, 290
Cormier, S., 197, 201
Cornell, S., 62
Correlational study: Designs that use continuous independent variables. 508
Correlations: Used to indicate the strength of the relation between two variables and to determine the extent to which the behavior of one variable can predict that of another variable. 444
Corsiglia, V., 396
Corsini, R. J., 251
Costa, P. T., Jr., 473, 474, 475

Costa, S. R., 98
Cost-containment case management: A model that allows case managers to develop treatment plans that take into account the client's social and medical needs. This may include authorizing services beyond the coverage of the plan, particularly if such treatment proves less costly. 738
Cottone, R. R., 587
Council for Accreation of Counseling and Related Educational Programs, 9, 15, 221, 659, 675
Council on Rehabilitation Education, 9
Counseling history, 3
Counseling theory: A framework for observing and understanding human behavior that also allows for making predictions about the concerns, actions, perceptions, emotions, and motivations of human beings. 195
Countertransference: Projections counselors cast on their clients. 15, 30
Cournoyer, B. R., 558, 559
Covariates: Confounding variables that can potentially influence the dependent variable. 444
Cowan, M., 204
Coward, R. L., 94
Coyne, J., 397
Cozolino, L. J., 607, 613, 615, 616, 617, 622
Crace, R. K., 331
Crawford, R. L., 41
Criminal law: Involves crimes punishable by fine, imprisonment, or death and is prosecuted by the government. 36
Crisis: The perception or experiencing of an event or situation as an intolerable difficulty that exceeds the resources and coping mechanisms of the person; unless the person gains relief, the crisis has the potential to cause severe affective, cognitive, and behavioral malfunctioning. 551–559
Crisis intervention, 559
  six-step model, 559–562
  trends, 564–566
  triage assessment, 562–564
Cristofalo, V. J., 130
Criterion-referenced test: Test that is used to determine if an individual demonstrates a predetermined standard of performance. 432
Criterion-related validity: A high association or correlation between the test score and some other measure of interest. 452
Critical friend: A trusted person who asks provocative questions, provides data to be examined through another lens, and offers critiques of a person's work as a friend. A critical friend takes the time to fully understand the context of the work presented and the outcomes that the person or group is working toward.

The friend is an advocate for the success of that work. 98

Critical period: Brief stage of development during which a developing child is predisposed to learn a specific ability or function because of heightened susceptibility to particular environmental stimuli. 113

Crnic, K., 589

Cronbach's alpha: A method of establishing internal consistency for test items that are not scored dichotomously, such as questionnaires. 448

Cross, W. E., 67

Cross-cultural career counseling: The study of how racial and ethnic minority groups adjust to White majority work environments. 342

Crouch, E. C., 280

Crystallized intelligence: Acquired skills and knowledge such as verbal abilities and general information that increase over time. 464

Cultural constructs, 60–63
  biases, 64
  discrimination, 64–66
  privilege, 66–67

Cultural context: The totality of the context in which people live, "including ethnographic, demographic, status and affiliation variables." 222

Cultural encapsulation: Counselors' reliance on a narrow model of helping that fails to account for cultural values, beliefs, and variables and interprets health and wellness the same across cultures. 57

Cultural heterosexism: The stigmatization, repudiation, subjugation, or defamation of sexual minorities within societal institutions. 65

Cultural identity: Involves taking account of cultural differences that may overlay other components and influence individual career development and vocational behavior. These differences typically surface in attitudes and discriminatory practices in the current job market and world of work. 354

Cultural identity development, 67–69
  R/CID model, 68

Cultural values: The worth, importance, or usefulness of something to a person that is aligned with the person's cultural background. Cultural values contain a historical component in that they are passed from one generation to another and are highly esteemed by the individual as well as the community from which the individual comes. 309

Culture: A combination of learned behaviors, thoughts, and beliefs as well as the results of learned behaviors, thoughts, and beliefs whose components and elements are shared and transmitted by the members of a particular society. 55

Culture-sensitive counseling, 54–55
  convergence, 55–56
  encapsulation, 57–58
  relativism, 55–56
  universality, 55

Cummings, N. A., 733

D

Dahir, C. A., 364, 365, 366, 372, 373, 374

Dahlstrom, W. G., 409, 473

Dandeneau, C. J., 83

Danger: Distress may be so severe that a person becomes a danger to himself or herself (suicide) or to others (homicide). 406

Daniels, J., 55

Daniels, T., 80

Dasen, P. J., 58

Dattilio, F. M., 379

Davidson, L., 614

Davis, J. H., 522

Davis, T., 15, 49, 50

Davison, R., 97

Dawis, R. V., 331, 484

Day, J., 391

Day, S. X., 343

de Perez, K. A. M., 518

deCharms, R., 596

Deci, E. L., 593, 594, 595, 596, 600, 601, 605

Deferred imitation: An infant's ability to imitate an adult's sounds or behaviors after a delay of several hours or days. 116

Deiter, P. J., 564

DeJong, P., 395

DeLucia-Waack, J. L., 276, 282, 299, 300

Delworth, U., 76, 77, 94

Deming, W. E., 530

Dendrites: Branches that extend from the cell body and receive signals from other neurons. 609

Denzin, N. K., 514

Dependent variable: Variable that is considered the consequence of the independent variable to the extent that it is predicted by the independent variable. 491

Descriptive statistics: Statistical inquiry that uses observations to describe or make summary statements about data. 436

DeShazer, S., 394

DeStafano, L., 733

DeTrude, J. C., 6

Deurzen-Smith, E., van, 271

Developmental Counseling and Therapy: an integrative theory that was developed within a counseling, wellness, developmental, and co-constructive framework and that brings all types of developmental theory into the counseling interview. 624
  consciousness models, 628–632
  historical context, 625–626

philosophy, 626–628

systemic cognitive therapy, 634–641

wellness, 632–634

Developmental crisis: Occurs when events in the normal flow of human growth are disrupted by a dramatic shift that precipitates a change in the way people function. 552

Developmental psychopathology: A combination of ecological and transactional theories that studies the contributions of the person and the environment to both adaptive and maladaptive developmental outcomes. 591

Deviance: Thoughts, emotions, or behaviors that are different for what is expected of that time and place. 406

Diagnosing: The process of matching an individual's observed and reported abnormal psychological symptoms to a cluster of symptoms known as a syndrome or a disorder. 408

Diagnosis: Statement made when psychological symptoms are consistent with a known mental health disorder or syndrome. 408

Diamond, G. M., 94

Dickerson, V. C., 384

Dickson, W., 565

DiClemente, C. C., 580

Dies, R. R., 293

Dietz, J., 62

Differentiation: In Bowenian family therapy, the process of becoming an individual self who is not defined by family roles or expectations; the outcome of this process is emotional and intellectual clarity and low levels of anxiety. In Holland's career theory, the difference between the highest and lowest interest. 381

Diffusion: A threat to internal validity that occurs when the treatment or control group becomes aware of the experimental treatment and because of the awareness does not respond as they normally would on the dependent variable. 496

Dinkmeyer, D. C., 531, 545, 546

Direct observation: Systematic observation of a person in a naturalistic setting in which the observer simultaneously considers the person's behavior and its environmental context. 476

Directional hypothesis: Specific statement about which group will exhibit more or less of a treatment effect. 487

Director: The psychodramatic group leader who encourages intense emotional participation by a protagonist, helps delineate what occurs after the psychodramatic enactment, and helps the protagonist gain insight and emotional resolution through group feedback. 255

Disability, *see* Ableism

Discontinuous development: Development occurs in distinct stages throughout the life span. 138

Discrimination: Unfair and unequal treatment that systematically prevents certain groups from being afforded opportunities that are provided to other groups. 79, 64

Dishabituation: An infant's restored interest in a known stimulus. 117

Disney, M. J., 95

Disorder: Abnormal psychological symptoms that tend to occur together, present to a marked degree, and last for a significant amount of time. 634

Displaced homemakers: Persons who find themselves leaving their responsibilities of taking care of the home and perhaps children to find paid work. 334

Dissonance: Occurs when there is inconsistency between two thoughts. 214–215

Dissymmetry: In Newcomb's model of attraction, the state that exists when either A or B have contradictory attitudes toward X; when dissymmetry exists, A and B change intensity of their attitudes toward X or their attraction toward one another until symmetry is reestablished. 216

Distress: Deviant thoughts, emotions, or behaviors that cause disruption and upset to the person experiencing them, and, at times, to others in contact with the individual experiencing distressing symptoms. 406

Diversity, *see* Multicultural realities

Doan, R., 94

Donigian, J., 299, 300

Dougherty, M. A., 531, 536, 538, 539, 540, 542, 547

Draguns, J. G., 221

Draper, R., 401

Drawing out: In group counseling, a technique the leader uses to invite group members who find it difficult to share or who only share at a superficial level to participate at a level of involvement of the member's own choosing. 294

Dreikurs, R., 249

Drummond, R., 410

Dryden, W., 261, 380

Dual diagnosis: Individuals who have some form of addiction, typically a chemical addiction, and an additional Axis I diagnosis. 581

Dual relationships: Any significantly different relationship a counselor has with a client outside of his or her counselor-client relationship. 29, 45–46

clients' emotional health, 46

Duffy, M., 37, 45

Duhl, B., 392

Duncan, B., 396, 398

Dunn, H. L., 644

Dunning, C., 565

Duties, 49–50

Duty to warn: Refers to the responsibility of a counselor or therapist to breach confidentiality if a client or other identifiable person is in clear or imminent danger. 49

Dye, H. A., 87

Dysfunction: Distress is so significant that it causes impairment in important daily activities (e.g., work or school) or relationships. 406

E

Echterling, L. G., 558, 565

Eclecticism: Borrowing from a variety of approaches depending on the presenting problem; the client's most important needs at a moment and time; how much time is available to initiate change; what objectives and goals have been agreed on; the preferences, styles, and mood of the helper; and the philosophy of the organization. 196

Eco, U., 519

Ecological-transactional counseling, 587–593, *see also* Self-determination theory

      Bowlby, 589

      Bronfenbrenner, 589–590

      Vygotsky, 588–589

Educational assessment: Methods for obtaining information relating to a student's overall academic progress and informal and formal learning. 468

Edwards, A., 344

Effective counselors, 7–8

Efferent neurons: Motor neurons that carry signals away from the central nervous system. 608

Egan, G., 99, 204, 207, 208

Eghrari, H., 601

Ego state: In transactional analysis, a system of feelings accompanied by a related set of behavior patterns. 165

Ego syntonic: Psychological symptoms that cause individuals little distress. 428

Ego: Component of personality that relies on the reality principle to weigh the desires of the id against the demands of the superego and the external world. 140

Egocentrism: A self-centered view of the world in which everything is perceived in relation to oneself. 120

Ehlers, A., 564

Eichhorn, K., 520

Eisenberg, N., 126

Eisler, R., 551

Elbert, S., 398

Eliason, G., 658, 661, 662, 663, 664, 674

Elkind, D., 128

Ellis, A., 78, 176, 177, 261, 262, 378, 627, 673, 674

Ellis, C., 521

Emic perspective: Suggests that cultural values, worldviews, and contexts all affect definitions of normal and deviant behavior. 56

Empathy: Ability of the counselor both to enter the world of the client without being influenced by his or her own personal values or beliefs and to communicate understanding genuinely and effectively. 186

Empirical dictates: Interventions clinically proven to alter problematic behavior or thoughts that are used during therapy. 378

Employee assistance programs (EAPs): Worksite-based programs designed to assist in the identification and resolution of productivity problems associated with employees impaired by personal concerns including, but not limited to health, marital, family, financial, alcohol, drug, legal, emotional, stress, or other personal concerns that may adversely affect employee job performance. 732

Empty chair technique: In Gestalt therapy, a technique designed to help members work through unfinished business. A member sits directly across from and speaks to an empty chair that he or she envisions holding the person with whom he or she is in conflict. 268

England, G., 484, 551

Engler, B., 667, 668, 669

Enns, C. Z., 387, 388

Epicurus, 22

Epstein, N. B., 379

Eriksen, K. P., 91

Erikson, E., 132, 142, 143, 665

Etaugh, C., 388, 389

Ethical codes: The written form of ethical conduct that is intended to improve professionals' ability to successfully and competently respond to clients' needs. 34–35

Ethical theory, 22

      Epicureanism, 22–23

      Kantianism, 23

      Situationalism, 23–24

      Utilitarianism, 23

Ethics: The standards governing the conduct of members of the counseling profession. 14–15, 19, 21

      ACA, 20–21

      and cultural diversity, 20

      codes, 19–20

      concerns, 28–31

Ethics and decision making, 24, 26–27

      autonomy, 25

      beneficence, 24–25

      fidelity, 25

      justice, 25–26

      nonmaleficence, 24

Ethnocentrism: The tendency to use one's own cultural standards as the standards by which to evaluate other groups and to rank these standards higher than all others. 58

Ethnography: A specialized form of field work that grew out of cultural anthropology and that should be conducted with as few presuppositions and as few predetermined goals as possible. 520

Etic perspective: Suggests that many aspects of human behavior are universal and counselors, therefore, can apply therapeutic techniques similarly across cultures and contexts. 56

Eurocentric perspectives, 53

Evaluation: The objective appraisal of the supervisee's performance based on clearly defined criteria that are realistic and attainable. 106

Everett, C. A., 400, 401

Existential crisis: Occurs when individuals become aware that an important intrapersonal aspect of their lives may never be fulfilled, which, in turn, has an impact on self-purpose and self-worth. 552

Existential-humanistic approaches, 184, 270–272
     gestalt, 187–189
     logotherapy, 190–192
     person-centered, 185–187

Exner, J. E., Jr., 472

Explore: Stage in the FERA inquiry learning model that involves encouraging the counselor to frame questions, develop hypotheses, and predict consequences of action that might be taken; issues and processes that are emerging in the counseling or supervisory relationships are also investigated. 100

External motivation: Initiatives that are characterized by a sense of pressure, coercion, and control. 597

External validity: Generalizability of the results or the extent to which results are replicable and can be generalized to other groups and contexts beyond the experimental setting. 496

Externalization: A technique in constructivist family therapy in which problems are conceptualized as separate from the family to free members from the belief that they are problematic. 384

Extinction: Withholding reinforcement from a formerly reinforced behavior. 145

F

Fabes, R. A., 126

Face validity: An informal assessment made by the person taking the test that the instrument measures what it appears to measure. 450

Facilitator: A leader who participates genuinely in the group process as a member of the group without using gimmicks or planned procedures. 266

Factor analysis: Statistical test used to analyze the effects of more than one independent variable as well as the interaction effects of the independent variables on a dependent variable. 451

Falendar, C., 90

Falicov, C. J., 55

Fall, K. A., 182, 183

Falvey, J. E., 95, 96

Family constellation: Variables such as personality, developmental issues, family attitudes and values, and structural factors that influence a child's interaction with and perception of the family compilation, and the ways in which a child views himself or herself outside of the family. 162

Family Education Rights and Privacy Act (FERPA): Federal legislation that governs education records and dictates how all written information on a student will be handled and disseminated for the protection of the student and his or her family. 42–43

Family map: A visual representation of three generations of the "star" or identified client's family that records adjectives to describe each person's personality or relationship to the larger family as well as general demographic information. 393

Family therapy
     behavioral, 378–380
     Bowenian, 380–382
     constructivist, 383–384
     experiential, 385–386
     feminist, 387–389
     psychodynamic, 389–391
     Satir growth model, 391–394
     solution-focused, 394–396
     strategic, 396–398
     structural, 398–400
     systemic, 400–402

Family time inventory: Family members track their activities throughout the day to facilitate the scheduling of family time for at least 1 hour per day. 393

Fast mapping: The ability to build vocabularies very quickly by learning to connect new words with their underlying concepts after only brief encounter. 121

Faust, N., 531

Feedback: A group member or leader's shared observations and reactions to another member's expressed feelings, thoughts, or behaviors. 292

Feller, R., 334, 336

Fetterman, D., 514

Fick, A. C., 589

Fidelity: The ethical precept stipulating that counselors act faithfully and honestly with their clients. 25

Finch, M. A., 213

Fine motor skills: Physical abilities that require the use of small muscles. 115

Fisch, R., 401

Fischer, L., 42

Fishman, H. C., 400

Fitzgerald, L. F., 342

Fixation: In psychoanalytic theory, the inability to move to a higher level of development because of excessive gratification. 140

Fixed battery: An instrument consisting of a number of standardized subtests administered in a determined fashion. 478

Fleming, A., 299, 300

Flexible battery: An instrument that consists of specific tests tailored to the examinee's apparent presenting problem. 485

Flores, L. Y., 343

Fluid intelligence: Abilities such as reasoning and concept formation that are related to mental operations and processes that decline over time. 464

Focus: Stage in the FERA inquiry learning model that involves engaging the counselor and determining what is known and what is not known about both content and process. The supervisor must listen for and determine what is explicit and what is implied in the counseling or supervision relationship. 105

Focusing: Paying attention to a problem as a whole within one's body, as these bodily shifts and responses to problems or solutions often go unrecognized. 211

Folstein, M. F., 478

Folstein, S. E., 478

Fong, 87

Foos, J. A., 731

Forced choice response: On an assessment instrument, the responder is forced to choose from the options given, such as never, sometimes, and always. 477

Forebrain: Comprised of the limbic system, the thalamus, the hypothalamus, and the basal ganglia, the forebrain lies below the cortex and contains communication, motor control, memory, and emotional processing centers of the brain. 610

Forester-Miller, H., 15

Formal norms: Group norms that are communicated and agreed on. 290

Forming: In group therapy, the initial stage during which members are getting to know each other, the group leader, and the group boundaries. 289

Forsyth, D. R., 214, 216, 276

Fouad, N. A., 341, 342, 343, 354

Foulkes, S. H., 248

Framo, J. L., 133, 385, 386, 389, 390, 391

Francis, M. K., 130

Frank, E., 397, 690

Frankl, V. E., 190, 668

Franklin, K. K., 230, 522

Frederickson, J., 391

Freedman, Z. R., 600

Freeman, M., 392, 394

Freire, P., 66

Fretz, B., 536

Freud, S., 247, 665, 666

Frontal lobe: The front-most and largest area of the cortex that contains the motor cortex and sensory cortex. 610

Fry, R. K., 621

Frye, N., 667

Fuhriman, A. J., 275, 280

Fuqua, D., 532, 545

Furman, W., 130

G

Gage, L., 645

Gagne, M., 600

Gale, A. U., 6, 8

Games: In transactional analysis, an ongoing series of complementary ulterior transactions progressing to a well-defined, predictable outcome. 253

Garmezy, N., 588, 592

Gatekeeper: Under some health insurance arrangements a primary care provider serves as the patient's agent, arranges for and coordinates appropriate medical services, laboratory studies, hospitalizations, and other necessary and appropriate referrals. 738

Gatson, S. N., 520

Gay, L. R., 496

Gazda, G. M., 275

Geertz, C., 519

Gelman, R., 125

Gelso, C., 536

Gender role stereotypes: Socially determined models that contain the cultural beliefs about what the gender roles should be. 61

Gender roles: Behaviors, attitudes, values, emotions, beliefs, and attire that a particular cultural group considers appropriate for males and females on the basis of their biological sex. 61

Gender: A system of sexual classification based on the social construction of the categories "men and boys" and "women and girls" and usually refers to a person's masculinity or femininity. 61

General intelligence (g): A construct used in the field of psychology that measures what is common to the scores of all cognitive intelligence tests. 464

Genetic determination theory, 151

Genotype: The underlying genetic makeup of an organism. 113

Genuineness: The congruence or "realness" of an individual counselor or group leader that increases the likelihood of growth and change in clients. 185

Gerler, E. R., 47

Gerrity, D. A., 276, 282

Gershenfeld, M. K., 281

Gestalt: A complete pattern or configuration. 267–270

Geuss, R., 519

Gevarter, W. B., 609, 612, 614, 616, 622

Giacino, J. T., 616
Gibson, R. L., 47
Gill, S., 94, 100
Ginter, E. J., 275, 732
Ginzberg, E., 319
Giordano, J., 226
Gladding, S. T., 19, 156, 157, 158, 166, 252, 254, 255, 382, 386, 389, 391, 393, 394, 399, 400, 401
Glaser approach, 523
Glaser, B. G., 513, 523
Glasser, W., 179, 180, 181, 263, 673
Gleitman, L. R., 121
Glisky, E. L., 619, 620, 621
Glisky, M. L., 619, 620, 621
Go around: A procedure during which group members are asked to either spontaneously or sequentially discuss what they learned, what they wish they had accomplished but did not, and how they will take their new knowledge and use it in the future. 296
Goals 2000, 363, 364
Goenjian, A., 558
Goh, M., 285, 286
Goldberg, A., 129
Goldner, V., 387, 389
Goldstein, A. P., 205
Goodman, P., 188, 267
Goodyear, R. K., 78, 79, 83, 87, 88, 93, 95, 100, 106
Gordon, R., 440
Gordon, T., 265
Gottesman, I. I., 113
Gottfredson, L. S., 322, 323
Graham, J. R., 409, 473, 474
Graun, K., 531
Gray-Little, B., 130
Green, M., 149, 150
Greenberg, K. R., 47
Grieger, T. A., 551
Grinder, J., 393
Grolnick, W. S., 600, 601
Gross motor skills: Physical abilities that require the use of large muscles. 120
Gross, D. R., 300
Groth-Marnat, G., 408
Group cohesiveness: The attractiveness of a group to the members that can be developed between individual group members, between the member and the group, and between the members and the group leader. 280
Group content: The words that are spoken between individuals in a group. 279
Group dynamics: The way in which the members interact with each other and mutually influence one another's perceptions and behavior. 278–281
Group leadership, 281–284
cultural considerations, 284–287

Group norms: Informal and formal beliefs about group behavior such as language, attendance, confidentiality, degree of self-disclosure, punctuality, content shared, and processes expected to occur. 290
Group process: Nature of the relationship between interacting individuals. 279
Group work: A broad professional practice involving the application of knowledge and skill in group facilitation to assist people in reaching mutual goals, which may be intrapersonal, interpersonal, or work related. 247–272
    fundamentals, 276–278
    history, 275–276
    multicultural, 300
    pregroup planning, 287–296
Grow, V. M., 600
Guba, E. G., 514
Guerney, B., 208, 398
Guth, L. J., 83
Guthrie, I. K., 126
Gysbers, N. C., 316, 325, 367

H

Habituation: An infant's waning interest in a stimulus that is repeatedly presented. 117
Hackett, G., 324, 343, 347, 348
Hackney, H. L., 78, 197, 201
Haddad, N. K., 601
Hadden, S. B., 275
Hafdahl, A. R., 130
Haley, J., 396, 397
Haley, T., 384
Halgin, R. P., 82
Hall, C. S., 160
Hall, D. L., 540, 542, 543
Hammer, A. I., 481
Hankin, S., 262
Hanley, C., 658
Hann, D. M., 589
Hanna, F. J., 6, 8, 542
Hansen, J. C., 259, 330, 481, 531
Hardin, E. E., 345, 353, 356
Hardy, E., 94
Hare, I., 50
Hare, P., 288
Hare-Mustin, R. T., 384, 388, 400
Harlow, H. F., 595
Harmon, L. W., 481
Harper, F. D., 225, 226, 228, 230, 231, 234
Harrington, T., 330
Harris-Bowlsbey, J., 316
Harrison, T. C., 540, 546
Hart, G., 87, 88

Harter, S., 129
Hartmann, D., 62
Hartung, P. J., 341, 351, 354, 356
Haskell, M. R., 256
Haskins-Herkenham, D., 50
Hatch, T., 364
Hathaway, S. R., 443, 473
Hattie, J. A., 647
Haughey, J., 290
Hawkins, P., 94
Hawthorne effect: Participants behave differently simply because they know they are being studied. 497
Haynes, R., 82, 89
Health and wellness, 15, 17, 57, 579, 643, 644
 burnout, 16–17
 countertransference, 15, 30–31
 networking, 17
 specialties, 4–5
Health Insurance Portability and Accountability Act (HIPAA): Federal legislation that emerged to address the substandard level of care in place with regard to sharing and releasing of client health and mental health information. 44
Health maintenance organization (HMO): A type of health care plan usually associated with specific geographical areas where members pay a flat monthly rate in return for health care services delivered by a group of mental health and medical professionals. 738
Heath, S. B., 521, 522
Hefferline, R. F., 188, 267
Heider, F., 214
Heider's balance theory, 215–216
Heiman, M., 133
Held, B. S., 384
Helms, J. E., 62, 68, 344, 350
Helping: A broad term that encompasses all the activities counselors use to assist others whether they have a professional relationship or not. 195
 diversity, 203
 effective helping, 199–202
 skills, 202–207
 social–psychological approaches, 211–217
 theories, 195–198
 training, 207–211
Henderson, D., 47
Henderson, P., 367
Hendricks, C. B., 94
Hendricks, C. G., 561
Hendricks, J. E., 561
Henly, G. A., 331
Henry, W. E., 133
Heppner, M. J., 487
Heppner, P. P., 316, 487
Herlihy, B., 21, 49, 664

Herma, J., 315
Herr, E. L., 361
Hess, A. K., 109
Hill, C. E., 99
Hill, G. W., 98
Hill, L. K., 731
Hill, M. R., 524
Himes, B. S., 531
Hindbrain: Found at the base of the brain between the cortex and the spinal cord, the hindbrain is the pathway between the brain and the rest of the body. 610, 612
Hippocampus: Part of the limbic system that is responsible for memory function, through involvement in the creation of new memories and recall of old memories. 611
Hirsch, S. I., 391
History: Threat to internal validity that refers to any event that is not part of the experimental treatment but occurs during the study and influences responses on the dependent variable. 495
HMO group practice: An HMO that contracts with a single multispecialty medical group partnership to provide services to its members on a preagreed per-capita rate, which the group distributes among its physicians. 739
HMO staff: A type of closed-panel HMO in which medical professionals are employed by the HMO to provide care to members in the HMO's own facilities. 739
Hobbs, N., 265
Hodder, I., 524
Hoff, L. A., 561
Holder, J. M., 182, 183
Holland, J. L., 318, 319
Hollander, M., 258, 259
Holloway, E. L., 75, 94, 99
Holophrastic: The expression of a complete thought as a single word. 117
Homan, M. S., 530
Homophobia: The expression of irrational fears about people who exhibit signs of accepting or using behaviors related to same-sex forms of sexual desire and orientation. 65
Horne, A. M., 256, 275
Howard-Hamilton, M. F., 55
Howatt, W. A., 577
Howieson, D. B., 610
Hoyt, M. F., 383, 384
Huck, S. M., 213
Hughes, T., 565
Human development: The phenomenon of continuity and change in the biopsychological characteristics of human beings both as individuals and as groups. The phenomenon extends over the life course across suc-

cessive generations and through historical time, both past and present. 137–140

Human growth and development
  adolescence, 125–128
  adulthood, 128–131
  approaches, 139–142
  behavioral theories, 143–145
  cognitive theories, 146–150
  continuity and discontinuity, 138–139
  death and bereavement, 131–133
  developmental domains, 139
  early childhood, 117–121
  ethological theories, 150–151
  humanistic theories, 152
  infancy, 112–117
  learning theories, 146
  maturational theories, 151
  middle childhood, 121–125
  nature vs. nurture, 137–138
  prenatal development, 111–112
  psychodynamic theories, 139–142

Hypothalamus: Part of the forebrain located beneath the thalamus that is important for control of autonomic nervous system responses and acts as the link between the neural and endocrine systems. 611

I

Ibrahim, F. A., 53, 69

Id: Structure of personality that is present at birth and may be considered the primitive, unconscious segment of personality that motivates individuals to seek immediate gratification of inherent desires (sexual, physical, emotional) without regard for potential consequences. 140

Identity, 4, 33
  and social work, 5
  legal issues, 34

Idol, L., 38

Ilardi, S. S., 613

Imaginary audience: A form of egocentrism that describes adolescents' impressions that they are the center of everyone's attention and judgment. 128

Imber, M., 42, 47

Imitation of treatments: *see* Diffusion.

Immanuel Kant, 23

Imprinting: A learning process driven by innate propensities to establish social bonds in the form of permanent attachments with the first living, moving organisms a young animal or human notices and shadows. 150

Indemnity health insurance: Through this type of plan, the patient or the provider receives reimbursement for services as expenses are incurred. 739

Independent practice associations (IPAs): Groups of independent medical practitioners who band together for the purpose of contracting their services to HMOs, preferred provider organizations (PPOs), and insurance companies to provide services to both HMO and non-HMO plan participants on an agreed, prepaid capitated rate. 739

Independent variable: Variable that is hypothesized to be responsible for the effect and also is called the treatment or experimental variable. 491

Individual values: The worth, importance, or usefulness of something to an individual. 309

Individuals with Disabilities Education Act, 760

Individuation: The movement of the personality toward its fullest creative potential. 160

Inferential statistics: Statistical inquiry that uses observations of a sample population to make predictions and generalizations about the wider population. 436

Informal norms: Group norms that influence individuals without the individuals necessarily being able to communicate the existence of the norms. 290

Informed consent: Disclosure to clients of what to expect from the counseling process. In research investigations, participants must be made fully aware of the scope of expectations surrounding their participation in and the procedures of the study, and then freely give their consent to participate. 28, 36–37

Ingersoll, R. E., 732, 733

Inhelder, B., 128

Instillation of hope: Members have a sense of hope that they can receive help and learn how to better deal with their problems. 289

Instrumentation: Data collection devices must be reliable and must be consistent across measuring occasions to avoid internal threats to validity. 495

Intention: Choosing the best potential response from among the many possible options. 80

Interest inventories: Inventories that identify an individual's self-reported interests according to categories or scales, career fields, and specific job titles. 329

Internal motivation: Refers to initiatives that are characterized by a sense of autonomy and choice. 597

Internal validity: The results of the experiment are attributable to the manipulated independent variable and cannot be explained by other factors. 495

Internalization: An aspect of socialization in which external values, norms, and regulations are taken in by the active, organismic self, and are experienced by that self as either endorsed and congruent or as alien and incongruent. 597

Interpersonal process recall (IPR), 82–83

Intersex: A person who was born with genitalia or secondary sexual characteristics of indeterminate sex, or with features combined from both sexes. A more archaic and less preferred term for people who are intersex is hermaphrodite. 61

Intersubjectivity: The process through which two individuals with differing views modify such views to come to a mutual understanding. 150

Interval scales: A form of measurement that also is rank ordered on a scale that contains equal intervals between numbers on the scale. However, there is no absolute zero point indicating that no mathematical calculations can be done with the data set. 437

Irrelevant: In conjoint family therapy, a communication style in which distracting the self and others by responding in a way that is not related to the context of the situation or to what is being felt, or to what has been previously said. 392

Isaacson, L. E., 317, 318, 323

Isabella, R. A., 589

Ivey, A. E., 6, 625, 627

Ivey, D., 346

Ivey, M. B., 6, 8, 625, 637

J

Jackson, B., 67, 531

Jackson, D. N., 68, 330

Jackson, J. S., 62

Jackson, M. L., 285, 287

Jacobs, E. E., 284

Jacobs, J. L., 666

James, R. K., 556, 557, 558, 559, 560, 562, 563, 565

James, W., 662

Jaschik, S., 237

Jennings, L., 6, 202

Jensen, M. A., 289

Job satisfaction: The pleasure that relates to one's occupational experience. 483

Jobes, D. A., 551

John Henry effect: *see* Compensatory rivalry.

Johnson, J. E., 280, 732

Johnson, M. J., 342, 349, 357

Johnson, R. L., 140, 142

Johnson, S. M., 484, 662

Johnson, S. W., 94

Johnston, J. A., 316

John Stuart Mill, 23

Joiner, T. E., Jr., 551

Joining: In structural family therapy, the process through which the therapist enters the family system to diagnose the source of dysfunction, understand the way the family perceives reality, and form therapeutic goals. 398

Jones, E., 231, 402

Joseph Fletcher, 23

Jung, C. G., 31, 159, 667

Juntunen, C. L., 224

Justice: The ethical precept that specifies counselors act fairly toward all potential, current, and past clients. 25

K

Kaemmer, B., 409, 473

Kaftarian, S., 514

Kagan, N., 82, 83, 210

Kahn, W. J., 539

Kallick, B., 98

Kalodner, C. R., 276, 378, 379, 380

Kane, R. A., 213

Karren, R. J., 292

Kasser, V. M., 601

Kaul, T. J., 288, 290

Keala, D. K., 382

Keith, D., 385, 386

Kell, B. L., 25, 30

Kelley, H. H., 217

Kelly, E. W., Jr., 662

Kelly, K. R., 732

Kemp, S., 480

Kenyon, B. L., 134

Kerr, M. E., 381

Kerwin, C., 68

Keyes, C. L., 645

King, C. A., 551

King, L., 646

Kinicki, A. J., 484

Kirk, U., 480

Kisch, J., 733

Kiselica, M. S., 29

Kitchener, K. S., 24, 26

Kivlighan, D. M., Jr., 280, 281, 289

Kjos, D., 195

Kleckner, T., 397

Kleespies, P. M., 551, 559

Kline, W. B., 284

Klos, D., 344

Knapp, L., 330

Knapp, R. R., 330

Knight, G. P., 68

Knudson-Martin, C., 380, 382

Kolski, T. D., 551

Konrad Lorenz, 150

Koper, R. J., 213

Korkman, M., 480

Kottler, J. A., 195, 196

Kratochwill, T. R., 531, 541

Kreidler, M. C., 551

Krumboltz, J. D., 323, 325, 379

Krushinski, M. F., 33

Kuder, F., 330, 681

Kuhl, J., 595

Kuhn, D., 128

Kurpius, D. J., 529, 530, 531, 532, 535, 543, 545

Kurtosis: The extent to which a frequency distribution of scores is bunched around the center or spread toward the endpoints. 440

Kvale, S., 518

L

La Guardia, J. G., 605

Laatsch, L., 619

Ladany, N., 88, 96, 99

Lafreniere, P. J., 150

Lallas, J. E., 362

Lambers, E., 94

Lancy, D. F., 513

Landauer, T. K., 621

Lane, G., 402

Lang, F. R., 133

Larson, D. D., 203, 204, 205, 206, 207, 209, 210, 211, 643

Lasky, G. B., 284

Latent content: In psychoanalytic theory, the unconscious meaning hidden behind the manifest meaning. 158

Latham, G. P., 292

Latner, J., 188

Law of effect: Behavior has a higher propensity to be repeated if the consequence of that behavior is positively reinforcing. 144

Law of exercise: A behavior will occur more frequently if connections between the behavior and reinforcer or consequence are routinely practiced; conversely, failure to support connections between the behavior and reinforcer through practice will result in weaker associations and a decreased likelihood of reoccurrence. 144

Law of reciprocity: Suggests that resource outputs must be balanced by inputs. 213

Law: The rule of conduct established by society and enforced by that society's government. 36

Lawe, C. F., 256

Lawless, L. L., 732, 733

Lawrence-Lightfoot, S., 522

Lazarus, A. A., 183, 672

Lazarus, B. N., 126

Lazarus, R. S., 126

Leary, M. R., 595

Lebovici, S., 589

LeCompte, M., 520

Leddick, G. R., 82

Lee-Borden, N., 94

Lent, R. W., 343, 347, 348, 349

Leone, D. R., 601

Leong, F. T. L., 341, 342, 343, 345, 347, 348, 349, 350, 351, 356, 357

Leung, S. A., 346, 347

Leventis, M., 658

Levers, L. L., 7

Levine, B., 622, 623

Levinson, D. J., 132, 698

Lewin, K., 275, 281, 282

Lewis, J., 55

Lewis, M., 55

Lezak, M. D., 610, 611, 612, 613

Liability: The legal responsibility one person has to another as a result of committing a negligent act. 34

Libow, J., 387, 388

Licensure, 9–10

Liddle, H. A., 94

Lieberman, M. A., 247, 282, 290

Liese, B. S., 94

Life fact chronology: A detailed history of the family, including the history of the parents' romantic relationship, their respective family histories, any previous unions and divorces or deaths, a history of extended family members living with the family, or others who contribute financially or in other ways and figure prominently. 393

Life scripts: Plans for life developed in early childhood that are reinforced by parents. 253

Lilienfeld, S. O., 559

Lincoln, Y. S., 514

Lindemann, E., 551

Lindle, S., 530

Lindzey, G., 160

Linking: An intervention used by group leaders to connect the concerns or behaviors of one member with those of one or more other members. 294

Lippitt, R., 281

Listening: Receiving what someone wishes to convey and saying it back to the person exactly as it was meant. 211

Litchy, M., 279

Littrell, J. M., 94

Liverpool, P., 254

Locke, D. C., 627

Locke, E. A., 292

Loftquist, L. H., 331

Loganbill, C., 94

Lohr, J. M., 559

Long, J. K., 94

Longitudinal study: Research design in which data are collected more than once over a period of time. 508

Lonner, W. J., 221

Lorenz, J. A., 94, 150

Loring, D. W., 610

Lovell, K., 378, 380

Lowry, C., 522

Luckmann, T., 513
Lunneborg, P. W., 343, 344
Luria, A. R., 616
Luthar, S. S., 593
Lynch, J. H., 596
Lynch, M. F., 588, 591, 592, 595

M

MacCluskie, K. C., 732, 733
Maccoby, E. E., 123
Macdonald, G., 197, 199, 201
MacKenzie, K. R., 280
Madanes, C., 396, 397
Maddox, G. L., 133
Maestas, M. V., 59
Main, M., 119
Malpractice, 41
Management services organization: An organization whose task is to provide business-related services, such as marketing and data collection to individual groups of providers. 739
Manaster, G. G., 251
Mandatory ethics: The level of functioning counselors must exhibit to fulfill the minimum ethical obligations. 21
Manifest content: In psychoanalytic therapy, refers to the obvious narrative of the dream. 158
Manipulation check: Process of examining the impact of the treatment to determine whether the outcome was expected or whether the outcome had unintended effects. 494
Manly, T., 620
Marcia, J. E., 129
Marcus, D. K., 278, 520
Marek, L. I., 94
Markland, D., 600, 602
Martin, D. G., 342
Martin, E., 610
Martin, F., 401, 402
Martin, J. A., 123
Martin, P., 375
Martin, S. D., 610
Maslow, A. H., 152, 198
Maslow's hierarchy of needs, 152
Mateer, C. A., 621
Mather, N., 467
Matthews, D. A., 660
Maturation: A threat to internal validity that occurs over time during which there is a chance that participants themselves undergo changes during the life of the study. 495
May, K., 388
May, R., 270, 271, 669

Mazur, C. S., 664
Mazur, J. E., 146
McAuliffe, G. J., 91
McCarroll, J. E., 551
McCaulley, M. H., 481, 482
McCrae, R. R., 473, 474, 475
McDavis, R. J., 54
McDermott, J. F., 382
McFadden, J., 225, 226, 228, 230, 231
McFarlane, A. C., 558, 559, 564
McGinn, L., 389
McGoldrick, M., 133, 226, 231, 232, 233, 234, 236
McGrew, 467
McHugh, P. R., 478
McIntosh, P., 67, 223
McKee, J. E., 484, 558
McKinley, J. C., 443, 473
McNally, R. J., 564
McNeill, B. W., 76
McWhinney, M., 50
McWilliams, N., 412
Mean: A measure of central tendency that is represented by the arithmetic average of a set of test scores from normally distributed interval or ratio data. 437
Measurement, *see* Psychometrics
Median: The measure of central tendency that represents the midway point in the distribution of data arranged in either ascending or descending order. 437
Medical staff organization: A group of physicians who have teamed together to contract with others for provision of services. 739
Medulla oblongata: Part of the hindbrain located at the base of the brain near the spinal cord, which is the control center for essential bodily functions such as breathing, blood pressure, heart rate, the gag reflex, and swallowing. 612
Meier, P. D., 666, 667, 668, 670, 671, 673
Meier, S., 531
Melnick, J., 290
Mendoza, D. W., 538
Mental health consultation: A process of interaction between two professional persons—the consultant, who is a specialist, and the consultee, who invokes the consultant's help in regard to a current work problem with which he or she is having some difficulty and which he or she has decided is within the other's area of specialized competence. 536
Mento, A. J., 292
Merkur, D., 666
Merriam, S. B., 521
Metacognition: The process of monitoring one's own process of thinking and memory. 121
Meyer, T., 98
Meyers, J., 547
Microcounseling supervision model (MSM), 80–82

Midbrain: A small section of the brain between the forebrain and the hindbrain whose primary function is sensorimotor integration. 612

Miles, M. B., 282

Miller, A., 598

Miller, G., 659, 660, 661

Miller, R. B., 382

Miller, W. R., 576, 602

Minirth, F. B., 666

Minuchin, P., 384, 398, 399

Minuchin, S., 398, 399, 400

Mitchell, D., 94

Mitchell, M. H., 47

Mitroff, I. I., 566

Mixed model: A prepaid system that combines features of more than one HMO model, without one particular model dominating another. 739

Mode: The measure of central tendency that represents the most frequently occurring score. 437

Modeling: A group leader or members exhibits behaviors and social skills that other group member can observe and then apply to their own lives. 259

Moderated management: Models of addiction treatment that see the goal of recovery as moderation rather than complete abstinence from the behavior or substance. 583

Moleski, S. M., 29

Moller, A. C., 605

Molnar, A., 394, 395

Montalvo, B., 399

Montgomery, M. L., 94

Montgomery, R. W., 559

Moore, E. J., 367

Moore, H., 565, 566

Moral development theory, 148–149

Moreno, J. L., 256

Mores: Convictions about the moral rightness or wrongness of behavior. 53

Morgan, C. D., 472, 473

Morgan, D. L., 310, 522

Morran, D. K., 279, 283, 292, 294, 296

Morris, J. R., 285

Mortality: *see* Attrition.

Morton, G., 68, 69

Motherese: Child-directed speech. 117

Motivational interviewing: An interview method in the addictions field that is founded on a high-quality clinical interview, incorporates many basic counseling skills (e.g., active listening, reflection of feeling and content, paraphrasing, etc.), and has a focus on an addict's motivation to engage in the change process. 576

Motor skills, 139

Moulton, P., 82

Moustakas, C., 519

Mowday, R. T., 484

Mullis, F., 540

Multicultural career counseling: The study of career counseling in many cultures. 69–71

Multicultural career development, 341–342

    models, 351–356

    theoretical approaches, 342–349

    variables, 349–351

Multicultural group work: The expansion of personal and group consciousness of self–in–relation by providing intentional, competent, and ethical helping behaviors that promote the mental health of group members. 300

    assessment, 305–311

    competencies, 301–303, 311–313

    history, 299–301

    theory, 303–305

Multicultural group worker competency: A framework used by group workers to anchor group goals, expectations, and processes that support and promote culturally relevant and sensitive group work. 301

Multicultural influences, 53–54

Multicultural realities, 220

    African Americans, 228–231

    Arab Americans, 236–238

    Asian Americans, 231–234

    children, 224–225

    elderly persons, 239–241

    gay, lesbian, or bi- populations, 243–244

    Latin Americans, 234–236

    Native Americans, 225–228

    relationship differences, 221–223

Murray, H. A., 472, 473

Myelin sheath: The insulated covering around axons that increases the speed at which signals travel. 609

Myer, R. A., 556, 557, 558, 560, 561, 562, 565, 566, 580

Myers-Briggs Type Inventory, 330–331

Myers, I. B., 481, 482

Myers, J. E., 6, 8, 15, 330, 633, 645, 646, 647, 648, 649, 650, 653

Myers, P., 625, 632, 647, 650

Mytton, J., 378, 379

N

N.C. v. Bedford Central School District, 769

Nachmann, B., 321

Nance, D. W., 87

Napier, A., 386

Napier, R. W., 281

Narrative reenactment: In constructivist family therapy, a technique in which clients tell the story of their lives and create new ones for a desired future; couples act out scenes written by their partners to share perspectives and create new outcomes. 384

Narrowband tools: Tools that measure a specific set of characteristics of only one disorder or syndrome. 409

National Board for Certified Counselors, 10, 316, 664

Naveh, D., 288

Negative reinforcement: The application of a desirable stimulus to decrease a behavior. 168

Negatively skewed data: Data contain few low scores and mostly are comprised of high scores. In this distribution, the tail of the curve goes out to the left. 440

Negligence: Any conduct that does not meet the minimum requirements for acceptable professional behavior. 37

Network: An HMO model that contracts with two or more independent group practices to provide services to HMO members, and may involve large single and multispecialty groups. 739

Neufeldt, S. A., 96, 97

Neugarten, B. L., 133

Neukrug, E. S., 73, 203, 535

Neural pathway: The pattern formed when a series of neurons fire or release electrical impulses in the form of neurotransmitters, that ultimately forms a permanent circuit. 609

Neuropsychological assessment: Used to draw inferences about brain functioning based on behaviors exhibited by the person under structured conditions. 478

Neuroscience, 607
    and psychotherapy, 607
    nervous system, 607–609
    neural change, 613–618
    processing deficits, 618–623
    the brain, 609–613

Neurotransmitters: Chemicals released by terminal buttons at the end of one neuron and received at receptor sites on the dendrites of other neurons. 609

Newcomb, T. M., 214, 216

Newcomb's A–B–X model of interpersonal attraction, 216

Newlon, B. J., 641

Ng, M., 351

Nichols, M. P., 378, 379, 380, 389, 390

Nichols, W. C., 400, 401

Niemic, C. P., 601

Niles, S. G., 316, 559

Nitza, A. G., 279

Nixon, S. J., 565

Nominal scales: The simplest form of measurement that assigns numbers to classify data into one or more categories (e.g., one type of nominal measurement is gender, and numbers can be assigned to the categories of male and female.) to make observations about the frequency with which data fall into each category. 437

Nondirectional hypothesis: Statement that there is simply a relation between variables or that groups differ on the variable of interest. 487

Nonmaleficence: The ethical precept stating counselors should do no harm. 24

Non-person-oriented career: The individual satisfies needs primarily by acting on things or ideas independently. 320

Norcross, J. C., 82, 157, 158, 580

Norming: The stage in group work when the members develop ingroup feeling and cohesiveness, new standards evolve, and new roles are adopted. 289

Norm-referenced test: Test that has been given in a standardized manner to a specific sample (group) of individuals, called the norm group. 432

Nugent, F., 73

Null hypothesis: States that in the population, there is no change, no effect, no difference, and no relation due to the effect of the treatment or condition. 488

Nykodym, N., 254

Nylund, D., 396

Nystul, M. S., 159, 162

O

O'Hanlon, B., 394

O'Hanlon, W., 385, 395, 396

O'Hara, R. P., 321, 710

Object permanence: The understanding that an object continues to exist even when it is out of sight. 116

Object relations theory: A means of explaining how people relate to others based on early attachment experiences with a caregiver. 389

Objective measures: Tools that evaluate personality through the use of forced choice responses to questions. 472

Occipital lobe: Part of the cortex located at the back of the head that is responsible for visual processing. 610

Occupational segregation: In Roe's career theory, the tendency for members of particular groups to be overrepresented in some occupations and underrepresented in others. 344

Office of Public Policy and Legislation, 770

Ohlsen, M. M., 256

Okech, J. E. A., 284

Okun, B. F., 201

Omer, H., 384

One-downmanship: The relationship between the consultant and the consultee as one of equals or peers. 538

One-way analysis of variance (ANOVA): Statistically equal to the t test, this statistical test can be used to test for true differences in two or more sample means on the same variable. 444

Open-ended or open panel HMO: An HMO that allows its members to utilize health care services from providers outside their own network of providers without referral authorization. 739

Operant conditioning: Learning that relies on consequences that follow behavior. 144

Oppression: The unjust or cruel exercise of authority or power that functions to crush or burden by abuse of power, privilege, or authority; oppression may also be an act of physical or psychological violence that hinders a person from being entirely human or alive. 66

Ordinal scales: Like the nominal scales, data are classified into categories, and they are also rank ordered. The distance between the rankings, however, is not known and rankings are not necessarily equidistant. 437

Organizational commitment: The degree to which one identifies with a particular organization. 484

Organizational consultation: The process in which a professional, functioning either internally or externally to an organization, provides assistance of a technical, diagnostic/perspective, or facilitative nature to an individual or group from the organization to enhance the organization's ability to deal with change and maintain or enhance its effectiveness in some designated way. 542

Organizational culture: The socially transmitted behavior patterns characteristic of a particular organization or company. 483–484

Organizational diagnosis: The process through which both the consultants and the consultees seek to grasp the dynamic, problematic, organizational situations. 543

Organizational structure: A strategic configuration of organizational functions, jobs, and policies in a pattern that best serves organizational goals. 483

Osborne, S. S., 529, 530

Osgood, C., 214, 216

Osipow, S. H., 345

Osofsky, J. D., 589

Ottens, A. J., 562, 731

Outcome expectations: Personal beliefs about the results of performance that are viewed as operating independently from efficacy expectations and dependent on actual performance. 348

Outcome goals: In behavioral family therapy, the desired changes that are clearly defined as the goals of therapy. 378

Overgeneralization: The tendency to apply conclusions or beliefs about a specific instance to other, nonrelated instances. 173

Overt aggression: Common in boys, and involves physically aggressive acts. 123

Overton, W. F., 594

P

Pack-Brown, S. P., 299, 300, 310, 311

Padilla, A. M., 349

Palmer, P. J., 40

Panel study: A study in which the same individuals are tested at successive points in time over the period of the study. 509

Panksepp, J., 617

Paradigm: A set of rules and regulations (written or unwritten) that does two things: (a) It establishes or defines boundaries; and (b) it tells you how to behave inside the boundaries to be successful. 6

Paradoxical intention: A technique used to aid group members to exaggerate or magnify the behaviors that are causing concern for the purpose of bringing awareness to the underlying feelings related to distressing behaviors. 269

Parallel process: The dynamic that occurs in the client-therapist relationship that is played out in the supervisee-supervisor relationship. 78

Parent ego state: In transactional analysis, this ego state consists of the critical parent and the nurturing parent. The critical parent acts to protect and is filled with values, shoulds, and ought tos. The nurturing parent acts as a nurturer and caregiver. 165

Parham, T. A., 53, 350

Parietal lobe: Part of the cortex found at the top of the head between the frontal lobe and the occipital lobe that contains motor and sensory processing areas. 610

Parker, W. M., 311

Parsons, F., 317–318

Parsons, R. D., 195, 198, 200, 539, 547

Parten, M., 122

Participant observation: Individuals make it clear to the community that they are researchers, but then try to partake, as much as possible and as much as allowed, in the daily and ordinary activities within that community. 519

Pastoral counseling: A process in which a pastoral counselor utilizes insights and principles derived from the disciplines of theology and the behavioral sciences in working with individuals, couples, families, groups, and social systems toward the achievement of wholeness and health. 659–660
    cognitive behavioral therapy, 673–674
    ethics, 663–665
    ideology, 660–663
    theories, 665–672

Pate, R. H., Jr., 49

Paton, D., 565

Patrick, B. C., 601

Patterson, C. H., 94

Patton, M. Q., 514

Pearce, J. K., 226

Pearlman, L. A., 564

Pedersen, P. B., 52, 60, 221, 222, 306

Pedhazur, E. J., 496

Peeks, B., 397

Peele, S., 574

Peirce, C. S., 515

Pelletier, L. G., 601

Percentiles: Describe the percentage of people whose score falls at or below a particular raw score. 440

Performing: Period of group work when the members have reconciled many of their differences and have developed enough trust and cohesion to examine themselves and their relationship to the group. 289

Peripheral nervous system (PNS): Comprised of nerves extending from the spinal cord to the rest of the body (e.g., organs and muscles). 608

Perls, F. S., 30, 187, 188, 267, 670

Perry, B. A., 379

Personal and social development: Strategies and activities implemented to provide personal and social growth experiences to facilitate students' progress through school and the transition to adulthood. 366

Personal fable: Adolescents' inflated opinion of themselves and their importance. 128

Personal responsibility: The concept that people have no power over others' behaviors, but they do have control over their own behavior, for which they are responsible. 180

Personality assessment: A method that counselors use to measure a variety of components of personality including: traits, states, identity, cognitive and behavioral styles, and other individual characteristics. 472

Personalization: Interpreting events and reactions as related to themselves even if there is no evidence of the connection. 174

Person-centered approach, 264–267

Person-oriented career: The individual satisfies needs primarily through interactions with people. 320

Peterson, S. E., 566

Pew, W. L., 249

Pfefferbaum, B., 565

Phenotype: A organism's manifest physical and psychological characteristics, which are determined by both genetic makeup and environmental factors. 113

Physical development: Involves growth of a physical nature, including muscular strength and fine and gross motor skills development. 139

Physiological dependence: Occurs when individuals experience tolerance and withdrawal in relation to a substance. 572

Piagetian theory of cognitive development, 146–148

Piel, J. A., 149, 150

Placating: In conjoint family therapy, a communication style in which a person denies the self to agree with someone else. 392

Plant, R. W., 600, 601

Plasticity: The ability of neurons and neural networks to change. 613

Point estimate: One statistic in the range of possible statistics within the confidence interval that estimates the population parameter. 490

Polarized thinking: The tendency to view events as either completely negative or positive or thinking that is dualistic and characterized by either-or traits. 174

Polite, C., 344, 522

Pons: Part of the hindbrain involved in posture, muscle movements, and coordination. 612

Ponterotto, J. G., 53, 68

Poortinga, Y. H., 58

Pope, M., 96, 285

Pope-Davis, D. B., 96

Porter, L. W., 484

Portraiture, 522

Positive reinforcement: Provision of a valued stimulus following a desired behavior. 144

Positively skewed data: Data contain few high scores and mostly are comprised of low scores. In this distribution, the tail of the curve goes out to the right. 440

Postconventional morality: The third level of Kohlberg's moral development theory in which moral conclusions are internalized and individuals make moral choices based on their evaluation of alternate moral codes and ultimate subscription to a personal moral code. 149

Prata, G., 401

Pratt, M. L., 275, 520

Precision Matching: 640

Preconventional morality: The first level of Kohlberg's moral development theory in which moral judgments reflect considerations for personal needs, but place little emphasis on societal needs. 148

Preferred provider organization: A health care delivery system that contracts with providers of medical care to provide services at discounted fees to members. Members may seek care from nonparticipating providers but generally are financially penalized for doing so by the loss of the discount and subjection to copayments and deductibles. 739

Prejudice: Generalizations or stereotypical beliefs about a group of individuals that are not grounded in empirical evidence. 64

Presbury, J. H., 558

Presbycusis: Hearing loss that usually affects a person's ability to detect higher frequencies. 131

Presbyopia: A major change in vision that results in diminished color discrimination, night vision, and visual acuity of marked decline between ages 70 and 80. 131

Pretending: A strategic family therapy technique that entails performing the problematic behavior or symptom in the session and practicing coping skills. 397

Pretest sensitization: A threat to internal validity that occurs when participants' performance on a test is improved because of having taken a pretest. 497

Principle of awareness: In Gestalt therapy, clients gain insight when they become aware of and take responsibility for their sensations, thoughts, and behaviors in the here and now. 188

Principle of figure-ground: In Gestalt therapy, clients address their most pressing needs first and as these are resolved, previously less evident needs emerge to be dealt with. 188

Principle of holism: In Gestalt therapy, clients experience a sense of completeness when they tie up problematic situations—"loose ends"—from the past that cause anxiety and prevent integration. 188

Principle of polarities: In Gestalt therapy, clients acknowledge the opposite or hidden aspects of a problematic situation to promote resolution of conflicts. 188

Principles, *see* Ethics

Privacy: The constitutional right of people to decide the time, place, manner, and extent of personal disclosures. 47–48

Privilege: The state of being preferred or favored in society combined with a set of conditions that systematically empower select groups based on specific variables such as race and gender, while systematically not empowering others. 66

Privileged communication: A legal concept that guards against compulsory disclosure in legal proceedings that breaks a promise of privacy. 47, 48–49

Probability: The likelihood that an occurrence will take place given all other chance factors. 441

Probert, B. S., 645

Process addiction: An addiction that does not require a substance to be ingested, but often presents similar problems as a substance-related addiction (e.g., shopping, sex, workaholism, etc.). 706

Processing: An activity in which individuals and groups regularly examine and reflect on their behavior to extract meaning, integrate the resulting knowledge, and thereby improve functioning and outcome. 279

Process-oriented consultation: A set of activities on the part of the consultant that help the client (consultee) to perceive, understand, and act on the process events that occur in the client's (consultee's) environment. 543

Prochaska, J. O., 157, 158, 580

Professional counseling paradigm: Approach to the helping relationship that pays particular attention to the interface between clients and their cultural and systemic connections, with strong emphasis on interpersonal relationships. 6

Professional counseling: The application of mental health, psychological, or human development principles, through cognitive, affective, behavioral, or systemic interventions, strategies that address wellness, personal growth, or career development, as well as pathology. 3

Professionalism, 8, 33, 35

Professional school counseling, 361–375
    ASCA model, 367–371
    ASCA standards, 364–367

Progression: The process whereby individuals experience an ever-increasing feeling of being out of control, increased consequences, and obsessive thinking related to their behavior. 570

Projective identifications: In psychodynamic family therapy, the ways in which parents project unwanted aspects of their personalities onto their children, who in turn accept that identity and unconsciously agree to act out in such a way as to uphold those expectations. 390

Projective measures: Allow for inferences about an individual's personality through responses to ambiguous or unstructured stimuli and are often used for educational, forensic, and therapeutic assessment. 472

Protagonist: In psychodramatic group therapy, the group member who has chosen to enact a life situation or relationship in an effort to experience a cathartic release of emotions, gain insight, and learn new and productive ways of managing future situations or relationships. 255

Protecting: A technique that is intended to protect a group member from too much self-disclosure and subsequent feelings of regret, as well as pressure from others in the group to reveal more than they may be comfortable with. 292

Protective factors: Those factors that can serve to buffer the individual from the influence of risk factors, such as the presence of a caring and nurturing adult. 590

Protinsky, H. O., 94

Prouty, A. M., 94

Proximodistal: The sequence of growth that occurs from the midline of the body outward. 115

Pryzwansky, W. B., 529

Psychoanalytic approaches, 247–249

Psychodramatic approach, 254–257

Psychodynamic approaches, 156
    analytic psychology, 159–161
    individual psychology, 161–164
    psychoanalysis, 156–158
    transactional analysis, 164–167

Psychoeducational tests: Take information from both cognitive and achievement measures to provide an overall picture of a student's abilities related to academic success and to measure academic achievement related to reading, math, and writing achievement. 471

Psychological dependence: Refers to individuals who remain dependent on a substance or behavior for reasons other than physiological ones. 572

Psychological emergency: Sudden event characterized by the presence of immediate danger and potential permanent psychological or physical damage. 555

Psychological heterosexism: The individual internalization of worldviews underlying cultural heterosexism resulting in prejudice against people who are not heterosexual. 65

Psychological paradigm: Approach to the helping relationship that emphasizes the etiology of psychopathology as intrinsic to the individual. 6

Psychometrics: Any form of mental testing or the branch of counseling and psychology that deals with testing. 435

    descriptive, 436–441

    inferential, 441–445

    reliability, 445–449

    statistics, 435–436

    test construction, 453–456

    validity, 449–453

Psychopathology, 406–412

    aging, 431–432

    anxiety, 412–415

    assessment, 407–411

    childhood, 428–430

    cognitive functions, 424–426, 431

    diagnostic system, 411–412

    eating disorders, 418–419

    gender identity, 421–424

    mood, 415–417

    personality, 426–428

    substance use, 419–421

Pugh, S. D., 62

Punishment: Applies an aversive stimulus to diminish the likelihood of occurrence of a behavior. 168

Pynoos, R. S., 558

Q

Qualitative Research: An approach to research that, at its core, can be described as an empirical inquiry into meaning. 512

    meaning, 514–515

    products, 520–524

    role in counseling, 524–525

    roots, 513–514

    techniques, 517–519

QUOID client: Acronym for "quiet, ugly, old, indigent, dissimilar" that refers to the type of client a counselor is least likely to want to work with. 245

R

Race: An inbreeding, geographically isolated population that differs in distinguishable physical traits from other members of the species. 62

Racial and cultural identity development: The processes used by individuals of minority groups and oppressed peoples to understand their own identity in light of their culture, the culture of dominant groups, and the convergence of the two cultures. 68

Racial salience: The degree to which an individual perceives race as a factor affecting workplace options. 350

Racism: The belief that racial or ethnic groups other than one's own are psychologically, intellectually, or physically inferior. 64

Random assignment: Individuals are assigned to either the experimental group or the control group, or some level of the treatment on the basis of chance. 492

Range: Provides a quick assessment of the variability in the data by describing the uppermost and lowermost scores among the data. 438

Raphael, B., 551

Rapin, L. S., 276

Raskin, N. J., 265

Raskin, P., 387

Ratcliff, D. E., 666

Rational-emotive behavior, 260–262

Ratio scales: Have all the properties of the interval scale of measurement and also have an absolute or true zero point. 437

Ray, W. A., 402

Reaction range: The range of possible phenotypes for a particular genotype across all environmental influences. 113

Reality therapy approach, 262–264

Reciprocal determinism: An individual's behavior is both influenced by and is influencing an individual's personal factors and the environment. 171

Record keeping, 42

Redding, S. G., 351

Reeve, J., 595, 601

Referral question: A statement given by the client or other parties close to the client about the area of concern that guides counselors in making informed decisions to ensure proper treatment. 411, 461

Reflect: Stage in the FERA inquiry learning model that uses dialogue to promote shared or mutual understanding and insight into the counseling and supervising experiences. New learning and the removal of blind spots help both the counselor and the supervisor gain different perspectives on the work and the relationships. 100

Reflecting team: In constructivist family therapy, a technique in which a team of clinicians observe family–counselor interactions and provide a diagnosis of family problems. 384

Reformity prescription: Seeks to make the therapy fit the client through structured learning therapy so that it can be more consistent with the client's styles. 205

Reframing: The counselor presents a different perspective, usually a positive interpretation, of what the client has presented. 384

Regression toward the mean: Occurs when participants scoring on the extremes on the pretest tend to move toward the middle or mean on the posttest. 496

Rehabilitation counseling: The maintenance of, or the improvement in, the physical, mental, and emotional states of a person, of any age, suffering from the effects of congenital mishap, crippling disease, injury, accident, or surgical intervention. 242

Reification: Treating concepts or abstractions as if they were real, concrete things. 120

Reinforcement: A behavior that is immediately followed by a positive event or experience; the likelihood of that behavior recurring is increased. 144

Reiser, M., 126

Reitan, R. M., 479

Relational aggression: More common in girls and involves the act of damaging social relationships and status. 123

Reliability: Provides an indication of the consistency of test scores over repeated test administrations. 445

Religion: The belief system and ritual practices of a sect or denomination of individuals that binds them together in worship, practice, and community. 63

Remley, T., Jr., 21

Repeated measures ANOVA: Used to analyze a single factor (independent variable) and a single dependent variable when the sample is the same for each treatment condition.

Research design, 487–490
    experimental research, 491–495
    experimental validity, 495–497
    nonexperimental, 507–510
    quasi-experimental, 507–510

Resentful demoralization: Occurs when the responses of the participants do not reflect their natural behaviors. 496

Resilience: Refers to positive or adaptive developmental outcomes, despite the presence of risk factors or adversity. 593

Reticular formation: Part of the hindbrain that regulates consciousness, which is a combination of alertness, attention, and awareness and also is involved with posture, smoothness of muscle movements, and maintenance of muscle tone. 612

Reynolds, C. R., 477

Richardson, M. A., 227

Richeport-Haley, M., 398

Ricoeur, P., 667

Ridley, C. R., 64

Rigazio-DiGilio, S. A., 625, 627, 634, 637

Risk factors: Those that have the potential to interrupt the individual's normal developmental pathway or trajectory, such as exposure to violence. 590

Risk of harm: Participants will incur no physical or psychological harm as a result of taking part in the study. 435

Rita, E. S., 94

Ritchie, M. H., 8, 49, 50

Riva, M. T., 276, 284, 290

Rivers, D. A., 57, 64, 197

Robbins, S. B., 609, 615

Robertson, I. H., 619, 620, 623

Robinson, D. T., 285

Robinson, S. E., 529, 530

Robinson, T. L., 55, 235

Rocha-Singh, I. A., 347

Rodin, G. C., 600

Roe, A., 315, 320, 321, 343, 344

Rogers, C. R., 101, 199, 208, 264, 266, 598, 669

Rohde, R. I., 290

Roid, G. H., 465

Rollnick, S., 576, 600, 602

Ronen, T., 94

Rønnestad, M. H., 6, 94

Rorschach, H., 472

Rose, S. D., 258, 259, 260

Rosenbaum, M., 94

Rosman, B., 398

Rounds, J. B., 331, 343

Rovine, M., 589

Rowntree, D., 436, 444

Roysircar-Sodowsy, G., 59

Rudd, M. D., 551

Rudolph, L. B., 47

Russell, R., 412

Russell-Chapin, L. A., 74, 75, 76, 80, 81, 82

Ruud, W., 254

Ryan, R. M., 593, 594, 595, 596, 597, 600, 601, 605, 645

Ryckoff, I. M., 391

Ryff, C. D., 645

S

Sacks, O., 521

Salter, A. C., 551

Samuel, D., 412

Sanchez, H. G., 551

Santrock, J. W., 118, 195

Satir, V., 392, 393

Sattler, J. M., 408, 461

Savickas, M. L., 342

Scaffolding: The altering degree of assistance that children receive from the skilled adults to suit their level of competence on which further development hinges. 589

Scarr, S., 113

Schein, E. H., 535, 543, 544

Scheiner, M. J., 605

Schemas: New ways of thinking that change with age, experience, and exposure to new environmental circumstances; ways of processing information for specific activities. 147

Schmidt, A. E., 562

Schmidt, J. J., 239, 241, 243

Schneider, J. P., 571

Schön, B., 90

School counseling initiative, 371–374

School counselors, 38–40

Schulte, A. C., 529

Schulte, E. H., 529, 530

Schutz, A., 513

Schwallie-Giddis, P., 364

Schwartz, B., 150

Schwartz, R. C., 378, 379, 380, 389, 390

Schwitzer, A. M., 203

Secondary victimization: Also known as vicarious trauma, this can occur when bearing witness to the results of extreme or unexpected harm or violence to another person. 16

Seely, M. F., 551

Segal, J., 390, 391

Segal, S. J., 321

Segall, M. H., 58

Seidman, I. E., 518

Selection: Inherent differences between groups at the outset of the study; is more likely to happen with intact groups. 496

Self-determination theory, 593–597

    and helping professions, 598–604

    motivation, 597–598

Self-efficacy: The individuals' judgments of their capabilities to organize and execute courses of action required to attain designated types of performances. 171

Self-report: Information gathering that relies on the client's input about behaviors of interest. 476

Seligman, L., 156, 157, 195, 200, 202, 329, 331, 641

Seligman, M. E., 199

Seltzer, W. J., 610, 611

Selvini Palazzoli, M., 401

Semantic bootstrapping: A process of relying on word meanings to learn grammatical rules. 121

Senescence: Genetically influenced declines in the performance of organs and systems. 130

Sensitive periods: In humans, the periods that are optimal but not exclusive for certain aspects of development. 113

Separation anxiety: Extreme stress experienced by infants or young children when they are separated from their mother. 151

Serafica, F. C., 348, 357

Seriation: In Piagetian cognitive theory, the arrangement of items on a quantitative dimension that occurs in the concrete operational phase. 148

Sex: The system of sexual classification based on biological and physical differences, such as primary and secondary sexual characteristics, which create the categories male and female. 60

Sexism: The belief that women and men are inherently and qualitatively different, with men being presumed superior to women. 65

Sexton, T., 97

Sexual misconduct, 29–30

Shalev, A. Y., 565

Shallice, T., 614, 622

Shank, G. D., 514, 517, 519

Shaping: Reinforcing behaviors that increasingly resemble the desired behavior until the desired behavior is attained. 145

Sharf, R. S., 321, 324

Shatz, M., 125

Shaver, P., 130

Sheldon, K. M., 594, 646

Sherman, N. E., 81

Shirk, S., 412

Shohet, R., 94

Sibling position: In Bowenian family therapy, personality characteristics that are consistent with birth order and used to describe sibling position; failure to display the expected personality characteristics of birth order is attributable to family projections and triangulations. 381

Silove, D., 555, 565

Simon, J., 465

Sink, C. A., 47

Situational crisis: Emerges with the advent of unexpected events that lie outside the realm of normal functioning; individuals neither anticipate nor have a way of controlling situational crises. 552

Skinner, B. F., 167, 168, 169, 257

Skovholt, T. M., 6, 57, 64, 94, 104, 197, 202

Skowron, E. A., 380, 381, 382

Skynner, R., 389, 391

Slaikeu, K. A., 565

Slawski, C., 212, 213, 214

Smart, D. W., 241, 242

Smart, J. F., 241, 242

Smedley, A., 62

Smedley, B. D., 62

Smith, E. J., 259

Smith, P. C., 484

Smith, P. L., 343, 348

Social clock: Refers to life events such as marriage, a first job, a first child, and so on, that follow age-graded patterns based on societal and cultural expectations. 133

Social convoy: The changes that occur in our social networks as people age. 133

Social interest: The need of human persons to experience a sense of belonging and emphasizes the overall concern for humanity that individuals possess. 146

Social learning theory, 146

Sociocultural context: A precise set of cultural, physical, socioeconomic, and historical circumstances that have an impact on variations in human development. 137

Sociocultural theory of development, 149–150

Socioemotional development: Involves changes in the ability to initiate and maintain interactions with others, changes in personality, and emotional regulation. 139

Sociological paradigm: Approach to the helping relationship that focuses on systems. 6

Soenens, B., 600

Sohlberg, M. M., 621, 623

Solomon, J., 119

Solovey, A., 396, 398

Sonstegard, M. A., 250

Sorenson, G. P., 42

Spark, G. M., 390

Speirs, K., 636

Sperry, L., 33, 195, 198

Spirituality: That which allows humans to transcend the corporeal body and to connect on many levels with that which is other. 659–660, *see also* Pastoral Counseling

Splitting: In psychodynamic family therapy, individuals perceive people as either good or bad if their early experiences are unresolved. 389

Spontaneous recovery: The premise on which moderated management is built; refers to the assumption that many individuals learn to manage their bad habit or addiction without any type of professional intervention. 583

Spradley, J. P., 518, 520

Sprinthall, R. C., 437, 440, 443, 445, 449

Spritz, B., 589

Stachowiak, J., 392

Stage: In psychodramatic groups, the formal stage area or large open room in which the enactment takes place. 255

Stake, R. E., 34, 521

Standard deviation (SD): The most commonly used measure of test score spread that indicates how far individual scores are from the mean. 438

Standard error of measurement: An estimate of how accurate the observed scores are at approximating the true score. 448

Steele, R. P., 292

Steer, R. A., 409

Steers, R. M., 484

Steffy, B. E., 530

Steinberg, L., 558

Stephens, A. M., 95

Sternberg, R. J., 133

Stimulus–response model, 143–144

Stockton, R., 278, 279, 283, 290, 292, 293, 294

Stoltenberg, C. D., 76, 77, 94, 109

Stone, C., 38, 39, 40, 45, 46, 47, 372, 373, 374, 375

Stone, G., 397

Storming: The stage of group work characterized by inevitable conflict, mild disagreements, and resistance that can have positive or negative implications. 289

Strauss, A. L., 513, 523, 524

Strong, E. K., 330

Structure: Encompasses many different techniques and interventions that have as their primary goal the development and maintenance of a healthy therapeutic group.

Structured learning therapy model, 205–206

Strunk, O., Jr., 662

Stuhlmiller, C., 565

Substance abuse: A pattern of use that is chronic and excessive, resulting in damage to relationships, work attendance or productivity, and health status. 419

Substance addiction: An addiction that requires the ingestion of a mood-altering substance (e.g., alcohol, drugs, etc.). 570

Substance dependence: Pattern of use where life activities are organized around the opportunity to consume a drug, and where psychological and physical tolerance (the need for more of the drug to get the same high) develops and withdrawal symptoms can result. 419

Sue, D. W., 54, 68, 69, 80, 222, 235, 284, 286, 341, 350, 354

Sue, S., 57, 68, 96, 222, 223, 235, 284, 286, 350, 354

Super reasonable: In conjoint family therapy, a communication style in which feelings are not acknowledged within the self or in others. 392

Super, D. E., 319–320

Superego: Structure of personality that serves as an individual's conscience, represents a moral code handed down from parent to child, and guides behavior to reflect rules that closely resemble societal norms or expectations. 140

Supervision: A distinctive, structured approach in which an often more experienced professional counselor responds to a counselor trainee or supervisee's needs with attention to the supervisee's differing developmental and competency levels. 73–75, 87–109

and professionalism, 73

collaborative model, 91–92, 97–98

credentialing, 88

ethical and legal considerations, 94–96

evaluation, 106–109
FERA learning model, 100–102, 105–106, 107–108
multicultural impact, 96–97
novice supervisors, 92–94, 97, 99
self-developed skills, 90
theories, 93–94
therapeutic working alliance, 101–104
training, 89
Supervision models, 75–84
developmental, 75–77
discrimination, 79–80
integrated model, 80–82
theory-specific, 77–78
videotaping, 82–83
Suzuki, L., 346
Swaney, K., 343
Sweeney, T. J., 6, 14, 625, 632, 633, 646, 647, 648, 649, 650, 653
Swerdlik, M. E., 439, 483

Switching addictions: Refers to the phenomenon often seen when individuals stop or reduce one addiction and trade it for another. 584

Symbolic substitution: The utilization of a word or other symbol in the place of a specific action. 147

Symmetry: In Newcomb's model of attraction, the state of balance among A, B, and X (two individuals and an object). 216

Synapse: The area between neurons, in which information is passed from the terminal buttons at the end of one neuron's axon to the dendrites of another neuron. 609

Syndrome: Abnormal psychological symptoms that tend to occur together, present to a marked degree, and last for a significant amount of time. 408

Syntactic bootstrapping: The process of discovering the meaning of words by observing how the words are used in syntax. 121

Systematic desensitization: The gradual exposure to an aversive stimulus that eventually allows a person to overcome a specific fear. 259

Systemic Cognitive Developmental Counseling: a therapeutic approach that adapts Developmental Counseling and Therapy constructs for work with families and wider networks by examining the internal meaning making of individuals, families, and institutional systems and the factors that influence exchanges across these systems. 634

evaluation, 640–641
fundamentals, 635–636
questioning strategies, 636–639

Systemic crisis: Occurs when an identifiable event ripples out into large segments of the population and the environment and has a psychological impact not only on the immediate victims, but on people throughout the world. 552

t test: A statistic that is used to determine whether or not there are true differences in two sample means for the same dependent variable. 444

T

Tang, M., 343
Tannenbaum, P., 214
Taschman, H., 392
Tata, S. P., 349
Tatar, M., 650
Taylor, D. G., 589, 658
Technical competencies, 7

Technical eclecticism: The idea that treatment can and should consist of techniques from a variety of theoretical perspectives without the therapist necessarily adopting a theoretical basis for those techniques. 184

Teed, C., 292
Teglasi, H., 473

Telegraphic: Expression of thought in two-word sentences. 117

Temperament: A child's typical way of behaving and responding to the environment. 118

Temporal lobes: Areas of the cortex located on the right and left sides of the cortex, in the area around the ear, and are important for language processing. 610

Teratogens: Environmental agents capable of causing developmental abnormalities in utero. 114

Terner, J., 249

Tests of linear regression: see Correlation.

Thalamus: Part of the forebrain that is a relay center in the brain, facilitating connections between the cortex and limbic system. 611

The ordeal: A strategic family therapy technique that entails changing the family structure in a way that is beneficial by prescribing a difficult activity that is more severe than the problematic behavior. The technique is useful in creating negative consequences for problem behavior and in reinforcing appropriate boundaries and authority roles. 397

Thematic communication: frequently observed styles of communication that are used within a particular ethnocultural community. 308

Theory: A set of principles that helps to explain a group of facts or a phenomenon and is used to make predictions. 195

Therapeutic contracts: Contractual forms completed by group members who indicate what it is they wish to accomplish as a result of participating in the group. Goals must be concretely defined so that group members can take responsibility for working toward them. 253

Therapeutic factor: An element of group therapy that contributes to improvement in a patient's condition and is a function of the actions of the group therapist, the group members, and the patient himself or herself. 280

Therapeutic working alliance: A supervisee-centered, collaborative relationship driven by the clinical and developmental needs of the supervisee, in which the process of identifying and addressing the supervisee's needs as they arise must be the mutual responsibility of both professionals. 101

Third-party administrators (TPAs): Individuals or firms that an employer hires to handle claims processing, reimburse providers, and deal with all other health-insurance-related matters. 739

Thomas, R. M., 149, 151

Thomas, V., 94

Thompson, B., 490

Thompson, C. L., 47

Tiedeman, D. V., 321, 680, 710

Tobin, V. J., 600

Tolerance: Either needing more of a substance to achieve intoxication or the desired effect, or a significant decrease in the effect of the substance when the same amount is used. 571

Tolin, D. F., 559

Tootle, A., 611, 612, 613

Torts: Civil wrongs recognized by law as grounds for a lawsuit. 37

Toth, P. L., 278, 290, 292, 293

Toth, S. L., 588, 591

Training, 8–9

Transactional analysis approach, 251–254

Transactional model: An approach to helping that acknowledges that people are active creators of their social environments and are in turn influenced by them. 206

Transfer of effect: What is learned in one situation should be transferred and used in future similar situations. 538

Transference: Projections clients cast on their counselors. 30

Transforming School Counseling: An initiative funded by the Dewitt Wallace-Reader's Digest Fund to create a new vision for school counseling that emphasizes leadership, advocacy, use of data, and a commitment to support high levels of achievement for all students. 371

Transgender: A person whose gender identity does not match her or his assigned gender (gender assignment is usually based on biological or physical sex). 61

Trauma: Occurs when an individual experiences or perceives an enormous sense of helplessness and physical threat that leads to the interruption of normal development. 558

Traupman, J. C., 661

Treatment group: In an experimental design, the group that receives the treatment. 491

Treatment integrity: Refers to the extent to which the treatment is the same for all groups across all contexts. 493

Trend study: Type of study in which the researcher takes a new sample of persons from the population of interest each year. All samples are asked the same questions or administered the same treatment. 509

Tresini, M., 130

Triangulation: In Bowenian family therapy, a basic, stable relationship system that can be healthy or unhealthy; unhealthy triangles form when family members lower stress by projecting the anxiety between two people onto a third person or thing. 381

Trimble, J. E., 221

Trochim, W., 435, 444

Truax, C., 199

Tucker, P., 484, 565

Tuckman, B. W., 288, 289, 295

Tuson, K. M., 601

Type I error: Occurs when a researcher finds a significant difference or relation when there is none. 489

Type II error: Occurs when the researcher fails to reject a false null when a significant difference exists. 489

U

Unconditional positive regard: The nonjudgmental, caring, and accepting attitude of the therapist toward the client. 186

Unconditioned response (UR): The natural response an organism makes to the unconditioned response. 143

Unconditioned stimulus (US): Stimulus that evokes an unconditioned response. 143

Unconscious: The largest part of the mind that contains thoughts and feelings of which a person is unaware or has repressed. 157

Unintentional racism: Occurs when White people ignore the reality of privilege and potentially can take part in oppressing people of color. 67

United States Census, 780

United States Employment Service, 330, 780

Universality: Group members come to understand that others have similar problems and they are not alone in their dilemma. 289

Ursano, R. J., 551, 565

Utilization management: The process of evaluating the necessity, appropriateness, and efficiency of health care services against established guidelines and criteria. 740

Utilization review: A formal process for reviewing the appropriateness and quality of health care services delivered to clients before, during, or after the delivery of the services. 740

V

Validity: Evidence that a psychological test measures the attribute or ability it purports to measure in the test manual. 449
Valliant, G. E., 132
Values, 7
van der Kolk, B. S., 558, 559, 564
Van Hesteren, F., 6, 8
Van Maanen, J., 519
Vandereycken, W., 600
Vandiver, B. J., 346
Vansteenkiste, M., 600
Variance: Describes the spread of a distribution of scores by indicating how much variation there is in a set of scores from the mean. 438
Vaslow, J. B., 62
Vernon, A., 47
Vicarious reinforcement: Learning that occurs as a result of watching someone model a particular behavior. 146
Violanti, J. M., 565
Vitz, P. C., 666, 667, 669, 670
Volker, C., 130
Voluntary participation: Participants are not coerced, forced, or deceived into participation. 435
Vontress, C. E., 284, 287
Vygotsky, L. S., 588, 589

W

Wachtel, M., 284
Waddington, C. H., 113
Walker, L. E., 551
Wallace, W. A., 540, 542, 543
Walz, G., 334, 336
Wandersman, A., 514
Wanlass, J., 280
Ward, C. M., 354, 355
Ward, D. E., 279
Ward, S., 620
Warner, R. W., 259
Watkins, C. E., Jr., 99
Watson, J. B., 671
Watzlawick, P., 401, 402
Weakland, J. H., 401
Webb, L., 540
Weber, A. L., 140, 142
Wechsler, D., 466, 467, 468, 479
Wegner, K. W., 362

Weiner-Davis, M., 385, 394, 395
Weinrach, S. G., 319
Weinstock, L. M., 379, 380
Weiss, D., 331, 484
Weiss, R. L., 379
Welfel, E. R., 26, 30
Wellness: A way of life oriented toward optimal health and well-being, in which body, mind, and spirit are integrated by the individual to live life more fully within the human and natural community. Ideally, it is the optimum state of health and well-being that each individual is capable of achieving. 643–645
   assessment tools, 648–650
   counseling, 650–656
   models, 645–648
Wessler, R. L., 262
West, C., 62
Wewers, S., 589
Wheel of influence: A visual representation of all the influential people in the client's life. 393
Whisman, M. A., 379, 380
Whitaker, C., 385, 386
Whitaker, D. S., 247, 290, 386
White privilege: An invisible knapsack of special provisions and unearned assets that put certain cultures at an advantage over others. 223
White, J. L., 53, 540
White, R. K., 281
White, V. E., 6
Whittingham, M. H., 294
Whittington-Clark, L. E., 310, 311
Whyte, W. F., 519
Wichern, F. B., 666
Widiger, T., 412
Wilk, J., 394
Wilkenson, G. S., 468, 469
Williams, C. L., 474, 600
Williams, G. C., 594, 600, 601
Williams, R. C., 562
Wilson, C., 619, 623
Wilson, G. T., 257, 258
Wilson, J. P., 551
Withdrawal: Physiological symptoms associated with a physical withdrawal (differs by substance), or the substance is used to relieve or avoid the withdrawal symptoms. 571
Witmer, J. M., 633, 646, 647, 649
Wolf, A., 248
Wolfson, D., 479
Wolpe, J., 671, 672
Wood, E. R. G., 671, 672
Wood, S. E., 671, 672
Woodcock, R. W., 467, 471
Woods, P. J., 78
Woollams, S., 252

Work Importance Locator, 331
Work Importance Profiler, 331
World Health Oganization, 408, 644
Worldview: A counselor's or client's presuppositions and assumptions about the makeup of her or his world. 299
Wrenn, C. G., 57, 58
Wykes, T., 618
Wynne, L., 391

Y

Yalom, I. D., 254, 279, 280, 282, 293
YAVIS client: Acronym for "young, attractive, verbal, intelligent and successful," the type of client a counselor is most interested in working with. 223
Yehuda, R., 558
Young, M. E., 196, 198
Youngson, H. A., 621

Z

Z score: Represents the number of standard deviations above or below the mean. 442
Zeran, F. N., 362
Zimbardo, P. G., 140, 142
Zimmerman, J. L., 384
Zimpher, D. G., 6
Zinker, J., 267
Zone of proximal development: The dynamic and interactive process between what a child is capable of doing by himself or herself and what a child can do with the assistance of a parent, teacher, or mentor. 149
Zuckerman, M., 62
Zunin, L. M., 263
Zunker, V. G., 319, 320, 324, 332
Zweerink, A., 521
Zytowski, D. G., 330